interact

INTERPERSONAL COMMUNICATION CONCEPTS, SKILLS, AND CONTEXTS

FOURTEENTH EDITION

KATHLEEN S. VERDERBER
Northern Kentucky University

ERINA L. MACGEORGE
Pennsylvania State University

RUDOLPH F. VERDERBER,
Author Emeritus
University of Cincinnati

with

DOUGLAS E. PRUIM
Purdue University, co-author Social Media Factor

NEW YORK   OXFORD
OXFORD UNIVERSITY PRESS

Oxford University Press is a department of the University of Oxford.
It furthers the University's objective of excellence in research,
scholarship, and education by publishing worldwide.

Oxford   New York
Auckland   Cape Town   Dar es Salaam   Hong Kong   Karachi
Kuala Lumpur   Madrid   Melbourne   Mexico City   Nairobi
New Delhi   Shanghai   Taipei   Toronto

With offices in
Argentina   Austria   Brazil   Chile   Czech Republic   France   Greece
Guatemala   Hungary   Italy   Japan   Poland   Portugal   Singapore
South Korea   Switzerland   Thailand   Turkey   Ukraine   Vietnam

For titles covered by Section 112 of the US Higher Education
Opportunity Act, please visit www.oup.com/us/he for the
latest information about pricing and alternate formats.

Published by Oxford University Press
198 Madison Avenue, New York, New York 10016
http://www.oup.com

Library of Congress Cataloging-in-Publication Data
Verderber, Kathleen S., 1949–
Inter-act : interpersonal communication concepts, skills, and contexts / Kathleen S.
 Verderber, Erina L. MacGeorge ; with Douglas E. Pruim. -- Fourteenth edition.
    pages cm
  Includes bibliographical references and index.
  ISBN 978-0-19-939801-0
 1. Interpersonal communication. 2. Interpersonal relations. I. MacGeorge, Erina L.
 II. Title. III. Title: Interact.
  BF637.C45V47   2016
  158.2--dc23
                                                          2015020042

Printing number: 9 8 7 6 5 4

Printed in Canada on acid-free paper

We dedicate this,
the fourteenth edition of Inter-Act to:

PROFESSOR RUDOLPH F. VERDERBER, PH.D., AUTHOR EMERITUS,

*who, though no longer able to do
that which he so truly loved,
has left his imprint on this book.*

*His influence on all basic
textbooks in our field will be
felt for many years to come.*

Brief Contents

Contents

▶ CHAPTER 10

USING INTERPERSONAL INFLUENCE   283

▸ CHAPTER 11

MANAGING CONFLICT   317

Part III: Using Communication Skills to Improve Relationships

▶ CHAPTER 12 COMMUNICATING IN INTIMATE RELATIONSHIPS: LONG-TERM ROMANTIC RELATIONSHIPS, FAMILY, AND FRIENDS 351

Preface

Welcome to the Fourteenth Edition of *Inter-Act!*

To Students Who Are About to Use This Text

Few courses you take in college can have as profound an impact on your life as a course in interpersonal communication. You are embarking on a course of study that will help you be a better friend, family member, lover, partner, employee, manager, co-worker, and leader. Today our rapidly changing technology and social media are presenting new challenges to how we manage effective relationships. This textbook, *Inter-Act,* will help you by introducing you to specific skills that you can use to overcome the complications that arise when our conversations are face-to-face and when they are mediated by technology. Each chapter explores concepts and current theories that explain how interpersonal communication processes work and the skills that help us to be effective.

You will be encouraged to practice, refine, and adopt specific skills that increase your capacity to communicate in different ways. This will increase your interpersonal competence and your ability to have healthy relationships. The basic skills you will learn include developing messages that effectively convey your thoughts and feelings, understanding the nonverbal behavior of others, listening effectively, managing conversations with strangers and acquaintances, providing support and comfort to others, dealing with conflict, and simply finding the most effective way to speak up for yourself. You will also practice more complex skills that help us to sustain intimate relationships with family members, close friends, intimate partners, and people in your workplace. Because how we communicate is embedded in culture, *Inter-Act* introduces you to some of the primary cultural differences that explain how and why specific communication behaviors are interpreted differently in different cultures.

Goals of *Inter-Act*

As with previous editions, this fourteenth edition of *Inter-Act* meets six specific goals that are essential to a basic course in interpersonal communication. These are:

1. To explain important communication concepts, frameworks, and theories that have been consistently supported by careful research so that you can understand the conceptual foundations of interpersonal communication;
2. To teach specific communication skills that research has shown to facilitate effective relationships;
3. To present ethical frameworks you can use to be a moral communicator in your relationships;

4. To sensitize you to ways that communication needs, rules, and processes differ between diverse cultural groups and among people in any particular cultural group;

5. To challenge you to think critically and creatively about the concepts and skills you learn;

6. To provide abundant practice activities that significantly enhance your learning.

To Instructors Who Have Selected This Text

The skills-based approach to interpersonal communication that was pioneered in *Inter-Act* and has remained so popular over the years has been expanded and reinforced with this new edition. These changes continue to be based on a message-centered approach to interpersonal communication (see Burleson, 2010). A message-centered approach allows us to explore how people form relationships and applies current theories and concepts as a framework for understanding interpersonal communication. The message-centered approach is consistent with the premise that there are basic universal message skills and guidelines that improve the likelihood of successful human interaction. This edition emphasizes both automatic and mindful processes involved in message preparation. Understanding these processes enables students to incorporate new skills into their behavioral repertoire and improve relationships. With this overview in mind, let's take a closer look at what is new in this edition.

New to This Edition

- **Explicit discussion of how our emotions affect our communication and our relationships:** In this edition, increased attention is given to theory and research on the role of emotions in our communication processes. Because emotions are integral to every aspect of interpersonal communication, this material is integrated in multiple chapters.

- **Continued and updated emphasis on social media:** Social media has become ubiquitous in our lives and the lives of our students, and has a profound effect on how we "do" our relationships. This edition has been strengthened with updated and expanded discussions of social media and interpersonal communication. Each chapter now includes a section called **The Social Media Factor** that discusses the newest practices, influential theories, current research findings, and practical guidelines for using social media related to the chapter's content. Additionally, the **Inter-Act with Social Media** marginal activities challenge students to apply what they learn about social media from their reading.

- **Expanded scholarship and theoretical profile:** Throughout, the fourteenth edition relies on current interpersonal communication theories that are well supported by programmatic research as the foundation for the concepts and skills students learn. We believe that the purpose of a textbook is to make these theories accessible to introductory students so that they understand why particular communication practices are more effective than others.

- **Streamlined chapter organization:** We have responded to feedback from our users by updating, reorganizing, redistributing, and removing some content. As a result we have been able to shorten the text to thirteen rather than fourteen chapters.

  - Chapter 1, "An Orientation to Interpersonal Communication," begins with an overview of a message-centered interpersonal communication model and includes discussion of how the message production, message interpretation, and message coordination processes work. This model is complemented by sections describing the purposes and characteristics of interpersonal communication, communication ethics, the dark side of interpersonal communication, and communication competence.

  - Chapter 2, retitled "Social Cognition: Understanding Others and Ourselves" has been substantially revised to provide a current overview of how we perceive and think about ourselves and others. This update incorporates substantial theory and research showing that attention, memory, and judgement processes have a profound influence on how we think about ourselves and interact with others.

  - Chapter 3, "Intercultural Communication," has been lightly revised. Updates include a discussion of cultural differences in displays of emotion.

  - Chapter 4, "Verbal Messages," has been lightly revised and streamlined. A new discussion of how to improve the semantic meaning of messages incorporates guidance on improving your emotional vocabulary and the skill of describing feelings. Grice's Cooperative Principle and maxims are now presented as explanations for how we interpret others' speech acts, and the skill of politeness is introduced as a means of avoiding damage to others' "face."

  - Chapter 5, "Nonverbal Messages," has been updated. The skill of perception-checking has been moved into this chapter, where it complements a recognition that nonverbal behavior can convey multiple messages.

  - Chapter 6, "Communication in the Life Cycle of Relationships," has been substantially edited to eliminate redundancy, simplify concepts, and improve the flow of ideas. Some content from this chapter was moved to other places in the text where it more naturally fits. Since relationships develop through disclosure, the discussion of self-disclosure and privacy in relationships has been moved here from a separate chapter in the last edition.

- Chapter 7, "Listening Effectively," has been updated to emphasize the four listening styles identified in recent research by Brodie and Worthington (2010).
- Chapter 8, "Holding Effective Conversations," has been streamlined and a section on using humor in conversations has been added.
- Chapter 9, "Supporting Others," has been reorganized, updated, and streamlined. The chapter explicitly deals with the importance of emotion in supportive interactions. New sections on creating supportive climates, validating emotions, and encouraging reappraisals couple contemporary theory with pragmatic strategies and skills.
- Chapter 10, "Using Interpersonal Influence," has been lightly revised with the addition of a section on interpersonal influence via social media.
- Chapter 11, "Managing Conflict," has been lightly edited, with the section on cyber-bullying expanded and updated to reflect new approaches to stopping it.
- Chapter 12, "Communicating in Intimate Relationships: Long-Term Romantic Relationships, Family, and Friends," has been substantially revised with new content. The chapter includes sections on long-term romantic relationships, families, and friendship. Each section explores the nature of these relationships, the challenges they face, and the role that communication plays in maintaining them.
- Chapter 13, "Communication in Workplace Relationships," has been refocused. Material on job searching has been updated by a senior human resources executive and moved onto the textbook website. The chapter now focuses on improving the effectiveness of our communication in our formal and informal workplace relationships: managerial, co-worker, client/vendor, mentor, and workplace friendships, including workplace romances. The section on how workforce diversity impacts communication has been updated. Finally, a new section thoroughly discusses how to improve workplace performance through giving and receiving feedback. The Social Media Factor has been completely rewritten with a focus on effective use of social media at work.
- **Revised and expanded suite of Analyze and Apply (formerly known as "Apply Your Knowledge") and Skill Practice activities:** Skill Practice exercises at the end of nearly every chapter reinforce *Inter-Act's* stature as the premier skills-based text. Exercises provide students with one or more activities for them to practice each skill discussed in the text.

Hallmark Features of *Inter-Act*—Strengthened and Revised

- **New chapter opening dialogues:** Each chapter opens with a new problematic conversation to set the scene for key ideas that are discussed in the chapter. These conversations are based on real ones reported by college students in Interpersonal Communication classes taught by the authors and contributors. At the end of each chapter, the opening dialogue is revisited, and students are asked to analyze the original dialogue using concepts and theories from the chapter. Then students are instructed to use what they have learned in the chapter to rewrite the dialogue so as to avoid some of the problems that occurred.

- **Running chapter features:** Each chapter includes several unobtrusive features that reinforce learning by engaging the student. *Key terms* and definitions are highlighted in the margins. *Observe and Analyze* activities ask students to observe common communication situations and analyze them using the concepts and theories that have just been presented in the text. *Inter-Act with Social Media* activities direct students to think about how basic interpersonal processes are affected when we use social or electronic media. Instructors can assign these activities as graded exercises or as prompts for journal entries.

- **Chapter box features:** A variety of special boxes highlight other perspectives on interpersonal communication. The popular feature *Diverse Voices* presents excerpts from previously published essays that shed light on the communication experiences of people from a wide range of backgrounds and cultures. Each feature includes a set of thought-provoking questions that will stimulate lively class discussions about diversity. *A Question of Ethics: What Would You Do?* are short case studies presenting ethical dilemmas that ask students to think critically about the situations and develop recommendations concerning the central issues. *Learn About Yourself* are self-administered attitude or behavior assessments that provide students with information about themselves that is related to the material in each chapter. All of these activities are based on research, and most illustrate well-respected ways of measuring a particular concept. While students often complete activities without prompting, instructors may choose to assign these and use them in class discussion.

- **Skill Builder charts:** Skill builder charts appear in the text near the discussion of the skill. They provide a graphic summary of the skill, including the definition, usages, message formation steps, and an example to illustrate its use.

- **End-of-chapter resources:** *Key Words* are lists with page numbers that provide students with an easy way to access chapter concepts. *Analyze and Apply* are activities that challenge students to use chapter concepts and skills to understand or improve a communication situation. These can be used as graded assignments, journal activities, or as in-class exercises. *Skill Practice* activities are short drills where students can practice forming messages using the communication skills presented in the chapter. These may be assigned as written activities or used as part of in-class activity. A *Communication Improvement Plan* helps students identify an area of their communication practice that they would like to improve and to design a program for meeting their objective. Students can download a form for making Communication Improvement Plans from the companion website. Instructors can create graded assignments based on these.

Supplementary Materials

As a reader of this text, you also have access to supplementary materials for both students and instructors.

Student Materials

- The companion website, www.oup.com/us/verderber, offers a wealth of resources for both students and instructors, study aids such as: practice quizzes, key term flashcards, discussion questions, journal prompts, review questions, communication improvement plans, and media examples, , links to a variety of communication-related websites, and a link to the latest *Now Playing*.
- *Now Playing: Learning Communication through Film*, available as an optional printed product, looks at more than 60 contemporary and classic feature films and television shows through the lens of communication principles. *Now Playing* illustrates a variety of both individual scenes and full-length films, highlighting concepts and offering discussion questions for a mass medium that is interactive, familiar, and easily accessible.

Instructor Materials

- **Ancillary Resource Center (ARC)** at www.oup-arc.com This convenient, instructor-focused website provides access to all of the up-to-date teaching resources for this text—at any time—while guaranteeing the security of grade-significant resources. In addition, it allows OUP to keep instructors informed when new content becomes available. The following items are available on the ARC:
  - The *Instructor's Manual* and *Test Bank* provide teaching tips, exercises, and approximately 400 exam questions in multiple-choice, true/false, and essay formats that will prove useful to both new and veteran instructors. The *Instructor's Manual* includes pedagogical suggestions, sample syllabi, content outlines, discussion questions, chapter activities, simulations, and journal assignments. A computerized test bank is also available.
  - Newly revised PowerPoint®-based lecture slides.
  - The Instructor's Companion Website at www.oup.com/us/verderber is a password-protected site featuring the *Instructor's Manual*, PowerPoint®-based lecture slides, and links to supplemental materials and films.
  - *Now Playing: Instructor's Edition*, an instructor-only print supplement, includes an introduction on how to incorporate film

and TV examples in class, more sample responses to the numerous discussion questions in the student edition of *Now Playing*, viewing guides, additional films, and references.

- Course cartridges for a variety of e-learning environments allow instructors to create their own course websites with the interactive material from the instructor and student companion websites. Contact your Oxford University Press representative for access.

Acknowledgements—Kathleen Verderber

First, I want to formally welcome Professor Erina MacGeorge of Pennsylvania State University to the author team. I have admired her scholarship for a long time and was delighted to have her help on the thirteenth edition. Her contribution to this, the fourteenth edition, has been substantial. Professor MacGeorge was responsible for developing the first draft of each chapter, and I think that her extensive knowledge of the field as well as her conversational writing style have produced a revision that is not only up to date, but also fun to read. Second, I would like to thank Doug Pruim of Purdue University, who worked with us to revise the Social Media Factor content. His knowledge of the growing literature in this area was most helpful. Finally, I would like to thank Christine Sheldon Fischer, retired regional vice president of Human Resources at Macy's, Inc., for updating and revising the material on job search strategies, which is available on our website.

During the revision, we worked with a dedicated team of professionals at Oxford University Press. I want to thank Thom Holmes, Development Manager, who helped us plan this revision, and Maegan Sherlock, who worked tirelessly as our Development Editor. While we were preparing this edition, Toni Magyar became the Communication and Journalism editor. Her work in launching this edition has been invaluable. Editorial assistants Paul Longo and Marie La Vina were instrumental in making the photo program a success and in obtaining permissions. I am also grateful for the fine job of the production group: our production manager, Lisa Grzan; project manager, Micheline Frederick; Christian Holdener, project manager at S4Carlisle Publishing Service; art director, Michele Laseau; and copyeditor Gail Cooper.

In addition, I'd like to thank others who helped in preparing the learning materials that accompany this edition, including Carlton Hughes and Beth Norton. We are also grateful to the following colleagues across the discipline who provided us with useful suggestions about how to improve this edition:

Shae Adkins, *Lone Star College – North Harris*
Shea Brooks, *Park University*
Anita P. Chirco, *Keuka College*
Erica Cooper, *Roanoke College*
Kelly Crue, *St. Cloud Technical and Community College*
Jean DeWitt, *University of Houston-Downtown*
Reginald Ecarma, *North Greenville University*
Meredith Frank, *La Salle University*

Lowell Habel, *Chapman University*

Daniel Hebert, *Springfield Technical Community College*

Jenny Hodges, *St. John's University*

Carlton W. Hughes, *Southeast Kentucky Community and Technical College*

Joy Jones, *Atlantic Cape Community College*

Melanie A. Lea, *Bossier Parish Community College*

Susan K. Minton, *Lindsey Wilson College*

Dante E. Morelli, *Suffolk County Community College*

Mark T. Morman, *Baylor University*

Beth Norton, *Madisonville Community College*

Marguerite Benjamin Parker, *Pitt Community College*

David Raskin, *Community College of Philadelphia*

Julie Simanski, *Des Moines Area Community College*

Lynn Stewart, *Cochise College*

Pamela Stovall, *University of New Mexico Gallup*

Matthew Taylor, *Lone Star College – Fairbanks Center*

Lindsay Timmerman, *University of Wisconsin-Milwaukee*

Judith Vogel, *Des Moines Area Community College*

Emanuelle Wessels, *Missouri State University*

Carleen Yokotake, *University of Hawaii/Leeward Community College*

Ibrahim Yoldash, *Indiana University Northwest*

Finally, on a personal note, I would like to thank my family and friends, who have always supported me in this work. I especially want to thank my daughter, Allison Verderber Herriott, whose love and encouragement has sustained me through various trials during these past few years; my mother and father whose 73 years of marriage continue to inspire me; and my husband, Rudy, who although no longer able to communicate, has left his wisdom and guidance etched in my memory.

—Kathleen S. Verderber

Acknowledgements—Erina MacGeorge

I am deeply grateful for Kathie's invitation to contribute to a textbook that has influenced so many students across the years, and like her, I appreciate Doug Pruim and all of the Oxford team members who helped make this work shine. My perspective on interpersonal interaction has been profoundly shaped by notable scholars and teachers, including Marcia Stratton (University of Alaska, Anchorage), Robert Arundale (emeritus, University of Alaska, Fairbanks), Daena Goldsmith (Lewis and Clark College), and Ruth Anne Clark (emerita, University of Illinois). I also want to thank my Interpersonal Communication students throughout my career, with a special acknowledgement to my classes in 2013–2014 whose comments on the prior edition informed revisions. I am thankful every day for interactions with my life partner, Jerry, and children, Jesalyn and Carson. They fill my life with purpose and joy.

—Erina MacGeorge

inter act

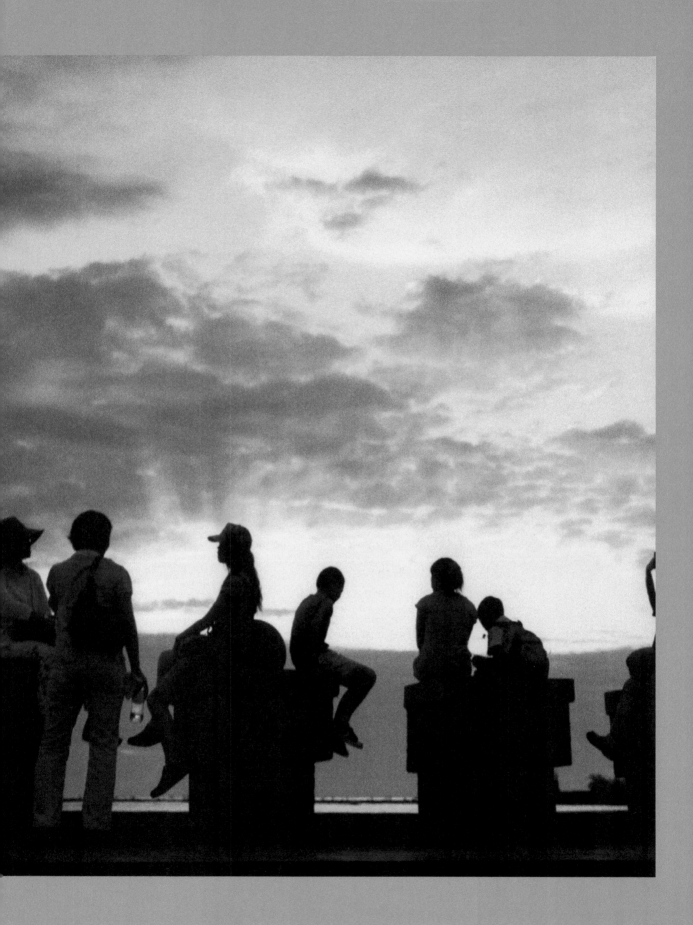

1

AN ORIENTATION TO INTERPERSONAL COMMUNICATION

Casey and Katherine are good friends who live together. Casey has been searching unsuccessfully in her closet for her favorite sweater. Just as she has given up hope of finding it, she sees Katherine walking past her room and then remembers . . .

Casey: Hey, Kath . . . didn't you take my sweater the other day?

Katherine: Um . . . no. I never wore it.

Casey: (in an exasperated tone) It's fine if you wore it. I just want to wear it today.

Katherine: But I didn't wear it! You must have left it somewhere . . . like you ALWAYS do.

Casey: No, you asked to borrow it! Fine . . . if you can't find it, can I borrow one of YOUR sweaters?

Katherine: (in a fake bored tone, with a smirk on her face): Sorry. You know I don't lend my clothes out . . . I might not get them back.

Casey: Seriously? Katherine, I know you took my sweater. Why are you lying to me?

Katherine: Excuse me? You're crazy. I don't even know what you're talking about!

Casey: (turns her back to Katherine) Whatever. Until you give me my sweater back, stay out of my room.

WHAT YOU SHOULD BE ABLE TO EXPLAIN AFTER YOU HAVE STUDIED THIS CHAPTER:

▶ The definition of interpersonal communication

▶ How messages are produced, interpreted, and coordinated

▶ The contexts for interpersonal communication

▶ The purposes of interpersonal communication

▶ The characteristics of interpersonal communication

▶ "Dark-side" messages

▶ Interpersonal communication competence and what it requires

▶ The five traits of social media

WHAT YOU SHOULD BE ABLE TO DO AFTER YOU HAVE STUDIED THIS CHAPTER:

▶ Write a Communication Improvement Plan (CIP)

Interpersonal communication—is the complex process through which people produce, interpret, and coordinate messages to create shared meanings, achieve social goals, manage their personal identities, and carry out their relationships

Communication theories—systematic and research-based explanations of how communication works

Communication skills—combinations of goals, plans, and scripts that are effective and appropriate for specific messages, interactions, and relationships

n the space of a brief conversation, not only have Casey and Katherine damaged their friendship, but Casey still doesn't have her sweater. Why do these kinds of interactions happen, and how can they be improved?

The purpose of this textbook, and your **interpersonal communication** class, is to help you become a more effective interpersonal communicator, by introducing you to well-established **communication theories**—systematic and research-based explanations of how communication works, and by developing your **communication skills**—goals, plans, and sequences of behavior that are effective and appropriate for particular contexts. You will find that some of the theories you will study will confirm personal theories that you have developed based on your experiences, but many will provide a more accurate understanding of what happens when people talk and why. Practicing a variety of communication skills in a safe classroom setting before trying them out in your "real" relationships can help you become a more effective interpersonal communicator. Let's get started by exploring the definition of "interpersonal communication."

INTERPERSONAL COMMUNICATION is the complex process through which people produce, interpret, and coordinate messages to create shared meanings, achieve social goals, manage their personal identities, and carry out their relationships.

We often take interpersonal communication for granted, but there's a lot going on. In this first chapter, we begin by looking at a model of interpersonal communication in order to help understand how this complex process works. We will then discuss the unique characteristics of interpersonal communication, the ethical standards that we expect in our own and others' interpersonal communication, and the ways that we can fall short of these standards. Next, we will describe what it means to be competent in interpersonal communication, the types of skills that can help you become more competent, and the steps necessary for learning new interpersonal communication skills. Finally, a significant amount of our interpersonal communication today is mediated. To end this chapter, we discuss the traits of social media that distinguish one type of communication from another and from face-to-face interactions. Throughout the text, there will be detailed discussions of how social media affects our interpersonal communication and relationships.

How does the social context of this photo explain the reactions of each person? How might a different context result in different reactions?

A Model of Interpersonal Communication

A model of interpersonal communication includes messages, their senders, and their receivers; the message production process used by senders; and the message interpretation process used by receivers. It also includes the interaction-coordination process they use during their conversation, and the communication context in which they exchange messages.

Messages

At the center of interpersonal communication is the exchange of messages. A **message** is a performance that uses words and/or nonverbal behaviors to convey the thoughts, feelings, and intentions of the speaker. In interpersonal communication, we typically alternate between sending messages and interpreting the messages we receive from others. Through **encoding** we create messages that convey our meanings and goals by selecting words and behaviors that we believe represent our ideas and feelings. The **message production process** encompasses both mental and behavioral steps that we use to form messages during encoding. Similarly, through **decoding**, we interpret both words and nonverbal behaviors in order to make sense of the messages we receive from others. Decoding is accomplished through the **message interpretation process**. When we talk with others, not only do we produce and interpret messages, we also have to adjust our messages to accommodate the messages of the person we are talking to, otherwise known as the **message coordination process.** Finally, the way senders and receivers produce, interpret, and coordinate interaction is influenced by the **communication context**, or background conditions surrounding the interaction.

Let's look at a simple message exchange as an example of what happens when two people interact. Suppose a toddler wants her bottle, which is sitting on a table next to her father. She may encode her desire by pointing to the bottle while crying out, "Da-da, ba-ba!" This message, comprising a nonverbal gesture and sounds, expresses what she wants. How the father responds to this message depends in part on how he decodes it—how he interprets the performance he has observed. He might hand her the bottle, smile, and say, "Here you go, little girl: Da-da and ba-ba are right here," or he may give her a puzzled look while raising his hands and shoulders, indicating that he doesn't understand what she wants.

Message—a performance that uses words, sentences, and/or nonverbal behaviors to convey the thoughts, feelings, and intentions of the speaker

Encoding—creating messages that convey our meanings and goals by selecting words and behaviors that we believe represent our ideas and feelings

Message production process—what we think and do to encode a message

Decoding—making sense of the messages we receive

Message interpretation process—what we think and do to decode a message

Message coordination process—adjusting messages to accommodate the messages of the person we are talking to

Communication context—the set of background conditions surrounding the interaction

His response, too, will be a message. Additionally, the father will coordinate his reply by purposefully directing his expression to his toddler, just as she coordinated her message by using her name for her father so that he would understand her message was meant for him. The messages that are produced, interpreted, and coordinated will be influenced by the context as well. If the father understands what his daughter means, how he responds is likely to depend in part on contextual factors, like how long it has been since she had her last bottle. Interpersonal communication is complicated because we produce and interpret messages while simultaneously adjusting and coordinating our messages with those of our partner, who is also juggling these processes, all within the specific context of the conversation (Burleson, 2010).

Now, let's look more closely at how the message production, message interpretation, and message coordination processes work, and then we will describe how contextual factors influence these processes.

Message Production

You've probably heard the term "producer" used to refer to people who generate the messages we receive through television, movies, and music. But you are also a producer—of messages during interpersonal communication. Message production is the process of encoding a message for the person you are talking with. While you may appreciate the complexity of producing a movie, have you ever thought about the complex process you manage as you produce a message in a conversation? Like movie production, in message production we have goals, plans, and actions that determine the messages we produce.

As Charles Berger (2002), a leading communication scholar, observes: "Social interaction is a goal-directed activity." Communication is motivated by **interaction goals**, the things we want to accomplish during a conversation. Your goals may or may not be complex or important, and you may not be fully aware of them, especially when they are routine. For example, Marko usually arrives home after his wife and children, and almost always asks his wife "How'd it go today, hon?" He might not be consciously aware that he has the goal of learning what has happened in his family's life that day, but if asked to explain his question, he would probably say something like, "I wanted to know what happened at my wife's work and how my sons did at school." Different goals result in different communication behaviors. Suppose one night Marko arrives home anxious to get everyone in the car so that they are not late for his son's Little League game. He may holler, "I'm home! Let's go!" and save the usual "How'd it go today?" for the drive. Our goals can, and often do, change quickly during conversation. If his wife replies, "The game is postponed to 6:30," Marko can relax, realizing that he doesn't have to get the family on the road as quickly, and may then encode a message that conveys his usual goal of catching up.

The **Goals-Plans-Action theory** of message production (Dillard, 2015) proposes that goals motivate us to communicate, but planning determines what we actually say. **Message planning** is identifying one or more strategies you can use that will accomplish the goal of your message. Some planning is done prior

---

Interaction goals—the things a message sender wants to accomplish through communication

Goals-Plans-Action theory—a theory of message production that posits that goals motivate us to communicate, but planning determines what we actually say

Message planning—identifying one or more message strategies you can use that will accomplish your interaction goals

to interaction. For example, you might spend time thinking through what you will say in a job interview if asked, "What is your greatest weakness?" Or you might plan how you are going to break the news to your mom that you are going to spend Thanksgiving with your dad and his wife. This kind of planning can be quite elaborate and may include contingencies or "if–then" plans, such as, "If I'm asked why I don't list my prior employer as a reference, I'll explain that I listed people who are more familiar with my skills relevant to this job." Or, "If Mom starts to cry, I'll give her a hug and promise to spend winter break with her." When the outcome of an interaction is important to you, this kind of pre-interaction planning can be very helpful.

However, we can't plan extensively for every encounter. In fact, most of our planning is far more spur-of-the-moment: it occurs just prior to and during interaction. How are we able to set goals, plan, listen, and speak more or less simultaneously? We get a lot of help by accessing our "canned" plans, stored in memory. A **canned plan** is a learned communication strategy for a specific type of situation. Canned plans come from reflecting on what repeatedly has worked for us or others in similar situations in the past, or by imagining and rehearsing what might work well in these types of situations (Berger, 1997). We remember these strategies and use them to guide our message production in future interactions where they appear to fit. We all have canned plans for the situations that we regularly encounter, such as making small talk, ordering food at a restaurant, or picking someone up in a bar. Beyond that, the kinds of canned plans you have and how detailed they are depend on the types of goals and situations you routinely encounter. For example, most of us have a canned plan for trying to persuade someone to do something. But if you are a salesperson, you probably have more elaborate canned plans for particular products, or for persuading specific kinds of customers—for example, for moms with kids, focus on moderate cost, parental controls, and ease of setup; for obviously wealthy customers, focus on brand prestige, new and unique features, and aesthetics.

Canned plans include **scripts**, which are sequences of communication behaviors or specific messages that are designed to carry out a plan. When you see a friend that you haven't seen in a while, do you have to stop and think about what to say? Probably not. You might say "Hey there!" or "What's up?" but whatever you says just pops out, because it is the start of one of your greeting scripts from your canned plan of how to acknowledge a friend. Many of our canned plans and scripts are acquired during childhood. For example, can you remember your mother admonishing you to "Wave, smile, and say 'Hi!'" as she modeled this behavior? As we grow, we add to and embellish these scripts. So, for example, as we learn to differentiate between different types of relationships, we expand our repertoire of greeting scripts. The variety of scripts you have stored in your memory will depend on the situations you most frequently encounter and your goals in those situations. Parents, teachers, and caregivers develop a repertoire of phrases for redirecting errant behavior in children ("Jackson, please stop. Let's do this instead"), and for rewarding good behavior ("Good job,

Canned plan—a learned communication strategy for a specific type of situation

Script—a sequence of communication behaviors or messages designed to carry out a plan

Jackson, what a big boy!"). People who work in a call center dealing with customer complaints are usually trained to say something like "How may I assist you today?" and once the customer has explained their complaint, respond, "I understand your concern. Let me see how I can help."

The point is that when we need to form a message, we don't usually have to start from scratch. Instead, knowing what we want to accomplish, we access the canned plans and associated scripts that are relevant to the goal and put them to work, customizing as we go in order to fit the unique context and other aspects of the current situation. For instance, you probably have a well-honed script you use to ask for a favor from a friend. But in a particular situation you will add that person's name, the specific favor requested, and anything you might be offering in return for the favor. All this mental activity typically happens automatically, in nanoseconds, so we are usually unaware of all the mental work going on that enables us to produce our messages. But think about it: How often is what you say similar to something you have said or heard said in a similar past situation?

At times, we need to produce messages for seemingly unfamiliar situations for which we don't have appropriate canned plans. In these cases, we search our mental library for canned plans that have similar goals and situations to the one we are currently facing, and modify them as best we can. For example, if, Jana's mother dies suddenly, and her friend Elyse has never comforted someone grieving the loss of a parent, Elyse may not have a plan for this type of situation. She will probably draw on her canned plans for comforting in other situations, like comforting someone who has lost a job. Elyse's success at comforting Jana will depend on the effectiveness of those plans and how well she succeeds at adapting them to the current goal and situation. For example, Elyse's comforting plan for a job loss may include a strategy of being optimistic ("Things will look up for you, I know they will"), but because this strategy is inappropriate for a recently bereaved person, she will need to adapt what she actually says.

The success of your communication depends on how well you are able to implement your goals, using plans and scripts. But frequently we need to meet several goals in the same conversation. For example, if you are interviewing to be a manager, you need to present yourself as cooperative and friendly, while at the same time conveying that you are someone who can take charge and make decisions. During the interview, there will be times when your messages convey that you are easy to get along with, while other messages will demonstrate your decision-making abilities. Sometimes you must choose between two mutually exclusive goals, and that choice can determine how effective you are. For example, in a conflict situation, your goal might be to compromise, or it might be to have your own way. We communicate better in challenging situations if we have done advanced planning and when we have more canned plans and scripts from which to choose. As you progress through this textbook, you will have the opportunity to reflect on your interaction goals and to develop more effective canned plans and scripts for common and important types of interpersonal communication situations.

Message Interpretation

During an interaction, you not only produce messages, you also consume them. **Message interpretation** is the process of understanding a message you have received. The process begins when you become aware that someone is trying to communicate with you. You observe the nonverbal behavior and listen to the words. Your inferences about the sender's message are influenced by how you perceive yourself and the sender, the goals and plans that you have for the interaction, and those you believe the sender to have. Then, based on your interpretation of the message, you prepare to respond, returning to the process of message production.

Like message production, much of message interpretation happens quickly and automatically, and we are often unaware of all the mental work we are doing unless we encounter behavior that is difficult to interpret. This is a good thing, because it would be hard to get anything accomplished if we had to stop and think carefully about every message we receive. However, there are times when it is valuable to slow down the process and give messages (and their senders) more thoughtful consideration. Your study of interpersonal communication will help you understand more about message interpretation, including developing your listening skills so that you are more likely to interpret others' messages as they are intended.

Interaction Coordination

A third process during interpersonal communication is **interaction coordination**, which is the activity that participants in a conversation perform to adjust their behaviors to that of the other party. We can think of interaction coordination as a dance where people's moves anticipate and respond to their partner's (Burgoon, 1998). While talking with someone, you anticipate how he or she is likely to act and respond. Additionally, each message you receive from the other person provides **feedback**, actual information about how your message was received. Your messages also provide feedback for your conversational partner; therefore, both of you adjust how you act and what you say depending on how your partner's actual messages and behavior match your expectations. For example, if your partner's messages are more positive than you expected, you may adjust your behavior by mirroring that positive behavior. Alternatively, if your partner's message or behavior is more negative than you expected, then you may also behave in a more positive way, hoping that your positive behavior will encourage your partner to reciprocate. Usually we try to adjust our behaviors so that our partner's behaviors more closely match what we would like them to be. At times you will adjust your behavior to match or mirror your partner's to show similarity or unity. At other times you may act or say things in a way that signals your individuality or distinctiveness from your partner. And your partner will make similar adjustments.

Let's look at an example of interaction coordination. Suppose that you go to see your instructor to discuss a paper on which you received a lower grade than you thought the paper deserved. Suppose you begin with a very assertive

Message interpretation—the process of understanding a message you have received

Interaction coordination—the activities participants in a conversation perform to adjust their behaviors to those of their partners

Feedback—information about how a message was interpreted by its recipient, conveyed in a subsequent message

How does it feel when you know that someone is really understanding what you are saying?

statement, such as, "I didn't deserve a 'C–' on this paper." Your instructor may then respond, "Well, I could have made a mistake. Let's talk about what you thought I missed." His openness to your point of view could be more positive than what you expected, which would lead you to adjust what you were saying to accommodate or match his tone. On the other hand, suppose your instructor mirrors your assertiveness with a more negative response than you expected, replying, "Well, you're not the one giving the grade, are you?" You may try to encourage a more cooperative stance by becoming less assertive and more accommodating, responding, "I'm sorry. I didn't mean to question your authority, but I don't understand what I did wrong." In so doing, you are attempting to coordinate the interaction by inviting your instructor to match your conciliatory message with one of his own.

Communication Context

Communication context—the set of background conditions surrounding an interaction, including the physical, social, historical, psychological, and cultural contexts

Physical context—the setting of a communication episode

Message production, message reception, and interaction coordination all take place in a **communication context**, which is the set of background conditions surrounding an interaction. The context includes physical, social, historical, psychological, and cultural factors that influence understanding in a communication encounter. The context may also include noise, which is stimuli that interfere with one or more of the three processes.

The **physical context** or setting of a communication episode is the place where you exchange messages. In many communication situations, you are talking with someone who is located in the same physical space. In these cases, the environmental conditions (e.g., temperature, lighting, noise level) and the physical space between you can affect the success of communication. For example, people sitting in a hot, noisy waiting room may have trouble focusing on each other. Increasingly, however, interpersonal exchanges do not occur face-to-face but are mediated by technology. And while mediated communication enables us to interact at a distance, the media we use may affect our ability to share meaning. Especially in those mediated contexts where nonverbal cues are limited or missing, message production, message interpretation, and interaction coordination can be tricky and lead to miscommunications that can create misunderstanding and damage relationships.

Social context—the type and closeness of the relationship that may already exist between the participants

The **social context** is the type and closeness of the relationship that may already exist between you and the person you are talking to. Most of us talk differently when we are speaking to our friends than we do when we are talking with our grandparents, professors, and managers. For example, when Trent talks with his friends, he often uses profanity. But when he visits his grandmother, interviews for a job, or speaks with his rabbi, he watches what he says and refrains from using inappropriate language. In addition, the social context also affects how accurately we interpret the messages we receive. Generally, we do a better job of understanding those with whom we have more in common. The **historical context** is the background provided by previous communication episodes

Historical context—the background provided by previous communication episodes between the participants

between you and the person you are talking to. For instance, suppose one morning Eduardo tells Anna that this afternoon he will pick up the draft of the report they had left for their manager to read. At 4:00 p.m., when Anna returns to the office, she sees Eduardo and simply asks, "Did you get it?" Someone eavesdropping would have no idea what the "it" is to which Anna is referring. Yet Eduardo has no problem understanding what Anna is talking about, and replies, "It's on my desk." Anna and Eduardo understand each other because of their shared history, the earlier exchange.

The **psychological context** includes the moods and feelings each person brings to the interpersonal encounter. For instance, suppose Corinne is under a great deal of stress during exam week. While she is studying, her friend Julia stops by and pleads with her to take a break and go to the gym with her. Corinne, normally good-natured, may snap at Julia in an irritated tone of voice, which Julia may incorrectly interpret to mean that Corinne is mad at her.

The **cultural context** is the set of beliefs, values, and attitudes common to the specific culture of each participant that influences how each produces and interprets messages, as well as how each tries to coordinate the interaction. We use our cultural expectations and behavior patterns when we talk with others. When two people from different cultures interact, misunderstandings may occur, because cultures differ in expectations and preferred communication behaviors. For example, while looking someone directly in the eye is a sign of respect in some cultures, in others, direct eye contact is considered rude. Everyone is a member of one or more cultural groups (e.g., racial, ethnic, and religious cultures; or cultures defined by other characteristics, such as region or country of birth, gender, sexual orientation, physical ability, etc.). We may differ in how much we identify with our cultures, but culture permeates every aspect of our lives, including our interpersonal communication.

Lastly, **noise**—any stimulus that interferes with sharing meaning—is also part of the context when we talk with others. Noise can be external, internal, or semantic. First, **external noise** is the physical sights, sounds, and other stimuli that draw your attention away from creating or interpreting a message. For instance, a pop-up advertisement may limit your ability to read a webpage or blog. Static or service interruptions can wreak havoc on cell phone conversations. The sound of a fire engine may distract you from a professor's lecture, or the smell of doughnuts may disrupt your train of thought during a conversation with a friend. Second, **internal noises** are mental thoughts and feelings that interfere with producing or interpreting messages. Have you ever stopped talking mid-message because you suddenly remembered something important that you have forgotten to do? When this happens, you become distracted by internal noise and are unable to finish your sentence. If you have a distracting emotional reaction to what someone is saying, you are also experiencing internal noise. Third, **semantic noise** is words in a message that interfere with or distort the meaning of a message for the receiver. Suppose that a doctor is advising a patient to have a screening CAT scan. If the physician says, "We need to rule out cancer, even though it's unlikely that your tumor is malignant," the patient may become

INTER-ACT WITH
SOCIAL MEDIA

Think for a moment about the different types of social media that you use on a daily basis—Facebook, Twitter, Instagram, Snapchat, YouTube, texting, talking on your cell phone, accessing the internet through your smartphone, listening to podcasts, etc. How do you use each form of social media to maintain your interpersonal relationships? Do you tend to favor one form of social media over another? What types of social media could you live without for 24 hours? Why is this the case?

Psychological context—the moods and feelings each person brings to an interpersonal encounter

Cultural context—the set of beliefs, values, and attitudes common to the specific cultures of each participant that influence how each interprets what is happening in a conversation

Noise—any stimulus that interferes with shared meaning

External noise—physical sights, sounds, and other stimuli that draw people's attention away from intended meaning

Internal noise—thoughts and feelings that interfere with producing or interpreting meaning

Semantic noise—words in a message that distort or interfere with the interpretation of the meaning of a message

frightened by the word "cancer" and miss the doctor's professional opinion that this diagnosis is unlikely. Racist and sexist language, profanity, and slang, are also powerful sources of semantic noise.

Figure 1.1 visually illustrates our model of interpersonal communication. The process begins when one person, whom we will call Andy, has an interaction goal he wants to achieve with Taylor, a girl he knows . Andy may want to persuade Taylor to go to a concert with him on Saturday. Andy reviews the situation, including the communication context, and selects from memory the canned plan that best fits his goal. Based on his prior experiences with asking for dates, Andy's plan may include things like, "Seem interested but casual," "Emphasize the fun we'll have," and "If Taylor says no, leave the door open for another time." The script he employs may go something like this: (1) Ask if the girl has plans for the date/time of proposed activity; (2a) If not, describe the proposed activity in positive terms; OR (2b) If she does, alter the date/time and try again; (3a) If she accepts, make arrangements for meeting; OR (3b) if she declines, express interest in the possibility of a future activity. Based on this script, he produces a customized message that includes appropriate words and nonverbal behaviors (e.g., friendly smile and eye contact): "Hey Taylor, do you have plans this weekend? A Grateful Dead cover band is playing at The Lounge on Saturday night. I know you like the Dead and wondered if you'd like to go with me to see them?" This message could be obscured by physical noise, but if Taylor hears the message, she will interpret it using her perceptions of the situation, herself, and Andy, including matching his message to plans and scripts

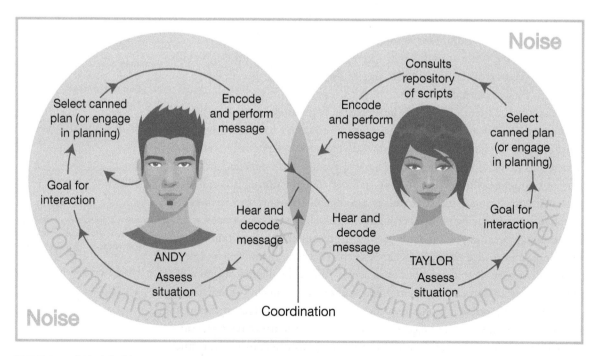

FIGURE 1.1 A Model of Communication between Two Individuals

of her own. Andy's intended meaning may be distorted during Taylor's decoding because of internal or semantic noise. It could also be distorted if Taylor's "asking for a date" canned plan is different from Andy's. Based on Taylor's interpretation of Andy's message, she will produce her own message, which Andy will interpret, and so forth.

The Purposes of Interpersonal Communication

To this point, we've focused on the first half of our definition of interpersonal communication. Now we turn our attention to the second half of our definition: why we engage in message production, interpretation, and coordination. You will recall that we exchange messages for four purposes: (1) sharing meaning, (2) meeting social goals, (3) managing our personal identities, and (4) conducting our relationships. Let's take a look at each of these.

We Share Meaning

Meaning is the significance that the sender and the receiver each attach to a message. **Shared meaning** occurs when the receiver's interpretation of the message is similar to what the speaker thought, felt, and intended. We can usually gauge the extent to which meaning has been shared by the sender's response to the feedback message. In other words, both people in the exchange determine shared meaning. For example, Sarah says to Nick, "I dropped my phone, and it broke." Nick replies, "Cool; now you can get the latest iPhone™." Sarah responds, "No, you don't understand. I can't afford to buy a new phone." It is Sarah's response to Nick's feedback message that lets Nick know that he understood what happened in the literal sense (she dropped and broke her phone), but did not share her meaning, her interpretation of the event, which for her is a problem that will be difficult to solve. The extent to which we are able to share meaning is affected by the communication context and noise.

> **Meaning**—the significance that the sender (speaker) and the receiver (listener) each attach to a message
>
> **Shared meaning**—when the receiver's interpretation of the message is similar to what the speaker thought, felt, and intended

We Meet Goals

Earlier, we discussed *how* our goals connect to our message planning. But we need to emphasize that a key purpose of interpersonal communication is to achieve specific primary goals, which may entail pursuing secondary goals as well. Any time we talk with someone, we have a **primary goal**—a need, want, or other desire motivating us to communicate that directs us to a canned plan (Dillard, 2015). Examples of primary goals include getting information about another person or something that they know, influencing another person to do something or think a certain way, and helping another person feel better. Primary goals can be general (have a pleasant conversation) or specific (get my friend to leave a bad relationship). At times we pursue several primary goals in the same interaction, or even simultaneously. Our primary goals direct us to the canned plans we have for attaining these goals.

> **Primary goals**—needs, wants, or other desires motivating a person to communicate that direct the person to a specific canned plan

Secondary goals—motivations that affect the specific script chosen to accomplish a primary goal

In addition to primary goals, we typically have **secondary goals**—additional motivations that affect the specific scripts we choose to use to accomplish our primary goals. For example, in a disagreement with her best friend Irene, Sofia's primary goal may be to convince Irene that she is wrong and Sofia is right. In her canned plan for convincing others she has several scripts, including scripts that insult, threaten, beg, reason with, and flatter the other person. If Sofia values her friendship with Irene, she will choose a script that is less likely to damage the relationship while still stating Sofia's point of view. It is a mistake to evaluate the success of an interpersonal communication encounter based solely on whether we have achieved our primary goals. If Sofia and Irene meet to discuss their disagreement, Sofia may not be able to change Irene's point of view, and so may fail to achieve her primary goal. Yet, if Irene had the goal of resisting Sofia's influence, she may rate the interaction a success. However, both of them are likely to think the interaction was somewhat successful if they managed the interaction so that their relationship remains intact.

We Manage Our Personal Identities

Personal identity—the traits and characteristics that, taken as a whole, distinguish you from other people

Relationship—a set of expectations that two people have for their behavior with respect to each other, based on the pattern of interaction between them

Your **personal identity** is made up of the traits and characteristics that, taken as a whole, distinguish you from other people. Personal identity has at least three facets: (1) Who you think you are; (2) who you want others to think you are; and (3) who you think others believe you are.

We learn who we are and how to be who we are through our interactions with others. Parents begin this when they interact with their infants, and the process continues throughout childhood and adulthood. As a child, you may have had a teacher who told you that you were smart. If you thought "smart" was a good thing to be, you incorporated "smart" into who you thought you were. Because of this, you may have behaved in ways that demonstrated you were smart so that other teachers would also believe this of you. You may even know that you are smart and love learning. But if your peers make fun of people who are smart, you may limit your vocabulary and what you say when you are with them so that they don't realize how smart you are and tease you.

Given that we are social animals, when we communicate, we usually try to manage our personal identity to encourage others to think of us in favorable terms and as we would like them to. Sometimes your messages reflect who you know yourself to be. At other times, how you want to be seen by your conversational partner is not who you are. So you consciously choose goals, plans, and scripts that portray yourself to be someone other than you are to gain the favor or avoid the ridicule of your conversational partner.

▶ **OBSERVE AND ANALYZE**

Managing Your Personal Identity

Recall a time when you were with someone you knew really well who chose to present himself or herself as someone who you knew the person was not. Describe the circumstances. What do you suppose was this person's motivation? Did it work? Did you ever confront this person about how he or she acted? If so, what happened? Did this incident alter how you viewed this person? If so, how?

We Conduct Our Relationships

Through interpersonal communication, we create and manage our relationships. Renowned relationship theorists have described a **relationship** as two individuals' sharing a degree of behavioral interdependence, which means that each person's behavior somehow affects the other's behavior (Berscheid & Peplau, 1983). Our interpersonal communication defines the nature of the current relationship between us, as well as what that relationship will become. As we communicate, we "do" our relationships. Is the relationship more personal or impersonal, closer or more distant, romantic or platonic, healthy or unhealthy, dependent or interdependent? The answers to these questions depend on how the people in the relationship talk to and behave toward each other. Think about this for a minute. You call someone your friend, romantic partner, or enemy because of the interactions you have had with that person. Some people have close relationships with their parents, while other people are estranged from theirs. Some people have sexual relationships that are close and loving, while other sexual relationships (like hook-ups) are emotionally distant, fraught with quarrels, verbal aggression, and even physical abuse. In each of these cases, the partners come to expect certain behaviors from the other based on the previous interactions that they have had.

Interpersonal communication helps us initiate, develop, maintain, repair, and end our relationships. When Mateo drops down into the chair in class, noticing an attractive woman sitting next to him, he will have to say or do something to begin a relationship. After class he may ask her if she wants to get a cup of coffee at Starbucks. If they find that they enjoy some of the same things and the conversation they have when they are together, they may become friends. If they continue to enjoy each other's company, they may become a couple. When they have their first fight, or when Mateo becomes jealous of the time she is spending with another man, they will repair their relationship by talking. And if one of them eventually wants to end the relationship, this will be done through communication as well.

Characteristics of Interpersonal Communication

Now that we have explored the definition of interpersonal communication, let's look at five characteristics of interpersonal communication.

Interpersonal Communication Is Transactional

In a business or consumer transaction, each person involved in the transaction gives and gets something. This is also true in an interpersonal communication episode where we give and receive messages, give and receive feedback, get our goals met, help others fulfill their goals, and give and receive information. It is impossible for only one of the parties to gain something from an interpersonal communication episode. Both parties get something, even if there are differences in what each person receives. For instance, even in a seemingly one-sided communication in which Greg's landlord angrily tells him that he must pay his rent on time or face eviction, and Greg merely responds, "Yes, I promise," Greg and his landlord both gain from the transaction. Greg and his landlord both receive messages and feedback, both give and receive information, and both fulfill goals. Greg's landlord may appear to be the only one in the exchange to fulfill his goal (i.e., getting Greg to pay rent on time), but Greg also fulfills a relationship goal (reacting positively and assuaging the situation).

The Colbert Report ✔
@ColbertReport

I am willing to show #Asian community I care by introducing the Ching-Chong Ding-Dong Foundation for Sensitivity to Orientals or Whatever.

What are the consequences of controversial tweets? Have you ever tweeted something you now regret?

Interpersonal Communication Is Irreversible

Once an interpersonal exchange has taken place, we can never ignore it, take it back, or pretend it did not occur. In other words, although we can wish we hadn't said something, we can never go back in time and reverse the communication. We might be able to repair any damage we have done, but the message has been communicated. When you participate in an online discussion or leave a post on a blog, you are leaving an electronic "footprint" that others can follow and read. Emails, instant messages (IMs), and text messages are not private, either. Once you click the "send" button, you lose control of that message. Not only can you not take it back, you can no longer direct where it goes.

Interpersonal Communication Is Situated

When we say that interpersonal communication is situated, we mean that it occurs within a specific communication setting that affects how the messages are produced, interpreted, and coordinated. Interpersonal communication doesn't occur in the abstract, but always in a specific, concrete situation (Burleson, 2010). For example, the interpretation of the statement "I love you" varies with the setting. If made during a candlelit dinner shared by a couple who have been dating each other since they were freshmen in college, it may be interpreted as a statement of romantic feelings and a deeper commitment to each other. If made by a mother as she greets her daughter who has come home for Thanksgiving, it can be interpreted as a confirmation of motherly love and approval. If made in response to a joke at a gathering of friends who are watching a football game, it will probably be interpreted as a compliment for being clever. Clearly, what is said and what that means depend on the situation.

Interpersonal Communication Reveals Relationship Qualities

Have you ever eavesdropped on a conversation between a couple you didn't know and concluded that they had a good relationship—or a bad one? You were able to discern this because interpersonal

When Pope Francis talks with a group of children his message to them is situated in the context of his role as pontiff and in the specific occasion.

communication reveals qualities about the relationship between the people interacting, at least at that particular time. According to Relational Framing Theory (McLaren & Solomon, 2015), two primary qualities of relationships that are observable in interaction are dominance and affiliation.

Dominance is the degree to which one person attempts to control the behavior of another, either directly or by establishing status over the other. Submission is the opposite of dominance. When Tom says to Sue, "I know you're concerned about the budget, but I'll see to it that we have money to cover everything," through his words, tone of voice, and nonverbal behavior, he is saying that he is "in charge" of finances; that he is dominant, at least in this area of their lives. The extent to which one person's dominance is contested or accepted is communicated through symmetrical or complementary behaviors. A **symmetrical message** is one that matches the dominance or submission implied in your partner's previous message. If Sue responds, "Excuse me, but I'm an accountant!" she is challenging Tom's dominance by asserting her own status. This is a symmetrical display of dominance because she matches Tom's dominance message with one of her own. A **complementary message** is one that is opposite to the dominance or submission implied in your partner's previous message. If Sue says, "Great, I'm glad you're looking after it," this is a submissive message that is complementary to Tom's dominant behavior.

Affiliation is the appreciation or esteem one person has for another; its opposite is disaffiliation. It is usually quite easy to tell whether two people appreciate one another, or not, by listening to what they say, how they say it, and what they are doing with their eyes, face, and body as they speak. You may even be able to get a sense of the type of affiliation is that is present, such as whether the relationship is romantic or platonic, personal or professional. When a little brother shouts "I hate you!" and his big sister responds "I hate YOU!" these messages show symmetrical disaffiliation. However, if the big sister responds, "I don't hate you. I don't like how you're behaving, but I love you," this message shows complementary affiliation.

Although interpersonal communication can reveal the quality of a relationship, what you observe in a single interaction may not be an accurate depiction of how that relationship operates over time. For example, if Tom and Sue are especially tense about finances, they may appear to be struggling for dominance when they ordinarily treat each other as equals. Two acquaintances who have had a lot to drink and are having a good time together may smile, laugh, and touch more than their level of affiliation would normally motivate them to do. To accurately gauge the quality of a relationship you need more than one snapshot.

Interpersonal Communication Is Continuous

While we have goals that drive our interpersonal communication, whenever we are in and aware of the presence of other people, there is the potential for unintended messages to be perceived and interpreted. For example, Ling is sitting

Who is dominant in this interaction? What cues did you use to arrive at this conclusion?

Dominance—the degree to which one person attempts to control the behavior of another; the opposite of submission

Symmetrical message—one that matches the dominance or submission implied in a partner's previous message

Complementary message—one that is the opposite to the dominance or submission implied in the partner's previous message

Affiliation—the appreciation or esteem one person has for another

▶ **OBSERVE AND ANALYZE**

Relationship Qualities in Communication

Record one episode of a television series that you aren't familiar with. Watch the episode and identify one relationship where the characters have a significant conversation. Then watch that portion of the episode again. This time, focus on what you can tell about dominance and affiliation in this relationship. Write a short paragraph describing your conclusions and what you observed in the messages that led to your assessment.

"This is the nicest conversation we've had in weeks. Let's not spoil it by talking."

in the break room staring into space when her co-worker Nadia comes in, sees Ling, and says, "Is everything okay? You look so sad." Ling did not intend to be sending a message, but nonetheless, Nadia interpreted her behavior as being a message. It is useful to remember that whether you intend to or not, someone can interpret your behavior as a message.

Ethics and Interpersonal Communication

Can people depend on you to tell the truth? Do you do what you say you will do? Can people count on you to be respectful? In any encounter, we choose whether we will behave in a way that others view as ethical. **Ethics** is a set of moral principles held by a society, a group, or an individual that provide general guidelines for acceptable behavior and are open to some interpretation and gradual change. An ethical standard does not tell us exactly what to do in any given situation, only what general principles to consider when deciding how to behave. Ethics directs your attention to the reasons behind the rightness or wrongness of any act and helps you make a decision recognizing how others may view you and your behavior. Your personal ethic reflects your acceptance of the societal standards you consider to be good. When we behave ethically, we voluntarily act in a manner that complies with societal standards. However, we interpret these societal standards in a way that serves not only the greater good, but also our own personal beliefs.

Ethics—a set of moral principles held by a society, a group, or an individual that provides guidelines for acceptable behavior

Every field of activity—from psychology and biology to sociology and history—also has its own general ethical principles designed to guide the practice of that field. Interpersonal communication is no exception. Every time we choose a canned plan to meet our interaction goals, we make choices with ethical implications, and those choices must fulfill both the greater good and our own personal interpretations of them. The generally accepted principles that guide ethical interpersonal communication include the following

1. Ethical communicators are truthful and honest. "An honest person is widely regarded as a moral person, and honesty is a central concept to ethics as the foundation for a moral life" (Terkel & Duval, 1999, p. 122). The fundamental requirement of this standard is that we should not intentionally deceive, or try to deceive, others. Messages that contain half-truths or lies are dishonest and unethical.

2. Ethical communicators act with integrity. Integrity is maintaining consistency between what we say we believe and what we do. The person who says, "Do what I say, not what I do," lacks integrity, while the person who "walks the talk" acts with integrity. Integrity, then, is the opposite of hypocrisy.

3. Ethical communicators behave fairly. A fair person is impartial and unbiased. To be fair to someone is to gather all the relevant facts, consider only

Does the fact that documentary film maker Michael Moore owns nine homes and is worth more than $50 million earned from his films affect his integrity when he condemns capitalism?

circumstances relevant to the decision at hand, and not be swayed by prejudice or irrelevancies. For example, if two of her children are fighting, a mother exercises fairness if she allows both children to explain their side before she decides what to do. Likewise, ethical communicators are evenhanded when presenting facts and arguments that support their goals and also when presenting those that do not.

4. Ethical communicators demonstrate respect. Respect is showing regard or consideration for someone else, that person's point of view, and that person's rights. We demonstrate respect through listening and understanding others' positions, even when they are vastly different from our own.

5. Ethical communicators are responsible. We act responsibly when we hold ourselves accountable for our actions. Responsible communicators recognize the power of words. Our messages can hurt others and their reputations. So we act responsibly when we refrain from gossiping, spreading rumors, bullying, etc. And if we unintentionally injure another person, then this ethical standard compels us to attempt to repair the damage.

6. Ethical communicators are empathetic. This ethical standard calls on us to acknowledge and honor the feelings of others when we communicate. When Tomas has to turn down Julian's request for vacation the week of Christmas, his communication is ethical if he conveys his understanding of how disappointing this is to Tomas.

In our daily lives, what is ethical is not always clear-cut. We often face ethical dilemmas and must sort out what is more or less right or wrong. As we make these decisions, we reveal our personal hierarchy of ethical standards. Resolving ethical dilemmas can be difficult. At the end of each chapter is a short case titled "A Question of Ethics," which presents an ethical dilemma related to the material in that chapter. As you work through these cases, you will gain clarity on what your own ethical standards are and how they differ from others.

The Dark Side of Interpersonal Communication

Dark-side messages—messages that are not ethical and/or appropriate

"The dark side" is a metaphor for inappropriate and/or unethical interpersonal communication (Spitzberg & Cupach, 2007). Hence, **dark-side messages** are those that fail to meet standards for ethical and/or appropriate behavior. Figure 1.2 illustrates four different types of messages based on the dimensions of ethicalness and appropriateness.

When Liz, who just spent a fortune having her hair cut and colored, asks, "Do you like my new hairstyle?" how do you respond if you think it is awful? A bright-side response would be one that is both ethical (honest, respectful, empathetic, etc.) and appropriate (sensitive to Liz's feelings and to maintaining a good relationship). A hard dark-side response would be ethical but inappropriate in that it is likely to hurt Liz and damage your relationship. An easy dark side response would be unethical but would be appropriate in

	Appropriate ◀▶ Inappropriate	
Ethical	Bright Side	Hard Dark Side
Unethical	Easy Dark Side	Evil Dark Side

FIGURE 1.2 Understanding Dark-Side Messages

INTER-ACT WITH
SOCIAL MEDIA

Pick up your cell phone and scan your history of sent and received text messages. Are any dark-side messages reflected in these past text messages? Can they be categorized into the blocks in Figure 1.2? Why did you send these messages to the people you did? How did these messages affect your relationships with these people?

that it will spare Liz's feelings and not damage your relationship. An evil dark side response would be both unethical and inappropriate. Let's look at how someone might respond to Liz:

Bright-side response: "Liz, it doesn't matter what I think. I can see that you really like how it looks, and that makes me happy." *(ethical and appropriate)*

Hard dark-side response: "Wow, Liz, it's a dramatic change. I liked your hair long, and I'd always admired the red highlights you had. But I'm sure it will grow on me." *(ethical and inappropriate)*

Easy dark-side response: "It looks great." *(unethical and appropriate)*

Evil dark-side response: "It doesn't matter what you do to your hair, you're still fat and ugly." *(unethical and inappropriate)*

As you can see from these examples, relationships may benefit from bright-side, hard dark-side, and easy dark-side responses, depending on the situation. But evil dark-side responses damage people and their relationships. In appropriate places in this book, we will discuss dark-side issues related to various aspects of interpersonal communication.

DIVERSE VOICES

Lessons from American Experience

BY HARLAND CLEVELAND

Harland Cleveland was a distinguished diplomat and educator. A Medal of Freedom winner, he was president of the University of Hawaii and the World Academy of Art and Science. Cleveland died in 2008 but left behind a legacy of books and articles. In this classic selection, Cleveland explains how Hawaii, the most diverse of our 50 states, is a model for managing diversity.

We Americans have learned, in our short but intensive 200-plus years of history as a nation, a first lesson about diversity: that it cannot be governed by drowning it in "integration."

I came face-to-face with this truth when I became president of the University of Hawaii. Everyone who lives in Hawaii, or even visits there, is impressed by its residents' comparative tolerance toward each other. On closer inspection, paradise seems based on paradox: Everybody's a minority. The tolerance is not despite the diversity but because of it.

It is not through the disappearance of ethnic distinctions that the people of Hawaii achieved a level of racial peace that has few parallels around our discriminatory globe. Quite the contrary, the glory is that Hawaii's main ethnic groups managed to establish the right to be separate. The group separateness, in turn, helped establish the rights of individuals in each group to equality with individuals of different racial aspect, ethnic origin, and cultural heritage.

Hawaii's experience is not so foreign to the transatlantic migrations of the various more-or-less white Caucasians. On arrival in New York (passing that inscription on the Statue of Liberty, "Send these, the homeless, tempest-tossed, to me"), the European immigrants did not melt into the open arms of the white Anglo-Saxon Protestants who preceded them. The reverse was true. The new arrivals stayed close to their own kind; shared religion, language, humor, and discriminatory treatment with their soul brothers and sisters; and gravitated at first into occupations that did not too seriously threaten the earlier arrivals.

The waves of new Americans learned to tolerate each other—first as groups, only thereafter as

Diversity and Interpersonal Communication

Diversity, the variations between and among people, affects nearly every aspect of the interpersonal communication process we have just discussed. Whether we understand each other depends as much on who we are as it does on the words we use. The United States is one of the most multicultural nations in the world. We have succeeded in making the diversity of our people the strength of the nation. Individuals are free to observe a variety of customs, traditions, religious practices, and holidays. Respecting diversity while learning from one another has made our nation vibrant. Nevertheless, when we interact with others, how we form our own messages and how we interpret the messages of others, as well as how we coordinate our interactions, depend on our cultural orientation. Intercultural communication scholar Peter Andersen asserts, "Every communicator is a product of

Courtney Stodden, then 16, and Doug Hutchison, then 50, caused a stir when they married in 2011. Many were not surprised when she cited their age difference as what caused them to separate in 2013. But they reconciled in 2014, so stay tuned.

individuals. Rubbing up against each other in an urbanizing America, they discovered not just the old Christian lesson that all men are brothers, but the hard, new, multicultural lesson that all brothers are different. Equality is not the product of similarity; it is the cheerful acknowledgement of difference.

What's so special about our experience is the assumption that people of many kinds and colors can together govern themselves without deciding in advance which kinds of people (male or female, black, brown, yellow, red, white, or any mix of these) may hold any particular public office in the pantheon of political power.

For the twenty-first century, this "cheerful acknowledgement of difference" is the alternative to a global spread of ethnic cleansing and religious rivalry. The challenge is great, for ethnic cleansing and religious rivalry are traditions as contemporary as Bosnia and Rwanda in the 1990s and as ancient as the Assyrians.

In too many countries, there is still a basic (if often unspoken) assumption that one kind of people is anointed to be in general charge. Try to imagine a Turkish chancellor of Germany, a Christian president of Egypt, an Arab prime minister of Israel, a Tibetan ruler of Beijing, anyone but a Japanese in power in Tokyo. Yet in the United States during the twentieth century, we have already elected an Irish Catholic as president, chosen several Jewish Supreme Court justices, and

racially integrated the armed forces right up to the chairman of the Joint Chiefs of Staff. . . .

I wouldn't dream of arguing that we Americans have found the Holy Grail of cultural diversity when, in fact, we're still searching for it. We have to think hard about our growing pluralism. It's useful, I believe, to dissect in the open our thinking about it, to see whether the lessons we are trying to learn might stimulate some useful thinking elsewhere. We still do not quite know how to create "wholeness incorporating diversity," but we owe it to the world, as well as to ourselves, to keep trying.

Excerpted from Cleveland, H. (2006). The Limits to Cultural Diversity. In L. A. Samovar, R. E. Porter, and E. R. McDaniel (Eds.), *Intercultural Communication: A Reader* (11th ed., pp. 405–408). Belmont, CA: Wadsworth. Reprinted by permission of the World Future Society.

FOR CONSIDERATION:

1. Does Cleveland's analysis about how new immigrants become "Americanized" hold true today?
2. How does interpersonal communication facilitate the manner in which America deals with the cultural differences between people?
3. Recall one of your first encounters with someone who was culturally distinct from you. Think about the interaction you had. How did this first interaction affect subsequent ones with people who were different from you?

Diversity—variations between and among people

his or her culture" (Andersen, 2000, p. 260). Thus, as we become an increasingly diverse nation, the study of intercultural communication is more important than ever. Because culture permeates our interpersonal communication, each chapter of this book will discuss the ways that culture impacts how people act in communication situations. In addition, the "Diverse Voices" articles provide opportunities for you to empathize with the communication experiences of a variety of individuals. In this classic Diverse Voice article, Harland Cleveland describes how diverse people in the United States have learned to live together.

Interpersonal Communication Competence and You

Communication competence—another person's perception that your messages are both effective and appropriate in a given relationship

Effective messages—messages that achieve the goals of their senders

Appropriate messages—messages that conform to the social, relational, and ethical expectations of the situation

Communication competence is *another person's perception* that your messages are both effective and appropriate in a given relationship (Spitzberg, 2000). Notice that your competence depends on how others think about your communication—you don't get to grade yourself! **Effective messages** achieve the goals of their senders. **Appropriate messages** conform to the social, relational, and ethical expectations of the situation. Some messages lack communication competence because they are effective but not appropriate, or vice versa. If Sam screams at her boyfriend, Carl, to stop smoking in the apartment, and he does, Carl will probably view the message as effective, but not appropriate; he may see Sam as less competent than if she had used a less confrontational and more appropriate message. According to Brian Spitzberg (2000), who studies interpersonal communication competence, your ability to produce, interpret, and coordinate your messages competently depends on three things: your personal knowledge of how interpersonal communication works, your skills, and your motivation. In other words, to be competent communicators, we have to (1) know what to say and do (knowledge); (2) know how to say and do it (skills); and (3) have a desire to apply our knowledge and skills (motivation).

Acquire Interpersonal Communication Knowledge

First, we need knowledge about the communication process. The more you understand how to behave in a given situation, the more likely you are to be perceived as competent. You can gain knowledge about how to interact by observing what others do, by asking others how you should behave, by learning through trial and error, and by studying theories of interpersonal communication that have been research-tested. For instance, if Emmie wants her manager to view her as competent during their conversation about increasing her responsibilities, she must know how to present her request in a way that her manager will find acceptable and persuasive. She may learn this by observing her manager's behavior in similar situations, asking coworkers how best to approach the situation, analyzing how similar communications with her boss went in the past, or researching persuasion and different approaches to influencing others.

Second, we need **emotional intelligence,** which is the ability to monitor your own and others' emotions and to use this information to guide your communications (Salovey & Mayer, 1990). People differ in the degree to which they are able to identify their own emotions and detect and interpret the emotions of others. In addition, people vary in their abilities to understand slight variations in emotion and to use these variations in communications. No one is born with emotional intelligence, but it can be learned and developed over time. At appropriate places in this book, we will describe concepts, theories, and skills that will help you increase your emotional intelligence, including how to identify, express, and respond effectively to different emotions.

> **Emotional intelligence**—the ability to monitor your own and others' emotions and to use this information to guide your communications

Increase Interpersonal Communication Skill

Knowledge is not enough. Competent communicators are also skilled. **Communication skills** are message scripts that are effective and appropriate for specific types of goals, interactions, and relationships. A large communication skill library increases the likelihood you will form messages that meet your goals while maintaining or improving your relationships. As your skill repertoire increases, you will be prepared for a wider variety of communication situations. For example, while Emma can read about persuasion and understand it, this knowledge will be of little help if she doesn't develop persuasion skills that she can use when she meets with her manager.

> **Communication skills**—the combinations of goals, plans, and scripts that are effective and appropriate for specific types of messages, interactions, and relationships

You will learn about two broad categories of interpersonal communication skills in this book. **Micro skills** are very specific skills for producing certain types of messages or brief sequences of messages. These skills can be used in many different situations. Micro skills emphasized in this text include active listening, making a request, asking a clarifying question, praising, paraphrasing, perception checking, describing feelings, and describing behavior. In this course you will want to assess how proficient you are at each of the micro skills. When you identify one that is new to you or difficult for you, focus on mastering it. **Macro skills** are more complex skills that help us generate longer sequences of messages and may apply to certain types of interactions. Macro skills often incorporate some micro skills. Macro skills emphasized in this book include connecting with others in conversation, creating and managing close relationships, supporting others, managing difficulties with others, influencing others, etc. In many of the chapters in this book we provide "guidelines" that can help you build these skills.

> **Micro skills**—very specific communication skills for producing certain types of messages or brief sequences of messages

> **Macro skills**—broader communication skills that apply to certain types of interactions and relationships and help us generate longer sequences of messages

Think of something you do well and how you acquired the skills to do it. Unless you were a natural talent, it probably took a lot of time and practice. Mastering communication skills is no different than mastering any other skill. Figure 1.3 enumerates the steps for developing interpersonal communication skills and identifies the activities in this book that you can use as you work through each step. Improving your communication skills is a lot like learning a new hobby or sport. If you are learning to play basketball, for instance, you will need to learn techniques that feel uncomfortable at first. You will find it difficult to determine what skills to use when, and how to use those skills smoothly and

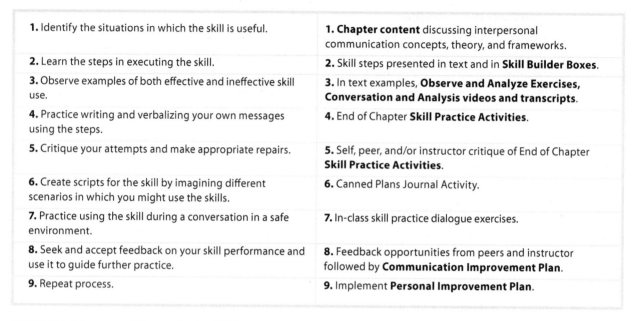

1. Identify the situations in which the skill is useful.	**1. Chapter content** discussing interpersonal communication concepts, theory, and frameworks.
2. Learn the steps in executing the skill.	**2.** Skill steps presented in text and in **Skill Builder Boxes**.
3. Observe examples of both effective and ineffective skill use.	**3.** In text examples, **Observe and Analyze Exercises, Conversation and Analysis videos and transcripts**.
4. Practice writing and verbalizing your own messages using the steps.	**4.** End of Chapter **Skill Practice Activities**.
5. Critique your attempts and make appropriate repairs.	**5.** Self, peer, and/or instructor critique of End of Chapter **Skill Practice Activities**.
6. Create scripts for the skill by imagining different scenarios in which you might use the skills.	**6.** Canned Plans Journal Activity.
7. Practice using the skill during a conversation in a safe environment.	**7.** In-class skill practice dialogue exercises.
8. Seek and accept feedback on your skill performance and use it to guide further practice.	**8.** Feedback opportunities from peers and instructor followed by **Communication Improvement Plan**.
9. Repeat process.	**9.** Implement **Personal Improvement Plan**.

FIGURE 1.3 Interpersonal Communication Skill Acquisition Steps and Text Activities

effortlessly. Because some communication skills may not be in your repertoire now, as you work on them, you are likely to feel awkward and to feel that your messages sound unrealistic or phony. Communication skills must be practiced until they feel comfortable and automatic—until you have created plans and scripts that work for you. The more you practice, the easier it will become to use a skill smoothly and with little conscious effort.

Be Motivated to Demonstrate Competence

You need two kinds of motivation if you are going to be a competent communicator. First, you need to be motivated to unlearn your old ineffective scripts and do the hard work required to replace them with better scripts. This means faithfully working on the skill-learning process that we just discussed. Second, you need to be motivated during an interaction to behave in a competent way. Being motivated during a conversation means saying "yes" to three questions: Do I want be perceived as competent? Do I know what will be considered competent in this situation? Have I mastered the skills I need to be competent? You are likely to answer "yes" to the first question if you think you will gain by being perceived as competent. If Emma thinks that talking with her manager will result in more challenging job responsibilities, then she will be motivated to have the conversation. Emma also needs to understand how her manager will view her in this particular situation. If Emma knows her manager well or has seen how others have successfully dealt with this situation, she will answer the second question "yes." Finally, Emma will be motivated if she can answer "yes" to the third question, confident in her mastery of the skills she will need to assertively influence her manager.

Develop Behavioral Flexibility

Because people, relationships, and conversations are unique, simple rote learning will not enable you to behave competently. Gaining knowledge and skill, however, will allow you to adapt to a unique situation and respond in more than one way. **Behavioral flexibility** is the capacity to react in a variety of ways to the same or similar situations. Let's look at a concrete example of behavioral flexibility. As her friend Grace is about to leave to go to the library, Tasha starts to emotionally recount a long list of problems to her. Grace must make many decisions and think about the various contexts in which the conversation is taking place. She may recall whether the historical context of their relationship suggests that this is really a serious situation or whether Tasha is just acting like her normal drama queen self. She may think about the social context and whether their relationship warrants her changing her study plans. She also may think about whether their location is the best physical context for this conversation and whether the psychological context leads her to feel that she is in the best psychological state to help Tasha at this time.

Suppose Grace decides to stay and talk with Tasha. If she is behaviorally flexible, she has many choices about what to say and how to behave. Grace can begin by listening actively. Later, after deciding that emotional support would be appropriate, she may form messages using her comforting skills. Then when she thinks Tasha is ready to hear her, she may give Tasha advice. With each new interpersonal skill she tries, Grace must analyze whether that skill is effective while adapting to what the situation requires, within the bounds of appropriateness and her own needs.

Behavioral flexibility—the capacity to react in a variety of ways to the same or similar situations

Create Interpersonal Communication Improvement Plans

Improving your communication practice is a lifelong journey. Realistically, during this course you are not going to master all the skills described in this book, yet study in this area will help you understand how interpersonal communication works and identify a few areas in which skill development would benefit you the most. Concentrate on systematically applying the skill-learning process to these skill areas during this term. Then, as a lifelong learner, you can take what you have learned in this course and continue to develop your skills. During this term and in the years to come, you are more likely to improve your skills if you write formal communication improvement plans. Figure 1.4 describes and provides an example of the contents of a good communication improvement plan.

At the end of each chapter of this book in which we introduce skills, you will be encouraged to form a communication improvement plan for those skills. Once you have written your plan, it is a good idea to work with another person as a consultant and coach—someone who will provide support and hold you accountable. During this term, you can partner with a classmate, with each of you serving as witness and consultant for the other. You can meet with this person periodically to assess your progress, troubleshoot problems, and develop additional procedures for reaching your goal.

STEP	DESCRIPTION	EXAMPLE
1. State the problem.	Start by writing down a specific communication problem that you have. This problem may affect only one relationship or it may be more general.	Even though my manager consistently overlooks me for interesting projects, leaving me with boring repetitive work that is not preparing me for promotion, I haven't spoken up because I'm not very good at standing up for myself.
2. State the specific goal.	A goal is specific if it is measurable and you know when you have achieved it.	To use assertiveness skills in a conversation with my boss so that she understands that I would like to be assigned interesting projects.
3. Outline a specific plan for reaching the goal.	Identify the skills you need. Adapt them to your situation. Mentally rehearse what you will say. Identify alternative responses. Practice role playing with a friend.	I will need to competently make a complaint, make a request, and use persuasion. I need to practice how to make a complaint both by myself and with someone who can give me feedback. When my partner gives me only positive feedback and I am confident that I can appropriately and effectively make this complaint, I will schedule a meeting with my manager.
4. Identify how you will know you have reached your goal.	Since a good goal can be measured, state how you will determine if you have achieved your goal.	Goal Test: I will know I have achieved my goal when I have finished the conversation with my manager, when my manager has paraphrased what I have said to my satisfaction, and when my manager has agreed to consider me for the next interesting project.

FIGURE 1.4 Writing a Communication Improvement Plan

THE SOCIAL MEDIA FACTOR

Understanding Social Media and Interpersonal Communication

Can you remember a time when you did not rely on some form of technology to communicate? Our world is filled with communication technologies, and chances are that you are just as comfortable with texting friends as you are with talking to them in person. You may even have friends and family you have not physically seen in years, but you still keep up with them through social media. We use **social media**—technologies that facilitate communication and interaction—to practice **digital communication**: the electronic transmission of digitally encoded messages. From texting and Tumblr to Facebook and Twitter, an endless list of social media helps us remain connected to others and the world in which we live. We use social media to remain connected with others in our **social network**—a digital web of people who are friends or share careers, organizations, family connections, and common interests.

Our social networks are larger now than ever before. This is due primarily to the evolution of technology that connects us to others. In the mid-1800s to mid-1900s, people usually had simple social networks made up of close friends and family whom they saw on a regular basis, and others with whom they

Social media—technologies that facilitate communication and interaction

Digital communication—the electronic transmission of messages

Social network—a group of individuals who are connected by friendship, family ties, common interests, beliefs, or knowledge

connected via postal mail or maybe with an occasional telephone call. When the first telephone call was made in the late 1800s, families and friends were quite excited because they were now better able to remain connected with others. But long-distance calling was expensive even into the second half of the twentieth century, so it was not a frequently used means of communication for most people. Since the first communication satellite (Telstar 1) was launched in 1962 and the first cell phone call was made in 1973, social media technology has evolved at a rapid rate. In the span of a few short years, the first text message was sent, Google launched, and Facebook, YouTube, and Twitter took off. Today our social

networks are significantly more complex than those of our grandparents. This is because of the global connectedness, portability, and instantaneous access provided by social media. No matter where we are, we are *plugged in* to our social networks and what is happening in the world. Using social media effectively, however, presents both challenges and opportunities when it comes to interpersonal communication.

Traits of Social Media Technology

The technology of social media has become so common that we barely give it a second thought when using it to communicate. Yet we should consider the unique ways that social media interactions differ from face-to-face communication, so we can use the technology more meaningfully and mindfully. Nancy Baym, a scholar in the emerging field of digital communication theory, has identified traits of social media that allow us to understand different types of social media by comparing them to each other and to face-to-face communication. Let's take a look at five of these traits (Baym, 2010).

Interactivity—the ability of a communication tool to facilitate social interaction between groups or individuals

1. **Interactivity** refers to the ability of a communication tool to facilitate social interaction between groups or individuals through inherent attributes that foster two-way communication or the capacity to "talk back." Like face-to-face communication, many forms of social media are highly interactive. Because social media enable interactivity across distances, we can remain connected and engaged with people who live in different cities, states, and countries. The portability of some social media devices enables us to remain connected no matter where we are. The downside to increased portability is that others expect us to be connected at all times, and some people become annoyed if we are not instantly responsive to their messages. Thus, with portability can come the troubling expectation that we are accountable to others at all times.

Temporal structure—the time it takes to send and receive messages or the time that elapses during a communication interaction

2. **Temporal structure** refers to the time that it takes to send and receive messages or the time that elapses during a communication interaction. Communication tools have varying lag times between the sending and receiving of messages. **Synchronous communication** occurs when participants are co-present and messages are exchanged in real time. **Asynchronous communication**

Synchronous—communication that occurs when participants are co-present and exchange messages in real time

Asynchronous—communication that occurs when participants are not co-present and where there are delays between sending, receiving, interpreting, and responding to messages

occurs when participants are not co-present and there is a lag in time between when a message is sent, when it is received and interpreted, and when it is responded to. For example, a telephone conversation is synchronous. Texting is almost synchronous if messages are received and responded to immediately after they are sent, but is asynchronous when they are not immediately responded to. Email and voice mail are asynchronous methods of communication because participants are not expected to be co-present; we expect a delay between when we send a message and when we receive a response.

3. **Social Cue Richness**. **Social cues** are the verbal and nonverbal aspects of a message that offer more information about the context, meaning, and identities of the involved parties. In face-to-face communication, social cues may take the form of facial expression, tone of voice, eye contact, inflection, hand gestures, and information about the other person's physical context. Many of the challenges we experience with social media stem from a lack of social cues. **Media richness theory** helps us better understand the social cues that accompany forms of social media. This theory proposes that certain media are better suited than others for some types of messages because social media vary in how well they reproduce the intended meaning (Daft & Lengel, 1984). Accordingly, some media are inherently richer in their social cues than others. Figure 1.5 displays common forms of social media by degrees of richness. You will note the position of face-to-face communication along the right side of the figure. As you scan further and further to the left, you will see how social media can become leaner (convey less of the message meaning) as the presence of rich social cues diminishes. Face-to-face is the richest form of communication. Bulk mail is a lean form of communication, while a handwritten note or an email is more robust and allows the sender to personalize a message for a specific receiver.

The richer the media, the more context cues are provided. For example, when you call a friend's cell phone, what is one of the first things you say after your friend answers the phone? More than likely, you will quickly say something to the effect of, "Hey, where are you?" You do this because the two of you are not sharing a physical context that can help you interpret your partner's social cues. When on the phone, you are unaware of these cues unless you ask. Social cues are even more limited in text-based social media. The more social cues available in a message, the more readily the receiver can understand the sender's intended

Social cues—verbal and nonverbal features of a message that offer more information about the context, meaning, and the identities of the involved parties

Media richness theory—the proposition that certain media are better suited than others for some types of messages due to differences in how accurately they reproduce intended meanings

Richness continuum

LEAN   **RICH**

| Bulk letters, posters | Letters, e-mail, texting | Facebook/ MySpace | Telephone | Skype | Face-to-face |

FIGURE 1.5 A Continuum of Media Richness

meaning. The richness of a given medium directly affects the degree to which social cues are available.

4. **Storage and replicability** refers to the extent to which a type of digital communication is preserved, can be continually accessed by others, and traced as to the time and place that a message was sent and who the participants in the exchange were. In 2013, Edward Snowden, a former government contractor, started a national conversation about privacy and security when he revealed that the U.S. government collected extensive data on the digital communications of both Americans and foreigners. Generally speaking, face-to-face conversations are gone forever once they are completed. At the other extreme, text-based social media are automatically recorded interactions and create a permanent storage space for digital communication. You should assume that every one of your text-based social media interactions—including email messages, posts to

Storage and replicability—the extent to which a type of digital communication is preserved, can be continually accessed by others, and traced as to the time and place that a message was sent and who the participants in the exchange were

---

A QUESTION OF ETHICS ▶ WHAT WOULD YOU DO?

Alisha and Rachelle became friends during high school and now live together in an off-campus apartment. Alisha, an only child, is a high-strung, anxious, and emotional person, while Rachelle, the oldest of six children, is easygoing and calm. Alisha depends on Rachelle to listen to her problems and to comfort and advise her; usually she is a good friend and supports Rachelle as well.

Currently, at work and at school, Alisha is under a lot of stress. Because of that, she hasn't had time to talk with Rachelle about what is going on in Rachelle's life. When they talk, the conversation is always about Alisha. Even when Rachelle tries to talk about what is happening to her, Alisha is distracted and manages to redirect the conversation back to her own problems. In the last two weeks, Alisha forgot that they had made plans to have dinner together, and another time she canceled their plans at the last minute.

This morning, Alisha told Rachelle, "I don't have time to pick up my prescription at the drugstore so you will have to do it, and my project group from biology is coming over to work this evening so I need you to straighten up this place. I don't have time to vacuum or dust, but I know that you have a break between classes and when you have to leave for work. Oh, and I'm really stuck in my Soc class. You know how slammed I am for time, and I have a one-page position paper due tomorrow. I know that you aced Soc last semester, so it

would be great if you would do a first draft for me. The assignment directions are on my desk." Before Rachelle could respond, Alisha continued, "Well, I've got to run. See you tonight."

After Alisha left, Rachelle plopped down in the chair and tried to sort out her feelings. As she talked to herself, she realized that while she was deeply concerned for Alisha, who seemed to be spinning out of control, she also believed that Alisha was taking advantage of her. It appeared to Rachelle that the relationship had become one-sided, with Alisha expecting Rachelle to serve her. Rachelle felt sad and abandoned as she recognized that Alisha had quit even trying to meet Rachelle's needs. "How," she asked herself, "has this happened?"

FOR CONSIDERATION:

1. How do the functions of interpersonal communication help you understand what is happening to Rachelle and Alisha?
2. How do the elements of the communication setting (the social, historical, psychological, and cultural contexts) help you understand?
3. Describe the levels of trust, control, and intimacy in the relationship. Be specific about what led you to your conclusions.
4. What ethical principles are involved in this case? Which principles does each woman violate?
5. What should Rachelle do now?

Facebook, photos that you upload, and tweets—are probably stored on a server somewhere and accessible to other people. These can be accessed, replicated, and distributed at a later time. This gives text-based interactions permanence in cyberspace that distinguishes them from the more transitive record of our voiced interactions.

Reach—the ability to connect with people in distant places

Viral message—a message whose reach is at a level unanticipated by its original sender

5. **Reach.** Face-to-face communication is limited to people who can fit in one particular space. Social media has tremendous **reach**, the ability to connect with people in distant places. The messages we send through social media travel quickly and widely. With a single keystroke or tap of a button, a message can be sent to thousands and maybe millions of people. A **viral message** is one whose reach is at a level unanticipated by its original sender. Viral messages reach or "infect" enormous audiences.

These five concepts help us understand how different social media technologies compare to each other and to non-mediated communication. In the following chapters, we'll build on this foundation by considering how social media connects with many aspects of interpersonal communication.

Summary

We have defined "interpersonal communication" as the complex process through which people produce, interpret, and coordinate messages to create shared meaning, meet social goals, manage personal identity, and carry out relationships. Messages are performances that use words, sentences, and/or nonverbal behaviors to convey the thoughts, feelings, and intentions of the speaker. The message production process consists of the activities that you undertake to encode and express a message. Based on our goals for interaction, we create communication plans or draw on "canned plans" in our memory and their associated scripts. We then adapt these plans and scripts to generate messages. The message interpretation process consists of the activities you undertake to decode a message and provide feedback. The interaction coordination process consists of the activities that you and your conversation partner use to adjust your messages to each other. Meaning is the significance that the sender and the receiver each attach to a specific message. Shared meaning occurs when the receiver's interpretation of the message is similar to what the speaker intended. Through interpersonal communication, we create shared meaning, pursue interaction goals, conduct our relationships, and manage our personal identities. Interpersonal communication is transactional, irreversible, and situated; reveals relationship qualities—including dominance and affiliation; and is also continuous. Ethics is a set of moral principles held by a society, a group, or an individual that provide guidelines for acceptable behavior. When we communicate, we make choices with ethical implications involving truthfulness and honesty, integrity, fairness, respect, responsibility, and empathy. The "dark side" of communication is a metaphor used to describe messages that are unethical and/or inappropriate. Diversity, variations between and among people, affects nearly every aspect of the communication process.

Communication competence is the impression that messages are both appropriate and effective in a given relationship. It involves increasing knowledge, skills, and motivation. Behavioral flexibility is the capacity to adapt messages to the same or similar situations. You can become a more competent communicator by studying interpersonal communication concepts, theories, and frameworks; by working to acquire new and improve existing interpersonal communication skills; and by desiring to communicate in ways that are effective and appropriate to the situation.

Increasingly, we communicate digitally using social media. The rapid evolution of social media technology has been widely adopted but poses special challenges to effective communication. We can compare various digital communication technologies by analyzing their interactivity, temporal structure, social-cue richness, storage and replicability, and reach.

CHAPTER RESOURCES

Key Words

Flashcards for all of these key terms are available on the *Inter-Act* website.

Analyze and Apply

The following activities challenge you to demonstrate your mastery of the concepts, theories, and frameworks in this chapter by using them to explain what is happening in a specific situation.

1.1 Rewind/Rewrite

Now that you have read the chapter, hit "rewind" on the opening dialogue between Casey and Katherine.

a. Use concepts from the chapter to explain what happened. Most of the concepts in the chapter are relevant in some way, but you may find that goals, identity management, relationship conduct, competence (effective and appropriate communication), and emotional intelligence are useful places to start.

b. Assuming that Katherine is telling the truth, rewrite the dialogue to produce a more positive outcome.

c. If Katherine is lying (or not telling the whole truth), how would that change the responsibility for improving this interaction? What responsibility does Casey have? What can you do to improve interpersonal communication when others engage in unethical behavior?

1.2 Interpersonal Communication Concepts

Rita and her daughter Jessica are shopping. As they walk through an elegant boutique, Jessica, who is feeling particularly happy, sees a blouse she wants. With a look of great anticipation and excitement, she exclaims, "Look at this, Mom—it's beautiful. Can I try it on?" Worried about the cost, Rita frowns, shrugs her shoulders, and replies hesitantly, "Well, yes, I guess so." Jessica, noticing her mother's hesitation, continues, "And it's marked down to twenty-seven dollars!" Rita relaxes, smiles, and says, "Yes, it is attractive—try it on. If it fits, let's buy it."

a. Use the definition of interpersonal communication to explain what is happening in this brief conversation between a mother and daughter.

b. How is each of the characteristics of interpersonal communication demonstrated in the conversation between Jessica and Rita?

c. Did Rita violate any ethical principle when she hesitantly responded, "Well, yes, I guess so." Was this a dark-side response? Explain your answer.

1.3 Social Media Analysis

Scott and Lynn have been dating for almost a year. As they approach their one-year anniversary, they begin drifting further and further apart. Right before their anniversary, Lynn finds out that Scott is cheating on her with one of her best friends. Lynn is furious. She immediately calls Scott and, in her rage, tells him that their relationship is over. After she hangs up on Scott, she texts her best friend and warns her to be on the lookout for revenge. Lynn then changes her relationship status on Facebook from "In a Relationship" to "Single." She tweets the following: "Scott is a huge jerk! And a certain girl better watch her back!"

Use the concepts that let us compare different types of social media to one another and to face-to-face communication to explain what is happening in this situation.

Communication Improvement Plan

Write a "Communication Improvement Plan" whose goal is to perfect scripts for turning down a date when you have a previous commitment but would like to see the person at some other time. As part of this activity, create at least three different response messages that meet your goal. You can download a Communication Improvement Plan form at the *Inter-Act* website.

State the problem: _____

State the goal: _____

Procedure: _____

Goal assessment method: _____

SOCIAL COGNITION: UNDERSTANDING OTHERS AND OURSELVES

"Welcome to the Junior Achievement Service Learning call-out," said Ryan. He strode calmly to the front of the room in his black Brooks Brothers suit, tie, and polished shoes. Confidently, he went on, "As you probably know, Junior Achievement brings a taste of the business world to K–12 students. I'm a senior, double majoring in finance and accounting. Last spring I was unanimously voted chairperson of this year's project." He smiled broadly. "Before I say more about how we will be working with our local schools this year, I'd like my co-chairs to introduce themselves."

Immediately, two young women, similarly attired in skirted black suits with brightly colored blouses, stylish haircuts, and perfect makeup jumped to their feet and started to talk simultaneously: "I'm Ashley!" "I'm Becca!" They stopped, looked at each other, and giggled.

Lynn, a scholarship volleyball player who was majoring in sports marketing, slouched in the back of the room in her sweats with her hair in a sloppy ponytail, and her arms crossed. She needed to complete her Service Learning requirement and had enjoyed coaching high school students in volleyball. So her advisor had suggested that serving as a Junior Achievement Advisor would be a good fit. But she was completely put off by Ryan, Ashley, and Becca. "Suits to a call-out?" she thought, feeling anxious and irritable. "Looks like they'll make all kinds of dress requirements that I can't afford. And all three of them are so cookie-cutter and full of themselves, I can't imagine how I'd fit in." With a heavy sigh, she got up and left before even hearing about the program.

WHAT YOU SHOULD BE ABLE *TO EXPLAIN* AFTER YOU HAVE STUDIED THIS CHAPTER:

▶ The difference between automatic and controlled social cognition

▶ How the attention process shapes what we notice and remember

▶ Processes and structures of memory

▶ The judgment processes of impression management, attribution, and stereotyping

▶ The relationship between self-concept and self-esteem

▶ How the self-concept develops

▶ Relationships between communication and the self-concept

▶ The connection between social cognition and emotion

▶ How to improve the accuracy of your social cognition

▶ How impressions are formed from social media

WHAT YOU SHOULD BE ABLE *TO DO* AFTER YOU HAVE STUDIED THIS CHAPTER:

▶ Improve the accuracy of your social perception

Social cognition—how we make sense of other people, ourselves, and our social world

Although Lynn didn't say a word to anyone, and Ryan and his co-chairs said very little, Lynn already has some very definite views of herself, the leaders of this Service Learning group, and the overall situation. These thoughts are the social cognitions that guide her behavior—in this case, her decision not to join Junior Achievement. In this chapter, we introduce you to the basics of **social cognition**, which is how we make sense of other people, ourselves, and our social world (Fiske & Taylor, 2013). Why study this? Simply put, because how we perceive ourselves and others affects our interpersonal communication with them. How you view your conversational partner will affect what you say, how you say it, and how you interpret what they say. Likewise, what you think of yourself will also influence how you talk with others. And there are things that are appropriate to say under some circumstances and in some situations that are not appropriate in others.

While social cognition is a type of *perception*, there are serious differences between perceiving objects and perceiving people that make accurate social cognition much more difficult. First, people try to control the situation; objects can't. For example, a college student who wants his professor to see him as a good student may arrive early, sit in the front of the class, and appear ready to take notes, whereas a red ball can't decide to appear to be green. Second, it's harder to prove that your perception of people is accurate than it is to confirm the accuracy of your perception of objects. You might think of Susan as unfriendly, but when you mention this to your sister, her impression of Susan may be different. Third, people perceive you back; objects don't. When Pete is talking, he is aware of how you are responding to his ideas. Fourth, people can change when they know they are being watched; objects can't. For example, when a child, intent on biting her older sister, notices her parent watching (perceives back), she may stop mid-bite to turn the bite into a kiss (change as a result of being watched). Finally, people change with time, so perceptions of people can become outdated.

We begin this chapter by describing the basic social cognition processes of attention, memory, and judgment, with a focus on how they relate to each other, and how they affect interpersonal communication. We also note the biases built into these processes, and provide several guidelines for overcoming them. Building on this foundation in the second half of the chapter, we discuss social cognition processes as applied to ourselves. We will see that our ideas about ourselves are strongly affected by what others think of us and by our culture. What we think about others is also colored by our emotions, so we will examine the interconnections between social cognition, emotion, and action. Finally, we will take a look at how social media affects what we think of others and ourselves.

Making Sense of the Social World

We develop an understanding of other people and ourselves through the mental or cognitive processes of attention, memory, and judgment. In other words, we notice things around us, draw on ideas in our memories to make sense of them, and evaluate what we see, both positively and negatively. These processes occur simultaneously and constantly influence each other. We'll define and discuss each process in turn, pointing out their connections and impact on interpersonal communication, but first we need to make an important distinction between *automatic* and *controlled* cognition. Think back to the first day of your Interpersonal Communication class, when many of your classmates were new to you. Within a few seconds of encountering other students, you decided whom you might want to study with, hang out with, or possibly avoid. Most of this process was **automatic social cognition**; you arrived at these conclusions without much consciousness, intention, or awareness of their future impact. This is not unusual. In fact, most of our social cognition occurs automatically. However, some social cognition is **controlled social cognition**, which means that you consciously and intentionally stop to think about something because you realize that how you think will affect what happens. For example, imagine that your instructor had told you that after a short "mixer," where you would have a chance to talk with your classmates, you were to nominate four of them to be your teammates for a final course project. In this circumstance, you are likely to carefully consider which of your classmates had the qualities you wanted in teammates.

Automatic social cognition is efficient—it gets the job done quickly, with minimal effort. In contrast, controlled social cognition consumes more time and energy, but can result in more accurate and complete perceptions of ourselves, others, and the situation at hand. As we examine the processes of attention, memory, and judgment, you will see that while these are often automatic, we can improve our communication by making the effort to control some of these processes.

Attention

When you interact with other people, or observe a social situation, your senses are bombarded with multiple stimuli. Fortunately, our minds are well adapted to

Automatic social cognition—arriving at conclusions about others, ourselves, or a situation without much consciousness, intention, or awareness of their future impact

Controlled social cognition—consciously and intentionally stopping to think about something because you realize that how you think will affect what happens

Attention—the process of focusing more closely on some of the stimuli in your environment

Salient—directing attention at people or things because they stand out in the social context, differ from our expectations, or are related to our goals

focus on some things while ignoring others. **Attention** is the process of focusing more closely on some of the stimuli in your environment. Although we can consciously give our attention to anything in our environment, we automatically attend to things that are **salient**, or noticeable.

People are social animals, so we tend to notice other people. But some people are especially salient, or more likely to get our attention, because they stand out in the social context, differ from our expectations, or are related to our goals. In social situations, we tend to notice people who are more talkative or more reserved than others. We also notice people who act differently than we expect them to. For example, we expect people at a formal wedding to dress in a way that is respectful of the occasion; therefore, we are likely to notice someone who arrives wearing flip-flops, jeans, and a T-shirt. Additionally, our personal goals affect what is salient to us. You may pay little attention to the employees in a department store—until you can't find something. Salience not only captures our attention, but also affects what we remember, and how we judge others' behavior. It probably won't surprise you that when other people stick out in some way, we are more likely to form memories of them. We also tend to perceive them as having more influence on what happens around them. For example, you may incorrectly assume that the biggest child in a group of misbehaving boys was the one who started the bad behavior. Generally speaking, we tend to evaluate salient people more positively or negatively than we would otherwise.

What you pay attention to also depends on what you have recently or frequently thought about. When you think about something, that idea becomes **primed**, or made ready in your memory to be thought about again. Once an idea has been primed, it will influence what you attend to. For example, it's only after you have bought a blue Ford Focus that you notice so many of them on the street. In another example, Keith, whose last girlfriend "played" him by dating several other guys when he thought they had an exclusive relationship, may be hyper-attentive to any sign that his current girlfriend is interested in another guy. He may even pay close attention to each guy she greets as they walk across campus. Here again, we can see the connection between attention and judgment. Since thoughts of his last girlfriend's betrayal are primed in Keith's memory, he consistently judges his new girlfriend's behavior on this basis.

Primed—attending to things that have recently been thought about

It can be difficult to control your attention when there are salient things in your surrounding environment, or when an idea has been strongly primed. Yet it isn't always necessary to completely control your attention during casual conversations. In fact, noticing things in the environment or commenting on what you're thinking may be quite appropriate, depending on the circumstances.

However, when your interactions have important outcomes, you'll want to exercise some conscious control over your attention. If Greta is interviewing for a job, it's important that she not be distracted by the attractiveness of the interviewer, or by worries about whether she is qualified for the position. Instead, she should focus on her goals: explaining her experience clearly, and conveying enthusiasm for the position. Sometimes you can alter the environment to remove salient distractions and help keep your attention focused on where it needs to be.

For example, if Ray comes to Arden with a problem, Arden can move their conversation to a private, quiet environment and turn off any electronic devices that may otherwise disturb them. Developing awareness of when your attention wanders and using conscious control when needed will help you be a more effective communicator.

Memory

You may think of **memories** as recollections of specific people and events that happened in the past. For example, you can probably remember your best friend from grade school, and the worst fight you had with that friend. For people you know well, you have thousands of specific memories, such as what your mom said the last time you talked, when your fiancé proposed, or the time you and your best friend laughed so hard you both wet your pants. Our memories are the basis of more abstract cognitive structures known as *schemas*. A **schema** is a memory structure that connects a concept to its related qualities. For example, your schema for the concept of a "best friend" might include shared secrets, inside jokes, and deep understanding. Schemas are based on our specific memories. So your schema for a best friend will be based on your memories of incidents you share with your best friends.

The essential point here is that your memory affects how you perceive others. We don't always see others exactly as they are; instead, we see them through the lenses of our schemas. This is especially true when you don't know someone well enough to have a lot of (or any) specific memories about him or her. Imagine that you have several different encounters with people who are multilingual and discover that they are all highly educated, involved in politics, and world travelers. From these experiences, you may form what is called an **implicit personality theory**, a specific kind of schema that connects a set of personality traits and behaviors. You are then introduced to Fara, and learn that she speaks French, Russian, and Farsi. Because of your implicit personality theory, you assume that Fara went to an elite school, is passionate about politics, and has traveled abroad. But it could be that Fara has learned these languages at home or in classes, is apathetic about politics, and has never traveled beyond the next state. Implicit personality theories often affect our judgments of others, causing us to leap from one or two observed behaviors, to a whole set of assumptions that may be inaccurate.

As we encounter new people and situations, things often happen that don't exactly fit our schemas. But once schemas are formed, they can be difficult to change. We have a strong tendency toward **assimilation**, which means forcing new information to fit a memory structure, or filtering it out because it doesn't fit. The fact that Fara hasn't traveled the world probably won't change your schema for multilingual people. Instead, you'll regard her as a minor exception to the schema. However, if you have many experiences that challenge an existing schema, you will eventually change your schema to reflect the consistent information these experiences provide. For example, if you meet a number of multilingual people who are not well traveled, you may form two multilingual sub-schemas, one for people who have traveled, and one for those who have not.

Memories—recollections of specific people and events that happened in the past

Schema—a memory structure that connects something or someone to its related qualities

Implicit personality theory—a specific kind of schema that connects a set of personality traits and behaviors

Assimilation—the tendency to force new information to fit a memory structure, or filtering it out because it doesn't fit

Which of these two young men would you be more likely to approach if you needed help? How would your impression of the man in the hoodie change if you learned that he was a dean's list student at a select university?

Stereotype—a schema in which the central concept is a category or group of people

A **stereotype** is a schema in which the central concept is a category or group of people. Your schema for a best friend is a stereotype, as are your schemas for soccer player, Russian-American, members of the Green Party, and professors. You have probably been taught that stereotypes are bad. But that isn't the whole story. We naturally form schemas to organize our specific memories, so forming stereotypes for categories of people is unavoidable and does not make you a bad person. In fact stereotypes serve an important function. They provide a preliminary basis for interacting with others until we come to know them as individuals. Does your stereotype for professors include "intelligent," "focused on ideas," or "expects a lot from students"? Then you probably weren't surprised by how your Interpersonal Communication instructor interacted with you during the first few days of class. However, there are significant problems with stereotypes, one of which is that a stereotype is only an approximation of any individual in a group. Does your stereotype for professor include "not handy"? Although some professors may have neglected to acquire practical skills in favor of dedication to their subject, others may be quite capable of working with their hands. You could easily underestimate or even insult a professor if you assumed that she or he couldn't cook or fix a toilet. Second, stereotypes that contain negative attributes, as many do, can lead to stereotyping, prejudice, and discrimination toward others. We will talk more about stereotyping, or inappropriate application of stereotypes, in the following section on judgment.

Judgment—evaluating people and their behaviors

Impression formation—the judgment process of developing an initial concept of another person

Judgment

The third social cognition process is **judgment**, or evaluating people and their behaviors. In everyday talk, you may hear people say, "Don't judge me!" when they mean, "Don't have a harsh, negative view of me." Here, "judgment" refers to evaluations that can be positive or negative, mild or intense. Like it or not, we are constantly evaluating others to determine what they are like and to predict what they will do. (We do the same for ourselves, trying to understand who we are and what we do.) Let's look at three judgment processes that are especially important for interpersonal interactions: impression formation, attribution, and stereotyping.

Assume that both of these women are Muslim. How does the way they are each dressed affect the judgments you make about them as individuals and as a group?

Impression Formation

Impression formation is the judgment process of developing an initial concept of another person. When you encounter someone for the first time, this cognitive process is especially active. You continue, however, to refine your impressions of others through repeated encounters. Although first impressions are formed quickly, they are surprisingly complex. They include assessments of physical appearance, observations of behavior, inferred personality traits, stereotypes, reactions, and relationships we expect to have (Wyer & Carlston, 1994). For example, upon first meeting Adam, Rudy might note that he is tall, freckled, and has very short, red, buzz-cut hair (physical appearance), and that he is carrying a baseball mitt and moves fluidly (behaviors). From these cues, he infers personality traits of "competitiveness" and "conservatism," and applies this stereotype to ballplayers, which also includes "dedicated" and "superstitious". Rudy may be mildly curious about Adam (reaction) and think he would be fun to hang out with (relationship). Notice how Rudy's impression (judgment) of Adam is strongly influenced by salient physical features (which grab attention) and by his own schemas (memory).

When we notice all of the details that are taken in when forming a first impression, it becomes easy to understand why first impressions have such a powerful influence on later interactions and relationship development. The power of impressions also leads us to try to influence or manage others' impressions of us, a topic we will discuss later on.

What is your first impression of this woman? How does the fact that she is smoking a cigarette inform your impression?

Making Attributions

A second component of judgment is attribution. **Attributions** are explanations we think of for why a particular person is behaving a certain way. When a behavior differs from what we expect, we often try to figure out the cause—something we can attribute the behavior to. Once we have made the attribution, we can use it to predict how that person will act in similar situations in the future. For instance, suppose the co-worker who was scheduled to relieve you at shift change is half an hour late. How do you explain this tardiness? One way is to assume that it's not her fault and figure out a reason that is beyond her control. A **situational attribution** is an explanation that puts the cause of the behavior outside the control of the person. In this case, you might assume that your co-worker was stuck in traffic, or that her car broke down. On the other hand, you may assume it is her fault and make a **dispositional attribution**, explaining the behavior as resulting from some cause that is under the person's control. For example, you may reason that your co-worker overslept her alarm, or didn't make allowances for how the recent snow would affect her commute. Both of these explanations attribute her lateness to something she could have prevented. Whether you make a situational or dispositional attribution, you are attempting to understand the behavior by answering the question, "Why is my co-worker late?"

The attributions you make have two important consequences. First, your attributions guide your immediate response to the behavior. When your co-worker finally arrives, if you made a situational attribution, you may ask, "Is everything all right?" Whereas, if you made a dispositional attribution, you might respond curtly or display your annoyance in other ways. Second, the attributions we make about people's behavior in one interaction set the tone for how we expect them to behave in the future. If your co-worker confirmed that she was late because she had an accident on the way to work, you will expect her

Attributions—explanations we think of for why a particular person is behaving a certain way

Situational attribution—an explanation that puts the cause of the behavior outside the control of a person

Dispositional attribution—an explanation that puts the cause of a behavior within the control of a person

Fundamental attribution error—the tendency to believe that others' negative behaviors result from their choices, whereas our own negative behaviors stem from conditions over which we have no control

Stereotyping—applying a stereotype to a particular individual, and treating that person as though he or she embodies all the characteristics associated with that stereotype

to be prompt the next time. Likewise, if your co-worker confirmed your hunch that she had overslept her alarm, the next time she's supposed to relieve you, you might send a text to remind her to put her alarm across the room instead of next to her bed, thus discouraging her from hitting the snooze button.

It would be nice if our attributions were 100% accurate, but as with other aspects of social cognition, we have predictable biases. The **fundamental attribution error** is the tendency to believe that others' negative behaviors result from their choices, whereas our own negative behaviors stem from conditions over which we have no control. For example, suppose that you go to the drugstore to pick up a prescription, and the pharmacy technician waiting on people is frowning and very abrupt with customers. You may explain this behavior to yourself by reasoning that he is naturally unhappy and rude. But just suppose that the tech is normally happy and polite to his customers but has just learned that his mother has been diagnosed with kidney cancer and his manager refused his request to leave work early to be with his mom. Your tendency to look for dispositional causes internal to the person will have biased your interpretation of his behavior.

Why does this happen? Part of the reason is that we know more about the actual reasons for our own behavior than we do about the reasons for others' behavior. We also prefer to think well of ourselves. Consequently, we usually interpret our own bad behavior in light of the situation. For example, have you ever been cut off by another car in traffic? Did you yell at the person and maybe even gesture rudely? Why? You probably would not say, "Because I'm really a hot-headed jerk." Instead, you are likely to interpret your behavior as being caused by the situation, explaining, "Well, I'm not normally like that, but I was really in a hurry, and this guy just cut me off. I couldn't help it. I mean, I almost got killed."

Since we often respond to others based on how we interpret their behavior, the fundamental attribution error can wreak havoc on our relationships. When Cassie doesn't call her mother for several days, her mother's attribution will drive the conversation with her daughter. Her mother's opening line might be, "I can see that the only person you ever think about is yourself. Otherwise, you would have called." Or it might be, "Honey, is everything okay? I was really concerned that something might have happened to you." Which of these responses is most likely to lead to a satisfying conversation that helps maintain a healthy relationship?

Stereotyping

A third judgment process is stereotyping. Recall that stereotypes are simply memory schemas in which the central concept is a group or category of people, and that the formation of stereotypes is largely unavoidable. However, **stereotyping** is applying a stereotype to a particular individual, and treating that person as though he or she embodies all of the characteristics associated with that stereotype.

There are at least two significant problems with stereotyping. First, the characteristics that your stereotype assigns to group members may be inaccurate for most members of the group. For example, while there are terrorists who are Muslims, the vast majority of Muslims are not jihadists bent on the destruction of Western civilization. Yet stereotyping would lead you to believe that all Muslims are terrorists. Second, the individual you are stereotyping may not have the characteristics that you associate with the group. Therefore, if being a terrorist is central to your stereotype of Muslims, then when you meet a moderate Muslim and assume he is a terrorist, your stereotyping will lead you to an inaccurate judgment and result in your treating this person with suspicion.

" *Are you sure he's a plumber ? I can't see his butt-crack .* "

Cartoonstock www.Cartoonstock.com

Prejudice is the emotional reaction to a stereotyped group or individual from that group. Prejudice can include positive emotions if your stereotype of a group has many positive attributes. For example, some teachers perceive girls as good students since they generally want to please and are able to sit still while in class. So teachers who have this stereotype are prone to like a new girl in their class. However, prejudice often gives rise to negative feelings, including anger, fear, disgust, anxiety, or other bad feelings toward individual members of stereotyped groups. For example, the 2014 shooting and death of Michael Brown, a young black man, by a police officer in Ferguson, Missouri, touched off nationwide protests. Some of the protesters not only demanded justice, but also demonstrated their prejudice (anger, hostility, and hatred) toward all law enforcement personnel, stereotyping all police as racists.

Prejudice—the emotional reaction to a stereotyped group or individual from that group

Prejudice often motivates **discrimination**, or acting differently toward a stereotyped group or individual. Teachers who stereotype girls as good students may call on girls more frequently or give a girl the benefit of the doubt when an essay answer is not quite on target. The cries for justice expressed around the country for Michael Brown were fueled by the perception that the police officer who shot Brown was acting on a stereotype of young black men and discriminating against Brown—shooting Michael simply because he fit the officer's stereotype.

Discrimination—acting differently toward a stereotyped group or individual

While some stereotyping is unconcealed, other stereotyping is less obvious. **Blatant stereotyping** occurs when people have extreme negative views of a certain group, are willing (even eager) to express and promote those views, and readily apply their stereotypes to members of the group. This type of stereotyping is associated with significant prejudice and conscious discrimination. Some people go so far as to join various hate groups, for whom blatant stereotyping and discrimination against certain groups and individuals is a prime motivation.

Blatant stereotyping—when people who have extremely negative views of out-groups express and promote those views, and readily apply their stereotypes to members of the out-groups

Most of us don't belong to hate groups. Many of us, however, engage in **subtle stereotyping**, which occurs when people who are minimally aware that they are basing their interaction on stereotypes nonetheless act toward someone on the basis of a stereotype. Subtle stereotyping influences how we talk to others, resulting in what psychologists call **microaggressions**, everyday insults, indignities, and demeaning messages sent to a member of a stereotyped group by well-intentioned others who are unaware of the hidden messages being sent (Sue et al., 2007). For example, when Jackson tried to flirt with Anita, a beautiful dark-haired woman, by saying, "Wow, you speak English really well, I can't even

Subtle stereotyping—when people who are minimally aware that they are basing their interaction on stereotypes nonetheless act toward someone on the basis of that stereotype

Microaggressions—everyday insults, indignities, and demeaning messages sent to a member of a stereotyped group by well-intentioned others who are unaware of the hidden messages being sent

DIVERSE VOICES

Just Walk on By

BY BRENT STAPLES

Brent Staples is an editorial writer for the *New York Times*. His memoir, *Parallel Time: Growing up in Black and White,* won the Anisfield-Wolf Book Award previously won by the likes of James Baldwin, Ralph Ellison, and Zora Neale Hurston. He holds a Ph.D. in psychology from the University of Chicago. While this article was originally published in 1986, its observations and the truths it conveys affirms the cost of microaggressions then and now.

My first victim was a woman—white, well dressed, probably in her early twenties. I came upon her late one evening on a deserted street in Hyde Park, a relatively affluent neighborhood in an otherwise mean, impoverished section of Chicago. As I swung onto the avenue behind her, there seemed to be a discreet, uninflammatory distance between us. Not so. She cast back a worried glance. To her, the youngish black man—a broad six feet two inches with a beard and billowing hair, both hands shoved into the pockets of a bulky military jacket—seemed menacingly close. After a few more quick glimpses, she picked up her pace and was soon running in earnest. Within seconds she disappeared into a cross street.

That was more than a decade ago. I was 23 years old, a graduate student newly arrived at the University of Chicago. It was in the echo of that terrified woman's footfalls that I first began to know the unwieldy inheritance I'd come into—the ability to alter public space in ugly ways. It was clear that she thought herself the quarry of a mugger, a rapist, or worse. Suffering a bout of insomnia, however, I was stalking sleep, not defenseless wayfarers. As a softy who is scarcely able to take a knife to raw chicken—let alone hold it to a person's throat—I was surprised, embarrassed, and dismayed all at once. Her flight made me feel like an accomplice in tyranny. It also made it clear that I was indistinguishable from the muggers who occasionally seeped into the area from the surrounding ghetto. That first encounter, and those that followed signified that a vast unnerving gulf lay between nighttime pedestrians—particularly women—and me. And I soon gathered that being perceived as dangerous is a hazard in itself. I only needed to turn a corner into a dicey situation, or crowd some frightened, armed person in a foyer somewhere, or make an errant move after being pulled over by a policeman. Where fear and weapons meet—and they often do in urban America—there is always the possibility of death.

In that first year, my first away from my hometown, I was to become thoroughly familiar with the language of fear. At dark, shadowy intersections in Chicago, I could cross in front of a car stopped at a traffic light and elicit the *thunk, thunk, thunk, thunk* of the driver—black, white, male, or female—hammering down the door locks. On less traveled streets after dark, I grew accustomed to but never comfortable with people who crossed to the other side of the street rather than pass me. Then there were the standard unpleasantries with police, doormen, bouncers, cab drivers, and others whose business it is to screen out troublesome individuals *before* there is any nastiness.

I moved to New York nearly two years ago and I have remained an avid night walker. In central Manhattan, the near-constant crowd cover minimizes tense one-on-one street encounters. Elsewhere— visiting friends in SoHo, where sidewalks are narrow and tightly spaced buildings shut out the sky—things can get very taut indeed.

Black men have a firm place in New York mugging literature. Norman Podhoretz in his famed (or infamous) 1963 essay, "My Negro Problem—and Ours," recalls growing up in terror of black males; they were "tougher than we were, more ruthless," he writes—and as an adult on the Upper West Side of Manhattan, he continues, he cannot constrain his nervousness when he meets black men on certain streets. Similarly, a decade later, the essayist and novelist Edward Hoagland extols a New York where once "Negro bitterness bore down mainly on other Negroes." Where some see mere panhandlers, Hoagland sees "a mugger who is clearly screwing up his nerve to do more than just ask for money." But Hoagland has "the New Yorker's quick hunch posture for broken-field maneuvering," and the bad guy swerves away.

I often witness that "hunch posture," from women after dark on the warren like streets of Brooklyn where I live. They seem to set their faces on neutral and, with their purse straps strung across their chests bandolier style, they forge ahead as though bracing themselves against being talked to. I understand, of course, that the danger they perceive is not a hallucination. Women are particularly vulnerable to street violence, and young black males are drastically overrepresented among the perpetrators of that violence. Yet these truths are no solace against the kind of alienation that comes of being ever the suspect, against being set apart, a fearsome entity with whom pedestrians avoid making eye contact.

It is not altogether clear to me how I reached the ripe old age of 22 without being conscious of the lethality nighttime pedestrians attributed to me. Perhaps it was because in Chester, Pennsylvania, the small, angry industrial town where I came of age in the 1960s, I was scarcely noticeable against a backdrop of gang warfare, street knifings, and murders. I grew up one of the good boys, had perhaps a half-dozen first fights. In retrospect, my shyness of combat has clear sources.

Many things go into the making of a young thug. One of those things is the consummation of the male romance with the power to intimidate. An infant discovers that random flailings send the baby bottle flying out of the crib and crashing to the floor. Delighted, the joyful babe repeats those motions again and again, seeking to duplicate the feat. Just so, I recall the points at which some of my boyhood friends were finally seduced by the perception of themselves as tough guys. When a mark cowered and surrendered his money without resistance, myth and reality merged—and paid off. It is, after all, only manly to embrace the power to frighten and intimidate. We, as men, are not supposed to give an inch of our lane on the highway; we are to seize the fighter's edge in work and in play and even in love; we are to be valiant in the face of hostile forces.

Unfortunately, poor and powerless young men seem to take all this nonsense literally. As a boy, I saw countless tough guys locked away; I have since buried

several, too. They were babies, really—a teenage cousin, a brother of 22, a childhood friend in his mid-twenties—all gone down in episodes of bravado played out in the streets. I came to doubt the virtues of intimidation early on. I chose, perhaps even unconsciously, to remain a shadow—timid, but a survivor.

The fearsomeness mistakenly attributed to me in public places often has a perilous flavor. The most frightening of these confusions occurred in the late 1970s and early 1980s when I worked as a journalist in Chicago. One day, rushing into the office of a magazine I was writing for with a deadline story in hand, I was mistaken for a burglar. The office manager called security and, with an ad hoc posse pursued me through the labyrinthine halls, nearly to my editor's door. I had no way of proving who I was. I could only move briskly toward the company of someone who knew me.

Another time I was on assignment for a local paper and killing time before an interview. I entered a jewelry store on the city's affluent Near North Side. The proprietor excused herself and returned with an enormous red Doberman pinscher straining at the end of a leash. She stood, the dog extended toward me, silent to my questions, her eyes bulging nearly out of her head. I took a cursory look around, nodded, and bade her good night. Relatively speaking, however, I never fared as badly as another black male journalist. He went to nearby Waukegan, Illinois, a couple of summers ago to work on a story about a murderer who was born there. Mistaking the reporter for the killer, police hauled him from his car at gunpoint and but for his press credentials would probably have tried to book him. Such episodes are not uncommon. Black men trade talks like this all the time.

In "My Negro Problem—And Ours," Podhoretz writes that the hatred he feels for blacks makes itself known to him through a variety of avenues—one being taken for a criminal. Not to do so would surely have led to madness—via that special "paranoid touchiness" that so annoyed Podhoretz at the time he wrote the essay.

I began to take precautions to make myself less threatening. I move about with care, particularly late in the evening. I give a wide berth to nervous people on subway platforms during the wee hours, particularly when I have exchanged business clothes for jeans. If I

(continued)

Just Walk on By (*continued*)

happened to be entering a building behind some people who appear skittish, I may walk by, letting them clear the lobby before I return, so as not to seem to be following them. I have been calm and extremely congenial on those rare occasions when I've been pulled over by the police. And on late-evening constitutionals along streets less traveled by, I employ what has proved to be an excellent tension-reducing measure: I whistle melodies from Beethoven and Vivaldi and the more popular classical composers. Even steely New Yorkers hunching toward nighttime destinations seem to relax and occasionally they even join in the tune. Virtually everybody seems to sense that a mugger wouldn't be warbling bright, sunny selections from Vivaldi's *Four Seasons*. It is my equivalent to the cowbell that hikers wear when they know they are in bear country.

Originally published in Ms. Magazine in 1986. Revised and published by Harper's the following year. Used with permission of _____.

FOR CONSIDERATION:

1. This article was written in 1986. Have the perceptions or experiences of young black men changed since then?
2. The author suggests that some thuggish behavior may be as a result of self-fulfilling prophecies. Does he have a point? If he does, what can be done to break the cycle of stereotyping-prejudice-discrimination-self-fulfilling prophecy-stereotyping…?
3. Can you identify stereotyping that leads you to treat someone differently just because they fit a category? Is your discrimination overt? Or are you apt to engage in microaggressions?

detect an accent," he drew on his stereotype of Hispanic people. Unfortunately, instead of complimenting her, he actually insulted Anita. His comment implied that she is "foreign," when in fact she is an American, the third generation of her family to be born and raised in New York. The "Diverse Voices" selection for this chapter, "Just Walk on By" by Brant Staples, was written in 1986 and is still relevant because unfortunately, the types of microaggressions depicted in this essay continue to reflect the experiences of black men today.

The persistence of subtle stereotyping contributes to ongoing disparities between majority and minority racial and ethnic groups because small but persistent forms of discrimination like microaggressions make it difficult for members of stereotyped groups to interact, pursue Goals, and succeed. Intentional or not, stereotyping often harms the self-concept and self-esteem of stereotyped individuals. In the following section, we will discuss ways of improving social cognition, including how to reduce the impact of subtle stereotypes.

Self and Social Cognition: Thinking About Yourself

Recall from the beginning of the chapter that social cognition is the set of cognitive (mental) processes we use to make sense of other people, ourselves, and our social world. We exercise attention, memory, and judgment as much on ourselves as we do on others. Strong emotions, or physical experiences such as pain or pleasure, absorb your attention and direct your behavior. The way you think about yourself (stored in your memory), affects how you present yourself and respond to others. As we reflect on our actions, we judge ourselves, asking internal questions such as "Why did I do that?" and "Did I do that well enough?" In this section, we will examine social cognition processes as applied to ourselves. We'll start by focusing on self-concept and self-esteem, examine how self-concept is developed and maintained, and then see how self-concept affects attention, judgment, and interaction.

Self-Concept and Self-Esteem

The **self-concept** is a very large schema in memory that is the collection of all the ideas you have about yourself, including your abilities, personality traits, and roles (Fiske & Taylor, 2013). Take a moment to write down the first five things you would choose to list in an honest description of yourself. Are you athletic or a great cook? Are you funny or pessimistic? Are you a parent or a member of the debate team? These choices are a window into your self-concept.

> **Self-concept**—a very large schema in memory that is the collection of all of the ideas you have about yourself, including your abilities, personality traits, and roles

Your self-concept schema is made up of many smaller, more specific types of self-schemas. These reflect different aspects of your understanding of yourself. Your **self-schema** is the qualities of yourself that you see as *most central* in defining or understanding who you really are. When you wrote down the first five things that came to mind about yourself, you probably named characteristics in your self-schema. Your **possible self-concept** is a set of ideas about what you *are capable of being*, whereas your **ideal self-concept** is the set of ideas about who you *would like to be*, recognizing that this may not be completely achievable. Your **ought self-concept** is your collection of ideas about what you *think you should be*, while your **feared self-concept** encompasses ideas about yourself that you don't want to be. For example, your self-schema may include "creative." Your possible self-concept could include "creative," "works in the film industry," and "mentors other artists." Your ideal self-concept might add to this list, "wins an Oscar" or "uses fame to stop bullying." Your ought self-concept could contain "takes care of my parents" and "pursues social justice." And your feared self-concept may contain, "I could compromise my artistic integrity for money."

> **Self-schema**—the qualities of yourself that you see as *most central* in defining or understanding who you really are
>
> **Possible self-concept**—a set of ideas about what you *are capable of being*
>
> **Ideal self-concept**—the set of ideas about who you *would like to be*
>
> **Ought self-concept**—the set of ideas about what you *think you should be*
>
> **Feared self-concept**—the set of ideas about yourself that you don't want to have

Other self-concept schemas operate in particular relationships and contexts. Your **relational self-concept** is the set of ideas you have about yourself *in a particular relationship or sets of relationships*. For example you may see yourself as assertive in your relationships with friends, but unassertive with your family members. Similarly, your self-concept varies depending on the context in which you find yourself. While you may see yourself as an accomplished singer, if you are asked to perform in an opera, you may lower your opinion of your talent in this context. Your **working self-concept** is the set of ideas about yourself that you are actively remembering *at any given time*. As you might expect, your working self-concept changes frequently as you move from situation to situation and relationship to relationship. For example, as Sarah leaves class one day and

> **Relational self-concept**—the set of ideas you have about yourself *in a particular relationship or in sets of relationships*
>
> **Working self-concept**—the set of ideas about yourself that you are actively remembering *at any given time*

heads off to her new job, her working self-concept may continue to include "dependable" but change from "understands what is expected" to "still trying to figure it out." Later, when she leaves work for her meeting at Hillel, a Jewish campus organization, her working self-concept will evolve to include "spiritual" and "socially conscious."

Self-esteem—our positive or negative judgment of the characteristics we think we have

Whereas the self-concept is the set of ideas we have about ourselves, our **self-esteem** depends on how we view the characteristics we think we have (Mruk, 2006). Having high self-esteem means that you value your own characteristics positively; this can also be described as having a positive self-concept. Low self-esteem means not valuing your characteristics, or seeing them as negative; this can also be described as having a negative self-concept.

Some of our characteristics influence self-esteem more than others. The more you value a part of your self-concept, the more impact it has on your self-esteem. Remember that a self-schema contains our defining characteristics, which we tend to value, therefore they are closely connected to self-esteem. Characteristics that are not part of the self-schema have less impact on self-esteem. For example, being a diehard Yankees fan is a central part of Chad's self-schema, so his self-esteem could drop dramatically if they have a poor season. But Dennis, who is not much of a baseball fan, only roots for the Yankees when he is watching a game with friends. Since "Yankees fan" is only part of his relational self-concept and accessed to his working self-concept only when he is in specific contexts, if the Yankees have a bad season, it is unlikely to have a lasting impact on Dennis's self-esteem.

Self-concept and self-esteem are closely intertwined, and some scholars combine them and talk about a "positive self-concept," which is having a positive judgment of your own qualities, and "negative self-concept," which is having a negative judgment of your own qualities.

Self-Concept Development

Your self-concept is a product of your experiences, especially your interactions with others. Beginning in our infancy, others' reactions to us inform us about our worth, our talents, and our shortcomings. Deon's view of himself as "good at math" might begin at home, where his parents notice and praise his efforts in grouping and reciting numbers. In kindergarten, Deon may notice that he knows more numbers than his classmates and that his teacher puts more stickers on his papers than on those of other students. If Deon says "I love math," a classmate may respond, "You're the best at math in our class." Through observation and interaction, Deon begins to understand his qualities and how they differ from those of others.

Like self-concept, self-esteem also depends heavily on experiences and interactions with others. What we see as worthwhile in ourselves is influenced by the ideas, morals, and values of our families and the groups to which we belong, and especially by people whom we respect and with whom we feel close (Rayner, 2001). Families and peer groups are especially important for the development of self-esteem and self-concept. If Deon, who is good at math, comes from a family

▶ **OBSERVE AND ANALYZE**

Reflecting on "At Seventeen"

Use the Internet to access and listen to "At Seventeen" by Janis Ian. Then download a copy of the lyrics to this song. Write a short essay in which you use the concepts in this chapter to explain the lyrics.

of engineers who value mathematics, he will probably feel more positive about having this ability than if he comes from a family of artists who aren't quite sure how to respond to a child who likes math. If Deon's friends dislike math and respond negatively to his achievements, this peer pressure could cause him to devalue his ability, leading to a less positive self-concept, and undercutting his motivation to improve his math skills.

What is this child learning to think about himself as a musician?

The development of self-concept and self-esteem continues throughout our lives, as interactions with others serve to validate, reinforce, or alter our perceptions of who we think we are and how good we are at something. These interactions sometimes include others making direct predictions about us, or treating us in ways that convey those predictions indirectly. Such predictions can become **self-fulfilling prophecies**, or predictions that become true because we act in ways consistent with the prediction.

Self-fulfilling prophecies—predictions that become true because we act in ways consistent with the prediction

Janelle is a talented pianist who is struggling to play the violin. If her teacher says, "I don't think you have the spatial ability to become a professional violinist," Janelle may stop practicing as hard, which will prevent her from becoming a professional violinist, thus making her teacher's prophecy come true. Not all self-fulfilling prophecies are negative, however. On the way back to their apartment after volunteering at the local Head Start center, Janet commented to her friend Madison, "You're a natural with kids. I can see you directing a center like that." Madison, who had been struggling to find a career direction, thought about Janet's comment and others like it that she had received over the years and therefore pursued a career in early childhood education.

The type of self-concept we develop depends on the culture in which we are raised (Chen & Starosta, 1998). Some cultures, like that of the United States, value behaviors that lead people to develop independent self-concepts; whereas in other cultures, like that of Japan and China, value behaviors that lead people to develop interdependent self-concepts (Markus & Kitayama, 1991). The differences between independent and interdependent self-concepts have critical implications for our interaction and self-esteem.

People from cultures that value independence are likely to have an **independent self-concept**, seeing themselves as distinct from others, with separate characteristics and abilities. In other cultures, people's sense of self depends on the situation at hand and how they perceive themselves in relationship to particular others. People who have a **interdependent self-concept** view their traits, abilities and characteristics within the context of a particular relationship. The goal is to maintain or enhance their relationships by using the appropriate abilities and characteristics for the given situation. Someone with an interdependent self-perception is unlikely to think, "I am really persuasive," but rather, "When I am with my friends, I am able to convince them to do what is good for all of us. When I am with my father, I do what he believes is best for the

Independent self-concept—culturally based self-perceptions in which people see themselves as distinct from others with separate characteristics and abilities

Interdependent self-concept—culturally based self-perceptions in which people view their traits, abilities, and characteristics within the context of a particular relationship

Asian children usually develop interdependent self-concepts.

good of our family." Such self-esteem is gained from behaviors that advance the interests of the relationship or group, not the individual.

Some people are members of more than one cultural group. If one of the cultures encourages interdependent self-perceptions while the other encourages independent self-perceptions, such people may develop characteristics of both types of self-perception. They can switch "cultural frames" and draw on self-perceptions appropriate to the situation. They are more likely to do this well when they have been able to integrate their bicultural identity by seeing themselves as part of both cultures and appreciating the strengths of both cultures (Benet-Martínez & Haritatos, 2005). For example, when Nori, a fourth-generation Japanese American, is with his non-Asian American friends, he enjoys showing off his quick wit and keen sense of humor by teasing them and is praised for his cleverness. But when Nori attends extended family get-togethers at his very traditional grandparents' home in the Japantown section of San Francisco, he is careful to show his relatives, whom he would never consider teasing, respect.

LEARN ABOUT YOURSELF ▶ INDEPENDENT AND INTERDEPENDENT SELF-CONCEPT

Take this short survey to learn something about yourself. Act on your first response. There are no right or wrong answers. Just be honest in reporting what is true for you. **For each question, select one of the numbers to the left that best describes how much you feel the statement describes you.**

0 = Strongly Disagree
1 = Disagree
2 = Agree
3 = Strongly Agree

_____ 1. I act the same way no matter who I am with.

_____ 2. It is important for me to maintain harmony within my group.

_____ 3. I enjoy being unique and different from others in many respects.

_____ 4. I often feel that my relationships with others are more important than my own accomplishments.

_____ 5. I am comfortable being singled out for praise or rewards.

_____ 6. I would stay in a group if they needed me, even if I were not happy with the group.

_____ 7. I'd rather say "no" directly than risk being misunderstood.

_____ 8. My happiness depends on the happiness of those around me.

_____ 9. My personal identity as independent of others is very important to me.

_____ 10. It is important to me to respect decisions made by the group.

_____ 11. I prefer to be direct and forthright when dealing with people I have just met.

_____ 12. I will sacrifice my self-interest for the benefit of the group I am in.

Scoring the Survey: This survey measures the extent to which your self-concept is primarily independent or interdependent. To get your independent score, add your answers to the odd-numbered questions (1, 3, 5, 7, 9, 11). To get your interdependent score, add your answers to the even-numbered questions (2, 4, 6, 8, 10, 12). Which of the two scores is higher? The higher of the two scores indicates your cultural orientation to your self-perceptions.

Adapted from Fernández, I., Paez, D., & González, J. L. (2005). Independent and interdependent self-construal and culture. *Revue Internationale de Psychologie Sociale / International Review of Social Psychology*, 18(1), 35–63.

Messages, Feedback, and Self-Concept

"Wherever you go, there *you* are." As you interact with others, you can't escape your self-concept. There are at least three distinct ways that your self-concept affects your interpersonal communication encounters: It directs your attention and affects your judgments of others; it results in messages that reflect and maintain your self-concept; and it motivates you to manage the impressions that others form of you.

Self-Concept Affects Our Attention and Judgment

In the first half of the chapter, we discussed attention and judgment as social cognitive processes we apply to others. But these processes are also influenced by our self-concepts. Because ideas about ourselves are easy for us to access in memory, we often use them to make sense of others. In other words, we pay attention to characteristics that are central to who we think we are. If Gina's self-schema includes: "pretty," "critical," and "ambitious," she will tend to notice others physical attractiveness, tolerance, and ambition. But Vincent will notice others' athleticism, spirituality, and warmth, because these are central to his self-schema. So when Gina and Vincent meet Ella, they each will judge her based on what they notice. Gina will notice that Ella is not particularly attractive but seems to be really career-oriented, while Vincent will be impressed with Ella's basketball prowess and her friendliness. Research has found that we have an overall tendency for **social projection**, or overestimating the similarity between our preferences, traits, opinions, and concerns and those of others (Fiske & Taylor, 2013). If Mason thinks of himself as an honest, hard-working environmentalist, and he meets Sam at the local Sierra Club chapter, Mason is likely to assume that not only is Sam an environmentalist, but that he is also honest and hard-working. Despite our tendency to assume similarity, we also use our self-concepts to judge others in more self-serving ways. For example, we are more likely to assume that others share our weaknesses, but not our strengths. Thus, if Mason's self-concept includes both "detail-oriented" and "procrastinates," he's more likely to think that Sam is a procrastinator than think he is detail-oriented.

Messages Reflect and Maintain Our Self-Concept

In general, we not only perceive, but also act and communicate in ways that reflect and maintain our self-concept. In other words, when you feel good about who you are, you tend to communicate in ways that display the positive feelings you have, thus supporting how you feel. We also tend to perceive, act, and talk

▶ **OBSERVE AND ANALYZE**

Independent and Interdependent Self-Concepts

Identify someone you know who is bicultural, with at least one of this person's cultures differing from your own. The two cultures that she or he experiences should have different approaches to self-perception. Make a date for an interview. Begin by sharing what you have learned about independent and interdependent self-perceptions. Then ask for a description of how your interviewee experiences self-perception and handles being part of two cultures with different approaches to self-perception. Write a short essay in which you present what you have learned, comparing and contrasting it with your own experience.

Social projection—overestimating the similarity between our preferences, traits, opinions, and concerns and those of others in ways that maintain a negative self-concept. What leads us to do this? Remember that self-concept is a schema, and schemas are resistant to change. We easily assimilate information that is consistent with a schema, but we have to work hard not to filter out information that is inconsistent. For example, suppose Marco has prepared a fund-raising plan for his service organization, and his colleague Olivia comments that he's a good organizer. If Marco's self-schema includes "disorganized," he may discount the remark by replying, "I'm not really good at organizing, but this was easy, anyone could have done it." However, if Marco has a positive self-concept, he is more likely to pay attention to the compliment and acknowledge its truth by saying, "Thanks, I'm pretty good at this stuff. I like it, whereas most folks don't, so I've gotten a lot of experience." In the first case, failure to assimilate the new, positive information leaves Marco's negative self-concept unchanged. In the second, assimilating affirms his positive self-concept.

Our messages based on negative or positive self-concept not only reinforce existing self-concepts, but also encourage others to treat us in ways that reflect how we regard ourselves. For example, Marco's replies do more than confirm his current positive or negative self-concept; they also help shape how Olivia will come to view Marco. If Olivia sees Marco's contributions to the organization as "nothing special," as his negative self-concept may lead her to believe, she may devalue and disrespect him. But if she comes to see Marco as an expert, as his positive self-concept would suggest, she will appreciate and respect him, thus supporting his positive self-concept. Similarly, if Ana perceives herself as socially awkward, she may think, "I bet I'll know hardly anyone at the party— I'm going to have a miserable time." Because Ana fears encountering strangers and sees herself as socially incompetent, she is unlikely to introduce herself to anyone at the party, and, just as expected, she will spend much of her time alone.

The tendency to assimilate consistent information and ignore inconsistent information sometimes results in **incongruence**, a situation in which there is a gap between perception and reality. If you are overly attentive to successful experiences and positive responses, you may see yourself as having traits or abilities that you do not actually possess, and develop an inflated self-esteem that is not really in line with your actual abilities and characteristics. If, however, you dwell on your failures while disregarding your successes, or if you remember only the criticism you receive, your self-concept may be distorted and your self-esteem poor. Incongruence is troublesome because our perceptions of ourselves are more likely to influence our behaviors and communication patterns than our true abilities (Weiten, Dunn, & Hammer, 2011). For example, Seamus may actually possess all of the competencies and personality traits needed for effective leadership, but if he doesn't perceive that he has these talents and characteristics, he won't step forward in a situation where leadership is needed.

Incongruence—a situation in which there is a gap between perception and reality

Self-Concept Affects Impression Management Strategies

Impression management is your attempt to protect your self-concept by influencing the perception that others have of you. People manage both the positive and negative aspects of their self-concept. Sometimes these strategies are automatic, or employed without much conscious awareness.

When trying to make a positive impression, people often unknowingly match their behaviors to those of their interaction partners so that they smile, laugh, lean forward, disclose, use formal or vulgar language, etc., to about the same extent as their partner. As a result of this , many of us have had someone who knows us well tell us that we were acting "strange" or "weren't being ourselves" when we were talking to a new acquaintance. Other positive impression-management strategies are more controlled, such as sharing positive information about ourselves, or offering compliments to others. When these impression-management strategies are successful, people perceive us as more "like them," so they like us better, which reinforces our positive self-concept. Of course, positive strategies can also backfire if they appear manipulative. For example, Kate is a crack marksman, having earned a Distinguished Rifleman Badge when she was in the Army; when she was flirting with Ron, who had done two tours of duty in Iraq, she downplayed her shooting abilities. When a mutual friend told Ron of Kate's expertise, Ron felt manipulated and broke their date.

We also use impression management to protect our self-concepts. Protective strategies include limiting the quantity and depth of our interactions, avoiding topics that threaten us in some way, and being overly modest about ourselves. For example, Amad, a devoted follower of Islam, becomes uncomfortable when a conversation turns to terrorism, so he remains silent and looks for ways to quickly change the topic. The problem with protective strategies is their potential for promoting negative impressions, such as being perceived as unfriendly or uninterested.

> **Impression management**—our attempt to protect our self-concept by influencing the perception that others have of us

Improving Self-Concept and Self-Esteem

While self-concept and self-esteem are enduring characteristics of self-perception, they can be changed through new social environments, therapy, and self-help techniques. Numerous research studies have shown that self-esteem is increased through hard work and practice (Mruk, 2006). When experiencing profound changes in their social environments, people are likely to hear new messages about themselves and assimilate information they would have otherwise filtered out. If you went to camp as a child, moved to a new community, or changed schools, you know that while these changes were scary, you probably learned a lot about yourself and experienced new things that helped you form new ideas about who you are. Starting college, beginning a new job, falling in love, committing to or dissolving a relationship, becoming a parent, retiring, and grieving the death of a loved one are important life events that help us acknowledge messages that may be at odds with our current self-concepts. For example, when Art died, his wife, Gloria, who had never managed the family's finances, found that, not only did she enjoy paying the bills, but she was also good at budgeting. As a result of new experiences, people change their picture of who they are and thus begin to predict new things for themselves.

Some of us have experienced abusive relationships in which our family, friends, or significant others have verbally or physically damaged us. These experiences can have profoundly negatively effects on our self-images and often require professional help to recover from the damage that was done, so that our self-concept accurately reflects our talents and characteristics. While seeking professional help was once taboo, today we recognize the value that "talk therapy" can have. For people whose self-image has been damaged by their interactions with others, getting professional help is an act of self-love.

There are also self-help techniques that we can use to improve our self-image. One small but powerful technique starts with being more mindful about your self-talk. **Self-talk** is the messages you send to yourself through your thoughts. For example, when you think to yourself, "I handled that situation well," that is self-talk. If we feel good about ourselves—that is, if our overall self-image is positive—then our self-talk is likely to be more accurate: we will notice our successes and acknowledge our failures. But when an overall self-image is negative, our self-talk may be inaccurately negative: we don't acknowledge our successes, even to ourselves, while dwelling on our failures and generalizing them with self-messages like, "I never do anything right." We can alter our self-talk by

Self-talk—the messages we send to ourselves through our thoughts

How can you replace negative self-talk with positive self-talk?

consciously reflecting on our self-conversations. If you make a mistake, what do you say to yourself? If it's overly negative, can you find better ways of talking to yourself? For example, when something doesn't go smoothly, self-talk such as, "I can learn from this situation and use that in the future," is not only better for your self-concept, but also more likely to result in a better performance next time. Likewise, make a conscious effort to notice your successes and compliment yourself. Seek honest feedback from people you trust and become attuned to the positive feedback you receive. If you begin to discount it, tell yourself, "This person really thinks this about me, and so should I." Unfortunately, some people with negative self-images use overly positive self-talk to compensate for their insecurities. Since the goal is to increase the accuracy of your self-image, you need to hear both positive and negative feedback from others.

Social Cognition and Emotion

Although the word *cognition* could suggest thinking that is "cold" and logical, the way we perceive others and ourselves is strongly influenced by our emotions. Our feelings motivate us to pay attention to some things and ignore others, are woven into memory, and strongly affect how we judge others. Throughout this book, we'll explore the connections between communication and emotion, including how we express and manage our own feelings, and how we attempt to produce or change emotions in others. As background for this exploration, we start with a brief look at what emotions are, and how they relate to one another.

Defining Emotion

Emotions are the positive and negative sensations we experience as a result of perceiving something in our environment that supports or threatens our well-being, which result in uncontrolled physical reactions expressed through verbal and nonverbal behaviors that motivate us to take action. From this definition, you can see that emotions have five major components (Moors, 2009). The **feeling component of emotion** is the positive or negative sensation that we recognize as happiness, anger, anxiety, contempt, pride, surprise, and so on. But emotions are much more than feelings. The **somatic component of emotion** is the physical experience of a feeling, such as blushing when you are embarrassed, or your heart pounding when you are anxious or afraid. The somatic aspect of emotion is largely uncontrollable and sometimes prevents us from hiding what we feel. The **motor component of emotion** is the expression of emotion through nonverbal and verbal behaviors, such as when you scream in fear at the sound of a gunshot, or your eyes and mouth open widely when you are surprised. Taken together, these three components (feeling, somatic, and motor) are what most people think of as emotions, but a greater appreciation for the power of emotions comes from understanding their cognitive and motivational components as well.

Emotions—the positive and negative sensations we experience as a result of perceiving something in our environment that supports or threatens our well-being, which result in uncontrolled physical reaction expressed through verbal and nonverbal behaviors that motivate us to take action

Feeling component of emotion—the positive or negative sensations that we recognize as happiness, anger, anxiety, contempt, pride, surprise, and so on

Somatic component of emotion—the physical experience of a feeling

Motor component of emotion—the expression of emotion through nonverbal and verbal behaviors

Cognitive component of emotion— the meaning or interpretation of the emotion-provoking event

The **cognitive component of emotion** is the meaning or interpretation of the emotion-provoking event. According to appraisal theories of emotion (Lazarus, 1991; Roseman, Antoniou, & Jose, 1996), emotional reactions start with cognition. When we perceive that there is something happening in our environment that either supports us or works against us achieving our goals, we become emotional. Screaming in fear at the sound of a gunshot is preceded by recognition of danger. And when Johanna makes a snide remark about Maddie's new hairstyle, Johanna is contradicting Maddie's goal of looking better, therefore Maddie feels hurt.

The specific emotion that results from having our goal threatened depends on how you perceive the threat. For example, when Amy's co-worker and friend Jonah is recruited by another company that has offered him a better salary, she may feel sad because she enjoyed working with Jonah, but understand his decision to take the job. But if Jonah transfers to another department within the same company for the same salary and benefits, Amy may be hurt and confused because she will miss working with Jonah and doesn't understand why he has transferred. In sum, as you think about the social world, you feel it, too.

Have you noticed that if you enjoy or are intrigued by certain people you want to continue talking to them? Or that being disgusted or hurt makes you want to end a conversation? The **motivational component of emotion** is the action that emotion encourages you to take. This component is central to understanding human communication, because the feelings we experience affect how we interact in the moment. Skillful communicators recognize the motivations produced by emotions and consciously choose to channel or inhibit those motivations rather than simply react to them. For example, your first reaction to end a conversation or change the subject when you become anxious or annoyed might be appropriate in some situations, but in others, you may damage your relationship if you continually choose to withdraw. Being conscious of your motivations can enable you to become a more mindful communicator and thus preserve your relationships with others.

Motivational component of emotion—the action that emotion encourages us to take

Types of Emotions

Some emotions are classified as *basic* emotions, including anger, fear, surprise, sadness, disgust, contempt, happiness, contentment, interest, and love (Ekman & Cordaro, 2011; Levenson, 2011). So, what makes these emotions "basic"? First, they are *discrete*, meaning that they are distinct from each other. Each has a profile of somatic, feeling, cognitive, motivational, and motor components that are different from the others. Second, these emotions are *universal*, meaning that they are experienced by all cultural groups, and also by primate species. Some of the evidence for universality comes from facial expressions, which are remarkably similar across cultures for these emotions. Third, they are *automatic*, which means that they are "hardwired," and we have relatively little control over experiencing them when the right kind of emotion-provoking event occurs. For example, when we encounter someone who smells bad, we feel disgust—

essentially without conscious thought. Finally, the basic emotions are thought to be *adaptive*, in that the actions they motivate have connections with the survival of the human species. For example, if love didn't motivate physical intimacy and nurturing, your ancestors might not have reproduced or survived to adulthood.

Most theorists describe the basic emotions as "families" of emotion that include variations in intensity. Thus, the "anger family" includes irritation or annoyance, usually described as less intense than anger, as well as the high-intensity emotion of rage; and the "happiness family" includes slight happiness, which might be called serenity, and extreme happiness, or ecstasy. In this way, the basic emotions actually capture a great deal of human emotional experience.

However, there are also many emotions that fail to meet one or more of the criteria for a basic emotion but are still important to understanding human interaction. For example, although guilt and shame may not be fully distinct from sadness (Ekman & Cordaro, 2011), there is no doubt that these emotions affect what we say and do, or that people try to manipulate these emotions to influence others (Miczo & Burgoon, 2008). In addition, some emotions seem to be culturally specific—shaped by cultural socialization—and are an important part of emotional life within those cultures. For example, in Malay there is no word that exactly means "anger." So Malaysians feel *marah*, which is a sullen brooding, or they can feel *amok*, which is a violent frenzy. Japanese can feel *fureai*, which refers to a feeling of connectedness (Markus & Kitayama, 1991).

Improving Social Cognition

In this chapter you have learned how we use the social cognitive processes of attention, memory, and judgment to make sense of others and ourselves. We discussed that some of our social cognitions are automatic while others are controlled. As you will have noticed from our discussion, our automatic cognitions are not always accurate, useful, or productive. But how can we overcome our tendencies to automatically process? The following guidelines can help you overcome this bias and work toward controlling how you perceive others and yourself.

1. Question the accuracy of your perceptions. Questioning accuracy begins by saying, "I might be wrong about this person, or about myself. What other information should I consider?" Maybe the person sitting next to you in class dresses in an unusual way that triggers one of your stereotypes. If you acknowledge the possibility that the stereotype doesn't fit this person, you will interrupt the process of subtle stereotyping and begin to consciously search out information that will give you a more accurate, individualized view of this person. In situations where accurate perception is important, take a few seconds to become conscious of what is happening. It will be worth the effort.

2. Seek more information to verify perceptions. If you are working with only one or two pieces of information about another person, you are more likely to project your ideas onto the other person. Set your implicit personality theory aside, and try to collect further information to better ground your perceptions. The best way to get additional information about people is to talk with them. Reach out to that unusually dressed classmate, introduce yourself, and see where the conversation takes you. It's okay to be unsure about someone you don't know well. But rather than letting structures in your memory cause you to judge others inappropriately, seek the information you need to make a better decision.

3. Realize that your perceptions of a person may need to be updated over time. Schemas are powerful. Once we have ideas about another person in our memory, we tend to stick with them. Not only are we powerfully influenced by first impressions, but we may also miss how people change over time. When you encounter someone you haven't seen for a while, you will want to become reacquainted and let the person's current behavior rather than past actions or reputation inform your perceptions. Have you changed since high school? A former classmate who was "wild" in high school may well have changed and become a mature, responsible adult. Similarly, you want to allow for the possibility that people you see regularly are growing and changing, too.

4. Monitor your messages for unintended effects. Because many social-cognitive processes that operate automatically are biased in various ways, skillful communicators monitor their messages to interrupt this process. For example, because all of us have stereotypes, it is inevitable that from time to time we will engage in subtle stereotyping. Remain mindful and silently edit your messages and behaviors to minimize the likelihood of creating microaggressions based on stereotyping.

5. Monitor your emotions so you can control your responses. Because emotions are powerful, we can be motivated to act in ways that are inappropriate and ineffective. When we pay attention to how we are feeling, we can usually control how we act. Specifically, by voicing our emotions, we can often defuse our urge to act out. For example, if and when you begin to feel threatened, telling your partner this may allow the two of you to change the dynamics and avoid violence.

THE SOCIAL MEDIA FACTOR

Forming Impressions on Social Media

Have you ever received a Facebook "friend" request from someone you didn't immediately recognize? If you are curious about the person, you will probably scan their profile, photographs, and other personal information to figure out who they are. Even if you decide you still don't "know" the person, you will develop an impression based on this information. Will your impression be accurate? What impressions do people form from your online communication?

During face-to-face interactions, we think about others based on how they look and act, but also based on ideas stored in our memories. When using social media, the social cognitive processes of attention, memory, and judgment still apply, but instead of seeing or hearing others directly, we process the information that is available to us on their webpages. Scholars of computer-mediated communication classify this information into three categories of cues: *self-generated, other-generated,* and *system-generated* (Tong, Van Der Heide, Langwell, & Walther, 2008). **Self-generated social media cues** are items of information that people post on their own profiles, such as status updates and profile pictures. Most of the time, users have full control over these cues. **Other-generated social media cues** are items that other people post on your page, like comments on Facebook or Twitter. While users may not have full control over these posts, they do control whether they stay up. **System-generated social media cues** are pieces of information that the system provides, such as the number of friends you have on Facebook.

When using social media, we pay attention to all three types of cues. But what if the cues are contradictory? Warranting theory explains that online information seems more credible when it cannot be easily manipulated by the person it describes (Walther, Van Der Heide, Hamel, & Shulman, 2009). For example, Gina's Facebook posts may suggest that she is successful at work and popular with a large group of friends, but if no one seems to "like" her posts about work achievements or tag her in photos of social gatherings, what will you conclude about Gina? Research shows that we view other-generated and system-generated cues as more credible than self-generated cues (Walther et al., 2009). Therefore, you are likely to conclude that Gina is less successful and popular than she claims. Similarly, if your photos show you studying and working, but your friends post photos of you partying, people viewing your site may be more likely to believe that you're the life of the party rather than a serious, goal-oriented student.

Because social media sites allow others to comment on our statuses and tag us in their photographs and posts, we have to be mindful of others' impact on our digital identities. One social media scholar advises users that, "to make a good impression, it is not enough to carefully construct one's profile; it is also wise to carefully select one's friends" (Utz, 2010, p. 329). At the very least, you may want to consider altering what you share, allow friends to share, or permit the social network site to share. You may also want to question the impressions you form of others. Perhaps Gina's posts about work aren't "liked" because she hasn't friended people she knows through work, or because her work associates are envious of her success. Someone whose self-, other-, and system-generated cues are highly consistent and positive could still be hiding things through careful editing. In all, it is important to remember that social cognition is as much a part of online interaction as face-to-face interaction and to communicate accordingly.

Self-generated social media cues—items of information that people post on their own profiles, such as status updates and profile pictures

Other-generated social media cues—items that other people post on our page like comments on Facebook or Twitter

System-generated social media cues—pieces of information that the system provides, such as the number of friends we have on Facebook

INTER-ACT WITH
SOCIAL MEDIA

Log in to your Facebook account and scan through your friends list. Select a few friends you haven't communicated with in a long time and look at their Facebook pages. Scan their posted photographs, examine their status messages, and check out their timeline postings and other information available on their pages. What is your impression of each friend? How has that impression changed since you last communicated with that person? What specific characteristics of his or her Facebook page led you to develop this impression? Now, look at your Facebook page. What impressions might others draw about you based on how you present yourself on Facebook?

Rustown is a small Midwestern factory town. Over the years the white, middle-class citizens have formed a close-knit community that prides itself on its unity. Corpex, a large out-of-town corporation, which had just bought out the town's major factory, recently decided to move its headquarters there and to expand the current plant, creating hundreds of new jobs. This expansion meant that the new people coming into Rustown to manage and work in the factory would spend money and build homes, but it also meant that the composition of the small community would change.

Rustown inhabitants had mixed reactions to this takeover. The expectation of increased business excited owners of land and shops, but most Rustown residents who had been born and raised there were pretty much alike—and liked it that way. They knew that many of the new factory managers as well as some of the new employees were African and Hispanic Americans. Rustown had never had a black or Latino family, and some of the townspeople openly worried about the effects the newcomers would have on their community.

Otis Carr, a Corpex manager, had agreed to move to Rustown because of the opportunities that appeared to await him and his family, even though he recognized that

as a black man he might experience resentment. At work on the first day, Otis noticed that the workers seemed very leery of him, yet by the end of the first week, the plant was running smoothly, and Otis was feeling the first signs of acceptance. On Monday morning of the next week, however, he accidentally overheard a group of workers chatting on their break, trading stereotypes about African Americans and Latinos and using vulgarities and racist slurs to describe specific new co-workers.

Shaken, Otis returned to his office. He had faced racism before, but this time it was different. This time he had the power and the responsibility to make a difference. He wanted to change his workers' attitudes and behavior for the sake of the company, the town, and other minority group members who would be coming to Rustown. Although he knew he had to do something, he realized that brute managerial force would get him nowhere. He was familiar with the prejudices but not with ethical ways to change them.

FOR CONSIDERATION
1. What are the ethical issues in this case?
2. What advice would you offer Otis if he asked you how he can ethically change the perceptions that must underlie the comments that he overheard?

Summary

Social cognition, a type of perception, is how we make sense of other people, our social world, and ourselves. Understanding social cognition is important to understanding interpersonal communication. We make sense of others and ourselves through the mental or cognitive processes of attention, memory, and judgment. Much of social cognition is automatic, but it is important to use controlled processing to counter the biases that arise when we think automatically.

Our memories form the basis of the cognitive structure known as a *schema*, which affects how we view others. Implicit personality theories and stereotypes influence how we interact with others. Judgment is the social cognition process whereby we evaluate others and ourselves. These judgments can be positive or negative, mild or intense. Three judgment processes that are important for interpersonal communication interactions are impression formation, attribution, and stereotyping.

Your self-concept, the very large schema in your memory, is the collection of all the ideas you have about yourself. It is made up of many smaller, more specific types of self-schemas, including your self-schema, your possible self-concept, ideal self-concept, ought self-concept, feared self-concept, relational self-concept, and working self-concept.

Self-esteem is your positive or negative judgment about the characteristics that are part of your self-concept. We form our self-concepts through our communication with others. The type of self-concept we form is also influenced by the culture in which we are raised.

Your self-concept affects your interpersonal communication by directing your attention, affecting your judgments of others, and motivating you to manage the impression others form about you. Self-concepts and self-esteem are enduring self-perceptions but can be changed through new social environments, therapy, and self-help techniques. Social cognitions are also strongly influenced by our emotions. You can improve your social cognition by: 1) questioning the accuracy of your perceptions; 2) seeking more information to verify your perceptions; 3) realizing the need to update your perceptions of others or yourself from time to time; 4) monitoring your messages for unintended effects; and 5) monitoring your emotions so you can control your responses.

We form impressions through social media based on self-generated, other-generated, and system-generated cues. Warranting theory claims that online information about the personal characteristics and behaviors of others will seem more credible when the person whom it describes cannot easily manipulate it.

CHAPTER RESOURCES

Key Words

Flashcards for all of these key terms are available on the *Inter-Act* website.

Analyze and Apply

The following activities challenge you to demonstrate your mastery of the concepts, theories, and frameworks in this chapter by using them to explain what is happening in a specific situation.

2.1 Rewind/Rewrite

Now that you have read the chapter, hit "rewind" on the chapter opening scenario at the Junior Achievement callout.

a. Use concepts from the chapter to explain how Lynn quickly became convinced that she should leave the meeting. The concepts of automatic processing, associative network, implicit personality theory, stereotype, impression formation, self-concept, and emotion may be especially useful.

b. Rewrite the scenario so that Lynn employs some controlled processing, stays at the meeting, and finds out more about Ryan, Ashley, Becca, and Junior Achievement. Recognizing that they may be making automatic judgments about her, what can Lynn do to help them form a good impression of her?

c. How might the leadership of Junior Achievement structure their call-outs to welcome, rather than intimidate, potential members?

2.2 Who Am I?

a. Make lists of all the attributes, competencies, and personality traits that you believe describe you. Try completing the following sentences:

1. I am skilled at…

2. I have the ability to…

3. I know things about…

4. I am competent at doing…

5. One part of my personality is that I am…

b. List as many characteristics in each category as you can think of. Then develop
    lists of answers to the same question, only preface them with the phrases:

    1. I would like to…

    2. I ought to be…

    3. I'm afraid I am…

    4. Pick a person and begin with "When I am with Person X, I am…

    5. Other people believe that I…

c. Look over your lists. What do you notice? Based on your observations, write an
    essay titled "Who I Am, and How I Know This."

INTERCULTURAL COMMUNICATION

Jamie had moved from Wichita, Kansas, to South Korea to attend Seoul National University. After a rough transition, she had settled into her dormitory and her classes, and had made several South Korean friends, including Kwan, whom she'd been dating for several months. One day as they were walking across campus, Jamie, who had recently lost five pounds, flirtatiously twirled around Kwan and playfully asked, "Do you think I look fat?" She was shocked and hurt when Kwan matter-of-factly replied, "Yes, you look big and your hair needs to be cut."

WHAT YOU SHOULD BE ABLE TO EXPLAIN AFTER YOU HAVE STUDIED THIS CHAPTER:

▶ The concept of culture

▶ The role of communication in defining, transmitting, and changing culture

▶ The relationship between dominant and co-cultures

▶ Seven systematic ways in which cultures differ and how that affects intercultural communication

▶ Barriers we face when communicating with others from different cultures

▶ How to develop intercultural communication competence

▶ How social media use differs across cultures

WHAT YOU SHOULD BE ABLE TO DO AFTER YOU HAVE STUDIED THIS CHAPTER:

▶ Develop a plan for acquiring intercultural competence

Culture shock—the psychological discomfort you experience when you must interact in a new culture

People are so familiar with their own culture, its language, gestures, facial expressions, conversational customs, and norms, that they may experience anxiety when these familiar aspects of communication are disrupted. Yet this occurs frequently when we interact with people from different cultures. Jamie was only flirting as any American girl might flirt, and Kwan was only being honest as any Korean man would be. **Culture shock** is the psychological discomfort you experience when you must interact in a new culture (Klyukanov, 2005). Culture shock results when taken-for-granted meanings and rituals are not shared by others. You are likely to feel it most profoundly when you are thrust into another culture through international travel, business, or study. Culture shock can also occur when you come in contact with people from co-cultures within your home country. For example, Brittney, who is from a small town in Minnesota, may experience culture shock on her first visit to see her sister who has moved to Miami, Florida. She may be overwhelmed by the distinctly Hispanic flavor of the city, by hearing Spanish spoken among people on the street, by the prevalence of Latin beat music, by the prominence of billboards in Spanish, and by the way people look and dress. Brittney is likely to be disoriented not only because of the prominence of the Spanish language but also because the beliefs, values, and attitudes of the people she encounters might seem quite foreign to her. If Brittney is to overcome her culture shock and enjoy the scene on South Beach, she will need to become adept at talking with people from this different culture.

Intercultural communication—interactions that occur between people whose cultures are so different that the communication between them is altered

Intercultural communication refers to interactions that occur between people whose cultures are so different that the communication between them is altered (Samovar, Porter, & McDaniel, 2013). In other words, when communicating with people whose beliefs, values, and attitudes are culturally different from our own, we are communicating across cultural boundaries, which can lead to misunderstandings that would not ordinarily occur between people who are culturally similar. It is important to recognize that not every interaction between persons of different cultures exemplifies intercultural communication.

For example, when Brittney is on the beach in Miami and joins a group of Latinos in a friendly game of beach volleyball, their cultural differences are unlikely to affect their game-related exchanges. However, when Brittney joins her sister for a night of club-hopping on South Beach, she is likely to experience conversations in which cultural differences lead to difficulty in understanding or interpreting what is said. The first step toward becoming effective at intercultural communication is to understand what a culture is and be able to identify how cultures systematically differ from one another and how that affects interpersonal messages.

In this chapter, we examine how culture affects our communication behaviors and how it influences our perception of the communication we receive from others. We begin by explaining culture and several basic culture-related concepts. Then we describe ways that cultures systematically differ in their values, attitudes, norms, orientations, and emotional expressions. Then we discuss cultural differences in the use of social media. We end the chapter by describing how to develop intercultural communication competence.

"I know we're on planet earth but what planet are you on?"

Cartoonstock www.Cartoonstock.com

Culture and Communication

Culture is the system of shared values, beliefs, attitudes, and orientations, learned through communication, that guide what is considered to be appropriate thought and behavior in a particular group of people. Culture is a way of life, the taken-for-granted rules of how and why you behave as you do. Your culture influences not only important behaviors and decisions, but also more trivial ones as well. For example, do you routinely address higher status people by a title like Ms., Reverend, Doctor, or Professor and feel uncomfortable when you don't? If so, you probably come from a culture where you learned to use titles to show respect.

At the heart of any culture are its values. **Values** are the commonly accepted preference for some states of affairs over others. They include agreed-on standards of what is considered right and wrong, good and evil, fair and unfair, just and unjust, etc. Although members of a culture may not be able to state these values, you can often observe these values in how people behave.

Cultures have both real and ideal values. Ideal values are those that members of a culture profess to hold, whereas the real values of the culture are those that can be seen guiding the actual behavior of members of that culture. For example, Iran is a Muslim state and Israel is a Jewish state. The constitutions of both offer protections for members of religious minorities (ideal value). But the legal systems and the everyday treatment of religious minorities in each country belie this ideal. Both countries routinely subject religious minorities to legal hassles and mistreatment by their fellow citizens (real value in action).

Communication plays a central role in culture. First, as the definition of culture makes clear, communication is the way that culture is transmitted to members. If you address higher status people by their title, you probably remember a parent or teacher prompting you to do this. In Western cultures, we eat using forks, knives, spoons, individual plates, and bowls that we learned to

Culture—the system of shared values, beliefs, attitudes, and orientations learned through communication that guides what is considered to be appropriate thought and behavior in a particular segment of the population

Values—the commonly accepted preference for some states of affairs over others

From our culture we learn even ordinary behavior. Do you eat your meals with chop sticks? Your fingers? Utensils? How do you hold your fork when you eat?

use in childhood. In China people eat with chopsticks, and in other cultures people use bread, or leaves, or eat with their fingers, and share a common bowl. All these dining rituals are culturally based and taught by one generation to the next through communication.

Not only is a culture transmitted through communication, but communication is also the mechanism through which a culture is modified. For example, two generations ago, most American children were taught to show respect by addressing adult family friends with a title and the friend's last name (Mr. Jones, Miss Smith, etc.). Today, it is commonplace for even young children to address family friends by their first name. How did this cultural custom change? In earlier generations, when a parent corrected a young child who had mimicked the parent's use of an adult friend's first name, the friend remained silent, reinforcing the correction. So, the child learned to say "Mr.," "Mrs.," "Doctor," etc. But during the last half of the twentieth century, adults began to communicate their permission for children to use their first name, stopping parents in mid-correction or correcting children who addressed them using a title with their last names. Over time, the cultural norm changed, and today it is common for American children to address all adult family friends as well as others by their first names. Communication is both the means by which culture is transmitted and the way that a culture is changed.

Dominant and Co-Cultures

Dominant culture—the learned system of values, beliefs, attitudes, and orientations held by the majority of people in a society

Although the United States is a diverse society, there are many attitudes, values, beliefs, and customs that the majority of people hold in common and that the minorities feel they must follow. The **dominant culture** is the learned system of values, beliefs, attitudes, and orientations held by the people who are in power in a society. Generally these people historically and presently have controlled the major institutions of the society (Samovar, Porter, & McDaniels, 2013). The less diverse the population of a society, the stronger is its dominant culture. In the United States, the dominant culture has evolved over time. It once strictly reflected and privileged the values of white, Western European, English-speaking, Protestant, heterosexual men. Before the 1960s, people coming to the United States from other cultural backgrounds were expected to assimilate into this dominant cultural perspective and to sublimate or abandon their native culture. In many cases, immigrants arriving from other countries changed their names to sound more American. They were expected to learn English as quickly as possible and follow the norms of conversation of the dominant culture.

While there is a dominant culture, many Americans also identify with one or more **co-cultures** that exist side by side with the dominant culture and are composed of smaller numbers of less powerful people who hold common values, attitudes, beliefs, and orientations that differ from those of the dominant culture. Co-cultural groups form around one or more shared demographic characteristics such as gender, race, ethnicity, sexual orientation/gender identity, religion, social class, and generation. Since the 1960s, the United States has experienced a cultural revolution that has resulted in an adjustment of the dominant cultural perspective to be more reflective of the diverse co-cultures with which its citizens identify. We have come to understand and expect that different people may follow different communication patterns learned from their co-culture and that if we are to be competent communicators we need to be able to adjust to diversity.

Co-cultures—cultures that exist side by side with the dominant culture and comprise smaller numbers of people who hold common values, attitudes, beliefs, and orientations that differ from those of the dominant culture

Gender

Most cultures differentiate between the behavior valued in men and the behavior valued in women. They socialize children in ways that lead girls and boys to act in accord with the roles that the culture expects them to play. Because they belong to different co-cultures, women and men communicate differently. For instance, research shows that, on average, women are more concerned with personal relationships when they communicate. They talk more about relationships and feelings, do more to include others in conversations, and respond more actively to what others say. Men more often focus on tasks or outcomes when they communicate. They talk more about activities and problem solving, tend to emphasize control and status, and are less responsive to others (Wood, 2012).

Race

The term "race" was traditionally used to classify people based on widely evident—or visible—biological traits, such as skin and eye color, hair texture, and body shape (Kottak, 2012). However, recent genetic studies such as the Human Genome Project (2001) show that racial groups are not biologically distinct (Smedley & Smedley, 2005). Yet race, as a social concept, is very

Codeswitch—to alter linguistic and nonverbal patterns to conform to the dominant or co-culture depending on the topics or the participants in a conversation

much a part of many cultures. People have experienced the social effects of perceived race and have formed communities and co-cultures based on racial experiences. If the racial group to which you belong is not the dominant culture of your country, you may have communication patterns that are distinct from those of the dominant group, so you may learn to **codeswitch**, altering your linguistic and nonverbal patterns to conform to either that of the dominant culture or of your co-culture, depending on the topics or co-participants in a conversation (Bonvillain, 2003). When Ling joins her family for dinner, she may speak Vietnamese and defer to her older relatives. At school, however, she may speak only English, and while hanging out at the local youth center with her friends from the neighborhood, she may speak a mixture of Vietnamese and English.

Ethnicity

Ethnicity—a classification of people based on shared national characteristics such as country of birth, geographic origin, language, religion, ancestral customs, and traditions

Like race, ethnicity is an inexact distinction. **Ethnicity** is a classification of people based on shared national characteristics such as country of birth, geographic origin, language, religion, ancestral customs, and tradition. People vary greatly in terms of the importance they attach to their ethnic heritage and the degree to which it affects their attitudes, values, and behaviors. Generally, the further you are from your family's immigrant experience, the less you will be influenced by your ethnic co-culture. Language or "mother tongue" is an obvious influence of ethnicity on communication. Immigrants bring with them the language of their original country and may or may not speak English when they arrive. Even after they learn English, many immigrants choose to speak their mother language at home, live in proximity to other people from their home country, and interact with them in their native language. Although the United States is considered an English-speaking country, it now has the third-largest Spanish-speaking population of any country in the world, and 75 percent of Latinos in the United States speak Spanish at home (US Census Bureau, n.d.). To accommodate Spanish speakers, businesses and government agencies offer automated phone services with bilingual menus and employ bilingual customer-service professionals.

Sexual Orientation and Gender Identity

In the United States, as in other countries, the dominant culture historically has valued and privileged heterosexuality and encouraged children to develop a gender identify that is consistent with their biological sex at birth. People who deviated from this preferred pattern of behavior were often severely mistreated. As a result, gay, lesbian, and transgender people formed underground communities that developed co-cultures where homosexual and transgender behaviors were valued and members received social support. Over the past 40 years, gay activism has modified the dominant culture so that homosexual and to some extent transgender people face less discrimination. Nevertheless, today there are still gay, lesbian, and transgender co-cultures that provide important social support to members.

Religion

A **religion** is a system of beliefs, rituals, and ethics based on a common perception of the sacred or holy. Although the ideal value of the dominant culture of the United States is religious freedom and diversity, historically its real values have reflected monotheistic Judeo-Christian perspectives. All observant practitioners of a religion participate in a co-culture. Those who strongly identify with a religious group outside the Judeo-Christian tradition will have different beliefs and attitudes that shape relationships and their communication behaviors. For example, Buddhism advises individuals to embrace rather than resist personal conflict. Adversity, emotional upheaval, and conflict are seen as natural parts of life (Chuang, 2004). Accordingly, a Buddhist is apt to communicate openly and calmly during an interpersonal conflict and embrace the positive aspects of conflict in strengthening interpersonal ties.

Religion—a system of beliefs, rituals, and ethics based on a common perception of the sacred or holy

Social Class

Social class is a level in the power hierarchy of a society whose membership is based on income, education, occupation, and social habits. Most Americans are uncomfortable talking about social class and identify with the middle class even though they may really be members of more elite or lower classes (Ellis, 1999). However, social classes exist in the United States just as they exist in all societies. In the United States, increasing educational and income disparity are making it more difficult for people to move into or stay in the middle class. Your social class often determines where you live, where you go to school, and with whom you come in contact. As a result, over time members of a social class develop and reinforce co-cultures with distinct values, rituals, and communication practices. Your accent, grammar, vocabulary, and the slang that you use are likely to be influenced by your social class. Likewise, how you celebrate and grieve are also influenced by your social class.

Social class—a level in the power hierarchy of a society whose membership is based on income, education, occupation, and social habits

Generation

The time period in which we are born and raised can have a strong formative influence on us. People of the same generation form a cultural cohort group whose personal values, beliefs, and communication behaviors have been influenced by the common life experiences and events they encountered as they aged (Zemke, Raines, & Fitzpatrick, 2013). Traditionalists, born before 1943, grew up influenced by the Great Depression and World War II; they value consistency, conformity, discipline, and logic. Baby Boomers, born 1943 to 1960, were strongly influenced by the counterculture of the 1960s, and are likely to judge, question, and compete. Those we call Generation X, born 1960 to 1980, who experienced latchkey childhoods and the consequences of widespread divorce, value self-sufficiency, informality, and diversity, and tend to be cynical. Millennials (also called Generation Y or the Echo Boomers), born after 1980, had more sheltered and scheduled childhoods than prior generations, were exposed to school and world violence at an early age, experienced the effects of globalization, and witnessed the failure of major corporations.

Is it rude to check messages, read social media feeds, etc. when you are with someone else?

Cultural identity—that part of your self-image that is based on the cultural group or groups with which you most closely associate and align yourself

▶ **OBSERVE AND ANALYZE**

Communicating within Co-Cultures

Attend an event of a co-cultural group on campus or in your community. Consider visiting an ethnic festival, an unfamiliar house of worship, or a senior center. Observe the behavior of others, and communicate with as many people as possible. Then write a paper describing the experience and discussing the concepts of intercultural communication, culture shock, ethnocentrism, and stereotyping. Provide specific examples of any of these concepts you experienced.

Nonetheless, as a generation, they are confident, optimistic, and collaborative. They are also Digital Natives, having grown up with computers, video games, internet, cell phones, and MP3 players. According to educational leader and learning software developer Marc Prensky, who coined the term:

> *Digital Natives are used to receiving information really fast. They like to parallel process and multi-task. They prefer their graphics before their text rather than the opposite. They prefer random access (like hypertext). They function best when networked. They thrive on instant gratification and frequent rewards. They prefer games to "serious" work. (Prensky, 2001)*

Scholars and social commentators are just beginning to define the qualities of the next generational cohort, Generation Z, born in 2005 or later (Emelo, 2013). This group, now in their tweens, will have lives influenced by continued globalization combined with economic downturn, terrorism, and school violence, and the infiltration of technology into virtually every aspect of life (e.g., "the internet of things"). Some predict they will be safety-conscious and conservative with money, but pragmatic and resilient (Anatole, 2013).

Whether in family relationships or in the workplace, when people from different generations interact, their co-cultural orientations can create communication difficulties. For example, when members of different generations work together, miscommunication, misunderstandings, and conflict are likely to occur more often than when people work with others of the same generation. Generally, people from the Traditionalist and Baby Boomer cohorts are less likely to question authority figures than those who came later (Zemke, Raines, & Fitzpatrick, 2013). One way they demonstrate their respect for authority is by using formal terms of address, referring to people as Mr., Ms., Dr., Sir, and so forth. Later generations tend to be more skeptical of authority and less formal in dealing with authority figures. They are more likely to question their managers and to openly disagree with decisions that are made by those in authority. Another line of division is between the Digital Natives (Millennials or Gen Y) and the earlier generations, who have been called "Digital Immigrants." For Digital Natives, connecting with others via technology is as real and significant as connecting face-to-face, whereas Digital Immigrants make stronger distinctions between the "real" and "virtual" worlds, and may resent Digital Natives' near-constant texting, tweeting, messaging, and other ways of communicating with non-present others.

Cultural Identity

In addition to the dominant culture, most of us belong to one or more co-cultures. Your **cultural identity** is that part of your self-image that is based on the cultural group or groups with which you most closely associate and align yourself. It is determined by the importance that you assign to your membership in a cultural group (Ting-Toomey et al., 2000). You may closely identify with one co-culture group into which you fit and not identify with another. You may choose to embrace a co-cultural identity at odds with the dominant culture, or you may work hard to distance yourself from a co-cultural group and adopt the values and mores of the dominant culture. You may be proud that you are a third-generation Polish American who embraces this heritage through your verbal and nonverbal mannerisms, your religion, your diet, and many other aspects of your identity. On the other hand, your roommate, also a third-generation Polish American, may be more assimilated to the dominant American culture, rarely thinking of or identifying herself as from a Polish background. She may not adhere to any of the cultural communication norms common to this ethnic background. When the dominant culture stigmatizes a co-culture, some members of the co-culture may downplay or obscure this part of their identity to fit into the dominant culture, or they may more closely identify with the co-culture and become activists or advocates for it.

How Cultures Differ

We may be able to figure out people's cultural background based on their language, dress, or personal artifacts, such as religious markers worn as jewelry or placed in the home. For example, when people meet Deen Singh, his turban tells them that he is a Sikh. But while these things may help you recognize that someone belongs to a specific culture, they do not help you understand the values or the communication practices you can expect from members of that culture. Sikhs wear turbans to identify themselves as part of a culture that practices gender and social class equality, values all life, stands strongly against injustice, and defends the weak and downtrodden.

The early work of Edward T. Hall and later work of Geert Hofstede give us a way to understand how cultures are similar to and different from one another

Many contemporary Muslim women honor their religious beliefs by wearing hijabs. Do you wear symbols of any religious affiliation?

How were you encouraged to maintain your ethnic or religious identity?

Individualism	High uncertainty avoidance	High power distance	Masculinity
X (1st)			
			X (15th)
		X (38th)	
	X (43rd)		
Collectivism	Low uncertainty avoidance	Low power distance	Femininity

FIGURE 3.1 Dimensions of Culture—U.S. Ranking Among 53 Countries/Regions.

and how cultural variation affects communication. Edward T. Hall, an anthropologist who is considered the father of intercultural communication, identified two ways in which cultures differ that have important implications for intercultural interaction: (1) cultural norms about time and (2) the importance of context for understanding a message (Rogers, Hart, & Miike, 2002). As a manager in the Personnel Research Department at IBM Europe, Hofstede (1980) conducted a large-scale research project that studied fifty countries and three regions. His work identified four ways in which cultures differ that are important for intercultural communication: (1) the extent to which the individual is valued versus the group or collective; (2) the extent to which predictability is valued versus tolerating uncertainty; (3) the extent to which the norms of the culture support equality or uneven distribution of power; and (4) the extent to which the culture is oriented to traditional masculine or feminine gendered behavior. Figure 3.1 shows where the United States falls on each of these dimensions. Finally, research suggests that cultures vary in their norms for expression of emotion. Let's look at each of these seven ways in which cultures may differ from one another.

Time Orientation

Edward T. Hall pioneered the field of **chronemics**, the study of how perception of time differs between individuals and cultures (Hall, 1976). Some people and cultures are **monochronic**, perceiving time as being small, even units that occur sequentially. Monochronic people adhere to schedule and do things one at a time. Monochronic cultures value punctuality, uninterrupted task completion, meeting deadlines, and following plans. For instance, when Margarite, who perceives time in a monochronic way, is interrupted by her sister, who is excited to share some good news, Margarite may snap, "Get out of here right now. You know it's my study time!" The dominant culture of the United States is monochronic.

Other people and cultures are **polychronic**, seeing time as a continuous flow. Polychronic people understand that appointment times and schedules are approximate and fluid. Rather than doing one thing at a time, they are comfortable

Chronemics—the study of how perception of time differs between individuals and cultures

Monochronic—a time orientation that views time as being small, even units that occur sequentially

Polychronic—a time orientation that views time as a continuous flow

doing several things at once, having flexible schedules or none at all, and disregarding deadlines and appointment times to satisfy task or relationship needs (Chen & Starosta, 1998). People who take a polychronic approach to time do not perceive interruptions as annoying departures from plans but as natural occurrences. Latin American, Arab, and southern European cultures are polychronic.

Differences in time orientation can make intercultural communication challenging. For example, Dante, who perceives time in a polychronic way, may show up for a noon lunch with Stephen at 12:47 and not think of that as a problem, since his co-worker stopped him to ask for help with a project. Stephen was annoyed and impatient, however, when Dante arrived more than forty-five minutes late to their planned lunch and then proceeded to ignore his attempts to quickly move the discussion to the business they needed to complete. Meanwhile, Dante found Stephen's attitude confusing and off-putting. Stephen's abrupt transition to business seemed rude to Dante. In polychronic cultures engaging in conversation to enhance the relationship is seen as much more important than quickly concluding business. Differences in time orientation make the lunch and conversation uncomfortable for both men. Like other cultural differences, monochronic and polychronic perceptions of time are only general tendencies of certain cultures and individuals, and one orientation is not better than the other.

The Importance of Context for Sharing Meaning

The difference between cultures perhaps most related to intercultural communication is the extent to which members rely on contextual cues to convey the actual meaning of a message. According to Edward T. Hall (1976), cultures differ not only in the languages spoken but also in the degree to which people rely on factors other than words to convey their meaning. In some cultures, the speaker's words convey most of the meaning. In other cultures, much of the speaker's message is understood from the context. Thus, cultures may be either high or low context.

A **low-context culture** is a culture in which message meanings are usually encoded in the verbal part of the message. The words spoken are more important in understanding the message than contextual cues like nonverbal behaviors, previous interactions, or cultural cues. Verbal messages are direct, specific, and detailed. Speakers are expected to say exactly what they mean and get to the point. In low-context cultures people use forceful verbal messages in persuading others. The United States, Germany, and Scandinavia are low-context cultures.

A **high-context culture**, on the other hand, is a culture in which much of the real meaning of a message is indirect and can only be accurately decoded by referring to unwritten cultural rules and subtle nonverbal behavior. In a high-context culture verbal messages are general and ambiguous, with the real meaning implied and understood by "reading between the lines." In high-context cultures speakers are cautious and tentative in their use of language. Most Native American, Latin American, and Asian cultures are high-context (Chen & Starosta, 1998).

INTER-ACT WITH
SOCIAL MEDIA

Various cultures treat time differently. Social media have changed how members of the American culture view time. Think for a moment about how quickly you respond to a friend's text message. Why might you feel a burning desire to respond so quickly? Does the same hold true for messages you receive through other forms of social media, such as email or Facebook? As you learn about culture in this chapter, think about how social media might influence how members of other cultures treat time. Is the burning desire to respond quickly to text messages unique to the American culture? Why or why not?

Low-context culture—a culture in which message meanings are usually encoded in the verbal part of the message

High-context culture—a culture in which much of the real meaning of a message is indirect and can only be accurately decoded by referring to unwritten cultural rules and subtle nonverbal behavior

When native Americans interact much of the meaning is embedded in the context. How do you suppose the context of this interaction is affecting what is communicated?

Effective communication between members of high- and low-context cultures is very difficult. Consider the following conversation between Isaac, a member of a low-context culture, and Zhao, a member of a high-context culture, who are trying to conduct business together.

Isaac: *Let's get right down to business here. We're hoping that you can provide 100,000 parts per month according to our six manufacturing specifications spelled out in the engineering contract I sent you. If quality control finds more than a 2 percent margin of error, we'll have to terminate the contract. Can you agree to these terms?*

Zhao: *We are very pleased to be doing business with you. We produce the highest quality products and will be honored to meet your needs.*

Isaac: *But can you supply that exact quantity? Will you commit to meeting all of our engineering specifications? Will you consistently have a less than 2 percent margin of error?*

Zhao: *We are an excellent, trustworthy company that will send you the highest quality parts.*

Isaac was probably frustrated with what he perceived as general, evasive language on Zhao's part. Zhao was probably offended by the direct questions and specific language, which he perceived as threatening and embarrassing.

Both Isaac and Zhao could have been more effective in this exchange if each had been mindful of how messages are formed and understood in the other's culture. When low-context communicators like Isaac interact with high-context communicators like Zhao, they should be aware that building a good relationship is important for long-term effectiveness. Therefore, polite social conversation should precede business; nonverbal messages and gestures will be as important as what is said; status and identity are communicated nonverbally and need to be acknowledged; face-saving and tact are important and can often supersede being frank; and indirect expressions must be interpreted within the context and rules of the speaker's culture. When high-context communicators like Zhao interact with low-context communicators like Isaac, they should recognize that what a low-context culture person says should be taken at face value rather than examined for underlying meaning. High-context people also need to remember that the direct questions, assertions, and observations made by a low-context person are not meant to be offensive. Finally, high-context people should recognize that low-context people usually do not interpret or understand indirect contextual cues.

The Value of the Individual vs. the Group

Hofstede found that cultures differed in the extent to which individualism or collectivism was valued (1997). An **individualistic culture** is a culture that values personal rights and responsibilities, privacy, voicing one's opinion, freedom, innovation, and self-expression (Andersen et al., 2003). People in individualistic

Individualistic culture—a culture that values personal rights and responsibilities, privacy, voicing one's opinion, freedom, innovation, and self-expression

cultures place primary value on the self and on personal achievement, which explains the emphasis on personal opinion, innovation, and self-expression. In individualistic cultures, people's connections to groups are loose. They consider the interests of others only in relationship to how those interests affect the interest of the self. If you come from an individualistic culture, you may consider your family and close friends when you act but only because your interests and theirs align. People in individualistic cultures also view competition as desirable and useful. Because of this, they value personal rights, freedom, and privacy as well as norms that support fair competition. According to Hofstede, individualistic cultures include those in the United States, Australia, Great Britain, Canada, and northern and eastern European countries.

In contrast, a **collectivist culture** is a culture that values community, collaboration, shared interests, harmony, the public good, and avoiding embarrassment (Andersen et al., 2003). Early in life, people in collectivist cultures are socialized into strong, close-knit groups that will protect them in exchange for loyalty. Collectivist cultures place primary value on the interests of the group and group harmony. An individual's decisions are shaped by what is best for the group, regardless of whether they serve the individual's interests. Collectivist societies are highly integrated, and the maintenance of harmony and cooperation is valued over competitiveness and personal achievement. According to Hofstede, collectivist cultures are found in South and Central America, East and Southeast Asia, and Africa.

Collectivist culture—a culture that values community, collaboration, shared interests, harmony, the public good, and avoiding embarrassment

The values of individualism and collectivism influence many aspects of communication, including self-concept and self-esteem formation, approaches to conflict, and working in groups (Samovar et al., 2013).

First, individualism and collectivism affect self-concept and self-esteem. You'll recall from our discussion of self-perceptions in Chapter 2 that people in individualist cultures form independent self-concepts and base their self-esteem on individual accomplishments. People in collectivist cultures form interdependent self-concepts and base their self-esteem on how well they fit into a group. If, for example, Marie, who was raised in an individualistic culture, is the highest-scoring player on her basketball team, she will feel good about herself and identify herself as a "winner," even if her team has a losing season. But if Marie is from a collectivist culture, the fact that she is the highest-scoring player will have little effect on her self-esteem. Her team's losing season will probably cause her to feel lower personal self-esteem.

Second, people from each of these cultural perspectives view conflict differently. The emphasis placed on the individual leads members of individualistic cultures to value and practice assertiveness and confrontational argument, whereas members of collectivist cultures value accord and harmony and thus practice collaboration or avoidance in arguments. In the United States, we teach assertiveness and argumentation as useful skills and expect them to be used in interpersonal and work relationships, politics, consumerism, and other aspects of civic life. In contrast, the collectivist culture of Japan has developed business practices that maintain harmony and avoid interpersonal clashes. For example, in

Individualism and Collectivism

BY MIN LIU, ASSISTANT PROFESSOR OF COMMUNICATION, SOUTHERN ILLINOIS UNIVERSITY AT EDWARDSVILLE

I was born and raised in China, which is a collectivist country. I arrived in the United States for the first time in August of 2002 when I entered the Ph.D. program as a graduate student at North Dakota State University (NDSU) in Fargo, North Dakota. I chose NDSU for a number of reasons, but one that stands out in my mind as important is the fact that Fargo was listed as one of the safest cities in the USA at the time. You see, my family was concerned about sending their daughter to study in the USA, which is the most individualistic country in the world. They felt a bit more at ease knowing I would be studying in one of the safest cities in that country. Even my decision to come to NDSU was influenced by my family and our collectivist ideals. Little did I know, however, how much "culture shock" I would experience beginning with the first day I set foot on the NDSU campus.

I officially became an international student studying communication at North Dakota State University in August of 2002. I felt prepared to study in the USA because I had learned English and was trained to become a college English instructor back in China. I had also aced the English proficiency test (TOEFL) required of international students. I remember feeling pretty confident about communicating with my American colleagues. As I walked across campus for my first day of orientation, I thought to myself, "Worst-case scenario I'll forget how to say something in English and that's what my digital Chinese-English dictionary is for."

I would soon learn, however, that the issue of translating vocabulary was not the worst-case scenario. For most of my communication struggles, I could not find an answer in the dictionary. For example, in one of the first graduate classes I took, the professor asked everyone to call her by her first name (Deanna). Without hesitation, all my American classmates began doing so. Calling a professor by her first name was unheard of for Chinese students like me! As a sign of respect, we always call our teachers by their titles—Dr. Sellnow, Professor Sellnow, or Teacher

Sellnow. Wherever you are on a college campus in China, it's clear who is the teacher and who are the students. I thought, "How I am to call a professor of mine by her first name?"

For a long time, I felt torn as to what to do—continuing to call her Dr. Sellnow may seem too distant and she might correct me. I want to honor her request out of respect for her authority. But, everything in my collectivist values suggested that calling her Deanna was simply too disrespectful. So, I simply avoided calling her anything. This solution worked fairly well in face-to-face communication situations—I would walk up to her, smile, and then start the conversation. This approach was working fairly well for me until the day came when I needed to email her. I remember sitting in front of my computer for almost an hour trying to fine-tune a one-paragraph email. Soon I realized the email message was fine. The reason I couldn't bring myself to press "SEND" was with the beginning of the email, which read, "Hello Deanna." I finally changed it to Dr. Sellnow, followed by an apologetic explanation asking her to understand my dilemma and why I addressed her in this way. To my surprise, she responded by saying there was nothing wrong in addressing her as "Dr. Sellnow" and that I should continue to do so if that is what feels most appropriate to me.

In another class, I studied intercultural communication concepts. What I learned there proved helpful to me in reconciling my collectivist-individualistic predicament and better understand the cultural shock I was experiencing. As a Chinese, I grew up in a high power-distance culture. Professors and teachers are seen as having more power than students because, in my culture, people hold more or less power depending on where they are situated in certain formal, hierarchical positions. Students are to respect and honor their teachers by acknowledging their higher position of authority and status. The United States, however, is a low power-distance culture. People demonstrate respect for one another by addressing each other more as equals regardless of the formal positions they may hold. So, as uncomfortable as I felt, I tried to call my professors by their first names when they suggested it was appropriate to do so. I reminded myself that, in the USA doing so was culturally appropriate and not a sign of disrespect.

Another culture shock experience I had to reconcile as a result of the differences between my collectivist values and the individualistic values of the USA had to do with disagreeing with my professor. In the USA, students learn to form opinions and defend their viewpoints and are rewarded for doing so in classroom presentations and debates. Professors perceive students who challenge their viewpoints with evidence and reasoning as intelligent and motivated. Students who do so are perceived very differently in the Chinese culture, where public disagreement with an authority figure is not only rare, but also inappropriate. Because of this value clash, I found it difficult to express and defend my opinions in class, especially if they differed from something the professor said. Doing so, it seemed to me, would be extremely disrespectful. Yet, I observed classmates doing so and being lauded for their comments. Many times, I chose not to say anything during a face-to-face meeting with a professor, but found the courage to write an email later. In the online environment, I found I could be honest and explain my disagreement with respect. Fortunately, many of my professors soon realized my cultural values dilemma and adapted their communication styles toward me. Still today, though, I prefer to present my viewpoints concerning controversial issues in a paper, a letter, an email message, or an online post, rather than in a meeting or other face-to-face discussion. I have found a way to honor my collectivist values in a way that also allows me to express myself in an individualistic cultural setting.

Finally, I recall struggling with how to behave in group settings as a result of the cultural differences along the individualism vs. collectivism continuum. When I first arrived in the USA, I was very conflict avoidant, probably because in collectivistic cultures maintaining the harmony of the collective is an important priority. The approaches I had learned to value and enact in small group settings were actually perceived negatively by my peers and professors in the USA. My conflict avoidant style—which I engaged in as a sign of respect—would actually frustrate some of my group members. They perceived it as a sign that I did not care about the group's success and was a "slacker." I felt frustrated, too, as I tried to help the group become more cohesive and successful by avoiding conflict! I eventually learned that, to be successful, we all had to begin by being upfront about where we come from and our values. Once we all understood the differences, we could create a workable plan for success.

I have been in the U.S. for seven years now, am married, and have a son. I have also earned my Ph.D. and am working as an Assistant Professor of Communication at the University of Southern Illinois at Edwardsville. Even now, I continue to learn new things about how to communicate best in this individualistic culture as compared to my collectivist home in China. Based on my experiences, I would have to say the most important thing for successful communication when interacting with people who come from a different place on the collectivism–individualism continuum is for all of us to always be mindful.

Originally published in: Verderber, K.S., Verderber, R.F., and Sellnow, D.D. (2014). *Communicate! 14th Ed.*, Boston, MA: Wadsworth Cengage Learning. pp. 61-62. Used with permission.

FOR CONSIDERATION:

1. In collectivist cultures respect is communicated by formalities like naming, unquestioning acceptance of the authority, and avoiding conflict. How is respect communicated in individualist cultures?

2. While the dominant culture in the United States seems to follow the patterns that Dr. Liu lays out in her essay, there are subcultures and family cultures that do not adhere to the patterns she describes. Were you raised to call your elders Mr., Mrs., Ms., Dr., etc.? Are you still most comfortable doing so? How questioning of authority are you? Does this reflect a cultural or family norm? Finally, how likely are you to directly express your disagreements with others? Is this pattern one that is valued by your culture or family?

Japanese business, an elaborate process called *nemawashii* (a term that also means "binding the roots of a plant before pulling it out") has evolved. In Japan, any subject that might cause conflict at a meeting should be discussed in advance so that the interaction at the meeting will not seem rude or impolite (Samovar et al., 2013). In collectivist societies like Japan, a communication style that respects the relationship is preferred to one that expedites the exchange of information. In collectivist societies, group harmony, sparing others embarrassment, and a modest presentation of self are important ways to show respect and avoid conflict. Direct speech that might hurt others in the group is discouraged.

Finally, individualism and collectivism influence how people work in groups. Because members of collectivist cultures consider group harmony and the welfare of the group to be of primary importance, they strive for consensus on group goals and may at times sacrifice optimal outcomes for the sake of group accord. In individualistic cultures, however, optimal outcomes are paramount, regardless of whether that results in group disharmony. Your cultural assumptions affect how you work to establish group goals, how you interact with other group members, and how willing you are to sacrifice for the sake of the group. Groups whose members come from both individualistic and collectivist cultures may experience difficulties because of their diverse cultural assumptions. In the Diverse Voices article, author Min Liu describes her experience of moving from a collectivist culture in her homeland of China to the individualist culture of the United States.

Attitudes Toward Predictability and Uncertainty

Hofstede found that cultures differed in their attitudes toward **uncertainty avoidance**, the extent to which people in a culture look for ways to predict what is going to happen as a way of dealing with the anxiety caused by uncertain situations or relationships. A **low uncertainty-avoidance culture** (such as the United States, Sweden, and Denmark) is a culture that tolerates uncertainty and is less driven to control unpredictable people, relationships, or events. As you might expect, the more diverse the people in a society, the more likely it is that the dominant culture will be low on uncertainty avoidance. People in low uncertainty-avoidance cultures tend to easily accept life's unpredictability and ambiguity, tolerate the unusual, prize initiative, take risks, and prefer as few rules as possible. People from these cultures are also more comfortable accepting multiple, diverse, and at times contradictory perspectives on "truth" rather than searching for one "truth."

A **high uncertainty-avoidance culture** is a culture characterized by a low tolerance for and a high need to control unpredictable people, relationships, or events. Societies whose members are more homogeneous are likely to be high on uncertainty avoidance, as there are usually fewer co-cultural groups with which they must interact. These cultures create systems of formal rules and believe in absolute truth as ways to provide more security and reduce risk. They also tend to be less tolerant of people or groups with deviant ideas or behaviors. Because their culture emphasizes the importance of avoiding uncertainty, they often view life as hazardous, experiencing anxiety and stress when confronted with unpredictable

Uncertainty avoidance—the extent to which the people in a culture look for ways to predict what is going to happen as a way of dealing with the anxiety caused by uncertain situations or relationships

Low uncertainty-avoidance culture—a culture that tolerates uncertainty and is less driven to control unpredictable people, relationships, or events

High uncertainty-avoidance culture—a culture characterized as having a low tolerance for and a high need to control unpredictable people, relationships, or events

people, relationships, or situations. Nations whose cultures are marked by high uncertainty avoidance include Germany, Portugal, Greece, Peru, and Belgium (Samovar et al., 2013). How our culture has taught us to view uncertainty affects our communication with others. It shapes how we use language and develop relationships.

First, uncertainty avoidance affects the use of language. People from high uncertainty-avoidance cultures use and value specific and precise language because they believe that through careful word choice we can be more certain of the meaning of a person's message. Imagine a teacher declaring to a class, "The paper must be well-researched, cite evidence, and be professional in format and appearance." Students from high uncertainty-avoidance cultures would find the teacher's remarks to be too general and vague. They would most likely experience anxiety and, to reduce their uncertainty, would probably ask a lot of questions about what kind of research is appropriate, how to cite evidence, how much evidence is needed, what writing style to use, and the desired length of the paper. These students would welcome a specific checklist or rubric that enumerated the exact criteria by which the paper would be graded. By contrast, students from a low uncertainty-avoidance cultural background would be annoyed by an overly specific list of rules and guidelines, viewing it as a barrier to creativity and initiative. As you can imagine, a teacher with students from both cultural backgrounds faces a difficult challenge when trying to explain an assignment.

Second, uncertainty avoidance influences how people approach new relationships and how they communicate in developing relationships. People from high uncertainty-avoidance cultures are wary of strangers and may not seek out new relationships or relationships with people they perceive as different from them, since these would be unpredictable. They generally prefer meeting people through friends and family, and they refrain from being alone with strangers. When developing relationships, people from high uncertainty-avoidance cultures tend to guard their privacy, to refrain from self-disclosure early in a relationship, and to proceed more slowly through relationship development. Members of low uncertainty-avoidance cultures, on the other hand, are likely to initiate new relationships with people who differ from them and enjoy the excitement of disclosing personal information in earlier stages of relationship development.

Attitudes About Social Power Distribution

How members of the culture view unequal distribution of power is a third way in which cultures differ that affects communication. **Power distance** is the extent to which members of a culture expect and accept that power will be unequally shared. A culture can be either a high power-distance culture or a low power-distance culture. A **high power-distance culture** is a culture in which both high- and low-power holders accept the unequal distribution of power. In these cultures the power imbalances are endorsed as much by less powerful members as they are by those with power. While no culture distributes power equally, in high power-distance cultures more inequality is seen by

Power distance—the extent to which members of a culture expect and accept that power will be unequally shared

High power-distance culture—a culture in which both high- and low-power holders accept the unequal distribution of power

members as natural. High power-distance cultures include most Arab countries of the Middle East, Malaysia, Guatemala, Venezuela, and Singapore. The recent "Arab Spring" political movements in Middle Eastern countries suggest that the acceptance of high power distance in a culture will only continue when less powerful people believe that the powerful are working in the collective best interest.

A **low power-distance culture** is a culture in which members prefer power to be more equally distributed. In cultures characterized as having low power-distance, inequalities in power, status, and rank are underplayed and muted. People know that some individuals have more clout, authority, and influence, but lower-ranking people are not awed by, more respectful toward, or fearful of people in higher positions of power. Even though power differences exist, these cultures value democracy and egalitarian behavior. Austria, Finland, Denmark, Norway, the United States, New Zealand, and Israel are examples of countries whose dominant cultures are characterized by low power-distance.

Our cultural beliefs about power distance naturally affect how we interact with others in authority positions. If you were a student, an unskilled worker, or an average citizen in a high power-distance culture, you would not argue with a person in authority. You would expect the more powerful person to control any interaction; you would listen with attention to what that person said to you; and you would do what was ordered without question. Proper and polite forms of language, and nonverbal signals of your status differences would be evident in the exchange. In contrast, if you come from a low power-distance culture, because differences in status are muted, you are more comfortable arguing with those in authority. When interacting with a higher-power person, you feel comfortable directing the course of the conversation, and you question or confront powerbrokers if needed. You do not feel compelled to use formal titles when addressing more powerful people.

Masculine vs. Feminine Orientation

A fourth way in which cultural differences affect communication is the extent to which traditionally masculine or feminine orientations are valued in a culture. Cultures differ in how strongly they value traditional sex-role distinctions. According to Hofstede, a **masculine culture** is a culture in which men are expected to adhere to traditional sex roles. Hofstede called these cultures *masculine* because, for the most part, groups that maintain distinct sex-based roles also value masculine roles more highly than feminine ones. If you come from a masculine culture like those dominant in Mexico, Italy, and Japan, you are likely to expect men to act assertively and dominantly and expect women to be nurturing, caring, and service oriented. Encounters with people who don't meet these expectations may make you uncomfortable. If you come from a masculine culture, your culture has probably taught you that masculine behaviors are more worthwhile, regardless of your own sex. Accordingly, you will probably value the traditionally masculine characteristics of performance, ambition, assertiveness, competitiveness, and material success more than you

Low power-distance culture—a culture in which members prefer power to be more equally distributed

Masculine culture—a culture in which men and women are expected to adhere to traditional sex roles

value traditionally feminine traits and behaviors that are relationship oriented such as nurturing and helping (Hofstede, 2000).

A **feminine culture** is a culture in which people regardless of sex can assume a variety of roles, depending on the circumstances and their own choices. Men as well as women in feminine cultures are accustomed to being nurturing, caring, and service oriented. If you are from a feminine culture, like Sweden, Norway, or Denmark, you will also value the traits that have traditionally been associated with feminine roles (Hofstede, 1998).

Whether you come from a masculine or a feminine culture has a significant effect on how much behavioral flexibility you demonstrate in communicating with others. People from masculine cultures have strict definitions of what behavior is appropriate for people of a particular sex. As a result, they learn and are rewarded only for those behaviors seen as appropriate for their sex. Men in these cultures may be unprepared to engage in nurturing and caring behaviors, such as empathizing and comforting, and women are unprepared to be assertive or argue persuasively. Both men and women in feminine cultures learn and are rewarded for demonstrating both traditionally masculine and feminine behaviors. Consequently, people from feminine cultures are more flexible in how they communicate. Both men and women learn to nurture, empathize, assert, and argue, although any single individual may still lack skill in one or more of these behaviors.

In feminine cultures like Denmark, people, regardless of sex, assume a variety of roles. Did your family tend to have a masculine or a feminine culture?

Feminine culture—a culture in which people regardless of sex can assume a variety of roles depending on the circumstances and their own choices

Norms About the Use of Emotions

In Chapter 2, you learned about emotion as an important component of social cognition. There we focused on the universal human experience of emotion, and indeed, human beings are similar across cultures in their experience of basic emotions, such as happiness, sadness, and anger. However, culture is also a powerful influence on emotion. Cultures provide **display rules**, or rules about when, why, and how different emotions are to be expressed (or not). Display rules can prescribe simulation (showing an emotion you do not feel), inhibition (suppressing an emotion you do feel), masking (showing an emotion that is different from what you feel), miniaturization (showing less emotion than you feel), or intensification (displaying more emotion than you feel). A study conducted in 32 different countries found that people in individualistic cultures believe they should be more expressive of their emotions than did people in collectivistic cultures, and especially the emotions of happiness and surprise (Matsumoto, Yu, & Fontaine, 2008).

Display rules—rules about when, why, and how different emotions are to be expressed (or not)

Culture can also affect what is actually felt, or identified as a distinct feeling. For example, the Japanese use the word *amae* (ah-may-eh) to refer to a complex set of feelings that close relationship partners experience when they make unnecessary or excessive demands on each other, or give in to these kinds of demands. Described in English, these feelings include affection, closeness, trust, happiness, and security. The person agreeing to the demands may also experience irritation or frustration. *Amae* is characteristic of traditional Japanese relationships between mothers and small children, in which the Japanese mother dotes on or spoils her child in ways

Observing Dimensions of Culture

Interview someone who was born and raised in a country other than yours. Explain the various dimensions of culture (monochronistic/polychronistic; high-context/low-context; individualist/collectivist; uncertainty avoidance; power distance; masculinity/femininity; and rules about emotional expression). After you describe each dimension, ask the interviewee to describe their culture using these dimensions. Also ask the interviewee to give you an example of typical behavior for each dimension. Compare this culture to your own. How are they similar and how are they different? How can this understanding help you when you interact with someone from this cultural group? Be specific.

that many American parents would view as excessive, and the child basks in this indulgence (Doi, 1973). But *amae* is also part of relationships between Japanese adults (Marshall, Chuong, & Aikawa, 2011). If Yui pleads for Masuyo to drive her to the airport when there is a very convenient, inexpensive shuttle and Masuyo recognizes the inappropriateness of this demand but feels good about helping Yui, she is experiencing *amae*. Similarly, if Shinobu persuades her boyfriend Daiki to watch a movie and cuddle when they both know he should be studying, her boyfriend will probably feel *amae* toward Shinobu. Experiencing *amae,* and creating situations in which *amae* will occur, is one way that the Japanese maintain and strengthen their interdependent relationships (Marshall, Chuong, & Aikawa, 2011). Like the Japanese, Americans report a mix of positive and negative feelings when seeking or granting unnecessary favors to close others (Niiya, Ellsworth, & Yamaguchi, 2006), but whereas Americans need multiple terms to describe how they would feel, the word *amae* represents this as a single feeling for the Japanese.

Barriers to Effective Intercultural Communication

As you have read this chapter, you have probably begun to realize how difficult it can be to effectively communicate with someone from a different culture. Yet you know that immigration, the internet, and increasing globalization of business require effective intercultural communication. Let's quickly look at several of the most common barriers to effective intercultural communication, and then

When you found yourself in the midst of others from a different culture, what was your initial feeling?

turn our attention to a model that describes how you can develop intercultural competence.

The most common barriers to effective communication between members of different cultures include anxiety, assuming similarity or difference, ethnocentrism, stereotyping, incompatible communication codes, and incompatible norms and values.

Anxiety

It is normal to feel some level of discomfort or apprehension when we recognize that we are different from almost everyone else or when entering a cultural milieu whose customs are unfamiliar. Most people experience fear, dislike, and distrust when first interacting with someone from a different culture (Luckmann, 1999). If you have ever traveled to a foreign country or been the only member of your cultural group in some setting, you probably experienced anxiety.

Assumed Similarity or Difference

When people enter an unfamiliar cultural environment, they often assume that the familiar norms that have always applied will apply in a new situation. When traveling internationally from the United States, for example, many people expect to eat their usual hamburgers and fries provided with rapid and efficient service. They may be annoyed with shops and restaurants closing during midday in countries that observe the custom of siesta. It can be just as great a mistake to assume that everything about an unfamiliar culture will be different. For example, Marissa, a Mexican American student from California who is studying at a small private college in Vermont, may feel that no one understands her and her experiences. As she makes friends, however, she may learn that while Rachel, who is Jewish, didn't have a *quinceañera*, she did have a bat mitzvah, and Kate, who is Irish Catholic, had a big confirmation party. While these occasions are different, each rite celebrates coming of age in their respective cultures. As Marissa makes these and other connections, she will be able to accurately notice similarities and then key in on real rather than apparent differences.

Ethnocentrism

We refer to other people as "egocentric" when they are self-centered, and see themselves as more important than others. Similarly, **ethnocentrism** is being focused on one's own culture and viewing it as more important than the cultures of others. People who are ethnocentric prefer their own culture over others, see their culture as superior, want to defend the "purity" of their culture against other cultural influences, and are willing to exploit people from other cultures to benefit their own. Not surprising, they also interact more cooperatively with people from their own culture, and are more loyal to them (Buzumic & Duckitt, 2012). In varying degrees, ethnocentrism is found in every culture, and can occur in co-cultures as well. An ethnocentric view of the world leads to attitudes of superiority and messages that are directly or subtly condescending in content and

Ethnocentrism—being focused on one's own culture and viewing it as more important than the cultures of others

tone. As you would expect, these messages are offensive to receivers from other cultures or co-cultures and get in the way of intercultural communication.

Stereotyping

As you will recall from Chapter 2, stereotyping is a perceptual shortcut in which we assume that everyone in a cultural group is the same. For example, thinking that a Chinese international student in your class will get the best grade in the course because all Asian students excel intellectually; assuming that Jean Marc, who is Haitian, is working in the United States as an undocumented worker; or anticipating that all European Americans are out to take advantage of people of color, are all examples of stereotyping. When we interact based on stereotypes, we risk creating inaccurate messages that damage our relationships. When we listen with our stereotypes and prejudices in mind, we may misperceive the intent of the person with whom we are talking.

Incompatible Communication Codes

When others speak a different language, it is easy to see that we have incompatible communication codes. But even among people who speak the same language, there will be cultural variations that result from the co-cultures to which they belong. For example, people from Great Britain take a "lift" to reach a higher floor and eat "chips" with their fish, while Americans ride an "elevator" and eat "french fries" with their burgers. Within the United States, Midwesterners drink "pop," while New Yorkers drink "soda." Co-cultural groups will often purposefully develop "in-group" codes that are easily understood by co-culture members but unintelligible to outsiders. Just try to have a conversation about your computer problem with your friend Sam, who is a "techno-geek." As an insider, Sam is likely to talk in a vocabulary as foreign to you as Icelandic. "BTW," "OMG," and other acronyms once confined to text messages are now sprinkled in the verbal messages of teens and other users of social media. To get past incompatible communication codes, we may use nonverbal signing in an effort to overcome the language barrier. However, significant differences in the use and meaning of nonverbal behaviors may also render those codes incompatible.

Incompatible Norms and Values

What is normal or of high value in one culture may be offensive in another. The Vietnamese, for example, consider dog a delicacy. Most Americans find this practice disgusting, yet think nothing of eating beef. Hindus, on the other hand, consider beef eating abominable, as the cow is sacred to their religion. Cultural incompatibilities can cause serious problems in personal relationships and even war on a societal level.

The Pyramid Mode of Intercultural Competence

Intercultural scholars define **intercultural competence** as "effective and appropriate behavior and communication in intercultural situations" (Deardorff, 2006). The Pyramid Model of Intercultural Competence (Deardorff, 2006) in Figure 3.2 depicts how the lifelong process of acquiring intercultural competence occurs. This tiered model indicates that competence begins with attitudes that support intercultural exchanges. Then you need to develop knowledge of the other culture and skills for communicating. This knowledge and skill will equip you with a cultural frame of reference that can guide you to communicate effectively and appropriately with people from another culture. Let's take a closer look at how this model works.

Intercultural competence—effective and appropriate behavior and communication in intercultural situations

Requisite Attitudes

According to the Pyramid Model, intercultural competence begins by having the right attitudes toward learning about another culture. These attitudes are respect, openness, and curiosity or discovery. When we respect another culture, we appreciate and try to see the value of the ways in which another culture differs from our own. This respect guides our desire to learn how to behave in culturally appropriate ways. For example, when Clarise, a store manager, wanted to reward

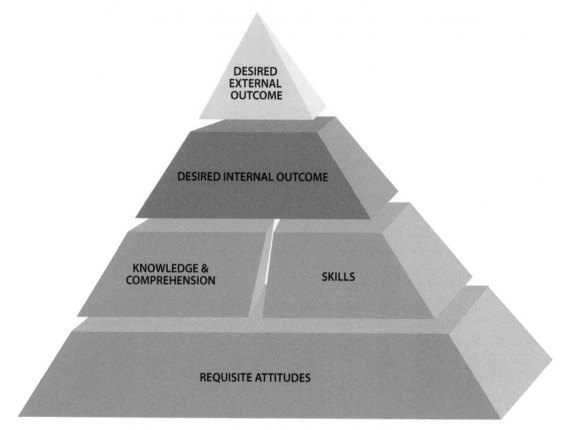

FIGURE 3.2 The Pyramid Model of Intercultural Competence.

her team with lunch, she chose a vegan restaurant because she respects the cultures of two members of her team, a conservative Jew and a Muslim who don't eat pork and are not allowed to eat meat unless the animal has been killed according to the dietary laws of each religion.

If you are to become effective in intercultural interactions, you must also be open to new ideas and to meeting people from other cultures. This requires that we withhold our judgements about their values, norms, attitudes, and orientations.

Finally, if we are to become effective, we must let our curiosity overcome our anxiety and fear of the unknown. We must work hard to tolerate the uncertainty and ambiguity that accompanies interacting with someone who is very different and in perhaps a foreign environment.

Developing Culture-Specific Knowledge and Skills

To become competent in intercultural interactions, we need to develop a deep understanding of the culture, including history, worldview, values, and customs. We also need to develop communication skills appropriate for the culture, which will often include new language, nonverbal behaviors, and rules for interactions and relationships. The more we know about other cultures, the more likely we are to be competent intercultural communicators (Neuliep, 2006).

There are various ways to learn about other cultures. These include observation, language study, formal cultural study, and cultural immersion.

1. Observation. You can simply watch members of another culture interact with each other. As you observe, you will notice how the values, rituals, and communication styles of that culture are similar to and different from your own and from other cultures with which you are familiar. Passive observers who study the communication behaviors used by members of a particular culture become better intercultural communicators as a result.

2. Language study. Because communication and culture are so closely intertwined, it is difficult to understand a culture without understanding its language. So it's not surprising to find that most adults who become proficient in a new language do so out of necessity; either because they move to a country where a different language is spoken, or because they need to speak another language as part of their work (Grosjean, 2010).

3. Formal cultural study. You can learn more about another culture by reading accounts written by members of that culture; looking at ethnographic research studies; taking courses; or interviewing a member of the culture about his or her values, rituals, and so on. Formal study and observation can go hand-in-hand, working together to help you achieve greater intercultural understanding.

4. Cultural immersion. Active participation is the best way to learn about another culture. When you live or work with people whose cultural assumptions are different from yours, you not only acquire obvious cultural information but also learn the nuances that escape passive observers and are generally not accessible through formal study. Study-abroad programs often include homestays to provide students the opportunity to be surrounded by the culture of the host country. We hope that you will consider participating in a study-abroad experience. The international or global studies office at your college or university can point you to a variety of study abroad opportunities and may even guide you to scholarships or grants to help pay your expenses.

Developing cultural knowledge and skill requires sustained motivation and effort, including the willingness to correct mistakes and misconceptions as you go. When Ian found out that in two months he was going to be transferred to Milan, Italy, for three years to work on a joint venture between an Italian company and his company, he knew that the success of the project depended on how well and how quickly he could understand Italian culture. Before he left, he read everything he could about Italian culture and history, used a Rosetta Stone® program to begin learning the language, and spent time with a co-worker's family who was from Italy.

Despite his efforts, when Ian arrived in Milan, he still felt like a fish out of water. As he interacted with his Italian neighbors and co-workers, he observed things about the culture that were foreign to him. For instance, he noticed that people adjourned for coffee or espresso at about 10 A.M. While he was used to the concept of a coffee break, he was surprised that instead of a ten-minute run to the company cafeteria, this was often an hour break taken at a local café. Moreover, it wasn't unusual for his co-workers to have a little *grappa* (a grape brandy) either alongside as a chaser or added to the espresso and called *caffè corretto* (corrected coffee). As an American, Ian was initially appalled until he noticed that his Italian co-workers extended or contracted their workday depending on how much time they had spent on breaks so that they always put in the expected eight hours of work. As for the *caffè corretto,* further observation showed that the typical barista added only a teaspoon of the liqueur to the espresso, enough to add flavor, but not enough to provide a buzz. After being in the country for six months, Ian's Italian had really improved, as had his understanding of northern Italian culture. When sent on a short business trip to Sicily, however, he once again experienced culture shock and had to refocus on using his skills to learn the subtle differences in Sicilian culture.

Internal and External Outcomes

The development of intercultural knowledge and skill results in a number of internal outcomes. First, the knowledge you gain is stored in your memory and may be linked to other knowledge and concepts you have about the culture, people, history, values, norms, and so forth. Second, the skills you practice become part of your "canned plan" and script library so you can behave automatically in a culturally appropriate way. For example, Allison has studied Japanese culture and understands that the Japanese use honorifics to show respect. When her Japanese client, who is around her age, addresses her as Allison-san, she knows that she should address him as Kaito-san. Third, cultural knowledge and skill usually bring increased confidence and **ethnorelativism**, a point of view that allows you to see the value in other cultural perspectives. It is much easier to replace ethnocentrism with ethnorelativism when you have developed some familiarity with a new culture.

The external outcome of becoming culturally competent is the ability to behave and communicate effectively and appropriately in the new culture. After being in Italy for a year and a half, Ian was still working on developing intercultural competence. One day after work, he stopped at his neighborhood bar for a drink. On his initial visit to the café, he had chosen to sit at a table (*al tavolo*), only to discover that his drink cost more than had he chosen to stand at the bar. This time, he sidled up to the bar to enjoy his drink and to talk with a couple of his neighbors. Like most people who are learning another language, Ian was still translating from English into Italian when he spoke and doing the reverse when he was listening. But this evening, as he was talking, Ian was amazed to realize that he had made a breakthrough. He was no longer translating; rather, he was thinking in Italian, the ultimate experience for someone learning a foreign language. But it came about because he had started with attitudes that supported his learning about Italian culture and trying to learn the language. He had not only read about Italy but had

Ethnorelativism—the point of view allows you to see the value in other cultural perspectives

immersed himself in Italian life, even choosing to live outside the normal districts frequented by Americans in favor of a "real" Italian neighborhood. Still, it took over a year and a half before Ian was able to be completely absorbed in the culture and think like an Italian. You may never have the opportunity to become so thoroughly immersed in another culture that you develop this level of cultural competence. But you can use the pyramid model of intercultural competence to identify ways to improve your intercultural communication. Ian is not entirely fluent in Italian culture, and having recently learned of his upcoming transfer to New Zealand to begin another project, he will continue his intercultural competence quest elsewhere.

Social Media Across Cultures

When most people in the United States think about social media, their first thoughts are usually about Facebook, Instagram, or Twitter. While these are currently the most popular social networking sites worldwide, there are many other ways that people connect online in different countries and cultures. Some countries have their own social networking sites, like Cloob in Iran, VKontakte in Russia, and Cyworld in South Korea. In addition, there are numerous co-cultural sites, such as G4Y5.com for gay males, asmallworld.com for millionaires (access by invitation only), and SNAAP for Asian American professionals. There are also social networking sites specifically for people looking to date Jews, Christians, farmers, vegans, geeks, and bicycle enthusiasts, just to name a few.

Culture not only drives the formation of culturally specific social networking sites, but also affects the way users communicate when using them. Recent research has examined cultural influences on Facebook and two sites similar to Facebook but based in collectivist countries: the South Korean site CyWorld, and the Chinese site RenRen (Kim, Sohn, & Choi, 2011; Qiu, Lin, & Leung, 2013). One study found that South Korean college students spend about the same amount of time using CyWorld as American college students spend using Facebook (around 1.5 hours daily; Kim, Sohn, & Choi, 2011). However, Korean students' online networks are smaller than those of American students (81 members vs. 412), while also containing much higher percentages of close friends and family (70% vs. 24%). In addition, South Korean students report spending more of their Cyworld time seeking support and information, whereas American students report spending more of their Facebook time looking for entertainment. Another study examined how Chinese students studying in Singapore use both Facebook (which is blocked in mainland China) and RenRen. These sites are perceived as having very similar

INTER-ACT WITH
SOCIAL MEDIA

How do people convey their feelings when they communicate via technology? Are there different display rules for communicating via Facebook, Twitter, or text message? Are cultural differences in emotional displays as obvious on social media as they are in person?

Tyler, Jeannie, Margeaux, and Madhukar are sitting around Margeaux's dining room table and working on a group marketing project. It was 2:00 A.M. They had been at it since 6:00 P.M. and still had several hours of work remaining.

"Oh, the agony," groans Tyler, pretending to slit his throat with an Exacto knife. "If I never see another photo of a veggie burger, it will be too soon. Why didn't we choose a more appetizing product to base our project on?"

"I think it had something to do with *someone* wanting to promote a healthy alternative to greasy hamburgers," Jeannie replies sarcastically.

"Right," Tyler answers. "I don't know what I could have been thinking. Speaking of greasy hamburgers, is anyone else starving? Anyone up for ordering a pizza or something?"

"Sorry, but no one will deliver up here so late," Margeaux apologizes. "But I have a quiche that I could heat up."

"Oh, oui, oui," Tyler quips.

"You wish," Margeaux says. "It came out of a box."

"Sure, it sounds great. Thanks," Jeannie says. "I'm hungry too."

"It doesn't have any meat in it, does it?" asks Madhukar. "I don't eat meat."

"Nope, it's a cheese and spinach quiche," Margeaux answers.

Tyler and Margeaux go off to the kitchen to prepare the food. Tyler takes the quiche, which is still in its box, from the refrigerator. "Uh-oh," he says. "My roommate is a vegetarian, and he won't buy this brand because it has lard in the crust. Better warn Madhukar. He's a Hindu, so I imagine it's pretty important to him."

"Shhh!" responds Margeaux. "I don't have anything else to offer him, and he'll never know the difference anyway. Just pretend you didn't notice that."

FOR CONSIDERATION:
1. What ethical principles are involved in this case?
2. What exactly are Margeaux's ethical obligations to Madhukar in this situation?
3. What should Tyler do now?

performance, security, and user-friendliness, but RenRen is viewed as being more collectivist—oriented toward sharing, conformity, and hierarchy (with users arranged according to status). Students shared more links and posts from others when on RenRen than on Facebook, codeswitching as they moved between the more individualistic culture of Facebook and the more collectivist culture of RenRen. These studies demonstrate how individualistic and collectivist cultures influence behavior on social networking sites. It will be possible to see other cultural influences in operation as researchers begin to examine social networking behavior across other sites, countries, cultures, and co-cultures.

Summary

Contact among people of diverse cultures is increasing. Culture is the system of shared values, beliefs, attitudes, and orientations learned through communication that guide what is considered to be appropriate thought and behavior in a particular segment of the population. Culture shock refers to the psychological discomfort people have when they attempt to adjust to a new cultural situation. Intercultural communication involves interactions that occur between people whose cultures are so different that the communication between them is altered. Within a society there are both dominant and co-cultures. A shared system of meaning exists within the dominant culture, but meanings can vary within co-cultures based on gender, race, ethnicity, sexual orientation and gender identity, religion, social class, and generation.

Cultures vary according to whether they are monochronic or polychronic; how important context is for understanding the meaning of verbal messages; how they value individualism versus collectivism, predictability versus tolerating uncertainty, equality versus an unequal distribution of power, and masculine versus feminine ways of behaving; and the experience and expression of emotions. Intercultural competence enables us to overcome common barriers to intercultural communication, including anxiety, assumptions about differences and similarities, ethnocentrism, stereotyping, incompatible communication codes, and incompatible norms and values. The Pyramid Model of Intercultural Competence depicts how you can develop intercultural competence. It begins with developing the requisite attitudes, which in turn support the acquisition of cultural knowledge and skill. Social media sites and norms for their use vary across cultures and co-cultures, so cultural knowledge and skill must be developed for online interactions as well as face-to-face interactions.

CHAPTER RESOURCES

Key Words

Flashcards for all of these key terms are available on the *Inter-Act* website.

Analyze and Apply

The following activities challenge you to demonstrate your mastery of the concepts, theories, and frameworks in this chapter by using them to explain what is happening in a specific situation.

3.1 Rewind/Rewrite

a. Using the concepts you have learned in this chapter, please explain why Jamie was shocked and hurt by Kwan's response to what she thought was a flirtatious question.

b. Korean culture prizes honesty. How does this cultural knowledge help you understand what happened in the exchange?

c. Rewrite the scenario creating additional dialog that help Jamie and Kwan each understand more of their cultural differences.

3.2 Understanding Your Culture

a. Name the co-cultural group with which you most identify. It might be your religious group, your sorority or fraternity, your ethnic group, etc

1. Describe this culture. Who belongs? How do you become a member? What are its top three ideal values? What are two of its real values? Cite at least one attitude widely shared by co-culture members. Describe two important rites or rituals in which members participate. What is the purpose of these? Identify at least one way that the communication in this co-culture differs from that in the dominant culture.

2. Locate this culture on each of the seven dimensions that differentiate cultural groups. Explain your reasoning.

3. On which of these dimensions is your co-culture most different from the dominant culture? How do you deal with these differences?

b. Recall a conversation you have had with someone whose culture or co-culture was very different from your own. Describe the difficulties you had in communicating with this person. Which of the barriers to intercultural communication seemed to be in play? How would better intercultural competence have helped you in this situation?

3.3 Cultural Competence

Identify a country where people speak a language you don't know and that you know very little about. Pretend that you have agreed to take part in a "sister cities" cultural exchange program in that country six months from now. You will be there for one month and will be staying in a home with citizens of that country. Use the pyramid model to help you develop a plan for acquiring as much cultural knowledge about this country as you can before you leave. Your plan should include a timetable.

Communication Improvement Plan:
Intercultural Communication

How would you like to improve your ability to communicate across cultures, as discussed in this chapter?

- Develop requisite attitudes
- Gain culture-specific knowledge and understanding
- Improve cultural learning skills

Pick the area in which you would like to improve and write a communication improvement plan. You can find a communication improvement plan worksheet on our website at www.oup.com/us/verderber.

4

VERBAL MESSAGES

Before their class "Major Novels" began, Molly, Nick, Tessa, and Natalya, who had met during orientation that semester, were chatting while the instructor readied the whiteboard.

"What did you all think of the first book we were assigned to read?" asked Natalya. She had arrived from the Ukraine on a study abroad program just two weeks before the semester had begun and was eager to make some American friends.

"A total walk in the park," Nick said.

"I enjoyed it, but I had to really rack my brain to write the first paper!" Tessa exclaimed.

"I feel you Tessa … personally I thought the book was sick," chimed in Molly.

"Way tighter than I had imagined," agreed Nick.

Natalya looked confused as she turned to each of them. "I'm sorry … I bought my book used, but it was not unhealthy … it was not overly loose or tight…. Why did you hurt your brain? How do you read while walking in the park?"

Her American classmates stared at her for a moment, and then broke out laughing. Natalya frowned at her desk, hurt and a little angry. If all American students were like this, how would she be able to fit in?

WHAT YOU SHOULD BE ABLE *TO EXPLAIN* AFTER YOU HAVE STUDIED THIS CHAPTER:

▶ How meaning is conveyed through verbal messages

▶ Differences between language, dialect, speech community, and "idiolect"

▶ How the meaning of a verbal message depends on the language itself

▶ How the conversational context affects the meaning of a verbal message

▶ How social or cultural contexts influence the meaning of verbal messages

▶ How online relationships are created and sustained with language

WHAT YOU SHOULD BE ABLE *TO DO* AFTER YOU HAVE STUDIED THIS CHAPTER:

▶ Use language to create messages that are precise and listener-adapted

▶ Produce messages that are appropriate and effective within a conversational context

▶ Tailor messages to diverse social and cultural contexts

A s this example illustrates, language can create both understanding and misunderstanding. The American students were able to draw on shared cultural interpretations of phrases like "walk in the park," "sick," and "rack my brain," but Natalya, who had less familiarity with American slang and culture, did not understand what her classmates were saying. In this chapter, we're going to look at the verbal parts of messages to help you understand how language is used to share meaning and how you can increase your ability to form and to interpret the verbal parts of messages. We begin by explaining several fundamental concepts regarding **verbal messages**, or messages conveyed using language. The bulk of this chapter is devoted to describing each of the levels of meaning in verbal messages as well as how you can improve your ability at each level.

Verbal message—a message conveyed using a language

Verbal Message Fundamentals

When we communicate with others, our messages are usually conveyed with both verbal and nonverbal behaviors. We'll talk about nonverbal behaviors, such as facial expressions and gestures, in Chapter 5. In this chapter, we focus on our use of verbal behavior, or language, to convey messages. We begin by examining language and its characteristics.

What Is a Language?

Language—a symbolic system used by people to communicate verbal or written messages

Lexicon—the collection of words and expressions in a language

Phonology—the sounds used to pronounce words

Syntax and grammar—the rules for combining words into larger units of expression

Language community—all people who can speak or understand a particular language

Language is a system of symbols used by people to communicate orally or in writing. Each language includes a **lexicon**, the collection of words and expressions; a **phonology**, the sounds used to pronounce words; and a **syntax and grammar**, the rules for combining words to form phrases, clauses, sentences, and larger units of expression. A **language community** includes all people who can speak or understand a particular language. For example, the English language community includes Australians, Scots, Irish, Canadians, Indians, and Americans, as well as others who speak English. The five largest language communities, in size order, are Chinese, Spanish, English, Arabic, and Hindi (Lewis, 2009). A quick look at the definition of "a language" makes it all seem so simple. But it is not. This definition implies that everyone in a particular language community knows all the words, pronounces them the same, and uses the same rules of grammar and syntax. But you know from experience that this is not the case. For example, you know that the English spoken in England is not the same as the English spoken in the United States. And the English spoken in Boston, Massachusetts, differs from that spoken in Biloxi, Mississippi, and in Fargo, North Dakota.

Languages are really collections of dialects. A **dialect** is a form of a more general language spoken by a specific culture or co-culture that, while differing from the general language, shares enough commonality that most people who belong to a particular language community can understand it (O'Grady, Archibald, Aronoff, & Rees-Miller, 2001). A **speech community** comprises members of a larger language community who speak a common dialect with a particular style and observe common linguistic norms or scripts. Dialects of the same language fall on a continuum of similarity, with some dialects being very similar, and other dialects being much less similar. If you are an American-born speaker of English and have had a conversation with someone from Scotland, you probably had trouble understanding this person. Even though you were both speaking English, the way that Scots pronounce most words is very different from the way Americans do. On the other hand, while Canadians pronounce a few words differently than Americans and use some different words, most Americans can easily understand English-speaking Canadians, and vice versa. On a dialect continuum, American and Canadian dialects are close, whereas Scottish dialects are more distant. In the "Diverse Voices" article, "Mommy, Why Does Raj Talk Funny?" you will read about how Indian English differs from the English spoken in America.

There are several common misconceptions about dialects, including the belief that they are substandard, incorrect, or slang. From a linguistic perspective, one dialect is not better or worse than another. They just have differences in lexicon, phonology, and grammar and syntax. Nevertheless, certain dialects are more privileged and perceived to be "better" than others because the power elite of a language group speaks them. Speaking a privileged dialect marks someone as part of the powerful "in-group" of the society or country. Those who speak other dialects, particularly if they are distant from the ones associated with the powerful people, are marked as the "out-groups," whose speakers are less likely to achieve positions of influence in the society or country. As the in-group solidifies its position, its dialect is idealized and seen as the "proper" or real form of a language, a power disparity captured by the old linguistic saying that "a language is a dialect with an army and a navy." People may, therefore, learn and use the in-group dialect to improve their opportunities or learn and use the out-group dialect to show solidarity with out-group co-cultures. As you will recall, from Chapter 3, this is called *codeswitching*.

What is called a language and what is called a dialect is usually a matter more political than linguistic, as the recent cases of the former Yugoslavia and

Dialect—a form of a more general language spoken by a specific culture or co-culture that, while differing from the general language, shares enough commonality that most people who belong to a particular language community can understand it

Speech community—the members of a larger language community who speak a common dialect with a particular style and observe common linguistic norms or scripts

"Mommy, Why Does Raj Talk Funny?"

BY RAJ GAUR, PHD, UNIVERSITY OF KENTUCKY

I grew up in India. In my home we spoke Hindi, but from the time I began school at five years old, I was also taught English. By the time I was fourteen years old I was fluent in English—at least what I thought of at the time as English. Ten years ago, I came to the United States and have since learned that the English I speak is somewhat different from the English that is spoken here in the United States. These differences sometimes make it difficult for me to be understood by some Americans. You see, the English I learned as a child is a *nativization* of English that might more accurately be called "Indian English." What is nativization?

Nativization is the unconscious process of adapting a foreign language so it conforms to the linguistic style and rhetorical patterns of the native language spoken in a particular culture. You are familiar with the ways American English differs between regions and among groups within the United States, as well as differences between British English and American English. If there are differences among native English speakers, imagine what happens when a cultural group like Indians whose native language is Hindi adopts English as a second language! As you would probably expect, they adapt English by using some of the grammar, syntax, and pronunciation rules that characterize their first language, as well as by adopting some of the rhetorical and idiomatic expressions that they use in their mother tongue. It's not that Indians consciously decide to make these changes. Rather, the changes simply occur as the new language, in this case English, is used in everyday conversations with other Indians.

Prior to coming to the United States, most of the people I knew spoke English just like I did, and I had no problem understanding them or being understood by them. So imagine my consternation when after arriving in the United States, some of my American colleagues, professors, and students had trouble understanding me when I spoke. What made this particularly interesting was that I didn't seem to have as much trouble understanding others or being understood when I wrote in English. Rather, it was when I spoke that I got quizzical looks and repeated requests to repeat myself.

What I now understand is that there are major differences between the way certain words are pronounced by those speaking American English and those speaking Indian English. Some of these differences are due to the rules each type of English uses for accenting the syllables within a word. In American English, as a general rule, words with more than one syllable alternate between accented and unaccented syllables. So if the first syllable is accented, the second is not, and vice versa. But in Hindi, whether a particular syllable is accented or not depends on the sounds in the word. Some sounds

China demonstrate. Serbo-Croatian, the official language of the former country of Yugoslavia, was composed of a variety of very similar dialects. But since the collapse of Yugoslavia in the mid-to-late 1990s, each of the former regions became a separate nation claiming its own unique language. Serbian is spoken in Serbia, Croatian in Croatia, Bosnian in Bosnia, and Montenegrin in Montenegro. Nevertheless, people from all these countries can still easily understand one another. So from a linguistic perspective, they all speak dialects of the same language (Cvetkovic, 2009).

always receive an accent and others do not, regardless of their position in a word. So in Indian English, "pho" is pronounced the same whether the speaker is using the word "photo" or "photography." If you speak American English, you are used to hearing "pho·TOG·gra·phy," but when I pronounce it in Indian English, I say "PHO·to·GRAPH·y." If you're an American English speaker and you hear me say this, you may not understand me or may think, "Oh he just mispronounced that word." But to me, your pronunciation sounds just as strange, because in India, that is how we pronounce the word.

There are also syntactic differences between Indian and American English. You will recall that syntax is the rules of a particular language for how words are supposed to be put together to form complete ideas. The syntactic issue that I have struggled most with is the use of articles (*a, an, the,* etc.). In Hindi, we may or may not use articles, and this practice also guides our Indian English. So an Indian English student may say, "I go to university in city of Mumbai," rather than "I go to *the* university in *the* city of Mumbai." Another syntactic difference that is common to speakers of Indian English is to form questions without using an auxiliary verb (*do, should, can, must,* etc.). In Hindi, auxiliary verbs are not required when forming an interrogatory sentence. So in Indian English I may ask "I know you?" rather than "*Do* I know you?" or "I finish it?" rather than "*Should* or *can* or *must* I finish it?"

Nativization of English can also be perceived at the idiomatic level when I attempt to express Indian sensibilities and Indian realities to my American friends. To clarify, as a speaker of Indian English, I sometimes exploit the syntactic structures of the language by directly translating Hindi idioms to English. For example, I might say "wheatish

complexion" in Indian English to mean "not dark skinned, tending toward light." Or I might use the phrase "out of station" to mean "out of town," which has its origins to denote army officers posted to far-off places during the British rule. Indians also commonly substitute "hotel" for "restaurant," "this side" and "that side" for "here" and "there," "cent per cent" for "100 percent," and "reduce weight" for "lose weight."

Any one of these English adaptations might not pose problems, but taken together they make the brand of English that I speak very different from that of my American friends. Indian English has evolved over a long period of time, and English is now integrated into much of Indian culture. English is taught in schools, business is conducted in English, and English is used in government dealings. Nonetheless, the English of Delhi is not the English of London, or Berlin, or New York, or Lexington, Kentucky. And I find it ironic that after living in the United States for nearly ten years now and struggling to be understood by Americans, my friends in India now complain about my English too. They say it's too American!

Originally published in: Verderber, K.S., Verderber, R.F., and Sellnow, D.D. (2014). *Communicate! 14th Ed.*, Boston, MA: Wadsworth Cengage Learning. pp. 61-62. Used with permission.

FOR CONSIDERATION:

1. How does this article help you to understand the variety within a "language?" How do the concepts of language communities aid this understanding?
2. Based on what you have learned in this article, is Black English (Ebonics) a nativization of American or British English? Argue your conclusion based on the characteristics identified in the article.

In contrast, the official language of China is, for political purposes, called "Chinese." All literate people in China use the same written symbol system developed in ancient times. In general, people from one part of the country can easily read writing from another part of the country, but the written symbols do not have a commonly shared pronunciation. Although the government of China considers the regional tongues of Mandarin, Wu, Cantonese, and Min to be dialects of Chinese, speakers of one dialect can't understand someone speaking another (Wright, 2010).

I take it you agree that there can be no *meaningful thought* without the existence of language?

CHRIS MADDEN

Idiolect—our personal symbolic system that includes our active vocabularies, our pronunciation of words, and our grammar and syntax when talking or writing

This linguistic situation is even more complex, however, for no one really speaks a dialect. Rather, each of us has our own personal symbolic system called an **idiolect** that includes our active vocabularies, our pronunciation of words, and our grammar and syntax when talking or writing (Higginbotham, 2006). We may have words in our lexicon that are understood by very few people, as well as words whose meaning is shared by many. We may pronounce words in an idiosyncratic way or use creative grammar and syntax. Those who know us well and talk with us frequently understand our idiolect best. That's why parents can understand the utterances of their own toddlers, whose speech is unintelligible to others. Those who speak a common dialect, those who speak similar dialects, and finally those who share a common language can also understand much of what we say.

With these background concepts in mind, let's consider some of the general characteristics of language that will help us understand why language is so useful, but also why sharing meaning through language can be tricky.

Characteristics of Language

All languages, dialects, and idiolects share six characteristics. They are arbitrary, ambiguous, abstract, self-reflexive, changeable, and revealing.

1. Language is arbitrary. The words used to represent things in all languages are arbitrary symbols. There is usually no physical connection between a word and its referent. The words used to represent objects, ideas, or feelings are arbitrary, yet for a word to have any meaning, it must be recognized by members of the language or speech community as standing for a particular object, idea, or feeling. Different language communities use different word symbols for the same phenomenon. Speech communities within a language community may also have words that differ from other speech communities within the language group. As long as members of the speech and/or language community accept the use of a particular word, it carries meaning. For example, the storage compartment of a car is called a "trunk" in America and a "boot" in England.

2. Language is ambiguous. No matter how specific you try to be with your verbal messages, there can always be multiple interpretations. This is because the real meaning being captured by the words in any utterance is not found in a *dictionary*, a written lexicon for the language community. Rather, the real meaning is conveyed by the person using the word as part of the lexicon, grammar, and syntax in her or his personal idiolect. Those same words, grammar, and syntax may have a different meaning for you, and you will interpret what is said using your idiolect. The ambiguity of language can be a source of fun and beauty, as occurs when jokes or poetry incorporate multiple meanings for words, but this ambiguity can also contribute to communication challenges.

3. Language is abstract. The word is not the thing that it represents. The words "I am so sad" represent your internal emotional state, but they are not your feelings. Another way to say this is that "the map is not the territory." Words vary in how abstract we perceive them to be. If Rema refers to her "pet," a fairly concrete word, her co-worker Margi may think of a dog, cat, snake, bird, or hamster. Even if Rema specifically mentions her dog, Margi still has many possibilities for interpretation, including dogs of various breeds, sizes, colors, and temperaments. If words that refer to tangible entities like cars and pets vary in abstraction, imagine all the possibilities of meaning for intangible concepts such as honesty, love, patriotism, or justice.

4. Language is self-reflexive. Not only does language refer to other things, but it can also refer back to itself. We can use language to talk about language itself and about its possible uses. In other words, it is self-reflexive. As a result of the reflexivity of language, humans are able to explore concepts that animals cannot. For instance, people have the capacity to think and talk about themselves, to speak hypothetically, to talk about past and future events, and to communicate about people and things that are not present. Language enables us to learn from others' experiences, to share a common heritage, and to develop a shared vision for the future. In addition, language, coupled with the ability to reflect on ourselves, allows for higher-order communication, or communication about communication. Think of the possibility for improving interpersonal communication when people can comment on the very process of communicating.

5. Language changes. Language changes over time in a number of ways. First, new words are constantly being invented. Younger generations and other subcultures invent new words (like "twerking," or "omnishambles") or assign different meanings to the words they learn (like "cookie"), use different grammars, and alter word pronunciation (like pronouncing "tame" and "time" the same as is done in some southern accents). New inventions produce new words (like "googling" or "selfies"). Words used by previous generations, such as "cassette tape," may fade from use over time and may even be removed from dictionaries. Members of a co-culture may redefine common words whose new meanings will initially be understood only by other speech community members. Finally, members of an ethnic subculture who also speak a heritage language may introduce parts of the heritage language into the common language. For example, you "take a *siesta*," or "live on a *cul-de-sac*," or "go to *kindergarten*."

6. Language reveals. Most of us do not realize the extent to which our word choice reveals our attitudes, judgments, or feelings. Imagine, for instance, that Shana routinely saves 60 percent of the money she earns. She lives in a very modest apartment, drives an old car, buys her clothes at resale shops, and rarely buys anything she doesn't absolutely need. What word comes to your mind to describe Shana's approach to money? Do you call her "thrifty," "budget-conscious," or "frugal"? Or do you select words such as "tightwad," "penny-pincher, "or "stingy"? Notice how the first set of words tends to leave a positive impression, whereas the second set seems negative. From the words you choose, a listener may infer your attitudes toward saving and spending.

As you can see from these characteristics, language is by nature an imprecise vehicle for transferring meaning from one person to another. The meaning of any verbal message is conveyed and understood as a result of: (1) the meaning of the language itself; (2) the meaning of the language in the verbal message within the context of the conversation; and (3) the meaning of the language in the verbal message within the social and cultural background of the interaction. In the next sections, we explain each of these and provide guidelines to help you form and correctly interpret the meaning of verbal messages.

▶ **OBSERVE AND ANALYZE**

Language and Dialects

Identify someone who comes from your language community but who belongs to a speech community that speaks a dialect different from yours. Arrange to interview this person about their dialect and idiolect. When did this person first notice that her or his dialect differs from that of others who speak the common language? What are some of the key differences between this person's dialect and the common language? Does he or she codeswitch, speaking the dialect when interacting with others in the speech community but speaking differently when interacting with others outside this group? If so, why does codeswitching occur, and how was it learned? Based on your interview, write a short paper describing what you have learned about how someone experiences language and dialect.

Meaning in the Language Itself

The **semantic meaning** of a message is the meaning derived from the language itself. At the semantic level of interpretation we understand a verbal message through its words and how the grammar and syntax of the language are used to combine them.

What do the words "I can't breathe" mean here?

Words are the arbitrarily chosen symbols used by a language or speech community to name or signify things and actions. Words allow us to identify parts of the world and to make statements about it (Saeed, 2003). Each of us has a lexicon of words for each of the languages that we speak. Although we learn new words, the size and accuracy of our vocabulary limit our ability to express what we are thinking and feeling, as well as our ability to understand the verbal messages we receive on a day-to-day basis. The extent to which you are able to share semantic meaning with someone depends on how much your personal lexicons overlap. As previously discussed, identifying word meanings can be tricky. This is because words have two types of meanings.

Denotation is the direct, explicit meaning of a word found in a written dictionary of the language community. Denotative meanings, however, diverge from dictionary to dictionary, change over time, and can vary by dialect. In addition, dictionaries use words to define other words that also depend on words for their meaning. Not only that, the lexicon of our idiolect rarely corresponds to the definitions of the same words found in formal dictionary definitions. Thus, your definition of a word may be different from mine. Suppose the president of our club says, "Please go upstairs and get a few more chairs for the meeting." When you hear the word "chair," you might picture a straight-backed, wooden object, whereas I picture something made of metal and plastic, with a slanted back. Our own idiosyncratic definitions, while similar, may or may not refer to the same real-world object.

Connotation is the feelings or evaluations we personally associate with a word. For example, think of the different meanings that people bring to the word "family" based on their positive or negative experiences growing up in their unique family situation. To you, a family may be a safe place where you are unconditionally loved, accepted, and cared for. To someone else with a different upbringing, a family may be a dangerous, brutal group in which everyone fends for himself or herself. There may be even greater variation of connotations for words that are more abstract and emotional, such as love, freedom, harmony, hate, oppression, and so on. So when we choose words or when we interpret the words of others, there is no guarantee that the representation intended by the person speaking the word will match that of the person who hears the word.

The meaning of the sentences in a verbal message is based not only on the words, but also on how those words are related to one another. You'll recall that grammar and syntax are the rules for combining words into meaningful phrases, sentences, and larger units of expression. Your vocabulary is somewhat set, but

Semantic meaning—meaning of a verbal message derived from the language itself

Words—the arbitrarily chosen symbols used by a language or speech community to name or signify

Denotation—the direct, explicit meaning of a word found in a written dictionary of the language community

Connotation—the feelings or evaluations we personally associate with a word

your ability to use the rules of grammar and syntax to create unique sentences is unlimited. For example, you might communicate the same meaning by saying:

"When he went to the pound, he adopted a three-pound puppy."
"He went to the pound and adopted a three-pound puppy."
"The three-pound puppy he adopted came from the pound."

These three sentences use different syntax and grammar and slightly different vocabulary but convey the same semantic meaning or "truth": Someone who was male procured a young canine weighing three pounds from a place where animals without an owner or whose owner is unknown are kept. But notice how we can alter the meaning of these words by changing the grammar and syntax and deleting one word:

"He, the three-pound adopted puppy, went to the pound."

Now the meaning in the semantics of the sentence is that an adopted, three-pound, immature canine went to the place where animals who are not owned or whose owner is unknown are kept. In addition, the meaning of a word may vary depending on its position in a sentence and the surrounding words. In the example above, the word "pound" is used twice in each sentence, but its meaning or sense changes. In one instance, it signifies a unit of weight, and in the other, it signifies a place. But you knew which meaning to apply by the syntactical context. With this in mind, what can we do to make it more likely that others will understand our semantic meaning? Let's look at several guidelines for forming verbal messages with clearer semantic meaning.

Guidelines for Improving Message Semantics

1. Use concrete and precise language along with details and examples to improve message specificity.

As we try to express our thoughts, we often use the first words that come to mind, which may be too general or ambiguous to convey meaning effectively. We can get a message across better if we use **specific language**. Specific language is language in an utterance that uses concrete and precise words as well as details and examples, combining them in accord with the rules of grammar and syntax for that language. Compare the speaker's use of language in the following three descriptions of a near-miss in a car:

1. "Some nut almost got me a while ago!"
2. "On my way here, someone driving crazy almost hit me!"
3. "An hour ago, an older man in a banged-up Honda Civic ran the red light at Calhoun and Clifton and almost hit me broadside while I was in the intersection waiting to turn left!"

Going from the first description to the third, the semantic meaning of the language becomes more and more specific. Consequently, the listener is likely to have a more accurate or "truer" understanding of exactly what happened. Let's

" WHEN YOU GUYS INVITED ME OVER FOR A JAM SESSION, I JUST ASSUMED.. "

Cartoonstock www.Cartoonstock.com

Specific language—language in an utterance that uses concrete and precise words, as well as details and examples, combining them in accord with the rules of grammar and syntax for that language

▶ **OBSERVE AND ANALYZE**

Language and Meaning

Answer the questions for each word or phrase that follows. Then ask someone who is at least one generation older than you to do the same without seeing your answers.

Expensive car: How much does it cost?

Staying up late on a weeknight: What time did you go to sleep?

Spending a lot of time writing a report: How much time did you prepare?

He's rich: How much money does he have?

She's liberal: What are her views on immigration, abortion, capital punishment, global trade, gay marriage?

(Continued)

▶ **OBSERVE AND ANALYZE**
(*Continued*)

He's got one of those hybrid cars: What make and model is the car?

They're tree-huggers: What environmental practices do they follow?

Compare the similarities and differences in the interpretation of these phrases between the two of you. Based on the meaning that you and your partner gave to these words, what can you conclude about idiolects and language denotation and connotation?

Concrete language—words that describe something that can be sensed

Precise words—words that identify a smaller grouping within a larger category

---

Qualifying language—language that indicates where a statement applies and does not apply, or indicates appropriate uncertainty about where it should apply

look more closely at what we mean by concrete words, precise words, details, and examples.

Concrete language is words that describe something that can be sensed: seen, heard, felt, tasted, or smelled. For example, instead of saying that Jill "speaks in a weird way," it is clearer to say, "Jill mumbles" (or whispers, or blusters, or drones). Each of these alternative words provides a specific description of the sound of Jill's voice.

Precise words are words that identify a smaller grouping within a larger category. For instance, notice the difference between

"Ruben is a blue-collar worker."
"Ruben is a construction worker."
"Ruben is a bulldozer operator."

Choosing concrete and precise words enables us to improve clarity, but there are times when a word may not have a more specific or concrete synonym, in which case a detail or an example may clarify or increase specificity. Suppose Lala says, "Rashad is very *loyal.*" Since the meaning of *loyal* (faithful to an idea, person, company, etc.) is abstract, Lala might add details: "I mean he never criticizes a friend behind her back," or examples: "Rashad stuck by me even when I was going through a hard time and wasn't very nice to him." By following her use of the abstract concept of loyalty with details or examples, Lala makes it easier for her listeners to ground their idea of this personal quality and see more accurately how it applies to Rashad. Figure 4.1 provides additional examples of how concrete and precise words and details or examples add semantic clarity to messages.

2. Use qualifying language to avoid overgeneralization.
Qualifying language is language that indicates where a statement applies and does not apply, or indicates appropriate uncertainty about where it should apply. Qualifying your message acknowledges that others' experiences may differ from the assertions you make. For instance, Jerome's statement to a friend, "With a degree in computer science you never have to worry about getting a job," is a

Message	Specified Message
The senator brought *several things* to the meeting.	The senator brought *recent letters from her constituency* to the meeting.
He lives in a *really big house.*	He lives in a *fourteen-room Tudor mansion.*
The backyard has *several different kinds of trees.*	The backyard has *two large maples, an oak, and four small evergreens.*
Morgan is a *fair grader.*	Morgan *uses the same standards for grading all students.*
Many students *aren't honest* in class.	Many students *cheat on tests* in class.
Judy *hits* the podium when she wants to emphasize her point.	Judy *pounds on* the podium when she wants to emphasize her point.

FIGURE 4.1 Improving Message Semantics through Specific Language

SKILL	USE	STEPS	EXAMPLE
Using language that is concrete and precise, and includes details and examples.	To improve message specificity.	1. Before you make a statement, consider the level of specificity that your listener needs in order to understand the meaning of your message. 2. Do one or more of the following: (a) Use concrete language to improve your listener's sensory interpretation of your message. (b) Use precise words to help your listener recognize the smaller groups within categories to which you are referring. (c) Use details and examples so that your listener understands the particular way you interpret more abstract concepts.	Describing a house, a realtor says "It's a cozy, family-friendly home in a two-story, Cape Cod style with a finished basement. It's around 2250 square feet, including three bedrooms and two-and-a-half baths. There is a screened porch looking out on the fenced-in back yard, which has a magnolia that produces huge blooms every spring. The owners' children and dogs spent their summers playing in the yard."

generalization to which there may be many exceptions. He can improve the semantic meaning of this statement by qualifying it, saying something like this: "With a degree in computer science you probably don't have to worry about getting a job. At least eleven of my friends who majored in computer science had no problem." The word "probably" indicates an appropriate degree of uncertainty, since Jerome does not actually control whether the friend gets a job. In addition, by mentioning his eleven friends, Jerome demonstrates that people with computer science degrees are indeed getting jobs, but that his actual knowledge is limited to this small set of people. All people generalize at one time or another, but by qualifying, we can avoid negative outcomes of overgeneralization. To qualify your verbal messages, first consider whether your intended message is about a specific object, person, or place, or whether it is a generalization about a class to which the object, person, or place belongs. If you are making a generalization, qualify your statement appropriately so that your assertion does not exceed the evidence that supports it.

One specific type of overgeneralization involves failing to specify *when* your statements apply. For instance, Parker says, "I'm going to be transferred to Henderson City. Do you know anything about the city?" Laura replies, "Yes I do.

SKILL BUILDER ▶ QUALIFYING LANGUAGE

SKILL	USE	STEPS	EXAMPLES
Mentally or verbally accounting for individual differences when generalizing.	To avoid overgeneralization that creates inaccurate meaning.	1. Before you make a statement, consider whether it pertains to a specific object, person, place, or time, or makes a generalization. 2. If you are making a generalization, qualify it appropriately so that your claim does not exceed the evidence that supports it.	"He's a politician and I don't trust him, although he may be different from most politicians I know." When Jake says, "How good a hitter is Steve?" Mark replies by date-stamping his evaluation: "When I worked with him two years ago, he couldn't hit the curve ball."

Let me just say that they've had some real trouble with their schools." On the basis of Laura's statement, Parker may worry about the effect the move will have on his children. What he doesn't know is that Laura's information about this problem in Henderson City is fifteen years old. Henderson City may still have problems, but then again, it may not. Had Laura assigned a time to her message and replied, "I know that fifteen years ago they had some real trouble with their schools. I'm not sure what the situation is now, but you may want to check," Parker would have received more accurate information. The skill of "date stamping" our messages requires that we consider and determine when the information was true and verbally acknowledge this time frame. This seems like a simple skill to put into practice—and it is. We cannot prevent circumstances from changing over time. But we can increase the semantic accuracy of our messages if we verbally recognize the reality of change by dating the statements we make. Figure 4.2 provides several examples of the skill of qualifying information to avoid overgeneralization, including date-stamping messages.

3. Adapt your language to your listeners.

Because we want to be understood, we need to choose our words carefully by using vocabulary our listener understands, using jargon sparingly, and using slang only when we are certain that the person whom we are communicating with not only understands the slang but will not be offended by our word choice.

People vary in the extent to which they know and use a large variety of words. The larger your vocabulary, the more choices you have for the language of your message. Having a larger vocabulary, however, can present challenges when you are communicating with people whose vocabulary is more limited. One strategy for assessing

Can you imagine how difficult it must be for scientists to adapt their language so that school children can understand scientific concepts?

Message	Qualified Message
Men are stronger than women.	*Most* men are stronger than *most* women.
State U must have a good economics department; the university is ranked in the top twenty in the U.S.	Because State U is among the top twenty schools in the nation, the economics program should be a good one, *although it may be an exception.*
Jack is sure to be outgoing; Don is, and they're brothers	Jack is likely to be outgoing because his brother Don is, *but Jack could be different.*
Your Sonic should go fifty thousand miles before you need a brake job; Jerry's did.	Your Sonic may well go fifty thousand miles before you need a brake job; Jerry's did, *but, of course, all Chevys aren't the same.*
Don't play the lottery; you won't win.	Don't play the lottery; *it's highly unlikely* that you will win.
Cancún is really popular with the college crowd.	When we were in Cancún *two years ago*, it was really popular with the college crowd.
Professor Powell brings great enthusiasm to her teaching.	Professor Powell brings great enthusiasm to her teaching—at least she did *last quarter* in communication theory.
You think Mary's depressed? I'm surprised. She seemed her regular high-spirited self when I talked to her.	You think Mary's depressed? I'm surprised. She seemed her regular high-spirited self when I talked with her *last month.*

FIGURE 4.2 Improving Semantic Accuracy by Qualifying Messages

another's vocabulary level is to listen to the types and complexity of words the other person uses—that is, take your signal from your communication partner. If you determine that your vocabulary is larger than your partner's, you can choose simpler synonyms for your words or use word phrases composed of more familiar terms. Adjusting your vocabulary to others does not mean talking down to them, however. It is merely polite behavior and effective communication to select words that others understand.

A second way to adapt to your listeners is to use jargon sparingly. **Jargon** refers to technical terminology whose meaning is understood by only a select group of people in a specialized speech community based on shared activities or interests. The key to effective use of specialized terms is to employ them only with people who use the same jargon. Among people who understand the same jargon, its use facilitates communication. If you must use jargon with people outside that specialized speech community, remember to explain the terms you are using. Without this explanation for outsiders, jargon becomes a type of foreign language.

A third way to adapt your language to your listeners is to use slang appropriately. **Slang** is the informal vocabulary developed and used by particular co-cultural groups in a society. Slang bonds those who use the same words by emphasizing a shared experience, simultaneously excluding others who don't share the terminology. Some slang words, which may be inoffensive when used by an in-group

Jargon—technical terminology whose meaning is understood by only a select group of people in a specialized speech community based on shared activities or interests

Slang—the informal vocabulary developed and used by particular co-cultural groups in a society

Linguistic sensitivity—using language that respects others while avoiding language that offends

with other in-group members, become highly offensive when used by non-members or when used outside the in-group speech community. The "N" word and many swear words exemplify this. Unless you want to risk offending your listener, use slang only with people who understand and appreciate it. If your communication goal is to be realized, your partner needs to understand you.

4. Demonstrate linguistic sensitivity.

Linguistic sensitivity is using language that respects others while avoiding language that offends. Some of our mistakes result from using expressions perceived by others as sexist, racist, or otherwise biased. Any language that is perceived as belittling any person or group of people can become the real meaning of our message, undermining our intended meaning.

Use inclusive language when you are referring to a wide swath of people. According to outdated rules of English usage, male references were employed as though they included both men and women. Masculine pronouns were used when referring to both men and women, as in the sentence, "When a person shops, *he* should have a clear idea of what *he* wants to buy." In modern English usage we are aware that this sentence is sexist because it encourages us to visualize a male person. Linguistic sensitivity means avoiding sexist language by using plurals or using both male and female pronouns. Stewart, Cooper, Stewart, and Friedley (2003) cite research to show that using *he or she* and to a lesser extent *they* alerts listeners to the importance of gender balance in both language and life.

In addition, English is rife with words that have single-sex markers for concepts that are really generic; for example, using "man" as a prefix or suffix (mankind, policeman, fireman, etc.). When some of these words were coined, a single-sex marker was appropriate since women or men were barred or discouraged from participating in those occupations or groups. Today, however, it is insensitive, for instance, to refer to a "flight attendant" as a "stewardess," and we recognize that it is more accurate to say "all people" rather than "mankind."

This is a police officer, not a policewoman. Can you think of other examples where single-sex labels have been replaced?

5. Improve your emotional vocabulary.

While emotions and feelings are often conveyed nonverbally through facial expressions, body language, and touch, there are also times when we need to talk about what emotions we are feeling. Many of us have difficulty doing this because we have been raised to mask our emotions. Likewise, some of us have trouble talking about our feelings because we don't have a rich vocabulary with which to do so. Often generic terms like "happy," "pissed," or "stressed" are not precise enough to convey what we are feeling and why we feel that way. For many of us, expanding our vocabulary would help us improve our ability to talk about what we are feeling. Table 4.1, A Vocabulary of Emotions, lists over 200 words that may help you expand your vocabulary so that you can more easily and accurately describe what you are feeling.

Describing feelings is the skill of verbally owning and explaining the precise feelings you are experiencing. Often people indicate that they have feelings, but are not very specific about what they are, or why they feel that way. If Nathan barks, "Who the hell asked you for your opinion?" he is probably experiencing negative feelings, but precisely what those feelings are and why he feels that way are much less clear. Similarly, when Shawna exclaims, "That's wonderful, Gabriella!" she may be experiencing positive feelings, but exactly what she feels and why are less clear. By describing negative feelings more effectively, we can reduce or avoid conflict, and be more successful at supporting each other. By describing positive feelings more effectively, we can increase our positive impact on others, and improve our relationships. For example, when LeRoy carefully and quietly tells Tony that he is annoyed that Tony borrowed his iPod without asking, Tony,

▶ **OBSERVE AND ANALYZE**

Building Your Emotional Vocabulary

Choose ten of the emotions in Table 4.1 that you don't usually use to describe your feelings. Say "I feel . . . ," and try to experience the feelings the word describes. Next make a list of the feelings that you recognize as ones that you have personally experienced. Then recall recent situations in which you could have used each of these words. Write the message that would have been appropriate for each situation. In those situations, did you choose the exact word you wanted to use, or were you inexact in your word choice?

Describing feelings—the skill of verbally owning and explaining the precise feelings you are experiencing

---

TABLE 4.1 A Vocabulary of Emotions

Words related to *angry*

agitated	hostile	offended
annoyed	incense	outraged
bitter	indignant	peeved
cranky	infuriated	resentful
enraged	irked	riled
exasperated	irritated	steamed
furious	mad	

Words related to *helpful*

agreeable	constructive	obliging
amiable	cooperative	supportive
beneficial	cordial	useful
caring	gentle	warm
collegial	kind	
compassionate	neighborly	

(Continued)

TABLE 4.1 (*Continued*)

Words related to *loving*

adoring	caring	heavenly
affectionate	charming	passionate
amorous	fervent	sensitive
aroused	gentle	tender

Words related to *embarrassed*

abashed	distressed	ridiculous
anxious	flustered	shamefaced
chagrined	humbled	sheepish
confused	humiliated	silly
conspicuous	jittery	troubled
disconcerted	overwhelmed	uncomfortable
disgraced	rattled	

Words related to *surprised*

astonished	flustered	rattled
astounded	jarred	shocked
baffled	jolted	startled
bewildered	mystified	stunned
confused	perplexed	
distracted	puzzled	

Words related to *fearful*

afraid	frightened	shaken
agitated	horrified	terrified
alarmed	jittery	threatened
anxious	jumpy	troubled
apprehensive	nervous	uneasy
bullied	petrified	worried
cornered	scared	

Words related to *disgusted*

afflicted	outraged	revolted
annoyed	repelled	sickened
nauseated	repulsed	

Words related to *hurt*

abused	forsaken	piqued
awful	hassled	rejected
cheated	ignored	resentful
deprived	isolated	rotten
deserted	mistreated	scorned
desperate	offended	slighted
dismal	oppressed	snubbed
dreadful	pained	wounded

Words related to *belittled*

betrayed	foolish	powerless
defeated	helpless	underestimated
deflated	inadequate	undervalued
demeaned	incapable	unfit
diminished	inferior	unworthy
disparaged	insulted	useless
downgraded	persecuted	

Words related to *happy*

blissful	exultant	jubilant
charmed	fantastic	merry
cheerful	giddy	pleased
contented	glad	satisfied
delighted	gratified	thrilled
ecstatic	high	tickled
elated	joyous	

Words related to *lonely*

abandoned	excluded	lost
alone	forlorn	rejected
bored	forsaken	renounced
deserted	ignored	scorned
desolate	isolated	slighted
discarded	jilted	snubbed
empty	lonesome	

Words related to *sad*

blue	gloomy	moody
crestfallen	heavyhearted	morose
dejected	joyless	pained
depressed	low	sorrowful
dismal	melancholy	troubled
dour	mirthless	weary
downcast	miserable	

Words related to *energetic*

animated	hardy	spirited
bold	inspired	sprightly
brisk	kinetic	spry
dynamic	lively	vibrant
eager	peppy	vigorous
forceful	potent	vivacious
frisky	robust	

How might the act of describing feelings prevent verbal abuse?

who didn't mean to offend LeRoy, is more likely both to respond without defensiveness and to ask LeRoy's permission the next time. When used effectively to show affection or approval, the skill of describing positive feelings can have beneficial effects on the relationship. For example, when Paul's *nana* tells him straightforwardly and without gushing how much she enjoys his emails, Paul is likely not only to have good feelings about his *nana* but also to write her more frequently.

Describing feelings can be a difficult skill to master. Simply beginning a sentence with "I feel" doesn't guarantee that you will end up actually describing a feeling. In many cases, statements beginning with "I feel…" actually end up evaluating, blaming, or scapegoating someone or something. Consider Jay's statement, "I feel like you insulted me when you said…." While Jay may believe that he has described a feeling, he has actually practiced blaming. The key to describing feelings is describing your own feelings, not labeling the person who made you feel that way or making assumptions about that person's intentions. Stop and think—If a person says something that you perceive as insulting, how might you *feel?* Perhaps you feel hurt, rejected, betrayed, or embarrassed. If so, then the descriptive statement might be "I felt hurt (rejected, betrayed, or embarrassed) when you said…." Suppose, for instance, that your brother screamed at you for something you did. If you said, "I feel that you're angry with me," your statement echoes what the other person said but does not describe your present feelings. To describe your feelings you might instead say, "When you talk to me in an angry tone of voice, I feel scared" (or hurt, pained, or distressed).

Describing feelings is a three-step process: (1) Identify what has triggered the feelings (a trigger is anything that causes a feeling or reaction); (2) identify the particular emotion you are experiencing accurately—this sounds easier than it sometimes is—use Table 4.1, A Vocabulary of Emotions, to help you name the specific emotion you are feeling; and (3) use an "I feel . . ." followed by naming the specific feeling. The following two examples describe feelings effectively:

> "Thank you for your compliment [trigger]; I [owning the feeling] feel gratified [specific feeling] that you noticed the effort I made."
> "When you criticize my cooking on days that I've worked as many hours as you have [trigger], I [owning the feeling] feel very resentful [specific feeling]."

If you are new to describing feelings, practice your skills by describing positive feelings: "You know, taking me to that movie really cheered me up," or "When you offered to help me with the housework, I really felt relieved." As you become more comfortable describing your positive feelings, you can try describing negative feelings attributable to environmental factors: "It's so cloudy that I feel gloomy," or "When we have a thunderstorm, I get really anxious." Finally, you can move to negative descriptions resulting from what people have said or done to you: "When you step in front of me like that, I really get annoyed," or "When you use a negative tone of voice while saying that what I did pleased you, I really feel confused."

SKILL	USE	STEPS	EXAMPLE
Verbally explaining and owning what you feel (or felt).	To effectively and appropriately express what you feel.	1. Identify what has triggered the feeling. 2. Identify what you are feeling—think specifically. Am I feeling amused? pleased? happy? ecstatic? 3. Own the feeling by using an "I feel" statement followed by naming the specific feelings.	"Because I didn't get the job, I feel depressed and discouraged." "The way you stood up for me when I was being put down by Leah makes me feel very warm and loving toward you."

Meaning Within the Conversational Context

The **pragmatic meaning** of the language in a verbal message is the meaning that arises from understanding the practical consequences of an utterance. At the semantic level, we are interested in what the words mean (Korta & Perry, 2008). At the pragmatic level, we are interested in what people mean; more specifically, we are interested in what a specific speaker talking to a specific other in a conversation means at a certain point in time. So, while the semantic meaning of a message remains the same across speakers and conversations, its pragmatic meaning changes. Understanding the context of individual speech acts and the cooperative principle help us determine the meaning of a message.

Pragmatic meaning—meaning of a verbal message that arises from understanding the practical consequences of an utterance

Speech Acts

A **speech act** is the action the speaker takes by uttering a verbal message. Typically, speech acts imply how listeners should respond. At the pragmatic level, when we *speak*, we *do*. At times, our speech acts are explicit, but in many instances what we are doing is implicit. As we search for the pragmatic meaning of the message, we ask ourselves, "What is the speaker doing by saying these words to me right now?" Similarly, when forming our message, we choose language intended to create a certain response in our listener. For example, suppose I say, "Karen, pass me the bowl of potatoes." This imperative statement directly orders Karen to pick up the bowl of potatoes and hand them to me. Instead, suppose I ask, "Karen, do you mind passing me the potatoes?" At the semantic level, this question appears to give Karen a choice, yet at the pragmatic level, what I am trying to do is the same: direct Karen to pass me the bowl of potatoes. We can accomplish the same pragmatic goal with either a direct/explicit or indirect/implicit speech act.

Speech act—the action that the speaker takes by uttering a verbal message

The meaning of a speech act depends on the context. We can use a verbal message whose semantic meaning is exactly the same to perform very different speech acts whose pragmatic meanings are quite different. Let's look at a simple example. One morning after his car failed to start, Harry made three phone calls:

Phone Call 1:
Harry: The car won't start.
Katie: Sorry about that. I'll just take the bus.

Phone Call 2:
Harry: The car won't start.
AAA Customer Service Representative: Where is the car, sir? I'll send a tow truck right away.

Phone Call 3:
Harry: The car won't start.
Previous owner, who recently sold the car to Harry: Wow, that never happened to me. But I told you I was selling the car "as is."

In all three cases, the verbal utterance and the semantic meaning of Harry's message is the same, but from a pragmatic standpoint, Harry performed three different speech acts. With Katie, he was expressing his feelings, apologizing and/or explaining. By this speech act, he implies that Katie should understand, comfort, and release him from his obligation to take her to school. With the AAA representative, Harry was directing him to act, calling in a promise of service that comes with his AAA membership. This speech act was a request for assistance. When Harry called the previous owner of the car, he was complaining and implying that the previous owner of the car should accept responsibility. In all cases there were the same words, same syntax, but three different speech acts.

Notice also that each of the people Harry talked to was able to understand the pragmatic meaning of his speech act and how Harry expected them to respond. Katie "read" what he said as frustration and that she needed to find her own way to school. So she offered a "sorry" and relieved him of the responsibility for getting her to class. The customer service rep at AAA expected that the person on the line would be calling to report car trouble and request that a tow truck be dispatched, so his response to Harry's speech act was to find out where the car was located. The previous car owner correctly understood Harry's speech act, but his response refused ownership of the problem.

How were Katie, the customer service rep, and the previous car owner able to recognize the speech acts being performed? You might say that these people interpreted the meaning of Harry's speech act within the situation or context, and you wouldn't be wrong. However, noted linguist Paul Grice has offered some more precise ideas about how we make sense of each other's speech acts in interaction. According to Grice, we make certain assumptions about how communication generally works, and we use those assumptions to make sense of each other's verbal messages.

The Cooperative Principle

Grice's **cooperative principle** states that conversational partners are able to understand what others mean to do with their verbal messages because they assume that their partners will cooperate to share meaning. In other words, they will create verbal messages that are in line with the shared purpose of the conversation (Grice, 1975). By assuming this level of cooperation, we can go beyond the semantic level of meaning and understand a speaker's goal for uttering a verbal message. Notice how all of the people Harry talked with assumed that his statement "The car won't start" made sense in their conversation. Even though there

are various ways this message could be interpreted, no one adopted an interpretation that was nonsensical in that interaction. Instead, they assumed that Harry was cooperating to create shared meaning and thus interpreted his message accordingly. In fact, we almost always assume that others are trying to cooperate to share meaning, regardless of whether or not our goals are the same. Even during conflict with others, we still assume that they are trying to make meaningful contributions to the interaction. If we couldn't make this assumption, it would be nearly impossible to communicate.

The cooperative principle is broken down into four **conversational maxims**, or specific assumptions that we rely on when interpreting messages. The **maxim of quality** is the assumption that others will tell the truth. The **maxim of quantity** is the assumption that others will provide an appropriate amount of information, neither too little nor too much. The **maxim of manner** is the assumption that others will say things in an orderly way. Finally, the **maxim of relevance** is the assumption that others will respond in coherent ways to what has been previously said, in line with the topic or purpose of the interaction. All of these maxims describe specific ways of following the cooperative principle.

Although Grice did not intend his maxims to be followed as rules, you might find them to be useful guides for effective communication. Certainly, it is both useful and ethical to speak in orderly, relevant, truthful, and sufficient ways. However, Grice's point was primarily that the cooperative principle and maxims guide the way we interpret messages. If a message appears to adhere to the maxims, we should be able to interpret it easily. However, if a message appears to violate one or more maxims, we can still assume that the general cooperative principle is in effect, and use that assumption to infer meaning from the violation. For example, if Barry asks, "Who's going to pick up Mom from work today?" and his brother answers, "I've got a big test tomorrow," this statement doesn't appear immediately relevant to Barry's question, because the question was about picking up Mom, and the answer he received was about a test. However, if Barry assumes his brother is following the cooperative principle, he can interpret the information about the test as being relevant and meaning, "I can't pick Mom up; I have to study." Similarly, when Jeremy asks his roommate, "What's for dinner?" and his roommate replies, "Ramen or filet mignon," his roommate violates the quantity maxim by not giving Jeremy the exact information, and probably the quality

Cooperative principle—the pragmatic principle that states that conversational partners are able to understand what the other means to do with their verbal messages because they assume that their partners are collaborating by sharing verbal messages in line with the shared purpose of the conversation

Conversational maxims—specific rules that cooperating partners count on others to follow

Maxim of quality—the assumption that others will tell the truth

Maxim of quantity—the assumption that others will provide an appropriate amount of information, neither too little nor too much

Maxim of manner—the assumption that others will say things in an orderly way

Maxim of relevance—the assumption that others will respond in coherent ways to what has been previously said, in line with the topic or purpose of the interaction

maxim as well, unless there is really filet mignon in their freezer. But Jeremy, assuming that his roommate is cooperating in the conversation, will probably interpret the comment as sarcasm meaning his roommate has no idea what they will eat. We make these kinds of interpretations all the time, often without realizing it, but we couldn't do it without relying on the cooperative principle.

Minor violations of Grice's maxims are common. Some of these are for sarcasm or other forms of humor, but more frequently we may be less relevant, sufficient, orderly, or truthful in our messages in order to be polite. Language does more than accomplish speech acts; it also conveys important information about how we view others, our relationships, and ourselves. For example, if Alicia comes out of the laundry room and admonishes her fiancé, Markus, "You've got to clean the lint screen on the dryer after each load!" the speech act of demanding compliance is clear. However, this clarity could harm Alicia's relationship with Markus and fail to change his behavior because it damages his face. **Face** is our public self-image, or how we want others to view us. According to face theorists Lim and Bowers (1991), we usually want others to view us as being independent (free to decide and act on our own), capable (able to do necessary and important things), and affiliated (connected with others who like us). When we feel that our face concerns are not respected, we tend to respond negatively. With her demand, Alicia implies that Markus needs to do what she wants, that he hasn't shown himself capable of doing a small task, and that he isn't very likeable (at least when he doesn't clean the lint screen). Due to the face implications of Alicia's demand, Markus may become upset and could also retaliate by refusing to clean the lint screen.

Consider how Alicia might have rephrased this message using **politeness**, or language strategies that show concern for face: "Hey, hon, I just restarted the load in the dryer. The lint screen was bulging again." Compared to the original statement, this one deviates from the maxims—it takes more words than are absolutely necessary, and Markus will have to do a little interpretation to see the

Face—our public self-image, or how we want others to view us

Politeness—language strategies that show concern for face

Message	Message with Politeness
Go talk to Professor Allen.	Maybe you can go talk to Professor Allen. You're such a dedicated student. I'm sure she'll see that. But you have to do what you're comfortable with.
Let me wear your orange sweater.	Bud, you know that orange sweater you've got? Could I borrow it, just for the game? No worries if you're planning to wear it, though.
This section should be cut back.	I'm such a big fan of your writing—you know that! I wonder if you could make this section shorter. Or, you may have some different ideas about how to improve it.
I want to break up with you.	I'm truly sorry to do this, Max, but I think we need to break up. You're a great guy, and you've been there through the good and bad for me. I care for you. I just need to be on my own right now.

FIGURE 4.3 Improving Message Pragmatics with Politeness

SKILL	USE	STEPS	EXAMPLES
Managing face concerns with polite language.	To avoid or reduce threats to another person's face, or public self-image.	1. As you interact, consider whether your speech acts could threaten your partner's face, making him or her feel less independent, capable, or affiliated (connected to and liked by others). 2. Use language that addresses these face concerns: (a) Show respect for the other person's independence from you; (b) show that you believe the other person is capable; and (c) show that you like and are connected to the other person.	Bethany and Dadrie are "Big Sister" and "Little Sister" in a sorority. Dadrie hasn't completed the T-shirt design she promised for the sorority's next dance, and with the deadline for orders approaching, Bethany needs Dadrie to finish it. She pops into Dadrie's room, gives her a warm smile and says "Da-da . . . ya know, the dance is only a month away? We are all counting on your talent for that T-shirt. I saw you were working on an incredible design. . . . I can't wait to see the finished product! Is it possible to wrap up in the next day or two?"

relevance of the last sentence. But by being less direct, Alicia treats Markus as more independent, competent, and likeable. Another alternative is for Alicia to say: "Hon, thanks for doing the laundry, I appreciate it. I just restarted the dryer and noticed the lint screen was bulging. Could you clean it whenever you switch loads?" Although this message is not as succinct or direct as it could be, and the first sentence might even be seen as irrelevant to the issue of cleaning the lint screen, compared to the original demand, it is far more protective of face, and consequently less likely to damage Alicia and Markus' relationship. Figure 4.3 provides several examples of using politeness to show concern for face.

Guidelines for Improving Pragmatic Understanding

1. Interpret a message within its context. The pragmatic meaning of a message is context-specific, so we risk misunderstanding a message when we fail to consider the people, their relationship to one another, and other context factors when we interpret a message. For example, while it is almost always considered inappropriate and offensive for white people to use the "N" word, there are times when African Americans will use one form of this word (N-a rather than N-r) as a way of referencing others in an affectionate or joking way (Motley & Craig-Henderson, 2007). So whether the "N" word is interpreted as offensive or endearing depends on the specific context.

▶ **OBSERVE AND ANALYZE**

Semantic Meaning vs. Pragmatic Understanding

An interesting place to observe the divergence between semantic meaning and pragmatic understanding is in the dialogues of situation comedies. Select an episode of *The Big Bang Theory* to analyze. Watch the show. Find three instances when a character correctly interprets the semantic meaning of the message while misinterpreting the pragmatic level of the message. Record what was said, what was meant, and what alternative pragmatic meaning was interpreted. For each case, explain why the misunderstanding occurred.

2. Avoid excessive maxim violation. All of us violate maxims in minor ways on a regular basis. Typically, our communication does not suffer, either because the violation goes unnoticed, or because others successfully rely on the cooperative principle and interpret our meaning correctly. However, excessive maxim violations could lead others to perceive us in negative ways. For example, you might be seen as ditzy if you often violate manner with disorganized messages, or dishonest if you often violate quality with exaggerations or equivocations. Maxim violations to produce sarcastic humor can be fun, but can also be annoying when they are too frequent.

3. Consider acknowledging that you are deliberately violating a maxim. If you are going to violate a maxim for deliberate effect, but are uncertain whether your partner will recognize what you are doing, consider doing something to signal that a maxim violation is coming. For example, saying "I don't know if this is true, but my sister said…" acknowledges that you may be violating the quality maxim. "If I told you, I'd have to kill you…" acknowledges violating the quantity maxim. "This may be beside the point, but…" acknowledges violating the relevancy maxim. And, "This is just off the top of my head…" acknowledges violating the manner maxim. When you recognize that your verbal message violates a maxim of the cooperative principle, you can still help your partner understand your intention if you acknowledge your violation. Similarly, pay attention when your partner acknowledges a violation so that you don't misinterpret what is being said.

4. Temper clarity with politeness. While at the semantic level we are working to achieve clarity, we also need to pay attention to the face needs of our partners. When a direct and clear message may create defensiveness, we should consider using more indirect language that conveys the same ideas but saves the face of our partners.

Meaning Within the Social and Cultural Context

In the last chapter we discussed how cultures vary and how this variation generally affects communication. The **sociolinguistic meaning** of a message is the meaning of a verbal message that varies according to the language norms and expectations of a particular cultural or co-cultural group. Since we learn to speak within the context of our culture and co-cultural groups, our "canned plans" and scripts come from modeling the verbal messages of others in our group. Sociolinguistic misunderstandings occur when we interact with someone from a different culture or co-cultural background. Cultures develop different norms and expectations about the way words are combined, about how to say what to whom and when, and about speech style.

First, cultures have norms that assign meaning to specific combinations of words that differ from the semantic meaning of those word combinations. For example, in English we associate the word "pretty" with women and "handsome" with men, even though both refer to physical beauty. So choosing to say

Sociolinguistic meaning—the meaning of a verbal message that varies according to the language norms and expectations of a particular cultural or co-cultural group

How might culture affect the conversation between the children in this picture?

"She is a pretty woman" sends a different message than "She is a handsome woman" (Chaika, 2007). In addition, all cultures develop **idioms**, expressions used by members of a language or speech community whose meaning differs from the usual meanings associated with that combination of words. Imagine how confusing it is to someone who is just learning the language to hear, "That test was *a piece of cake,*" which literally means the test was a slice of baked goods. In French, someone might say "Il s'est jeté *à corps perdu* dans son nouveau projet." This literally means "He threw himself *with body lost* into his new project." Both the French and the English use the idiom "to throw oneself into something," but the French use the expression *à corps perdu* to signify what in English would be idiomatically expressed as "body and soul," "wholeheartedly," or "headlong." It is necessary to understand French cultural idioms to correctly translate and interpret this statement as "He threw himself wholeheartedly into his new project."

Second, cultures develop different norms about what language should be used to convey certain meanings, what it means when a particular person uses a specific verbal message, and what it means when a specific language is used in addressing a particular person. For example, complimenting others and accepting compliments are common to all language communities, but the sincerity of the compliment can depend on the language employed. In American culture, our compliment messages often use hyperbole or exaggerations. For instance, you might compliment your new Japanese friend by saying, "Miki, this is the *best* miso soup I have ever tasted." To Miki, a new Japanese exchange student, your compliment sounds insincere because in Japanese culture the language of compliments is less effusive. To mitigate your error, she may reply, "Oh, it's nice of you to say that, but I am sure that you have had better miso soup at sushi

Idioms—expressions used by members of a language or speech community whose meaning differs from the usual meanings associated with that combination of words

LEARN ABOUT YOURSELF ▶ VERBAL STYLE

Take this short survey to learn about your preferred verbal style. There are no right or wrong answers. Just be honest in reporting how you act in most situations. **For each item, select the number to the left that best reflects how you talk.**

1 = **Rarely**

2 = **Occasionally**

3 = **Frequently**

4 = **Most of the time**

_____ 1. I tell the truth regardless of the consequences

_____ 2. When I want something, I drop a hint and expect the other person to figure out what I need.

_____ 3. If a conversation becomes heated, I join in, or tell them to cool it.

_____ 4. If a conversation becomes heated, I change the subject.

_____ 5. I like to hear a clear "no" if someone disagrees with me.

_____ 6. When people dispute what I have said, I acknowledge the point they have made but do not directly disagree with them.

_____ 7. I enjoy a good verbal argument.

_____ 8. If I don't want to do something, I say "maybe" rather than hurt someone with my refusal.

_____ 9. If I see people make a mistake, I immediately tell them what they did and how to correct it.

_____ 10. If I see people make a mistake, I take them aside and ask them what they were trying to do.

_____ 11. If someone compliments me, I acknowledge it by saying, "Thank you."

_____ 12. If someone compliments me, I point out how what I did was not exceptional.

Scoring the survey: Add up your scores on the odd-numbered items for your direct verbal style score. Then add up your scores on the even-numbered items to get your indirect verbal style score.

Direct Verbal Score: _____   Indirect Verbal Score: _____

Both scores can range from 6 to 24. The more divergent your scores, the more you rely on either a direct or indirect verbal style; the more similar your scores, the more flexible your style. Take a moment to think about how your style affects the people with whom you interact. Do most of your family and friends have similar styles? Can your style create problems for a relationship?

restaurants in the city." Similarly, in the American Midwest, we often smile and say "Hi" to strangers on the street as a way of being friendly. In China, acknowledging a stranger in this way assumes a familiarity that is unwarranted and even rude.

Third, different cultures also prefer different verbal styles. These may vary in a number of ways, but the degree to which the style is direct or indirect has the greatest effect on sociolinguistic meaning (Ting-Toomey & Chung, 2005).

A **direct verbal style** is characterized by language that openly states the speaker's intention and by message content that is straightforward and unambiguous. An **indirect verbal style** is characterized by language that masks the speaker's true intentions, and by roundabout, vague content whose real meaning is embedded in the social or cultural context. As you have probably inferred, low-context cultures value direct verbal styles, while high-context cultures value indirect styles. Let's look at an example of how these diverse styles can create difficulty in interpreting the language that people use to express their meaning.

> College roommates Jorge and Kevin are from the same hometown as Sam, who lives across the hall and has a car. Thanksgiving is fast approaching, and both men need to find a ride home. One night while watching a football game in Sam's room, the following conversation occurs:
>
> Jorge says to Sam: "Are you driving home for Thanksgiving?" [Maybe he'll give me a ride.]
>
> Sam: "Yep." [If he wanted a ride, he'd ask.]
>
> Kevin: "Well, I'd like a ride home."
>
> Sam: "Sure, no problem."
>
> Jorge: "Are you taking anyone else?" [I wonder if he still has room for me.]
>
> Sam: "Nope. I'm leaving early, after my last class on Tuesday and not coming back until late Sunday evening." [I guess Jorge already has a ride home.]
>
> Jorge: "Well, enjoy Thanksgiving." [If he wanted to give me a ride, I gave him several opportunities to offer. I guess I'll take the bus.]

In this conversation, Jorge, the son of Nicaraguan immigrants, uses the indirect style he learned as a child growing up in the Latin American neighborhood of the city they all come from. His questions were meant to prompt Sam to offer him a ride. But Sam, whose parents grew up in New York, where being direct is the preferred style, completely misses what Jorge meant. Consequently, Jorge will ride the bus, even though Sam would have driven him home had he just asked in a way that Sam understood.

Evidence supports differences in the verbal styles of ethnic, national, cultural, and co-cultural groups; however, current scholarship challenges the earlier research findings of distinctly masculine and feminine verbal styles. Still, the popular and online media continue to erroneously report widespread differences. Today linguistic scholars emphasize that language use is so particular to the conversational context that few reliable differences appear to exist between men and women in the same cultural or co-cultural group. Rather, the differences that are sometimes observed may be due to unequal power, conversational topic, individual identity, and same-sex or mixed-sex groups (Freed, 2003).

Guidelines for Improving Sociolinguistic Understanding

1. Develop intercultural competence. In the last chapter, we described how to develop intercultural competence. The more you learn about other cultures, the better you will be able to form messages whose sociolinguistics align with

Direct verbal style—language that openly states the speaker's intention and content that is straightforward and unambiguous

Indirect verbal style—language that masks the speaker's true intentions and roundabout, vague message content whose real meaning is embedded in the social or cultural context

How can practicing mindfulness help you when you are talking with someone from a different culture?

Mindfulness—the process of drawing novel distinctions

your intended meaning, and the better you will be able to understand the socio-linguistic meaning of others' messages.

2. Practice mindfulness. Mindfulness is the process of drawing novel distinctions (Langer & Moldoveanu, 2000). If we are mindful when interacting with others, we are focused on the present moment and noticing how we are similar to and different from our conversational partners. How do our partners differ in this moment from how they were in the last moment? How does what is happening now differ from what has happened or from what we expected to have happen? How are our partners' verbal messages distinct from other things they have said or from what we would have said? In other words, when we practice mindfulness, we pay close attention to what is happening in the conversation at that moment and work hard to understand both our partners and ourselves.

3. Recognize, respect, and adapt to the sociolinguistic practices of others. As the old saying goes, "When in Rome, do as the Romans do." If, for example, you travel to Jakarta or are invited to your Indonesian American friend's home for the weekend, you should adapt your verbal style to that of your hosts. Or if you are from a low-context culture and are talking with someone who you think is from a high-context culture, be sensitive to the indirect meaning of verbal messages. Fluency in more than one language, or in more than one dialect of a language, allows you to codeswitch and to use the dialect of your conversational partner.

Using Language to Relate Online

As communication technologies become increasingly more integrated into our daily lives, many of us have relationships in which communication takes place largely, or even exclusively, online. Many of us communicate frequently through texts, emails, and social media sites like Facebook and Twitter, with people that we see only infrequently, if at all. In the terms of "media richness theory" (Daft & Lengel, 1984), these are **lean media** because they rely heavily on language and other symbols, such as emoticons or emojis, to convey meaning, whereas the telephone, videoconferencing, and face-to-face interactions are **rich media** because meaning can be conveyed through both verbal and nonverbal behavior. When we conduct relationships largely online, are these inferior because of our reliance on language to develop and maintain connection?

Back when the internet was still in its infancy, most computer-mediated communication took place via email. The idea that people could conduct relationships online, through language, seemed ridiculous to many. In 1992, however, Joseph Walther, a professor of interpersonal, computer-mediated communication, proposed the theory of "social information processing" (SIP), which claimed that people could form relationships despite the leanness of online interaction, and that these relationships could be at least as meaningful as those conducted in face-to-face interactions. But in order for this to happen, people had to adapt their use of language so that it could do the work that nonverbal behavior normally did. Indeed, Walther's research revealed that people were quite capable of showing that they felt positively toward others through language strategies that included giving personal information, offering encouragement, expressing joy, and making statements of affection, including using emoticons (Walther, Loh, & Granka, 2005). Other studies indicate that it can take more time to develop closeness online, but that if you are willing to "SIP" rather than gulp, it will still occur (Peter, Valkenburg, & Schouten, 2005). Walther argues that if people are interested in making a personal connection, they will find a way to do so, regardless of the medium.

Beyond simply finding ways to manage with digital communication, Walther found that people can potentially form deeper relationships than traditional encounters using just verbal communication. Walther (1996) describes this phenomenon in an extension of SIP called the "hyperpersonal model." The hyperpersonal model argues that relationships actually benefit from the peculiarities of online interaction. Asynchrony, or not having to respond immediately, allows people to communicate at their own tempo and convenience. Asynchrony allows senders to edit their verbal messages for optimal effectiveness, while receivers have time to interpret messages carefully before creating new ones themselves. In addition, receivers often idealize senders

Lean media—media that rely heavily on language and other symbols, such as emoticons or emojis, to convey meaning

Rich media—media where meaning can be conveyed through both verbal and nonverbal behavior

Abbie, who was from San Antonio, Texas, was adding sweetener to her iced latte in the coffee bar when she spied Ethan and Nate, two friends she knew from the gym. She flounced over to their table in the corner, dropped into the empty seat, and greeted them cheerily: "Hi, guys. How y'all doin'?"

"Not bad. Ethan and I were just chillin' between classes. What about you?"

"Well, I'm really annoyed," Abbie replied. "It took that guy behind the counter three times to get ma order. I mean, if you cain't understand English, I don't thank you should be workin' in a customer service position. And after he finally understood what I was sayin', he started to rattle off somefen in what I guess he thought was English. But damned if I could understand a word he said. You'da thank with all the people out of work that they could find someun who spoke good English."

"Who are you talking about, Abbie?" asked Ethan.

"That guy over yonder with the green shirt and the little bitty mustache at the second cash register."

"Abbie, that's Jean-Paul. He's French Canadian, and he speaks excellent English. Yes, he has an accent, but so do you," Ethan pointed out.

"Ah don't have an accent!" Abbie drawled. "I talk just fine. Both'a y'all have accents, but I understand you just fine. It's just those quote unquote immigrants who come over here and expect us all to put up with 'Press one for Spanish, two for English.' I mean come on, if ya cain't speak the language, don't 'spect us to cater to ya. I'm just sick of all of it. And. . . ."

"Well," Nate interrupted. "You're right. I do have an accent—a Boston accent—and I'm proud of it. It lets people know where I'm from. And I have no problem understanding Jean-Paul, but I sure don't understand you sometimes."

FOR CONSIDERATION:
1. What ethical principle is at issue in this case?
2. What do you think about the issues that Abbie raises?
3. Based on what you have learned about language in this chapter, what could you tell Abbie that might help her become more tolerant of others?

because the messages are better-crafted than they would be face-to-face, and because there is no contradictory information coming from nonverbal behavior. Together, these circumstances make it easy to disclose and reciprocate personal information, leading to strong emotional connections. Although there are certainly disadvantages to relationships conducted solely online, such as lack of physical contact and increased potential for dishonesty, our ability to feel a strong relationship with another person is not impaired, and may even be enhanced.

Summary

We use verbal behavior, or language, to convey messages. Language is a symbolic system that includes a lexicon, phonology, and syntax and grammar. A language community includes all the people who can speak or understand a particular language. Languages are really collections of dialects, and a speech community is composed of language users who speak a common dialect. None of us speaks a language or a dialect; rather, we have our own personal idiolect. All languages, dialects, and idiolects share six common characteristics. They are arbitrary, ambiguous, abstract, self-reflexive, changing, and revealing. To understand the full meaning of a verbal message, you need to interpret its semantics, pragmatics, and sociolinguistics. The semantic meaning of a message is contained in the language itself. You can improve a message's semantic level of verbal meaning by using specific language, qualifying information, adapting your language to your listener, and demonstrating linguistic sensitivity. The pragmatic meaning of a verbal message is the practical meaning of the language within the context of the conversation. Our messages are actually speech acts designed to elicit a specific response from the listener. We rely on the cooperative principle and conversational maxims to make sense of speech acts. It is important to balance the clarity of a speech act with politeness. The sociolinguistic meaning of a verbal message varies from culture to culture depending on its norms and expectations about verbal message forms. You can improve a message's sociolinguistic level of verbal meaning by developing intercultural competence, practicing mindfulness, and recognizing, respecting, and adapting to the sociolinguistic practices of others. Because we can adapt language to substitute for missing nonverbal behaviors, relationships developed and maintained online can be as close as face-to-face relationships.

CHAPTER RESOURCES

Key Words

Flashcards for all of these key terms are available on the *Inter-Act* website.

Analyze and Apply

The following activities challenge you to demonstrate your mastery of the concepts, theories, and frameworks in this chapter by using them to explain what is happening in a specific situation.

4.1 Rewind/Rewrite

Now that you have read the chapter, hit "rewind" on the opening dialogue between Natalya and her American classmates and answer the following questions.

a. Use concepts from the chapter to explain how a misunderstanding occurred. The concepts of language community, speech community, dialect, slang, and idiom may be especially relevant.

b. Rewrite the dialogue so that the American students show more mindfulness and respect for Natalya, and do a better job of adapting their language to her as a listener.

c. During her stay in the United States, Natalya will probably encounter other language that confuses her. How do you recommend she manage these situations?

4.2 Demonstrating Semantics, Pragmatics, and Sociolinguistics

Write a short dialogue that demonstrates the unique ways in which semantics, pragmatics, and sociolinguistics each contribute to the meaning of verbal messages. Annotate your dialogue to explain what is happening at each level in each turn.

Skill Practice

Skill practice activities give you the chance to rehearse a new skill by responding to hypothetical or real situations. Additional skill practice activities are available at the companion website.

4.3 Clarifying Language

Reword the following messages to make the language more specific with concrete and precise words, details, or examples.

a. "You know that I really love baseball. Well, I'm practicing a lot because I'm hoping to get a tryout with the pros."

b. "I'm really bummed out. Everything with Corey is going down the tubes. We just don't connect anymore."

c. "She's just a pain. Ya know, always doing stuff to tick me off. And then just acting like, ya know."

4.4 Qualifying Language

Improve each of the statements below by qualifying the information:

a. "The Mortensons always drive a new car."

b. "Grady is always on Facebook. He has more "friends" than anyone I know."

c. "The Scoop has the best ice cream in Southwest Florida."

d. "Just watch, when Cameron walks in he'll look like he just walked off the set of a *GQ* shoot."

e. "He'll be on time. He was in the military."

f. *"Law and Order: Los Angeles* is going to be a hit. It's a Dick Wolf show."

Communication Improvement Plan:
Verbal Communication

How can you improve your ability to use language in producing or interpreting the meaning of verbal messages? Identify a problem you have forming or understanding verbal messages. Review the guidelines for improving the semantic, pragmatic, and sociolinguistic meanings of verbal messages. Select at least one of these as a goal. Then using the interpersonal communication skills you have studied in the course, write a communication improvement plan. You can find a communication improvement plan worksheet on our website at www.oup.com/us/verderber.

NONVERBAL
MESSAGES

Jen and Mel are best friends who share an apartment. One morning, Jen had an interview for a summer internship with the company she really wanted to work for after graduation. In the week leading up to the interview, she talked with Mel nonstop about her hopes and fears. When she left for her interview, she hollered "Hey, Mel, wish me luck!"

After her afternoon class, Mel returned to their apartment, where she saw Jen slumped on the couch, still in her suit, staring at the television with the sound off. Consumed with frustration and annoyed by her professor, Mel tossed her backpack by the door and burst out, "Jen, you would not believe how BORING class was today! Professor Juarez went on and on about the only thing she thinks matters."

"Uh huh." Jen replied quietly, twirling a piece of her hair and looking miserable. Jen glanced in Mel's direction, hoping that Mel would notice her obvious distress, but Mel was busy pushing her coat into the closet and didn't even look in Jen's direction.

"Yeah! I mean, I know the class is earth science, but do we reeeeeally have to talk about the Andean Volcano Belt ad nauseam just because it's the focus of her research?" Mel complained. This time, Jen didn't even nod or look up. Her eyes filled with tears. Mel, who was heading toward the kitchen, didn't seem to notice. "I know you've complained that some of your professors are boring, but you have no idea what boring is until you have had Jensen. Today was way beyond annoying," Mel said, with an exaggerated sigh.

131

(Continued)

"You're right, I have no idea," Jen quietly replied, her voice dripping with sarcasm. When Mel disappeared into the kitchen, Jen got up from the couch, went to her room, and slammed the door. That startled Mel, who called out, "Hey, Jen? What's going on? … Are you OK?"

WHAT YOU SHOULD BE ABLE TO EXPLAIN AFTER YOU HAVE STUDIED THIS CHAPTER:

▶ The characteristics and functions of nonverbal messages

▶ The types and meanings of body language, paralanguage, physical space, and self-presentation cues in messages

▶ Culture and gender differences in nonverbal behavior

▶ How to improve your encoding and decoding of nonverbal messages

▶ How nonverbal messages are conveyed in text

WHAT YOU SHOULD BE ABLE TO DO AFTER YOU HAVE STUDIED THIS CHAPTER:

▶ Improve your encoding and decoding of nonverbal messages

▶ Use the skill of perception checking

It's clear that something went wrong at Jen's interview—and that Mel, consumed with her own day, was oblivious to any of Jen's nonverbal behaviors signaling her obvious distress. Consequently, Jen, who was already hurting, became further upset with Mel's insensitivity, while Mel remained clueless about what was going on with her friend. In the last chapter, we focused on how we use language—our verbal behavior—to share meaning. In this chapter, we will examine how we use nonverbal behaviors to create messages or augment verbal ones. This study is important because research indicates that our nonverbal behavior conveys as much as 65 percent of the social meaning we share in face-to-face interactions (Burgoon and Bacue, 2003). As we can see from the example of Jen and Mel, noticing and correctly interpreting others' nonverbal messages is critical to understanding what someone is "saying." We begin this chapter by first identifying the characteristics and functions of nonverbal behaviors. Second, we describe the types of nonverbal behavior, including body language, paralanguage (nonverbal sounds), spatial cues (use of space during interaction), and self-presentation cues. Third, we explain how nonverbal behaviors vary with culture and gender. Fourth, we examine what happens in our interactions when our expectations about appropriate nonverbal behavior are not met. Fifth, we offer suggestions for improving the ways you send and interpret nonverbal messages, including how you can use the skill of perception checking to improve your interpretation of ambiguous nonverbal behavior. Finally, we take a closer look at what happens to the nonverbal part of messages when we use social media.

Characteristics and Functions of Nonverbal Messages

Regardless of the type of nonverbal behavior, all nonverbal messages share common characteristics and functions. Understanding these commonalities provides a foundation for our study of nonverbal messages.

Characteristics of Nonverbal Communication

Nonverbal communication is all human communication that transcends spoken or written words. It has five distinct characteristics.

1. Nonverbal communication can be *intentional* or *unintentional*. Sometimes we are aware of the nonverbal messages we are sending, but most often we are not consciously aware of them. For example, Zach smirks when he is nervous, taps his foot when impatient, speaks forcefully when angry, and stands tall when confident. Although he consistently uses these behaviors, he may be unaware of them, but people close to him "read" his emotional state by noticing these mannerisms. Because we are generally unaware of our emotional signals, many of us react to seeing video of ourselves, saying things like, "I didn't know that I sounded like that, frowned so much, walked like that, gestured like that, or stood that close to people." While we may be acting naturally and without any conscious intent to send nonverbal messages, the people we talk with often interpret nonverbal behaviors as intentional—they interpret them as *communication*.

2. Nonverbal messages are *primary*. We interpret how speakers feel about what they are saying based on the nonverbal messages in the utterance. In other words, nonverbal communication is primary, taking precedence over verbal communication. For instance, when Janelle frowns, clenches her fists, and forcefully says, "I am *not* angry!" her sister Renée ignores the verbal message in favor of the contradicting nonverbal behaviors, which indicate that Janelle is, indeed, very angry. In addition, the nonverbal message is usually perceived to be more believable than the verbal. It is easy to deceive others with our scripted words. Nonverbal behavior, however, is harder to fake because it is less easily controlled. Was your gut-level response to someone you encountered ever discomfort or distrust? The other person's verbal messages may have seemed friendly or kind, but your reaction was based on nonverbal cues. Though you may not have been conscious of or able to pinpoint the person's nonverbal behaviors that bothered you, you were reacting more strongly to these subtle signals than to the content of the verbal message.

3. Nonverbal communication is *continuous*. Although your verbal messages start and stop, as long as you are in the presence of another person, your nonverbal behavior may be noticed and interpreted as having meaning. You never stop communicating nonverbally. For instance, when Austin yawns and nods off during a meeting

Nonverbal communication—all human communication that transcends spoken or written words

In negotiations, he appeared to have ice in his veins, but his tail betrayed him.

Cartoonstock www.Cartoonstock.com

at work, his co-workers will notice this behavior and make assumptions about him. Some may think he is rude; others, bored. Paul, however, may correctly recognize that his friend Austin is exhausted from studying for exams. Meanwhile, Austin snoozes, unaware of the various meanings he is sending with his nonverbal "message."

4. Nonverbal messages are *multi-channeled*. When interpreting someone's nonverbal behavior, we use a variety of cues or channels to make sense of what is happening. These cues include the vocal tone, body position, gestures, facial expressions, and the general appearance of the other person. For example, when Alisha first meets her new neighbor, Mimi, she may notice Mimi's smile, twinkling eyes, fast rate of speech, erect posture, designer suit, perfume, and apartment décor. Alisha will use this package of information about Mimi as she interprets Mimi's comments about other neighbors. We generally interpret multiple cues together, simultaneously, rather than one by one. This helps reduce the ambiguity of any single nonverbal behavior. Thus, although Mimi's smile and twinkle may signal friendliness, the entire set of behaviors may alert Alisha to Mimi's tendency to be critical of others.

5. Nonverbal behavior is frequently *ambiguous*. Most nonverbal behaviors are not codified; that is, there is no agreed-on lexicon of definitions for what it means to behave a certain way. For example, the word "smile" means a pleasant facial expression in which the corners of the lips turn up and the outside of the eyes crinkles. When we say, "She was smiling," we are describing her facial expression. But the nonverbal meaning of that same smile is ambiguous. It can depend on the smiler's personality, culture, the conversational context, and the relationship of the nonverbal behaviors to the verbal message. The nonverbal act of smiling may convey nervousness, happiness, or excitement. A smile can also be used to mask anger, hatred, boredom, or embarrassment. Ambiguity can make it difficult to interpret the meaning of nonverbal behaviors, especially when you do not know someone well.

Functions of Nonverbal Messages

In addition to having the characteristics we just discussed, nonverbal messages serve five primary functions.

1. Nonverbal behaviors *provide information*. Our nonverbal behaviors provide information by repeating, substituting for, emphasizing, or contradicting our verbal messages. First, we may use nonverbal cues to *repeat* what we have said verbally. For instance, if you say "no" and shake your head at the same time, your nonverbal message repeats what you have said verbally. Second, some nonverbal behaviors *substitute* for words. A wave, for example, has the symbolic meaning of "hello" or "good-bye." In some cultures, curling your index finger and motioning toward yourself substitutes for the verbal message "come here," but in other cultures, the same gesture carries the nonverbal message meaning "go away" or "good-bye." Third, nonverbal behaviors can *emphasize* a verbal message by accenting, complementing, or adding information to the words. For instance, a teacher may smile, clap, or pat a student on the back when saying, "Good job on the test." In this case, facial expression, body motions, and voice volume emphasize the verbal praise message. Finally, nonverbal behaviors may send messages that *contradict* the verbal message. This can confuse the listener. For example, when Sadie says in a quiet, monotone voice, "I am really interested in your project," while avoiding eye contact and moving away, her nonverbal message has contradicted her verbal message. Remember, nonverbal behavior is primary, so people who receive mixed messages typically use the nonverbal message to interpret the actual meaning of the verbal message.

2. Nonverbal behaviors *regulate interaction.* We manage a conversation through both subtle and more obvious nonverbal cues. We use shifts in eye contact, slight head movements, posture changes, raised eyebrows, and nodding to tell another person when to continue, to repeat, to elaborate, to hurry up, or to finish what he or she is saying. Think of the times you have used nonverbal cues in an attempt to end a conversation. You may have decreased the amount of eye contact you gave the other person, given abrupt or abbreviated responses, shown less animated facial expression, or turned away from the other person. Students in a classroom regularly signal to the instructor that class time is nearly over by packing away their laptops, putting on their coats, fidgeting in their seats, or mumbling to each other. Effective communicators learn to adjust their contributions to a conversation based on the behaviors of others.

3. Nonverbal behaviors *express emotions.* While we may be able to hide from others the things we are thinking, it is more difficult to hide what we are feeling. As we experience them, our emotions may be instantaneously conveyed by our nonverbal behavior, including facial expressions, vocal cues, and body language. For example, pride may be expressed bodily through raised arms and hands, back head tilts, and expanded chests, whereas shame is expressed with slumped shoulders and narrowed chests (Tracy & Matsumoto, 2008). People use our nonverbal expressions of emotion to interpret our verbal messages. So, if you knit your brows together, tighten your jaw, and scream at your mother, "I'm not angry," your nonverbal expressions of emotion will drown out your verbal message. As we discussed in Chapter 3, we learn cultural display rules for expressing emotions in socially appropriate ways. Thus, we sometimes miniaturize or downplay emotional expression and mask what we are actually feeling by showing a different emotion, or simulate (pretend) emotions that we don't actually feel. Our success at doing this varies; you may know people you can "read like a book," and others who have "poker faces." Sometimes we can detect falseness in facial expressions of emotion because they are longer or shorter than the usual duration (somewhere between half a second and four seconds) (Schmidt, Cohn, & Tian, 2003). We are also better at interpreting the facial expressions of people from our own cultures than those of other cultures (Dovidio, Hebl, Richeson, & Shelton, 2006).

4. Nonverbal behaviors *manage impressions and identities.* Much of our effort to influence the ideas that others have about us is accomplished

What are other common nonverbal behaviors used to regulate interactions?

INTER-ACT WITH
SOCIAL MEDIA

You might use social media to remain connected with your romantic partner throughout the course of a day. Since we are likely to experience a stronger emotional connection with romantic partners than we do with our friends, we often want to convey that emotion through social media—perhaps through a text message or Facebook message. How do you communicate emotion in the messages that you send through social media? What are some of the challenges associated with using certain forms of social media—such as texting, Facebook, and videoconferencing services (e.g., Skype)—to fully express how you are feeling?

Immediacy behaviors—nonverbal actions that signal warmth, communicate availability, decrease distance, and promote involvement between people

nonverbally. When you are introduced to new co-workers, and want to convey a good first impression, it isn't really appropriate to tell them, "Hi, I'm friendly, cooperative, and enthusiastic!" Instead, you use **immediacy behaviors**, or nonverbal actions that signal warmth, communicate availability, decrease distance, and promote involvement between people (Burgoon et al., 2011). For example, you will probably orient your body toward these co-workers, smile, make plenty of direct eye contact, and offer your hand for a shake. People also use nonverbal behavior to convey identify or self-concept. Do you wear sweatshirts or hats that display your affiliation with a school, club, or sports team? Do you wear jewelry or clothing that indicates your religious beliefs? Clothing, grooming, jewelry, and personal possessions are commonly used to signal, "This is who I am." Even seemingly mundane things like the way people handle, accessorize, and wear their cell phones can say something about them and their lifestyles (Kleinman, 2007).

5. Nonverbal behaviors *express dominance and affiliation.* As you will recall, interpersonal communication reveals qualities of the relationship between two people, including dominance and affiliation. Many nonverbal behaviors are signs of dominance. Consider how a high-level manager conveys status and how subordinate employees acknowledge that status through nonverbal behavior. The manager may dress more formally, have a larger and more expensively furnished office, and walk and speak authoritatively. Subordinates may show respect to the manager by using eye contact and listening attentively when the manager speaks, by not interrupting, and by seeking permission (appointments) to enter the manager's office. Of course, nonverbal behavior also speaks volumes about the closeness or distance in the relationship between two people. Sometimes we even use nonverbal behavior intentionally. If you are at a party, and someone is flirting with your significant other, you might move in close, put an arm around his or her hips, and give a kiss as a way of saying, "This one's mine, back off."

Both Miley Cyrus and Taylor Swift have faced the challenge of defining a more adult public image. How are the images the two women are projecting similar and different? Can you speculate on why each made the choices she did?

Types of Nonverbal Communication

Nonverbal behaviors used in messages can be classified into four general categories or types. These categories are body language (body motions used in communication, such as eye contact, facial expressions, gestures, posture, and touch), paralanguage (nonverbal sounds such as pitch, volume, rate, quality, and intonation that accompany words), use of space (personal space, acoustic space, and territory), and self-presentation cues (physical appearance, artifacts, scents and odors, and use of time).

Body Language

Of all the categories of nonverbal behavior, you are probably most familiar with **body language**, the movement of various body parts. Body language is also known as **kinesics**, and includes eye contact, facial expression, gesture, posture, and touch.

What emotions is this child conveying through his eye contact?

Body language—the intentional or unintentional movement of various body parts that sends nonverbal messages

Kinesics—the study of body language

    1. Eye contact (or gaze) refers to the focus of the eyes, and especially to looking at each other's eyes simultaneously. Eye contact conveys meanings that vary with person, situation, and culture, but often has something to do with attention, emotional response, or dominance. When your professor, looking out over the class, sees that most of the students are not looking back, she knows that they are not paying attention to her lecture. If you inappropriately mention at dinner with his parents that your friend is contemplating dropping History this semester, he may glare at you, whereas a declaration of love for your girlfriend may earn you a long, loving gaze. Intense eye contact may be an attempt to dominate (Pearson, West, & Turner, 1995). Accordingly, we speak of "looks that could kill" or "staring another person down." Indeed, in some segments of society, a prolonged stare may be an invitation to a physical fight. Yet, ironically, not making any eye contact at all can also be seen as a sign of dominance. The dominant person in an exchange, such as a boss, an interviewer, a teacher, or a police officer, has the freedom to maintain eye contact or look away at will, but the subordinate person in the situation is expected to maintain steady and respectful eye contact.

    2. Facial expression is the arrangement of facial muscles that can convey an emotional state or reaction. Three groups of muscles are manipulated to form facial expressions: those in the brow and forehead; those surrounding the eyes, eyelids, and root of the nose; and those in the remainder of the nose, the cheeks, mouth, and chin. You will recall that facial expressions are especially important in conveying the six basic emotions of happiness, sadness, surprise, fear, anger, and disgust. Facial expressions also frequently provide nonverbal feedback to speakers. For instance, people knit their brows and squint their eyes into a quizzical look when they don't understand what someone is saying, or they purse their lips and raise one eyebrow to convey skepticism.

INTER-ACT WITH
SOCIAL MEDIA

When we have a face-to-face conversation with another person, we are expected to make eye contact to indicate that we are attentive and fully engaged in the conversation. In a face-to-face conversation with one person, however, we can simultaneously use social media (such as texting and Facebook) to communicate with another. How often do you find yourself in this situation, either as the person communicating with two people at once, or as the person conversing with someone who is using social media at the same time? How does your use of social media affect the quality of the face-to-face conversations that you have with others?

▶ OBSERVE AND ANALYZE

Facial Expressions and the News

Record and watch a half hour of *Morning Express* with Robin Meade on CNN Headline News and a half hour of the *PBS News Hour* with Gwen Ifill and Judy Woodruff. Describe how the facial expressions of each of these women affect your impression of them and of the messages that they are delivering.

Eye contact—using eye focus to signal attention, respect, emotional reactions, or dominance

Facial expression—arranging facial muscles to communicate emotion or provide feedback

Gesture—using hand, arm, and finger movement to replace, complement, and augment a verbal message

Emblems—gestures that substitute completely for words

Posture—the position and movement of the whole body

Body orientation—your position in relation to another person

Touch—putting part of the body in contact with something or someone

Haptics—of or relating to the sense of touch

3. Gesture is using hand, arm, and finger movement to replace, complement, and augment a verbal message. Just as we learn what words mean, we also learn what certain gestures mean. **Emblems** are gestures that substitute completely for words. To Americans, an upward-pointing thumb gesture used by a person on the side of the road indicates that they are hoping for a ride. Likewise, in many cultures, a finger placed vertically across the lips means "Be quiet."

Gestures can also complement a verbal message. For example, when a person says "about this high" or "nearly this round," we need to see a gesture accompanying the verbal description to understand the height or size of the object. Gestures can also augment or add to a verbal message by conveying emotional information. When the verbal message, "I told you not to do that," is accompanied by the speaker's repeatedly slamming the fist of one hand into an open palm of the other, the extreme frustration of the speaker becomes evident.

4. Posture is the position and movement of the whole body. Your posture is erect when you straighten your spine, open your chest, and settle your shoulders down and apart, with your head and neck aligned with your spine. Your posture is slouched when your spine curves in, your chest and shoulders roll forward, and your head and neck are forward of your spine. **Body orientation** refers to your position in relation to another person. Like eye contact, it can be described as direct or indirect. Facing another person squarely is called direct body orientation. When two people's postures are at angles to each other, this is called indirect body orientation. The combination of posture and body orientation can convey information about attentiveness, respect, and power. Consider, for example, how you would sit in a job interview. You are likely to sit up straight and face the interviewer directly because you want to communicate your interest, respect, and confidence, while the interviewer may also sit up straight, face you directly, and possibly lean forward to signal dominance. Interviewers tend to interpret a slouched posture and indirect body orientation as lack of interest, disrespect, and lack of confidence, while interviewees may interpret a slouched, indirectly oriented, and backward-leaning interviewer as not only uninterested and disrespectful, but also a pushover. In other situations, such as talking with friends, a slouched posture and indirect body orientation may simply convey that a person is relaxed, and may not carry any messages about attention, respect, or power. This difference in meaning based on various situations demonstrates the ambiguous nature of nonverbal communication. Rarely does any one posture or body orientation absolutely mean any one thing.

5. Touch is putting part of the body in contact with someone or something, and is also known as **haptics**. We use our hands, our arms, and other body parts to pat, hug, slap, kiss, pinch, stroke, hold, embrace, and tickle, communicating a variety of emotions and messages. Our touching can be gentle or firm, perfunctory or passionate, brief or lingering. Like many of the other types of body motion, touch can convey messages about dominance. Usually, the higher-status person in a situation is the one to initiate touch. Managers are more likely to touch their employees than vice versa, and faculty members are more likely to touch their students than vice versa.

There are three types of touch: spontaneous, ritualized, and task-related. *Spontaneous touch* is touch that is automatic and subconscious. Patting someone on the back when you hear that he or she has won an award, for example, is spontaneous touch. In addition, there are many forms of *ritualized touch,* touch that is scripted rather than spontaneous. Handshakes or high-five slaps of the hands, for example, are forms of ritualized touch that have rather definite meanings as greeting rituals and are expected in certain situations. *Task-related touch* is touch used to perform a certain unemotional function. For instance, a doctor may touch a patient during a physical examination, or a personal trainer may touch a client during a workout at the gym. We do not attach the same meanings to task-related touch as we do to spontaneous or ritualized touch. We see task-related touch as part of the professional service we are receiving. There is also a type of touch that combines spontaneity and task-related touch to convey messages of closeness. In public, when someone adjusts your coat collar or removes some lint from your clothing, the person is not only doing a task-related favor for you but is also signaling, perhaps inadvertently, a degree of closeness between the two of you that they would not signal to a complete stranger or a casual acquaintance.

What is this man conveying with the caress of his hand on his partner's face?

People differ in their touching behavior and in their reactions to unsolicited touch from others. Some people like to touch and be touched; other people do not. Although American culture is relatively non–contact-oriented, the kinds and amounts of touching behavior within our society vary widely. Touching behavior that seems innocuous to one person may be perceived as overly intimate or threatening to another. Moreover, the perceived appropriateness of touch differs with the context. Touch that is considered appropriate in private may embarrass a person in public or with a large group of people.

Paralanguage

The second category of nonverbal communication is paralanguage. **Paralanguage** (also known as *vocalics*) is variation in the voice. There are five vocal characteristics that compose paralanguage: pitch, volume, rate, quality, and intonation. By controlling these, we can complement, supplement, or contradict the meaning conveyed by the language of our message.

Paralanguage—using the voice to convey meaning

1. Pitch is the rate of vibration of your vocal cords. The faster your vocal cords vibrate, the higher the pitch of your voice; the slower they vibrate, the lower the pitch of your voice. We raise and lower our vocal pitch to emphasize ideas, indicate questions, or show nervousness. Our pitch may rise when we are nervous and drop when we want to be forceful.

Pitch—the rate of vibration of your vocal cords

Volume—the loudness of a person's vocal tone

2. Volume is the loudness of a person's voice. Whereas some people have naturally loud voices that carry long distances, others are normally soft-spoken. Regardless of our normal volume level, most of us vary vocal volume depending on the situation or topic of discussion. For example, people may talk loudly

Rate—the speed at which a person speaks

Quality—the sound of a person's voice

Intonation—the variety, melody, or inflection of a person's voice

Vocal interferences—extraneous sounds or words (fillers) that interrupt fluent speech

Proxemics—the study of personal space

Personal space—the area that surrounds a person, moves with that person, and changes with the situation as well as moment-to-moment

when they wish to be heard in noisy settings, raise their volume when angry, or speak more softly when being romantic or loving.

3. Rate is the speed at which a person speaks. While some people's normal rate is faster than that of others, people tend to talk more rapidly when they are happy, frightened, nervous, or excited, and they tend to talk more slowly when they are problem-solving out loud or trying to emphasize a point.

4. Quality is the sound of a person's voice. Each human voice has a distinct tone. Some voices are raspy, some smoky, some have bell-like qualities, and others are throaty. But regardless of voice quality, each of us uses a slightly different quality of voice to communicate a particular state of mind. We may convey a complaint with a whiny, nasal vocal quality; a seductive invitation with a soft, breathy quality; and anger with a strident, harsh quality.

5. Intonation is the variety, melody, or inflection of a person's voice. Some voices have little intonation and sound monotonous. Other voices are very melodious and may have even a childlike singsong quality. People prefer to listen to voices with a moderate amount of intonation.

Pitch, volume, rate, quality, and intonation add nonverbal shades of meaning to words. **Vocal interferences**, however, are extraneous sounds or words that interrupt fluent speech. These vocalized sounds add little or no meaning to the verbal message and may even interfere with understanding. They are sometimes used as "place markers" designed to fill in momentary gaps in a verbal message while we search for the right word or idea. These place markers indicate that we are not done speaking and that it is still our "turn." The most common interferences that creep into our speech include "uh," "er," "well," and "okay," as well as "you know" and "like." Excessive vocal interferences can lead to the impression that you are unsure of yourself or confused about what you are attempting to say.

Use of Space

When interacting with others, we use space in ways that convey meaning. This type of nonverbal behavior is also known as **proxemics**. Specifically, we send nonverbal messages through the use of personal space and acoustic space, the space we claim as territory, and the arrangement of furnishings to affect the space between people.

1. Personal space is the area that surrounds a person, moves with that person, and changes with the situation as well as from moment to moment. Have you ever been speaking with someone and become aware that you were uncomfortable because the other person was standing too close to you? Or maybe you've found yourself starting a conversation and then moving closer to someone as you begin to share an embarrassing story. If you have experienced either of these situations, you are already aware of the way that the space between conversational partners influences their interaction. We adjust our personal space depending on the conversation. Research suggests that most Americans comfortably converse at

WHY DO PEOPLE WITH LOUD ANNOYING VOICES AND NOTHING INTERESTING TO SAY INSIST ON TALKING CONSTANTLY?

one of four distance ranges determined by the nature of the relationship and the topic of conversation (Hall, 1969):

- *Intimate distance,* up to 18 inches, is comfortable spacing for private conversations among intimates.
- *Personal distance,* from 18 inches to 4 feet, is comfortable spacing for casual conversations with a normal amount of background noise.
- *Social distance,* from 4 to 12 feet, is comfortable spacing for impersonal or professional interactions such as a job interview or team meeting.
- *Public distance,* anything more than 12 feet, is comfortable spacing for people in a public forum where interaction and conversation is not desired.

Of greatest concern to most people is the intimate distance—the distance we regard as the appropriate distance between people when we have a very personal conversation with close friends, parents, and younger children. People usually become uncomfortable when "outsiders" violate this intimate distance. For instance, in a movie theater that is less than one-quarter full, people will tend to leave one or more seats empty between themselves and people they do not know. If in such a setting a stranger sits right next to you, you are likely to feel uncomfortable or threatened, and you may even move away. Intrusions into our intimate space are acceptable only in certain settings, and then only when all involved follow the unwritten rules. For instance, people will tolerate being packed into a crowded elevator or subway car, making physical contact with people they do not know, provided those involved follow the "rules." The rules may include standing rigidly, looking at the floor, and not making eye contact with others. In essence, we cope with this space violation by turning other people into objects. Only occasionally will people who are forced to invade each other's intimate space acknowledge the other as a person. Then they are likely to exchange sheepish smiles or otherwise acknowledge the mutual invasion of intimate distance.

2. Acoustic space is the area over which your voice or other sounds can be comfortably heard. Competent communicators adjust the volume of their voices so that their conversations can be easily heard by their partners but not be overheard by others who are not part of the conversation. Speaking too loudly or too softly can annoy both your conversational partner and those around you. Mobile phone conversations and excessively loud car or headphone music can be seen as an acoustic invasion of space. This is why some communities have ordinances prohibiting loud music from cars and restaurants, hospitals and theaters have rules against cell phone use, and public transportation passengers are increasingly bold about asking other passengers to turn down their music and keep their cell phone conversations to themselves.

3. Territory is the space over which we claim ownership, either permanently or temporarily. With real estate, people use locks, signs, and fences to communicate ownership of their territory. In day-to-day interactions, the signals may be

Have you ever had a stranger strike up a conversation with you on a crowded bus, train, or elevator? How did you feel? What did you do?

Acoustic space—the area over which your voice or other sounds can be comfortably heard

Territory—the space over which we claim ownership

▶ **OBSERVE AND ANALYZE**

Intruding on Personal Space

Find a crowded elevator. Get on it, and face the back. Make direct eye contact with the person you are standing in front of. Note their reaction. On the return trip, introduce yourself to the person who is standing next to you and begin an animated conversation. Note the reaction of others around you. Get on an empty elevator and stand in the exact center. Do not move when others board. Note their reactions. Be prepared to share what you have observed with your classmates. Also, be prepared to apologize and explain if someone becomes upset or angry about your behavior!

We learn to mark our territory early in life.

more subtle, but are still powerful. When Regan eats lunch in the company cafeteria, the space at the table becomes her temporary territory. If she gets up to get butter for her roll, she is likely to leave her coat on her chair and her tray of food on the table, indicating that the chair and the space around her tray are "hers." If she returns to find that a stranger has sat in the next seat, or has moved a dish close to her tray, she is likely to feel resentful. At home, Regan may assert the kitchen as her permanent territory by creating an organizational scheme for the food and housewares. She is likely to be upset if anyone rearranges the layout without her permission.

Territoriality often involves a claim to dominance. Higher-status people generally claim larger, more prestigious, and more protected territory (Henley, 1977). A top-level executive may have a large, expensively decorated, top-floor office with a breathtaking view, as well as one or more people to protect the space from intruders. An entry-level employee in the same organization may have a small cubicle that is neither private nor protected. Think of all the messages that we get from the amount and type of territory that someone claims. For instance, in a family, who shares bedrooms and who gets the largest one? Who sits where when the family members are watching TV? Who generally sits at the "head" of the dinner table?

4. Furnishings can be arranged to affect the space between people, and consequently convey messages about identity and interaction. The chairs and couch in your living room may approximate a circle that invites people to sit down and talk. Or the seating in a room may be theater style and face the television, thereby discouraging conversation. A manager's office with a chair facing the manager across the desk encourages formal conversation. It says, "Let's talk business—I'm the boss and you're the employee." A manager's office with a chair at the side of the desk (absence of a physical barrier) encourages more informal conversation. It says, "Don't be nervous—let's just chat."

Furnishings—furniture and other decorative accessories for a house or room, which can be arranged to affect the space between people, and consequently convey messages about identity and interaction

Self-Presentation

A fourth category of nonverbal behaviors includes your physical appearance, artifacts, use of smells and scents, and approach to time. Although different in many ways, these behaviors are grouped together because they have a strong impact on how others perceive us, and we can manipulate these in order to present ourselves in particular ways.

1. Your **physical appearance** is how you look to others, including your race, gender, body type, facial features, clothing, personal grooming, and body art/ tattoos. You control some parts of your physical appearance, while other parts you inherit from your family. In our sex- and race-conscious society, others use your gender, race, and ethnicity to form impressions of you. Although someone may claim to be "color-blind," the first thing people notice about others is their race (DiTomaso, Parks-Yancy, & Post, 2003). The size and shape of your body are taken into consideration when people are trying to figure out who you really

Physical appearance—how you look to others, including your race, gender, body type, facial features, clothing, personal grooming, and body art or tattoos are, with some body types held in higher regard than others. American society places so much emphasis on physical appearance that entire industries are devoted to changing one's physical appearance through cosmetic surgery, weight loss, and grooming products. In addition, many people go to great lengths to select clothing to manage the impressions they portray. Brands and styles of clothing convey certain images. How you wear your hair and whether and how you use makeup and body art also convey something about you to others, though the exact "message" will depend on another person's frame of reference. Spiked and magenta-tinted hair together with large tattoos and earlobe "gauging" may be read by one person as "He's really slammin'" and by another as "He's sure a loser." Since choice of clothing and personal grooming will communicate messages about us, most of us modify our dress and grooming to the situation. For example, at work, Tiffany dresses conservatively, carefully covers her tattoo by wearing sleeved tops, and pulls her hair up into a neat ponytail or back in a barrette. These nonverbal behaviors convey the message, "I am a serious, intelligent professional whom you can trust to perform my job well." But on the weekends when Tiffany goes out, she chooses short, tight skirts, stiletto heels, and halter tops that show off her tat. She also wears her hair long and loose. These nonverbal behaviors convey, "I am confident, sexy, and ready to have a good time."

2. Artifacts are the objects we select for personal use. We own and display things in our rooms, offices, and homes, not just for their functions, but also for their qualities we find pleasing. As a result, other people looking at these artifacts come to understand something about us. Consider the many types of cars and the identities these cars help to project for their owners. Someone driving a Cadillac Escalade˚ is likely to convey a different identity than someone driving a new Chevy Volt˚ or a Jeep˚. Also think what your home, apartment, or room says about you. You probably accumulated the objects in that space over a period of time, but together they provide information to others about who you are and what you think is important, beautiful, and so on.

3. Your intentional or unintentional odor and intentional use of scents either on your body or in your territory also send messages to others. **Olfactory cues** are messages sent through smells and scents. If you do not think that smells and scents have the power to communicate, think of the beauty care industry in the United States designed to manufacture and market scent-related products for both women and men. We buy not only perfumes and colognes, but also scented soaps, shampoos, air fresheners, candles, cleaning products, and pet products, to name a few. Often we go to great lengths to influence the odors associated with our bodies, our cars, and our homes. Aromatherapy is used to relieve stress and alter mood (Furlow, 1996). Homeowners sometimes bake cookies or bread before holding an open house so that prospective buyers will perceive the house to be "homey." The meanings attached to certain odors and scents as well as other nonverbal behaviors are firmly based in culture, as we will see in the next section.

Artifacts—the objects we use to adorn our territory

Olfactory cues—messages sent through smells and scents

▸ **OBSERVE AND ANALYZE**

Communicating with Artifacts

Find a dormitory, office, or apartment building where the rooms, offices, or cubicles are identical in size and shape. Visit at least five different rooms/cubicles that are occupied by five different people. Describe the person you believe occupies each space. Then notice and catalog the different artifacts in each space. Analyze how the artifacts inform your description of the occupant.

"The boss finally noticed me today. He said I should wear deodorant."

Cartoonstock www.Cartoonstock.com

LEARN ABOUT YOURSELF ▶ ORIENTATION TO TIME

Take this short survey to learn something about your perception of time. Answer the questions honestly based on your initial response. There are no right or wrong answers. For each question, select one of the numbers to the left that best describes your behavior.

1 = Always False

2 = Usually False

3 = Sometimes True, Sometimes False

4 = Usually True

5 = Always True

_____ 1. I do many things at the same time.

_____ 2. I stick to my daily schedule as much as possible.

_____ 3. I prefer to finish one activity before starting another one.

_____ 4. I feel like I waste time.

_____ 5. I would take time out of a meeting to take a social phone call.

_____ 6. I separate work time and social time.

_____ 7. I break appointments with others.

_____ 8. I prefer that events in my life occur in an orderly fashion.

_____ 9. I do more than one activity at a time.

_____10. Being on time for appointments is important to me.

Scoring the survey: To find your score, first reverse the responses for the odd-numbered items (if you wrote a 1, make it a 5; 2 = 4; leave 3 as is; 4 = 2; and 5 = 1). Next add the numbers for each item. Scores can range from 10 to 50. The higher your score, the more monochronic you are. The lower your score, the more polychronic you are.

Adapted from Gudykunst, W. B., Ting-Toomey, S., Sudweeks, S., & Stewart, L. P. (1995). *Building Bridges: Interpersonal Skills for a Changing World.* Boston: Houghton Mifflin.

4. Use of time. In Chapter 3 we discussed how cultures differ in their approach to time. Just as cultures are monochronic or polychronic, so, too, are individuals. If your approach to time matches that of the people with whom you interact, they probably won't notice it, or will view you as being appropriate. On the other hand, if your approach to time is different, your behavior will be viewed as inappropriate and will strain your relationship. For example, Carlos, a Brazilian national who is polychronic, often arrives late to meetings with his North American project team. His teammates resent his tardiness and see him as arrogant and self-important. The example of Carlos illustrates how different expectations for nonverbal behavior can lead to negative perceptions and poor outcomes for communication and relationships. We address this issue of expectations in more detail in the next section.

Culture and Gender Differences in Nonverbal Communication

As we saw in the previous sections, there are many different nonverbal behaviors, and each behavior can mean very different things, depending on who uses it, who interprets it, and the context in which it is used. In this section, we consider culture and gender, both of which are significant influences on nonverbal behavior and its interpretation.

Cultural Differences

Cultural groups vary widely in their use and interpretation of body language and paralanguage. When it comes to eye contact, in the United States and other Western cultures, talkers hold eye contact about 40 percent of the time, and listeners nearly 70 percent of the time (Knapp & Hall, 2006). People also generally maintain better eye contact when discussing topics with which they are comfortable, when genuinely interested in another person's comments or reactions, or when trying to influence the other person. Conversely, they tend to avoid eye contact when they are discussing topics that make them uncomfortable; when uninterested in the topic or the person talking; or when embarrassed, ashamed, or trying to hide something. However, these U.S. or Western norms are not considered universal (Samovar, Porter, & McDaniel, 2010). For example, in Japan, people avoid direct eye contact, directing their gaze to a position around the Adam's apple. Middle Easterners, in contrast, look intently into the eyes of the person with whom they are talking for longer periods than is usual for people in the U.S.—to them, direct eye contact demonstrates keen interest. Chinese people, Indonesians, and rural Mexicans lower their eyes as a sign of deference; too much direct eye contact is a sign of bad manners. There are also differences in the use of eye contact among co-cultures within the United States. For instance, African Americans tend to use more continuous eye contact than European Americans when they are speaking, but less when they are listening (Samovar et al., 2010).

Cultures also differ significantly with regard to touch, paralanguage, and gestures. Latin American and Mediterranean countries have high-contact cultures. Northern European cultures are medium to low in contact. And Asian cultures are, for the most part, low-contact cultures. The United States, a country of immigrants, is generally perceived to be in the medium-contact category, though there are wide differences among individual Americans because of variations in family heritage (Ting-Toomey & Chung, 2011). All languages use pitch and tone to convey both literal and emotional meaning. However, some languages are called *tonal* languages because the pitch at which a word is spoken is integral to its meaning, conveying among other things the part of speech of each word in an utterance. Asian languages are highly tonal, so the average pitch of an utterance is higher than that of the average message spoken in a non-tonal language like English. The tonal nature of these languages gives an utterance a singsong staccato quality that is missing from non-tonal languages. Yet, there are also non-linguistic cultural variations in the use of paralinguistics. For example, in Middle Eastern cultures, speaking loudly signifies being strong and sincere. What we would call vocal interferences in the United States are not considered interferences in China, where using fillers signals wisdom and attractiveness (Chen & Starosta, 1998). When communicating with people from cultures other than your own, be especially careful about the gestures you use, as they are by no

Latin American and Anglo American Use of Personal Space in Public Places

BY ELIZABETH LOZANO

How we use space and how we expect others to treat the space around us are determined by our culture. In this excerpt, the author focuses our attention on the ways in which the body is understood and treated by Latin Americans and Anglo Americans and the cultural differences that become apparent when these two cultural groups find themselves sharing common space.

It is 6:00 P.M. The Bayfront, a shopping mall near a Miami marina, reverberates with the noise and movement of people, coming and going, contemplating the lights of the bay, sampling exotic juice blends, savoring the not-so-exotic foods from Cuba, Nicaragua, or Mexico, and listening to the bands. The Bayfront provides an environment for the exercise of two different rituals: the Anglo American visit to the mall and the Latin American *paseo*, the visit to the outdoor spaces of the city.

Some of the people sitting in the plaza look insistently at me, making comments, laughing, and whispering. Instead of feeling uneasy or surprised, I find myself looking back at them, entering this inquisitive game and asking myself some of the same questions they might be asking. Who are they, where are they from, what are they up to? I follow their gaze and I see it extend to other groups. The gaze is returned by some in the crowd, so that a play of silent dialogue seems to grow amidst the anonymity of the crowd. The crowd that participates in this complicity of wandering looks is not Anglo American. The play of looks described above has a different "accent," a Hispanic accent, which reveals a different understanding of the plaza and public space.

The Anglo American passers-by understand their vital space, their relationship with strangers, and their public interactions in a different manner. If I address them in the street, I better assume that I am confronting them in an alley. But when I am walking by myself along the halls of a Hispanic mall, I am not alone. I do not expect, therefore, to be treated by others as if they were suddenly confronting me in a dark alley. I am in a crowd, with the crowd, and anyone there has access to my attention.

Anglo Americans are alone (even in the middle of the crowd) if they choose to be, for they have a guaranteed cultural right to be "left alone" on their way to and from anywhere. To approach or touch someone without that person's consent is a violation of a fundamental right within Anglo-Saxon, Protestant cultural tradition. This is the right to one's own body as private property. Within this tradition, touching is understood as an excursion into someone else's territory. With this in mind then, it is understandable that Anglo Americans excuse themselves when they accidentally touch someone or come close to doing so. To accidentally penetrate someone else's boundary (especially if that person is a stranger) demands an apology, and a willingness to repair the damage by stepping back from the violated territory.

One can see how rude a Latin American might appear to an Anglo American when the former means universal. For example, making a circle with the thumb and forefinger signifies "okay" in the United States, "zero" or "worthless" in France, money in Japan, and something vulgar in Germany and Brazil (Axtell, 1998). So when you know that you will be interacting with others from a different culture, plan to learn about how that culture's use of emblems differs from that of yours.

distractingly touches another person without apologizing or showing concern. But within Latino and Mediterranean traditions, the body is not understood as property. That is, the body is not understood as belonging to its owner. It does not belong to me or to anyone else; it is, in principle, public. It is an expressive and sensual region open to the scrutiny, discipline, and sanction of the community. It is, therefore, quite impossible to be "left alone" on the Latin American street. For Latin Americans, the access to others in a public space is not restricted by the "privacy" of their bodies. Thus, the Latin American does not find casual contact a form of property trespassing or a violation of rights. Walking the street in the Anglo United States is very much an anonymous activity to be performed in a field of unobstructive and invisible bodies. Since one is essentially carrying one's own space into the public sphere, no one is actually ever in public. Given that the public is private, no intimacy is granted in the public space. Thus while the Latin American public look or gaze is round, inquisitive, and wandering, the Anglo American is straight, nonobstructive, and neutral.

Civility requires the Anglo American to restrict looks, delimit gestures, and orient movement. Civility requires the Latin American to acknowledge looks, gestures, and movement and actively engage with them. For the Latin American, the unavoidable nature of shared space is always a demand for attention and a request to participate. An Anglo American considers "mind your own business" to be fair and civil. A Latin American might find this an unreasonable restriction. What takes place in public is everybody's business by the very fact that it is taking place in public.

One can understand the possible cultural misunderstandings between Anglo Americans and Latin Americans. If Anglo Americans protest the "impertinence" of Latin Americans as nosy and curious, Latin Americans would protest the indifference and lack of concern of Anglo Americans. The scene in the Miami mall could happen just as easily in Los Angeles, Chicago, Philadelphia, or New York, cities in which Latin Americans comprise an important segment of the population. The influence of this cultural heritage is going to have growing influence in the next few decades on the Anglo American scene, as Hispanics become the largest ethnic and linguistic minority in the United States. The more knowledge we can gain from what makes us culturally diverse, the more we will be able to appreciate what unifies us through the mixing and mutual exchanges of our cultures.

Excerpted from Lozano, E. (2007). The cultural experience of space and body: A reading of Latin American and Anglo American comportment in public. In A. Gonzalez, M. Houston, & V. Chen (Eds.), *Our Voices: Essays in Culture, Ethnicity, and Communication: An Intercultural Anthology* (4th ed., pp. 274–280). New York: Oxford University Press.

FOR CONSIDERATION:

1. How comfortable would you be on South Street in Miami? Would you be more or less comfortable having read this article?
2. What do you think about the author's following statement?
   But within Latino and Mediterranean traditions, the body is not understood as property. That is, the body is not understood as belonging to its owner. It does not belong to me or to anyone else; it is, in principle, public. It is an expressive and sensual region open to the scrutiny, discipline, and sanction of the community.
   How well does that reaction map onto the author's dichotomy that contrasts Anglo American concepts of space with Latin American ones?

On the other hand, some facial expressions appear to be universal. These include the standard expressions for the six basic emotions (happiness, sadness, fear, anger, disgust, and surprise; Samovar et al., 2010), and the eyebrow raise to communicate recognition (Martin & Nakayama, 2006). However, as discussed in Chapter 3, cultures have different display rules that affect when emotional expressions should be inhibited, miniaturized, simulated, or intensified. People in individualistic cultures typically believe they should reveal more of their emotions, especially positive emotions, than do people in collectivistic cultures (Matsumoto, Yu, & Fontaine, 2008).

Cultures also differ considerably in their norms for use of space. Recall that in the dominant culture of the United States, the closest boundary of personal space is about 18 inches, although men are usually more comfortable being further apart. In Middle Eastern cultures, however, men move much closer to other men when they are talking (Samovar et al., 2010). Thus, when an Egyptian man talks with an American man, one of the two is likely to be uncomfortable. Either the American will feel uncomfortable and encroached upon, or the Egyptian will feel isolated and too distant for serious conversation. Latin American and Anglo American spatial usage also differs, as described in the "Diverse Voices" box in this chapter. Differences in the use of space extend to the arrangement of furnishings and environments. In the United States, where many people live in single-family homes or in large apartments, we expect to have greater personal space. In other countries, where population densities in inhabited regions are high, people live in closer quarters and can feel "lonely" or isolated in larger spaces. In Japan and Europe, most people live in spaces that by American standards would be called cramped.

Standards for physical appearance vary widely by culture, as does the use of artifacts and scents. For example, in India and Pakistan, both females and males who are more heavyset in appearance are considered more attractive than in the United States, where being thin and/or physically fit is considered the standard of physical attractiveness. Conversely, in Japan, even more emphasis is placed on being thin than in the United States. When it comes to clothing and adornments, cultures assign different meanings to color, often connected with religious beliefs. This influences what people wear and their choice of artifacts. To illustrate, white not black, is the color of mourning in India, and Hindu brides wear red. In Latin America, purple signifies death, and in Japan, green denotes youth and energy. Religious culture may dictate standards for modest dress, hairstyles, and head coverings for both women and men. In some cultures, artificial scents from colognes and perfumes are considered annoying, while in other cultures, such as the dominant United States culture, natural body odors are perceived to be offensive.

Differences in the use and interpretation of nonverbal behavior contribute substantially to the challenge of communicating cross-culturally. Consequently, if you want to communicate effectively with people whose cultures are different from yours, study and practice of culturally appropriate nonverbal behaviors is a must.

Gender Differences

Gender is also a source of considerable variation in nonverbal behavior, in all of the categories previously discussed (Burgoon, Guerrero, & Manusov, 2011). In the category of body language, women use more eye contact as both speakers and listeners than do men, are more facially expressive (including smiling more often), and are more prone to touch the other person. Women also exhibit less dominance in posture and gesture, and show less anger. With regard to paralanguage, women's voices are higher pitched than men's, they are more vocally expressive, and they use more rising or "questioning" intonations. Women's use of space is different from that of men, too: they occupy less territory, tolerate more intrusion into their personal space, and are more likely to move aside for others. During interaction, women accommodate their partners more so than men, talking less and listening more, and interrupted more often.

Aside from these specific behavioral differences, men and women also differ in their average levels of nonverbal skill. Several decades worth of studies consistently show that women are better at both encoding and decoding of nonverbal messages. In other words, they are better at expressing meaning nonverbally in ways that others will understand, and at correctly interpreting the nonverbal messages sent by others (Burgoon et al., 2011). This skill difference between men and women is greatest for nonverbal behaviors that are positive, can be seen, and are not deceptive. It is important to keep in mind that these gender differences in nonverbal skill are not large; women on average are just a bit better at producing and receiving nonverbal messages. Individuals also vary widely in nonverbal skill, so you may know men who are excellent nonverbal communicators, and women who struggle in this area. Men, however, do seem to exhibit superior skill in one area: controlling their emotional expressions.

There are many explanations for gender differences in nonverbal behavior, most of which involve some combination of biology, socialization, and power. Some differences have a clear biological basis. For example, adult women have smaller and thinner vocal cords than adult men, which accounts for the higher pitch of their voices. The configuration of the female brain may help women more accurately interpret nonverbal behavior. Yet, socially transmitted norms for masculine and feminine behavior also play an important role. For example, before puberty, the vocal cords do not differ, but boys frequently speak in a lower pitch than do girls (Wood, 2013), suggesting that they become aware of expectations for masculine and feminine behavior. Women's greater willingness to allow others into their personal space and accommodate during interaction may reflect a combination of biological and social influences. According to social role theory (Eagly & Koenig, 2006), women are socialized to be more nonverbally sensitive and responsive than men, but this socialization is built on a biological foundation. Over thousands of generations, women who were naturally more nonverbally sensitive and responsive to others may have been more likely to mate and have children who survived to adulthood, gradually resulting in the gender difference we observe today.

Some gender differences in nonverbal behavior have no clear connection to biology, but are rooted in history, culture, and gender differences in status and power. In contemporary Western cultures, many women take their equal status with men for granted, forgetting that throughout most of recorded history (and still in most parts of the world today), women have lived within cultures that prescribe greater status and power to men. Thus, gender differences that now seem innocent, or even positive, sometimes stem from inequality (Wood, 2013).

In the United States and Western countries, women's clothing and accessories are more decorative, while men's clothing and accessories are more functional. Historically, most men's occupations required functional rather than fanciful clothing, and women had few options to provide for themselves financially aside from marrying and becoming homemakers. The need for women to make themselves attractive to potential spouses and providers promoted a focus on decorative clothing. This was especially true in the middle and upper classes where servants and appliances were available to perform manual labor in the home and there was disposable income to spend on women's clothing. In the last century, as women have achieved greater power, status, and independence from men, they have become more able to dress functionally, suited to their varied occupations and individual preferences. For example, Angela, who works as a construction engineer, spends her time in jeans, hard hats, and steel-toed boots, while Ellen, a school principal, wears suits with pants and flexible, flat-soled shoes. Men's options for dress have also expanded considerably. But time spent in any department store or reading a fashion magazine will convince you that there is still far more emphasis on women's dressing in ways that emphasize their physical attractiveness and sexuality.

Nonverbal Expectations

As emphasized earlier in the chapter, nonverbal behavior can be naturally ambiguous, which creates a variety of challenges for us when we are creating and trying to understand messages. We've looked at how cultural, gender, situational, and individual variability can make it difficult to understand what others mean by their behaviors. Yet there is an additional problem that we also confront. Sometimes nonverbal behaviors are not what we expect them to be. This can lead to misinterpretations.

Most of the time, before or during an interaction, we anticipate what the nonverbal behaviors of others are likely to be, and we expect them to follow our script. When they do, the conversation goes smoothly. But sometimes others behave in ways we don't anticipate, which can lead us to negatively interpret the meaning of the unexpected behavior and respond accordingly. Expectancy violations theory proposes that we form our expectations for the nonverbal behavior of others based on such things as their gender, age, personality, the relationship we have with them, and the context of interaction, which includes both the social situation and cultural influences (White, 2015). For example, if you were introduced to an older male engineer, you might expect him to be stone-faced and unlikely to smile or crack jokes. Your expectations would be based on a stereotype drawn from your previous experiences with older male engineers and from popular culture's representation of these people. However, if the engineer were your father, who you knew was quirky, witty, and quick to joke around, your expectations for smiles and laughter from him would be different. But if you happened to be with your father at a memorial service for a much-loved rabbi who died suddenly, you would probably expect your dad to speak and act in a more sober manner.

When people act in ways that are different from what we anticipate, these **expectancy violations** create uncertainty for us. Expectancy violations theory proposes that in trying to figure out how to react, two things influence us: how we interpret the violation itself, and how we perceive the person who committed it.

Expectancy violations—behaviors that are different from what we expect

Interpreting a Violation

When someone acts in an unanticipated way, we try to make sense of the violation behavior: was the violation positive or negative, and what does it mean? Imagine that Glen and Donnice are both divorced and currently unattached, and have met several times at their children's sports events. At a party given by a mutual friend, they end up sitting together on a small couch, drinking and sharing stories. As they talk, Glen is surprised when Donnice casually scoots a little closer to him than he normally associates with casual conversation, puts her hand on the couch, grazing his leg, and smiles a little more broadly at him than before. How will Glen respond? Because they are at a party, Glen may interpret Donnice's unexpected behaviors collectively as *flirting*, an indication of romantic interest, or he may think it is just an accident resulting from sitting together on a small couch. If Glen interprets that behavior as flirting, since he wasn't expecting these behaviors, he may also be uncertain about whether to view them as positive or negative. Flirting behavior can be flattering, but also uncomfortable. In this situation, expectancy violations theory predicts that Glen will take into account what he thinks about Donnice. If Glen considers Donnice attractive and fun to be with (rewarding), he will view her behavior as a positive expectancy violation and may reciprocate by casually putting his arm behind her, or taking her hand. But if he doesn't find her appealing and has only been tolerating her stories for lack of anything else to do (unrewarding), he'll find a way to exit the interaction.

An important point made by this theory is that intentional expectancy violations are risky. If you are going to do something that might violate someone's expectations, it's best to consider whether the behaviors are likely to be interpreted positively, and whether your "reward" for that person is likely to motivate a positive response. Understanding expectancy violation theory helps you recognize when you may have behaved in a way that was not expected of you, and can help you decide how to repair the violation. For example, if Glen abruptly ends their conversation, Donnice should consider the possibility that her nonverbal behavior made Glen uncomfortable. If she recognizes that what she was doing could have been construed as flirting, she might repair the relationship by offering an apology and/or a brief explanation.

Guidelines for Improving Nonverbal Messages

Sending Nonverbal Messages

1. Be mindful of the nonverbal behavior you are displaying. Remember that you are always communicating nonverbally. Some nonverbal cues will always be subconscious, but you should work to bring more of your nonverbal behaviors into your conscious awareness. Pay attention to what you are doing with your eyes, face, posture, gestures, voice, use of space, and appearance, as well as your handling of time and scents. To help you develop mindfulness, you might ask a friend to give you feedback about how well your nonverbal behaviors complement your verbal messages.

2. Adapt your nonverbal behaviors to your purpose. Choose to display nonverbal behaviors that are appropriate to your interaction goals. For instance, if you want to persuade your partner to your way of thinking, you should adopt nonverbal cues that demonstrate confidence and credibility. These may include direct eye contact, a serious facial expression, a relaxed posture, a loud and low-pitched voice with no vocal interferences, and professional clothing and grooming. If you want to communicate empathy and support, you would use different nonverbal behaviors, including a moderate gaze, caring facial expressions, posture in which you lean toward the other, a soft voice, and touch.

3. Adapt your nonverbal behavior to the situation. Situations vary in their formality, familiarity, and purpose. Just as you would select different language for different situations, you should adapt your nonverbal messages to the situation. Assess what the situation calls for in terms of body motions, paralanguage, spatial usage, artifacts, physical appearance, and use of time and scents. Of course, you already do some situational adapting with nonverbal communication. You wouldn't dress the same way for a wedding as you would to walk the dog. You would not treat your brother's territory the same way you would treat your doctor's territory. But the more you can consciously adapt your nonverbal behaviors to what seems appropriate to the situation, the more effective you will be as a communicator.

4. Align your nonverbal cues with your verbal communication. When we presented the functions of nonverbal communication, we explained how nonverbal behaviors may contradict verbal messages, creating a mixed message. Effective interpersonal communicators try to avoid mixed messages. It is important to make your verbal and nonverbal messages match, yet it is also important that the various types of nonverbal cues should complement each other. If you are telling your friend that you feel sad, a soft and less expressive voice will complement your words. Similarly, your friend will expect your facial expression to convey sadness and will be confused if you smile brightly, using the facial signals for happiness. People get confused and frustrated when they have to interpret inconsistent verbal and nonverbal messages.

5. Eliminate nonverbal behaviors that distract from your verbal message. Fidgeting, tapping fingers or feet, pacing, mumbling, head nodding, and vocal interferences (e.g., *um, er, you know*, etc.) send messages that influence the way your

After the intramural mixed-doubles matches on Tuesday evening, most of the players adjourned to the campus grill to have a drink and chat. Although the group was highly competitive on the courts, they enjoyed socializing and talking about the matches for a while before they went home. Marquez and Lisa, who had been paired together at the start of the season, sat down with another couple, Barry and Elana, who had been going out together for several weeks. Marquez and Lisa had played a particularly grueling match that night against Barry and Elana, a match that they lost largely because of Elana's improved play.

"Elana, your serve today was the best I've seen it this year," Marquez said.

"Yeah, I was really impressed. And as you saw, I had trouble handling it," Lisa added.

"And you're getting to the net a lot better, too," Marquez added.

"Thanks, guys," Elana said with gratitude. "I've really been working on it."

"Well, aren't we getting the compliments today," sneered Barry in a sarcastic tone. Then after a pause, he said, "Oh, Elana, would you get my sweater? I left it on that chair by the other table."

"Come on, Barry. You're closer than I am," Elana replied.

Barry got a cold look on his face, moved slightly closer to Elana, and said emphatically, "Get my sweater for me, Elana—now."

Elana quickly backed away from Barry as she said, "Okay, Barry—it's cool." Then she quickly got the sweater for him.

"Gee, isn't she sweet?" Barry said to Marquez and Lisa as he grabbed the sweater from Elana.

Lisa and Marquez both looked down at the floor. Then Lisa glanced at Marquez and said, "Well, I'm out of here— I've got a lot to do this evening."

"Let me walk you to your car," Marquez said as he stood up.

"See you next week," they said in unison as they hurried out the door, leaving Barry and Elana alone at the table.

FOR CONSIDERATION:
1. What ethical principles are violated in this case?
2. Analyze Barry's nonverbal behavior. What was he attempting to achieve?
3. How do you interpret Lisa's and Marquez's nonverbal reactions to Barry?
4. Was Barry's behavior ethically acceptable? Explain.

partner interprets your message. While controlling the nonverbal cues that telegraph nervousness, impatience, and disapproval can be difficult, it is important to try so that our conversation partners are not distracted from our meaning.

Interpreting Nonverbal Messages

1. Be mindful that most nonverbal behaviors are not emblems. Most gestures have no set meanings. They vary from person to person and culture to culture. Just because you fidget when you are lying doesn't mean that others do. What is a loud, angry tone for one person may be normal volume and pitch for another person. The more you interact with someone, the more you learn how to read that person's nonverbal cues. Even then, quick interpretations and rapid conclusions about the meaning of another's nonverbal cues can lead to misunderstandings.

2. Recognize culture, gender, and other diversity when interpreting nonverbal cues. As you gain intercultural competence, you will become more accurate in interpreting others' nonverbal cues.

Cultural Differences in Nonverbal Behavior

Interview or talk with two international students from different countries. Try to select students whose cultures differ from each other and from the culture with which you are most familiar. Develop a list of questions related to the material discussed in this chapter. Try to understand how people in the international students' countries differ from you in their use of body language, paralanguage, space, and self-presentation cues. Write a short paper explaining what you have learned.

Perception checking—sharing your perception of another's behavior to check its accuracy

3. Attend to all of the nonverbal cues and their relationship to the verbal message. Do not take nonverbal cues out of context. In any one interaction, you are likely to get simultaneous messages from a person's eyes, face, gestures, posture, voice, spatial usage, and touch. Most nonverbal cues occur in conjunction with verbal messages. By taking into consideration all the channels of communication, you will more effectively interpret the messages of others.

4. Use the skill of perception checking. Perception checking is sharing your perception of another's behavior to see if your interpretation is accurate. It involves describing your perspective on what you have observed, and asking for feedback. By doing a perception check, you can verify or correct the interpretations you make. You can check your perceptions of either verbal or nonverbal behavior, but the skill is especially important for ambiguous nonverbal behavior. For example, imagine that Donnice was trying to flirt with Glen, and that Glen left the couch quickly thereafter. Although Donnice may interpret his behavior as rejection, this may not be correct. Even if he was rejecting her advance, Donnice will probably encounter Glen again at her children's activities, so it might be useful for her to find out what happened, and smooth things over. Donnice could catch up with Glen as they leave the party, and say "Glen, it seemed like we were having a good time talking, but then you left. I think I may have upset you. If so, I'm sorry." Notice that she describes Glen's nonverbal behavior ("then you left") without evaluating it by voicing her approval or disapproval, and then provides her interpretation. Using the skill of perception checking, Donnice reopens communication between them and gives Glen the opportunity to say, "No offense, I'm just not

SKILL BUILDER ▶ PERCEPTION CHECKING

SKILL	USE	STEPS	EXAMPLE
A statement that expresses the meaning you perceive from the behavior of another.	To determine the accuracy of our perceptions of others' behavior.	1. As you observe someone's behavior, determine what you think the behavior means. 2. Describe the behavior objectively, without approval or disapproval. 3. Explain your perception of the behavior. 4. Be prepared to alter your perception, based on the response to your perception checking.	As Dale frowns while reading Paul's first draft of a memo, Paul says, "From the way you're frowning, I take it that you're not too pleased with the way I phrased the memo."

ready for that right now," or "Yeah, I'm sorry, too, I'm a little skittish, but I enjoyed talking to you. Maybe we can get coffee on Saturday while the kids are practicing?"

Because perception checking enables you to clarify ambiguous nonverbal messages, it is especially useful when someone acts in an unexpected way, the person's verbal message and nonverbal cues contradict each other, or when you are not sure of the cultural or gender norms surrounding specific nonverbal cues.

THE SOCIAL MEDIA FACTOR

Nonverbal Communication in Text

If you ask someone why communicating via social media is different (and possibly worse) than communicating face-to-face, people often note the absence of nonverbal behaviors. As discussed in Chapter 4, text-based communication is "leaner" than face-to-face interaction: it relies heavily on language to convey meaning. However, text-based communication is less lean than you may think, because people can use symbols to convey meaning normally conveyed through facial expressions, body movements, vocalics, and other nonverbal behaviors.

Gestures are not absent in digital communication, but are translated into text-based symbols (Schandorf, 2013). We embed and embody our gestures in our language, finding ever-new ways of "keeping in touch" in digital environments. The following are examples of text-based gestures.

- Pointing to things (e.g., poking, liking, favoriting, tagging, etc.)

- Imitating hand gestures (e.g., digital high five, *slow clap*, or symbols like -------->)
- Text expressions of emotions or cognitive states (e.g., <3 [heart], hahahaha, WHHAAATTTHHEEE....?!)
- Culturally specific nonverbal messages in text format (e.g., acronyms like LOL or SMH, and hashtags like #FAIL)
- Rhythmic gestures mimicking normal speech patterns (e.g., ellipses ... or punctuated phrases like 'BEST. TEXTBOOK. EVER!').

One of the most obvious ways to express nonverbal behaviors in digital interaction is use of the "emoticon," or emotion icon. In all likelihood, you have used these in texts and emails. Early on, these were keyboard-created images that were read sideways: ;-) , : -(, etc. Today, you probably use "emojis," which are cartoonlike pictographs that can express a wider range of nonverbal message content. Some versions are even animated, so that they show gradual changes in facial expression, such as blushing.

Research shows that when we add emoticons to text, we increase our receivers' ability to correctly interpret our emotions and attitudes (Lo, 2008). So the next time you wonder whether you should use the winky-face emoticon to let your friend know you're just kidding, the research says, "Yes!" ;-)

Summary

Nonverbal communication is the term commonly used to describe all human communication events that transcend spoken or written words. It includes how actions, vocal tone, and other things create meanings that stand alone, support, modify, or contradict the meaning of a verbal message. Important characteristics of nonverbal communication include that it varies in intentionality, and is primary, continuous, multi-channeled, and ambiguous. The functions of nonverbal communication are that it provides information, regulates interactions, expresses or hides emotions, manages impressions and identities, and conveys dominance and affiliation.

There are different types of nonverbal communication. Perhaps the most familiar type of nonverbal communication is body language—how a person communicates using eye contact, facial expression, gesture, posture, and touch. A second type of nonverbal communication is paralanguage, which includes our use of pitch, volume, rate, quality, and intonation to give special meaning to the words we use. A third type of nonverbal communication is spatial usage. People communicate through the use of physical space, acoustic space, posture and body orientation, and territory. The final type of nonverbal communication is self-presentation cues, including personal appearance, artifacts, use of time, and choice of scents and smells.

The use and interpretation of nonverbal communication vary considerably, depending on an individual's culture and gender. Expectancy violations theory describes how nonverbal behavior may violate expectations and result in difficult communications. You can improve the nonverbal messages that you send by being mindful of the nonverbal behavior you are displaying, adapting your nonverbal behaviors to your purpose, adapting your nonverbal behavior to the situation, aligning your nonverbal cues with your verbal message, and eliminating nonverbal behaviors that distract from your verbal message. You can improve the accuracy of your interpretations of others' nonverbal communication by being mindful that most nonverbal cues are not emblems; by recognizing culture, gender, and other diversity in the use of nonverbal cues; by attending to all the nonverbal cues and their relationship to the verbal message; and by using the skill of perception checking. Symbolic nonverbal behaviors such as emoticons and emojis help us adapt effectively to the leanness of text-based interactions.

CHAPTER RESOURCES

Key Words

Flashcards for all of these key terms are available on the *Inter-Act* website.

Acoustic space, pp. 141
Artifacts, pp. 143
Body language, pp. 137
Body orientation, pp. 138
Emblems, pp. 138
Expectancy violations, pp. 151
Eye contact, pp. 138
Facial expression, pp. 138
Furnishings, pp. 142
Gesture, pp. 138

Haptics, pp. 138
Immediacy behaviors, pp. 136
Intonation, pp. 140
Kinesics, pp. 137
Nonverbal communication, pp. 133
Olfactory cues, pp. 143
Paralanguage, pp. 139
Perception checking, pp. 154
Personal space, pp. 140
Physical appearance, pp. 142

Pitch, pp. 139
Posture, pp. 138
Proxemics, pp. 140
Quality, pp. 140
Rate, pp. 140
Territory, pp. 141
Touch, pp. 138
Vocal interferences, pp. 140
Volume, pp. 139

Analyze and Apply

The following activities challenge you to demonstrate your mastery of the concepts, theories, and frameworks in this chapter by using them to explain what is happening in a specific situation.

5.1 Rewind/Rewrite

Now that you have read the chapter, hit "rewind" on the opening dialogue between Mel and Jen and answer the following questions.

a. Use concepts from the chapter to explain how misunderstanding was created. The concepts of body language, paralanguage, using nonverbal behavior to express emotion, and expectancy violation may be especially useful.

b. Rewrite the dialogue so that Mel and Jen do not end up in a conflict with each other. Keep in mind that both Mel and Jen have responsibility for how the conversation turns out.

c. At points in the future, either Mel or Jen may find that their nonverbal behaviors do not convey their intended messages effectively. What recommendations can you give for handling those situations?

5.2 Diversity and Nonverbal Behavior

Drawing on your own experiences, write a dialogue that illustrates how culture, gender, or individual differences in nonverbal behavior can make communication more difficult. Annotate your dialogue to explain what happens and why.

Skill Practice

Skill practice activities give you the chance to rehearse a new skill by responding to hypothetical or real situations. Additional skill practice activities are available at the companion website.

5.3 Perception Checking

Review the perception checking Skill Builder before beginning this activity. Write a well-phrased perception check for each of the following situations.

a. Christie, dressed in her team uniform, with her hair flying every which way, charges into the room, and announces in a loud voice, "I'm here, and I'm ready."
   You say:

b. Franco comes home from the doctor's office with a pale face and slumped shoulders. Glancing at you forlornly, he shrugs his shoulders.
   You say:

c. As you return the tennis racket you borrowed from Liam, you smile and say, "Here's your racket." Liam stiffens, grabs the racket, and starts to walk away.

   You say:

d. Natalie dances into the room with a huge grin on her face.

   You say:

e. Larry walks into the cubicle, throws his report across the desk, smiles, and loudly proclaims, "Well, that's that!"

   You say:

f. It's dinner time, and Anthony is due home from work. Suddenly the door flies open, banging against the wall, and Anthony stomps in. Crossing the room in three long strides, he plops onto the sofa, folds his arms, and with a sour expression stares straight ahead.

   You say:

Communication Improvement Plan: Nonverbal Communication

How can you improve your nonverbal behavior? Identify a problem you have with nonverbal message cues. Review the guidelines for improving nonverbal messages. Select at least one of these as a goal. Then, using the interpersonal communication skills you have studied in the course, write a communication improvement plan. You can find a communication improvement plan worksheet on our website at www.oup.com/us/verderber.

6

COMMUNICATION IN THE LIFE CYCLE OF RELATIONSHIPS

Yvonne, Alex, and Wendy are close friends in their second semester of their freshman year of college. Yvonne and Wendy came from the same town and have known each other since middle school. Alex met them both during freshman orientation, and the threesome bonded during long, late-night talks about careers, family, guys, and their futures. Alex and Wendy, who are both art majors, have two studio classes together, so lately they have been spending more time together without Yvonne. Today, though, Yvonne met Alex at the student center for lunch.

"Hey Alex, do you know what's up with Wendy?" Yvonne asked, sitting down with her pizza and salad.

"What do you mean?" Alex frowned.

"Well, yesterday I asked her what classes she was planning to take next year and she acted like it was top secret information," Yvonne complained.

"Well, she probably doesn't know yet." Looking up to see Yvonne staring at her with a puzzled expression, Alex went on. "You know . . . she has to decide about the Art Institute."

"What are you talking about?" Yvonne exclaimed, nearly spilling her drink.

"Oh!" Alex said. "I thought you knew. She got into that design program that wait-listed her last year. But she isn't sure . . . she's worried about the extra cost."

161

(Continued)

Yvonne frowned at her plate. "I can't believe she didn't tell me. We've been friends for so long."

Later that day, Alex received the following text from Wendy:

"Why'd u tell Yvonne??? It was PRIVATE."

WHAT YOU SHOULD BE ABLE *TO EXPLAIN* AFTER YOU HAVE STUDIED THIS CHAPTER:

▶ The functions communication plays in relationships

▶ Types and dimensions of relationships

▶ How relationships change

▶ How relationships begin and develop

▶ How relationships are sustained

▶ The dialectical tensions in relationships and how to manage them

▶ How relationships deteriorate and end

▶ How to manage self-disclosure and privacy

▶ How social media blur the public–private boundary

▶ Rules for effective social media engagement

WHAT YOU SHOULD BE ABLE *TO DO* AFTER YOU HAVE STUDIED THIS CHAPTER:

▶ Self-disclose appropriately and effectively

▶ Successfully manage private information for yourself and others

Relationship—exists when two individuals are interdependent, so that each person's behavior affects the other

People need people. At heart, we are social animals. So we crave relationships with others. A **relationship** exists when two individuals are interdependent, so that each person's behavior affects the other. In a good relationship, people are interdependent in ways that are satisfying and healthy for the two individuals who are involved. Most people value the companionship, support, affection, and fun they obtain from such relationships and therefore try to keep them healthy. In the chapter opening dialogue, we see how unique relationships can be and how complicated it can be to successfully manage them. Although all three women are close, they each have distinct relationships with one another. The relationship between Wendy and Yvonne is not the same as the one between Alex and Wendy, and these are both different from the relationship between Yvonne and Alex. Although Wendy was comfortable telling Alex that she was considering transferring colleges, she didn't want Yvonne to know. Perhaps her reluctance to share her problem with Yvonne was that she didn't want Yvonne's opinions to influence her decision. Wendy disclosed her dilemma to Alex because she believed that Alex would be supportive and understanding. She purposefully chose not to tell Yvonne, thinking that if she decided to stay, she would avoid a potentially unpleasant confrontation that might damage their relationship. Unfortunately, Alex was unaware of the persuasive dynamic between Wendy and Yvonne when she shared Wendy's news. Have you ever experienced a situation like that of Alex, Wendy, and Yvonne's? If so, like Alex, were you blind to the dynamics of your relationships or those of others?

Communication is the mechanism through which we have relationships. If you didn't communicate with others, you couldn't have relationships with them. Not only that, but our relationships differ in systematic ways and can be categorized by the types of communication that relationship partners share. Communication serves several important functions in our relationships. Through communication, relationships are changed as partners manage their closeness, becoming more or less intimate with each other. This process is described as the "life cycle" of relationships. Relational partners manage their intimacy levels through their decisions about what to disclose and what to keep private.

Because humans are social animals, we all want to have relationships that are satisfying. But good relationships do not just happen, nor do they grow and sustain themselves automatically. Partners must invest time and effort in their relationships or they will fall apart (Canary & Dainton, 2002). The interpersonal skills you will learn in this course will help you start, build, and sustain healthy relationships with others and, when necessary, they can help you more gracefully end relationships that are no longer satisfying. With this in mind, let's look at the roles that communication plays in our relationships.

The Functions of Communication in a Relationship

In Chapter 1, we said that one of the primary functions of interpersonal communication was to help us conduct our relationships. But how does communication do this? First, communication is how we "do" our relationships—it forms or constitutes them. Second, communication is instrumental in our relationships: we use it to get things done with our relationship partners. Third, the content and tone of our communication is a measure or index of how close or distant, healthy or unhealthy, satisfying or unsatisfying our relationship is at any point in time. Let's take a closer look at each of these functions.

The Constitutive Function

How do you "do" or perform your relationships? At first glance, this may seem like a strange question. But what is a relationship if not the sum of all of the messages partners exchange? In a very real sense, it is your messages that make or constitute your relationships. So when we say that communication serves a **constitutive function**, we simply mean that the messages that are exchanged in a relationship form that relationship. If we use a piece of cloth as a metaphor for a relationship, then the relationship has been woven from the messages that have been exchanged. Each time you send or receive a message, you add a thread to the fabric of your relationship. Just as each thread adds color and texture and affects the strength of the fabric, so, too, our messages interweave to create the type and quality of the relationship we have with someone. Think about the two people whom you consider closest to you. Are your relationships the same? No. Each relationship is unique. Why? Because the sum and

Constitutive function—the communication messages exchanged in a relationship form the relationship

substance of what you have shared differs from person to person, from relationship to relationship, and within one relationship, from one time to another. Some of our relationships are characterized by rich, confirming interactions that are healthy for both partners. Other relationships are punctuated with tense interactions and unresolved arguments that create friction between partners. Each time you talk with a partner, you continue to define, refine, and redefine your relationship.

The Instrumental Function

How do you get your relationship partner to do something you want done? You tell or ask, beg or threaten, promise or ingratiate. In this way, our communication serves an **instrumental function**. Our messages are the means through which we accomplish our personal and relationship goals.

Our personal goals vary from simple to difficult, such as conveying information, planning activities, negotiating expectations and responsibilities, managing conflict, and conveying support when our partners face difficulties. If a metaphor for the constitutive function of communication is weaving cloth, then a metaphor for the instrumental function would be a toolbox with different tools that we pull out at the appropriate time to accomplish our purposes. Our communication scripts and plans are the tools that we can use when we need them. When we have incorporated effective communication skills into our repertoire, we are better equipped to craft messages that will accomplish our goals. For example, Zack needs to go home because his dad is having surgery next week. But he can't take his dog because his younger sister is allergic to dogs. He would like to leave his dog with Maggie, his girlfriend. How does he make this happen? He might try promising, bargaining, appealing to her emotions, or some other script to persuade her to keep the dog. But to accomplish his purpose, his message will have to effectively communicate his need. How competently he communicates his desire will not only determine whether his girlfriend agrees to keep his dog, but it may also affect their relationship.

We also use communication as the instrument to change our relationships. For example, if you become sexually attracted to a friend, you might initiate a "relationship talk" with the hope of changing it from a platonic friendship into a romantic relationship. You mend a relationship that has been damaged by talking through problems and transgressions. And, when you don't want to continue a romantic relationship, you will accomplish this goal through the messages you exchange with your partner.

The Indexical Function

How do you figure out what type of relationship you and others have, and how healthy it is? When we say that communication serves an **indexical function** in relationships, we mean that the interaction between relationship partners measures or indicates what their relationship is like; in other words, it "indexes" it. We introduced this idea in Chapter 1 when we said that communication

Instrumental function—the communication messages exchanged in a relationship are the means through which we accomplish our personal and our relationship goals

Indexical function—the interaction between relationship partners indicates what the relationship is like, including the partners' dominance and affiliation toward each other

reveals relationship qualities, especially dominance and affiliation (McLaren & Solomon, 2015).

Exchanges of dominance messages indicate whether partners agree about who is in charge of the relationship at that point in time. For example, Leon demands of his high school son, "I need to see your homework." The content of the message is that this father wants his son to show him the homework that he was supposed to have completed. But on another level, the father is asserting dominance over his son. Notice that he doesn't ask to see the homework, he makes a demand. If the son responds, "Okay, here it is," then the form of this exchange demonstrates submission—the son accepts his father's control of the relationship. If, however, the son replies, "I don't need you looking over my work. I'm almost 18," then the son has rejected his father's control move and is signaling his own desire to control the relationship.

Messages index not only who is dominant or whether there is a power struggle in the relationship, but how close and warm relationships are. By demanding to see his son's homework, Leon also signals that he is engaged in this detail of his son's life. An acquaintance or stranger would not have the right to make this demand, and a father who was detached from his son's life probably would not care about homework. However, we would agree that a father who said, "I'd like to help you get a good grade on your test, so please let me look over your homework" has a more respectful and closer relationship with his son. Of course, from a single message we can't accurately gauge the quality of a relationship. Leon may not normally try to dominate his son, but may have spoken abruptly because he was in a hurry or having a bad day. To get a sense of what a relationship is like, whether someone else's or your own, it is necessary to pay attention to the quality and type of multiple interactions over time. A metaphor for the indexical function of communication is a thermometer that measures the temperature of relationships. A relationship may change slowly or abruptly. It may vary only slightly from one time to another, or it might have wide swings. And the average "temperature" of different relationships is likely to differ. But in all cases, the communication messages that partners exchange provide the best index of the dominance arrangement and the affiliation ties in the relationship.

In sum, communication functions to constitute, be instrumental in, and index our relationships. With this understanding, let's look at how relationships systematically differ from one another.

Describing Relationships

We use many terms to describe the different types of relationships we have with others: "He's my buddy," "She's my old lady," "We're cousins," or "They're besties." These and other descriptors we use to identify the nature of a relationship convey information about three basic qualities of the relationship: whether it is romantic or platonic, voluntary or involuntary, and intimate or distant. For example, when Phoebe describes Sam as a "friend," we probably assume that the relationship is **platonic**, meaning without romantic or sexual involvement. In a

Platonic relationship—a relationship in which partners are not sexually attracted to each other or choose not to act on their sexual attraction

Romantic relationship—relationships in which partners act on their mutual sexual attraction to each other

Voluntary relationship—a relationship in which we freely choose the people with whom we interact

Involuntary relationship—a relationship in which we have no choice about the other people with whom we interact

Interdependence—a dimension of relationships that gauges the extent to which partners rely on each other to meet their needs

Commitment—a dimension of relationships that gauges how dedicated or loyal partners are to each other

Understanding and predictability—a dimension of relationships that gauges how well partners understand and can predict each other's behaviors

romantic relationship there is a sexual attraction. Additionally, we may add prefixes, suffixes, or other descriptors to clarify the nature of our relationships. For example, we can have platonic "friends," but may use the terms "boyfriend" or "girlfriend" to differentiate romantic from platonic friendships. Other relationship terms help us to understand how much choice the partners had in creating the relationship. Spouses and friends are **voluntary** relationships, meaning that these were chosen by the partners. In contrast, most family relationships (e.g., mother, brother-in-law, cousin) are **involuntary**, because they are created by biological relatedness or the choices of others. Relationship terms also help distinguish between relationships that vary in closeness, or intimacy. For example, a "best friend" is usually closer than a "friend," and friends in turn are closer than "colleagues" or "mates."

While we intuitively understand these distinctions, there are five other important but subtle and complex differences that help us distinguish between relationships.

1. Interdependence. Relationships vary in the extent to which partners rely on each other to meet their needs. The more interdependent the partners, the more each partner's behavior will affect the other. When you first meet someone, you are independent. Neither of you expects the other to go out of his or her way to help. Likewise, as you are just getting to know people, you are less likely to be swayed by their opinion, adapt your behavior to please them, or depend on them to meet your needs. But as you get to know someone better, you become more intimate, and you are both more likely to consider each other's preferences, make joint decisions, and mutually rely on the other. You become interdependent. Sometimes one partner may become overly dependent on the other, which can create tension in the relationship. An appropriate level of interdependence, however, characterizes a healthy relationship.

2. Commitment. Relationships vary in terms of how much the partners feel obliged or emotionally motivated to continue the relationship. In a relationship, you may feel committed to your partner because you enjoy being with him or her; therefore, you have a personal desire to continue the relationship. In addition, you may feel a moral commitment to the relationship and feel guilty if you think about ending it. For example, if you have had a friend since grade school, you may feel compelled to continue your relationship. At times there can be external forces or structural reasons to be committed to the relationship. For instance, a legally binding relationship such as a marriage or a shared apartment lease may increase your sense of commitment. If you have a child with someone, even if your romantic relationship ends, for the sake of your child, you may feel committed to maintaining a good relationship with the other parent.

3. Understanding and predictability. Relationships vary in how well partners understand and can predict each other's behaviors. As you become closer and get to know a person better, this knowledge reduces your uncertainty and enables you to predict how that person is likely to feel and act in a particular situation. Over time, you may share so much that you become experts about

LEARN ABOUT YOURSELF ▶ TRUST IN A CLOSE RELATIONSHIP

Take this short survey to learn something about one of your close relationships. Answer the questions based on your first response. There are no right or wrong answers. Just be honest in reporting your beliefs. Respond to these items with one relationship in mind. Choose someone you are close to, such as a romantic partner. For each question, select one of the numbers to the right that best describes your assessment:

_____1. My partner is primarily interested in his (her) own welfare.

_____2. There are times when my partner cannot be trusted.

_____3. My partner is perfectly honest and truthful with me.

_____4. I feel that I can trust my partner completely.

_____5. My partner is truly sincere in his (her) promises.

_____6. I feel that my partner does not show me enough consideration.

_____7. My partner treats me fairly and justly.

_____8. I feel that my partner can be counted on to help me.

7 = Very Strongly Agree
6 = Strongly Agree
5 = Mildly Agree
4 = Neutral
3 = Mildly Disagree
2 = Strongly Disagree
1 = Very Strongly Disagree

Scoring the Survey: This survey measures the trust you have in your partner. To find your score, first reverse the response scores for Items 1, 2, and 6 (if you wrote 7 make it a 1, 6 = 2, 5 = 3, 4 = 4, 3 = 5, 2 = 6, and 1 = 7). Now add up your numbers for all eight items on the survey. Total scores can range from 8 to 56. The higher your score, the more you trust your partner; the lower your score, the less you trust your partner. You can compare your score to those of people who took this survey when it was developed.

Score	Percentile
< 40	Bottom 25%
40–47	26%–50%
48–52	51%–75%
53–56	76%–99+%

Based on Larzelere, R. E., & Huston, T. (1980). The dyadic trust scale: Toward understanding interpersonal trust in close relationships. Journal of Marriage and Family, 42, 595–604.
The Dyadic Trust Scale is copyrighted by R. E. Larzelere and used with permission.

each other's feelings and behaviors. This is why couples who have been married for many years are able to anticipate each other's needs and wants and can even finish the other's sentences.

4. Interpersonal trust. Relationships vary in interpersonal trust, or the extent to which people believe that their relationship partners will not intentionally harm them. Interpersonal trust increases as partners believe that they know what to expect from the relationship partner, know how they are supposed to act, and know that they want to act according to expectations (Pearce, 1974). Trust is lowest with strangers, and it increases or decreases depending on how

Interpersonal trust—a dimension of relationships that gauges the extent to which partners believe that they know what to expect from each other, know how they are supposed to act, and know that they want to act according to expectations

Johari Windows

Working with a friend, each of you should draw a window that represents your perception of the relationship with the other person. Then each of you should draw a window that represents what you perceive to be the other person's relationship with you. Share the windows. How do they compare? If there are differences in the representations, talk with your friend about them.

Self-disclosure—verbally sharing personal, private information, and feelings

Feedback—providing verbal and nonverbal responses to relationship partners and their messages

Johari window—a visual framework for understanding how self-disclosure and feedback work together in a relationship

Open pane—a pane of the Johari window that contains the information about you that both you and your relationship partner know

Secret pane—a pane of the Johari window that contains all those things that you know about yourself, but have chosen to keep private from your relationship partner

reliably our partners meet our needs and act in ways that enhance the relationship. Because trust is a belief, by nature it involves some level of risk that your partner will disappoint you. Research suggests that four characteristics of partners lead to trust (Boon, 1994): dependability, responsiveness, collaboration, and faithfulness. Dependable partners can be relied on to behave in consistent and expected ways. Responsive partners recognize and act to meet each other's needs. Collaborative partners resolve conflicts using problem-solving approaches that result in win-win situations. Faithful partners are loyal to the relationship by honoring each other's privacy wishes; by defending each other's reputation even when it is personally inconvenient; and in romantic relationships, by refraining from sexual behavior with others.

5. Self-disclosure. Relationships vary in self-disclosure, or the extent to which partners share with each other their personal and private information and feelings, as well as the **feedback** that partners give in response to these disclosures. If you meet someone on a blind date to a movie that your friend set up for you, your conversation may focus on what you have heard about the film, other movies you've enjoyed, and favorite actors. If you disagree with the other person's opinion, you will probably keep it to yourself. If you get to a second and subsequent dates or find yourselves so attracted to each other than you extend your first date into an all-night conversation, you will probably share your political and moral viewpoints and talk about your families, personal histories, and even previous relationships. As you share, the feedback you give and receive will let you assess how well your perspectives align, and where they are different.

The **Johari window** (named after its two originators, Jo Luft and Harry Ingham) is a visual framework for understanding how self-disclosure and feedback work together in a relationship (Luft, 1970). The entire window represents all of the information about you that there is. In every relationship you have, you and your partner each know some (but not all) of this information. The window has four "panes," or quadrants, as shown in Figure 6.1. The **open pane** contains the information about you that both you and your partner know. The **secret pane** contains

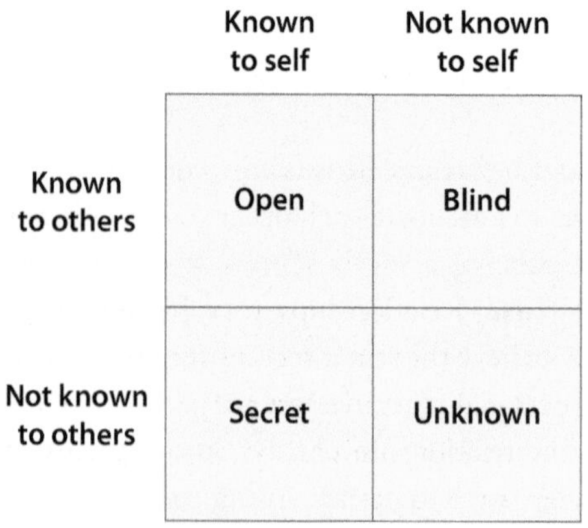

FIGURE 6.1 The Johari Window.

A 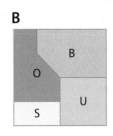 **B** 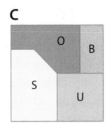 **C** 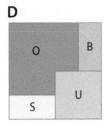 **D**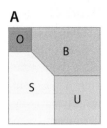

FIGURE 6.2 Sample Johari windows: (A) low disclosure, low feedback; (B) high disclosure, low feedback; (C) low disclosure, high feedback; (D) high disclosure, high feedback.

all the things that you know about yourself but have chosen to keep private from your partner. As you disclose to your partner, the open pane increases in size and the secret pane decreases. The **blind pane** contains the information that the other person knows about you but of which you are unaware. As you interact with your partner and receive feedback, the size of this pane decreases. The **unknown pane** contains information about you of which neither you nor your partner is aware. New experiences and reflections, with or without your partner, may give you more self-awareness, reducing the size of this pane. As shown in Figure 6.2, your Johari windows for different relationships will look different, depending on how much you disclose, and how much feedback is provided by your partners. Johari windows help us understand how the quantity of disclosure and feedback change our relationships, but self-disclosure and privacy management are complicated, and we will discuss them in more depth later in this chapter.

How Relationships Change: Relationship Life Cycles

Relationships move through identifiable stages of beginning, developing, maintaining, and degenerating. The process and pattern of changes in a relationship is referred to as its **life cycle** (Knapp, Vangelisti, & Caughlin, 2014). Relationship life cycles vary: they may be linear and sequential, progressing in stage-by-stage fashion, or unevenly paced, accelerating through some stages and jumping over others. Back and forth movement between several stages characterizes most relationship life cycles, and each relationship has a unique life cycle. You probably know someone who became deeply involved with another person very quickly, seeming to jump from barely acquainted to highly committed. And you have seen couples who develop a seemingly warm romantic relationship, then cycle through big fights, break-ups, time apart, and reconciliation. At times, our relationships may evolve so slowly that we don't recognize that we have moved from one stage to another. But if we reflect back on our relationship, we can probably identify specific **turning points**, or crucial events that changed the nature of the relationship and its future.

Any event can be a turning point, if it is seen by relationship partners as marking a significant change in the relationship. Studies of turning points in

Blind pane—a pane of the Johari window that contains the information that your relationship partner knows about you, but of which you are unaware

Unknown pane—a pane of the Johari window that contains information about which neither you nor your relationship partner is aware

Life cycle—the process and pattern of changes in a relationship

Turning point—any event or occurrence that marks a relationship's transition from one stage to another

▶ **OBSERVE AND ANALYZE**

Turning Points in Relationships

Select one long-term relationship in which you have been or are currently involved. Identify what you consider to be the turning points in that relationship. For each turning point, indicate whether in your opinion this was a positive event that strengthened the relationship or a negative event that weakened relationship intimacy. Indicate whether you discussed these turning points with the other person.

How will deployment change the nature of this couple's relationship?

romantic relationships (Baxter & Bullis, 1993; Baxter & Erbert, 1999) show that these markers often include responding to online dating inquiries, first phone calls, first dates, first kisses, meeting the family, dealing with rivals, engaging in sexual activity, vacationing together, deciding to be exclusive, having a big fight, making up, separating, living together, getting engaged, marrying, separating, and divorcing. The effect of a particular turning point depends on how it is perceived by the people in the relationship. In this chapter's "Diverse Voices" selection, Saba Ali explains how simply holding hands ended a promising romantic relationship for her.

With this general background in mind, let's explore how communication functions and differs in each stage of a relationship's life cycle.

Stage One: Beginning Relationships

For most of us, starting a new relationship is scary because we are uncertain about how we should act, how our partner will act, and how the relationship will develop (Knobloch & Miller, 2008). In most cases, our first few conversations involve finding out more about our partner to reduce some of our uncertainty. **Predicted outcome value theory** suggests that we use our early conversations with potential relationship partners to gather information that allows us to predict whether the benefits of future interactions will outweigh the costs (Sunnafrank, 1990). The conversations that occur at the beginning of relationships actually progress through three identifiable phases (Berger & Calabrese, 1975).

During the first or entry phase, we follow the norms of our culture, sharing appropriate basic demographic and interest information ("Where are you from?" "Do you have any brothers or sisters?" "What is your major?" "Do you follow sports?" etc.). After initial conversations, we decide whether or not spending additional time with someone will be worth it. We start by excluding people we dislike or don't think are appropriate partners (Fehr, 2008). For example, when Kelly joined the marching band at college, she didn't know anyone, so she was interested in finding others who might become friends. At the first practice, after talking with six of the band members, Kelly decided to avoid two of the guys because they were loud and obnoxious. She also ruled out one girl who openly bragged to anyone who would listen that she could "hook them up with a supplier." That left three possibilities for developing relationships.

After we have excluded people we don't like or don't think appropriate, we continue to evaluate the people we have talked with based on their physical attractiveness, social skills, and responsiveness to our overtures (Fehr, 2008). Kelly found that while all of the remaining three people she had met were good looking, one of the women was really shy and difficult to talk with. Another guy seemed interesting, but when she tried to continue talking with him, he seemed distracted and aloof. That left her with one woman who was easy to talk with and seemed to enjoy Kelly's company. So Kelly asked her if she wanted to get a bite to eat.

Predicted outcome value theory—the claim that in our early conversations with potential relationship partners, we gather information to predict whether the benefits of future interactions will outweigh the costs

Modern Love: Close Enough to Touch Was Too Far Apart

BY SABA ALI

Who knew that holding hands, the very act that signals the start of so many relationships, would be the end of mine? It seems the mullahs were onto something when they wagged their fingers against premarital relations, of any kind.

Born in Kenya, I came to the United States at age six, settling with my family in upstate New York. Growing up Muslim, I missed out on the "Dawson's Creek" method of courtship.

For scarf-wearing Muslims like me, premarital interaction between the sexes is strictly controlled. Men and women pray, eat and congregate separately. At private dinner parties, women exit the dining room so the men can serve themselves. Boys sit on one side of the hall, girls on the other, and married couples in the middle.

When out in public interactions with non-Muslim boys, we tend to be less constrained but still formal. A playful push from a boy would bring an awkward explanation of how touching is against my religion.

So my friends and I had high expectations for marriage which was supposed to quickly follow graduation from college. That's when our parents told us it was time to find the one man we would be waking up with for the rest of our lives, God willing. They just didn't tell us how.

There were no tips from our mothers or anyone else on how to meet the right man or to talk to him. It's simply expected that our lives will consist of two phases: unmarried and in the company of women, and then married and in the company of a man.

It's all supposed to start with a conversation, but not a private one. My friends and I call them "meetings." The woman comes with her chaperone, a family member, and the man comes with his. Talking points include such questions as "What do you expect from your husband?" and "Would you mind if my parents were to move in with us after the reception?"

Yet now, at 29, despite all of my "meetings," I remain unmarried. And in the last five years I've exhausted the patience of my matchmaking aunties and friends who have offered up their husbands' childhood playmates.

All I wanted was to feel secure, to look forward to spending my days and nights with my match. Which is why my interest was piqued last year when a friend from college told me about a radiologist in his early 30s who was also frustrated by the challenges of the contemporary Muslim hookup. We lived hours from each other, but I agreed to do the traveling for our first get together, which we decided would be for brunch at a little French café near Central Park. I listened as he talked about his past relationships. Not the most appropriate topic for a first date, perhaps, but more comfortable for me than some typical pressurized questions: "Do you cook?" and "How many children do you want?"

After brunch, we walked through the park. I spoke with ease about my own confusions, ambitions, faith and fear of making the wrong decision about marriage. I told him I wanted someone who liked eating out. He said he wanted a wife who wasn't conservative and could fit in with his non-Muslim friends.

After meeting him, we kept getting to know each other by phone, often talking for hours at a time. If I was driving when he called, I would roam around aimlessly just so our exchange wouldn't end when I reached my destination. I hadn't yet told my parents about him, not wanting to get my mother's hopes up.

Our lingering problem, however, was the difference in how religious we each were; he hadn't planned on marrying someone who wore the traditional head scarf. His ideal woman was less strict, more secular. But I reveled in the recognition. Covering was a choice I had made in high school, partly out of a need for identity, and partly out of fear. The fear came from what I had heard at Muslim summer camp, which scared me enough to start covering and praying.

In the years since, that fear has evolved into understanding. Most girls will say the scarf is for modesty. I see it as a protection. It keeps me from making stupid decisions.

In order to get him over his hesitation, I planned our dates to take place in very public places. We played miniature golf, ate out at restaurants and went

(continued)

Modern Love: Close Enough to Touch Was Too Far Apart (*continued*)

blueberry picking. I had my own doubts, although I was afraid to admit them: Namely, why should I push forward with this when we weren't aligned in terms of our faith? How could we be a good match if he didn't approve of my hijab? Would I have to change? Should I?

One evening he called to tell me he had gone to a lounge with a few of his buddies. "I visualized what it would feel like to have you sitting next to me," he told me.

"And how did I feel?" I asked.

"Pretty good," he said. "Manageable."

After, I finally called my mother and told her about him.

Before him, I had never gone past the second date. But by now he and I were approaching our fourth date—plenty of time, in my mind, to decide whether a man is right for you.

And then came the night of the movie, his idea. I'm a movie fanatic and remember the details of almost every movie I've ever seen. I can't remember the title of the one we saw that night. I looked over at him and smiled, convincing myself that the weightiness I felt was because I was in uncharted territory. We were moving forward, talking about meeting each other's families. So when he leaned over and asked, "Can I hold your hand?" I didn't feel I could say no. I liked him for taking the risk.

Nearly 30 years old, I had thought about holding hands with a boy since I was a teenager. But it was always in the context of my wedding day. Walking into our reception as husband and wife, holding hands, basking in that moment of knowing this was forever.

Non-Muslim girls may wonder about their first kiss or, later, about losing their virginity. I thought I was running the same risk, though for me it would be the first time actually touching the hand of a potential husband. How would it feel? Would it convince me that he was the one?

A lifetime's worth of expectations culminated in this single gesture in a dark theater over a sticky armrest. I'm not sure it's possible to hold hands wrong, but we were not doing it right. It felt awkward with my hand under his, so we changed positions: my arm on top, his hand cradling mine. It was still uncomfortable, and soon my hand fell asleep, which was not the tingling sensation I was hoping for. Finally, I took it away.

But the damage had been done. We had broken the no-contact rule, and in doing so, I realized I wasn't willing to be the kind of girl he wanted. I believe in my religion, the rules, the reasons and even the restrictions. At the same time, I've always wanted to be married, and the thought of never knowing that side of myself, as a wife and a mother, scares me. Being with him made me compromise my faith, and my fear of being alone pushed me to ignore my doubts about the relationship.

When we took it too far, I shut down. It wasn't supposed to happen that way. So after the date, I split us up. And I never saw him again.

FOR CONSIDERATION:

1. There are a variety of opportunities for turning points in a relationship. On their first date, the doctor told Saba that he was interested in finding someone "who wasn't very conservative." How could Saba have used this comment as a turning point that perhaps would have led to a different outcome later?

2. Have you ever faced a relationship turning point where continuing the relationship meant that you would have compromised your values or beliefs? If you have, did you choose to compromise? What impact did your decision have on the relationship long term? Do you regret your choice?

After one or more entry-stage conversations, we move to the second or personal phase of beginning the relationship. Conversations in this phase move beyond basic demographic information exchange as we begin to disclose somewhat more personal stories and relate critical incidents in our lives. From these more personal disclosures, we can learn about the attitudes, beliefs, and values of our partner and judge whether they are compatible with our own. During dinner at the Union Café, Kelly learned that both she and the other woman held similar political views, were close to their families, were majoring in public relations, and were avid environmentalists. It appeared that they had a lot in common and even had a similar sense of humor. So at the end of the meal, they made plans to meet again for coffee before the next band practice.

At some point, partners will transition into the third or exit phase of the beginning relationship stage. If the former strangers decide that they like each other, that they have enough in common, and that the advantages of pursuing the relationship outweigh the disadvantages, they will continue to meet and invest in the relationship with self-disclosures. Or one or both of them may choose not to pursue a deeper relationship. After meeting and talking together several more times, Kelly recognized that although she had initially enjoyed the other woman's company, the more she got to know her, the less she liked her. Consequently, Kelly continued to talk with her bandmate at rehearsals and games, but she made excuses to avoid her outside of this context, and the women remained simply acquaintances.

Stage Two: Developing Relationships

We develop our relationships by choosing to continue investing our time in pursuing conversation, sharing joint activities, and engaging in deeper, reciprocated self-disclosure with our partner. Why do we continue to invest in and develop some relationships yet not others?

Choosing Which Relationships to Develop

Two theories can help us understand how and why we choose to develop a specific relationship. According to **interpersonal needs theory**, all of us have inclusion, affection, and control needs that we try to meet through our relationships, although our need for each of these varies in degree from person to person and over time (Schutz, 1966). **Inclusion need** is our desire to be in the company of other people, which stems from our nature as social animals. But people differ in how much interaction they need and with how many people they need to have social relationships. Some people are happy spending time with one or two others and enjoy spending many hours alone. Other people enjoy having many relationships of varying intensities and find they are happiest if they spend most of their time with others. Most of us find ourselves somewhere between these

Interpersonal needs theory—the premise that all of us have inclusion, affection, and control needs that we try to meet through our relationships, although our need for each of these varies in degree from person to person

Inclusion need—our desire to be in the company of other people

When you meet someone new, how do you decide if you like the person enough to spend more time with him or her?

Affection need—our desire to love and be loved

Control need—our desire to influence the events and people around us and to be influenced by others

Social exchange theory—the premise that we continue to develop a relationship as long as we feel that its rewards outweigh its costs and we perceive that what we get from a particular relationship is more than we would be able to get if we invested elsewhere

Relationship costs—negative outcomes to a relationship, including the time and energy we spend developing a relationship and the negative experiences that may arise, like hurt feelings, conflict episodes, jealousy, etc.

Relationship rewards—positive outcomes to a relationship, including having basic relationship needs for affection, control, and inclusion met

two extremes. **Affection need** is our desire to love and be loved. The people you know probably run the gamut of this scale. Some people tend to avoid close ties, seldom show their loving feelings, and shy away from people who try to show them affection. Other people thrive on developing close and loving relationships with many others. They enjoy developing deep friendships, both verbally and nonverbally display their loving feelings, and thrive on the affection others show them. Again, you may find yourself somewhere between these two extremes. Finally, **control need** is our desire to influence the events and people around us and to be influenced by others. Like the other two needs, people also vary in their need for control. Some people feel a strong need to be in charge of the situation, calling the shots, organizing their own lives and the lives of those around them; whereas other people seem happiest when someone else is making the decisions, taking charge, and being responsible. Most of us need to be in control some of the time when the outcome of events is important to us, but we also need to have our relationship partners "step up" and take control of other situations and decisions.

A second theory, **social exchange theory**, proposes that we continue to develop a relationship as long as we feel that its rewards outweigh its costs, and we perceive that what we get from a particular relationship is more than we would be able to get if we invested elsewhere (Thibaut & Kelley, 1986). **Relationship costs** include the time and energy we spend developing a relationship and the negative experiences that may arise like hurt feelings, conflict episodes, jealousy, and so forth. **Relationship rewards** include having basic relationship needs for affection, control, and inclusion met. As long as we perceive that a relationship's benefits are worth its costs, we will continue to develop it.

Let's look at an extended example of how interpersonal needs and social exchanges affect our decision to develop relationships. Zeke met Madison and Hailey during freshman orientation week. Since then, he had texted with Madison several times and recently spent an entire night hanging out with her at her dorm, where they talked into the early hours of the morning. He found that Madison was an only child whose parents were divorced. She was easy to talk with, enjoyed several of his favorite bands, and laughed at his jokes. He was also pleased when she seemed to be fine after they didn't talk for a couple of days. He also had several long conversations with Hailey, and they had actually had a date that she initiated. While the date was okay, Hailey had annoyed him by calling several times a day, including very late every night, and texting him almost every hour. A couple of times she woke him up, and at other times she interrupted his study time. He concluded that Hailey was too needy. Madison, on the other hand, seemed to be a good fit, and he found that he looked forward to seeing her. As the semester progressed, Zeke spent more time getting close to Madison, and although he continued to be pleasant when he saw Hailey, he avoided answering her calls, didn't respond to her text messages, and turned down her requests for another date. When his roommate asked him why he was pursuing Madison and keeping Hailey at arm's length, he explained: "Madison gets me. She understands that my classes and labs take a lot of time, and I need my space [meets my inclusion need/reward]. Because we share so many common interests, she's always willing to do what I want to do [meets my control need/reward]. And I can tell that she likes me, yet she's not overly expressive or possessive and recognizes that I'm not yet ready to declare my undying love [meets my affection need/reward]. Hailey just didn't get me. She needed much more attention than I have time to devote to anyone [too inclusive/cost] and wanted to take over my life [too controlling/cost]. She had already told me how much she liked me and expected me to reciprocate, but I just didn't have those kinds of feelings for her [too affectionate/cost]. So compared to Hailey, Madison and I are just more compatible [weighing the alternatives and choosing the most rewarding]."

Throughout our relationships, we continue to compare our costs to the rewards that we receive. As long as we feel that what we are getting from the relationship is worth what we are giving, and we don't see another relationship where our outcomes would be better, we continue developing or sustaining the relationship that we are in.

Communication in Developing Relationships

The developing stage of the relationship life cycle is a very intense period that results in our feeling closer and more committed to our partner. During this phase, we increase the time we spend together while merging some of our daily activities, sharing more intimate disclosures, and testing the relationship. For example, Zeke and Madison began to study together in the late afternoon, followed by having dinner in the cafeteria. During dinner one Friday, Madison mentioned that she was going to do her wash Saturday morning, and Zeke, who hadn't done laundry in two weeks, joined her. This became a Saturday morning "date," which they laughed about but continued to observe. As they spent more time together, each learned a great deal about the other. Among other "secrets," Zeke shared the painful breakup he had had with his longtime girlfriend, who dumped him two days before their senior prom. Madison confided that she worried about her father, who drank too much and had lost his driver's license but continued to drive. Over the next three months, both Zeke and Madison tested the relationship. Madison, who had trouble trusting others, was pleased when Zeke kept what she had told him about her dad to himself. Several times Zeke purposely didn't follow his tradition of calling Madison to say goodnight to see how she would react. They also tested their chemistry and quickly agreed that although they really cared about each other, neither was physically attracted to the other. Consequently, they became really close friends in a platonic rather than romantic relationship. Rather than calling Zeke her "boyfriend," Madison referred to him as her "friend guy." When she marries she wants Zeke to be her "man of honor," and when he marries, Zeke wants Madison to be his "best woman."

Like Zeke and Madison's experience, developing any relationship occurs over time and through the self-disclosure process. As we disclose more and learn that our partner is trustworthy, we deepen our relationship. As long as we perceive that on balance the relationship's rewards outweigh its costs, we will continue to invest in it. The more we have invested, the more we become committed to our partners. Over time, many relationships we develop become social friendships, some become close friendships, and a few become platonic or romantic intimate relationships.

Stage Three: Sustaining Relationships

The periods during which we are developing a close relationship can be very exciting. Getting to know someone, learning to trust him or her, and sharing activities are heady stuff. But once the relationship has stabilized, it cannot be taken for granted. Relationships that last are those in which the partners continue to emotionally invest in the relationship and maintain their commitments while managing the tensions inherent in any relationship. Let's look at the behaviors that characterize healthy ongoing relationships, and then discuss the tensions that arise in all relationships and how you can effectively handle these.

Communication Behaviors That Sustain Relationships

People use various types of behaviors to maintain healthy relationships (Canary, Stafford, & Semic, 2002; Dindia & Baxter, 1987). First, people continue to use prosocial behaviors. They are friendly and polite to one another, and they avoid becoming overcritical of their partner. Unfortunately, it's very easy to begin to take a partner for granted. For example, instead of politely asking our roommate to pick up a needed item, we may phrase this request as an order: "Stop by Kroger on your way home and pick up a loaf of bread."

Second, people who sustain a relationship continue to observe ceremonial occasions like birthdays and anniversaries. They share vacations and spend time together recounting pleasant, memorable events from their common past. When one of our daughters was in college, she developed a very close group of friends. They are now spread out across the country, yet they continue to exchange emails, keep up with each other on Facebook, send birthday cards, and get together either at a college reunion or for group vacations with spouses, significant others, and kids. During these times, they relive their favorite memories from college as well as make new memories.

Third, partners who sustain relationships make it a habit to spend time together as a couple and with mutual friends. Many happily married couples have a weekly "date" night when they go out to have fun, seeing a movie, sharing a quiet dinner, or just taking a long walk. These planned times allow them to withdraw from the busyness of day-to-day living and to focus on each other. Also, doing things together with mutual friends can help sustain a relationship since it provides an opportunity for partners to observe each other in a social setting and to privately discuss what happened at the gathering.

Fourth, partners who sustain relationships communicate frequently and talk about deep and everyday topics. Their communication is characterized by honesty and openness. While frequent communication is the norm, there are those special relationships that are maintained even when partners have extended times where they don't communicate. These are usually long-standing relationships where the partners have shared a common history and know each other intimately. But these relationships are the exception. Most relationships require continuing communication.

Fifth, those who sustain relationships exchange words and actions that acknowledge their continuing commitment, affection, discretion, and trustworthiness. "You're my best friend," "I really can't imagine not having you to talk with," and "I love you" exemplify statements that reassure a partner of the relationship's status.

Finally, relationships are sustained when partners share the tasks that must be done. For example, Chas and Raj share an off-campus apartment, and both men do household chores and contribute to a household fund from which they pay joint expenses. All these behaviors are investments in the other person and the relationship. Just like a checking account, when the relationship account is flush, the relationship is healthy, but when one or both members continually make relationship withdrawals that exceed relationship deposits, the reward/cost ratio tilts, and the partners may look for alternative relationships in which to invest. The deposits that we make in our relationship are what keep it from stagnating or deteriorating. Not only will you need to be proactive in your relationships, but you will also need to manage the relationship tensions that inevitably arise.

Understanding and Managing Dialectical Tensions in Relationships

Have you ever wanted two opposing things—at the same time—in your relationship? Have you and your partner ever struggled over competing wants and needs, like how much time was the right amount to spend together, what things should be kept private between you or shared with your friends and family, or whether to try something new? If so, you've experienced a relational dialectic. **Relational dialectics** are opposing forces or tensions that affect relationships and can never be fully eliminated. At any one time, one or both people in a relationship may be aware of these tensions. The challenge for relationship partners is managing the dialectics in ways that satisfy the needs of both partners.

A primary tension in relationships is the **dialectic of expression**, which is also known as the **openness–closedness** dialectic. It is the tension you feel at a specific point in time between sharing intimate ideas (being open with your partner) and the conflicting feelings of maintaining privacy (being closed). When getting to know each other, both Zeke and Madison disclosed quite a bit about themselves. But Zeke always told Madison more than she told him. Madison comes from an alcoholic family, so she has learned to keep secrets, making disclosure harder for her. In other words, the open quadrant of Zeke's Johari window in their relationship is quite large, whereas Madison's is smaller. As their relationship stabilized, Zeke continued to disclose but noticed that Madison seemed to be withdrawing and not sharing as much as he was. The fact that Zeke and Madison differed in their preferred levels of self-disclosure was one source of tension they needed to manage to sustain the relationship. But Zeke did not

Relational dialectics—the conflicting pulls or tensions that exist in relationships as well as within each individual in a relationship

Dialectic of expression—the tension we feel between sharing intimate thoughts with a partner and maintaining our privacy

Openness—the desire to share intimate ideas and feelings with your relationship partner

Closedness—the desire to maintain privacy

Dialectic of integration—the tension between the desire to be connected to your partner versus being independent from your partner

Connection—the desire to link your actions and decisions with those of your relationship partner

Autonomy—the desire to act and make decisions independent of your relationship partner

Dialectic of certainty—the tension between wanting your partner to behave in predictable ways versus wanting your partner to act in new and delightfully surprising ways

always want complete openness, feeling that at times it is appropriate to be closed or to refrain from self-disclosure with Madison. He sought both openness and closedness in this relationship. Madison, while wanting more closedness than Zeke, still wanted some openness. So, like Zeke, she experienced opposite forces occurring simultaneously in their relationship.

A second tension in relationships is the **dialectic of integration**, which is the tension we feel between our desire for **connection** or interdependence with our partner versus our need for **autonomy**, or separateness and independence of our partner. Imagine that Madison and Zeke have been best friends for about a year. At this point in their relationship, Zeke wants to spend most of his free time with Madison and enjoys talking with her before acting or making decisions, but Madison has begun to feel hemmed in. For example, she wants to spend some time hanging out with her roommates, her new boyfriend, or studying alone. At the same time, however, she doesn't want to hurt Zeke's feelings or ruin the closeness in their relationship. Although Zeke is at peace and may not recognize any tension between autonomy and connection in the relationship, Madison is feeling the conflict of wanting to be more autonomous but without jeopardizing her connection to Zeke. If Madison begins to act autonomously, she may relieve her own tension, yet she may create tension in the relationship.

The third primary relational tension is called the **dialectic of certainty**, which is tension between wanting your partner to behave in predictable ways versus wanting your partner to act in novel and delightfully surprising ways. People in relationships frequently feel tension between these competing desires. While Madison and Zeke know each other well, can predict much about each other, and have several routines in their relationship, they also want to be surprised and have new experiences with each other. Madison and Zeke may differ

How does this image illustrate the dialectic of integration?

in their needs for **novelty** and **predictability**. Zeke may wish that Madison would surprise him by proposing that they try something different ("Let's go parasailing!"), or he may shock Madison by spontaneously breaking into her favorite song in the middle of campus. At this point in their relationship, Madison may be comfortable operating by the routines they have established, and given her father's erratic behavior, she may appreciate that she can count on Zeke to behave in predictable ways. As a result, his spontaneous song may shock and embarrass her. Zeke may need more novelty at this moment, and eventually Madison may experience this as well. But to effectively sustain their relationship, they will need to adjust their behavior to relieve the tensions that arise between their needs for novelty and predictability in the relationship.

It is important to remember that dialectical tensions exist in all relationships, and they are ongoing and changing. Sometimes these dialectical tensions are active and in the foreground; at other times, they are not prominent and are in the background. Nevertheless, when these tensions are experienced, they change what is happening in the relationship (Wood, 2000).

Not only do dialectical tensions exist between relationship partners, but they also exist between pairs and the network of family and friends that surround them. The openness-closedness tension between a couple and their social network concerns what information about the relationship should be made known to others and what should be kept private. Madison and Zeke need to agree about and manage the tension surrounding how much of the particulars of their relationship they want to share with their friends and family. They may quickly agree to conceal that they had a brief sexual relationship before deciding they were not romantically attracted to each other, while freely disclosing their growing attachment to each other as friends. Relationship partners also feel integration tensions between their desire to include others in their time together versus their desire to be secluded, spending time alone as a couple. Zeke would like to spend more time with Madison without her boyfriend or other friends around, but Madison would like Zeke and her boyfriend to become friends, and for Zeke to find a girlfriend so that they could do things as a foursome. The couple may also feel a tension between being seen as predictable or conventional by others and being recognized for the novelty or uniqueness of their relationship. By having such a strong, platonic relationship, Zeke and Madison are somewhat unique within their social networks given that male–female friendships are usually romantic. However, they are also conventional because in their college student social networks, members of the opposite sex spend a lot of time together platonically.

After reading about dialectical tensions, you are probably asking yourself, "How can I cope with dialectical tensions in my relationships?" "How can I satisfy opposite needs at the same time?" Several scholars (Baxter & Montgomery, 1996; Wood, 2000) have studied how people actually manage the dialectical tensions in their relationships. People report using four strategies to manage these dialectics: temporal selection, topical segmentation, neutralization, and reframing.

Novelty—the desire for originality, freshness, and uniqueness in your partner's behavior or in your relationship

Predictability—the desire for consistency, reliability, and dependability in your partner's behavior or in your relationship

Temporal selection—the strategy of dealing with dialectical tensions by choosing one side of a dialectical opposition while ignoring the other for a period of time

Topical segmentation—the strategy of dealing with dialectical tensions by choosing certain areas in which to satisfy one side of a dialectical tension while choosing other areas to satisfy the opposite side

Neutralization—the strategy of dealing with dialectical tensions by compromising between the desires of those in the relationship

Reframing—the strategy of dealing with dialectical tensions by changing perceptions about the level of tension

**INTER-ACT WITH
SOCIAL MEDIA**

We often experience relational dialectics in our use of social media. What personal rules do you have for what you disclose or keep private about yourself and about your relationships when you are Tweeting, posting on Facebook, etc.? What do these rules tell you about your willingness to take risks?

1. Temporal selection is the strategy of dealing with dialectical tensions by choosing one side of a dialectical opposition while ignoring the other for a period of time. For example, perhaps you and a friend realize that you have spent too much time apart lately (autonomy), so you make a conscious decision to pursue connection. That is, you agree that over the next few months, you will make a point of spending more time together. You schedule many activities together to be more connected. Over time, however, if you feel that you are spending too much time together, you may find yourself canceling dates. Seesawing back and forth like this is one way to manage a relational dialectic.

2. Topical segmentation is the strategy of dealing with dialectical tensions by choosing certain areas in which to satisfy one side of a dialectical tension while choosing other areas to satisfy the opposite side. For instance, if you and your mother want more openness in your relationship, you may choose to be open about certain topics or aspects of life, such as feelings about school, work, or politics, but remain closed about your sex lives. This segmentation can satisfy both parties' needs for balance in the openness-closedness dialectic.

3. Neutralization is the strategy of dealing with dialectical tensions by compromising between the desires of those in a relationship. This strategy partially meets the needs of both people in the relationship but does not fully meet the needs of either. For example, a couple might pursue a moderate level of novelty and spontaneity in their lives, which satisfies them both. The degree of novelty in the relationship may be less than what one person would ideally want and more than what the other would normally desire, but they have reached a middle point comfortable to both.

4. Reframing is the strategy of dealing with dialectical tensions by changing perceptions about the level of tension. Reframing involves putting less emphasis on the dialectical contradiction, looking at your desires differently so that they no longer seem quite so contradictory. For instance, maybe you are uncomfortable because you perceive that you are more open and your partner is more closed. As a result, you think about how much you disclose to him and how little he discloses to you. You might even discuss this issue with your partner and begin to realize the times that you have held back (closedness) as well as the instances where he was open. After the conversation, you no longer see such a strong contradiction. You see yourselves as more similar than different on this dialectic. You have reframed your perception of the tension.

In most cases, when you are trying to sustain a relationship by managing dialectical tensions, it helps if you and your partner talk about the tensions that you are feeling and come to an agreement about how you will manage the dialectic going forward. By disclosing your anxiety and receiving your partner's feedback, you and your partner may be able to negotiate a new balance satisfying to you both. When tensions cannot be managed and/or when partners quit investing in the relationship, it will begin to decline and may eventually end.

Stage Four: Relationship Decline

Less well-developed relationships like those with acquaintances, casual friends, co-workers, and neighbors are more likely to easily devolve than are highly developed relationships (Parks, 2007). Yet any relationship can decline. As a relationship declines, interdependence, commitment, understanding and pre-dictability, trust, and disclosure all decrease. Several scholars have offered descriptive stage models of how relationships decline and end (Duck, 1987; Knapp, Vangelisti, & Caughlin, 2014), but there is little research to support any one model. Nevertheless, relationship decline is obviously a process that at its most basic level involves the following: one or both partners' recognizing that the relationship is somehow less satisfying than in the past; they make a successful attempt to repair the relationship; and/or they take a series of steps to disengage from the relationship that results in either a less intimate relationship or a com-plete break in, or end to, the relationship. Let's look at these processes.

Your relationships are like living things that need to be continually fed if they are to flourish. When they are neglected or conflict-laden, you or your part-ner eventually notice that the relationship has become dissatisfying—that the rewards you are receiving from the relationship are not worth the costs you're paying. This may be caused by unmet interpersonal needs, unresolved dialectical tensions, benign neglect, or by continual unresolved conflict (including nagging and fighting). At this point, there are three choices. First, you can ignore what you are feeling and hope that the relationship spontaneously improves. Perhaps it will, but more likely, it will not, since your partner will remain unaware of your dissatisfaction, or your partner will sense it but not really understand what is happening. Ignoring your dissatisfaction may be a temporary strategy, yet in the long run you will end up doing something else.

Second, you can decide to talk with your partner about your dissatisfaction. People tend to take this route when they have heavily invested in the relationship and don't have readily available alternative relationships that are promising. When someone who has been married for a long time and has small children feels dissatisfied with the marriage but doesn't have immediate romantic op-tions, he or she will probably opt for talking with his or her spouse. Choosing this option means that you honestly disclose what you think is causing your dissatisfaction. If your partner is receptive to your message, then the two of you may decide to work on your relationship and try to reestablish the level of inti-macy, trust, and closeness that you previously felt. Your conversations about your relationship may include discussions of how to better meet each other's in-terpersonal needs and resolve the dialectical tensions you are experiencing, as well as acknowledging and apologizing for trust violations and attempting to resolve other issues in the relationship.

For example, Danita and Faith had been best friends since childhood, shar-ing everything with each other and spending most Saturdays shopping and taking in a movie—that is, until Faith started going out with Troy. Then it seemed to Danita that Faith didn't need or have time for her. Over the last two months, Faith had cancelled their Saturday plans five times. But Danita, who didn't have many friends, wasn't willing to let her relationship with Faith deteriorate, so she sent Faith an email asking to see her to talk about their relationship. When they met, Danita was careful to just describe what she perceived to be happening, indicating that although she was happy that Faith was with Troy, Danita missed their talks and time together. Faith acknowledged that she had been taking Danita for granted. She explained that Saturdays were the only day Troy had off work and that she wanted to spend time with him but didn't want to lose her great relationship with Danita, and she certainly didn't want to have to choose between them. After a lengthy conversation, they agreed to move their shopping day to Sunday afternoon, and Faith also suggested that Danita join Troy and her for coffee tomorrow.

At times a moderator for these conversations can be useful. Impartial outsiders and professional counselors can offer a different perspective, helping partners listen and respond to what is being said. Many relationships can be repaired when both partners decide to reinvest in them.

Third, one or both partners may begin consciously disengaging from the relationship. Disengaging partners may feel less connected to the other, share fewer activities, and communicate less frequently. They may begin to emphasize the other's faults and downplay virtues. Some subjects (which once inspired deep, private, and frequent communication) may become off-limits or sources of conflict. As the relationship begins to be characterized by more touchy subjects and more unresolved conflicts, partners become increasingly defensive and less able to foster a positive communication climate. Statements such as "I don't want to talk about it anymore (or right now)," or "Stop bugging me," become more frequent. For example, if roommates Walt and Mark have been arguing about the cleanliness of their room, frequency of visitors, and unpaid personal loans, they may begin to avoid any discussion of these subjects.

As the relationship continues to deteriorate, people disengage from each other or drift apart. They become less willing to sacrifice for or forgive each other. Their communication patterns change from a pattern of sharing ideas and feelings to a pattern of mostly small talk and other "safe" communication, and finally to a pattern of no significant interaction at all. It may seem strange that people who once had so much to share find themselves with nothing to talk about. They may begin to avoid each other altogether and seek out other people with whom to share interests and activities. They may depend less on each other and more on other people for favors and support. Hostility need not be present; rather, the overriding emotional tone is usually indifference.

Sometimes, rather than end their relationship, partners may agree to a **relationship transformation**, where they continue to interact and influence a partner but in a different type of relationship. Romantic relationships may transform into friendships; best friends may become casual friends. Even people who end their marriage through divorce may continue on friendly terms or develop a type of "business" relationship that coordinates child-rearing practices and expenses (Parks, 2007). For example, R. J. and Liz are divorced but work with a counselor to develop a functional joint-custody parenting relationship, which

Relationship transformation—continuing to interact and influence a partner through a different type of relationship after one type of relationship has ended allows them to be cordial, make joint decisions about the children, and even share important events with them. Likewise, although arguing and mistrust damaged the intimate relationship of former roommates Whitney and Madeleine, who decided to no longer share an apartment, they may continue to talk when they run into each other on campus.

When a relationship can't be maintained at a less developed level, it ends. A relationship has ended when the people no longer interact with each other at all. People give many reasons for terminating relationships, including poor communication, lack of fulfillment, differing lifestyles and interests, rejection, outside interference, absence of rewards, and boredom (Cupach & Metts, 1986). Unfortunately, many people who want a relationship to end don't want to be seen as the person who makes the first move. These people are likely to use strategies of manipulation, withdrawal, and avoidance (Baxter, 1982). Misguided and inappropriate, manipulation involves being indirect and failing to take any responsibility for ending the relationship. Manipulators may purposely sabotage the relationship in the hope that the other person will break it off. Withdrawal and avoidance, also less-than-competent ways of ending relationships, involve taking a passive approach, which leads to a slow and often painful death of a relationship.

The most competent way to end a relationship is to be direct, open, and honest. It is important to clearly state your wish to end the relationship while being respectful and sensitive to the resulting emotions. If two people have had a satisfying and close relationship, they behave ethically by being forthright and fair about communicating during its final stage. Whitney and Madeleine, mentioned above, may have decided separately that their friendship has reached an end and that they both want to room with different people next year. As effective communicators, they should discuss this sensitive topic with each other without blame or manipulation, acknowledge that their relationship is less close than it once was, and agree perhaps to move in with new roommates the following year.

While we have discussed these stages in a sequential order, it is important to remember that over their lifespans many relationships cycle back and forth between stages, transforming themselves through the messages that partners exchange.

Self-Disclosure and Privacy in Relationships

Central to how our relationships develop and decline are the decisions we make to disclose things to our partner or to keep them private. Earlier in the chapter, we learned that self-disclosure varies in relationships, and contributes to relationship development. We've also seen that maintaining relationships requires management of the openness-closedness dialectic. In this section, we explore the topics of self-disclosure and privacy in more detail, with an emphasis on becoming more skillful at communicating about our own personal information and that of our relationship partners.

Social penetration theory—the premise that self-disclosure is integral to all stages of relationships, but the nature and type of self-disclosure change over time, as people move from being strangers to being intimates

Generally, our self-disclosures increase in frequency, breadth, and depth as we move from being strangers to intimates. According to the **social penetration theory** of self-disclosure and relationship development (Altman & Taylor, 1973), we can think of personalities as being like onions. On the outside are the public layers that contain factual information like your major, where you grew up, how you like your steak cooked, etc. Deeper in the onion of your personality are the layers of your inner self that house your attitudes, beliefs, and feelings. Finally, we all have an inner core that consists of our values, deep emotions, and self-concept. When we meet someone, our initial conversations expose the public layers of our personality. If our disclosures are reciprocated, we quickly disclose this outer layer. People who know us at this level are our long-term acquaintances. Most of our relationships remain at this level. As we begin to trust our partners, we will allow them to penetrate our outer layers and begin to share our inner self. During this time, our disclosures become somewhat deeper and riskier, and we make them less frequently as we gauge the trustworthiness of our partners. People with whom we share this type of information become our casual friends. Few relationships ever go past this point. But if we trust our partners and choose to disclose private and very personal things, we vastly increase the depth of our disclosures and share our inner core. When these types of disclosure are reciprocated, the relationship becomes intimate. We develop emotional attachments, and if partners are sexually attracted to one another, the relationship may become physical. Although truly intimate relationships are rare, they also tend to be deeply meaningful and stable.

Once relationships are established, we do not continue moving toward ever-greater intimacy. Instead, influenced by the openness-closedness dialectic, relationship partners tend to cycle between periods of significant disclosure, and periods in which less information is shared. Reciprocation also tends to be less immediate in established relationships, because partners don't need to match each other's disclosures in order to show liking and trust. Instead, one partner can disclose when they have information to share, knowing that the other partner will be able to disclose in the future.

Although self-disclosure is critical to relationship development, privacy also affects the development and success of relationships. **Privacy** is withholding confidential or secret information to enhance one's autonomy and/or minimize vulnerability. The concept of privacy rests on the assumption that people *own* their personal information and have the right to control it by determining whether that information may be communicated to others (Petronio & Durham, 2015). Individuals may choose privacy over disclosure for many legitimate reasons, including protecting another person's feelings, avoiding unnecessary conflict, being sensitive to the face needs of another person, and protecting a relationship. In newer relationships, people may manage their privacy to control the pace at which a relationship develops. If a casual dating relationship seems to be moving too quickly toward greater emotional attachment, the relational partners may, for a certain period of time, avoid communicating on topics such as the state of the relationship, expectations of each

Privacy—withholding confidential or secret information to enhance autonomy or minimize vulnerability

other in the relationship, prior romantic relationships, and extra-relationship activity (Knobloch & Carpenter-Theune, 2004).

Self-disclosure and privacy connect in important ways when people share information from the inner layers of their "onions." For example, suppose Jim, while telling his new girlfriend Bella about his childhood, reveals that he was a bed-wetter until he was in the sixth grade. This was something that only his parents knew until he told Bella. Jim has engaged in self-disclosure to Bella because he has revealed information about himself. By disclosing, he has made Bella a co-owner of this private information. **Information co-owners** are people who share private information because one person has shared it with the other (or because both persons have shared the same experience).

Later, Jim and Bella attend a party. Over drinks, people begin sharing their childhood secrets, and Bella comments playfully that Jim used to be a bed-wetter. While Bella is disclosing information, it is not *self*-disclosure, because she is disclosing Jim's private information, not her own. Jim feels embarrassed and betrayed because Bella has breached his privacy, and is cold to Bella for the rest of the evening. Bella is at first confused, then hurt, and finally becomes angry because she didn't realize that Jim considered the information highly private, and Jim didn't say that she couldn't share the information. Because neither Bella nor Jim thought to engage in **boundary management**, or discussion of who else is allowed to co-own the information, they are experiencing **boundary turbulence**, or interpersonal difficulty associated with violation of a privacy boundary. These kinds of problems can arise when two (or more) people have differences in their rules for managing disclosure and privacy, and haven't made the necessary effort to understand each other's rules, or negotiate new rules that are comfortable for both (Petronio & Durham, 2015).

The terms *information co-owner, boundary management*, and *boundary turbulence* come from **communication privacy management (CPM) theory**, which provides a framework for understanding the decision-making processes people use to manage private information. CPM theory says we each have our own rules about when to disclose or conceal personal information about ourselves and others. These rules are designed to help us maximize the benefits of disclosure, while minimizing risks (Petronio & Durham, 2015). Although the rules are individual and vary from person to person, they are also influenced by culture, gender, motivation, and context. Let's see how these four factors may have helped create Bella's and Jim's personal rules.

1. Culture. Our rules about privacy and disclosure are influenced by how our culture values privacy. In some cultures, a person's privacy is highly respected, and people who choose to disclose information generally regarded as confidential violate cultural norms. Members of these cultures are less likely to disclose personal information to anyone but

Information co-owners—people who share private information because one person has shared it with the other, or both have shared the same experience

Boundary management—discussion of who is allowed to co-own private information

Boundary turbulence—interpersonal difficulty associated with violation of a privacy boundary

Communication privacy management (CPM) theory—a framework for understanding the decision-making processes people use to manage private information

When you share private information you run the risk of your partner sharing it with others. Have you ever had someone disclose information you had shared but thought would be held in private? How did you handle this breach of confidentiality? What was the long-term effect on your relationship?

close intimates. As you might expect, individualistic cultures value privacy more than collectivist cultures do. For instance, British and German people are less inclined to disclose and more likely to be protective of their privacy. The United States is an individualistic culture where privacy is also valued, yet it is also less formal than other individualistic cultures (Samovar & Porter, 2001, p. 82). As a result, Americans tend to disclose more about themselves than people from many other individualistic cultures, especially individualistic European cultures. If Bella and Jim are from cultures that place different values on privacy, this may help explain why she thought it was all right to share Jim's bed-wetting, but he did not. Families can also develop their own subcultures with regard to privacy. Because Jim's parents did not share the information with others, Jim learned that bed-wetting was viewed as highly private information within his family culture.

2. Gender. Men and women who strongly identify as masculine or feminine are likely to use rules for disclosure and privacy that correspond to sex-role expectations. The expectation for men throughout much of the world includes being "strong and silent" and competitive characteristics. Consequently, men may keep their feelings to themselves and avoid disclosing private information that might be used against them in a competitive situation. For example, if Horst sees himself as very masculine or macho, he probably won't disclose that as a child he studied ballet, fearing that if he discloses this event from his past, he will be ridiculed. The expectation for women throughout much of the world is that women are nurturing and sensitive. Therefore, women who identify with these characteristics are more likely to disclose personal information. If Bella considers herself very feminine, she may easily share her innermost feelings or disclose information about someone else as a way of strengthening her self-image and relationships with others, not realizing that Jim does not view disclosure in the same way. People whose identities are not strongly rooted in gender roles are less likely to ground their disclosure-privacy rules in gendered expectations.

3. Motivation. People differ in how eager they are to disclose to someone (Petronio & Durham, 2015). Motivation to disclose or to maintain privacy is influenced by our risk–benefit analysis. In **risk–benefit analysis**, we weigh what advantages we might gain by disclosing private information or maintaining private information against the dangers. Figure 6.3 lists the benefits and risks of both disclosure and privacy. Jim viewed disclosure of his childhood bed-wetting as embarrassing and creating vulnerability for himself, so it was risky for him. Sharing the information with Bella initially helped him build his relationship with her,

Risk–benefit analysis—weighing advantages and disadvantages (of disclosing private information)

Risks of Disclosure	Risks of Privacy	Benefits of Disclosure	Benefits of Privacy
loss of control	social isolation	building relationships	control
vulnerability	being misunderstood by others	coping with stress	independence
embarrassment		emotional or psychological relief	

FIGURE 6.3   Risks and Benefits of Disclosure and Managing Privacy

through reciprocal disclosure of their childhood experiences. Unfortunately, due to Bella's violation of his unstated private rules, he now feels the embarrassment and vulnerability even more acutely, along with the loss of control over this information. Bella did not view Jim's disclosure as being nearly so risky as Jim did, which led to her decision to share it.

4. Context. Privacy and disclosure rules, like other communication rules, are influenced by the circumstances in which people find themselves. For Bella, the party context in which others were sharing their childhood secrets contributed to her feeling that it was acceptable to share Jim's bed-wetting. You may disclose private information to a therapist or counselor to help you cope with a difficult situation. Likewise, in times of crisis, you may need to adjust your need for privacy and open up to people to whom you would not normally disclose. Disclosure during times of stress contributes to physical and mental health (Smyth et al., 2012). Circumstances related to a relationship sometimes influence people to disregard others' privacy rules. If, for example, Sal tells Greg that he's extremely depressed and has been thinking about dying, Greg may tell one or two of Sal's close friends about this disclosure to get their help dealing with this potentially dangerous situation.

Bella and Jim's privacy boundary turbulence was created when different privacy rules, influenced by culture, gender, motivation, and context, led Bella to share Jim's childhood secret. Understandable as this may be, damage has been done to their relationship. How could this have been avoided? The following guidelines for self-disclosure and privacy are designed to help you manage information in ways that is effective and appropriate for you and your relationships.

Guidelines for Self-Disclosure

While self-disclosure helps us develop our relationships, indiscriminate self-disclosure can be damaging to people and relationships. So it's important to make appropriate disclosures. The following guidelines can help you decide when and what to disclose.

1. Self-disclose the kind of information that you want others to disclose to you. Since we expect self-disclosures to be reciprocated, you should only share the type of information that you would like others to share with you. For example, if you want to know about your partner's previous romantic partners, you should be willing to talk about yours.

2. Self-disclose information appropriate for the type of relationship you have. Disclosures about fears, loves, and other deep or intimate matters are most appropriate in close, well-established relationships. When people disclose deep secrets to acquaintances, they are engaging in potentially threatening behavior. Making such disclosures before a bond of trust is established risks alienating the other person. Moreover, people are often embarrassed by and hostile toward others who saddle them with personal information in an effort to establish a relationship where none exists.

3. Self-disclose more intimate information only when you believe the disclosure represents an acceptable risk. There is always some risk involved

INTER-ACT WITH
SOCIAL MEDIA

Scan your Facebook newsfeed or Twitter feed throughout the course of your day. Look at the information that your friends and followers are sharing with others. Do they appear to be following the guidelines for self-disclosure and privacy explained in this chapter? As you reflect on your use of social media, have you been following these guidelines?

in disclosing, but as you gain trust in another person, you perceive that the disclosure of more revealing information is less likely to have negative consequences. We might expect this to occur in the context of an ongoing relationship, yet people sometimes inappropriately disclose very personal information to strangers because they perceive the disclosure to be safe since they will never see the person again.

4. Be sensitive to your partner's ability to absorb your disclosure. Because receiving self-disclosure from a partner can be as threatening as making the disclosure, be sensitive to your partner's capacity to handle what you might disclose. This means that you should avoid dumping deep and potentially disturbing disclosures without first considering your partner and even asking if your partner is willing to hear what you want to reveal. For example, B.J., who had fathered a child when he was in high school, had been seeing Julia for a while and wanted to tell her about his son. But he didn't know if Julia could accept knowing this about him and how that would affect their promising relationship. So, one evening after dinner, he said, "Julia, there is something that happened when I was in high school that is important to me, but that you may not like. I'd like to share it with you. Are you willing to hear it?"

5. Continue intimate self-disclosure only when it is reciprocated. We expect a kind of equity in self-disclosure. When it is apparent that self-disclosure is not being returned, you should not continue to self-disclose. Lack of reciprocation generally suggests that your partner does not feel that the relationship is intimate enough for the type of disclosures you are making.

Guidelines for Privacy

Just as indiscriminate self-disclosure can be damaging to people and relationships, so can our insensitivity to important privacy concerns. The following guidelines can help you honor the privacy needs of others and protect your privacy as well.

1. Recognize that others' rules for privacy may be different from your own. As we've seen, there are many factors that influence our individual rules for privacy. If you assume that others share your rules, you are likely to share others' information when you shouldn't—or have yours shared when you want it to remain private.

2. Treat co-ownership of information as a privilege, not a right or opportunity. No matter how close your relationship to another person, there can still be things they want to keep to themselves, and a lot of information they don't want shared outside your relationship. If you act as though you are entitled to someone else's private information, or seek their information to use for your own benefit, you are likely to damage the relationship.

3. Respect others' stated (and implied) privacy boundaries. When someone tells you not to share information, don't. In addition, when someone acts as though the disclosure is risky, ask before sharing. The only time to consider violating someone else's privacy boundaries is when the disclosure indicates the intention to harm himself or herself or someone else.

It was like he could read my mind.

Cartoonstock www.Cartoonstock.com

4. Ask to determine others' privacy boundaries. If you have any uncertainty about whether another person's private information can be shared, you should ask before you do.

5. Communicate your personal privacy boundaries. When you are sharing private information with another person and want to control further co-ownership of that information, you need to state your wishes directly. "Please keep this information to yourself." Or "I don't mind if you talk to X about this, but no one else, please." Keep in mind that communicating your privacy boundaries does not guarantee they will be respected, so you still shouldn't disclose unless you believe you can trust the recipient of your disclosure to do as you ask.

When other people express interest in your private information, but you don't want to share it, you can communicate your boundaries in one of several ways. One option is to share the level of information you are willing to share. For example, if someone is asking you how much money you make, you might say "I'm solidly middle-class," or "I'm grateful to have a comfortable living." Many people will recognize that you haven't been more specific because you don't want to be, and that they have trespassed on your privacy.

A second option is to use the skill of describing feelings that is discussed in Chapter 4 to share how efforts to invade your privacy make you feel. When used to protect your private information, a general form of this message might be, "When you ask me about [private topic], I feel [emotion] and [emotion], because I [have the following reason for not wanting to talk about it]." So if a friend is pumping you for information about whether you are sexually intimate with your boyfriend or girlfriend, you may say, "When you ask me about how sexually active we are, I become annoyed with you. I believe that relationship intimacies are private, and while I value our friendship, I won't be talking with you about this."

A third option is to directly communicate your privacy boundary. When you communicate privacy boundaries, you politely tell your partner your policy about disclosing a particular type of information. This approach has the advantage of clarifying exactly what the boundary is, and why you enforce it. To communicate a boundary: (1) identify the personal privacy policy that guides your decision not to share the information; (2) preface your boundary statement with an apology or some other statement that helps your partner save face; (3) make an "I" statement that politely indicates your desire to keep the information private; and (4) briefly explain your privacy policy. For example, "Mom, I know that you love me and are excited to have grandchildren, and I don't want to hurt you. But when you continually pester us about when we are going to have children, you make both of us uncomfortable. Emmett and I decided that we are not going to discuss our plans for children with our family and friends. I hope I can count on you to respect this decision."

6. Repair boundary turbulence with sincere apologies and assurances of future care with private information. Violating a relationship partner's privacy boundaries damages trust, which in turn will affect intimacy and future self-disclosure. Repairing this kind of relational damage requires a sincere apology, assuring your partner that you will treat future disclosures with greater care.

SKILL BUILDER ▶ COMMUNICATING A PERSONAL BOUNDARY

SKILL	USE	STEPS	EXAMPLE
Politely tell someone your policy regarding disclosing a particular type of information	To help others understand your policy about the privacy of certain information.	1. Identify your privacy policy that guides your decision. 2. Preface your boundary statement with an apology or some other statement that helps your partner save face. 3. Form a brief "I" message that diplomatically informs the person that you wish to keep that information private. 4. Briefly explain your privacy policy.	"Paul, I know that you are curious about how much money I make. While a lot of people are okay with sharing salary data, I'm not. It's not you, I just don't tell anyone what I make. I hope you understand."

If the violation was severe in your partner's eyes, you should expect that it could take a lot of time and repeated demonstrations of trustworthiness before your partner feels comfortable revealing private information again. (Skills for repairing relationships are discussed in more detail in Chapter 12.) Of course, the best way to "repair" boundary turbulence is to avoid causing it in the first place.

THE SOCIAL MEDIA FACTOR

Public and Private Online

Communication technologies that allow us to carry on private conversations in public spaces have blurred the line between private and public communication (Gumpert & Drucker, 2007). Scholars describe us as living in a world of **"collapsed contexts"** (Baym & boyd, 2012) in which public and private are much less separate than they once were. How many times in the last few days have you overheard a person's "private" cell phone conversation? Engrossed in their conversations, these people may not recognize that they are revealing private information to complete strangers as well as to the person on the other end of the phone. Often, these conversations are annoying to bystanders, who feel uncomfortable hearing information they would not ordinarily hear. It is also possible that bystanders could use your private information to do harm (e.g., learning gossip that could get back to people who know you, or finding out where you live in order to steal from you). Do you want to assume these

Collapsed contexts—the merging of public and private contexts as a consequence of social media

risks of sharing your private information with strangers? If not, the next time you need to have a private cell phone conversation, ask the person on the other end if others are within earshot. If so, arrange the call for a time when both of you can be alone.

Indeed, as communication technologies have changed when and where we share private information, social media have also changed *what* information we view as private and public. Did you or someone you know keep a paper diary growing up? Chances are, these personal thoughts were kept under lock and key and tucked under a mattress or in a dresser drawer. You know that reading another person's diary is considered taboo because diaries protect the private information we ink onto the pages. Today, however, digital diaries— often in the form of blogs—are purposely made accessible to friends, acquaintances, and thousands of strangers online. Posts on Facebook and other social media sites go out to hundreds, sometimes thousands, of "friends." You probably know some people who ignore the distinction between public and private altogether. These over-sharers write absolutely everything they think on Facebook, post pictures of every meal on Instagram, and Snapchat while in the bathroom. They don't seem to realize that most of us are thinking "TMI!" (too much information!). In these collapsed contexts, how can we manage our private information appropriately?

How does this woman's cell phone use illustrate "collapsed contexts"?

Effective communicators develop and follow rules of social media engagement that protect themselves and others. In one study (Bryant & Marmo, 2012), researchers asked users to describe their rules for Facebook use, and they compiled a list of best practices, including: (1) Share information with close friends before posting it on Facebook. (2) Do not confront anyone using a public component of Facebook. (3) Only comment on a friend's photos if you are actually friends with them offline. And (4) if a friend deletes or untags a photo or post, do not repost it. It is also important to think about potential audiences beyond those you have chosen as friends. Potential employers, enemies, or even identity

A QUESTION OF ETHICS ▶ WHAT WOULD YOU DO?

Grant and Amy have been in a committed relationship for two years. They maintain their relationship by spending almost all their free time together and having a common circle of friends. They are each other's best friends, share many hobbies and interests, and confide in each other on virtually all topics. A few months ago, Grant met Devon online through Facebook because of a common childhood friend. They began to exchange messages on Facebook and text each other on a daily basis. Occasionally, they would Skype or talk on the phone. Recently, when Devon was in town, they met at Starbucks for coffee and ended up spending the day together. Their relationship seems to be developing such that they share personal information, connect with each other easily, interact frequently, and expect the relationship to continue. Amy and Devon do not know about each other.

FOR CONSIDERATION:
1. What, if any, ethical principles is Grant violating?
2. What is likely to happen if Amy and Devon find out about each other?
3. What should Grant do?

thieves can often access writings, photos, videos, and other information that you post online. In sum, always consider the potential risks that accompany the rewards of disclosing private information through social media.

Summary

A relationship exists when two people are interdependent. Communication serves constitutive, instrumental, and indexical functions in relationships. We can describe relationships in several ways: intimate or distant, voluntary or involuntary, platonic or romantic. Relationships vary on five dimensions: interdependence, commitment, understanding and predictability, trust, and self-disclosure. The Johari window is a visual framework for understanding how self-disclosure and feedback work together in a relationship.

Relationship life cycles include beginning, developing, sustaining, and perhaps deteriorating and ending stages. Relationship stage changes are marked by turning points. Beginning relationships pass through three phases: an entry phase when we exclude people we don't like, a personal phase when we use midlevel disclosures to probe and assess our compatibility, and an exit phase when partners determine whether to invest in developing the relationship. We choose to develop relationships with people who can meet our interpersonal needs for inclusion, affection, and control and with whom social exchanges are more beneficial than costly, and are better than our other options. We sustain relationships by continuing to invest in them through prosocial behavior; by observing ceremonial occasions; by spending time together; by conversing frequently about day-to-day and intimate topics; by verbally and nonverbally reassuring our partners of our continuing affection, discretion, and trustworthiness; and by successfully managing relationship dialectics. Relational dialectics are the conflicting pulls that exist in a relationship; for example, the tugs between openness and closedness, autonomy and connection, and novelty and predictability. We can manage these tensions through temporal selection, topical segmentation, neutralization, and reframing. Relationships decline and perhaps end when one or both partners, recognizing that the relationship is less satisfying, unsuccessfully attempt to repair the relationship or begin to disengage from the relationship, which results in either its transformation or its termination. At all times, communication skills or lack of communication skills affect how relationships move through their life cycle.

Relationship partners have to manage both self-disclosure and privacy. Social penetration theory holds that self-disclosure is integral to all stages of relationships but that the nature and type of self-disclosure change over time. Maintaining privacy is withholding confidential or secret information to enhance autonomy and/or minimize vulnerability. Communication privacy management theory provides a framework for understanding the decision-making processes people use to manage private information. Following guidelines for self-disclosure and privacy will help reduce negative consequences from inappropriate self-disclosure and privacy violations. When sharing information on cell phones and social media, it is essential to remember your audience and consider the risks as well as the benefits of disclosure.

CHAPTER RESOURCES

Key Words

Flashcards for all of these key terms are available on the *Inter-Act* website.

Affection need, pp. 174
Autonomy, pp. 178
Blind pane, pp. 169
Boundary management, pp. 185
Boundary turbulence, pp. 185
Closedness, pp. 177
Collapsed contexts, pp. 190
Commitment, pp. 166
Communication privacy management theory, pp. 185
Connection, pp. 178
Constitutive function, pp. 163
Control need, pp. 174
Dialectic of certainty, pp. 178
Dialectic of expression, pp. 177
Dialectic of integration, pp. 178
Feedback, pp. 168
Inclusion need, pp. 173

Indexical function, pp. 164
Information co-owners, pp. 185
Instrumental function, pp. 164
Interdependence, pp. 166
Interpersonal needs theory, pp. 173
Interpersonal trust, pp. 167
Involuntary relationship, pp. 166
Johari window, pp. 168
Life cycle, pp. 169
Neutralization, pp. 180
Novelty, pp. 179
Openness, pp. 177
Open pane, pp. 168
Platonic relationship, pp. 165
Predictability, pp. 179
Predicted outcome value theory, pp. 170
Privacy, pp. 184
Reframing, pp. 180

Relational dialectics, pp. 177
Relationship, pp. 162
Relationship costs, pp. 174
Relationship rewards, pp. 174
Relationship transformation, pp. 182
Risk–benefit analysis, pp. 186
Romantic relationship, pp. 166
Secret pane, pp. 168
Self-disclosure, pp. 168
Social exchange theory, pp. 174
Social penetration theory, pp. 184
Temporal selection, pp. 180
Topical segmentation, pp. 180
Turning points, pp. 169
Understanding and predictability, pp. 166
Unknown pane, pp. 169
Voluntary relationship, pp. 166

Analyze and Apply

The following activities challenge you to demonstrate your mastery of the concepts, theories, and frameworks in this chapter by using them to explain what is happening in a specific situation.

6.1 Rewind/Rewrite
Now that you have read the chapter, hit "rewind" on the opening dialogue between Yvonne and Alex, and answer the following questions.

a. Use concepts from the chapter to explain why Yvonne became upset when she learned that Wendy was thinking of transferring to another college, and why Wendy was upset with Alex for sharing this information. The concepts of intimacy, understanding and predictability, self-disclosure, co-ownership, and privacy boundary may be especially useful.

b. Rewrite the dialogue between Yvonne and Alex so that Alex doesn't end up in trouble with Wendy. Alternatively, create a dialogue between Wendy and

Alex that leaves Alex clearer about what she can and shouldn't share with Yvonne.

c. Assume that Wendy still feels close to Yvonne, and just didn't want to upset her by talking about the transfer until she made a decision. How could she have handled this situation more effectively? How can she improve things now? If Wendy didn't disclose because she no longer feels as close to Yvonne, is there anything she should have done differently, or can do to improve the situation?

6.2 Identifying Personal Self-Disclosure Guidelines

The following exercise will help you recognize the types of self-disclosures you consider risky. Label each of the following information as **L** (low risk), meaning you believe that it is appropriate to disclose this information to almost any person; **M** (moderate risk), meaning that you believe this information is appropriate to disclose to people you know fairly well and consider friends; or **H** (high risk), meaning that you would disclose such information only to the few friends you trust deeply and to your most intimate friends; or **X** (unacceptable risk), meaning that you would not disclose this information to anyone.

_____ a. Your hobbies or how you like to spend your free time.
_____ b. Your music likes and dislikes.
_____ c. Your educational background and your feelings about it.
_____ d. Your views on current political issues, including your opinion on the president.
_____ e. Your personal religious beliefs and the nature of your religious participation.
_____ f. Your habits and reactions that bother you.
_____ g. Your accomplishments and personal characteristics in which you take pride.
_____ h. Your most embarrassing moment recounted in detail.
_____ i. Your life's unhappiest moment.
_____ j. Your life's happiest day.
_____ k. Your deepest regret.
_____ l. Your fondest wish and biggest dream.
_____ m. Your views on an ideal marriage.
_____ n. Your physical fitness routine.
_____ o. Your physical features that make you proudest.
_____ p. Your physical features that most displease you.
_____ q. Your most resented person and why you feel as you do.
_____ r. Your use/abuse of alcohol, drugs, gambling, or sex.
_____ s. Your opinions on "hooking up" and friends-with-benefits relationships.
_____ t. Your personal hook-up and friend-with-benefits experiences.

Review your responses. What do you conclude about your willingness to disclose? Write a set of personal self-disclosure guidelines based on what you have learned about yourself.

6.3 Relationship Development

Describe one of your relationships that has not progressed beyond an acquaintanceship even though you have known the person for a long time. Use the concepts in this chapter to explain why this relationship has not developed.

6.4 Ending Relationships

Think about one of your relationships that ended badly. Considering what you have learned about relationship endings, how would you change the way that relationship ended if you could end it again? Write a script of the key parts of the final conversation you would like to have had.

Skill Practice

Skill practice activities give you the chance to rehearse a new skill by responding to hypothetical or real situations. Additional skill practice activities are available at the companion website.

6.5 Communicating Personal Boundaries

Review the "Communicating a Personal Boundary Skill Builder" before beginning this activity. Write a well-phrased response for each of the following situations.

a. *In your line of work, almost everything about what you do has to be kept confidential, or you could lose your position. A new acquaintance asks you a specific question about your work that you're not allowed to answer.*

   You say:

b. *Your spouse has a serious but invisible medical condition and prefers that no one else know. Talking to your child's teacher, you accidentally let it slip that you had to go to a doctor's appointment with your spouse. The teacher innocently asks about your spouse's health.*

   You say:

c. *A friend of yours went to a prestigious college as a freshman, but ran into academic trouble and was expelled after making the poor choice to cheat. She is at home working and preparing to apply to another school, and has asked you not to tell people why she left college. One of your mutual friends keeps bugging you for information.*

   You say:

d. *One of your co-workers wants to know more about the details of your day-to-day life than you think is necessary (where you do your shopping, what television shows you watch, etc.).*

   You say:

e. *You and your spouse have been trying to get pregnant, and on the advice of your doctor, are now thinking about in vitro fertilization or adoption. Your mother has religious objections to IVF, and will be overly anxious about adoption, so you do not want to talk with her about these choices. She keeps asking pointed questions about when you and your spouse are going to "give her a grandbaby."*

   You say:

Communication Improvement Plan: Relationships

Relationships are developed through self-disclosure and feedback. Do you have problems either disclosing personal information or providing your relationship partner with feedback? Using the interpersonal communication skills you have studied in the course, write a communication improvement plan. You can find a communication improvement plan worksheet on our website at www.oup.com/us/verderber.

LISTENING EFFECTIVELY

Lucy, Ryanne, Cecelia, and Amy recently joined a student service organization. Leaving a meeting about an upcoming dance-fundraiser, the four women were discussing their responsibilities.

"I can't believe the event is only two weeks away!" exclaimed Lucy nervously. "I think we should have started planning sooner. How many people are we supposed to get to attend? Aren't you guys worried about this?" she asked, looking closely at her friends.

Ryanne shrugged. "Yeah, so the whole meeting I was trying to figure out the pricing. With $750 to rent the barn and $350 for the deejay, and that doesn't include the decorations, we're going to have to get a LOT of people to come. And buy food. Did they even talk about food?"

Cecelia nodded vigorously. "Yeah, I'm not sure this event is really going to make money. The committee seemed so disorganized. Like, they weren't sure if the DJ was $350 or $400. And then the one with the really curly hair—what's her name? I can't remember—said we would have pizza, but then Elise was talking about wanting tacos."

"Yeah, and they all seemed so stressed, how are we going to—" Lucy started, but was cut off by Amy, who spoke with an exasperated tone.

"Look, the point is that we have to do our jobs, not whine about them. Ryanne, you and I are on decorations, so let's you and I get that figured out. Cecelia and Lucy, you're doing the Facebook announcement, right?

197

(Continued)

Ryanne and Cecelia looked startled, and Lucy looked hurt. "Amy," Ryanne said, "you're not listening. I don't want to start anything until I understand what the budget is."

"Not listening?" exclaimed Amy. "I'm listening … but we don't have time to get hung up on details!"

WHAT YOU SHOULD BE ABLE TO EXPLAIN AFTER YOU HAVE STUDIED THIS CHAPTER:

▶ The definition of listening

▶ The challenges to effective listening

▶ The personal styles of listening

▶ Listening apprehension

▶ The dual approaches we use when we listen

▶ The processes we use when we actively listen, and ways to improve them

▶ Principles guiding effective digital listening

WHAT YOU SHOULD BE ABLE TO DO AFTER YOU HAVE STUDIED THIS CHAPTER:

▶ Attend, understand, remember, evaluate, and respond more effectively

▶ Ask questions to clarify understanding

▶ Paraphrase a message to demonstrate what you have understood

Listening is a fundamental communication activity. How well we listen affects the quality of our conversations and shapes the course of our relationships (Halone & Pecchioni, 2001). In fact, listening creates reality. We listen and create reality based on what we hear in each moment (Ellinor & Gerard, 1998). If we are poor listeners, the personal reality we create may be very different from the one that others are trying to help us understand.

Of the basic communication skills (reading, writing, speaking, and listening), we use listening the most. What is listening? According to the International Listening Association, **listening** is the process of receiving, constructing meaning from, and responding to spoken and/or nonverbal messages.

According to one study, from 42 to 60 percent (or more) of communication time is spent listening. This percentage varied with the occupation of the listener, whether they were students, managerial trainees, doctors, counselors, lawyers, or nurses (Purdy, 1996). Unfortunately, after 48 hours, many listeners can remember only about 25 percent of what they heard (Steil, Barker, & Watson, 1983). And listeners who heard the same message may remember different things. Considering the importance of listening, it is unfortunate that we don't spend more time trying to understand and improve this important skill. To that end, this chapter is devoted to listening. We begin our study by looking at three challenges that make it difficult for us to effectively listen. Then we describe each of the steps in the active listening process (attending, understanding, remembering,

Listening—the process of receiving, constructing meaning from, and responding to spoken and/or nonverbal messages

What style of listening do you think is taking place in this conversation?

critically evaluating, and responding) and present guidelines and skills that can help you improve your ability to listen at each.

Challenges to Effective Listening

Even before we hear a message, three things can affect how we listen to it: our personal style of listening, our level of listening apprehension, and which of the dual processes of listening we adopt in a specific situation.

Personal Styles of Listening

Most often when we listen, we do so based on our personal habits or style. Your **listening style** is your favored but usually unconscious approach to attending to others' messages (Watson, Barker, & Weaver, 1995). It reflects your preferences, attitudes, and predispositions about the how, where, when, who, and what of receiving messages (Sargent & Weaver, 2007). Research suggests that there are four styles of listening and that most of us favor one, though some people have two, and a few can switch between all four (Weaver & Kirtley, 1995). We also know that it is difficult to adapt your listening style even when another one would be more effective (Wolvin & Coakly, 1992). Current research has identified four styles of listening (Bodie & Worthington, 2010).

Some of us are inclined to have a **relational listening style**, which means that when we listen to a message we tend to focus on what it tells us about our conversational partners and their feelings. For example, we notice whether our partners are pleased or upset about the message that they are sending. Others have an **analytical listening style**, which means that we listen to gather information, and tend to think carefully about what we hear. Analytical listeners try

Listening style—your favored but usually unconscious approach to attending to your partner's messages

Relational listening style—a personal listening style that focuses on what a message tells us about our conversational partners and their feelings

Analytical listening style—a personal listening style with a focus on gathering information and thinking carefully about what is said

LEARN ABOUT YOURSELF ▶ PERSONAL LISTENING STYLE PROFILE

Below are several items that people use to describe themselves as listeners. Assess how each statement applies to you by marking your level of agreement or disagreement with each item. Please do not think of any specific listening situation, but of your general ways of listening; how you typically listen in most situations.

1 = Strongly disagree

2 = Disagree

3 = Somewhat disagree

4 = Unsure

5 = Somewhat agree

6 = Agree

7 = Strongly agree

_____ 1. When listening to others, it is important to understand the feelings of the speaker.

_____ 2. I wait until all the facts are presented before forming judgements and opinions.

_____ 3. I am impatient with people who ramble on during conversations.

_____ 4. When listening to others, I focus on any inconsistencies and/or errors in what's being said.

_____ 5. When listening to others, I am mainly concerned with how they are feeling.

_____ 6. I tend to withhold judgement about another's ideas until I have heard everything they have to say.

_____ 7. I get frustrated when people get off topic during a conversation.

_____ 8. I often catch errors in other speakers' logic.

_____ 9. I listen to understand the emotions and mood of the speaker.

_____ 10. When listening to others, I attempt to withhold making an opinion until I've heard their entire message.

_____ 11. When listening to others, I appreciate speakers who give brief, to-the-point presentations.

_____ 12. I tend to naturally notice errors in what other speakers say.

_____ 13. I listen primarily to build and maintain relationships with others.

_____ 14. When listening to others, I consider all sides of the issue before responding.

_____ 15. When listening to others, I become impatient when they appear to be wasting time.

_____ 16. I have a talent for catching inconsistencies in what a speaker says.

_____ 17. I enjoy listening to others because it allows me to connect with them.

_____ 18. I fully listen to what a person has to say before forming any opinions.

_____ 19. I prefer speakers who quickly get to the point.

_____ 20. When listening to others, I notice contradictions in what they say.

_____ 21. When listening to others, I focus on understanding the feelings behind words.

_____ 22. To be fair to others, I fully listen to what they have to say before making judgements.

_____ 23. I find it difficult to listen to people who take too long to get their ideas across.

_____ 24. Good listeners catch discrepancies in what people say.

Scoring the survey: This survey identifies your personal listening style. Sum your responses to Items 1, 5, 9, 13, 17, and 21. This is your relational listening style score. Sum your responses to Items 2, 6, 10, 14, 18, and 22. This is your analytical listening style score. Sum your responses to Items 3, 7, 11, 15, 19, and 23. This is your transactional listening style score. Sum your answers to Items 4, 8, 12, and 16, 20, and 24. This is your critical listening style score. The style for which you have the highest sum is your preferred personal listening style. Some people have one dominant style, while others will have two with close scores. A few people do not have a dominant style and can switch listening modes as needed.

Based on: Bodie, G. D., Worthington, D. L., & Gearhart, C. G. (2013). The Revised Listening Styles Profile (LSP-R): Development and validation. *Communication Quarterly, 61*, 72–90. doi: 10.1080/01463373.2012.720343. Used with permission.

to truly understand what speakers are saying, taking a thoughtful, logical approach to what they hear. The **transactional listening style** involves wanting speakers to remain on task and "get to the point." Transactional listeners dislike listening to speakers who take too long to express their ideas, or who they view as going off on tangents. Finally, people who have a **critical listening style** focus a lot of attention on the accuracy and consistency of speakers' messages. These listeners evaluate closely, and assess how often speakers make errors, or say things that don't fit together. You can learn about your own listening style by completing the Personal Listening Styles Profile.

Each listening style has its advantages and disadvantages. Relational listeners pay close attention to the emotional tone of a message, and therefore tend to be good at empathy, comfort, and support. But relational listeners can also become too involved with a speaker's feelings and may miss inconsistencies in what has been said or fail to be critical enough of what others say. Because they enjoy listening, they may also devote too much time to it when there are more important things to do. Being an analytical listener is a distinct advantage for gathering and making sense of information, but analytical listeners may not attend as much as they should to others' feelings, and their focus on understanding others may prevent them from evaluating as carefully or skeptically as they should. Critical listeners have no difficulty evaluating, but may "miss the forest for the trees," becoming hung up on minor errors or inconsistencies and failing to recognize the overall quality of what someone says. Finally, transactional listeners can be excellent at getting things accomplished in conversations and meetings, but tend to dislike listening fully, and run the risk of offending others when they ignore their feelings or try to rush them into action.

Because each listening style has strengths and weaknesses, we should train ourselves to move between the different styles so that we can listen in the way that is most appropriate to the situation (Bodie & Worthington, 2010). For example, using a relational style would be ideal when a friend is sharing a personal experience. Being an analytical listener would help you when your professor is reviewing a concept during office hours. The critical style could be very helpful when you listen to a sales pitch or watch political discussions on television talk shows. Using the transactional style can help both you and team members when

Transactional style—a personal listening style that prefers speakers who remain on task and "get to the point"

Critical listening style—a personal listening style that focuses attention on the accuracy and consistency of speakers' messages

▸ **OBSERVE AND ANALYZE**

Listening Styles

Identify six people you talk with daily. What personal listening style do you think each uses most often? During the next few days, note whether each of their listening behaviors corresponds to your original perception. Then have a short conversation with each person. Begin by quickly explaining the four personal listening styles and ask them to identify the one they believe they use most frequently. Write a paragraph explaining what you have learned.

How I Learned to Shut Up and Listen

BY EILEEN SMITH, BEARSHAPEDSPHERE.COM

Living in the "wrong" country for nearly seven years now, Eileen bikes, photographs, writes, eats, and talks about language, but not in that order. Chile is her home now, and probably will be for a while. She was raised in Brooklyn, New York.

I sat at a table of no fewer than fifteen people on the street Pio Nono, entry to Bellavista, the down-home party section of Santiago, Chile. I'd been invited to go out for a beer after the monthly critical mass bike ride. We sat at a long series of card tables extending down the street, serving ourselves beer from the liter bottles of Escudo on the center of the tables. Some, drinkers of fan-schop (a Chilean specialty), mixed theirs with Fanta. I drank mine plain, and listened.

I arrived to Chile in 2004, with way more than a passing knowledge of Spanish. Between high school and a couple of travel and study stints in the *mundo hispanohablante* (Spanish-speaking world), I could express myself fairly well, if not cleverly. Hadn't I explained the Electoral College to a group of teachers in Antigua, Guatemala, in the '90s? Wasn't it me who grabbed other travelers by the hand to take them to the post office, the bus station, to get their hair cut? I enjoyed helping, expressing, being in charge. I could get you a seat on the bus, a doorstop, tape to fix a book—you name it. I could ask for it directly or circumlocute it. I spoke, and people understood. At the time, I felt that this was the only necessary linguistic accomplishment. You listen to me. And then it was over.

While output was the feather in my linguistic cap, my listening wouldn't have won any awards. Still, I was skilled enough (or so I thought). Ask a predictable question while travelling, and get a predictable answer. "Where" questions should lead to a location. "When" questions should yield a time, or a day. "I don't know" might come up at any time, so be prepared. Other times you might get a "probably," or "No, we're out of that (on the menu), what about this?" These little sayings are repetitive, predictable, often accompanied by hand and head motions, and occasional pointing. Understandable.

But what happens when you get out of the predictable, and put fifteen of your new closest friends on a loud sidewalk, add an unfamiliar accent, country-specific slang and not just a touch of cheap beer? As an ESL [English as a Second Language)] teacher I'd seen students reduced to frustration, to squinching their eyes shut against visual input while they leaned their heads closer to the audio, hoping that the problem wasn't their ear for English, but their hearing. Try as I might there on the sidewalk, no matter of eye squinching or head leaning was going to fix the fact that I was simply not up to the task. My Chilean friends could understand me, but of the reading/writing/listening/speaking quadrifecta that make up second-language learning, clearly my listening was the weakest. I'm loquacious at the best of times, grate-on-your-nerves chatty when it's worse. But here, on the street in Santiago, 5,000 miles from a place where I could understand easily (and foolishly had taken this for granted), I was relegated to good listener status.

you have an important project deadline looming. All of us need to work on our listening skills. We will complete this chapter by suggesting specific ways you can adapt your listening to specific situations.

Listening Apprehension

Listening apprehension—the anxiety we feel about listening that interferes with our ability to be effective listeners

Listening apprehension, the second challenge to effective listening, is the anxiety we feel about listening that interferes with our ability to be effective listeners.

It wasn't that I couldn't exactly understand what anyone was saying. I could understand enough to follow, kind of, but not fast enough to say anything relevant to the conversation while the topic was still hot.

I was also in Chile, which, with the exception of not letting people off the metro before getting on, is one of the most polite places I'd ever been. What this means is that any time I so much as appeared to want to say anything, a hush would fall over the string of tables. People knew they might not understand me easily, so they wanted to give me their complete attention.

Between the hot topic issue and the *plancha* (embarrassment) I felt at having all eyes on me, the venerable communicator, I simply had to take a different tack. No longer was I Eileen, wordsmith extraordinaire. I was Aylín, the good listener. I was polite. It was cute. People described me as quiet. Not being able to participate in a conversation is like being in disguise. I would sit there in my shy suit and let the words whirl around me, swirl past me. For the first time in my life I was getting to know the patient people, the ones that reach out to quiet ones. I'd never met them before because I was so busy with my soundtrack. It made people want to take me into their confidence, their inner circle. I was not a person who repeated private information. As far as they could tell, I didn't even speak.

After several months of more listening than speaking, I took it up as a new challenge: To follow every conversation with surgical precision, and say nothing, or nearly nothing. I could feel the cloud of wonder and panic lifting, and still I chose to stay quiet. I learned about body language and turn-taking, Chilean social niceties, and watched the other quiet people to see what they were doing. Following along

as well, in most cases. They weren't bland, just quiet. It was a revelation.

Nearly five years later, I don't have to just listen any more. I can exchange jokes and fling around slang with abandon. But what I've found is that I often don't want to. I'm often happy to let events take place without interrupting them, just listening to people say what they have to, what they want to. I don't interrupt as much and I've discovered this whole new world, even among my very own family, the self-professed masters of interrupting and simultaneous yammering (I blame Brooklyn). Sometimes I just try to let them talk themselves out before chiming in. Because when people are talking, they tend not be great listeners. I'd rather have their attention before saying something.

I'm often told I've changed quite a bit since being in Chile. Years have passed, and in that time we've all changed. But what I learned here is that you don't have to be on your game at every possible second. You can watch from the sidelines and participate at the same time. Sometimes the story we tell when we're not saying a word is the most important story of all.

Originally posted April 2, 2009, at Travelblogs.com. Used with permission of the author.

FOR CONSIDERATION:

1. Have you ever been in a similar situation where you couldn't really follow a conversation because it was in a different language or dialect? Did you respond as this author did?

2. The author describes how not being able to be verbally active in conversations taught her to enjoy a whole different part of interaction. Can you list the benefits she described? Which of these benefits would enrich you the most?

Listening apprehension may be due to our fear of misinterpreting the message, our fear of not being able to understand the message, or our fear of how the message may psychologically affect us (Brownell, 2006; Wheeless, 1975). For example, if you are in an important meeting or job training, you may feel undue stress about having to absorb all the important technical information that you know you need to remember to do your job well. Or your anxiety may escalate if you find yourself in a situation where the material you need to absorb is difficult or confusing.

"Being open-plan allows us to bounce ideas around and communicate more freely as a group."

Cartoonstock www.Cartoonstock.com

Passive listening—the effortless, thoughtless, and habitual process of receiving the messages we hear

---

Active listening—the skillful, intentional, deliberate, conscious process of attending to, understanding, remembering, critically evaluating, and responding to messages that we hear

Likewise, your anxiety may increase when you have to listen closely to a message but are feeling ill, tired, or stressed. Or suppose that your spouse confronts you with a lie that you told. You may experience listening apprehension that stems from the emotionally charged atmosphere, from the psychological turmoil caused by being confronted with your own ethical lapse, or from your concern about how what you are hearing will affect your relationship. Whatever the reasons for listening apprehension, anxiety makes it more difficult for us to focus on what we are hearing. In the "Diverse Voices" selection, "How I Learned to Shut Up and Listen," blogger Eileen Smith describes how her listening apprehension taught her the value of listening.

Dual Processes in Listening

You may recall from Chapter 2 that we use one of two approaches to process the information that we receive—automatic or conscious. **Passive listening** is the effortless, thoughtless, and habitual process of receiving the messages we hear. When we listen this way, we are on automatic pilot. We may attend to only parts of the message and then assume that what our conversational partner is saying is predictable from one of our scripts. Passive listening is the default setting of our listening behavior. Sometimes we passively listen because we aren't really interested in the subject. At other times we passively listen because we are multitasking—trying to do several things at once. Think of how you normally listen to music or watch television. Most of us are passive listeners to these media. Some of us have either music or TV on when we are doing other activities. Some of us will continue to "listen" to music or podcasts even when talking with others. If asked about what we are hearing on this background media, we may be able to give the title of the song playing, but unless we know the song, we usually will be unable to report its lyrics accurately.

By contrast, **active listening** is the skillful, intentional, deliberate, conscious process of attending to, understanding, remembering, critically evaluating, and responding to messages that we hear. Active listening is a fundamental communication skill that requires mindfulness and practice. Although we usually passively listen to music, you may have actively listened to a song so you could learn its lyrics. When you did this, you listened differently than you normally do. The process you used was intentional and aimed at attending to, understanding, and remembering the words, phrasing, and tone of the lyrics. If you succeeded in learning the words, you understand how much work is involved in active listening.

As you have seen, our ability to be effective listeners is challenged by our listening style, our level of listening anxiety, and our tendency to use a passive listening approach. If we are to improve our listening effectiveness, we must understand the active listening process and master and use listening skills. In the rest of this chapter, we will look at each step in the active listening process and suggest guidelines and listening skills that will help you overcome listening challenges.

The Active Listening Process

The active listening process includes five steps: attending, understanding, remembering, critically evaluating, and responding to the messages we receive.

Attending

Active listening begins with **attending**, the process of willfully striving to perceive selected sounds that are being heard (O'Shaughnessey, 2003). To get a clearer idea of what attending is, stop reading for a minute, and try to become conscious of all of the sounds you hear around you. Perhaps you notice the humming of an electrical appliance, the rhythm of street traffic, the singing of birds, footsteps in the hall, a cough from an adjoining room. Yet while you were reading, you were probably unaware of most of these sounds. Although we physically register any sounds emitted within our hearing range, we exercise psychological control over the sounds to which we attend. Improving your listening, then, begins with attending—learning to keep your mind on or pay attention to what you hear in a more focused manner. Attending is especially challenging for people with a transactional listening style, or with high listening apprehension, but all of us can benefit from the following guidelines.

> **Attending**—the process of willfully striving to perceive selected sounds that are being heard

Guidelines to Improve Attending

1. Get physically and mentally ready to attend. To get ready to attend, good listeners prepare physically and mentally. Physically, good listeners create an environment conducive to listening, and they adopt a listening posture. It is easier to pay attention to what someone is saying when you have eliminated possible sources of distraction. For example, turning off music before you answer the

In class, how does your posture change when the instructor says, "Now this will be on the test..."?

Experimenting with Attending Techniques

Select an information-oriented program on your local public television station (such as *NOVA, PBS NewsHour,* or *Wall Street Week*). If possible, record it before you watch it. Watch at least fifteen minutes of the show while lounging in a comfortable chair or while stretched out on the floor with music playing in the background. After about fifteen minutes, stop the playback and quickly outline what you have learned. Now, make a conscious decision to follow the guidelines for improving your attending skills during the next fifteen minutes of the show. Turn off the music and sit in a straight-backed chair as you watch the program. Your goal is to increase your attentiveness so that you can absorb the information from the program as effectively as possible. You need, therefore, to eliminate distractions and put yourself in an attentive position. After this fifteen-minute segment, you should again outline what you remember. Watch the program a second time and make note of how your attentiveness affected your memory.

Compare your notes from the two listening sessions. Is there any difference between the amount and quality of the information you retained? Be prepared to discuss your results with your classmates. Are their results similar or different? Why?

phone creates a better environment for you to focus on the caller's message. You can also improve your attention if you align your body so your senses are primed to receive messages. Moving toward the speaker, adopting a more upright stance, and making direct eye contact with the speaker are all physical actions that stimulate your senses and prepare you to perceive. You've probably noticed that when the professor tells the class that the next item of information will be on the test, students adjust their posture, sitting upright in their chairs and leaning slightly forward. They stop any extraneous physical movement and look directly at the professor. Their bodies are poised to attend to what will be said.

Attending to unrelated and competing thoughts and feelings rather than your partner's message is one of the leading causes of poor listening. Accordingly, active listeners also mentally prepare to attend. Active listeners make a conscious decision to ignore competing stimuli and focus on what the speaker is saying. If their minds wander, they quickly refocus on their partner's message. They deliberately block out miscellaneous thoughts that compete for their attention and put aside emotional distractions.

2. Make the shift from speaker to listener a complete one. In conversation, you are called on to quickly switch back and forth from being a speaker to being a listener. As a result, at times you may find it difficult to completely shift roles. We passively listen when we rehearse what we're going to say as soon as we have a chance, rather than focus on what our partner is saying. We actively attend when we discipline our thoughts so that we pay attention to what our partner is saying. Especially when engaged in a heated conversation, take a second to check yourself: Are you preparing your next remark instead of listening? Shifting completely from the role of speaker to listener requires continuous effort.

3. Stay tuned in. Far too often, we stop attending before our partner has finished speaking because, based on our scripts, we "know what they are going to say." "Knowing" what a person is going to say is really only a guess, and failing to attend may cause you to miss something important, or to interrupt them before a useful thought is fully expressed. Active listeners cultivate the habit of waiting for the speaker to finish before searching their mental script library.

Understanding

The second part of active listening, **understanding**, is the process of accurately decoding a message so you comprehend the semantic, pragmatic, and sociolinguistic meaning of a message. Having attended to and perceived the message being sent, you are now ready to understand, or "make sense" of it. People with an analytical listening style may find this step natural and easy, but most of us can improve our understanding skills by using the following guidelines and skills.

Guidelines and Skills for Improving Understanding

1. Identify the speaker's purpose and key points. Even in casual social conversations, speakers have some purpose or point they are trying to make. Sometimes people's thoughts are spoken in well-organized messages whose purposes and key ideas are easy to follow and identify. At other times, however, we must work harder to grasp the essence of what the speaker is trying to get across. If you can't figure out the speaker's purpose or key ideas, you will have trouble understanding the message. As you listen, ask yourself, "What does the speaker want me to understand?" and "What is the point being made?" For example, if Manuel spends two minutes talking about how much he likes the Cubs and asks Corella about her interest in baseball, casually mentioning that he has tickets for the game this weekend, Corella may recognize that he would like her to go with him.

Because speakers use messages to do things, you need to understand the pragmatic meaning of a message. When the speaker's purpose is to persuade you to think or do something, you will also want to identify what specific arguments the speaker is making. For instance, when Marlee, who is running for a city council seat, asks Joanna what she thinks about the plan for the new arts center and begins to talk about some of its pros and cons, Joanna understands that Marlee is not making idle conversation. Beneath the surface of what Marlee is saying, she is attempting to persuade Joanna to vote for her.

2. Interpret nonverbal cues. In Chapter 5 we noted that up to 65 percent of the meaning of a message is transmitted nonverbally. Therefore, to understand what a speaker means, you need to understand, not only what is said verbally, but also the nonverbal behaviors that accompany what is said. For instance, if Deborah says to Gita, "Go on. I can walk home from here," what do these words mean? Without understanding the message cues transmitted through her tone of voice, body language, and facial expression, Gita can't really tell if Deborah truly prefers to walk or if she's just being polite but would really like a ride. Whether you are listening to a coworker describing her stance on an issue, a friend explaining the process for hanging wallpaper, or a loved one expressing why he or she is upset with you, you must look to how something is said as well as to what is said if you want to understand the real message.

Sometimes there is a message in silence, which can be the subtlest form of nonverbal communication that needs to be understood.

3. Ask clarifying questions. The skill of asking a clarifying question provides an easy way to better understand what a speaker is saying to you. A **clarifying question** is a response designed to get further information or to remove uncertainty from information already received. It also encourages the speaker to continue speaking. In addition to helping the listener, good clarifying questions help speakers sharpen their thinking about the points they make. Although you may have asked clarifying questions for as long as you can remember, you may notice that at times your questions either failed to yield the information you wanted or, worse, provoked an unwanted

Understanding—accurately decoding a message so you comprehend the semantic, pragmatic, and sociolinguistic meaning of a message

Clarifying question—a response designed to get further information or to remove uncertainty from information already received

Listening means paying attention to nonverbal as well as verbal cues. What message is the speaker conveying through nonverbal cues?

response—perhaps the other person became irritated, flustered, or defensive. To become skilled at questioning, you should follow these procedures:

- *Be specific about the kind of information you need to increase your understanding.* Suppose Maria calls you and says, "I am totally frustrated. Would you stop at the store on the way home and buy me some more paper?" At this point, you may be somewhat confused and need more information to understand what Maria is telling you. Yet if you respond by simply saying, "What do you mean?" you are likely to add to the confusion, because Maria, who is already uptight, won't know precisely what it is you don't understand. So be more specific by asking for details, definitions, and causes. You might ask:

  "What kind of paper would you like me to get, and how much will you need?"
  (*clarify the important details*).
  "What do you mean by 'frustrated?'" (*clarify the definition*).
  "What is it that's frustrating you?" (*clarify the cause of the feelings the person is expressing*).

- *Deliver questions in a sincere tone of voice.* Ask questions with a tone of voice that is sincere—not a tone that could be interpreted as accusing, affected, sarcastic, cutting, superior, or judgemental. We need to remind ourselves that how we ask a question may be more important to getting a useful answer than the way we phrase the question.

- *Limit questions or explain that you need to ask multiple questions.* Sometimes asking several clarifying questions in a row can seem like an interrogation. If you can, limit your number of clarifying questions to the most appropriate ones. But if you need to ask several, you might explain why you are asking them. For instance, Vanessa could say to her dad, "I really want to understand why you won't pay my tuition this year, so I need to ask a few questions to get more information. Is that okay?"

- *Put the "burden of ignorance" on your own shoulders.* To minimize unplanned or unwanted reactions, phrase your clarifying questions in a way that puts the burden of ignorance on your own shoulders. Preface your questions with a short statement that suggests that any problem of misunderstanding may be the result of *your* listening skills. For instance, when Drew says, "I've really had it with Malone screwing up all the time," you might say, "Drew, I'm sorry. I'm missing some details that would help me understand your feelings better. What kinds of things has Malone been doing?"

Let's look at two examples that contrast inappropriate with more appropriate questioning responses.

I. Tamara: They turned down my proposal again!
Art: Well, did you explain it in the way you should have?

SKILL BUILDER ▶ QUESTIONING

SKILL	USE	STEPS	EXAMPLE
Phrasing a response designed to get further information or to remove uncertainty from information already received	To help get a more complete picture before making other comments; to help a shy person open up; to clarify meaning	1. Be specific about the kind of information you need to increase your understanding of the message. 2. Deliver questions in a sincere tone of voice. 3. Limit questions or explain that you need to ask multiple questions. 4. Put the burden of ignorance on your own shoulders.	When Connie says, "Well, it would be better if she weren't so sedentary," Jeff replies, "I'm not sure I understand what you mean by 'sedentary'— would you explain?"

(Inappropriate: Tamara is likely to view this question as an attack.)
Art: Did they tell you why?
(Appropriate: This question is a sincere request for additional information.)

II. Renée: With all those executives at the party last night, I really felt weird.
Javier: Why?
(Inappropriate: With this abrupt question, Javier is making no effort to be sensitive to Renée's feelings or to understand them.)
Javier: What is it about your bosses being there that made you feel weird?
(Appropriate: Here the question is phrased to elicit information that will help Javier understand and may help Renée understand as well.)

Note how the appropriate, clarifying questions are likely to get the necessary information while minimizing the probability of an unplanned or unwanted reply. The inappropriate questions, on the other hand, may be perceived as an attack. To become skillful at questioning, follow the steps in the Skill Builder on Questioning.

4. Paraphrase what you hear. Another way to affirm your understanding of what others say is to paraphrase what you hear. A **paraphrase** is an attempt to verify your understanding of a message by putting it into your own words and sharing it with the speaker. When you paraphrase, you don't just repeat what the speaker has said. Rather, you convey and try to verify the ideas and emotions you have perceived from the speaker's message. For example, during an argument with your sister, you might paraphrase what she said as follows: "So you are saying that you think I try to act superior to you when I talk about my successes at work?" Your sister can respond by saying, "Yes, exactly! It feels like you are trying to put me down when you do that." Or she may correct your paraphrase

Paraphrase—an attempt to verify your understanding of a message by putting it into your own words and sharing it with the speaker

Cartoonstock www.Cartoonstock.com

SKILL BUILDER ▶ PARAPHRASING

SKILL	USE	STEPS	EXAMPLE
Verifying your understanding of a message by putting it in your own words	To increase listening efficiency; to avoid message confusion; to discover the speaker's motivation	1. Listen carefully to the message. 2. Notice what ideas and feelings seem to be contained in the message. 3. Determine what the message means to you. 4. Create a message in your own words that conveys these ideas and/or feelings.	Grace says, "At two minutes to five, the boss gave me three letters that had to be in the mail that evening!" Bonita replies, "I understand; you were really resentful that your boss dumped important work on you right before quitting time, when she knows that you have to pick up the baby at daycare."

Content paraphrase—a feedback message that conveys understanding of the denotative meaning of a verbal message

Feelings paraphrase—a feedback message that conveys understanding of the emotional meaning behind a speaker's verbal message

by saying, "Well, actually, I'm not feeling that you are trying to act like a big shot. It just makes me feel bad about the fact that I got laid off."

There are two types of paraphrases: a **content paraphrase** conveys your understanding of the denotative meaning of a verbal message; a **feelings paraphrase** conveys your understanding of the emotional meaning behind a speaker's verbal message. You can also combine these into a paraphrase that conveys one's understanding of both the denotative and emotional meaning of your partner's verbal message. Whether a content or feelings paraphrase is most useful for a particular situation depends on what you perceive as the pragmatic meaning of the message. Let's look at an example.

> *Statement:* "Five weeks ago, I gave the revised paper for my independent study to my project advisor. I felt really good about it because I thought the changes I had made really improved my explanations. Well, yesterday I stopped by and got the paper back, and my advisor said he couldn't really see that this draft was much different from the first."
>
> *Content paraphrase:* "So you really thought that you had provided more depth and detail to your explanations, but Professor Delgato didn't notice."
>
> *Feelings paraphrase:* "You seem really frustrated that Professor Delgato didn't notice the changes you'd made."
>
> *Combination:* "So Professor Delgato told you that he didn't notice the work you had done. What a bummer. No wonder you sound so disgusted."

Common sense suggests that we need not paraphrase every message we receive, nor would we paraphrase after every few sentences. So when should you use the skill of paraphrasing to better understand what you hear? We suggest that you paraphrase when you need a better understanding of a message's content, feelings, or both; when misunderstanding the message will have serious consequences; when the message is long and contains several complex ideas;

when the message seems to reflect emotional strain; and when you are talking with people whose native language is not English.

To become skillful at paraphrasing, follow the steps in the Skill Builder on paraphrasing.

Remembering

The third step of the active listening process is **remembering**, the process of moving information from short-term memory to long-term memory. Too often, people almost immediately forget what they have heard. Several things make remembering difficult. First, we often filter out the parts of the message that don't fit our personal listening style. As a result, this information, which is not stored in short-term memory, cannot be transferred to our long-term memory. For example, a relational listener may be able to recall how someone felt about what she or he said but be unable to recall the details of the message. Second, when we are listening anxiously, we may be so stressed that we are not able to recall anything we have heard. Some of us who become anxious when introduced to a large number of people at one time may be unable to remember any of their names five minutes later. Third, when we passively listen to a message, we don't really pay attention to what is being said, so we don't remember it. Fourth, we are also selective in what we remember, finding it easier to recall messages that support our positions and to forget information that contradicts our beliefs. For instance, if we watch a debate on television, we tend to recall the arguments for our point of view but forget some equally valid opposing arguments. Fifth, we are more likely to remember information at the beginning or end of a message and forget what comes in between. The **primacy effect** is the tendency to remember information that we heard first over what we heard in the middle, and the **recency effect** is the tendency to remember information that we heard last over what we heard in the middle. This explains why we are likely, when given directions, to remember the first few street names and turns as well as the last few, but fail to recall the street names or turns in the middle of the route.

Let's look at several guidelines that can help you remember what has been said to you.

Guidelines for Improving Remembering

1. Repeat what was said. Repetition—saying something two, three, or even four times—helps you store information in long-term memory (Estes, 1989). If information is not reinforced, it will be held in short-term memory for as little as twenty seconds and then forgotten. The key to repetition is silently or vocally repeating something multiple times to aid the remembering process. When you are introduced to a stranger named Jon McNeil, if you mentally repeat, "Jon McNeil, Jon McNeil, Jon McNeil, Jon McNeil," you increase the chances that you will remember his name. Similarly, when a person gives you the directions, "Go two blocks east, turn left, turn right at the next light, and it's in the next block," you should immediately repeat to yourself, "Two blocks east, turn left, turn right at light, next block—that's two blocks east, turn left, turn right at light, next block."

Remembering—the process of moving information from short-term memory to long-term memory

Primacy effect—the tendency to remember information that we heard first over what we heard in the middle

Recency effect—the tendency to remember information that we heard last over what we heard in the middle

Mnemonic device—a learning technique that associates a special word or short statement with new and longer information

2. Create mnemonics. A **mnemonic device** is a learning technique that associates a special word or short statement with new and longer information. One of the most common ways of forming a mnemonic is to take the first letter of each of the items you are trying to remember and form a word. For example, an easy mnemonic for remembering the five Great Lakes is HOMES (Huron, Ontario, Michigan, Erie, Superior). When you want to remember items in a sequence, try to form a sentence with the words themselves, or assign words using the first letters of the words in sequence and form an easy-to-remember statement. For example, when you studied music the first time, you may have learned the notes on the lines of the treble clef (EGBDF) with the saying, "Every good boy does fine." Or to help students remember the colors of the visible light spectrum in sequence, science teachers often ask them to remember the name "Roy G Biv," standing for red, orange, yellow, green, blue, indigo, violet.

3. Take notes. Although note-taking may not be an appropriate way to remember information when you are engaged in casual interpersonal encounters, it is a powerful tool for increasing your recall of information in telephone conversations, briefing sessions, interviews, and business meetings. Note-taking provides a written record that you can revisit while promoting a more active role in the listening process (Wolvin & Coakley, 1992). In short, when you are listening to complex information, take notes.

What constitutes good notes will vary with the situation. Useful notes may consist of a brief list of main points or key ideas, plus a few of the most significant details. Or the notes may take the form of a short summary of the entire concept; a type of paraphrase written after the message has been delivered. For lengthy and rather detailed information, however, good notes are best written in outline form, including the overall idea, the main points of the message, and key developmental material organized by category and subcategory. Good outlines are not necessarily long. In fact, many classroom lectures can be reduced to an outline of one page or less.

Critically evaluating—the process of determining how truthful, authentic, or believable you judge the message and the speaker to be

Critically Evaluating

The fourth step of the active listening process is critically evaluating. **Critically evaluating** is the process of determining how truthful, authentic, or believable you judge the message and the speaker to be. This may involve ascertaining the accuracy of facts, the amount and type of evidence supporting a position, and the relationship of a position to your own values. For instance, when you get a tweet directing you to vote for a particular candidate for office or to sign a petition to add a skateboard park to the neighborhood, you will want to critically evaluate the message. Have supporting facts been presented for what you are being asked to do, and are they true? Have you been provided with the supporting

What are the advantages and disadvantages of taking notes during a meeting?

information you need to make a judgement? Do you fundamentally agree with the basic idea? Critically evaluating also means assessing the speaker's credibility, including his or her expertise and character. People with a critical listening style may have the edge with this skill, but even if we are inclined to other styles, we can improve our ability to critically evaluate messages by using the following guidelines and skills.

Guidelines for Improving Critical Evaluation

1. Separate facts from inferences. Facts are statements whose accuracy can be verified or proven; **inferences** are claims or assertions based on the facts presented. Separating facts from inferences requires us to distinguish between a verifiable observation and an opinion related to that observation. Too often, people treat inferences as factual. Let's clarify this distinction with an example. If we can document that Cesar received an A in geology, then saying that Cesar received an A in geology is a fact. If we go on to say that Cesar studied very hard, without knowing that this was the case, our statement is an inference. Cesar may have studied hard to receive his grade, but it is also possible that geology comes easily to him or that he had already learned much of the material in his high school physical science course.

Separating facts from inferences is important because inferences may be false, even if based on verifiable facts. Making sound judgements entails basing our inferences on facts whose correctness we have evaluated. Consider the following statements: "Better watch it. Carl is really in a bad mood today. Did you see the way he was scowling?" or "I know you're hiding something from me. I can hear it in your voice"; or "Olga and Kurt are having an affair—I've seen them leave the office together nearly every night." Each of these conveys an inference, which may be—but is not necessarily—true.

2. Probe for information. Sometimes, to critically evaluate a message, we need to encourage the speaker to delve deeper into the topic. Or we may need to challenge the information to see if it holds up under scrutiny. To do this, we can ask **probing questions**, questions that search for more information or try to resolve perceived inconsistencies in a message. For example, suppose that Jerrod's landlord was talking with him about the need to sign a lease. Before signing this legally binding document, Jerrod should ask the prospective landlord probing questions, such as the following:

> "You said that I would need to sign a lease, but you did not state the term of the lease. What's the shortest lease I could get?"
>
> "Your ad in the paper said that utilities would be paid by the landlord, but just now you said that the tenant pays the utility bill. Which way will it work with this apartment?"

Facts—statements whose accuracy can be verified or proven

Inferences—claims or assertions based on the facts presented

Probing questions—questions that search for more information or try to resolve perceived inconsistencies in a message

How do members of a jury make sure that they consider only the facts and not the inferences drawn by the attorneys who are presenting the case?

"Is there a deposit, and if so, what must I do to get my deposit back when the lease is up?"

With questions like these, Jerrod is testing what the landlord has said and is trying to resolve inconsistencies.

When we ask probing questions, our nonverbal communication is especially important. We must pay attention to our tone of voice and body language so we do not appear arrogant or intimidating. Too many probing questions accompanied by inappropriate nonverbal cues can cause the other person to become defensive.

Responding

Responding—the process of providing feedback to your partner's message

The final step of the active listening process is **responding**, the process of providing feedback to your partner's message. You can listen without providing any external cues that would indicate to others that you are listening (Bostrom, 2006). If you have ever talked with someone who appeared totally unresponsive to what you were saying, you can appreciate the importance of responding to messages you hear. The active listening process is not complete without responses on the part of the listener to indicate that he or she hears the speaker, understands the message, and is willing to comment on what has been understood. In fact, responding, both verbally and nonverbally, is central to what people usually mean when they say that someone is a "good listener" (Bodie, St. Cyr, Pence, Rold, & Honeycutt, 2012). You can more effectively respond if you adopt the following guidelines.

Guidelines to Improve Responding

Back-channel cues—verbal and nonverbal signals that indicate you are listening and attempting to understand the message

1. Provide back-channel cues. One way to indicate that you are listening to the message is to provide **back-channel cues**, verbal and nonverbal signals that indicate you are listening and attempting to understand the message. These cues include nodding, head shaking, smiling, laughing, head cocking, frowning, eyebrow knitting, or saying "huh?" "uh huh," "yeah," or other short vocalized utterances. Back-channel cues are useful and appropriate when they provide feedback to the speaker without becoming distractions.

2. Reply only when the message is complete. Except for back-channel cues, listeners should respond to a message only when the speaker has finished talking. One of the most common signs of poor listening is interrupting. A study of college students cited interrupting as the behavior that most interferes with really listening to what another person is saying (Halone & Pecchioni, 2001). Learning to wait can be especially challenging for those with a time-oriented listening style, when a group of people is talking, when you are in a heated conversation, or when you are excited and enthusiastic about what you have just heard. With concentration and practice,

How are these women responding to each other?

however, you can become better at waiting until a speaker is finished talking and you have had a chance to understand, remember, and critically evaluate what he or she is saying.

3. Respond to the previous message before changing the subject. Abrupt topic changes are inappropriate because they don't acknowledge what your partner has said. It is important to acknowledge your partner's message before changing the subject. Besides asking questions or paraphrasing what was said, you might respond to a message by agreeing or disagreeing with what was said, expanding on the ideas, challenging some of the message, indicating empathy or support, and offering advice. Let's look at an example that demonstrates different ways to respond to the same message from a friend:

> **Message:** "I need to look for a better job, and I'm probably going to quit school. I'm in a major financial mess with credit card debt, monthly living expenses of $1200, and late child support payments. And on top of all of this, my hours at work are being cut back. I'm in deep trouble here and pretty stressed out. I don't know what to do. Got any ideas?"
>
> **Paraphrase:** "So you're having trouble paying your bills at the same time that your paycheck is being reduced."
>
> **Question:** "What's the difference between your bills and your take-home pay each month?"
>
> **Agreement:** "Yeah, it makes sense to look for a higher-paying job."
>
> **Challenge:** "Is there a way that you can continue to make progress toward your degree even though you have to work more?"
>
> **Advice:** "You may want to meet with a debt consolidator who could help you work on a long-term plan for getting back into good financial shape."
>
> **Support:** "Wow, off the top of my head I can't really think of any, but I'm willing to talk with you about things, and maybe together we can figure this out."

As you can see, some responses are aimed at developing a clearer understanding of the original message, whereas others focus on helping the speaker. As we discussed in Chapter 1, it is important for you to develop behavioral flexibility so that you are skilled at responding in a variety of ways.

THE SOCIAL MEDIA FACTOR

Digital Listening Skills

Some of you may wonder what "listening" has to do with social media. Rest assured that the listening skills discussed in this chapter apply not only to face-to-face conversations, but to conversations that you have using social media. As communication technologies improve, sending messages becomes easier; yet effectively dealing with all of the various messages we receive presents formidable challenges. In 2012, researchers with the Pew Research Center reported that the typical teenager sends an average of 30 text messages a day (Lenhart, 2015).

Think about how many digital messages you receive each day. There are texts, emails, voicemails, and Facebook posts. Then add to that all the messages you get through Tumblr, Instagram, GroupMe, Snapchat, Vine, Twitter, and other social media you use. All of these messages beckon you to attend to them, make sense of them, respond appropriately to them, and in some cases, remember them. Being an effective digital listener requires **digital communication literacy**— the ability to critically attend to, analyze, evaluate, and express digital messages. Let's briefly look at some of the problems and the solutions to the unique challenges we face when it comes to digital listening.

Digital communication literacy— the ability to critically attend to, analyze, evaluate, and express digital messages

Attending to and Understanding Digital Messages

Digital communication technologies affect what we pay attention to and what we ignore. Some of this is largely outside our control: our email provider may set spam filters, Facebook chooses what it thinks we'd most like to see, and our smartphones tell us who is calling or texting before we answer. In other cases, we make active selections: we mark things as "junk" and delete them, we change the notification settings on Facebook and our smartphones, or we assign special ringtones to our friends so we know when to pick up (or not). It's important to recognize that these selections have implications for our relationships. If you are seeing more posts from some friends than others, you know more about them and may feel closer to them. If you routinely answer some calls immediately, but ignore others until it's more convenient for you, you are probably conveying messages to these friends about the value you place on those relationships.

Attending to digital messages becomes more complicated when they compete with offline messages, and with each other. How many times have you texted a friend while talking to another friend face-to-face? Or responded to texts while messaging on Facebook or writing an email? When this occurs, you may not be paying sufficient attention to each of your messages. People who are physically present with you may be especially annoyed if your attention is constantly divided. Research indicates that even the presence of a cell phone on a table during a conversation can interfere with a relationship (Przybylski & Weinstein, 2013). You can improve both your digital and face-to-face interactions by attending to each separately. This may require some explanation and restraint, such as telling your friends that you won't respond to texts at certain times, and putting your digital devices away so that you won't be tempted by them.

Keep in mind that people who receive your digital messages may be distracted by other messages and tasks as well. To help them attend and understand when you are communicating, strive for clarity. One simple typographical error can communicate a completely different message, and many smartphones automatically "correct" an unfamiliar word to something very different. The internet abounds in examples of auto-correct "fails," and although these can be funny, they can also create miscommunication, embarrassment, and even hurt feelings. If you receive a message that seems "off," don't respond until you can focus on the message. Then, if you are still concerned about what your partner said, help your partner clarify the message with a question or paraphrase.

Another thing to remember is that digital media aren't as rich as face-to-face interactions. As a result, even when we try to be skillful at digital listening, some of the sender's meaning may be difficult to determine without nonverbal cues. When your girlfriend sends an unusually short text message, how should you interpret this? Do you automatically think she is mad at you? Or do you keep in mind that she may have other things competing for her attention? It is important to focus carefully on the message, ask questions, and consider the possibility of multiple, alternative meanings. Do not jump to conclusions because a smiley face is omitted, or a reply is brief. Similarly, consider how the leanness of digital media may affect the interpretation of your own messages. If you are angry with your significant other, do not try to resolve the conflict via text messaging. This medium is not well suited to conveying complex emotions, or negotiating difficult issues. Your messages may be grossly misinterpreted and cause more harm. Use a "richer" media and talk to your significant other in person.

A QUESTION OF ETHICS ▶ WHAT WOULD YOU DO?

Janeen always disliked talking on the telephone—she thought that it was an impersonal form of communication. Thus college was a wonderful respite, because, when her friends would call her, instead of staying on the phone, she could quickly run over to their dorm or meet them at the campus coffeehouse.

One day, during a reading period before exams, Janeen received a phone call from Barbara, a childhood friend. Before she was able to dismiss Barbara with her stock excuses, Janeen found herself bombarded with information about old high school friends and their whereabouts. Not wanting to disappoint Barbara, who seemed eager to talk, Janeen tucked her phone under her chin and began to check her email, answering Barbara with the occasional "uh huh," "hmm," or "Wow, that's cool!" As the "conversation" progressed, Janeen signed on to her Facebook account and became absorbed in reading posts. After a few minutes she realized there was silence on the other end of the line. Suddenly very ashamed, she said, "I'm sorry, what did you say? Our connection went bad . . . and I couldn't hear you."

Barbara, seeing through Janeen's lie, replied with obvious hurt in her voice, "Yeah, right. I'm sorry I bothered you; obviously you must be terribly busy."

Embarrassed, Janeen muttered, "I'm just really stressed, you know, with exams coming up and everything. I guess I wasn't listening very well. What you were saying wasn't really all that important, right?"

"Right, nothing 'important,'" Barbara answered. "I was just working up to telling you about my brother Billy. You remember him, the guy you dated in high school? Well, I'm sure it's really unimportant compared to whatever was taking your attention, but you see, we just found out yesterday that he's terminal with a rare form of leukemia. So you're right, not important." With that, she hung up.

FOR CONSIDERATION:

1. Which of the ethical principles did Janeen violate by how she listened to Barbara? Explain how each of these principles applies to listening.
2. Although Barbara was the one hurt by Janeen's comment about the importance of the call, did she violate any ethical principles by how she ended the call?
3. What could each of the women have done to make this conversation more effective?
4. How has this case helped you understand the ethical obligations of listening?

Critically Evaluating Digital Messages

Being a digitally literate communicator via social media requires us to be able to critically evaluate the digital messages we encounter. Since information is so easy to share online, sometimes false information is unintentionally shared, posted, and retweeted without much consideration. Unfortunately, some people intentionally share misinformation. That being said, it is important to critically evaluate the digital messages that you "listen" to. If a new friend's Facebook profile contains unfamiliar information that piques your curiosity, ask the person questions, as long as you are comfortable discussing the topic. Then you will be better able to separate facts from inferences you may make about your new friend. As you may well know, computer hackers sometimes spread viruses through social media. For example, in 2011 a "news" story appeared throughout Facebook falsely reporting that actor Charlie Sheen had died. It turned out the "story" was actually a virus that was transmitted through social media (Kanalley, 2011). Therefore, if it appears that a Facebook friend has posted an odd item on his page, or uploaded bizarre photos that are uncharacteristic of his personality, those strange postings may be a computer virus in disguise. In addition, some information that circulates on the web as "facts" is really urban legend—stories that may have a basis in fact, but as told are grossly or partially inaccurate. So before you act on or pass along inaccurate information, check it out. One useful place to check out the accuracy of information is at Snopes.com, an award-winning website dedicated to ferreting out the truth of "urban legends."

Summary

Listening is the process of receiving, constructing meaning from, and responding to spoken and/or nonverbal messages. There are three primary challenges to our listening effectiveness: our personal listening style, our listening apprehension, and the dual approach we can take to listening. Our personal listening style may be relational, analytical, transactional, or critical. Each style has advantages and disadvantages. Listening apprehension is the anxiety we feel about listening that interferes with our ability to be effective listeners. We use a dual-process approach to listening. Most of the time we are passive listeners, automatically processing what we hear, but making little effort to focus on the message. Alternatively, we may use the active-listening process of attending, understanding, remembering, critically evaluating, and responding to the message we heard. Attending is the process of willfully striving to perceive selected sounds that are being heard. To improve your attending skills, get physically and mentally ready to attend, make the shift from speaker to listener a complete one, resist tuning out, and avoid interrupting. Understanding is the process of accurately decoding a message so that you share its meaning with the speaker. To increase your understanding skills, identify the speaker's purpose and key points, interpret nonverbal cues, ask clarifying questions, and paraphrase what you hear. Remembering is the process of moving information from short-term memory to long-term memory. To be more skilled at remembering, repeat what was said to you, use mnemonic devices, and take notes. Critically evaluating is the process of interpreting what you have understood to determine how truthful, authentic, or believable you judge the meaning to be. To improve your critical evaluation skills, separate facts from inferences and probe for information. Responding is the process of reacting to what has been heard while listening and after listening. To improve your responding skills, provide back-channel cues, and reply when the message is complete. Listening skills need to be applied in the digital context as well as face-to-face.

CHAPTER RESOURCES

Key Words

Flashcards for all of these key terms are available on the *Inter-Act* website.

Active listening pp. 204
Analytical listening style pp. 199
Attending pp. 205
Back-channel cues pp. 214
Clarifying question pp. 207
Content paraphrase pp. 210
Critical listening style pp. 201
Critically evaluating pp. 212
Digital communication literacy pp. 216

Facts pp. 213
Feelings paraphrase pp. 210
Inferences pp. 213
Listening pp. 198
Listening apprehension pp. 202
Listening style pp. 199
Mnemonic device pp. 212
Paraphrase pp. 209
Passive listening pp. 204

Primacy effect pp. 211
Probing questions pp. 213
Recency effect pp. 211
Relational listening style pp. 199
Remembering pp. 211
Responding pp. 214
Transactional listening style pp. 201
Understanding pp. 206

Analyze and Apply

The following activities challenge you to demonstrate your mastery of the concepts, theories, and frameworks in this chapter by using them to explain what is happening in a specific situation.

7.1 Rewind/Rewrite
Now that you have read the chapter, hit "rewind" on the opening dialogue between Lucy, Ryanne, Cecelia, and Amy and answer the following questions.

a. Use concepts from the chapter to explain why these young women "heard" different things at the meeting, and why they may not be "hearing" each other. The types of listening style and components of active listening may be especially useful.

b. Based on what you have learned in this chapter and book, write a short memo to each of the women suggesting how she might improve her listening, both in the meeting they attended and in their conversation with each other.

7.2 Listening Styles and Careers

Should you consider your preferred listening style when thinking about what career to pursue? Should employers consider these styles when hiring? Explain.

7.3 Listening and Situations

Does the importance of different listening skills vary in different situations, or relationships? Explain.

Skill Practice

Skill practice activities give you the chance to rehearse a new skill by responding to hypothetical or real situations. Additional skill practice activities are available at the companion website.

7.4 Writing Questions and Paraphrases

Provide an appropriate question and paraphrase for each of the following statements. To get you started, the first conversation has been completed for you.

a. *Luis: It's Dionne's birthday, and I've planned a big evening. Sometimes, I think Dionne believes I take her for granted—well, I think after tonight she'll know I think she's someone special!*

 1. **Question:** What specific things do you have planned?

 2. **Content paraphrase:** If I understand you, you're planning a night that's going to cost a lot more than what Dionne expects on her birthday.

 3. **Feelings paraphrase:** From the way you're talking, I get the feeling you're really proud of yourself for making plans like these.

b. *Angie: Brother! Another nothing class. I keep thinking one of these days he'll get excited about something. Professor Romero is a real bore!*

 1. **Question:**

 2. **Content paraphrase:**

 3. **Feelings paraphrase:**

c. *Jerry: Everyone seems to be talking about that movie on Channel 5 last night, but I didn't see it. You know, I don't watch much that's on the idiot box.*

 1. **Question:**

 2. **Content paraphrase:**

 3. **Feelings paraphrase:**

d. **Kaelin:** *I don't know if it's something to do with me or with Mom, but lately she and I just aren't getting along.*

   1. **Question:**

   2. **Content paraphrase:**

   3. **Feelings paraphrase:**

e. **Aileen:** *I've got a report due at work and a paper due in management class. On top of that, it's my sister's birthday, and so far I haven't even had time to get her anything. Tomorrow's going to be a disaster.*

   1. **Question:**

   2. **Content paraphrase:**

   3. **Feelings paraphrase:**

7.5 Creating Mnemonics

Practice remembering the four personal listening styles and the steps in the active-listening process by creating a mnemonic for each. Record your mnemonics. Tomorrow morning while you are dressing, see whether you can recall the mnemonics you created. Then see how many of the personal listening styles and active-learning steps you can recall using the cues in your mnemonics.

Communication Improvement Plan: Listening

Would you like to improve the following skills discussed in this chapter?

- Questioning

- Paraphrasing

Pick a skill, and write a communication improvement plan. You can find a communication improvement plan worksheet on our website at www.oup.com/us/verderber.

8

HOLDING EFFECTIVE CONVERSATIONS

Susan and Samuel are both second-year resident assistants (RAs) in a large university dormitory. They trained and worked together last year, but this year they live on different floors, and consequently they haven't seen much of each other. One evening they happened to run into each other in the lobby. Samuel had a student on his floor who had been behaving oddly, and Samuel was concerned about how he should handle the situation. He knew that Susan had had to deal with a similar issue on her floor last year, so seeing her, he decided to get her take on the situation.

"Hey, Susan!" Samuel shouted across the lobby.

Susan looked over, saw Samuel, smiled, turned, and walked toward him. "Wow," she exclaimed, "long time no see! I can't believe we still live in the same building! Remember we used to always have rounds together?"

"Yeah, it was almost every night for . . ." Samuel started, but Susan interrupted excitedly.

"You know that time we were going up the stairs and I fell because my slippers were really slick? And that guy we found sleeping on the roof?" Susan laughed, pointing up.

"Sure, I remember," said Samuel. "And that girl that was. . . ."

Susan cut in again. "It was so much fun! My floor is boring this year, but at least it's easy. Only one problem resident so far this year."

223

(Continued)

"That's good. My residents are fine except—" Samuel started to share the story about his odd resident, but Susan interrupted.

"So, how are you?" Without even waiting for an answer, Susan continued: "I've been so busy! My classes are super hard. I had an exam today, I have two exams tomorrow, a group project Wednesday, and then a lab due Friday. And I still have to do next semester's roommate agreements, bulletin boards, and smoke detector checks before Saturday."

At this point, Samuel was trying to remember whether he had ever really liked Susan when they worked together, and completely abandoned the idea of getting her input on his problem resident. "Yeah, it's a lot," he said shortly, edging toward the elevator.

Susan continued, not noticing Samuel's discomfort. "Oh my gosh, Samuel this is my sixth cup of coffee today and I haven't slept in two days—ha ha! I'm going to be up late tonight studying, but then I can get some sleep."

The elevator bell sounded, and the doors began to open. Samuel moved purposefully toward it, saying over his shoulder, "Good luck! Gotta go!" Looking a little surprised, Susan waved after him, shrugged, and walked away. "That's odd," she thought, "I could swear he wanted to talk to me."

WHAT YOU SHOULD BE ABLE *TO EXPLAIN* AFTER YOU HAVE STUDIED THIS CHAPTER:

▶ What defines a conversation

▶ The characteristics of conversation

▶ Six ways that conversations vary

▶ How to become a more effective conversationalist

▶ Message strategies to initiate, sustain, and close conversations effectively

▶ Cultural variations in conversation

▶ Factors influencing your ability to engage in effective digital conversations

WHAT YOU SHOULD BE ABLE *TO DO* AFTER YOU HAVE STUDIED THIS CHAPTER:

▶ Use effective turn-taking in a conversation

▶ Comfortably initiate a conversation with a stranger

▶ Skillfully sustain and close conversations

Conversations are the stuff from which our relationships are made. All relationships are initiated, developed, sustained, and terminated through conversations, which may be face-to-face or mediated. Conversing is one of the primary activities between friends and romantic partners (Duck, 2007). When our conversations go well, they are interesting, informative, stimulating, and just plain fun. Yet we experience some conversations as awkward and uncomfortable, even difficult. By examining how conversations work, we can see how much they depend on the collaborative effort of two (or more) participants. We can also learn to converse in ways that increase our ease and enjoyment.

In this chapter, we explore conversation in detail. We begin by defining the word "conversation," using the definition to investigate the characteristics of conversation, and then we consider some important ways in which conversations vary: type, purpose, sequence, tone, participants, and setting. Next, we present general guidelines to help you become a more effective conversationalist and specific skills for improving first-time conversations with strangers, since this is a type of conversation that many people find challenging. Finally, we summarize how culture and technology affect conversation.

Conversation—an interactive, extemporaneous, locally managed, and sequentially organized interchange of thoughts and feelings between two or more people

Turn-taking—alternating between speaking and listening in an interaction

Extemporaneous—uttered in the spur of the moment without lengthy preplanning

Conversations: Characteristics and Variations

A **conversation** is an interactive, extemporaneous, locally managed, and sequentially organized interchange of thoughts and feelings between two or more people. While all conversations have these characteristics, no two conversations are identical – we have wide variations in our conversations.

Characteristics of Conversations

You probably noticed that our definition of conversation is pretty lengthy. This is because the list of adjectives in the definition is the characteristics that differentiate conversations from other forms of communication like speeches, interviews, group meetings, or debates. Let's look a bit closer at each of these characteristics.

1. Conversations are interactive. Conversations involve **turn-taking**, alternating between speaking and listening in an interaction. A turn can be as short as one word or as lengthy as a monologue. In ordinary conversation, people often overlap or speak "on top of" each other for brief segments. This can make it difficult to identify where one person's turn begins and another's ends. Nevertheless, the concept of a turn is significant for people conversing. For example, when you and your partner both try to take a turn speaking at the same time, various behaviors can occur that demonstrate that you both understand the importance of turn-taking. You may back down and let the other person speak. Or both of you may back down through a polite negotiation in which each says, "I'm sorry. You go ahead." Or both may continue trying to speak until the more persistent one "wins" a turn and the other gives way, though this can result in the "loser" feeling frustrated or annoyed by being interrupted.

2. Conversations are extemporaneous. Much more than presentations or interviews, for example, our social conversations are **extemporaneous**, with messages uttered in the spur of the moment without lengthy preplanning. For an ordinary or typical conversation, we do not script exactly what we will say at each

Recall a recent conversation you had that you thoroughly enjoyed. What made it such a positive experience?

turn. Instead, we reference our "canned plans" and scripts as the conversation unfolds and create messages based on them to pursue our goals. This makes conversation spontaneous and, in some ways, more creative than other forms of communication. The ability to move from one topic to another as the mood strikes is one of the characteristics that most of us find enjoyable about conversation. Still, you have undoubtedly also had conversations that were rather painful, a struggle to find things to talk about. Extemporaneous talk, despite its apparent effortlessness, is actually a skillful form of communication to master.

Local management—the way that conversational partners produce and monitor every aspect of the conversational give-and-take

   3. Conversations are locally managed. Local management is the way that conversational partners produce and monitor every aspect of the conversational give-and-take, including not only turn-taking but also topic changes (Nofsinger, 1991). If Hector and Desirée are chatting casually before class, Desirée may introduce a topic based on their common ground, such as an upcoming exam in the class. They may briefly converse about that until subtle nonverbal cues signal that this topic is winding down. Each person's voice may become softer and less animated, and there may be shorter remarks and more pauses between turns. Hector may notice this and make a conscious (or semiconscious) decision to introduce a new topic, such as the behavior of another student in the class. They may converse on that topic until nonverbal cues indicate the need for a further change. Or Desirée may abruptly change the topic while Hector is speaking by asking, "Have you had lunch yet?" Topic change can be gradual, following a natural progression from one topic to the next, or it can be abrupt and unpredictable, changing from one unrelated issue to the next. Regardless of how it is accomplished, topic change in conversation has to be locally managed by the interactors themselves. In contrast, topics and turns are often scripted beforehand at group presentations or meetings, for example, and participants follow a preplanned outline or agenda. In these settings, there may even be group sanctions for deviating from preset rules.

Sequential organization—the identifiable beginnings (openings), middles (bodies), and ends (closings) of conversations

   4. Conversations are sequentially organized. Sequential organization means that conversations have identifiable beginnings (openings), middles (bodies), and ends (closings), similar to other forms of communication. Unlike communication in other settings, however, the sequential organization is not planned in advance but instead unfolds, turn by turn, through extemporaneous and locally managed talk.

   With these characteristics defined and explored, it becomes more evident that the most ordinary conversation is actually a complex form of communication. You can compare it to improvised music or dancing: conversational partners exchange the roles of leader and follower, make different moves, "dance" with quick or slow turns and topic changes, and so forth, all under their own direction. Most of us, much of the time, do a fairly good job of conversing. However, some conversational issues can be difficult to manage. Later in this chapter, we'll discuss some ways to improve your conversational dancing. But first, let's continue exploring conversation by looking at some of the ways that conversations vary.

LEARN ABOUT YOURSELF ▶ HOW CONVERSATIONS WORK

Take this short survey, which will help you get a better idea of how conversations work by exploring an actual conversation you have had. Pick a recent conversation (satisfactory or unsatisfactory) with a friend, colleague, family member, or anyone else, and then answer the following questions. There are no right or wrong answers, so answer the questions using your first instinct. For each question, select one of the numbers to the left that best describes your attitude toward the conversation you chose to explore.

_____ 1. I would like to have another conversation like this one.

_____ 2. I was very dissatisfied with this conversation.

_____ 3. During this conversation, I was able to present myself as I wanted the other person to view me.

_____ 4. The other person expressed great interest in what I had to say.

_____ 5. We talked about things I was not interested in.

_____ 6. I was annoyed by the other person's interruptions of me.

_____ 7. Turn-taking went smoothly in this conversation.

_____ 8. There were many uncomfortable moments during this conversation.

_____ 9. I did not get to say what I wanted in this conversation.

_____ 10. I was very satisfied with this conversation.

1 = Strongly Agree

2 = Agree Somewhat

3 = Neutral

4 = Disagree Somewhat

5 = Strongly Disagree

Scoring the survey: To find your score, first reverse the responses for the odd-numbered items (if you wrote a 1, make it a 5; 2 = 4; leave 3 as is; 4 = 2; and 5 = 1). Next add the numbers for each item. Scores can range from 10 to 50. The lower (closer to 10) your score, the more satisfied you were with the conversation. The higher (closer to 50) your score, the less satisfied you were with the conversation. Keep your score in mind as you work through this chapter and learn how to improve your conversational skills. If your conversation got a low satisfaction score, what could the participants have done to improve the conversation? If your conversation got a high satisfaction score, what did the participants do right?

Note: After an important conversation, it would be useful for both you and your partner to complete this survey separately, then compare and discuss your scores.

Adapted from Hecht, M. L. (1978). Measures of communication satisfaction. *Human Communication Research, 4,* 350–368.

Variation in Conversation

Conversations are like snowflakes—no two are exactly alike. We can appreciate how conversations vary by understanding conversational types, purposes, sequence, tone, and humor, along with the influence that participants and setting have on your conversational behavior.

"...AND THAT'S ABOUT IT– HOW WAS YOUR DAY?"

Cartoonstock www.Cartoonstock.com

Small talk—a type of conversation focused on inconsequential topics such as the weather, uncontroversial news topics, harmless facts, and predictions

Gossip—discussion of people who are not present for the conversation

Conversation purpose—what the conversation is intended to do

Conversational Types

There are many different types of conversation. Some are common enough that we have shared names for them. **Small talk**, for example, is a type of conversation focused on inconsequential topics such as the weather, uncontroversial news topics, harmless facts, and predictions. We are familiar with small talk and use it to initiate conversations with strangers, break the ice with new acquaintances, or even begin conversations with intimates. **Gossip** is another easily recognized form of conversation, involving the discussion of people who are not present for the conversation. Statements such as "Do you know Armando? I hear he has a really great job" and "Would you believe that Mary Simmons and Tom Johnson are going out? They never seemed to hit it off too well in the past," are both examples of gossip.

One study identified twenty-nine distinct types of conversation common in friendships and romantic relationships (Goldsmith & Baxter, 2006). Along with small talk and gossip, the most-reported types were making plans, joking around, recapping the day's events (i.e., reviewing what happened to each person that day), and catching up (i.e., going over what has happened in each person's life since the last meeting). Other common types included complaining, talking about problems, decision making, conflict, making up, and relationship talk (Goldsmith & Baxter, 2006). Figure 8.1 presents a list of all twenty-nine types.

Purposes

Conversational types differ, in part, because they have distinct purposes. The **conversation purpose** is what the conversation is intended to do. Some conversations are intended to entertain, but others might be meant to persuade, inform, or comfort. Conversations can and do have multiple purposes, such as when we converse to pass time as well as to get acquainted with another person. The purpose of a conversation is typically linked to the goals of the individual participants. What each participant is trying to achieve during the conversation will obviously influence the direction of the conversation as a whole. Because conversation is interactive, however, the purpose of the conversation is not necessarily identical to either participant's goals. Instead, the purpose is "negotiated" by the participants as they interact. Usually the negotiation isn't obvious, because the participants' goals are compatible and result in a mutually agreeable purpose. The fact that we negotiate our goals to arrive at the purpose of the conversation becomes more evident when our goals are incompatible with our partner's goals. For example, if Adrianne meets Micah at a club and is physically attracted to him, she may have the goal of "hooking up," but the conversational purpose won't become a "pickup" if Micah isn't also interested in hooking up or isn't attracted to Adrianne.

The purpose of an interaction is usually evident in the type of messages exchanged and after the fact by what has happened as a result of the conversation. A conversation's purpose can be identified as "joking around" partly because of

1. **Asking a favor:** talk with the specific purpose of getting someone to do something for you.

2. **Asking out:** the kind of talk one person uses when asking another out on a date.

3. **Bedtime talk:** the kind of routine talk you have right before you go to bed.

4. **Breaking bad news:** a conversation in which one person reveals bad news to another.

5. **Catching up:** the kind of conversation you have when you haven't talked with someone recently, and you talk about the events in your lives that have occurred since you last spoke.

6. **Class information talk:** informal conversations in which you find out about class assignments, exams, or course material.

7. **Complaining:** expressing frustrations, gripes, or complaints about some common experience, directing negative feelings toward the topic but not the other people in the conversation.

8. **Conflict:** conversations in which the two people disagree.

9. **Current events talk:** a conversation whose topic is limited to news and current events.

10. **Decision-making conversation:** a conversation whose goal is making a decision about some task.

11. **Getting to know someone:** the kind of small talk you have when you want to be friendly and get acquainted with someone.

12. **Giving and getting instructions:** a conversation in which one person gives another information or directions about how to do some task.

13. **Gossip:** exchanging opinions or information about someone else who isn't present.

14. **Group discussion:** group talk to exchange information, persuade other people, or make decisions.

15. **Interrogation:** a one-way kind of conversation in which one person grills another with questions.

16. **Joking around:** a playful kind of talk to have fun or release tension.

17. **Lecture:** a one-way kind of conversation in which one person tells another how to act or what to do.

18. **Love talk:** talk that has little content but gives attention and expresses love and affection.

19. **Making plans:** talk to arrange a meeting or an activity with someone.

20. **Making up:** a conversation in which one person or both apologize for violating expectations.

21. **Morning talk:** the kind of routine talk you have when you first wake up in the morning.

22. **Persuading conversation:** conversation in which one person aims to convince the other to do something.

23. **Recapping the day's events:** discussing what's up and what happened to each person during the day.

24. **Relationship talk:** talking about the nature and state of a relationship.

25. **Reminiscing:** talking with someone about shared events you experienced in the past.

26. **Serious conversation:** a two-way, in-depth discussion or exchange of feelings, opinions, or ideas about some personal and important topic.

27. **Small talk:** a kind of talk to pass time and avoid being rude.

28. **Sports talk:** the kind of talk that occurs while playing or watching a sporting event.

29. **Talking about problems:** a conversation in which one person talks about some problem he or she is having and the other person tries to help.

▶ **OBSERVE AND ANALYZE**

Conversational Profiling

Look at the list of conversation types in Figure 8.1 and think about the conversations you had yesterday. Which of the twenty-nine types did you participate in? Which did you have most frequently? Were there any types of conversation that don't fit in these categories? Now choose two different relationships in your life and go through the list, thinking about the conversations you've had with these two people over the past week. How does the "conversational profile" differ between the two relationships? In Chapter 6, you learned about the indexical function of communication in relationships. What do the two different conversational profiles tell you about dominance and affiliation in these two relationships?

FIGURE 8.1 Twenty-nine types of conversations. Adapted from Goldsmith, D. J., & Baxter, L. A. (2006). Constituting relationships in talk: A taxonomy of speech events in social and personal relationships. *Human Communication Research, 23,* 87–114.

What portion of the conversations you have had today have been somewhat entertaining?

the teases and jibes that the participants exchange, but also because, looking back later, they observe that nothing consequential occurred because of that conversation. Sometimes the purpose of a conversation isn't evident until it's over and both participants can see what it has accomplished. This may be especially true when a conversation is a turning point in a relationship. Have you ever said, "That conversation was when we became friends" or "I knew when we finished the conversation that the relationship was not going to last?" A particular outcome may help you realize that the conversation had a different purpose than you intended when you were engaged in it.

Sequence

While all conversations have openings, bodies, and conclusions, the turn-by-turn sequence of any conversation is unique. Much of the sequential variation is linked to the type and purpose of the conversation. Consider joking around and recapping the day's events, two types of conversation that occur frequently in the relationships of college students. The opening of a joking-around episode often involves some form of teasing, which will typically be returned in kind. Subsequent acts may include a combination of jokes, banter, humorous put-downs, amusing anecdotes, and so forth. A very different sequence is involved in "recapping the day's events," whose opening would be something like "So . . . how'd it go today?" The sequence for this episode involves each person talking about what happened, punctuated by questions and comments from the other party; and the ending might be a transition to another activity ("Let's get dinner started") or to another type of conversation such as planning ("What do you want to do tomorrow?").

Scripted—highly routinized

In some types of conversation, the sequence becomes **scripted** or highly routinized. People adhere to their canned plans without much conscious thought or choice. For example, consider brief conversations whose only purpose is to greet and acknowledge someone you know. If Kimiko and Jesse have not seen each other for some time but bump into each other while jogging, the following conversation would follow a greeting script.

> **Jesse:** Hey, it's been a long time. How are you doing?
>
> **Kimiko:** Yes, it's been forever since we've seen each other. I'm doing fine. How about you?
>
> **Jesse:** I'm good. Can't complain. How is work going?
>
> **Kimiko:** Work's keeping me busy. Are you still with KDC Software?

Notice the reciprocal exchange of acknowledgements and inquiries in this conversation. Jesse greets Kimiko and asks a question; after acknowledging the greeting and answering the question, Kimiko asks the same question of Jesse.

Certain topics are standard in a greeting script. We are likely to chat about health, work, school, and common friends rather than world politics, serious crises, or our financial status. Notice also how turns are very short. Greeting conversations have a quick give-and-take to them. Other scripted conversations might relate to giving and receiving compliments or the annual phone call to your great aunt to thank her for your birthday present.

A unique type of conversational scripting occurs between two individuals who have been interacting for a long time. **Co-narration** is a specific type of conversational sequencing in which people finish each other's sentences because they have intimate knowledge of the topic and each other's style (Sawyer, 2001). So they share a script. For example, if Dana and Armand have lived together for many years and Armand says, "In 1999, we went out West for a trip," Dana will say, "It was spring and we drove our RV." When Armand adds, "That RV always gave us trouble because . . ." Dana will finish, "the engine would overheat when you drove fast." Because this conversation is so routine and scripted, Armand and Dana may not perceive that they are interrupting each other. Instead, they are cooperating in narrating the story.

Tone

The **conversation tone** is its emotional and relational quality, or how it feels "inside" the interaction. Imagine you are at a social event and are forced into conversation with a former boyfriend or girlfriend who really hurt you by abruptly ending your relationship to be with someone else. Neither of you really wants to be interacting with the other, and your distaste for the situation (and for each other) will be indexed nonverbally through behaviors like limited eye contact and lack of facial expressiveness, and verbally through very short and impersonal messages. These behaviors will create a conversational tone that is cold and "stiff." In contrast, a conversation with a friend you hadn't seen recently and were delighted to encounter would probably have a warm, easy tone.

One important dimension of tone is **formality**, the degree to which a conversation follows scripted norms, rules, and procedures. The formality of a conversation is strongly influenced by the participants' characteristics and their relationship to each other, especially their relative status and familiarity. Typically, when there is a recognized status difference between the participants, the tone of the conversation will be more formal. For example, if you were speaking to the president of your college or your company, the conversation tone would probably be formal. You might shake the president's hand rather than hug or slap hands. You would defer to the president and accept the president's topic choice. You would self-monitor so that you didn't interrupt the president and would

Co-narration is expected of identical twins, but it is also experienced by others who are intimate. Do you know any couples that co-narrate?

Co-narration—specific type of conversational sequencing in which people finish each other's sentences because they have intimate knowledge of the topic and each other's style

Conversation tone—emotional and relational quality, or how it feels "inside" the interaction

Formality—degree to which a conversation follows scripted norms, rules, and procedures

self-censor to avoid using profanity. When participants are more familiar with each other, conversations are more informal. When you talk with a close friend, you stand or sit closer together. You both introduce topics. Interruptions are acceptable, and—depending on the sensitivity of the participants—profanity may be used and intimate topics discussed.

Participants

Obviously, conversations vary with the participants. This is because how conversational partners talk to each other is fundamentally influenced by their roles, their relationship to each other, and their individual characteristics and personality traits. Imagine an older married couple who have been regular customers at a small restaurant for several years. Because of their role as "regulars," they are likely to have conversations with the wait staff that are more extended and personal than the conversations that would occur with casual customers. For example, the regulars and the employees would probably have learned things about each other's families and pets, activities away from work, and some likes and dislikes, all of which would provide material for their conversations. If the couple had not come to the restaurant for a longer than usual period, the employees would almost certainly inquire about what they had been doing in their absence.

The audience for a conversation is not necessarily limited to the participants who speak. The couple who are regulars at the restaurant may be talking directly to one employee, but other customers and employees who are nearby are likely to overhear. These others might be "candidates" to participate actively in the conversation, depending on their interest and whether the current participants encourage them, by making eye contact and smiling in their direction rather than avoiding eye contact and leaning in toward each other to signal that others are not welcome to contribute.

Setting

How we experience any conversation is influenced by the setting or physical environment in which it occurs, and the setting often influences our perception of the kinds of conversation that are appropriate. Few people engage in casual joking around in a funeral parlor (though funeral home employees would certainly do it when mourners were not around), nor would many people choose a crowded fast-food restaurant for a conversation that involved emotional reminiscing about someone who had died. Even when the physical setting remains the same, the "scene" within that setting can change, with consequences for the type of conversation that occurs. For example, the scene is different in an apartment when roommates are getting ready for work or school from when they are hosting a party.

How does the formality of a State Dinner affect the subjects of conversation?

In the first scene, conversation will probably focus on mundane morning activities such as making breakfast, finding misplaced keys or phones, or planning for events that will take place later in the day. In the second scene, there is likely to be a much wider range of topics, greater volume and more energetic expression, and the sense that the conversation is a key part of the fun rather than a way of getting things done.

Guidelines for Effective Conversationalists

Because conversations are highly varied, the kinds of skills necessary to be an effective conversationalist also vary according to type of conversation, setting, participants, and so forth. In the remainder of this chapter we will describe general guidelines you can use to become a better conversationalist. Then we will present specific skills that will help you when you converse with someone you don't really know.

General Conversation Guidelines

There are several general guidelines you can follow as you work to be a better conversational partner: develop an other-centered focus, engage in appropriate turn-taking, maintain conversational coherence, protect privacy, and engage in ethical dialogue.

1. Focus on your partner. Focusing on your partner in conversation means listening carefully to what they are saying rather than being consumed by your own agenda, asking questions, and introducing topics that interest your conversational partner. Focusing on your partner also requires you to fully participate in the conversation. For example, looking at your partner rather than watching others who are entering or leaving the room, silencing cell phones and not responding to vibration, and not multitasking are all ways to be other-centered. Being other-centered does not mean leaving yourself out. If you are focused on others, you can still talk about yourself when the conversation naturally moves to your interests or when your conversational partner asks you for information.

2. Engage in appropriate turn-taking. Effective conversationalists show respect and consideration for others in the way they take turns. Two major elements of appropriate turn-taking are distributing the talk time evenly and avoiding interruption. **Talk time** is the share of time participants each have in a conversation. Generally, you should balance speaking and listening, and all participants should have

Talk time—the share of time participants each have in a conversation

How can you tell that these people are focusing on each other?

roughly the same opportunity to talk. Certainly, it is acceptable to allocate more floor time to higher-status people and to accommodate those whose conversational style is more outgoing or reserved. However, people are likely to tune out or become annoyed at conversational partners who make speeches, filibuster, or perform monologues rather than engage in the ordinary give-and-take of conversation. Similarly, it is difficult to carry on a conversation with someone who provides one- or two-word replies to questions designed to elicit meaningful information. Turns do vary in length depending on what is being said, but if your statements average much longer or much shorter than your conversational partners, you probably need to adjust. If you discover that you are speaking more than your fair share, try to restrain yourself by mentally checking whether anyone else has had a chance to talk once you talk a second time. On the other hand, if you find yourself being inactive in a conversation, try to increase your level of participation. In group conversation, you can help others who are unable to get enough talk time by saying something like "Donna, I get the sense that you've been wanting to comment on this point," or "Tyler, what do you think?"

A second critical element of turn-taking is learning to wait for others to finish speaking. Some people are chronic interrupters and do not realize it. Pay attention to your turn-taking behavior to make sure that you are not seizing the conversational floor from others. Interrupting for "agreement" (confirming) or clarification is generally considered to be interpersonally acceptable (Kennedy & Camden, 1983). For instance, if you say, "Good point, Max," or "Exactly!" most people won't object, even if you are talking right on top of them. Similarly, you can usually interrupt with questions or paraphrases to better understand what

---

SKILL BUILDER ▶ **TURN-TAKING**

SKILL	USE	STEPS	EXAMPLE
Engaging in appropriate turn-taking	Determining when a speaker is at a place where another person may talk if he or she wants	1. Take your share of turns. 2. Gear the length of turns to the behavior of partners. 3. Give and watch for turn-taking and turn-exchanging cues. Avoid giving inadvertent turn-taking cues. 4. Observe and use conversation-directing behavior. 5. Limit interruptions.	When John lowers his voice as he says, "I really thought they were going to go ahead during those last few seconds," Melissa, noticing that he appears to be finished, says, "I did, too. But did you notice...."

another person is saying without offending. For example, you could interrupt to ask, "What do you mean by you were 'on the struggle bus?'" or say "'On the struggle bus'—oh, you mean it was a tough day." If, however, your interruptions involve changing the subject, minimizing the contribution of the interrupted party, disagreeing, or attempting to turn conversational attention to yourself, they are likely to be viewed as disruptive and impolite.

3. Maintain conversational coherence. Conversational coherence is the extent to which the comments made by one person relate to those made previously by others in a conversation (McLaughlin, 1984). It is a way to create clear meaning in conversation. The more directly messages relate to those that precede them, the more coherent or meaningful the conversation. If what you want to say is only tangentially related or unrelated to what was said before, then you should probably yield your turn to someone else who may have more relevant comments and wait for a lull in the conversation to introduce your new topic. If only two people are conversing, then the listener should at least respond to the speaker's message before introducing a change in topic. If at any point you must introduce a completely unrelated topic, it will appear somewhat more coherent if you acknowledge what you're doing, such as, "Sorry to change the subject, but did you hear that . . .?"

4. Protect privacy. Being an effective conversationalist also includes protecting privacy. One aspect of protecting privacy is keeping confidences. If someone reveals private information in a conversation and asks you not to share this information with others, it is important to honor this request. Another aspect of protecting privacy is paying attention to any unintended audience to the conversation. To avoid revealing private things to strangers who don't need to know them and probably don't want to know them, you may need to move a conversation to a more secluded location, speak more softly, or have the conversation at another time.

5. Engage in ethical dialogue. The final guideline followed by effective conversationalists is to engage in ethical dialogue. **Ethical dialogue** occurs when conversational partners act in ways that are authentic, empathic, confirming, present, equal, and supportive (Johannesen, Valde, & Whedbee, 2008). Not all of these characteristics need be present in every conversation. For example, while you would be hurt if your closest friends were inauthentic, in certain situations you probably don't need or even want to know what others really think.

6. Choose appropriate humor. Humorous messages are designed to create amusement. Do you enjoy conversations that feel "fun" and make you laugh? Most people do. Humorous conversations can encourage feelings of cohesiveness and satisfaction among conversational partners. Laughing together helps deflect negative feelings and create a sense of belonging (Maki, Booth-Butterfield, & McMullen, 2012). People who are good at creating lighthearted, entertaining conversations are usually well-liked and make friends easily. With care and practice, you may be able to use humor to improve your conversational skills.

Theorists Peter McGraw and Caleb Warren (2010) have defined humor as a **benign violation**, meaning that we become amused when we observe

Cartoonstock www.Cartoonstock.com

Conversational coherence—the extent to which the comments made by one person relate to those made previously by others in a conversation

Ethical dialogue—a conversation characterized by authenticity, empathy, confirmation, presentness, equality, and supportiveness

Benign violation—the idea that humor is created from behavior that is unexpected, but not harmful

Analysis of a Media Conversation

Analyze a conversation between two people in a television show or movie. Evaluate the communicators according to the guidelines for effective conversationalists. To what extent do the people show an other-centered focus, take turns appropriately, maintain conversational coherence, protect privacy, and engage in ethical dialogue? Provide examples of the characters following or violating these guidelines. If this is a comedy, how do violations add to the humor? If this is a drama, how do violations affect the emotional tone of the conversation?

something unexpected but not harmful. For example, imagine seeing a pig wearing a sweater. Most of us have never seen a pig in clothes, so this is unexpected. It also isn't harmful, so we may smile or chuckle. If you can introduce something unexpected but benign to your conversations, you may create humor that others will enjoy. For example, in a conversation with a stranger, you could notice something odd but unthreatening in the surroundings, comment on something silly that you thought or did, or relay an absurd story you heard about a celebrity. As you get to know people, you often discover what kinds of benign violations they find especially humorous.

However, humor must always be handled with care. Something you consider to be unexpected may be taken for granted by others, making your attempts at humor seem boring or childish. We also don't always know what others consider harmful. For example, people often underestimate the hurtfulness of "humor" based on gender, ethnicity, or sexual orientation (Alberts & Drzewiecka, 2008), so these are generally not good topics on which to create conversational humor. When you use humor it's important to monitor others' reactions to see how your humor is being received and if it is having its intended effect.

Skills for Conversing with Strangers

Conversations often seem to have a life of their own, and when they're going well, they seem effortless. But as you have seen, creating a satisfying conversation is a complex and sometimes difficult activity. In particular, many of us find it challenging to talk to people we are meeting for the first time or don't know very well. You want to be able to converse successfully with strangers or acquaintances for many reasons. These include the need to network with others who might be good career contacts, to develop friendships in your new neighborhood, or to simply pass the time more pleasantly while waiting in the airport lounge for a delayed flight. Although many people avoid conversation with strangers and view it as effortful, talking can generally make you happier. In one recent experiment, people who carried on a conversation with a coffee shop barista were happier afterward than people who placed their order as efficiently as possible (Sandstrom & Dunn, 2014).

To help you get the most from your conversations, this section focuses on developing skills for conversing with someone you do not know well or at all. The skills discussed will help you initiate, continue, and close conversations, leading to more enjoyable and effective interactions. Even if you typically like talking with unfamiliar people, you may find some suggestions that will make your first-time conversations flow more easily or that apply to other kinds of conversation.

Starting a Conversation

Are you comfortable initiating a conversation with a complete stranger? Many of us feel that just getting started is the most awkward part. Fortunately, four easy strategies can help break the conversational ice: Make a comment, ask a question, introduce yourself, and pay attention to nonverbal cues.

1. Make a comment. One simple approach is to make a comment that invites the other person to respond. You might comment on your surroundings or situation, such as "Well, I guess the bus is running late this morning," or mention something you find interesting about the other person, such as "That's a unique book bag. I haven't seen one like that before." Yet another possibility for opening conversation is to notice something you and the other person have in common—"Looks like we're both headed up to campus"—or possibly something that's different about you, particularly if the other person would find the comparison positive. For example, if it's raining and the other person has an umbrella and you don't, a conversation starter might be "You're a lot more organized than I am. I never remember to bring an umbrella!" A note of humor, especially at your own expense, can also help get things off to a good start. Researchers have found that a shared laugh can ease the initial awkwardness between strangers (Fraley & Aron, 2004). For example, if you got wet in the rain, you could say, "The drowned rat look is *always* in fashion!" or "I used to laugh when Grandma said I should take an umbrella. Guess who's laughing now?"

2. Ask a question. Another general strategy is to ask a question. Generally, this should be a **ritual question**, a question about the other person or the situation that is easy to answer and doesn't pry into personal matters (Gabor, 2001). For example, if you're in line at a smoothie shop, you might ask the person in front of you, "Do you recommend a particular flavor?" or if it's the first day of class and the professor hasn't arrived yet, you could ask, "Is this class for your major?" or "Do you know the instructor for this class?" It can be useful to pair comments and ritual questions, especially when the comment makes the question seem more natural or less intrusive. For example, just blurting out "What's your major?" to someone at a campus bus stop is rather awkward, but if you comment on something you see that gives a clue about the person's course of study ("That's a really nice portfolio. Are you in Fine Arts?"), the observation creates a basis for asking the question.

3. Introduce yourself. Make a greeting, state your own name, and directly or indirectly ask for the other person's name. For example, "Hi. My name is Brianna. What's yours?" A variation on this approach is to add a simple disclosure that helps explain why you're introducing yourself: "Hello. My name's Evan. I just got added to this class. What's your name?" The introduction approach probably works best in situations where you expect to interact with the other person again (such as a classroom or work context), which makes an exchange of names highly appropriate. If you're talking to someone you probably won't see again (e.g., at the bus stop or smoothie shop), you could still use this strategy to open the conversation, but it could be seen as pushy because the other person will feel pressure to offer his or her name and may not want to do so. In such situations, you will probably get a more positive reaction if you start with a comment or ritual question and delay the introduction until some conversation has taken place. Once the conversational ball is rolling, there may not be an obvious time to introduce yourself, but you can always slide it in with a comment that indicates you know you're changing the topic: "I don't think I mentioned this,

Ritual question—a question about the other person or the situation that is easy to answer and doesn't pry into personal matters

Snapshots

"Like to read, huh? Me, too. I'm a big reader. I just finished a book by Brown. You know Dan Brown? Great writer..."

Cartoonstock www.Cartoonstock.com

but my name's Brianna." You may also find this opening helpful in situations where you know you have talked with people before, but can't remember their names. Saying something like, "It's good to see you again, my name is Brianna, and forgive me, but I can't recall your name," is a polite way to truthfully acknowledge the situation, and provide an opportunity for people to tell you their names.

4. Pay attention to nonverbal cues. Paying attention to nonverbal as well as verbal behavior will enhance your success at getting a conversation started. You are much more likely to have a positive interaction with someone who appears receptive to conversation. Clues that someone might be interested in talking with you include open arms, eye contact, and a smile. If someone does not look interested in conversation, this doesn't mean you can't or shouldn't try to talk to her or him, but it may take more skill and effort on your part, and you should be prepared for the other person to close the conversation quickly. Your own nonverbal behavior also matters. To show your interest in interaction, you can smile, keep your arms uncrossed and relaxed, approach to a distance that's appropriate for conversation (or, if seated, lean slightly forward toward the other person), and make eye contact.

Sustaining a Conversation

Once a conversation is underway, how do you keep it going? Several specific strategies facilitate conversation: using free information, asking questions, seeking topics of interest to the other person, providing self-disclosure, and listening.

1. Use free information. One essential strategy for keeping a conversation going is making use of **free information**, information volunteered during conversation rather than specifically required or requested (Gabor, 2001). For example, if you asked, "Where are you headed after class today?" the person might respond, "Downtown. I have a job interview." The information about the interview is "free" because it isn't strictly necessary to answer your question. This

Free information—information volunteered during conversation rather than specifically required or requested

---

SKILL	USE	STEPS	EXAMPLE
Initiating conversation with a stranger	To start an interaction with someone you don't know	Do one or more of the following: 1. Make a comment about the situation, the other person, or yourself. 2. Ask a ritual question. 3. Introduce yourself.	Jenna is waiting in line at the grocery store. The woman in front of her is looking at the candy bars. Jenna says "Don't those look good? I always seem to end up at the store when I'm hungry."

information provides a natural basis for your next contribution to the conversation, enabling you to ask something like, "Oh, where are you interviewing?" or "I noticed you had a suit on. Interviewing makes me so nervous. How do you handle it?" Keep in mind that you need to provide free information for others to use, too. If you give only minimal responses to others' questions or comments, you are depriving them of material that will help them sustain the conversation with you.

2. Ask questions. Questions can open new topics of conversation, demonstrate interest in the other person, and ensure that all parties to the conversation get opportunities to speak. Skilled conversationalists use a mix of **closed-ended questions**—questions that can be answered with "yes," "no," or a few words, and **open-ended questions**, questions that require answers with more elaboration and explanation (Garner, 1997). Closed-ended questions are good for eliciting specific information ("Where are you headed?"), but if you use exclusively closed-ended questions, your conversation can end up feeling like an interrogation, especially if your conversational partner provides only the required information ("Where are you headed after class today?" "Downtown." "What takes you downtown?" "Shopping."). When you follow a closed-ended question with an open-ended question, you create a space for your conversational partner to expand. For example, "Hmm . . . why do you shop downtown rather than around here?" Notice how these open-ended questions would encourage disclosure of your conversational partner's thoughts and feelings.

3. Seek out topics of interest to the other person. Most people will jump at the chance to talk about things that they find personally interesting and important. If you can identify one of these topics and get the other person going, the conversation will practically run itself for a while. Often, what other people are wearing or items they are carrying will provide clues about where they devote their time, energy, and money, including their jobs, affiliations or associations, and hobbies or other activities. A brief comment such as, "Looks like you're a Cubs fan!" can stimulate subsequent discussion. Free information also provides good clues about topics that others find interesting. For example, if you ask, "What neighborhood do you live in?" and the response is, "Well, because we have little kids . . . ," or "You know, with our dogs, we decided we had to . . ." you can bet that it won't take much prompting to get that person talking about his or her kids or dogs. You can also use direct questions to elicit another person's high-interest topics, such as, "What do you do when you're not working?" As you seek out another person's high-interest topics, don't forget that your own interests can be part of the conversation, too. For example, if you've been talking with another person about his or her work, sharing something about your work or school can be a good way to continue the conversation. For example, "It sounds like you have a good time with your work. I like my job, too, especially interacting with the public. . . ." If you have indicated interest in things that matter to someone else, that person will be likely to show you the same respect. Even better, as each of you reveals some of what's interesting and important to you, you may have the joy of discovering that you have something in common.

Closed-ended questions—questions that can be answered with "yes," "no," or a few words

Open-ended questions—questions that require answers with more elaboration and explanation

Self-disclosure—verbally sharing personal ideas and feelings with others

4. Self-disclose appropriately. Self-disclosure involves verbally sharing personal ideas and feelings with others. Although you don't want to disclose highly intimate or risky information to people you've just met, a willingness to share some of your personal experiences and perspective can result in more stimulating and meaningful conversation. So, with new acquaintances, disclose factual information about yourself. For example, if you've been chatting with someone about the stores and restaurants in your neighborhood, you might disclose that you prefer to buy locally and support merchants who live near you rather than spending your money at national chains. This disclosure reveals something about your perspective and values, creating an opportunity for your conversational partner to know you a little better, reveal a shared—or different—point of view, or ask you questions about the practice of buying locally. At the same time, this disclosure would not be perceived as overly intimate, put your privacy at risk, or embarrass you. Overall, the best approach to self-disclosure in initial interactions is to disclose gradually, making sure that the thoughts and feelings you reveal are relevant to whatever topic is under discussion and appropriate to sharing with a stranger (or whatever relationship you may have with the other person). You should also observe whether your self-disclosure is reciprocated or matched by your conversational partner. If he or she doesn't reveal thoughts or feelings similar in quality and quantity, you may want to scale back on your disclosure so that both of you are comfortable.

5. Actively listen. Use the listening skills you learned in Chapter 7. If you are prone to worrying about what you will say next, paying close attention to

SKILL BUILDER ▶ SUSTAINING CONVERSATION

SKILL	USE	STEPS	EXAMPLE
Sustaining conversation	To sustain a first-time conversation, pass time enjoyably, and get to know someone	Do the following throughout the conversation: 1. Use and provide free information. 2. Ask closed-ended and open-ended questions. 3. Seek high-interest topics. 4. Make appropriate self-disclosures. 5. Listen actively.	Roger and Eduardo are chatting while waiting for treadmills to become available at the gym. Roger says, "Man, I wish this place had more treadmills. I really need to step up my workouts." Eduardo replies, "Are you training for something in particular?" "Yes," says Roger. "I've signed up for a half-marathon in a couple of months." "Phew," Eduardo comments. "That's a lot of miles. What got you into running races?"

what the other person is saying will make coming up with a response less of a problem. Also, if your nonverbal behavior suggests that you're listening (eye contact, nodding, positive facial expression, etc.), you will probably encourage the other person to continue talking, making your side of the conversation that much easier.

Closing a Conversation

Knowing how to close a conversation smoothly is just as important as being able to get one started. A graceful exit leaves a good impression, which is valuable even if you don't expect to encounter the other person again. Also, on occasion you may be uncomfortable continuing to talk with someone, in which case knowing how to bring a conversation to a close quickly can be useful. Four strategies are useful for closing a conversation: Notice and use nonverbal leave-taking cues, verbalize your desire to end the conversation, ask to see the other person again if appropriate, and close with a brief stock message.

1. Notice and use leave-taking cues. Leave-taking cues are nonverbal behaviors that indicate someone wants to end the conversation. These include changes in eye contact and body position and movement. One nonverbal leave-taking cue is shifting eye contact from looking mostly at your conversational partner to scanning the scene around the two of you. Similarly, if someone you've been talking with rises, turns away, or begins rapidly nodding as you're talking, these are probably kinesic (bodily movement) cues of the desire to end the conversation. You can use these cues to signal your desire to end a conversation, and when you observe your partner using these cues, you should quickly finish talking and allow your partner to exit.

2. Verbalize your desire to end the conversation. You need to complement your use of nonverbal leave-taking cues with verbal indicators that the interaction is nearing its end. You can do this indirectly by summarizing something interesting that has been talked about: "Alex, I'm glad I had the opportunity to learn about your work with the Literacy Center. You're making an important contribution to our community." You can thank or compliment the other person for the interaction: "I really enjoyed talking to you!" Or you can be more direct by stating your need to end the conversation: "I really need to get going." "Please excuse me, but I see someone I need to talk with."

3. Ask to see the person again if appropriate. If you are interested in seeing the other person again, this is the time to inquire about whether the other person is also interested, and if so, exchange phone numbers or email addresses, or agree on a specific date and time. For example, you might say, "Would you like to get together for coffee? I'm free during the week most afternoons after 3:00"; or "It was fun talking to you! I'm going to take my kids to the park Saturday morning. Would you and your kids like to join us?"

4. Close with a brief stock message. Just as there are ritualized ways to open a conversation, there are recognized messages to end a conversation. To politely close an interaction, say something like, "Take care," or "Have a great day, okay?" Or, if you have learned and remember the person's name, using it as

Leave-taking cues—nonverbal behaviors that indicate someone wants to end the conversation

▶ **OBSERVE AND ANALYZE**

Making Conversation

At your next opportunity, make a point to strike up a conversation with a stranger. (Do this in a safe, public place with someone you feel comfortable approaching). Try out the strategies for initiating, sustaining, and closing the conversation. Then reflect on the experience. Was this conversation different from other first-time interactions? Did you feel more or less effective as a conversationalist? What will you do next time?

SKILL BUILDER ▶ CLOSING CONVERSATION

SKILL	USE	STEPS	EXAMPLE
Closing conversation	To end a conversation	Do one or more of the following: 1. Use and respond to others' nonverbal leave-taking cues. 2. Use verbal leave-taking cues such as summarizing something interesting in the conversation and thanking the other person for the opportunity to talk. If desired, make plans to talk again. 3. Use a brief closing statement. 4. Verbalize your desire to end the conversation.	Elena and Danh have been talking in the hallway of a campus building, but it's almost time for Danh to go to class. He picks up his backpack and says, "Hey, it's been fun talking. I have to go to class now, but you can look me up on Facebook. It's like "Dan," but with an 'h' on the end, and my last name is just Ng." Elena says, "Yeah, I'll do that. Bye now!" "Bye!"

you say goodbye adds a personal touch and shows respect: "Have a great afternoon, Marissa!"

Cultural Variations in Conversation

Throughout this chapter, we have assumed a Western cultural perspective on effective conversation: specifically, the perspective of "low-context" cultures (See Chapter 3). Verbal and nonverbal rules vary from low-context to high-context cultures, as do the guidelines for effective conversation. For example in the "Diverse Voices" article in this chapter, Nancy Masterson Sakamoto discusses how a conversation in Japan can be a very different experience from a conversation in the United States. Four differences in conversational patterns between people from low-context and high-context cultures have been observed (Gudykunst & Matsumoto, 1996).

First, conversations in low-context cultures (like the U.S.) are likely to include greater use of direct categorical words such as *"certainly," "absolutely,"* and *"positively,"* whereas in high-context cultures (like China), conversations rely on indirectness, using verbal qualifiers such as *"maybe," "perhaps,"* and *"probably."*

Second, low-context cultures have a strong expectation that conversational contributions will be overtly relevant—clearly on topic with whatever has been talked about up to that point. In high-context cultures, however, individuals' responses are likely to be more indirect, ambiguous, and apparently less relevant because listeners rely more on nonverbal cues to help them understand a speaker's intentions and meaning.

Third, in low-context cultures, there is an expectation of verbal directness and honesty. People are expected to communicate their actual feelings verbally, regardless of how this affects others. Effective conversationalists in high-context cultures, however, put a high priority on maintaining harmony with others, and so conversationalists will sometimes send messages that mask their true feelings.

Fourth, in low-context cultures, periods of silence are perceived as uncomfortable because when no one is speaking, little information is being shared. In high-context cultures, silences in conversation are often meaningful. When three or four people sit together and no one talks, the silence may indicate agreement, disapproval, embarrassment, or disagreement, depending on the context.

In this chapter, you have learned a number of guidelines for conducting effective conversations. But because of these and other cultural variations, adhering too closely to particular guidelines may sometimes be ineffective. In other words, different cultures have different standards for what constitutes an effective conversation. For example, people from other cultures observing a conversation between people from southern Europe or Middle Easterners may misinterpret an interaction to be an argument, because in these cultures conversational style is animated. People converse by talking loudly, yelling, confronting, interrupting, abruptly changing topics, and being passionately involved (Sawyer, 2001). Members of these cultures view this as part of a lively, engaging conversation and would see rules of politeness, turn-taking, topic changing, and conversational coherence as uninvolving and ineffective. Instead, a good conversationalist would be expected to discuss multiple topics at once, jump into the conversation without waiting for a turn, speak in a loud and emotional tone, and disagree strongly with others. So be aware that there are cultural norms but no absolute rules regarding conversation. By understanding and appreciating cultural variation in conversations, we can avoid judging others' conversational styles when they do not conform to our own rules. There are many ways to have a conversation.

THE SOCIAL MEDIA FACTOR

Digital Conversation Skills

Daily conversations have traditionally been viewed as taking place face-to-face or over the telephone, but now they are increasingly conducted through social media. The effectiveness of these digital conversations depends strongly on **social presence**, which is our sense that conversational partners are immediately available to us—even if they really aren't (Biocca, Harms, & Burgoon, 2003). If you've been chatting online and felt as though you were face-to-face, you've experienced strong social presence. But you've probably also experienced weak social presence, or the sense that someone else isn't "really there," even though

Social presence—your personal sense that in a particular moment your conversational partners are immediately available to you—even if they aren't

Conversational Ballgames

BY NANCY MASTERSON SAKAMOTO

Nancy Masterson Sakamoto is Professor of American Studies at Shitennoji Gakuen University, Hawaii Institute; and coauthor of *Mutual Understanding of Different Cultures* (1981). A former English teacher and teacher trainer in Japan, she co-wrote (with Reiko Naotsuka) a bilingual textbook for Japanese students called *Polite Fictions: Why Japanese and Americans Seem Rude to Each Other* (1982). "Conversational Ballgames" is excerpted from this book.

After I was married and had lived in Japan for a while, my Japanese gradually improved to the point where I could take part in simple conversations with my husband and his friends and family. And I began to notice that often, when I joined in, the others would look startled, and the conversational topic would come to a halt. After this happened several times, it became clear to me that I was doing something wrong. But for a long time, I didn't know what it was.

Finally, after listening carefully to many Japanese conversations, I discovered what my problem was. Even though I was speaking Japanese, I was handling the conversation in a Western way.

Japanese-style conversations develop quite differently from Western-style conversations. And the difference isn't only in the languages. I realized that just as I kept trying to hold Western-style conversations even when I was speaking Japanese, so my English students kept trying to hold Japanese-style conversations even when they were speaking English. We were unconsciously playing entirely different conversational ballgames.

A Western-style conversation between two people is like a game of tennis. If I introduce a topic, a conversational ball, I expect you to hit it back. If you agree with me, I don't expect you simply to agree and do nothing more. I expect you to add something—a reason for agreeing, another example, or an elaboration to carry the idea further. But I don't expect you always to agree. I am just as happy if you question me, or challenge me, or completely disagree with me. Whether you agree or disagree, your response will return the ball to me.

And then it is my turn again. I don't serve a new ball from my original starting line. I hit your ball back again from where it has bounced. I carry your idea further, or answer your questions or objections, or challenge or question you. And so the ball goes back and forth, with each of us doing our best to give it a new twist, an original spin, or a powerful smash.

And the more vigorous the action, the more interesting and exciting the game. Of course, if one of us gets angry, it spoils the conversation, just as it spoils a tennis game. But getting excited is not at all the same as getting angry. After all, we are not trying to hit each other. We are trying to hit the ball. So long as we attack only each other's opinions, and do not attack each other personally, we don't expect anyone to get hurt. A good conversation is supposed to be interesting and exciting.

If there are more than two people in the conversation, then it is like doubles in tennis, or like volleyball. There's no waiting in line. Whoever is nearest and quickest hits the ball, and if you step back, someone else will hit it. No one stops the game to give you a turn. You're responsible for taking your own turn.

But whether it's two players or a group, everyone does his best to keep the ball going, and no one person has the ball for very long.

A Japanese-style conversation, however, is not at all like tennis or volleyball. It's like bowling. You wait for your turn. And you always know your place in line. It depends on such things as whether you are older or younger, a close friend or a relative stranger to the previous speaker, in a senior or junior position, and so on.

When your turn comes, you step up to the starting line with your bowling ball, and carefully bowl it. Everyone else stands back and watches politely, murmuring encouragement. Everyone waits until the ball has reached the end of the alley, and watches to see if it knocks down all the pins, or only some of them, or none of them. There is a pause, while everyone registers your score.

Then, after everyone is sure that you have completely finished your turn, the next person in line steps up to the same starting line, with a different ball. He doesn't return your ball, and he does not begin from where your ball stopped. There is no back and forth at all. All the balls run parallel. And there is always a suitable pause between turns. There is no rush, no excitement, no scramble for the ball.

No wonder everyone looked startled when I took part in Japanese conversations. I paid no attention to whose turn it was, and kept snatching the ball halfway down the alley and throwing it back at the bowler. Of course the conversation died. I was playing the wrong game.

This explains why it is almost impossible to get a Western-style conversation or discussion going with English students in Japan. I used to think that the problem was their lack of English language ability. But I finally came to realize that the biggest problem is that they, too, are playing the wrong game.

Whenever I serve a volleyball, everyone just stands back and watches it fall, with occasional murmurs of encouragement. No one hits it back. Everyone waits until I call on someone to take a turn. And when that person speaks, he doesn't hit my ball back. He serves a new ball. Again, everyone just watches it fall.

So I call on someone else. This person does not refer to what the previous speaker had said. He also serves a new ball. Nobody seems to have paid any attention to what anyone else has said. Everyone begins again from the same starting line, and all the balls run parallel. There is never any back and forth. Everyone is trying to bowl with a volleyball.

And if I try a simpler conversation, with only two of us, then the other person tries to bowl with my tennis ball. No wonder foreign English teachers in Japan get discouraged.

Now that you know about the difference in the conversational ballgames, you may think that all your troubles are over. But if you have been trained all your life to play one game, it is no simple matter to switch to another, even if you know the rules. Knowing the rules is not at all the same thing as playing the game.

Even now, during a conversation in Japanese I will notice a startled reaction, and belatedly realize that once again I have rudely interrupted by instinctively trying to hit back the other person's bowling ball. It is no easier for me to "just listen" during a conversation than it is for my Japanese students to "just relax" when speaking with foreigners. Now I can truly sympathize with how hard they must find it to try to carry on a Western-style conversation.

If I have not yet learned to do conversational bowling in Japanese, at least I have figured out one thing that puzzled me for a long time. After his first trip to America, my husband complained that Americans asked him so many questions and made

him talk so much at the dinner table that he never had a chance to eat. When I asked him why he couldn't talk and eat at the same time, he said that Japanese do not customarily think that dinner, especially on fairly formal occasions, is a suitable time for extended conversation.

Since Westerners think that conversation is an indispensable part of dining, and indeed would consider it impolite not to converse with one's dinner partner, I found this Japanese custom rather strange. Still, I could accept it as a cultural difference even though I didn't really understand it. But when my husband added, in explanation, that Japanese consider it extremely rude to talk with one's mouth full, I got confused. Talking with one's mouth full is certainly not an American custom. We think it very rude, too. Yet we still manage to talk a lot and eat at the same time. How do we do it?

For a long time, I couldn't explain it, and it bothered me. But after I discovered the conversational ballgames, I finally found the answer. Of course! In a Western-style conversation, you hit the ball, and while someone else is hitting it back, you take a bite, chew, and swallow. Then you hit the ball again, and then eat some more. The more people there are in the conversation, the more chances you have to eat. But even with only two of you talking, you still have plenty of chances to eat.

Maybe that's why polite conversation at the dinner table has never been a traditional part of Japanese etiquette. Your turn to talk would last so long without interruption that you'd never get a chance to eat.

Excerpted from Sakamoto, N. M. (1995). Conversational ballgames. In R. Holton (Ed.), *Encountering Cultures* (pp. 60–63). Englewood Cliffs, NJ: Prentice-Hall. Used with permission.

FOR CONSIDERATION

1. How do the conversational ballgames that Japanese and Americans play relate to their cultural characteristics? In other words, what in the culture of Japan leads them to bowling-style, and what in the culture of America leads to tennis-style conversations?

2. Write two short scripts (one an American-style tennis match and the other a Japanese-style bowling game) for a conversation between an American and a Japanese student who have been assigned to work on a term paper together and must decide on a topic. Which was harder to write? How did the Japanese approach yield a decision?

you are interacting. Different types of media affect our sense of social presence and the ability to create it. For instance, we are more likely to perceive our partners as fully present in conversations through Skype, SnapChat, FaceTime, or iChat than through text messages or emails, because the latter are more asynchronous and do not convey many of the nonverbal cues that signal engagement. To converse effectively, we need to recognize how the media we use to communicate influence our awareness of audience, management of multiple conversations, and abruptness of disengagement.

Awareness of Audience

When you practice face-to-face communication, you know exactly who your conversational partner is when you begin the interaction. But when you send a tweet or post to a blog or your Facebook page, you can't always be sure who your conversational partner will be. For example, you may text your boyfriend about your upcoming date, but what if your boyfriend's roommate picked up your boyfriend's cell phone and jokingly responded to your message? If you are upset over a co-worker's attitude, you may send your close friend a private email that explains your frustration in detail, only to find out that your friend forwarded your email to many other people. As you interact with others through social media, always remember that your message can make its way into the hands of an unintended recipient. Even though you expect certain people to visit your Facebook page, it is also open for the world to examine. Facebook can become a platform for creating many unplanned digital conversations (Engdahl, 2007). Communicating through some forms of social media is equivalent to inviting thousands of people into a conversation with you. Always keep your intended audience (and *unintended* audiences) in mind.

Multiplicity of Conversations

Without a doubt, more than one face-to-face conversation can occur at any one time. Consider a class project group that is working on an upcoming assignment. If everyone is interacting face-to-face, members of the group can easily determine when multiple conversations are occurring simultaneously, and who is participating. However, when conversations take place digitally, who is participating and which conversation takes precedence can be problematic. For instance, while the group is meeting face-to-face, Melissa may briefly disengage from the group to take a quick phone call; Sean may exchange text messages with friends he plans to meet afterwards; Chrissy may use her laptop to reply to an email from her mom; and Darren may be looking up his grades online. Many people have come to see this kind of divided attention as acceptable, but it can create significant problems. If you are paying more attention to your online interactions, you are likely to miss important information, or fail to have your input included in the face-to-face discussion. You also run the risk of conveying that the people with you are not as important or interesting as those not physically present. The same kinds of issues can arise within online interactions if you are

Does it bother you when someone you are talking with interrupts your conversation to answer a cell phone call, check texts and e-mails, or engage in other technology-mediated communication?

primarily focused on your face-to-face interaction. Despite the temptation of "multi-tasking," you will be a more competent communicator if you handle face-to-face and digital interactions separately. If you must take a phone call or respond to a text, politely put your face-to-face conversation on hold. Deal with your digital interaction efficiently, and then thank your conversational partner for his or her cooperation and patience. When we practice interpersonal communication in face-to-face or digital contexts, each person that we communicate with deserves our full attention. Avoiding the problem of "split attention" will lead others to perceive you as a competent communicator.

Abruptness of Disengagement

Digital conversations often lack the clear beginnings and endings that characterize face-to-face conversations, such as "Hello" and "See you later." Have you ever been instant-messaging with someone only to have the person quickly type "brb" (be right back) or "gotta go, bye"? Or maybe your friend disappeared from your online list altogether without even saying goodbye. These abrupt endings can be frustrating because we often expect our digital conversational partners to follow the rules that typically apply to face-to-face conversations. Understanding that digital conversations can be terminated suddenly is one requirement for practicing effective conversations through social media. We know that the digital communication context is different from face-to-face settings, so we may consider abrupt endings acceptable for digital conversations. If you are messaging with a friend on Facebook, and you notice that the person has stopped

▸ **OBSERVE AND ANALYZE**

Face-to-Face vs. Mediated Conversations

For one day, keep a log of your face-to-face conversations and your mediated conversations. Referring to the list of conversation types in Figure 8.1, identify each type of conversation you had, and whether it occurred face-to-face or via communication technology. Tally your results. Are your face-to-face and mediated conversations achieving the same purposes, or different ones? If so requested by your instructor, bring your findings with you to class so that they may be compared to those of your classmates. Are your patterns similar to or different from those of the entire class?

INTER-ACT WITH
SOCIAL MEDIA

When we use social media, it is not always clear to everyone which conversations are taking place with whom. Consider a recent Facebook status update that garnered over thirty comments. Or scan your Twitter feed and examine a series of posts pertaining to a single topic. Can you clearly follow the conversation flow? How might you evaluate each user's ability to respond appropriately to the comments of another user?

responding to your messages, don't be frustrated. Although it can be easy to perceive your friend's lack of response as rude, he or she may have had to quickly step away from the computer, take a phone call, or may have lost an Internet connection altogether. If your friend goes offline, try following up with an email or text message. Chances are your friend meant no harm by not responding, but a follow-up message can ease any feelings of frustration you may have and clarify any misunderstandings.

Summary

Conversations are interactive, extemporaneous, locally managed, and sequentially organized interchanges of thoughts and feelings between two or more people. Conversations vary in type, purpose, sequence, tone, participants, and setting.

Good communicators follow the general guidelines for conducting effective conversations, which include focusing on others, taking turns appropriately and avoiding interruptions, maintaining conversational coherence, and engaging in ethical dialogue.

A QUESTION OF ETHICS ▶ WHAT WOULD YOU DO?

Tonia is her Uncle Fred's only living relative, and he has been her favorite relative for as long as she can remember. About three years ago, Fred was diagnosed with lung cancer that eventually led to surgery and a round of radiation and chemotherapy. At that time, Fred made out his will, naming Tonia as his executor and giving her his medical power of attorney. Recently, he also signed a waiver so that his medical team would be able to disclose all his medical information to Tonia even though he has been feeling great.

Uncle Fred has worked hard all his life and has talked about, dreamed about, and saved for a trip to visit his mother's hometown in northern Italy. Last week he called Tonia very excited, and told her that he had just finished making all his reservations and was scheduled to leave for Italy in two weeks. While Tonia was really happy for him, she wondered if his doctor had approved his trip.

Reluctant to rain on his parade, Tonia nonetheless phoned the doctor to see if Uncle Fred had told him about the trip. She was alarmed to learn that not only had Uncle Fred not mentioned the trip to his doctor, but also his latest follow-up CT scan showed that the cancer was growing aggressively. The doctor believed that Fred needed to cancel his trip and immediately begin another round of chemotherapy. When Tonia asked about the likelihood of the treatments bringing the cancer back into remission, the doctor said, "To be perfectly honest, there is only a 10 percent chance that the chemo will work. But without treatment, the cancer is sure to kill him in less than six months." Then the doctor implored Tonia to talk with her uncle and persuade him to cancel his plans and begin treatment.

FOR CONSIDERATION

1. Was it ethical for Tonia and her uncle's doctor to have this conversation?
2. Is it ethical for Tonia to try to persuade her uncle to stay and have chemotherapy?
3. Should Tonia agree to talk with her uncle? If so, what ethical issues will she confront?
4. If she chooses to have this conversation with her uncle, how can Johannesen's guidelines for ethical dialogue—authenticity, empathy, confirmation, presentness, equality, and supportiveness—help her create an effective conversation?

To improve conversation when you interact with someone for the first time, there are strategies for initiating, sustaining, and ending conversation. The strategies for initiation are making a comment, asking a ritual question, and introducing yourself. You can sustain conversation more effectively if you use free information, ask questions (both closed-ended and open-ended), seek high-interest topics, self-disclose in appropriate ways, and actively listen. Terminating conversation goes most smoothly if you pay attention to and use both verbal and nonverbal leave-taking cues, verbalize a desire to end the conversation, and conclude with a simple parting comment. Humor can be used to enhance conversation, but it must be handled carefully to avoid offense. Skilled communication requires adaptation to cultural differences in conversational style.

The effectiveness of digital conversation largely depends on social presence, or the perception that our conversational partners are near us in space and time. Mediated communication technologies vary in their capacity to enhance our feelings of social presence. To communicate effectively, digital communicators must remain aware of their audience, manage multiple conversations appropriately, and accommodate abrupt disengagement.

CHAPTER RESOURCES

Key Words

Flashcards for all of these key terms are available on the *Inter-Act* website.

Benign violation pp. 235
Closed-ended questions pp. 239
Co-narration pp. 231
Conversation pp. 225
Conversation purpose pp. 228
Conversation tone pp. 231
Conversational coherence pp. 235
Ethical dialogue pp. 235

Extemporaneous pp. 225
Formality pp. 231
Free information pp. 238
Gossip pp. 228
Leave-taking cues pp. 241
Local management pp. 226
Open-ended questions pp. 239
Ritual question pp. 237

Scripted pp. 230
Self-disclosure pp. 240
Sequential organization pp. 226
Small talk pp. 228
Social presence pp. 243
Talk time pp. 233
Turn-taking pp. 225

Analyze and Apply

The following activities challenge you to demonstrate your mastery of the concepts, theories, and frameworks in this chapter by using them to explain what is happening in a specific situation.

8.1 Rewind/Rewrite

Now that you have read the chapter, hit "rewind" on the opening dialogue between Samuel and Susan, and answer the following questions.

a. Use concepts from the chapter to explain why Samuel became eager to end the conversation. Talk time, turn-taking, nonverbal cues, and other-centered focus may be especially relevant.

b. Rewrite how the dialogue could have unfolded if Susan had exercised better conversational skills.

c. Sometimes we have to deal with people whose conversational behavior is frustrating, but exiting the conversation isn't an option. Is there anything Samuel could have done to participate more fully in the conversation with Susan, and maybe get the input he wanted on his problem resident?

8.2 Local Management of Conversation

Think about a recent time when you temporarily misunderstood what someone was saying (or they misunderstood you). How did you discover the misunderstanding? How did you correct it? What does this show you about the "local management" of conversation?

8.3. Conversational Violations

Have you laughed out loud in a recent conversation? Apply the concept of "benign violation" to explain why you laughed.

Skill Practice

Skill practice activities give you the chance to rehearse a new skill by responding to hypothetical or real situations. Additional skill practice activities are available at the companion website.

8.4 Practice Initiating Conversation

For each of the following scenarios, come up with a way to initiate conversation using at least two of the three strategies described in this chapter (make a comment, ask a ritual question, or introduce yourself).

a. *You've just moved to a new town. You love to swim and play racquetball, so you decide to join the nearest health club. Today, after finishing your first workout at the gym, you see someone in the locker room who looks like a regular.*

   Your Opening:

b. *You are at the mall with your eight-year-old daughter. You are in Gap Kids, and she is whining because you don't want to purchase a frivolous item that isn't on sale. Another parent grins in your direction.*

   Your Opening:

c. *You are a new employee at a company. Tonight is the mid-year company party at a downtown hotel. You're in a long line for drinks. The person in front of you is someone you've seen in the hallway at work but have never talked with.*

   Your Opening:

d. *You're at a friend's Super Bowl party. You're getting settled on one of the couches and someone you don't know sits down on the loveseat opposite you.*

   Your Opening:

e. *You're bored on the bus home from work, and your smartphone's battery is dead. The person sitting next to you is staring off into space.*

   Your Opening:

f. *You're walking your dog on a leash in the park. When you stop at a drinking fountain, your dog starts sniffing a dog whose owner is sitting on the bench next to the fountain.*

   Your Opening:

Communication Improvement Plan: Conversation

How would you like to improve your conversational skills as discussed in this chapter?

• Developing an other-centered focus

• Engaging in appropriate turn-taking

• Maintaining conversational coherence

• Protecting privacy

• Engaging in ethical dialogue

Pick a skill, and write a communication improvement plan. You can find a communication improvement plan worksheet on our website at www.oup.com/us/verderber.

SUPPORTING OTHERS

Melanie, Jenna, and Becca are all reporters for the student newspaper and share a tiny office in the basement of the Student Union. One evening, while Melanie is struggling with a feature story, Jenna stops in, looking pleased.

Jenna: "Hey, Melanie, guess what?"

Melanie (glancing up from her work): "Yo, Jenna."

Jenna: "You know that big midterm project I stayed up all night for last week? I just got it back, and I got an A!"

Melanie (smiles, but without much enthusiasm): "Awesome, way to go."

Jenna (smiling broadly): "Yeah, I am still in shock! I mean, it was a third of my grade! I'm sooooo happy! Best. Day. Ever."

Melanie (now scowling at her computer): "Yeah, that's real nice."

Jenna (looking puzzled and hurt): "Yeah . . . Well, okay, gotta go now."

Melanie (continuing to look at her computer): "Kay."

An hour later, Becca stops by the office. She finds Melanie staring at her computer, looking tearful.

Becca: "Hey Mel. Something wrong?"

Melanie: "I'm so frustrated with this story. It's just not coming together. I'm going to miss my deadline."

253

(Continued)

Becca (in a bored tone): "Oh. Well, if you sit there, it just gets worse, you know! When I'm stuck, I just start writing anything and eventually it starts making sense."

Melanie (in a defensive tone): "I've been writing and writing! The interviews were good. But the story doesn't fit together. Maybe I wasn't cut out to be a journalist."

Becca (breezily): "Well, hang in there, right? What doesn't kill you makes you stronger. Gotta go!"

Melanie (under her breath, glaring at Becca's back as she leaves): "Please do!"

WHAT YOU SHOULD BE ABLE *TO EXPLAIN* AFTER YOU HAVE STUDIED THIS CHAPTER:

▶ Types of empathy and ways to improve it

▶ Four phases of supportive interaction

▶ Creating a supportive climate

▶ Why validating emotions is important to providing support

▶ How support can encourage reappraisal of emotionally difficult situations

▶ How to encourage action with advice

▶ The role of celebratory support in the process of capitalization

▶ Gender and cultural similarities and differences in supportive communication

▶ Advantages of using social media to seek and provide support

WHAT YOU SHOULD BE ABLE *TO DO* AFTER YOU HAVE STUDIED THIS CHAPTER:

▶ Create a supportive conversational climate

▶ Validate the emotions of others

▶ Encourage reappraisals

▶ Give effective advice

▶ Offer celebratory support

Have you ever been really happy about something, only to have another person's response bring you down from your high? Or maybe you really needed some sympathy or an ego boost, but it just wasn't there? Most of us understand the importance of providing support for our friends and family members through both the good and the bad. But too often our efforts fall short because, like Melanie and Becca, we don't fully understand how to effectively support others. Research consistently links social support with important health outcomes, including longer life, reduced incidence of disease, better recovery from illness, improved ability to cope with chronic illness, and better overall mental health (MacGeorge, Feng, & Burleson, 2011). In addition, support contributes to healthier relationships, with such benefits as marital satisfaction, healthy family interactions, strong friendships, and amicable work relationships (Brock & Lawrence, 2010). These are just a few of the reasons that make it important to become skillful at providing support to people who live, work, and interact with you.

In this chapter, you will study the supportive communication process and how to become more proficient at supporting others. We begin by explaining the concept of empathy and describing how to increase your ability to empathize. Then we describe supportive interactions, including the four phases typical of these interactions. This is followed by attention to four skills essential to providing support: creating a supportive climate, validating emotions, encouraging reappraisal, and promoting action. We then examine the idea of providing support for positive as well as negative emotions. The chapter concludes with discussions of gender and cultural differences in support, and supportive interactions via social media.

Empathizing

The foundation of supporting others is **empathy**—the cognitive and affective process of perceiving the emotions others are feeling and then acting on our perception (Preston & de Waal, 2002). Scholars recognize that empathy is an important element in understanding and maintaining good interpersonal relationships (Omdahl, 1995). When you empathize, you attempt to understand or experience what your partner understands or experiences; in effect, you put yourself in the other person's shoes. It obviously requires effort to empathize with someone who is very different from you or with someone who is experiencing something that is out of your realm of experience. But giving support effectively begins with your ability to empathize with what another person is experiencing. In this section, we discuss the three types of empathy and steps you can take to improve your ability to empathize.

Empathy—the cognitive and affective process of perceiving the emotions others are feeling and then acting on our perception

Three Types of Empathy

Scholars who study empathy have identified three different ways that people empathize: perspective taking, sympathetic responsiveness, and empathic responsiveness (Weaver & Kirtley, 1995).

Perspective taking is empathizing by using everything we know about our partner and our partner's circumstances to help us understand how he or she is feeling. This is the most "logical" or "cold" form of empathy, because it doesn't require you to have an emotional response. All it requires is careful thinking about what the other person is experiencing, and what he or she is likely to be feeling because of that experience. For example, suppose that Jackson tells James that he is in really serious financial trouble. James, who has known Jackson since grade school, understands that he is very conservative and was raised by parents who were frugal and paid their bills on time. Because of what he knows about Jackson, James understands that he must be panicked about his accumulating debt. When we don't know others very well, we can still consider how most people would feel in a given situation. So, if James didn't know Jackson well, he could still reflect on how increases in debt make people anxious.

Perspective taking—empathizing by using everything we know about our partners and our partners' circumstances to help us understand how they are feeling

LEARN ABOUT YOURSELF ▶ EMPATHY TENDENCIES

Take this short survey to learn something about yourself. Answer the questions honestly based on your first responses. There are no right or wrong answers. For each item, use the following scale and provide a number score to indicate how well the item describes you:

0	**1**	**2**	**3**	**4**
Does not describe me well				**Describes me very well**

_____ 1. Before criticizing people, I try to imagine how I would feel if I were in their place.

_____ 2. I sometimes try to understand my friends better by imagining how things look from their perspective.

_____ 3. I believe that there are two sides to every question, and I try to look at them both.

_____ 4. I find it easy to see things from another person's point of view.

_____ 5. I try to look at everybody's side of a disagreement before I make a decision.

_____ 6. When I'm upset at someone, I usually try to put myself in his or her shoes for a while.

_____ 7. When I see someone being taken advantage of, I feel protective of this person.

_____ 8. I often have tender, concerned feelings for people less fortunate than me.

_____ 9. I would describe myself as a pretty soft-hearted person.

_____10. Sometimes I feel sorry for other people when they are having problems.

_____11. Other people's misfortunes usually upset me a lot.

_____12. I am often quite touched by things that I see happen.

_____13. When I see someone who badly needs help in an emergency, I go to pieces.

_____14. I sometimes feel helpless when I am in the middle of a very emotional situation.

_____15. In emergency situations, I feel apprehensive and ill at ease.

_____16. Being in a tense emotional situation scares me.

_____17. When I see someone get hurt, it freaks me out.

_____18. I tend to lose control during emergencies.

Scoring the survey: This survey measures your tendencies to use each of the three types of empathy. Add your scores for items 1 through 6. This indicates your tendency to use perspective taking when you empathize. Add your scores for items 7 through 12. This indicates your tendency to use sympathetic responsiveness when you empathize. Add your scores for items 13 through 18. This indicates your tendency to use empathic responsiveness when you empathize.

Adapted from Davis, M. H. (1980). A multidimensional approach to individual differences in empathy. *JSAS Catalog of Selected Documents in Psychology, 10,* 85.

Sympathetic responsiveness is empathizing by feeling concern, compassion, or sorrow for another person because he or she is in a distressing situation. This kind of empathy is "warmer" than perspective taking because it requires an emotional response to another person's plight. Some scholars call this "emotional concern" (Stiff et al., 1988), while others use the term "sympathy" (Eisenberg & Fabes, 1990). In the previous example, James could recognize how stressed and worried Jackson felt, and feel concerned for his friend. Sympathetic responsiveness does not require personal experience of the other person's problem, or feeling what the other person feels. For example, if James always pays his bills on time and can't imagine being in financial difficulty, he can still empathize with Jackson through a sympathetic response. Recognizing that Jackson is stressed and worried, James can feel compassionate toward him, even though James does not feel financial stress or worry himself.

Empathic responsiveness (which has also been called empathic distress) is the "warmest" or most emotional form of empathy. It involves personally experiencing an emotional response that is parallel to another person's actual or anticipated display of emotion (Omdahl, 1995; Stiff, Dillard, Somera, Kim, & Sleight, 1988). For instance, if James not only senses the stress and anxiety that Jackson is feeling but also feels stress and anxiety himself, we would say that James has experienced empathic responsiveness. Empathic responsiveness is most common when there is a close or intimate relationship between the person in need of support and the person called on to provide it. Because of the strong relational bond, you are more likely to identify closely with the emotions of a close friend, family member, or intimate partner than with someone you know less well. Similarly, empathic responsiveness is more likely when you have personally experienced something similar to what the other person is going through (e.g., if James had at one point experienced a period of financial stress).

> **Sympathetic responsiveness**—empathizing by feeling concern, compassion, or sorrow for another person because he or she is in a distressing situation

> **Empathic responsiveness**—personally experiencing an emotional response that is parallel to the other person's actual or anticipated display of emotion

What kind of empathy do you think these children are experiencing?

You might think that empathic responsiveness is the best form of empathy, but this isn't necessarily true. Experiencing something parallel to what others feel can help you give effective support (because you understand what they are feeling). But if your own feelings are too intense, you may end up focusing more on soothing yourself and not do a very good job of supporting the other person. If you have a very strong emotional reaction to someone else's problem, you may not be the best person to provide support, or you may need to consciously engage in sympathetic responsiveness (feeling concern and sympathy for the other person rather than whatever you are feeling along with them). Making an effort to understand the other person's perspective by thinking through the situation is always valuable, too.

Guidelines for Improving Empathy

While some people seem to have an inherent capacity to empathize, most of us need to improve our ability. As you can guess, successful empathizing demands active listening. In addition, the following three guidelines can help you improve your ability to empathize.

1. Pay attention to nonverbal and paralanguage cues. What people feel about what they are saying is usually conveyed in the nonverbal parts of the message. These cues are your best indication of what they are feeling. How well you empathize depends on how clearly you observe and read the nonverbal messages others send. Research studies have shown that when people concentrate, they can do well and are adept at recognizing such primary emotions as happiness, sadness, surprise, anger, and fear (greater than 90 percent accuracy) and are good at recognizing contempt, disgust, interest, determination, and bewilderment (80 to 90 percent accuracy; Leathers, 1997). The research also suggests that recognizing facial expressions is the key to perceiving emotion (Leathers, 1997). To improve your understanding of nonverbal messages, try mentally answering two questions when talking with others: "What emotions do I believe the person is experiencing right now?" and "What cues am I seeing to draw this conclusion?" Consciously raising these questions can help you focus your attention on the nonverbal aspects of messages, which convey most of the information regarding the person's emotional state.

2. Pay attention to the emotional content of the verbal message. Although most of the emotional message will be conveyed in the paralinguistic and nonverbal portions of a message, your partners will also provide cues about how they are feeling by the specific language that they use, as well as their direct statements about their feelings. For example, when your friend tells you what his grandmother sent for his birthday, he might say, "She only sent me fifty bucks," or he might say, "She sent me fifty dollars, which is a lot since she is retired." In the first case, the language suggests your friend may be disappointed, whereas in the second, the language indicates your friend feels grateful, or maybe even concerned that his grandmother has been too generous for her budget.

3. Use the skill of perception checking. As discussed in Chapter 5, perception checking allows you to determine whether you have correctly understood

▶ **OBSERVE AND ANALYZE**

Empathizing Effectively

Describe the last time you effectively empathized with another person. Write a short summary of the episode. Be sure to cover the following: What was the person's emotional state? How did you recognize it? What were the nonverbal cues? Verbal cues? What type of relationship do you have with this person? How long have you known the person? How similar is this person to you? Have you ever had a real or vicarious experience similar to the one the person was reporting? Did you use perspective taking, sympathetic responsiveness, or empathic responsiveness? Why? What was the outcome of this communication episode?

someone else's perspective. If uncertainty about what another person is feeling is making it difficult to empathize, you can describe your perception and ask for feedback. So, you might say to your friend whose grandmother sent him $50, "You seem disappointed in the birthday present. Am I right?" or "Do you feel that she spent too much on you?" By doing a perception check, you can verify or correct the interpretations you make, and have a stronger foundation for providing effective support.

Supportive Interactions

Social support is the assistance we provide to others who we believe need our aid. Social support includes providing for tangible or physical needs, such as helping with money, food, or transportation, and the intangible or psychological needs of others, such as comfort, advice or companionship. Social support is typically given and received in closer relationships, and is usually distinguished from assistance that is paid for, or given in the context of a professional relationship. However, strangers and acquaintances do sometimes provide social support, and paid helpers can provide social support in addition to their paid services. For example, your hairstylist may help cheer you up while she cuts your hair, or your accountant may provide useful information about schools or real estate while reviewing your taxes.

Communication is essential to providing intangible social support: You can't comfort, advise, motivate, or otherwise help someone with their psychological needs if you don't interact with them. Tangible support often requires communication as well, in order to offer it and carry it out. Such communications are known as **supportive interactions**, conversations in which the goal is to provide emotional support for a partner.

As you may know from your own experiences, supportive interactions can be either relatively simple and brief, or complex dialogues that take place over time. Some provider and recipient turns will be nothing more than brief nonverbal cues or short verbal messages, whereas others may be lengthy narratives complete with subplot digressions. Some of this variation in communication will be due to the nature of the problem, the level of distress, and the needs involved. For example, consider the difference between trying to help someone who needs a ride while his or her car is being repaired, versus helping comfort someone who is grieving the death of a loved one. Although both cases involve offering social support, a grieving person is likely to need a deeper and ongoing level of supportive interaction.

Additionally, what one person perceives as helpful social support may be perceived by another as demeaning or meddling. While we may be comfortable and skilled at providing social support in some situations, we may be uncomfortable and bumbling in others. For example, in this chapter's "Diverse Voices" selection, "Which Is My Good Leg?" the authors describe the difficulties that disabled and able-bodied people have when interacting with each other.

Social support—the assistance we provide to others who we believe need our aid.

Supportive interactions—conversations in which the goal is to provide emotional support for one partner

DIVERSE VOICES

"Which Is My Good Leg?"

BY DAWN O. BRAITHWAITE AND CHARLES A. BRAITHWAITE

Jonathan is an articulate, intelligent, 35-year-old professional man who has used a wheelchair since he became a paraplegic when he was 20 years old. He recalls inviting a non-disabled woman out to dinner at a nice restaurant. When the waitress came to take their order, she looked only at his date and asked, in a condescending tone, "And what would *he* like to eat for dinner?" At the end of the meal the waitress presented Jonathan's date with the check and thanked her for her patronage.

Kim describes her recent experience at the airport: "A lot of people always come up and ask can they push my wheelchair. And I can do it myself. They are invading my space, concentration, doing what I wanted to do *on my own*. . . . And each time I said, "No, I'm doing fine!" People looked at me like I was strange, you know, crazy or something. One person started pushing my chair anyway. I said, [in an angry tone], 'Don't touch the wheelchair.' And then she just looked at me like I'd slapped her in the face."

Jeff, a non-disabled student, was working on a group project for class that included Helen, who uses a wheelchair. He related an incident that really embarrassed him. "I wasn't thinking and I said to the group, 'Let's run over to the student union and get some coffee.' I was mortified when I looked over at Helen and remembered that she can't walk. I felt like a real jerk." Helen later described the incident with Jeff, recalling:

> **"At yesterday's meeting, Jeff said, 'Let's run over to the student union' and then he looked over at me and I thought he would die. It didn't bother me at all. In fact, I use that phrase myself. I felt bad that Jeff was so embarrassed but I didn't know what to say. Later in the group meeting I made it a point to say, 'I've got to be running along now.' I hope that Jeff noticed and felt okay about what he said."**

Although it may seem hard for some of us to believe, these scenarios represent common experiences for many people with physical disabilities and are indicative of what often happens when people with disabilities and non-disabled others communicate.

For people with disabilities, personal control and independence are vitally important, and "maintenance of identity and self-worth are tied to the perceived ability to control the illness, minimize its intrusiveness, and be independent" (Lyons et al., 1995, p. 134). This does not mean that people with disabilities deny their physical condition, but rather that they find ways to manage it, to obtain whatever help they need and to lead their lives. Although it is possible to identify and find accommodations for physical challenges associated with mobility, self-care, and employment, the two key life functions of social relationships and communication often present much more formidable challenges. It is often less difficult to detect and correct physical barriers than it is to deal with the insidious social barriers facing people with disabilities.

When people with disabilities begin relationships with non-disabled people, the challenges associated with forming any new relationship are often greater. For non-disabled people, this may be due to lack of experience interacting with people who are disabled, which leads to high uncertainty about how to react with a person who is disabled. Non-disabled persons may be uncertain about what to say or how to act. They are afraid of saying or doing the wrong thing or of hurting the feelings of the person with the disability, much as Jeff with his group member Helen. As a result, non-disabled persons may feel self-conscious, and their actions may be constrained, self-controlled, and rigid. Their behavior, in turn, may appear as uninterested or unaccepting to the person who is disabled. The non-disabled person will need to figure out how to communicate appropriately, and sometimes these communication attempts are not successful. At times their attempts to act in ways that are acceptable to a disabled person will be perceived as offensively patronizing disabled people with unwanted help or sympathy. Even when a non-disabled person tries to "say the right thing" and wants to communicate acceptance to the person with the disability, his or her nonverbal behavior may communicate rejection and avoidance instead. For example, people with disabilities have observed that many non-disabled persons may keep a greater physical distance, avoid eye contact, avoid mentioning the disability, or cut the conversation short. These non-disabled persons may be doing their best not to show their discomfort or not "crowd" the person with the disability. However, the outcome may be that the person with the disability perceives they do not want to interact. In this case, a person's disability becomes a handicap in the social environment as it can block the development of a relationship with a non-disabled person who finds the interaction too uncomfortable.

When non-disabled persons make the effort to overcome discomfort and stereotypes to interact with people from the disabled culture, they often find themselves with conflicting expectations. On the one hand, Americans are taught to "help the handicapped." At the same time, Americans conceptualize persons as "individuals" who "have rights" and "make their own choices" and thus are taught to treat all people equally. However, when non-disabled persons encounter a person with a disability, this model of personhood creates a real dilemma. How can you both help a person and treat that person equally? For example, should you help a person with a disability open a door or try to help him up if he falls? If you are working with a blind person, should you help her find a doorway or get her lunch at the cafeteria? These dilemmas often result in high uncertainty for non-disabled people, who often end up trying to give more help than people with disabilities want or need.

It should not be surprising to learn that most people with disabilities are well aware of the feelings and fears many non-disabled persons have. In fact, disabled people report that they believe that they can just "tell" who is uncomfortable around them, and they develop communication strategies to help them interact in these situations. For example, people with disabilities when meeting non-disabled persons will communicate in ways designed to get the discomfort "out of the way." They want the non-disabled person to treat them as a "person like anyone else," rather than focus solely on their disability. One man told the following story: "Now there were two girls about eight playing and I was in my shorts. And I played a game with them and said, 'Which is my good leg?' And that gets them to thinking. 'Well this one [he pats his artificial leg] is not nearly as old as the other one!'" Not only may disabled people use humor, but they may talk about topics they believe they have in common with the non-disabled person, such as cooking, sports, or music. They also plan ahead and develop strategies to help when they may need help from non-disabled persons and at times accept help they do not need because they understand that refusing

help might increase the discomfort and uncertainty of the non-disabled person. In closing, we suggest the following practical proscriptions and prescriptions:

DON'T:
- Avoid communication with people who are disabled simply because you are uncomfortable or unsure.
- Assume the people with disabilities cannot speak for themselves or do things for themselves.
- Force your help on people with disabilities.
- Use terms such as "handicapped," "physically challenged," "crippled," "victim," and the like, unless requested to do so by people with disabilities.
- Assume that a disability defines who a person is.

DO:
- Remember that people with disabilities have experienced others' discomfort before and likely understand how you might be feeling.
- Assume that people with disabilities can do something, unless they communicate otherwise.
- Let people with disabilities tell you if they want something, what they want, and when they want it. If a person with a disability refuses your help, don't go ahead and help anyway.
- Use terms such as "people with disabilities" rather than "disabled people." The goal is to stress the person first, before the disability.
- Treat people with disabilities as persons first, recognizing that you are not dealing with a disabled person but with a person who has a disability. This means actively seeking the humanity of the person with whom you are speaking and focusing on individual characteristics instead of superficial physical appearance. Without diminishing the significance of the person's disability, make a real effort to focus on all of the many other aspects of that person as you communicate.

Excerpted and adapted from Braithwaite, D. O., & Braithwaite, C. A. (2012). "Which Is My Good Leg?": Cultural communication of persons with disabilities. In L. A. Samovar, R. E. Porter, & E. R. McDaniel (Eds.), *Intercultural Communication: A Reader* (13th ed.). Boston, MA: Wadsworth. Used with permission.

FOR CONSIDERATION
1. How does your need to maintain "face" affect your interactions with disabled people?
2. How does this article help you better understand the face needs of disabled people? How can you use this to avoid face-threatening acts and support the face needs of disabled persons?

Typically, there are four phases to social support interactions: support activation, support provision, recipient reaction, and provider response (Barbee & Cunningham, 1995). These phases recur frequently in more complex interactions, but we will describe them separately here.

1. Phase one: support activation. Supportive interactions begin when something happens to trigger an initial supportive response, such as the words or behaviors of the person needing support. Alternatively, a relational partner who perceives a need to support the other can trigger support activation. For example, if Brianne comes home, walks into the kitchen, and finds her mother slumped over the sink silently sobbing into her arm, she is likely to activate support by rushing over, putting her arms around her mom, and asking, "Mom, are you all right? What's happened?" Either the provider or the recipient, then, can activate support. The support activation phase can be relatively brief if the need is obvious or quickly disclosed, but it can also occupy a more extended period if the provider must coax the recipient to disclose information about the problem.

2. Phase two: support provision. During the second phase of a supportive interaction, support providers enact messages designed to support their partner. Once Brianne's mother shares that she is crying because she has been laid off from her job, Brianne may say, "I'm so sorry. Are you frightened about paying the rent? I've been saving a little. I can help." In this message Brianne combines support for her mother's feelings with an offer to help address part of the problem. In the next section of this chapter, we'll examine support provision in detail, focusing on different types of support messages and how to make them more effective.

3. Phase three: recipient reaction. Once support has been provided, the recipient will react to what the provider has said or done. This reaction will often give some indication of whether the support provided was helpful to the recipient. However, it is rarely the case that one supportive message will immediately reduce all of the recipient's distress, or completely solve the problem. For example, Brianne's mother may be somewhat soothed by Brianne's message and stop crying long enough to respond, "I'm not just worried about the rent. There's the car payment, and I just finished paying off the credit card bill. I don't know if I can face going into debt again."

4. Phase four: provider response. The fourth phase of supportive interactions consists of the provider's response to the recipient's reaction. If the recipient's response shows a continuing need for support, the interaction will cycle back to a previous phase and continue until one of the partners changes the subject or ends the conversation. In this example, since Brianne's mother has begun to explain the breadth of the problem caused by her job loss, Brianne may respond by acknowledging her mother's continued distress, and cycle back to phase two to continue her support efforts. Because job loss is a complex problem that will continue to have an impact over time, Brianne and her mother are likely to have repeated conversations, returning to phase one and reactivating the support interaction as needed.

Supportive interactions like the one between Brianne and her mother signal interest, care, compassion, and even love. For this reason, our relationships often grow from times when we have offered or received support. Yet not all efforts to provide support are effective. Most of us can recall interactions in which we sought support and left the interaction feeling unsupported, hurt, or even angry. And you may be able to recall interactions in which you tried to help someone, but knew (or felt) that you failed. It is important to recognize that the outcome of a support interaction depends on many factors, including not only what is said and intended, but the problem and its context, the relationship and prior interactions between the provider and recipient, and even other people who may be involved. In the following section, we will discuss how people can provide support more effectively in many different kinds of supportive interaction.

Supportive Messages

Supportive message skills include creating a supportive climate, validating emotions, encouraging reappraisal, effectively offering advice, and providing celebratory support. We present these skills in that order because supportive-communication scholars believe they function best when you use them one by one: starting with creating a supportive climate, validating emotions as they are revealed, then encouraging reappraisal, and only later offering advice if appropriate (Burleson & Goldsmith, 1998). If you have a firmly established supportive relationship with another person, using these skills out of order might be equally effective because your support recipient will infer that the missing aspects of support are still there. But when you know someone less well, or have less of a history of supporting each other, you are likely to do better working through these skills sequentially.

Creating a Supportive Climate

People who are experiencing emotional turmoil can have trouble reaching out to and fully trusting those whose support they seek. Support providers need to create a **supportive climate**, or a conversational environment in which recipients will feel comfortable disclosing their problems and emotions. The following five elements are key to creating a supportive climate. These should be employed from the beginning of a supportive interaction and reinforced throughout.

1. Emphasize your desire and availability to help. Most people don't like to burden others with their problems, and may be reluctant to seek the support they need. By emphasizing that you are willing and available to help, you can make opening up less threatening. For example, you might say "I'd like to help you. What can I do?" or "Sometimes it helps to have someone to listen, and I'd like

▶ **OBSERVE AND ANALYZE**

Supportive Interaction Phases

Recall the last time you received emotional support from someone. Describe the situation that led to this interaction and the emotions you felt. Describe how well this interaction passed through the four supportive interaction phases. How does this analysis help you understand how supported you felt? In which of the phases did your comforter excel, or where could he or she have improved the way in which support was provided?

Supportive climate—a conversational environment in which recipients will feel comfortable disclosing their problems and feelings

Have this young woman's friends created a supportive climate for talking about her troubles? What makes you feel comfortable disclosing your problems and feelings?

to do that for you." If the person seems concerned about the amount of time required to discuss the problem, you can emphasize that your availability is open-ended ("You know that I'm going to be here for you for as long as it takes.") or that you are willing to talk more than once about the problem ("Call me tonight so we can talk some more").

2. Promise—and keep—confidentiality. Support seekers are often concerned that their private problems not be shared with others. Address this concern by promising to keep what you discuss between the two of you, or with whomever the support recipient specifies. Of course, you should only make promises you intend to keep, and certain kinds of disclosures should prompt you to seek help from health professionals or law enforcement (e.g., intention to commit suicide or harm another person).

3. Convey acceptance and affiliation. If you've ever been embarrassed or ashamed about a problem that you were having, you know how difficult it can be to ask for support. In Chapter 4, we discussed the idea of "face," or public self-image. Revealing a problem threatens your face because it suggests that you aren't as capable or independent as you could be—otherwise you wouldn't have a problem and you wouldn't need help. As a support provider, you can help reduce recipients' concerns for face by showing that you are accepting of the problem, whatever it may be, and happy to affiliate with the support recipient. With a close friend, it might be, "I love you no matter what!" whereas with a co-worker you might say, "I'm honored that you trusted me with this."

4. Convey warmth and caring nonverbally. Your nonverbal behavior needs to complement, not work against, what your words are saying. Leaning in toward the other person, touching as appropriate for the relationship (patting, hand holding, hugging, etc.), and facial expressions that parallel those of the support recipient are important because they demonstrate solidarity. For example, when Brianne arrived home to see her mother in tears, her first move was to immediately hug her.

5. Promote elaboration with questions and brief responses. As the interaction unfolds, help the support recipient share his or her situation fully by asking questions ("Really, what happened then?" "What are you planning to do now?") and brief responses that indicate your interest in what is being said without interrupting the flow ("Wow." "I see." "Tell me more.")

Validating Emotions

An essential part of supporting others is acknowledging what they are feeling and their right to feel that way. The skill of validating emotions is essential to being an effective support provider. This skill

If your anger is validated by others, how do you feel?

SKILL BUILDER ▶ CREATE A SUPPORTIVE CLIMATE

SKILL	USE	STEPS	EXAMPLE
Create messages designed to promote a safe conversational space for a person needing comfort.	To let people in need of support know that you are on their side, that they can safely discuss their situation, and that your motive is simply and solely to help them.	1. Emphasize your desire and availability to help. 2. Promise—and keep—confidentiality. 3. Convey acceptance and affiliation. 4. Convey warmth and caring nonverbally. 5. Promote elaboration with questions and brief responses.	After listening to Sonja describe her frustration with her parents' inability to let her be independent, her friend Deepak gave her a quick hug and replied: "Oh, Sonja, maybe I can help you sort through this. I understand your frustration. I went through the same thing with my parents who just don't get that we want to be American, not Indian. Why don't you tell me what happened? Trust me, I won't share this with anyone, and I'd like to help."

has three elements: (1) acknowledging the negative emotion, (2) legitimating the experience of emotion, and (3) encouraging discussion of the emotion.

Consider the following example:

Bill: *My sister called today to tell me that Mom's biopsy came back positive. She's got cancer, and it's untreatable.*

Dwight: *Bill, you must be in shock. This is such difficult news … devastating, really. Do you want to talk about it?*

Dwight's response acknowledges what Bill is probably feeling (shock), legitimates his experience of shock by describing the event as difficult and devastating, and invites Bill to talk.

For many of us, this kind of response to another person's negative emotion is difficult to master. We may have been raised in families or come from cultures that have taught us not to dwell on negative feelings or pry into the business of others. Consequently, even when a friend or intimate is upset, our instinct may be to change the topic or make light of the situation. We may even believe that we are being helpful by distracting the other person from the distressing situation. Yet this approach can do harm rather than good.

Encouraging Reappraisals

Emotion theory helps explain why ignoring or dismissing negative feelings does not make them go away, and why validating emotion is a more successful

SKILL BUILDER ▶ VALIDATE EMOTIONS

SKILL	USE	STEPS	EXAMPLE
Acknowledging what someone is feeling and his or her right to feel that way.	To provide comfort by acknowledging what someone is feeling and his or her right to feel that way.	1. Acknowledge the negative emotion. 2. Legitimate the experience of emotion. 3. Encourage discussion of the emotion.	"Oh, Jamie, it sounds like you're really angry. I think I understand why you would feel that way, but can you tell me more about how you're feeling?"

Appraisal theories of emotion—theories that hypothesize that what we feel arises from what we think

How does the way you think affect the way you feel?

approach to comforting. It also suggests that an emotional reaction will change only if the person who is experiencing it begins to perceive the situation differently.

Appraisal theories of emotion (Smith & Kirby, 2009) explain that what we feel arises from what we think. People experience negative emotions when they appraise (perceive) events as relevant to their goals and in opposition to them. The nature and intensity of the negative emotion depends on the importance of the goals, the type of opposition created by the event, and the person's coping resources. For example, Elaine may need to finish a research paper by a deadline in order to avoid taking a 10% grade deduction. If Elaine has trouble finding the sources she needs, she is likely to become anxious and anticipate being unable to meet the deadline. In order for her feelings to change, something has to change about the situation or how she thinks about it. If the professor emails the class acknowledging the difficulty of the assignment, extends the deadline, and offers help during extra office hours, or if Elaine makes an appointment to meet with a reference librarian, this may alter the situation and alleviate some of Elaine's anxiety.

Alternatively, Elaine might also reduce her anxiety by changing the way she thinks about the situation. She could remind herself that she has been successful at completing difficult assignments in the past or start planning a different direction for the paper that would allow her to make use of sources she already has. She could also decide that it is more important to write a good paper and take a deduction than to submit it on time. When Elaine's negative feelings change, the situation changes, and vice versa.

Imagine now that Elaine's friend Tyler calls while she is fretting about the assignment. If Tyler downplays the importance of the paper ("Don't worry about it, it's just a paper! You'll be fine"), will this change her feelings? Possibly, but only if Elaine agrees with Tyler's perspective and actually changes the way *she* thinks about the paper. If her goal is to complete the paper on time, and she still has insufficient sources, her anxiety is likely to remain unchanged. Tyler's "comforting" will be at best, ineffective, and may even be harmful if it makes Elaine feel that Tyler doesn't understand or care. What if Tyler instead used the strategy of validating Elaine's feelings? "I can tell you're really anxious about this paper.

After all, it's a big chunk of the grade. What do you think will help?" This strategy recognizes Elaine's feelings, treats them as a normal response to the situation, and opens the door for reflection and discussion. If Elaine begins discussing with Tyler why she feels anxious, she can start to identify different ways of thinking about the situation, and things she can do to improve it.

The **theory of conversationally induced reappraisals** (Burleson & Goldsmith, 1998) explains that when we have a conversation with someone who validates what we are feeling, there is relief that comes simply from having our emotions recognized and understood. This recognition and understanding helps us temporarily stop reacting emotionally to the situation, and instead begin examining our feelings and the situation provoking them. Examining those feelings can help us accept them, and begin to **reappraise**, or revise our perspective. Although the steps of acknowledging, legitimating, and encouraging discussion are relatively simple, there are a few things to consider so that your efforts at validating emotion are as successful as possible. First, when acknowledging, keep in mind that empathy isn't perfect: you may sometimes misjudge a support recipient's emotional state. However, incorrect acknowledgement can still serve the important purpose of getting a person to think and talk about what he or she is feeling. If you're really uncertain of what someone else is feeling, use perception-checking. Second, support providers can use their own experiences to help legitimate what support recipients feel, but need to be careful about keeping the focus on the recipient. Using a response like, "I was in a similar situation and was SO disappointed," can be a good strategy, but discussing the details of that situation is not. Finally, even with clear invitations to discuss a problem, some people will resist talking about their feelings. Support providers need to be sensitive to and acknowledge the fine line that exists between encouraging someone to open up and invading that person's privacy to satisfy their own curiosity. Even if your only motive is to help the other person, there will be times when you should not pursue the matter. If you have taken steps to create a supportive conversational climate (e.g., emphasizing your desire to help, conveying warmth and caring nonverbally), and validated emotions, but your support recipient doesn't want to talk, you must respect his or her wishes. One way to conclude this kind of interaction is to say "Okay, I understand that you may not want to talk, but if you change your mind, I'm always here for you. Just call or text me."

Sometimes simply validating emotions is not enough to start the reappraisal process. When people's emotions are running high, they are especially

Theory of conversationally induced reappraisals—the theory that having our emotions recognized and understood results in relief, which allows us to look for other explanations for how we feel and steps we can take to make the situation better

Reappraise—revise one's perspective

How does conversation help us feel better?

Encouraging reappraisal—offering information, observations, and opinions that help the support recipients reframe the situation so that they see it in a different light that is not associated with strong emotion

likely to perceive events in very limited ways and become stuck in that specific way of thinking and feeling. The skill of **encouraging reappraisal** offers information, observations, and opinions that help the support recipient reframe the situation so that they see in a different light that is not associated with strong emotion. Consider the following situation:

> After class, Travis announces to his roommate, Abe, *"Well, I'm flunking calculus. It doesn't matter how much I study or how many of the online problems I do; I just can't get it. This level of math is above me. I might as well just drop out of school before I flunk out completely. I can ask for a full-time schedule at work and not torture myself with school anymore."*

In this example, Travis has not only described his situation but has also interpreted it in a limited way to mean that he is not smart enough to handle college-level math courses. Yet there could be information that Travis doesn't have or hasn't thought about that would lead to other interpretations. For example, Abe might remind Travis that he has been putting in a lot of hours at his part-time job this term, which may be interfering with his studies. Or Abe might tell Travis that he heard the calculus instructor likes to scare the class into working harder by grading hard at the beginning of the semester, but curving the grades at the end. In this way, Abe suggests a reappraisal, or a new way of thinking about the situation. If Travis adopts this reappraisal, he is likely to feel better, and it may encourage him to take useful actions, such as reducing his work hours, or talking with the instructor about how to succeed in the class.

To encourage reappraisal effectively, you need to (1) listen to how your partner is interpreting events; (2) notice information that your partner may be overlooking or overemphasizing in the interpretation; and (3) clearly present relevant, truthful information, observations, and opinions that enable your partner to reframe what has happened. In the following example, notice how Shelby suggests an alternative interpretation of Deon's behavior that may help Karla feel better.

> Karla: *"I'm just furious with Deon. All I said was, 'We've got to start saving money for a down payment or we'll never get a house.' And he didn't say a word. He just got angry and stomped out of the room."*
>
> Shelby: *"Yes, I can see what you mean, and I'd be angry, too. It's hard to work through issues when someone up and leaves. But maybe Deon feels guilty about not being able to save. You know his dad. Deon was raised to believe that the measure of a man is his ability to provide for his family. So, when you said what you did, unintentionally, you may have hurt his male ego."*

As a support provider, it's important to remember that you can't make reappraisal happen. You can offer potential ways of reframing the situation, but the actual change in appraisal has to come from your support recipient. If a recipient indicates resistance to the reframing you've offered, what you've suggested may not be a comforting or useful way of rethinking the situation for that person. Or, the recipient may simply not be ready to adopt a different way of thinking. Try

SKILL BUILDER ▶ ENCOURAGE REAPPRAISAL

SKILL	USE	STEPS	EXAMPLE
Offering information, observations, and opinions that help support-recipients reframe a situation so that they see it in a different light that is not associated with strong emotion.	To support others by providing alternative explanations for situations in which the emotions experienced by the support-receiver limit their ability to reappraise the situation.	1. Listen to how your partner is interpreting events. 2. Notice information that your partner may be overlooking or over-emphasizing in the interpretation. 3. Clearly present relevant, truthful information, observations, and opinions that enable your partner to develop a less ego-threatening explanation of what has happened.	Pam: "Katie must be really angry with me. Yesterday she walked right by me at the market and didn't even say 'Hi.'" Paula: "Are you sure she's angry? She hasn't said anything to me. And you know, when she's mad I usually hear about it. Maybe she just didn't see you."

not to become discouraged or resentful, as these reactions will only get in the way of helping. Instead, continue to create a supportive climate, validate emotions, and look for other beneficial ways to reframe.

Encouraging reappraisal is a useful support skill for any kind of emotional upset, but it is especially important when support recipients are dealing with lost self-esteem. When people make embarrassing blunders, experience failure or rejection, or do something they shouldn't have done, they often feel bad about themselves. Low self-esteem can prevent them from taking useful steps to improve the situation. The **cognitive-emotional theory of esteem support messages** (Holmstrom & Burleson, 2011) explains that support providers can help restore self-esteem and promote problem-solving by encouraging more positive reappraisals. For example, people who have lost their jobs report higher self-esteem when their support providers emphasize the recipient's positive, job-relevant traits, ability to cope with the situation, and the stability of the relationship between the provider and recipient, regardless of employment status (Holmstrom, Russell, & Clare, 2013). For example, Joel might say to his buddy, Mac, "Your resume shows good experience and a real work ethic. I know this is hard on you and your family, but I also know you'll pull through. I don't care what job you have—I'll always be your bro." Job seekers' esteem also benefits when support providers point to causes of the job loss that are likely to change. For example, Joel might also say, "The economy was a big part of your layoff. Things are getting a little better out there, and employers are looking for people who know how to work."

Cognitive-emotional theory of esteem support messages—the theory that support providers can help restore self-esteem and promote problem-solving by encouraging more positive reappraisals

Why is job loss so emotionally painful?

As support recipients begin to reappraise their situations and feel better, they often start to see for themselves how they can take action to address their current problems, or prevent them from happening in the future. However, as a support provider, you may also want to promote useful actions by giving advice.

Promoting Action with Advice

Advice—recommendation about actions to take in response to a problem

Advice is a recommendation about action to take in response to a problem (MacGeorge, Feng, & Thompson, 2008). Advice can be highly supportive, but it needs to be presented thoughtfully. Unfortunately, support providers often rush to provide advice before developing the rapport that allows support recipients to see the advice as helpful, or before they really understand the problem from the recipient's perspective. Sometimes nothing can be done about a problem, and sometimes advice isn't wanted or needed. When you give advice in these circumstances, it is likely to be ignored or even resented. Before giving advice, consider whether you've created a supportive climate, validated emotion, and encouraged reappraisal. Advice should be offered after recipients have had enough time to understand, explore, and make sense of what has happened to them—and to plan actions for themselves. Advice is also better received if it is requested or desired, so if possible, wait until you are asked (Goldsmith, 2000).

Research indicates that support recipients are especially concerned about the efficacy of the advice, whether it will really help, and the feasibility of the advice, whether realistically it can be accomplished (MacGeorge et al., 2013). If you don't think an advised action will make the situation better, or don't believe you can do it, it's unlikely that you will appreciate the advice, much less try the advised action. Support recipients may also be highly sensitive to the potential limitations or drawbacks of advice because they don't want to do something to make a situation worse. For these reasons, you should carefully consider what your support recipient is likely to think about the actions you advise, explain why you think the advised action will work, and discuss how to manage any possible limitations or drawbacks. For example, if Justice is struggling to choose a major, Kaylee might say, "I suggest going to the career center (advice). Any student can go (feasibility), and the counselors there have lots of ways to help you figure out what you're good at (efficacy). The only hitch is that you have to make an appointment, but you can do that online (managing limitations)."

Support recipients also prefer advice that is polite, or face-saving. Because advice is about what the recipient should do, it can easily come across as bossy, patronizing, or critical. Unless you have been asked directly for advice, demonstrate politeness by asking for permission to give it. For example, you might say, "Would you like to hear my ideas on this?" Then, make clear that your advice is a recommendation, not an order. One way of doing this is to acknowledge that your partner is a competent decision maker who is free to accept or reject the advice. "This is just a suggestion; you are the one who has to deal with this," is a message that expresses deference to your partner's opinions and preferences. Another way to manage the other's face needs is to hedge and qualify your opinions and advice, making it easier for your partner to disagree with you. For instance, you might say, "I can't be 100% certain this will work (hedge), but if I were in a situation like this, I might think about doing. . . ."

Finally, you can propose actions indirectly by relating what others have done in similar situations or by offering hypothetical suggestions. For instance, you might say, "You know, when my friend Tom lost his job, he . . ." or "Maybe one option to try might be. . . ." Always remember that advice is a form of persuasion. It can influence what a support recipient actually does, which could turn out to be either good or bad. Thus, it is wise to let recipients have the final say in what they do.

Another thing to consider when giving advice is whether you are qualified to give it. Not surprisingly, we evaluate advice more positively when it comes from people we consider experts. If you have limited knowledge about or experience with a situation, it can be more helpful for you to ask questions that allow your partner to find his or her own solutions. If you do have expertise, but your support recipient doesn't know that, it is a good idea to briefly mention what gives you that expertise. When Kaylee spoke with Justice about the career center, she could have indicated her expertise by saying, "I had a consultation there as a freshman," or, "I learned about career counseling in my human services class." Support recipients also respond better to advisors they trust and like. If you don't know someone very well, you should be especially reserved about giving unsolicited advice.

Keeping these recommendations in mind, you can skillfully give advice by following these procedures: (1) Ask for permission to give advice, (2) briefly describe any expertise relevant to the advice, (3) explain why you believe the advised action is effective and feasible, (4) address any limitations or drawbacks, and (5) phrase your recommendation as a suggestion. For instance, suppose

"Forget everything I told you about flying."

Cartoonstock www.Cartoonstock.com

SKILL BUILDER ▶ GIVE ADVICE

SKILL	USE	STEPS	EXAMPLE
Make recommendations about actions to take in response to a problem.	To comfort our partners after a supportive climate has been established and our partners are unable to find their own solutions.	1. Ask for permission to give advice. 2. Briefly describe any expertise relevant to the advice. 3. Explain why you believe the advised action is effective and feasible. 4. Address any limitations or drawbacks. 5. Phrase your recommendation as a suggestion.	After a friend has explained a difficult situation she is facing at work, Sam might say, "I faced something similar a while ago where I worked. I have a suggestion if you'd like to hear it." When the friend nods "yes," Sam continues: "As I see it, one way you could handle this is to talk directly to your co-worker about how to share the work more fairly. He might not realize how uneven things have become. And then you wouldn't have to involve your manager and be perceived as a trouble-maker. Of course, your co-worker may blow you off and do even less than he's doing now."

▶ OBSERVE AND ANALYZE

Supporting

Recall the last time you provided support to someone. Describe the situation. Do you think you were successful at supporting your partner? How did you use each of the support skills in this situation? Which of the skills do you feel most comfortable using? Which are more difficult for you? How did your use of the skills help or hinder your success at supporting your partner? If you had a chance to redo how you supported this person, what would you do differently?

Shawn is aware that his manager relies on him to help solve major problems that confront their work team. Yet on two occasions when positions that pay much more than Shawn's have opened up, his manager has recommended others who are less qualified. When Shawn shares his frustration with his friend Marino, Marino responds by acknowledging Shawn's frustrations and posing questions to help him better understand the problem. Then he asks permission to give advice and makes reference to his expertise: "Shawn, over the last year you've told me a lot about your situation at work, so I think I understand all the players. Are you interested in hearing my ideas about what you could do?" When Shawn nods, Marino continues, offering thoughtful, polite advice: "I know you have many choices. You could get a different job. But if I were in your shoes, before I did anything radical, I would make a point of seeing my manager. I would tell him how much I appreciate his confidence in me. Then I'd tactfully describe my disappointment at not being promoted and ask him why he hasn't suggested me for these jobs." Marino then discusses the efficacy, feasibility, and limitations of the advice: "It won't be easy to have this conversation, but I know you'll handle it well. I also think that if you don't let him know how you perceive this situation, you will begin to resent him and may begin to dislike your job." Finally, Marino indicates that the advice is a suggestion, while still conveying confidence about his recommendation: "Still, it's your decision, and there are probably other ways to go about it. But I hope you'll consider my suggestion."

When others are feeling bad, giving effective support requires several skills, including creating a supportive conversational climate, validating emotions, facilitating reappraisal, and promoting action with useful advice. If you develop these skills, you will provide higher quality support, which will benefit your relationships. You can also enhance your relationships by learning to support others when they are feeling good.

Supporting Positive Feelings: Celebratory Support

We all like to treasure our successes and make the most of the good feelings that come from them. When good things happen to us, we like to share them with others. **Capitalization** is the process of sharing our successes and leveraging the good feelings that come from them by telling others, with the expectation that they will celebrate with us (Langston, 1994). When we share our successes, we don't want them belittled by listeners' inappropriate or insensitive responses. Rather, we disclose these events in the hope that our partner's response will magnify how good we are feeling about what has happened (Gable, Reis, Impett, & Asher, 2004). This is where celebratory support becomes important. **Celebratory support** is helping others capitalize on their success. When our relationship partners offer celebratory support, they help us continue to feel good about what has happened and about our relationships (Gable et al., 2004). When we see that a partner can be counted on to positively support us, we feel more intimacy, trust, and commitment (Gable, Gonzaga, & Strachman, 2006).

What is the best way to provide celebratory support? Although "Congratulations!" may be a good initial response, research indicates that support providers can do more to promote capitalization. The skill of celebratory support is more effective when it includes at least two elements: (1) Affirming the positive emotions and (2) offering to celebrate with the person. Affirming positive emotions is very similar to validating negative emotions. It involves acknowledging what the person is feeling and legitimating the experience. For example, if Kendra's hoped-for application for a business loan has been approved, Selena could affirm her positive emotions by saying, "Wow! Way to go! In this economy, that's a terrific accomplishment. All the work you put into your business plan really paid off. You must be so pleased and excited." Notice how Selena's message not only highlights Kendra's feelings, but legitimates those feelings by pointing out the reasons for her success. Offering to celebrate is exactly what it sounds like: suggest a way of celebrating that is appropriate to the original positive event and the relationship between you and the other person. Doing this not only extends the

Capitalization—the process of sharing our successes and leveraging the good feelings that come from them by telling others, with the expectation that they will celebrate with us

Celebratory support—the skill of helping others capitalize on their success

What can you say and do to help your friends capitalize on their accomplishments?

positive event into the future, but shows that you value the person enough to spend time (and probably money, too) focusing on something of importance to them. Selena might say "Kendra, we have to go out! Drinks on me!" or "Let's get the gang together at my house to celebrate."

Gender and Culture in Supportive Interactions

According to popular belief, men and women value support differently, the common assumption being that women expect, need, and provide more support than men. Yet a growing body of research indicates that both men and women of various ages place a high value on support from their partners in a variety of relationships (Burleson, 2003). Studies also find that men and women have similar ideas about what makes messages supportive. Both men and women find that messages validating emotions and encouraging reappraisal provide more support than messages that lack these elements. Both men and women also respond positively when support-providers work to create a supportive climate. And both men and women are concerned that advice be effective, feasible, and polite. The biggest difference between men and women is that men are (on average) less likely to validate emotions or encourage reappraisal. This suggests that we need to focus greater attention on enhancing men's abilities in the comforting realm (Kunkel & Burleson, 1999).

Research has also been directed toward understanding cultural differences in supportive situations. While studies have found some differences, Burleson (2003) reports that, for members of multiple cultural groups, support strategies that involve validating emotion and encouraging reappraisal are regarded as highly sensitive ways of providing support. Recent research has examined the influence of culture on giving and responding to advice. For example, Russians routinely give more advice to family and friends and see advice as more supportive than do people in the United States (Chentsova-Dutton & Vaughn, 2012). In addition, Chinese people appear to be more strongly influenced by advisor characteristics like expertise, trust, and liking than are people in the United States (Feng & Feng, 2013). This is probably because the Chinese in their collectivist culture are more relationship-oriented and rely more heavily on relational cues when communicating than do people in more individualistic cultures such as the United States.

THE SOCIAL MEDIA FACTOR

Using Social Media to Offer Empathy and Support

When we face stress or crises in our lives, we naturally turn to close friends and family with whom we have strong interpersonal relationships. Traditionally, we used face-to-face communication to seek and to offer support and comfort.

Today, however, people who experience stress and crises are increasingly turning to social media as new avenues of support (Bambina, 2007). In some situations, providing support through digital communication has some advantages, such as increased social distance, increased presence of others, benefits for apprehensive individuals, ease of management, and opportunities for dealing with loss (Wright, 2015).

Increased Social Distance

Digital support creates a social distance that frees some people to disclose problems that they would be uncomfortable talking about in face-to-face contexts. Through social media, people can even remain anonymous and receive comfort from a stranger. Although social media can bring us closer together, the increased social distance also created by technology allows individuals to participate in the support process from the comfort of their computer. Although she is friends with Carla, Jill may feel more comfortable disclosing her health diagnosis to everyone via Facebook because the social networking site offers a bit of social distance between her and her friends. Although Jill can find support in talking about her illness with others face-to-face, those rich interactions may lead Jill to cry and become even more upset. Oftentimes, we widely share information through social media to reach a large audience of people very quickly and distance ourselves from any potential outpouring of face-to-face support.

Increased Presence of Others

The number of individuals who participate in an online support group enhances opportunities to receive support from people who have experienced the same situation (Mirivel & Thombre, 2010). In Alcoholics Anonymous group meetings, members sit in a circle, share personal information, and receive support from others in the same room. Even though fellow group members may have experienced similar struggles with alcohol, the presence of others in the room may cause some participants to hesitate to disclose their experiences with alcohol use and sobriety. Now, anonymous online support groups exist that enable participants to actively send and receive empathic and supportive messages. While close friends and loved ones may try to put themselves in your situation, being able to chat with people who are in your exact situation can provide more meaningful comfort and support. Individuals who struggle with an eating disorder or a rare illness may turn to online support groups as the only way to find others who can truly empathize. In addition, the increased presence of others through social networking sites such as Facebook provides additional opportunities for a person to receive support from others. Consider a Facebook friend who frequently posts status messages that highlight their life's latest misfortunes. How often have you read a status message from a friend who vents about difficult college classes, unhelpful professors, or struggles with landing a job? Those support-seeking status updates are often followed by a host of Facebook friends who comment and offer support, empathy, and comfort.

INTER-ACT WITH
SOCIAL MEDIA

People frequently use Facebook as a forum for social support. Scan your Facebook newsfeed for friends who post supportive messages. Pay careful attention to the comments posted in response to a friend's support-seeking message. Evaluate the nature of the support communicated through Facebook in light of the characteristics of effective and ineffective support messages discussed in this chapter.

▶ OBSERVE AND ANALYZE

Support on Social Media

Read at least fifteen postings of any online support group. Identify examples of perspective taking, sympathetic responsiveness, empathic responsiveness, validating emotions, encouraging reappraisal, or giving useful advice. How do people create a supportive conversational climate online? What conclusions can you draw about giving and receiving support online?

Benefits for Apprehensive Individuals

Individuals who are apprehensive about communicating in face-to-face settings benefit greatly from receiving support through social media. Digital support can be particularly advantageous for people who are extremely introverted, shy, or prone to loneliness (Segrin, 1998). Individuals who experience anxiety when communicating face-to-face often turn to social media as outlets for empathy and support. If Jimmy has difficulty initiating relationships in face-to-face contexts, the relationships that he develops online may be his primary source of receiving supportive messages. However, the digital supportive messages that Jimmy receives through social media may be free of the rich social cues that are often present in face-to-face interactions. In many ways, those cues may be what cause Jimmy to experience apprehension and uncomfortable feelings when he communicates with others in face-to-face settings. The sheer absence of these cues through social media may attract Jimmy to Facebook, texting, or email as outlets for receiving support. If you are shy in face-to-face settings, know that you can receive support from others through social media. Your support providers will need to work hard to communicate their thoughts and feelings as they comfort you during your difficult time.

Ease of Management

Comforters, too, may more easily manage the sending of empathy and support through social media. When we digitally send support, we can carefully choose our words and craft the most effective and helpful messages possible. In face-to-face contexts, we have all served as the go-to support person for a particular friend experiencing stress or a life crisis. These repeated interactions require significant emotional energy to demonstrate to the support seeker that we care enough about him or her to offer adequate comfort. Unlike our face-to-face interactions, we can choose when to begin and end digital supportive interactions without the support seeker assuming that we are annoyed, frustrated, or bothered by his or her need for comfort. Even though we are able to carefully craft supportive messages through social media, we must give extra effort to communicating care and concern through those messages. Remember that certain forms of social media—such as texting—lack the social cues that are present in face-to-face interactions. When you offer digital support through social media, remember to choose your words wisely and position them alongside smiley faces and other emoticons that communicate empathy and warmth.

Memorializing Others Through Digital Communication

The rapid development of social media has generated new ways to help others cope with the loss of a dear friend or loved one. Increasingly, one or more family members may honor their loved one by preparing a commemorative web page that memorializes the life of the departed. Websites such as Legacy.com, MyDeathSpace.com, and Memory-Of.com have been around for over a decade to facilitate the creation of interactive online memorials. An article in the *Boston Globe* described Shawn Kelley's "moving tribute" to his brother Michael, a National Guardsman killed in Afghanistan. The 60-second video featured a picture slideshow of Michael growing up while quiet classical music played softly and a voice-over recounted Michael's attributes and interests. Shawn reported that it made him feel good to be able to "talk" about his brother, and over a year later, he was still visiting the site to watch the video and to view the messages left by family members and friends (Plumb, 2006). In many ways, Facebook and other social networking sites have taken the form of "electronic grief counselor" (Stingl, 2007). How many Facebook memorial groups have you seen in recent months? Chances are, you've seen quite a few. We use these groups to post messages to our deceased friends to cope with loss and offer others support.

Interactive memorial websites have become places where mourners can connect with other mourners, express condolences, and share stories about the deceased, activities that traditionally occurred at a funeral or memorial service. Communicating on social network memorial walls and groups reconnects the living with the deceased and helps us make sense of our lives without these friends and loved ones. Denise McGrath, a mother who created "R.I.P. Tony," a memorial web page for her teenage son on MySpace, explained that it was "just a place for his friends to go" (Plumb, 2006). Today Legacy.com hosts permanent memorials for over two-thirds of the people who die in the United States and is visited by over 14 million users each month (Legacy.com, 2011). People can visit with their departed loved one and even leave messages directed to him or her. Sending such a digital message through a website or social networking site is called **transcorporeal communication**, "trans" indicating beyond and "corporeal" indicating the physical, material body (DeGroot, 2012).

When President John F. Kennedy was assassinated decades ago, citizens turned to television and radio and gathered together with family members to cope with the tragedy. But when nine black Christians were massacred at Mother Emmanuel A.M.E. church during a Bible study, citizens took to social media to grieve this act of terrorism. Although our methods of grieving and seeking support have expanded over the years, one thing remains constant: Effective communication that comforts and supports other people is a key part of developing our relationships.

> **INTER-ACT WITH**
> ## SOCIAL MEDIA
> Think about the last Facebook memorial group you visited. Go to that Facebook page. Spend some time looking through and reflecting on the postings that others made to honor the deceased person. How would you describe the comments that people made on this page? Did you post on this page? If so, what motivated you to make a comment? Think about the relationship that you had with the deceased person. Write a short paragraph describing your relationship with the person. In another paragraph, describe the types of comments that people made on this page. In a final paragraph, explain how this Facebook page might have been used as an outlet for grieving individuals to seek empathy and support over the loss of their friend or loved one.

Transcorporeal communication— a process through which a living person sends a digital message to a deceased person through a website or social networking site

Summary

Supporting others begins with being able to empathize. Empathizing is the cognitive and affective process of perceiving the emotions others are feeling and then acting on our perceptions. It is shown through perspective taking, sympathetic responsiveness, and empathic responsiveness. Empathizing requires that we pay attention to the nonverbal and verbal paralanguage cues of our partners, recognize the emotional content of verbal messages, and use the skill of perception checking. Social support is the assistance we provide to others we believe

Kendra and Emma are roommates and have been best friends since grade school. For the past three years, Kendra has been dating Emma's older brother, Dominic. Dominic finished college recently and moved to Chicago, about an hour away from where Kendra and Emma go to school. This past weekend, Dominic invited Kendra to visit him. She even told Emma that she was sure he was going to ask her to marry him. Emma gently tried to discourage her from expecting that, but Kendra remained convinced that this was the purpose for the invitation.

Far from proposing, Dominic spent the weekend watching TV and picking fights with Kendra. By the end of the weekend, Kendra was miserable, hurt, and worried about their relationship. She decided to test him by remarking, "Well, it just seems like you aren't very glad to see me, so maybe we should just forget it and start seeing other people." She was dumbfounded when Dominic replied, "Well, if that's what you want, okay," turning his attention back to the football game on TV. In shock, Kendra quickly gathered her things and left.

By the time she got back to the apartment she shared with Emma, she was a mess. Crying and screaming, she called Dominic every name she could think of as she walked in the front door. When Emma raced into the room, Kendra exclaimed, "I can't believe you let me go up there and be so humiliated! What kind of a friend are you? You're just like your brother—mean." Stunned by Kendra's outburst, Emma asked, "Kendra, what are you talking about? What happened? Is Dominic okay?"

Kendra: "Oh sure, you worry about Dominic, but what about me? Sure, take your brother's side. I don't know

what else I should have expected from you. You were probably in on it. It's just not fair."

Emma: "Wait a minute, Kendra, in on what? What happened?"

Kendra: "Dominic broke up with me."

Emma: "He did? I can't believe it."

Kendra: "Well . . . no, but, yeah, well kind of. . . ."

Emma: "Kendra, you're not making any sense. Did Dominic break up with you or not? Tell me. What happened?"

Kendra: "Well, he made it pretty clear that he didn't really want to be with me anymore."

Emma: "Kendra, did he or did he not break up with you?"

Kendra: "Well, he certainly didn't propose marriage."

Emma: "Is that what this is about? Kendra, what made you think he was ready to propose? He just finished school. He has a ton of college debt, and he's still looking for a job. He can't help it if you got it in your head that he was going to propose. But I can't believe that he broke up with you. So what really happened?"

Kendra: "Emma, I don't want to talk about it, especially not with you. Now would you please just leave me alone? Your family has done enough damage to me today."

With that, Kendra stomped into her bedroom and slammed and locked the door.

FOR CONSIDERATION

1. What ethical principles were violated in this encounter?
2. Is it ethical for Kendra to expect Emma to support her if this means disowning her brother?
3. How can Emma support Kendra and not violate the ethical call to speak the truth?

need our aid, both tangible and intangible. Supportive interactions, conversations whose goals are to provide emotional support for one partner, have four phases: support activation, support provision, recipient reaction, and provider response. Although most supportive interactions use the phases sequentially, sometimes they are used out of order; in difficult situations they may be cycled through several times. Although we may try to comfort a person with a single supportive comment, more often our support requires a longer conversation, or series of conversations over days, weeks, months, and even years. Supportive message skills include creating a supportive climate, validating emotions, encouraging reappraisal, offering advice, and providing celebratory support. The desire to be comforted appears to be universal, with few substantial differences reported across cultures and between men and women.

People who experience stress and crises are increasingly turning to social media as new avenues of support. Digital support creates a social distance that frees some people to disclose problems that they would be uncomfortable talking about in face-to-face contexts. The number of individuals who participate in an online support group enhances opportunities to receive support from people who have experienced the same situation. Individuals who are apprehensive communicating in face-to-face settings benefit greatly from receiving support through social media.

CHAPTER RESOURCES

Key Words

Flashcards for all of these key terms are available on the *Inter-Act* website.

Analyze and Apply

The following question challenges you to demonstrate your mastery of the concepts, theories, and frameworks in this chapter by using them to explain what is happening in a specific situation.

9.1 Rewind/Rewrite

Now that you have read the chapter, hit "rewind" on the opening dialogue between Jenna, Melanie, and Becca and answer the following questions.

a. Use concepts from the chapter to explain why Jenna is hurt by Melanie's response, and why Melanie becomes angry with Becca. The concepts of capitalization, celebratory support, validating emotion, encouraging reappraisal, and advice may be especially relevant.

    b. Rewrite the dialogue so that Melanie does a better job of supporting Jenna, and Becca does a better job of supporting Melanie.

    c. Challenge: Exchanging support effectively is more difficult when one person is stressed and the other is happy (like Melanie and Jenna), or when both people are highly stressed. Should Melanie put her own needs aside to show more enthusiasm for Jenna's success, or should she describe her own situation so Jenna understands? What are some good ways of handling a situation in which you are temporarily unable to provide effective support for someone else, such as not having time to talk, or being too upset yourself?

9.2 Reflect on Support

    a. What is the best support you ever received?

    b. Do you remember a time when someone tried to give you support, but it wasn't helpful?

    c. What concepts from this chapter help explain the difference(s) between these experiences?

Skill Practice

Skill practice activities give you the chance to rehearse a new skill by responding to hypothetical or real situations. Additional skill practice activities are available at the companion Inter-Act website.

9.3 Practice Providing Support

For each of the following situations, write a multi-turn dialogue/script in which you are the support provider. Demonstrate the four phases of supportive interactions and your supportive message skills. Use a two-column format. In the left-hand column, write your dialogue. In the second column, identify what phase of the supportive interaction is being enacted and which message skills are present in the turn.

    a. Your best friend walks into the restaurant, flops down in the booth, and sighs, *"My manager is trying to fire me or get me to quit. He told me that my error rate was higher than average, so he wants me to drive all the way downtown to headquarters and take another ten hours of training on my own time."*

    b. As you turn the corner at work, you spy your co-worker Janet leaning against the wall, silently sobbing into her hand.

    c. Your sister (or brother) storms in the front door, throws her (or his) backpack on the floor, and stomps upstairs.

    d. As you are watching TV, your roommate bursts into the room exclaiming, *"I did it. I did it. I really did it! I got accepted to law school! Woohoo!"*

Communication Improvement Plan: Empathizing and Supporting

Would you like to improve your use of the following skills discussed in this chapter?

- Empathizing

- Creating a supportive climate

- Validating emotions

- Encouraging reappraisals

- Giving advice

- Providing celebratory support

Pick a skill, and write a communication improvement plan. You can find a communication improvement plan worksheet on our website at www.oup.com/us/verderber.

10

USING INTERPERSONAL INFLUENCE

Alan and Brad are sophomores who share an on-campus apartment. Alan likes living with Brad, but is tired of living in a small, old apartment while still paying a premium price for being on campus. Brad, on the other hand, thinks the convenience of their current digs is worth the price, especially since his girlfriend lives close by. Alan wants to look for an off-campus apartment for the next school year, with the idea of getting something larger, nicer, and/or cheaper. He tells Brad what he intends to do, and explains that Brad is welcome to join him. At the time, Brad says very little in response. Over the course of the week that follows, Alan notices that Brad lets his chores slide, leaving the dishes and trash for Alan to deal with. Sunday morning, Alan gently confronts Brad about his slacking. After staring at the table for a few seconds, Brad blurts out irritably:

Brad: "Why are you being such a jerk? What happened to wanting to live with friends? I want to live on campus, and I don't know why you wouldn't."

Alan (sighs): "Look, man, I told you, it's not personal. I just would like to live in a nicer, bigger apartment next year, and the newer and nicer on-campus apartments are too expensive."

Brad: "It's so dumb to live off campus. You'll be so far from the parties. And classes, too."

Alan: "With work and my additional studio hours next year, I won't be able to party too much. Plus, I can park on campus for parties on

(Continued)

the weekends. I really don't mind it taking longer to get to class if I can have a better space to work on my projects, study, and hang out when I'm home."

Brad: "C'mon. Don't be a pain. We can get a bigger TV here and a better cable package. My dad will probably buy me a new gaming system this summer, if I work for him."

Alan: "Brad, you're not hearing me. I want a better apartment, not a better Xbox. If you'd look with me, I'll bet we could find something off-campus that would work for both of us."

Brad (turns away and sulks): "Nah. Not so much."

WHAT YOU SHOULD BE ABLE _TO EXPLAIN_ AFTER YOU HAVE STUDIED THIS CHAPTER:

▶ The concept of interpersonal influence

▶ Interpersonal power and its five sources

▶ The four principles of power

▶ The concept of persuasion and two approaches to processing a persuasive message

▶ The six heuristics for automatically processing persuasive messages

▶ The three types of appeals analyzed when extensively processing persuasive messages

▶ What constitutes passive, aggressive, and assertive messages

▶ How to create assertive messages

▶ The impact of electronic persuasive messages

WHAT YOU SHOULD BE ABLE _TO DO_ AFTER YOU HAVE STUDIED THIS CHAPTER:

▶ Make an assertive complaint

▶ Skillfully ask for a change in behavior

▶ Effectively refuse a request

Interpersonal influence—the act of changing the attitudes or behaviors of others

In this brief conversation, Brad is trying to get Alan to reconsider his decision to look for apartments off campus; in other words, he is trying to influence him. At the same time, Alan is also trying to get Brad to see his point of view—and maybe change his mind about staying on campus. Could Brad handle this interaction more effectively? Could Alan? This chapter explores **interpersonal influence**, the act of changing the attitudes or behaviors of others (Dillard & Knobloch, 2011).

Because our individual goals and preferences often differ from those around us, interpersonal influence is an essential skill. In addition to influencing decisions, some of the most common interpersonal influence goals are to gain assistance, give advice, share activities, get permission, change attitudes, and alter relationships (Dillard & Knobloch, 2011). All of these types of influence are part of everyday interactions and messages. This chapter explores what we currently know about interpersonal influence, including interpersonal power as the basis of influence, the processing of influence attempts, the types of effective persuasive messages, and forming messages that assert our rights and expectations without damaging our relationships.

Interpersonal Power

Power is the potential that you have to influence the attitudes, beliefs, and behaviors of someone else. Whether we are conscious of it or not, power dynamics are a part of all our relationships (Guerrero, Andersen, & Afifi, 2013). In some relationships, one person has relatively more power than the other, while in other relationships, power is more equally distributed. And the way power is distributed between the people in relationships can change over time. Let's look at the five sources of power in relationships and the four principles that explain power dynamics.

Power—the potential that you have to influence the attitudes, beliefs, and behaviors of someone else

Sources of Power

Research suggests that influence can stem from five distinct roots or sources of power (French & Raven, 1968; Hinken & Schriesheim, 1980).

1. Coercive power. **Coercive power** is the potential to influence rooted in our ability to physically or psychologically punish our partner. The playground bully and the abusive spouse clearly exemplify the use of coercive power. A playground bully may get his or her way by taunting another child psychologically or because he or she has demonstrated physical aggressiveness. Similarly, an abusive spouse may get his or her way because his or her partner fears further verbal or physical abuse. These are extreme examples of the direct use of coercive power. But this type of power may also be indirect, humorously illustrated in the old vaudeville joke, "Where does a gorilla sit when it enters the room? Anywhere it wants." Whether we use coercive power intentionally or unintentionally, if our partners perceive that we have the capacity to punish them in some way, they will be vulnerable to our attempts to influence them.

Coercive power—the potential to influence rooted in our ability to physically or psychologically punish our partner

2. Reward power. Reward power is the potential to influence rooted in our ability to provide something our partner values and cannot easily get from someone else. Influence attempts based on reward power include the following statements: "I'll give you your allowance when you clean your room," and "If you don't tell Mom that I went to that party, you can use my iPad." Like coercive power, influence rooted in reward power may be direct, as in these two examples, or indirect. For example, you might agree to take your co-worker's shift on Friday night because you know that she belongs to a sorority that you would like to join. Your reward power depends on how much your partner values the rewards you control, how scarce they are, and how likely your partner believes you are to provide the rewards if they were to comply with an influence attempt. For example, suppose Maggie really wants to attend the sold-out Katy Perry concert, and her brother Mitchell, who just broke up with his girlfriend, has an extra ticket. If Mitchell asks Maggie to take his turn picking up their younger brother

Reward power—the potential to influence rooted in our ability to provide something our partner values and cannot easily get from someone else

Legitimate power—the potential to influence others rooted in the authority granted to a person who occupies a certain role

Expert power—the ability to influence rooted in someone's subject-specific knowledge and competence

after soccer practice, she may comply, hoping that Mitchell will reward her by taking her to the concert.

3. Legitimate power. Legitimate power is the potential to influence others rooted in the authority granted to a person who occupies a certain role. The power is called "legitimate" because it is officially bestowed and upheld by laws or rules that dictate how that power is used. Elected officials (regardless of whether you voted for them or agree with their election) are the most obvious example of people who hold legitimate power. Other people who hold a position of authority have legitimate power. For example, teachers have legitimate power with respect to their students, parents with their minor children, managers with employees, and non-elected government officials with citizens. If your instructor tells you that class attendance is mandatory, if your parents tell you that you have to get a summer job, if your manager suggests that you need to work overtime during inventory, or if you are speeding and a police car signals to pull you over, you comply because some authority you recognize and accept has given them the right to influence your behavior.

4. Expert power. Expert power is the potential to influence rooted in someone's subject-specific knowledge and competence. For example, if you want to get a divorce and your friend is a family law attorney, she has the ability to influence your decisions about your divorce settlement because of her expertise. Since she doesn't have children and has little other experience with kids, however, she has little expert power over your child-rearing decisions. Class

In the doctor-patient relationship, the doctor is normally thought to have expert power. How is the availability of medical information on the Internet changing this?

instructors can influence your thinking about what they are teaching because they usually have more subject-specific knowledge and expertise than you. Similarly, when a physician tells you to take a specific medication for your migraines, you are probably persuaded because your doctor has medical expertise and you do not. Even though someone may not actually be an expert, if we believe this person knows more than we do, she or he has the potential to influence us. For instance, when shopping for a water heater, sales associates can persuade us to buy a specific model. They may or may not be experts on water heaters. But if customers perceive them to be, then they have the potential to influence purchase decisions.

5. Referent power. Referent power is the potential to influence rooted in liking, respect, or admiration. Let's face it. We want to be liked and to impress those we like, respect, or admire. As a result, we are susceptible to their influence attempts. If your best friend raves about an obscure art film showing at the local theater, you are likely to go see it, even though you've never heard of it and don't know any of the actors in it. Even when they don't try to exert influence, celebrities have this power because their fans admire them. For example, in an April 2011 interview with *GQ* magazine, Bruno Mars, commenting on his arrest for cocaine possession, echoed other celebrities when he said, "I'm not a role model, I'm a f****** musician." Nonetheless, he added, "I learned people are watching, so don't do nothing stupid" (Gratereaux, 2011). Most of us aren't celebrities, yet we still have referent power when someone likes us.

Principles of Power

Research has identified a number of basic principles of power dynamics (Guerrero et al., 2013).

1. Power is a perception, not a fact. While you may believe that you are powerful with the potential to influence your partner, if your partner doesn't perceive you as having power, you don't.

2. Power exists within a relationship. Power is not a personality trait or a behavior that you can learn and perform. Rather, the sources of power available to you are specific to each relationship and can change over time. For example, Joshua, who has taken a class on personal finance, may be perceived by his younger sister to be an expert on consumer credit, and she may take his advice when selecting a credit card. But Joshua is unlikely to be perceived as an expert in finance by his friend who is a stockbroker.

3. Power is not inherently good or bad. In and of itself, power is neither good nor bad, but the use of power can lead to positive or negative outcomes for people or relationships. Whether the power dynamic in a relationship is healthy or sick will depend on the communication skills of both partners and the ethical use of power by the more powerful partner.

4. The person with greater power in a relationship can make and break the rules for the relationship. In families or in workplaces, parents or managers

Referent power—the potential to influence rooted in liking, respect, or admiration

What is the power dynamic in your relationship?

make and break the rules that children and employees must follow, because they have more power. Likewise, in social groups, the more popular members may dictate how group members are expected to act and yet violate the very norms they have established.

Interpersonal Persuasion

Persuasion—the use of verbal messages designed to influence the attitudes and behaviors of others

Persuasion is using verbal messages designed to influence the attitudes and behaviors of others. We are using persuasion when we use words to directly attempt to influence someone. To understand how messages can influence, you first need to appreciate how we mentally process persuasive messages.

Processing Persuasive Messages: The Elaboration Likelihood Model (ELM)

Can you remember times when you carefully and thoughtfully listened to someone who was trying to convince you of something? Do you remember consciously thinking over what your partner had been saying, critically considering the basis of his or her appeal? Can you remember other times when you did what someone was advocating without really thinking much about it?

Elaboration likelihood model (ELM) of persuasion—a theory that posits people will use either heuristics or more elaborate critical thinking skills when processing persuasive messages

What determines how closely we listen to and how carefully we evaluate the hundreds of persuasive messages we hear each day? In Chapter 2, we learned that thinking can be either automatic or controlled. We can process persuasive messages automatically, responding without much conscious thought, or we can process them deliberately, thinking more thoroughly and slowly about what is being said. The **elaboration likelihood model (ELM) of persuasion** explains that people can use either heuristics—mental shortcuts—or more elaborate critical thinking skills when processing persuasive messages (Petty & Brinol, 2012). The ELM posits that people use one of two routes to process persuasive messages. With the **peripheral route**, we automatically process the persuasive message, using shortcut heuristics that save us time and mental energy. With the **central route**, we consciously process the persuasive message, critically evaluating the logic, credibility, and emotional appeals of the sender. Obviously, the central route consumes more time and energy; rather than taking mental shortcuts, we carefully assess and mentally elaborate on the message to fully understand the basis on which our partner is trying to influence us.

According to the ELM, when the issue is vital to us, we are willing to expend the energy necessary for processing on the central route. When there is much at stake, we will pay attention to the speaker's arguments, evidence, and logic. We will carefully consider the speaker's credibility and use of various emotional appeals. But when the issue is less important to us, we will process the message on the peripheral route, using persuasive heuristics as shortcuts. For example, suppose that you are healthy and take a job at a company that offers several healthcare insurance options at a similar cost. If the friendly woman in human resources who is about your age mentions that she has Plan C and likes it, you may decide to bypass the pages and pages of information on all the plan options and immediately enroll in Plan C. But suppose you have a chronic illness that is expensive to treat. Because choosing an appropriate plan is much more important to you in this case, you will centrally process the information on each of the plans. You will carefully wade through all the material, evaluating each proposal to select the one that best meets your particular needs.

In addition, we are more likely to use extensive processing when we feel that we are capable of analyzing and understanding the information. Otherwise, we will use shortcuts and base our decisions on one or a limited number of factors that we do understand. For example, when Jason went shopping for an engagement ring, he didn't really know much about diamonds. So he went to a jewelry store recommended by a friend, told the attractive salesperson, who reminded him of his girlfriend, how much he could spend, and bought the first ring the salesperson showed him because she said it was the best one. On the other hand, Rob, a diamond cutter by trade, examined over 250 diamonds offered to him by various sales reps to find the perfect one, then cut it himself, and designed the setting before he proposed. Both men ended up spending about the same amount of money, but because Rob had expertise, he figured he was the best judge of a diamond's quality.

The ELM also suggests that when we form attitudes based on centrally processed persuasive messages, we are less likely to alter them than when we form attitudes based on peripherally processed persuasive messages. You can probably remember a time when you quickly agreed to something without really thinking it through. Later on, after thinking about it or living with the consequences of your hasty decision, you regretted being swayed by the message and changed your mind. You also probably have some strongly held beliefs that are the result

Peripheral route—automatically processing persuasive messages by using shortcut heuristics that save time and mental energy

Central route—consciously processing persuasive messages by critically evaluating the logic, credibility, and emotional appeals of the sender

of carefully processing persuasive information. For example, many of us have religious beliefs we accept and whose tenets guide our behavior. Some of us have "inherited" our beliefs, accepting them because our parents, whom we admire and respect, passed them on to us. We may have never bothered to really study the assumptions that underlie our beliefs. Others have come to their religious beliefs after periods of doubt and intense spiritual searching. According to the ELM, those who have engaged in the personal search are less likely to change their beliefs or to act contrary to them. But those of us who have inherited a set of religious principles can be easily swayed to think and act in ways inconsistent with the beliefs.

With the ELM in mind, let's look at the heuristics people use when automatically processing persuasive messages. Then we will discuss the factors that make messages persuasive when they are extensively processed.

Persuading Automatic Processors

When we are processing persuasive messages on the peripheral route, people can influence us by phrasing their requests in ways that trigger a particular heuristic. There are six heuristics whose triggers can be woven into our persuasive messages (Cialdini, 2009).

1. Repay in kind. When you comply with someone's influence attempt because you believe that you are indebted to or obligated to him or her, you are operating from the **reciprocity heuristic**. We will believe or do what another person advocates as a way of repaying another person. This rule of thumb is deeply ingrained in the social contract of all cultures. If in the past someone has done something for you, you will feel obligated to reciprocate. For example, your brother loaned you his car last month when yours was in the shop. Today, when your brother says, "Hey, can I borrow your car? I don't want to put gas in mine," you may not really think about his driving record or whether his explanation is a good one. Instead, you may automatically answer, "Sure," as you toss him the keys. Notice that he didn't even have to remind you about your "debt." The need to reciprocate is so ingrained that we respond automatically to relieve the discomfort that being indebted causes. Therefore, if you want to be able to influence someone, give what you want to receive (Cialdini, 2001). Giving gifts or doing favors for others obligates them to you. The more someone is indebted to you, the more likely she or he is to comply with your persuasive messages.

2. Do what others do—follow the crowd. Being influenced by what others think or do is the **social proof heuristic** rule of thumb used during peripheral processing of persuasive messages. This following-the-crowd rule is especially powerful in social situations where we are unsure of how to act. The old sayings "When in Rome, do as the Romans do" and "There is safety in numbers" reflect the logic of this heuristic. Simon, for instance, is responding to the social proof heuristic when he asks the waiter if the cheeseburgers are good, and the waiter replies, "Well, they're okay, but our pulled pork sandwich is the best seller," and Simon says, "Well, I don't usually eat pork, but I'll try it." The fact that the pork

Reciprocity heuristic—being influenced by a perceived debt or obligation to someone else during peripheral processing of persuasive messages

Social proof heuristic—being influenced by what others think or do during peripheral processing of persuasive messages

"You scratch my back, I'll scratch yours is just a figure of speech, Ned. A little left, and higher."

Cartoonstock www.Cartoonstock.com

sandwich is a best seller is social proof that it is a good choice. Children and teenagers routinely try to influence their parents using the social proof message script, "Well, everyone is going, or doing it, or saying it," and so forth.

3. Do what your friends do. Being influenced to believe or do what people we like advocate is the **liking heuristic** rule of thumb used during peripheral processing of persuasive messages. When friends make a persuasive appeal, we are likely to comply with what they are saying just because we like them. Have you ever been on a diet yet agreed to buy overpriced candy bars from a friend at work whose child's school was selling them as a fundraiser? Did you want the candy bars? Probably not, but you didn't want to disappoint your friend, and you didn't want your friend to stop liking you. In 1936, Dale Carnegie published a book called *How to Win Friends and Influence People.* His recipe for influencing is simple: Be friendly. The book details ways to get others to like you, including smiling, calling others by name, listening, showing interest in what others are interested in, refraining from criticizing, and making other people feel important (Carnegie, 1936). People who like you are more likely to comply with your attempts to influence them.

> **Liking heuristic**—being influenced to believe or do what people we like advocate during peripheral processing of persuasive messages

4. Do what the experts advise. Being influenced by what knowledgeable professionals believe or advocate is the **authority heuristic** rule of thumb used during peripheral processing of persuasive messages. You'll recall that one factor that encourages us to short-circuit how we process a persuasive message is our belief that the information is too difficult or complicated for us to understand. So when someone whom we recognize as an expert advocates that we adopt a particular idea or behavior, we may do so without critically evaluating the evidence. When the service representative at the local car dealership calls me to say that the mechanic thinks I need new brake pads, I may unquestioningly give them the go ahead to make this repair. Because I don't know anything about brake systems and I couldn't tell a brake pad that needed to be replaced from one that was okay, I automatically defer to the mechanic's authority.

> **Authority heuristic**—being influenced by what knowledgeable professionals believe or advocate during peripheral processing of persuasive messages

5. Be consistent. Being influenced by our past active, voluntary, and public commitments is the **consistency heuristic** rule of thumb used during peripheral processing of persuasive messages. Because we like to believe that our behavior is consistent with our beliefs and principles, we can be influenced to comply with persuasive messages that are or appear to be consistent with our previously stated positions or actions. Zeke has volunteered for a local environmental watch group that has been taking monthly water samples from a local creek for the last two years. He was wearing his local group's T-shirt in the student center on campus when he was approached by someone he didn't know who commented that Zeke must be an environmentalist. When he nodded, the other student explained that he was raising money for the World Wildlife Fund. Without hesitating, Zeke reached in his pocket and gave the guy a twenty. Later he had to borrow money from a friend for bus fare home. Knowing what others are committed to can be used to influence them by linking our requests to their beliefs or past actions.

> **Consistency heuristic**—being influenced by our past active, voluntary, and public commitments during peripheral processing of persuasive messages

6. Get what is in short supply. Being influenced by the rarity or availability of something is the **scarcity heuristic** rule of thumb used during peripheral processing of persuasive messages. Believing scarce things to be more valuable, we can be influenced by how plentiful or rare something is portrayed to be. For example, suppose you call to schedule a physical. If the doctor's receptionist tells you that the only appointment available for the next month is on Tuesday at 10:00 a.m., and you have a breakfast meeting with your class project group scheduled at that time, what do you do? Without even thinking about it or checking your calendar, you may quickly accept the appointment time. Later you apologize to the group for having double-booked yourself, explaining, "It was the only appointment I could get." Buying into your scarcity appeal, your group agrees to move the meeting. Making appeals advocating what appears to be exclusive or less available can influence others. Anyone who shops on eBay is also subjected to a constant barrage of language declaring the scarcity or rarity of an item for sale, all for the purpose of boosting its potential auction price.

We use these six heuristics to automatically process and respond to persuasive messages because they are based on principles that generally hold true. For example, reciprocity is an ingrained social norm that enables humans to specialize their labor, share resources with others, and thus create a civilization. And as these heuristics are deeply ingrained, we automatically respond to appeals based on them. In most cases, this isn't a problem: The heuristic is appropriate for the situation, and the person with whom we are interacting has good intentions. But the automatic nature of heuristic use can allow people to take advantage of or manipulate us with persuasive appeals that directly or indirectly evoke these heuristics. The intentions of the person appealing to us determine whether these messages are ethical or unethical. For example, the parent who tells a child, "If you pick up your toys, I'll read you an extra bedtime story," is using the reciprocity heuristic, but since teaching a child to be responsible for cleaning up and reading stories are both good for the child, the appeal is ethical.

Let's look at a different example. Joshua, who is culturally Jewish but religiously agnostic, and Miriam, his Orthodox Jewish girlfriend, have been invited to the wedding of a Christian friend of Joshua's. Miriam agrees to go to the wedding, but wants Joshua to ask the bride to accommodate her dietary restrictions by providing a kosher meal. Joshua thinks that would be embarrassing, so he tries to persuade Miriam by saying, "Miriam, just this one time, can't you please make an exception and eat what everyone else does? Please, just this once, do this for me?" Because Joshua is using Miriam's feelings for him as a way to get her to reject her religious practice, his use of this heuristic is unethical, as it does not respect Miriam's beliefs. Unscrupulous use of these heuristics is not just unethical; it is also shortsighted. Although people may comply with the immediate request, if the outcome is harmful to them, you lose their trust and willingness to comply with your persuasive attempts in the future.

Cars are expensive so most people use extensive processing when evaluating the persuasive messages of salespeople.

Persuading Extensive Processors

When an issue is important to us, we will take a central route to process the persuasive messages that we receive. As we analyze the message, we will evaluate (1) the quality of the reasoning, (2) the credibility of the speaker, and (3) the legitimacy of appeals to our emotions. Let's look at each of these.

1. Quality of the reasoning. Because people pride themselves on being rational—that is, they like to think that they seldom believe or do anything without a reason—you increase the likelihood of persuading extensive processors if you can provide them with reasons rather than just claiming something. **Claims** are simple statements of belief or opinion. They don't answer the "Why?" question. You can probably think of many times that you made a claim to which a person in effect responded, "I can't accept what you've said on face value—give me some reasons!" **Reasons** are statements that provide valid evidence, explanations, or justifications for a claim. They answer the question "Why?" by providing information to back up your position. Let's look at a simple example to illustrate the relationship between claims and reasons. Suppose you're talking with a friend about movies. You might ask, "Have you seen *12 Years a Slave?*" If your friend says "No," you might then make the claim, "It's great. You really need to see it." If your friend asks "Why?" you might explain, "Well, it tells the story of Solomon Northrup, a free Negro who was unlawfully re-enslaved. It won the 2013 Academy Award for Best Picture!" Your reasoning could be outlined as follows:

> **Claim:** You need to see the movie *12 Years a Slave*. (Why?)
> **Reason 1:** Because it portrays the life of Solomon Northup, a free Negro, who was unlawfully re-enslaved.
> **Reason 2:** Because it won the 2013 Academy Award for Best Picture.

Claims—simple statements of belief or opinion

Reasons—statements that provide valid evidence, explanations, or justifications for a claim

Ethical communicators give good reasons to back up their claims so that their partners are able to weigh and evaluate for themselves the substance of the influence attempt. Having heard the reasons, they may accept or reject it based on how they evaluate the reasons. Now let's consider what makes a reason a good or effective reason.

- *Good reasons are relevant to the claim.* As you consider the reasons that you might provide to support a claim, you'll find that some are better than others because they relate more directly to the issue at hand. For example, the reasons just offered for seeing *12 Years a Slave*—"real person who was unlawfully re-enslaved" and "won an Academy Award"—are relevant criteria that people are likely to look for in movies, unlike the reason "It's only showing this week."

- *Good reasons are well supported by valid evidence.* You need to support your reasons with some type of **evidence**—facts, expert opinions, and relevant personal narratives that support the truth of a reason. Your friend may find those reasons relevant but still want additional information that justifies your position. As a result, you'll also need to provide specific support or evidence. For example, in support of "portrays the life of...." you could report that (1) *12 Years a Slave* (the book upon which the movie script was based), originally published in 1853, was Northup's memoir told to an editor, David Wilson; (2) the accuracy of this account was verified by two modern historians, Joseph Logsdon and Sue Eakin.

- *Good reasons are meaningful to the person you're trying to persuade.* There are times when you know something about your conversational partner that calls for you to give more weight to one particular reason than to another. Therefore, you also need to tailor your reasoning to make your assertions meaningful to the person you are trying to persuade. For instance, suppose the friend to whom you recommended *12 Years a Slave* is a film buff who is a fan of Spike Lee and other black filmmakers. In this case, you might want to add as a third reason that Steve McQueen, the director of *12 Years a Slave*, was the first black filmmaker to win an Academy Award for Best Picture.

2. Source credibility. Good reasons may be persuasive, but they are more powerful when presented by a credible source. **Credibility** is the extent to which your partner believes in your competence, trustworthiness, and likability. Automatic processors may mindlessly believe influence attempts by those claiming to be authorities, but extensive processors will critically examine your credibility. You may be able to recall times when no matter how logical the information appeared, you didn't believe it because you didn't trust the person presenting it. Whether your conversational partner has confidence in who you are as a person may determine whether your persuasive messages are effective. Three factors affect your credibility.

Evidence—facts, expert opinions, and personal narratives that support the truth of your reason

Credibility—the extent to which your partner believes in your competence, trustworthiness, and likability

- *Competence* is the perception that you are credible because you are well qualified to provide accurate and reliable information. The more people perceive you as knowledgeable on a particular subject, the more likely they are to pay attention to your views on that subject. For example, if Reggie knows that his friend Gloriana has attended all of the meet-the-candidate sessions and has read candidate websites and party platforms, he will consider her competent, and her reasons may persuade him to vote for a particular candidate.

- *Trustworthiness* is the perception that you are competent because you are dependable, honest, and acting for the good of others. Your intentions or motives are particularly important in determining whether others will view you as trustworthy. For instance, if a sales clerk who is working on commission says to you, "Wow, you look terrific in those jeans," you may not give the opinion much weight. If your mom, however, looks at you and says, "Now those jeans really fit. They don't gap in the back at the waist, and they don't pull across your stomach," you are likely to accept her reasoning because you trust your mom to tell you the truth.

- *Likability* is the perception that you are credible because you are congenial, friendly, and warm. Automatic processors readily believe what those they like tell them, but extensive processors carefully assess the likability of speakers so that they don't succumb to scam artists and other unethical operators who cultivate likability to persuade others to do things not in their best interests.

Competence—the perception that speakers are credible because they are well-qualified to provide accurate and reliable information

Trustworthiness—the perception that speakers are credible because they are dependable, honest, and acting for the good of others

Likability—the perception that speakers are credible because they are congenial, friendly, and warm

You can become an expert in areas that you would like to have influence. You can also behave in ways that earn trust and work to cultivate pleasant relationships. By doing these things, you enhance your credibility and are ethical in your persuasive attempts.

3. Honest emotional appeals. The third component of persuasive messages, **emotional appeals** are persuasive messages that influence others by evoking strong feelings in support of what the speaker is advocating. Messages from a credible source that provide good reasons are likely to influence others' attitudes and ideas. But when you're trying to influence others to *act*, you can increase the persuasiveness of your message by appealing to people's emotions (Jorgensen, 1998). Those who *believe* they should do something still may be reluctant to act on their belief without an additional appeal. For instance, Jonas may believe that people should donate money to worthy causes, but he may not do so; Gwen may believe that people should exercise three times a week for forty-five minutes, but she may not do so. Often what motivates people to act on a belief is the degree of their emotional involvement. Appeals to negative emotions like fear, shame, anger, and sadness, as well as appeals to positive emotions like happiness, joy, pride, relief, hope, and compassion nudge us from passive belief to overt action. When Jonas, for instance, is shown graphic photos of a town torn apart by a tornado, his feelings of compassion may prompt him to donate to the Red Cross.

Emotional appeals—persuasive messages that influence others by evoking strong feelings in support of what the speaker is advocating

Is it ethical for the ASPCA and other animal rescue organizations to use photos of abused animals to appeal to the emotions of potential donors?

The effectiveness of emotional appeals depends on the mood and attitude of the person you are persuading and the persuasive language being used. Suppose, for example, you are trying to convince your brother to loan you money to buy textbooks for the semester without waiting for your grant money to be released. In addition to your rational approach, you may want to include several appeals to his emotions using specific examples and experiences, such as, "I'm sure you remember how tough it is to understand the lectures when you haven't looked at the book," or "Mom will be on my back if I don't do well in this class," or "I know you want to be a nice guy and help your little brother here." Or even better, you may want to employ an emotional appeal that evokes stories from the past. For instance, instead of saying, "I thought you might be interested in going hiking and rock climbing with me tomorrow—it will be fun," you might say, "I thought you might be interested in going hiking and rock climbing with me. It will be like old times when we would spend the whole day at the gorge, just two brothers, bonding. Remember how much fun we had on our hike to Clear Creek Canyon?"

Asserting Rights and Expectations

So far, our discussion of social influence has focused on general approaches to changing others' beliefs, attitudes, or behaviors through persuasion. Now we want to turn our attention to situations in which we want others to show greater

LEARN ABOUT YOURSELF ▶ ASSERTIVENESS

Take this short survey to learn something about yourself. This is a test of your passive, assertive, and aggressive behaviors. Answer the questions based on your first response. There are no right or wrong answers. Just be honest in reporting your true behavior. For each question, select one of the numbers to the left that best describes your behavior.

_____ 1. I am aggressive in standing up for myself.

_____ 2. If a salesperson has gone to a lot of trouble to show me merchandise that I do not want to buy, I have no trouble saying "no."

_____ 3. If a close and respected relative were bothering me, I would keep my feelings to myself.

_____ 4. People do not take advantage of me.

_____ 5. If food in a restaurant is not satisfactory to me, I complain and insist on a refund.

_____ 6. I avoid asking questions for fear of sounding stupid.

_____ 7. I would rather make a scene than bottle up my emotions.

_____ 8. I am comfortable returning merchandise.

_____ 9. I find it difficult to ask friends to return money or objects they have borrowed from me.

_____10. If I hear that a person has been spreading false rumors about me, I confront that person and talk about it.

_____ 11. I can yell at others when I feel that I have been wronged.

_____ 12. I get anxious before making problem-solving business phone calls.

1 = Strongly Agree

2 = Agree Somewhat

3 = Neutral

4 = Disagree Somewhat

5 = Strongly Disagree

Scoring the Survey: Add your scores for items 3, 6, 9, and 12. Your score will range from 4 to 20. The lower (closer to 4) your score, the more you tend to engage in passive behavior.

Add your scores for items 2, 4, 8, and 10. Your score will range from 4 to 20. The lower (closer to 4) your score, the more you tend to engage in assertiveness.

Add your scores for items 1, 5, 7, and 11. Your score will range from 4 to 20. The lower (closer to 4) your score, the more you tend to engage in aggressive behavior.

Adapted from Rathus, S. (1973). A 30-item schedule for assessing assertive behavior. *Behavior Therapy, 4,* 398.

respect for our rights and expectations. Communicating in these situations can be difficult or risky, given the potential to upset others and damage relationships. We need strategies that help us pursue what we need, want, and deserve, while still respecting others' differences. In this section, we discuss the difference between passive, aggressive, and assertive communication. Then we focus specifically on how to skillfully complain, request that other people change their problematic behavior, or refuse a request. Each of these situations involves asserting our own rights and expectations.

Approaches to Communicating Rights and Expectations

We can take three approaches when faced with a situation in which we feel someone has violated our rights or not met our expectations. We can behave passively, aggressively, or assertively. Let's look at each of these approaches and their interpersonal effectiveness.

The Passive Approach

The **passive approach** is concealing your feelings rather than voicing your rights and expectations to others. We may remain passive when someone violates our rights or expectations or comply with requests that are not in our best interests, for several reasons. First, we may not believe that we have rights. Second, we may fear that if we complain or don't comply, we will damage or lose our relationship. Third, we may lack self-esteem and consequently believe that we don't deserve to be treated well. Finally, we may be passive because we don't have the social skills we need to stand up for ourselves. Obviously, passive behavior is not influential, and those who use this method end up submitting to other people's demands, even when doing so is inconvenient, demeaning, or not in their best interests. For example, suppose that when Sergei uncrates the new plasma television he purchased at a local department store, he notices a deep scratch on the left side. If he is upset about the scratch but doesn't try to get the store to replace the expensive item, he is exhibiting passive behavior.

At times, behaving passively is an appropriate response. If someone who is normally considerate of our rights and expectations inadvertently violates them, we may overlook the transgression and chalk it up to our friend's having a bad day. In such cases we put our friend's needs ahead of our own, recognizing that what has occurred is not intentional and is unlikely to be repeated.

In most cases, however, passive behavior is ineffective because it fails to protect our interests and may also damage our relationships. Suppose that Alicia doesn't say anything to her ex-husband when he is late to pick up the children since it was the first time it had happened. Alicia's ex-husband may interpret her silence as indifference to the pick-up time. So the next time, he figures that he will just pick them up an hour later than the original agreement, which is more convenient for him. If Alicia chooses not to comment on his tardiness a second time, she will be teaching him that it is okay to pick the kids up an hour later, and this is likely to become a pattern, as he doesn't see any problem with the new "arrangement."

Not only may passive behavior thwart our interests, but it may also damage our relationships, because when we are passive, we are also private. When we don't share our honest reactions with our partner, we deprive them of the opportunity to meet our needs and to know us better. Marriages have dissolved because one partner was unable to voice his or her needs, protest violations of rights and expectations, or refuse the spouse's requests. The sad thing in these cases is that partners may be totally unaware of their spouse's unhappiness. Although there are situations in which passive behavior is useful, in the long run, passive behavior is not in our own or our relationship's best interests.

Passive approach—concealing your feelings rather than voicing your rights and expectations to others

---

INTER-ACT WITH
SOCIAL MEDIA

Review the last week of Twitter feeds you follow. Select five incidents each of a passive, aggressive, and assertive response to an original tweet. How did the people posting after the identified responses react? Was there any pattern?

The Aggressive Approach

Verbal aggression is sending messages that attack another person's self-esteem or express personal hostility for perceived violations of rights or expectations (Infante & Rancer, 1996). Verbally aggressive messages display our strong feelings, overstating our opinions in a manner that shows little regard for the situation or for the feelings, needs, or rights of others. Aggressive messages include name-calling, threatening, judging, or fault-finding. Verbal aggression is different from **argumentativeness**, which refers to defending our own ideas or questioning the reasoning of others while still according them respect. Research has found that argumentativeness can actually enhance relationships, but verbal aggression is harmful and can be a precursor to physical violence.

Suppose that, after discovering the scratch on his new television set, Sergei storms back to the store, confronts the first salesperson he finds, and loudly demands his money back while accusing her of intentionally selling him damaged merchandise. Such aggressive behavior may or may not result in getting the damaged set replaced, but it will certainly damage his relationship with the salesperson. Even in a professional scenario, most receivers of aggressive messages are likely to feel hurt by them (Martin, Anderson, & Horvath, 1996). While Sergei may not care about his relationship with the salesperson, if he is prone to aggression as a means of communicating his rights and expectations, he is likely to damage other, more intimate relationships. Studies have found that verbal aggression leads to less satisfying relationships, family violence, and lower credibility, and it causes employees to lose respect and loyalty for managers (Hample, 2003). Today, certain textual, visual, and audio forms of online messages have the potential to harm others because they employ aggressive messages (O'Sullivan & Flanagin, 2003). **Flaming** is sending an aggressive message using social media.

Verbally aggressive messages may be overtly hostile, but aggression may also be characterized by **passive-aggressive behavior**, exhibited in messages that indirectly express hostility. Examples of passive-aggressiveness include being stubborn, being unresponsive, intentionally refusing to help, and not owning up to one's responsibilities. For example, after Sergei finishes ranting at the salesperson, she takes his information, appears to apologize, and promises Sergei that she will rectify the situation. But once Sergei leaves, she behaves passive-aggressively by calmly throwing his contact information in the wastebasket and doing nothing.

Passiveness, verbal aggression, and passive-aggressive behavior are far too common, and most of us have probably used these approaches at some point in time. But the third approach to communicating our rights, expectations, and refusals is more likely to achieve our short-term goals while enhancing or maintaining our relationships.

Verbal aggression—sending messages that attack another person's self-esteem or express personal hostility for perceived violations of rights or expectations

Argumentativeness—defending our own ideas or attacking the reasoning of others while according them respect

Flaming—sending an aggressive message using social media

Passive-aggressive behavior—messages that indirectly express hostility

The Assertive Approach

Assertiveness is the skill of sending messages that declare and defend personal rights and expectations in a clear, direct, and honest manner, while respecting the preferences and rights of others. In contrast to passive behavior and aggressive messages, which are self-oriented, assertive messages focus simultaneously on both our interests and those of others. Unlike the passive approach, assertiveness respects and expresses our own rights and dignity by verbalizing our honest thoughts, feelings, and preferences. Unlike the aggressive approach, assertiveness also respects the rights and dignity of others by avoiding hostile and inflammatory language and nonverbal behavior (Alberti & Emmons, 2001). In short, assertive messages allow us to stand up for ourselves rather than acting passively or aggressively.

Assertive messages have the following characteristics:

1. **Owning.** The purpose of assertive messages is to directly and respectfully represent your position or needs, so your message should be "owned" and include "I" statements like "I think . . . ," "My opinion is . . . ," "I feel . . . ," and "I would like. . . ."
2. **Describing behaviors and feelings.** If we want others to honor our rights and expectations, then we should provide them with specific descriptive information to justify our requests. We do this by describing the feelings we have, as well as the behaviors and outcomes we desire.
3. **Doing facework.** The goal of assertive messages is to influence others without damaging relationships. Messages should be formed in ways that both meet the face needs of others and assert your rights and expectations.
4. **Using appropriate nonverbal behaviors.** As you know, nonverbal behavior conveys much of a message's emotional meaning. We can reflect our self-confidence and our respect for the other person by using steady eye contact, a calm and sincere facial expression, relaxed and involved posture, and appropriate paralanguage, including fluent speech, and appropriate volume, intonation, and firmness (Rakos, 2006).

The difference between an assertive approach and a passive or aggressive approach is not in how we think and feel, but in how our feelings work in conjunction with the thoughts and feelings of others. To return to our example, if Sergei chooses an assertive approach to handling the problem of the damaged television, he will still feel angry. But instead of either doing nothing and living with the damaged merchandise, or verbally assaulting the salesperson, Sergei might call the store, describe the condition of the TV to a customer service representative, share his feelings on discovering the scratch, and state what he would like to see happen now. He might request that the store exchange the damaged set for a new one, or he might ask for a refund. Sergei's assertive messages should accomplish his own goals without annoying or hurting anyone else.

It's important to recognize that you will not always achieve your goals by being assertive, and that being assertive involves risks. For instance, some people, not knowing the difference between assertiveness and aggressiveness, are inclined to view assertive messages as aggressive. Nonetheless, the potential benefits of assertiveness far outweigh the risks. Remember, our behavior teaches people how to treat us. If we are passive, people will ignore our feelings because we have taught them that it's okay to do so. If we are aggressive, we teach people to respond in kind. By contrast, if we are assertive, we can influence others to treat us as we would prefer to be treated. If you have trouble taking the first step to being more assertive, try beginning with situations in which your potential for success is high (Alberti & Emmons, 2001).

Since assertiveness is concerned, not only with your own needs, but also with maintaining your relationship, assertive messages are most effective when they are well timed, when they ask for the "minimal effective response" from a partner, and when they are politely pursued if a partner does not immediately comply (Rakos, 2006). When asserting your rights and expectations, it's important that your partner be prepared to hear you. Choosing a time and place that allow for discussion and privacy is critical. In addition, assertiveness is not the same as taking advantage. You will be more successful if you ask for a **minimal effective response**, which is what you need to feel that your rights and expectations are respected, not everything you might want. Finally, it may take a longer conversation or several conversations to persuade your partner. So be prepared to persist.

Assertive Message Skills

In the remainder of this chapter, we are going to apply the principles of assertive communication skills to three specific occasions: when we complain about how we are being treated, when we request that someone change a problematic behavior, and when we refuse a request that someone has made of us.

Is it more difficult for you to be assertive when you deal with strangers or with people you love?

Complaint—a message telling someone that what is or has occurred is unacceptable because it has violated your rights or expectations

Making a Complaint

A **complaint** is a message telling someone that you find what is happening or has occurred unacceptable because it has violated your rights or expectations. A good complaint script assumes that the violation was unintentional and that your partner will want to cooperate with you in correcting the problem. Let's look at an example of how to make an assertive complaint.

Tanisha is the only woman in a professional role in her department. Whenever her manager has an especially interesting and challenging job, he assigns it to one of the men in the department. Despite consistently good performance reviews, Tanisha is stuck with routine assignments that are not challenging her or preparing her for promotion. She could respond passively by saying nothing, continuing to be frustrated and believing that she is being discriminated against. Or she could storm into her manager's office and accuse him of discrimination. But, alternatively, Tanisha decides to assertively complain. She begins by asking her manager if they can meet to discuss work assignments. To begin the meeting, she might say something to this effect:

> *"I know it must be hard to balance work assignments. So I'm not sure you are aware that during the past three months, every time there was a really interesting or challenging job to be done, you gave it to Tom, Rex, or Jamal, while you have assigned me all of the routine tasks. To the best of my knowledge, you believe that Tom, Rex, Jamal, and I are equally competent. You've never said anything to suggest that you thought less of my work. So I would expect that we would each get opportunities to work on the more challenging and less routine assignments. But when you give the all the work that I perceive as interesting to my colleagues and continue to give me only the routine stuff, I feel really frustrated and discouraged. Do you understand what I'm saying?"*

Tanisha's message followed these guidelines for making effective complaints:

1. *Begin by doing "facework."* Tanisha begins by acknowledging that the manager's job is difficult, and that the manager has not been overlooking her intentionally: "I know it must be hard to balance work assignments. . . ."
2. *Describe what has happened that you believe violates your rights or expectations.* Tanisha continues by specifically describing how the manager has behaved without using any evaluative language: "During the last three months, every time there was an interesting. . . ."
3. *Explain why what has happened violates your rights or expectations:* Tanisha explains, "I would expect that. . . ."
4. *Describe how you feel about what has happened.* Tanisha describes, "I get really frustrated and discouraged."
5. *Invite the person to comment on or paraphrase what you have said.* Tanisha concludes, "Do you understand. . . ?"

SKILL BUILDER ▶ COMPLAINING

SKILL	USE	STEPS	EXAMPLE
"Sending" or "communicating" messages that tell someone that you find what is or has occurred unacceptable because it has violated your rights or expectations.	To assert your rights and expectations when they have been violated.	1. Begin by doing facework. 2. Describe what has happened that you believe violates your rights or expectations. 3. Explain why what has happened violates your rights or expectations. 4. Describe how you feel about what has happened. 5. Ask the person to comment on or paraphrase what you have said.	Colin ordered his food over twenty minutes ago. The people at two tables seated after him have eaten and left. Colin decides to complain, saying, "Excuse me. I can see that things are really busy, but I ordered my food about twenty minutes ago, and two tables of people who ordered after me have come and gone. I expected that our food would be served in order. I'm really annoyed. Do you understand my position?"

Requesting a Change in Problematic Behavior

We make simple requests all the time: "Could you stop on the way home and pick up my prescriptions?" "Will you tell your brother that dinner is ready?" "Would you take out the garbage on your way out?" Other requests are harder to make. **Change requests** are messages that ask others to change their behavior in ways that show more respect for our rights, or do a better job of meeting our personal expectations. These messages teach others how to treat us. A good change request assumes that our partners are willing to change their current behavior if they understand that it is a problem and that we find it unacceptable. For example, Margarita has invited two of her best friends, Nicole and Ramona, to hang out at her residence hall suite for the evening and watch a movie. When they arrive, they introduce her to Nick, Ramona's friend from high school. Shortly after the movie begins, Nick lights a cigarette. Margarita hates the smell of smoke and doesn't want her clothes to reek. Also afraid that someone will complain, as smoking in dorms is banned, she makes the following request:

> "Nick, please put your cigarette out. You probably forgot that dorms are non-smoking areas. I could get kicked out. I also don't want my place and clothes to smell. When you need to smoke, I'll pause the movie so you can go outside. Thanks for understanding."

Change requests—messages that direct others how to change their behavior to show greater respect for our rights or expectations

Margarita's message followed these guidelines for making effective personal requests:

1. *Politely but directly describe what you want the other person to do.* "Nick, please put your cigarette out." In this statement, Margarita does not ask Nick to stop smoking, she directs him to. Asking a question gives the person a choice and implies that we will accept a refusal. Suppose Margarita had asked, "Will you please put out your cigarette?" and Nick had said, "No." Now what does she do?

2. *Do facework.* When Margarita says, "You probably forgot that . . ." she is providing a face-saving explanation for Nick's violation.

3. *Describe how the behavior violates your rights or expectations.* Margarita's message notes two violations. First, she has the right to require legal behavior in her space. Second, she has a reasonable personal expectation that guests in her space will not be the source of offensive odors.

4. *When possible, offer an alternative to your partners' unacceptable behavior that meets their needs while not violating your rights and expectations.* Margarita tells Nick where he can smoke and offers to accommodate his need by pausing the movie.

5. *Assume that your partners will comply with the personal request and thank them.* Margarita closes her message by thanking Nick for understanding.

SKILL BUILDER ▶ REQUESTING A CHANGE IN PROBLEMATIC BEHAVIOR

SKILL	USE	STEPS	EXAMPLE
Showing others how to respect your rights or expectations.	To produce a change in behavior that fails to respect your rights or reasonable expectations.	1. Politely but directly describe what you want the other person to do. 2. Do facework. 3. Describe how the behavior violates your rights or expectations. 4. When possible, offer an alternative to your partners' unacceptable behavior, which meets their needs while not violating your rights and expectations. 5. Assume that your partners will comply with the personal request and thank them.	"Rahm, don't criticize me in front of your children. If you don't agree with what I am doing, please tell me later when we can talk it out. I know you don't mean to undermine my authority, but when you interrupt me and contradict what I have said, that's what happens. It's hard to be a stepparent, but I think it's important for both sets of kids to see us as a team. I know you understand. Thanks, honey."

Refusing a Request

People make requests of you every day. Some requests are simple and easy to comply with, but others are inconvenient, difficult, and at times not in line with your own values, beliefs, or interests. All of us can think of times we regretted having done what someone asked us to. Often we comply with these requests because we don't know how to turn them down in a way that will not damage our image or relationship. Not only do we end up agreeing to something we later regret, we may even resent the person who made the request. We comply with uncomfortable requests when we feel indebted to someone, when we like someone, when we don't want to disappoint someone, and when there is group pressure. Overcoming these powerful and often indirect pressures is challenging. But you can use the communication skills that you have studied to develop a general script for turning down requests in a way that serves your interests and maintains your relationships.

Let's look at an example of how Carl dealt with pressure from his friend Reece. Carl and Reece are next-door neighbors who have become friendly. One night Reece invites Carl to go clubbing with several friends who work as roadies for a touring rock band in town for the night. Carl initially hesitates, but after some waffling, he reluctantly agrees to go, even though he is in alcohol recovery and tries to avoid the whole club scene—something he is not yet comfortable sharing with Reece. When the bartender asks for their order, Reece replies, "We'll have beers all around. What have you got on tap?" Carl quickly corrects Reece, saying to the bartender, "Make mine a Coke." Reece then turns to Carl, raises his eyebrows, and loudly says, "Hey, bro, loosen up, forget the Coke, let me buy you a beer." Carl sighs then says, "Hey, man, thanks for the offer, but no beer for me. You guys go ahead, but I never drink when I'm driving. I appreciate you springing for the round, but make mine a Coke."

Notice that in turning down Reece's offer, Carl maintains privacy concerning his chemical dependency, offering a generalized statement as an explanation. He also doesn't judge Reece and his friends or insinuate that there is anything wrong with their drinking beer. Carl just politely refuses Reece's request, then offers another valid an alternative explanation with which he is comfortable.

Carl's message followed these guidelines for effectively refusing requests:

1. *If it's appropriate, thank people for what they are asking you to do.* Carl begins, "Hey man, thanks for the offer," later adding, "I appreciate you springing for the round."
2. *Directly own that you are not willing to agree to the request.* Carl turns down the offer, saying ". . . no beer for me."
3. *State a generalized reason or alternative explanation for your refusal, but don't feel obligated to disclose something that you want to remain private.* Carl states, "I never drink when I'm driving."
4. *When possible, offer an alternative to which you can agree.* Carl offers, ". . . make mine a Coke."

SKILL BUILDER ▶ REFUSING A REQUEST

SKILL	USE	STEPS	EXAMPLE
Messages that decline to act or believe as others would like you to.	To inform others that we don't want to do or think what they want us to.	1. When it's appropriate, thank people for what they are asking you to do. 2. Directly own that you are not willing to agree to the request. 3. State a generalized reason for your refusal, but don't feel obligated to disclose something that you wish to keep private. 4. When possible, identify an alternative to the request that you could agree to.	"Would you take my shift next Friday? I'd really appreciate it." "Thanks for offering it to me, but sorry, I already have plans. Check with Heather, though, when she comes in. I think she was interested in picking up a shift."

One assertive message may accomplish your goal, but at other times, your assertion may lead to a conflict. In the next chapter you will learn how to use assertive message skills in combination with other communication skills to effectively resolve interpersonal conflicts.

Assertiveness in Cross-Cultural Relationships

Assertiveness, like other communication skills, is valued by some cultures more than others. As Samovar, Porter, and McDaniel (2013) observe, "Communication problems can arise when someone from a culture that values assertiveness comes in contact with a person from a culture that values social harmony" (p. 313). The standard of assertiveness considered appropriate in the dominant American culture can seem inappropriate to people with other cultural frames of reference.

Asian cultures, for example, clearly differ from American culture regarding assertiveness. Asian cultures value harmony, so direct assertiveness can cause problems, as it can be perceived as leading to conflict and discord. Research has shown that Japanese, Malaysian, and Filipino adults are less likely to engage in assertiveness than their Western counterparts (Niikura, 1999). Likewise, research has demonstrated that Turkish adolescents are less likely to engage in assertiveness than Western adolescents (Eskin, 2003). In contrast, men in Latin and Hispanic societies are frequently taught to exercise a form of self-expression that goes far beyond the guidelines presented here for assertiveness. In these societies, the concept of *machismo* often guides male behavior. Though not exactly aggressive, machismo is more focused on the self than on a balance between the self and the other.

Thus, when we practice assertiveness—like any other skill—we need to be aware that no single standard of behavior ensures the achievement of our goals. Although what is labeled "appropriate" behavior varies across cultures, the results of passive and aggressive behavior seem universal. Passive behavior fails to communicate problems, generating resentment in the person behaving passively toward others; aggressive behavior also fails to communicate problems effectively, creating fear and misunderstanding of the person exhibiting the aggressive behavior. When talking with people whose cultures, backgrounds, or lifestyles differ from your own, you may need to observe their behaviors and their responses to your statements before you can communicate with them in a persuasive manner.

How can understanding the cultural norms about assertiveness in African American and policing cultures help us understand some of the problems that occur when members of each group interact?

THE SOCIAL MEDIA FACTOR

Electronic Influence

We communicate to influence others online as well as offline. If you think back over the past week, you can probably identify many instances of persuasive messages that you either produced or received electronically. You might have texted a friend with an appeal for help moving furniture, emailed your professor to request a deadline extension, or posted an announcement on Facebook about a play that your cousin will appear in. The success of these influence attempts will depend largely on the same factors that affect unmediated persuasion. If the message recipient processes them via the central route, then your credibility, the quality of your arguments, and the effectiveness of your emotional appeals will all influence the outcome. If your recipient processes them via the peripheral route (thinking less carefully about your message), he or she might still be persuaded through one or more heuristics. For example, your friend might say yes to helping you move furniture just because he likes you (liking heuristic), or your professor may agree to the deadline extension because you offered to be a teaching assistant next semester (reciprocity heuristic). Being assertive, whether in complaints, change requests, refusals, or other persuasive messages, can be accomplished online following the same principles as those discussed for face-to-face interactions.

Cassie and Pete have been very lucky. They both have well-paying jobs that they dearly love. Having worked hard and saved money during college, they had enough money to buy a house two years after graduating. Their first home has needed a lot of remodeling, but Cassie and Pete have found that they enjoy working together and learning how to do various projects. So far they have refinished the floors, repaired some drywall, removed the old wallpaper, and repainted every room in the house. Now it is time to tackle the kitchen.

The current kitchen is a mess. The cabinets are scratched, and several doors are loose. The flooring is discolored and coming up in places, and the appliances are from the 1970s. The more they have discussed the kitchen, the more they have found that they disagree on what needs to be done. Pete wants them to tackle the project themselves and believes that they can make the kitchen serviceable by removing the current floor, putting down ceramic tile, painting the current cabinets, and buying new appliances, phasing in the purchases over several years. Cassie, who loves to cook, wants the kitchen to be the centerpiece of the home. She wants to hire a kitchen designer to plan and execute a complete kitchen remodel. Pete adamantly refuses to consider spending the thirty thousand dollars or more that this would take. Having stated his position, Pete considers the conversation over and done. During their most recent discussion of the issue, Pete walked out of the room, turned on the TV, and refused to say any more on the matter.

Recently, Cassie decided to take a different approach, asking, "Pete, do you really love me?" to which he replied, "Of course I love you. Do you really need to ask?"

"Well, I was wondering if, for our anniversary, we could take a couple of weeks and go to Europe? It would be expensive, but it would be such a wonderful treat."

"Hey, that's a great idea," Pete replied. "I'll talk to a travel agent tomorrow."

"Well, are you sure?" Cassie asked. "I mean, it's going to cost a lot, since we already used up our frequent flier miles."

"Don't worry, babe. We've got the money in the bank, and you know I only live to make you happy."

"Really?" Cassie pounced. "Then why can't we hire a designer and have the kitchen done first-class? You know I hate to travel, but I love to cook. Why are you willing to pay for an expensive trip but not pay for my dream kitchen?"

FOR CONSIDERATION

1. What ethical issues do Cassie and Pete confront in this situation?
2. Analyze the conversation between Cassie and Pete. Is Cassie's approach an ethical use of interpersonal influence or a manipulative trap?

One thing that is different about persuasion via social media is the capacity to extend ordinary interpersonal influence attempts beyond the individual or small groups. Prior to digital technologies, if you wanted to get people to attend your cousin's play, you would have had the options of talking to individuals in person or by phone, sending flyers by mail, or perhaps distributing flyers around campus. Now, with social networking sites like Facebook and Twitter, your appeal can be made to your entire network simultaneously, reaching hundreds or more. On a small scale, this mimics traditional television advertising: You are able to "broadcast" your influence effort to your "audience." Yet it retains an interpersonal element because the message originates from you, even if the announcement was originally created by your cousin or the theatrical group. Some scholars use the term **masspersonal** to describe media that disseminate personal communication to a large audience in this way (Sullivan, 2005).

Masspersonal—a term used to describe media such as Facebook that disseminate personal messages to a large audience

Businesses have long known that "word of mouth" (WOM) advertising is essential to their success, and seek to encourage clients to tell others about the products and services they purchase. Today, businesses continue these efforts online, seeking "likes" and positive comments, posts, and shares on Facebook and Instagram that others in your network will view and be influenced by. Research indicates that businesses benefit from this **electronic word of mouth** (eWOM), or electronically distributed information, opinion, and advice about organizations' products or services (Chu & Kim, 2011). For example, imagine that you are a runner. Your friend posts a photograph on Instagram of her new running shoes and tags the location of the photograph as her local gym. The post's caption contains hashtags and a link to the shoes' manufacturer, as well as the gym your friend belongs to. Research suggests you are more likely to be influenced by these posts than by advertising that came directly from the manufacturer or gym. Why? Because we trust our friends and are more open to influence from them than to direct influence from companies (Chu & Kim, 2011). However, a recent study of restaurant word of mouth reported that traditional WOM was stronger than eWOM (Meuter, McCabe, & Curran, 2013). Perhaps people receiving eWOM are more aware that businesses promote eWOM and profit from it, whereas people receiving traditional WOM are less aware that the business stands to benefit. Alternatively, traditional WOM may be better tailored to its recipients. For example, if you speak with your friend about her new shoes, she might tell you details that matter specifically to you, such as how the shoes help prevent knee pain.

> **Electronic word of mouth (eWOM)—** information, opinion, or advice about an organization's products or services that is electronically shared by an individual consumer

Summary

Interpersonal influence is the act of changing the attitudes or behaviors of others. It is a core element of our interpersonal relationships. Power is the potential you have to influence someone else. There are five sources or roots of power that we may have with respect to our partner: coercive power, reward power, legitimate power, expert power, and referent power.

Research suggests that there are several principles of power: power is a perception, not a fact; power exists within a relationship; power is not inherently good or bad; and the person with more power in a relationship can make and break the relationship rules.

Persuasion is the use of verbal messages designed to influence the attitudes and behaviors of others. The elaboration likelihood model is a theory that explains that people will use either heuristics or more elaborate critical thinking skills when processing persuasive messages. When we receive persuasive messages that we believe are important, or about which we feel knowledgeable, we take the central route and extensively process them, evaluating the arguments, credibility, and emotional appeals of the sender. When we think the issues are unimportant, we process them peripherally, using heuristics that shortcut our need to think.

We can use social influence not only to change the general attitudes and behavior of others, but also to teach others how to treat us. We can take three approaches when we think our rights and expectations have been breached. We can behave passively, aggressively, or assertively. Assertive communication requires owning, doing facework, describing behavior and feelings, and using appropriate nonverbal behaviors. Assertive communication is important to making effective complaints, requests for behavior change, and refusing the requests of others.

The appropriateness and form of assertiveness varies with culture. While assertiveness is not valued in some cultures, it is valued in most Western cultures.

CHAPTER RESOURCES

Key Words

Flashcards for all of these key terms are available on the *Inter-Act* website.

Argumentativeness pp. 299
Assertiveness pp. 300
Authority heuristic pp. 291
Central route pp. 289
Change requests pp. 303
Claims pp. 293
Coercive power pp. 285
Competence pp. 295
Complaint pp. 302
Consistency heuristic pp. 291
Credibility pp. 294
Elaboration likelihood model (ELM) of persuasion pp. 288

Electronic word of mouth (eWOM) pp. 309
Emotional appeals pp. 295
Evidence pp. 294
Expert power pp. 286
Flaming pp. 299
Interpersonal influence pp. 284
Legitimate power pp. 286
Likability pp. 295
Liking heuristic pp. 291
Masspersonal pp. 308
Minimal effective response pp. 301
Passive approach pp. 298

Passive-aggressive behavior pp. 299
Peripheral route pp. 289
Persuasion pp. 288
Power pp. 285
Reasons pp. 293
Reciprocity heuristic pp. 290
Referent power pp. 287
Reward power pp. 285
Scarcity heuristic pp. 292
Social proof heuristic pp. 290
Trustworthiness pp. 295
Verbal aggression pp. 299

Analyze and Apply

The following activities challenge you to demonstrate your mastery of the concepts, theories, and frameworks in this chapter by using them to explain what is happening in a specific situation.

10.1 Rewind/Rewrite

Now that you have read the chapter, hit "rewind" on the opening dialogue between Alan and Brad and answer the following questions.

a. Use concepts from the chapter to explain why Brad is having difficulty influencing Alan. The liking and consistency heuristics, quality of reasoning, and aggressive and passive-aggressive behavior may be especially relevant.

b. Assuming that Brad might still have a chance to change Alan's mind, rewrite how the dialogue could have unfolded if Brad had exercised better influence skills.

c. Assuming that Alan is certain he won't remain in the current apartment, rewrite the dialogue to show how he could do a better job of refusing Brad's request and getting Brad to consider an off-campus apartment.

10.2 Inter-Action Dialogue: Interpersonal Influence

Interpersonal influence occurs when one person attempts to change another person's attitudes or behaviors. As you read the following dialogue, do a line-by-line analysis of this conversation and indicate where you see evidence of the participants' exerting power, using heuristics to influence, or providing logical reasons, appeals to credibility, or appeals to emotion, as well as instances of responding passively, aggressively, or assertively. You can watch a video of this conversation on the Inter-Act website and use a form provided to write down your own analysis of the conversation.

DIALOGUE

Paul's friend Hannah stops by his dorm to show him what she has done.

Hannah: Hey, Paul. Take a look at my term paper.

Paul: (*quickly reading the first page*) Wow, so far this looks great. You must have put a lot of time into it.

Hannah: No, but it should be good. I paid enough for it.

Paul: What?

Hannah: I got it off the Internet.

Paul: You mean you bought it from one of those term paper sites? Hannah, what's up? That's not like you—you're not a cheater.

Hannah: Listen—my life's crazy. I don't have time to write a stupid paper. And besides, everyone does it.

Paul: What's stupid about the assignment?

Hannah: I think the workload in this class is ridiculous. The professor acts as if this is the only class we've got. There are three exams, a team project, and this paper. What's the point?

Paul: Well, I think the professor assigned this paper for several reasons, to see whether students really know how to think about the material they have studied and to help us improve our writing.

Hannah: Come on, we learned how to write when we were in elementary school.

Paul: That's not what I meant. Sure, you can write a sentence or a paragraph, but can you really express your own ideas about this subject? What the professor is doing is putting us in a position where we can show not only our understanding of the material but also our ability to phrase our thoughts in a sophisticated manner. By writing a term paper, we have the chance to develop our own thinking about a topic. We can read a wide variety of sources and then make up our own minds and in our writing explain our thoughts. And the neat thing is, we'll get feedback about how we did.

Hannah: Yes, but you're not listening—I just don't have time.

Paul: So you believe the best way to deal with the situation is to cheat?

Hannah: Man, that's cold. But like I said, I'm not the only one doing this.

Paul: Are you saying that since some people cheat, it's okay for you to cheat? Like people take drugs or sleep around, so it's okay for you?

Hannah: No, don't be silly, but I told you I'm up to here in work. I've got no time.

Paul: Right. So remind me what you did last night.

Hannah: You know. I went to Sean's party. I deserve to have a little social life. I'm only twenty after all.

Paul: Sure, point well taken. So what did you do the night before?

Hannah: Well, I worked until 8:00. Then Mary and I grabbed a bite to eat and then went clubbing.

Paul: So, for two nights you chose to do no schoolwork, but you had time to socialize? And you're saying you're "up to here in work." Hannah, I'm just not buying it. Your workload is no different from mine. And I manage to get my work done. It's not perfect—like your Internet paper. But it's mine. So who do you hurt when you cheat? Besides your own character, you hurt me.

Hannah: Hey, chill. You've made your point. But what can I do now? The paper's due in two days and I haven't even begun.

Paul: Do you have to work tonight?

Hannah: No.

Paul: Well, then you still have time. It will be a couple of long, hard days, but I'll bring you coffee and food.

Hannah: What a friend. Well, okay, I guess you win.

Paul: Hey wait. Let's seal it by tearing up that bought paper.

Hannah: What! You mean I can't even borrow a few ideas from it?

Paul: Hannah!

Hannah: Okay. Okay. Just kidding.

Skill Practice

Skill practice activities give you the chance to rehearse a new skill by responding to hypothetical or real situations. Additional skill practice activities are available at the companion Inter-Act website.

10.3 Identifying Heuristic Triggers in Messages

For each of the following messages, identify the heuristic that the sender is using.

a. *"Well, I've been selling cell phone plans for three years, and I think that Verizon is the way to go if you want to get a smart phone."*

   Heuristic:

b. *"I don't know anyone who enjoyed that class. You don't want to take it."*

   Heuristic:

c. *"I really want to see you, but I'm leaving tomorrow morning. Can we have dinner together tonight?"*

   Heuristic:

d. *"I loved my Zumba exercise class. And we both like exercising to music. You just have to try it. I know you'll love it."*

Heuristic:

e. *"Hey, man. Can I borrow twenty bucks until payday? You know I'd loan it to you if the situation was reversed."*

Heuristic:

f. *"Last time we went out, you didn't mind the fact that Justin came with us. So is it okay if I ask him again?"*

Heuristic:

10.4 Creating Persuasive Messages

For each of the following situations, develop a message script that uses logical reasoning, credibility, and valid emotional appeals.

a. *You are going to run in the Relay for Life cancer fundraiser and want to persuade your friend to support you with a $25 donation.*

Message:

b. *You are an Environmental Studies major at college and want to persuade your parents to put solar panels on their roof.*

Message:

c. *Your best friend has put on a lot of weight. Because heart disease runs in his family, you're worried about him and want to persuade him to stop eating a high-fat diet.*

Message:

d. *You want to study abroad next semester, but your parents, whose help you need to fund the trip, aren't onboard with the idea. The tuition for the program is about the same as what it would be if you stayed at your college, but there are some additional expenses. You are hoping that a semester abroad will not only improve your language skills, but also give you a leg up on others in the job market when you graduate.*

Message:

10.5 Assertiveness

For each of the following situations, write an assertive message. Indicate what type of assertion you are making: a complaint, a change request, or a refusal.

a. *The woman who works the next shift is consistently five to twenty minutes late, and you can't leave until she gets there, even though you are off the clock and not paid.*

Type of Assertion:

Message:

b. *For five years, you have been a vegan, the only one in your family. Your older sister has invited you to a family dinner to celebrate your mother's sixty-fifth birthday. You'd like to go, but in the past her menus haven't accommodated your diet.*

Type of Assertion:

Message:

c. *Three weeks ago, you took a test in your family communication course, which the instructor has still not graded. She has offered one excuse after another, promising that she will have them for the next class. You have a comprehensive final in this class next week. A few minutes ago, she came into class, again without the tests.*

Type of Assertion:

Message:

d. *As a committed Christian, you are offended when others swear using the name of God or Jesus. You have a new co-worker who swears frequently.*

Type of Assertion:

Message:

e. *At a restaurant, the steak you ordered rare arrives medium well.*

Type of Assertion:

Message:

f. *Your best friend from childhood is getting married in Aruba and has asked you to be in the wedding party. Your friend has indicated that you will have to pay your own expenses. You are struggling to pay your rent and tuition, and you have maxed out your credit cards. In addition, you think destination weddings are selfish because they require friends and family to take vacation time and spend a lot of money going somewhere they might not have chosen to go.*

Type of Assertion:

Message:

g. *You are living rent-free with your mom, who has asked you to babysit for your niece so she can go shopping with your sister. After an exhausting week, you had planned to take a nap and then go out with friends.*

Type of Assertion:

Message:

h. *The woman who lives in the apartment next door stops by and asks you to turn your music down as it is disturbing her. It's the middle of the day, and you don't think your music is too loud.*

Type of Assertion:

Message:

i. *You are proud of your yard and spend a lot of time working in it. The people who recently moved in next door have two large dogs. Although they walk their dogs on leashes and pick up after them, you have noticed that both dogs urinate on one of your bushes, which is turning yellow, dropping leaves, and looking sickly.*

Type of Assertion:

Message:

j. *You're out with a group of guys, one of whom points at a man who has just walked into the club and says, "Well, there's one of Tinkerbell's helpers." Everyone else nervously laughs, but you can't even feign amusement.*

Type of Assertion:

Message:

k. *Your roommate is supposed to do the dishes on the nights you cook, and vice versa. You always clean up right away, but your roommate sometimes waits until the next day to take the dishes off the table. Or she stacks them by the sink without even cleaning them off. In the morning, you are the first one up, and it makes you sick to your stomach to walk into the kitchen and smell last night's dinner.*

Type of Assertion:

Message:

Communication Improvement Plan: Assertive Communication

Would you like to improve your use of the following skills discussed in this chapter?

- Making a complaint
- Making a change request
- Refusing a request

Choose the skill(s) you want to work on, and write a communication improvement plan. You can find a communication improvement plan worksheet on our website at www.oup.com/us/verderber.

MANAGING CONFLICT

Keisha, Sasha, and Tara are sorority sisters who live together in a large and active sorority house. Keisha and Sasha are co-leaders for the committee of juniors planning the initiation ceremony and breakfast for new freshmen, which will take place in a few days. Tara is a senior, and the House Marshall, which gives her final decision-making authority for house events. Unfortunately, Keisha and Tara have never really gotten along, and they have clashed throughout the planning process. Tara believes that Keisha tries to take authority she doesn't have, and Keisha resents Tara's insistence that the seniors should have the final say in everything. During their final meeting before the event, the following conversation takes place:

Tara, looking down at her notes, says, ". . . So, after the ceremony, the new initiates and their Big Sisters will go to the dining room for their formal brunch. I told our Housemother, Mrs. B., to buy you juniors bagels, so you can eat in the "bum room." When you finish cleaning up, you guys are good to go."

Surprised and annoyed, Keisha asks, "Wait . . . no brunch for us?"

Showing no sympathy, Tara responds "Sorry, there isn't enough space in the dining room for juniors."

Raising her voice in frustration, Keisha replies, "So? That's not the point. We can eat anywhere in the house! We just want some decent food after all the work we've done."

(Continued)

Sasha quietly adds, "That's kind of disappointing, Tara."

Tara firmly declares: "You're getting bagels and cream cheese. I talked to Mrs. B. and she agreed."

Keisha, who is livid, exclaims, "Why? So you seniors can have a bigger dinner at graduation? Of course Mrs. B. agreed, you always suck up to her."

Tara frowns, and in a threatening tone of voice slowly responds, "What—ever. If *you* don't want to do this, I can certainly find someone to replace you."

Sasha, trying to make peace, quietly interjects: "C'mon, you two."

Keisha glares at Tara for a second, gets up, walks toward the door, turns, and in a voice dripping with sarcasm says: "Oh, ex—*cuse* me, no problem, Tara. I'll just make sure all the juniors know who to thank for BAGELS."

Looking distraught, Sasha looks down at her hands and quietly says to herself, "I can't believe this, there has to be a better way...."

WHAT YOU SHOULD BE ABLE *TO EXPLAIN* AFTER YOU HAVE STUDIED THIS CHAPTER:

▶ The definition and six types of interpersonal conflict

▶ The five conflict styles

▶ Face negotiation theory

▶ Destructive conflict patterns and how to break them

▶ How to skillfully initiate, respond to, and mediate conflict

▶ How to repair relationships damaged by conflict

▶ How to respond to aggressive behavior online

WHAT YOU SHOULD BE ABLE *TO DO* AFTER YOU HAVE STUDIED THIS CHAPTER:

▶ Skillfully initiate and respond to conflict

▶ Mediate a conflict

▶ Apologize effectively

Interpersonal conflict—disagreement between two interdependent people who perceive that they have incompatible goals

Interpersonal conflict may be defined broadly as disagreement between two interdependent people who perceive that they have incompatible goals (Guerrero, Andersen, & Afifi, 2013). In this conflict, Tara's goals of saving money and not overcrowding the dining room are at odds with Keisha's and Sasha's goal of having their class recognized and rewarded for their hard work on this event.

Conflict may be neither good nor bad, but it is inevitable. Although it can damage people and relationships, it can also help expose important issues and develop learning, creativity, trust, and openness (Brake, Walker, & Walker, 1995). Whether conflict hurts or strengthens a relationship ultimately depends on how those involved manage it. When conflict is managed appropriately, it is possible to satisfy your own goals and those of others, while maintaining relationships. Understanding conflict and developing conflict management skills will make you a more effective interpersonal communicator, able to deal with conflict episodes in your relationships.

In this chapter, we begin by looking at six types of interpersonal conflict. Next, we discuss the five communication styles that people use to manage conflict. Then we describe how face is negotiated during conflicts, and how this

LEARN ABOUT YOURSELF ▶ CONFLICT MANAGEMENT

Take this short survey to learn something about yourself. This is a test of your conflict management style. Answer the questions honestly, based on your first response. There are no right or wrong answers. For each of the following statements, select one of the numbers to the right that best describes your behavior:

_____ 1. I try to avoid conflicts whenever possible.	**1 = Always**
_____ 2. I will give up my own desires to end a conflict.	**2 = Often**
_____ 3. It is important to win an argument.	**3 = Sometimes**
_____ 4. I am willing to compromise to solve a conflict.	**4 = Rarely**
_____ 5. It is important to discuss both people's point of view in a conflict.	**5 = Never**
_____ 6. I am stubborn in holding to my position in a conflict.	
_____ 7. In conflicts, I give up some points in exchange for other points.	
_____ 8. I try to avoid conflicts.	
_____ 9. I give in to others during conflict.	
_____ 10. It is important to regard conflicts as problems to be solved together.	
_____ 11. I strongly assert my views in a conflict.	
_____ 12. I withdraw from disagreements.	
_____ 13. I try to find the middle-ground position in a conflict.	
_____ 14. I will give in to the other person to end an argument.	
_____ 15. I try to be cooperative and creative in finding a resolution to a conflict.	

Scoring the Survey: Add your scores for items 1, 8, and 12. Your score will range from 3 to 15. The lower (closer to 3) your score, the more you tend to use withdrawal as a conflict management style.

Add your scores for items 2, 9, and 14. Your score will range from 3 to 15. The lower (closer to 3) your score, the more you tend to use the accommodating style of conflict management.

Add your scores for items 3, 6, and 11. Your score will range from 3 to 15. The lower (closer to 3) your score, the more you tend to use the competing style of conflict management.

Add your scores for items 4, 7, and 13. Your score will range from 3 to 15. The lower (closer to 3) your score, the more you tend to use the compromising style of conflict management.

Add your scores for items 5, 10, and 15. Your score will range from 3 to 15. The lower (closer to 3) your score, the more you tend to use the collaborating style of conflict management.

Does the game "Rock, paper, scissors" resolve conflict?

Pseudo conflict—disagreement that is caused by a perceptual difference between partners and is easily resolved

Fact conflict—disagreement that is caused by a dispute over the truth or accuracy of an item of information

Value conflict—disagreement caused by differences in partners' deep-seated moral beliefs

Policy conflict—disagreement caused by differences over a preferred plan or course of action

Ego conflict—disagreement that results when both parties insist on being the "winner" of the argument to confirm their self-concept or self-esteem

differs across cultures. With this understanding in mind, we describe destructive conflict patterns that damage relationships. Then we introduce guidelines for effective conflict management, including how to initiate, respond to, and mediate interpersonal conflicts. We end the chapter by discussing the process of forgiveness, which helps repair relationships that have been damaged by conflict.

Types of Interpersonal Conflict

There are six broad categories of conflict: pseudo conflict, fact conflict, value conflict, policy conflict, ego conflict, and meta conflict. Some conflicts fit one category, while others may fit two or more.

1. Pseudo conflict. A **pseudo conflict** is disagreement that is caused by a perceptual difference between partners and is easily resolved. Pseudo conflicts usually occur in three situations: when communication partners ascribe different meanings to words; when partners have goals or needs that appear to be incompatible but are not; and when one partner badgers (teases, taunts, mocks) the other. Pseudo conflicts can be resolved through paraphrasing to elucidate word meaning, clarifying goals, and asserting boundaries for appropriate teasing.

2. Fact conflict. Simple or **fact conflict** is a disagreement caused by a dispute over the truth or accuracy of an item of information. These conflicts can be resolved by consulting an external source. If you find yourself in a fact conflict, suggest to your partner that together you consult a source that can verify what is true or accurate.

3. Value conflict. A **value conflict** is a disagreement caused by differences in partners' deep-seated moral beliefs. Conflict stemming from differences in value systems can be difficult to resolve, and at times we must simply be content to respect each other but agree to disagree.

4. Policy conflict. A **policy conflict** is a disagreement caused by differences over a preferred plan or course of action. Given that both culture and situation determine what is perceived to be an appropriate policy, this type of conflict is common in most relationships. Because policy conflicts are based on highly personal considerations, there is no "right" or "wrong" way to resolve them; the best policy depends on what both parties feel personally comfortable with and agree to.

5. Ego conflict. An **ego conflict** is a disagreement that results when both parties insist on being the "winner" of the argument to confirm their self-concept or self-esteem. When both people already engaged in a conflict see it as a measure of who they are, what they know, how competent they are, or how much power they have, an ego conflict may accompany and complicate other types of conflict. Ego conflicts are more likely to develop when one or both partners to a conflict make personal, negative, and judgemental statements. These often cause others to ignore the central disagreement to defend themselves.

Conflicts in which values or egos are at issue often escalate. How can we manage conflicts of these types?

6. Meta conflict. Meta conflict is a disagreement over the process of communication itself during an argument (Guerrero et al., 2013). It is conflict *about* the conflict. In a meta conflict, we may accuse our partner of pouting, nagging, name-calling, not listening, showing too much emotion, fighting unfairly, or a variety of other negative behaviors related to the conflict communication process. Once we introduce meta conflict into the conversation, we then have two conflict issues to address: the original area of incompatibility and the conflict process itself. Meta conflict complicates our interpersonal communication, making it more difficult to find a satisfactory resolution to our conflict.

Meta conflict—disagreement over the process of communication itself during an argument

Styles of Managing Interpersonal Conflict

Think about the last time you experienced a conflict. How did you react? Did you try to avoid it? Did you give in? Did you force the other person to accept your will? Did you compromise, getting part of what you wanted and giving the other person part of what he or she wanted? Or did the two of you find a solution with which you were both completely satisfied? These styles differ in the amount of cooperation and assertiveness the participants display. The extent to which we are willing to cooperate when managing a conflict depends on how important we believe the relationship and the issue are to us. We each have one or two styles of conflict that are our default way of behaving, but if we are mindful, we can use other styles when they are more appropriate. Let's take a closer look at five

TABLE 11.1 Styles of Conflict Management

Approach	Characteristics	Goal	Outlook
WITHDRAWING	Uncooperative Unassertive	To keep from dealing with conflict	"I don't want to talk about it."
ACCOMMODATING	Cooperative Unassertive	To keep from upsetting the other person	"Getting my way isn't as important as keeping the peace."
COMPETING	Uncooperative Assertive	To get my way	"I'll get my way regardless of what I have to do."
COMPROMISING	Partially cooperative Partially assertive	To get partial satisfaction	"I'll get part of what I want and other people also have part of what they want."
COLLABORATING	Cooperative Assertive	To solve the problem together	"Let's talk this out and find the best solution for both of us."

different styles: withdrawing, accommodating, competing, compromising, and collaborating (Thomas, 1976). As you read through this section, you can refer to Table 11.1, which summarizes the characteristics, goals, and outlooks of each conflict management style.

Withdrawing

Withdrawing—resolving a conflict by physically or psychologically removing yourself from the conversation

Certainly one of the easiest ways to deal with conflict is to withdraw. **Withdrawing** is resolving a conflict by physically or psychologically removing yourself from the conversation. This style is both uncooperative and unassertive because at least one person involved in the conflict refuses to talk about the issue at all. A person may withdraw physically by leaving the site, or psychologically withdraw by ignoring what the other person is saying.

From an individual satisfaction standpoint, withdrawing typically creates a lose/lose situation because neither party to the conflict really accomplishes what he or she wants. Withdrawing from a conflict provides a temporary escape from a potentially uncomfortable situation, but in an ongoing relationship, the issue will come up again. Meanwhile, your partner experiences frustration on two levels: Not only does the conflict not get resolved, but also your partner feels ignored and slighted. Recurring withdrawal hurts relationships in at least two ways. First, the conflict eventually resurfaces and is usually more difficult to resolve at that time (Roloff & Cloven, 1990). Second, withdrawal leads to mulling over or brooding about issues and behaviors to the point where they become bigger than they actually are. This can generate enduring ill feelings about the relationship.

Although habitually withdrawing from a conflict can result in dissatisfying relationships, withdrawing may be an appropriate style

What motivates people to withdraw? What's lost as a result?

in at least three circumstances. First, withdrawal can be appropriate when neither the relationship nor the issue is really important to you. Second, when an issue is unimportant to you but the relationship is important, you might simply choose to hide your objections to your partner's position and go along with what he or she says, which can have a positive effect on your relationship (Caughlin & Golish, 2002). Third, withdrawing permits a temporary disengagement allowing you to check your strong emotional reactions. If both an issue and a relationship are important to you, you may find that temporarily withdrawing from the argument allows you to calm down and renew the discussion at a later time when you are able to approach the issue with a clear head.

Accommodating

Accommodating is resolving a conflict by satisfying the other person's needs or accepting the other person's ideas while neglecting one's own needs or ideas. This approach is cooperative but unassertive. It preserves friendly relationships but fails to protect your personal rights. When we feel insecure with others, we may accommodate to ensure that we don't lose the relationship. Considered from an individual satisfaction standpoint, accommodating creates a lose/win situation. When you accommodate, you choose to lose while you give in to what your partner wants. From a relational satisfaction standpoint, habitual accommodation creates two problems. First, accommodation may lead to poor decision making because you do not voice important facts, arguments, and positions that might lead to a better decision. Second, habitual accommodation risks damaging your self-concept and making you resentful, which can undermine the very relationship you were hoping to maintain.

There are also situations, of course, in which accommodating is appropriate and effective. When an issue is not important to you but the relationship is, accommodating is the best style. It may also be useful to accommodate from time to time to build "social credits" or goodwill that you can draw on later.

Accommodating—resolving a conflict by satisfying the other person's needs or accepting the other person's ideas while neglecting one's own needs or ideas

Competing

Competing, sometimes called "forcing," is resolving a conflict by satisfying your own needs or advancing your own ideas with little concern for the needs or ideas of the other person or for the relationship. Competing is uncooperative but assertive. You are competing when you insist on your own point of view, refuse to consider others' perspectives, demand a particular outcome that benefits you, and generally "plan to win." Competing can include coercion, manipulation, threats, or other forms of verbal aggression, though it does not have to. If your partner accommodates, the conflict episode ends. If, however, your partner also responds by competing, your conflict escalates. Competing creates an "I win/ you lose" situation. You may win the conflict episode and get your way, but at your partner's expense. From a relational satisfaction standpoint, episodes of competing usually hurt relationships, at least in the short term. If competing is your preferred style, you are likely to have trouble maintaining relationships that are healthy for you and your partner.

Competing—resolving a conflict by satisfying one's own needs or advancing one's own ideas with little concern for the needs or ideas of the other person or for the relationship

There are circumstances when competing is an effective means of resolving conflict that does not damage a relationship. In emergencies, when quick and decisive action must be taken to ensure safety or minimize harm, taking a forceful position can be useful. Firefighters, paramedics, and police officers, for example, use this style during crises to ensure the safety of the public. There is no value in compromising with someone trying to enter a burning building or a crime scene unnecessarily.

Compromising

Compromising—resolving a conflict by bargaining so that each partner's needs or interests are partially satisfied

Compromising is resolving a conflict by bargaining so that each partner's needs or interests are partially satisfied. With this approach, both you and your partner give up part of what you really want or believe, or trade one thing you want or believe, to get something else. Compromising is an intermediate tack between assertiveness and cooperativeness: Both you and your partner have to be somewhat assertive and somewhat cooperative, and both of you end up partially satisfied. From an individual satisfaction standpoint, compromising creates neither a lose/lose nor a win/win situation because you both lose something even as you win something else. From a relational satisfaction standpoint, compromise may be seen as neutral to positive since each partner is satisfied to some extent. Compromising is appropriate when the issue is moderately important, when there are time constraints, and when attempts at competing or collaborating have not been successful. Although compromising is a popular and at least partially satisfying conflict management style, significant problems can be associated with it. Of special concern is the possibility that you may trade away a better solution to reach a compromise. When possible, seek to move beyond compromising to collaborating.

Collaborating

Collaborating—resolving a conflict by using problem solving to arrive at a solution that meets the needs and interests of both parties in the conflict

Collaborating is resolving a conflict by using problem solving to arrive at a solution that meets the needs and interests of both parties in the conflict. Treating your disagreement as a problem to be solved, you and your partner discuss the issues, describe your feelings, and identify the characteristics of an effective solution. Collaborating is assertive and cooperative, assertive because you both voice your concerns, cooperative because you both work together to find a resolution.

From an individual satisfaction standpoint, collaborating creates a win/win scenario because the needs of both partners are met completely. From a relational satisfaction standpoint, collaboration is positive because you both feel heard. You get to share ideas, weighing and considering information in a way that satisfies both of you individually and strengthens your relationship as a result. However, it requires time, effort, and problem-solving skills.

Using Problem Solving to Collaborate

Managing conflict through collaboration requires some of the communication skills we have discussed in earlier chapters. For

Cartoonstock www.Cartoonstock.com

example, you must use accurate and precise language to describe your ideas and feelings, and you must empathetically listen to your partner's ideas and feelings. In addition, you will need to follow five problem-solving steps: (1) Define the problem: What's the issue being considered? (2) Analyze the problem: What are the causes and symptoms of the issue? (3) Develop mutually acceptable criteria for judging solutions: What goals will a good solution attain? (4) Generate solutions and alternative solutions: What do you think about this idea, and what is another approach you could take if that other idea doesn't work? (5) Select the solution or solutions that best meet the criteria identified: What do you say we go with this solution and that one, too, since we both seem to agree that these are the most realistic ones?

Let's apply these five steps to a conflict example: Justina and Eduardo are a young couple whose financial situation is precarious. Justina is worried that they may have to declare bankruptcy. Eduardo thinks that things are difficult, but that they can manage. Because this issue is important to them both, and because they really love each other, they sit down to talk things over. They begin by listening to each other's position, defining and analyzing the problem. Justina describes the threat she has received from the landlord about possible eviction if the rent checks continue to be late, and she expresses her anxiety about not paying the other bills on time. Eduardo may remind her that money is tight because he recently took a pay cut to start a new job with more potential. From this baseline, they can work together, creating a list of guidelines or criteria for a solution acceptable to them both. Justina asks that the solution allow them to pay bills on time, whereas Eduardo wants any option they pursue to lower their monthly costs. Once they have agreed on these two criteria, Justina might propose that they save money by eating out only once a month and using Netflix rather than going to movies. Eduardo might suggest that they have a yard sale and use the proceeds as a cushion that would allow them to pay bills on time, replenishing it when they get their paychecks. Once they have a satisfying list of options that they can both live with, they can then complete the collaborative problem-solving process by selecting the solution or solutions on which they agree. They might decide to go with three of the four ideas they came up with, such as paying more than the minimum credit card balances, eating out only once a month but still going to the movies occasionally, and having the yard sale.

Collaboration is hard work. When you and your partner commit to trying, however, chances are that, through discussion, you can arrive at creative solutions that meet your needs while simultaneously strengthening your relationship. As stated earlier, no single conflict style is best; all five are useful in some settings. Developing behavioral flexibility will allow you not only to use your couple of default modes, but also to switch between styles. In so doing, you will be able to competently handle the situations you face. As we will see next, an effective conflict style also depends on cultural considerations.

Joint problem solving is a collaborative activity. Can you think of a time when you solved a problem with the help of someone else?

Face Negotiation in Conflict

Face—how we want our partners and others who are present to view us, our public self-image

When you engage in conflict, your style affects "face" for you and your partner. **Face** is public self-image, or how we want our partners and others who are present to view us. In any interaction, either partner can grant face to the other or cause him or her to lose face. Thus, in addition to resolving the specific issues in a conflict, we are also negotiating issues of face. When people in conflict attack each other's face, they damage the relationship. For example, when Cindy's manager called a meeting thirty minutes before her usual arrival time to work, Cindy had trouble getting there, and arrived fifteen minutes late. Her frustrated manager confronted Cindy in front of everyone, saying, "You're stealing from the company when you're late. Next time, I'll write you up." As someone who prided herself on her work ethic and honesty, Cindy was humiliated by her manager's criticism. By attacking her publicly, and labeling her lateness as "stealing," her manager added loss of face to a conflict that could have been limited to the issue of timeliness.

Face Negotiation Theory

Face negotiation theory—proposes that in conflict settings we prefer conflict styles consistent with our cultures and the face-orientations most consistent with those cultures

Self-face orientation— the inclination to uphold and protect our self-image in our interactions with others

Face negotiation theory proposes that, in conflict settings, we prefer conflict styles consistent with our cultures and the face-orientations most consistent with those cultures (Ting-Toomey & Chung, 2011; Zhang, Ting-Toomey, & Oetzel, 2014). According to this theory, people from individualist (and low-context) cultures, such as the dominant American culture and other Western Hemisphere cultures, are more likely to have a **self-face orientation**, which is the inclination to uphold and protect their self-image in interactions with others. For example, if Cindy has a self-face orientation to conflict, she may perceive her manager's tirade as a direct attack on her self-esteem, which she might protect with her own competing response, exclaiming: "Well, you don't have to worry about me 'stealing' anymore. I don't need this abuse. I quit." Competing is their default style, as this serves our self-face interests and may resolve the issue in their favor. They often produce conflict messages that directly pursue their own interests, with relatively little attention to their relationship implications. When they successfully force their will on others, they feel that they have defended their rights. Because the fact that they may have damaged the face of their partner doesn't really enter their consciousness, they can be surprised when their victory damages their relationships. Cindy's angry response to her manager's public reprimand was her way of protecting her face and asserting her rights. Recounting this incident later, she may even say, "Well, I showed *him*, he had no *right* to talk to me that way, especially in front of my colleagues." Her spur-of-the-moment resignation probably caught her manager off guard. Reflecting on what happened, he might not even consider that his tirade shredded Cindy's face. Instead, he may rationalize his behavior by concluding that Cindy was just a disgruntled employee.

On the other hand, people who come from collectivist cultures (many in the Eastern and Southern Hemispheres) that are high-context, often high-power,

Conflict can be damaging to the face of our partner. How can we mend the damage to another's face that we might do during an argument?

and with high distance orientations, sometimes believe that their responsibilities to others supersede their own rights. In conflicts, these people have an **other-face orientation**, the inclination to uphold and protect the self-images of their partners and other people affected by the conflict even at the risk of their own face. If possible, they adopt an avoiding style. When verbal expression of conflict simply can't be avoided, they typically employ a style that is consistent with the relationship and the conflict issue. They will accommodate those of higher status, and compromise or collaborate with peers and people of lower status. If an issue is important, they prefer collaborating, considering the time it takes to reach consensus a wise investment. If Cindy was from a collectivist culture, she would probably have an other-face orientation during conflict. This orientation would help her empathize with the emotional responses of her manager and fellow employees (Zhang et al., 2014). She would recognize that her lateness was disappointing and frustrating to her manager, and possibly irritating to her peers, and she would likely to be motivated to accommodate and apologize. Although Cindy and her peers would consider the manager's harsh and public reprimand rude, they would also view her tardiness as having caused loss of face for everyone. Consequently, Cindy would accommodate, apologizing to the group and her manager, an act of self-deprecation that would help her regain face (assuming that they all shared a collectivist culture).

> **Other-face orientation**—the inclination to uphold and protect the self-images of our partners and other people affected by the conflict, even at the risk of our own face

Co-Cultures and Individual Differences in Conflict

Conflict styles in American co-cultures may be complex mixtures of dominant and co-cultural influence. For example, both the collectivist and high-power distance values of African culture and the individualist values of the dominant American culture influence African American conflict styles. Within the family or community, younger African Americans are likely to accommodate older or more respected family members, giving them their "propers" (proper respect). In other circumstances, the typical African American mode of conflict is assertive, competitive, and emotionally expressive, which stems not only from their ethnic cultural background, but also from a long history of experiencing racism and oppression. An upfront, animated style during conflict is a cultural norm, not a sign of aggression (Ting-Toomey & Chung, 2011). Due to experiences with racism, African Americans can be especially sensitive to loss of face. This makes facework very important when working through conflict with most African Americans.

Hispanic or Latino/a American values are collectivist with high-power distance, cultural norms that dictate an other-face orientation. When the conflict is of little or no importance, Latinos who identify with the co-culture will use avoidance and accommodation as their default strategies. When, however, the conflict is important and their partner is of equal or lower status, Latinos who identify with the co-culture are more likely to use an emotionally animated, competing style than Latinos who do not strongly identify with the co-culture (Garcia, 1996; Ting-Toomey, Oetzel, & Yee-Jung, 2001).

Asian American conflict styles reflect the collectivist, high-context cultures of their ethnic heritage, influenced by Confucianism, a philosophy that values collective face-saving. Asian Americans who strongly identify with their co-culture are likely to use avoiding and accommodating styles of conflict management. With important issues, these Asian Americans may seek the help of a respected third party to mediate the conflict. Asian Americans who identify more with the dominant American culture favor collaborating for managing conflict (Ting-Toomey, Oetzel, & Yee-Jung, 2001).

The more that members of an ethnic group identify with their ethnic cultures, the more likely they are to see conflict through their particular cultural lens. You can be more effective at resolving conflict with people who identify with a different ethnic group if you understand that they are working to resolve the conflict in what for them is the culturally appropriate way. Of course, within cultures and co-cultures, individual values and behaviors still vary, because our approach to conflict is influenced by our families, education, professional and social groups, religious beliefs, and a host of other factors. Thus, people in the dominant American culture do not always adopt a competing style even though the culture is individualistic, and people in dominant Chinese or Japanese cultures, for instance, may adopt a competing style even though their culture is collectivistic.

Self-construal—how you see yourself

According to face negotiation theory, some of this variation within cultures results from differences in **self-construal**, or how you see yourself. If your self-construal is more independent, you see yourself as distinct from others and value your own unique perspective, which typically leads to higher self-face orientation and competing in conflict. If your self-construal is more interdependent, you see yourself as connected with others and value their perspective, which typically leads to higher other-face orientation and adopting more other-friendly conflict styles (e.g., accommodating, avoiding, compromising, or collaborating). Going back to the example of Cindy, if she is from a collectivist culture but higher in independent self-construal, she might apologize, but do so in a way that shows her disdain for the manager's authority, or she might write an anonymous complaint to her manager's supervisor.

In conflict situations, people may behave in accord with their cultural and co-cultural norms, or they may not. Nevertheless, you will be more effective at resolving interpersonal conflict if you are mindful that your partner's orientation toward conflict and her or his expectations for facework may differ from your own.

Destructive Conflict Patterns

Principle of negative reciprocity—the proposition that we repay negative treatment with negative treatment

As was stated at the beginning of this chapter, conflict is a fact of life in any relationship. It can be beneficial, drawing you and your partners closer together, or it can damage or end your relationships. Conflict that seriously damages relationships usually follows the **principle of negative reciprocity**, or the tendency to repay negative treatment with negative treatment. In a conflict conversation, it is easy to fall into a back-and-forth pattern of answering one partner's hurtful message with another, in a spiraling vortex of negative reciprocity. When this occurs, the likelihood of successfully resolving the conflict decreases as the likelihood that our relationship will be damaged increases. Furthermore, conflicts that follow patterns of negative reciprocity damage our physical and mental well-being (Roloff & Reznik, 2008). Notice that what causes the damage is not a single message but rather the tendency to reciprocate a negative message in what becomes a pattern of interaction. A number of these patterns can occur when we disagree with our partners. Let's look at five of the most common: serial arguing, counterblaming, cross-complaining, demand-withdrawal, and mutual hostility.

Serial Arguing

Most of us have experienced **serial arguing**, a conflict pattern in which partners argue about the same issue two or more times (Roloff & Johnson, 2002). In serial arguing, both partners are focused on the issue but disagree about how it should be resolved, exchanging messages that either defend their position or attack their partner's. As these conversations end without resolving the differences between partners, the issue has to be re-argued when it comes up again. For example, newlyweds Michaela and Carl have a recurring argument about Carl's participation in three evening basketball leagues that he had been playing in since before they knew each other. Since their engagement, Michaela has been arguing with Carl, urging him to give up at least one league. About once a month as Carl prepares to leave for a game, Michaela initiates this argument by telling Carl that it is not normal for a married man to spend so many evenings away from home playing ball with the guys. The back-and-forth arguing usually ends in Michaela crying and Carl stomping out of their apartment, returning long after Michaela is in bed. As you can see, this pattern of conflict is unlikely to be resolved unless one or both partners do something to break the pattern.

> **Serial arguing**—a conflict pattern in which partners argue about the same issue two or more times

Counterblaming

A second destructive conflict pattern, **counterblaming**, is a conflict pattern in which you blame your partner for being the cause of what he or she has accused you of doing, shifting responsibility and leaving the original issue unresolved. Instead of resolving an argument, counterblaming only escalates a back-and-forth series of attacks. For example, suppose that Nicole says to her sister Stacey, "I can't believe you just took my new black skirt and wore it without asking." Here Stacey should respond to the issue at hand (unauthorized borrowing) by defending herself: "But you said I could always borrow anything from you," or she might apologize for what she did: "I'm sorry, but I needed something nice to wear to work." If, however, Stacey replies, "Well, it's your own fault, I would not have had to borrow your skirt for work today if you had done the laundry like you promised," she is counterblaming. Nicole may either respond appropriately, "Stacey, the issue is not why you needed to borrow the skirt, but that you did it

> **Counterblaming**—a conflict pattern in which you blame your partner for what he or she has accused you of doing, shifting responsibility and leaving the original issue unresolved

Cartoonstock www.Cartoonstock.com

Cross-complaining—a conflict pattern in which partners trade unrelated criticisms, leaving the initial issue unresolved

Demand-withdrawal—a conflict pattern in which one partner consistently demands while the other consistently withdraws

without asking me," or she may take the bait and also counterblame: "I couldn't do the laundry because you didn't buy any laundry detergent when you went shopping, as usual." And Stacey may reciprocate Nicole's negativity: "Well, duh, how can I know that we need detergent when you don't bother to put it on the shopping list?" Notice how a counterblaming exchange strays further and further away from the original issue.

Cross-complaining

Similar to counterblaming, **cross-complaining** is a conflict pattern in which partners trade *unrelated* criticisms, leaving the initial issue unresolved. For example, Mia, irritated by her roommate Sasha for not putting his dishes in the dishwasher, says to him, "Sasha, I really get annoyed when I come home at night and your breakfast dishes are still on the counter. Is it asking too much for you to rinse them off and put them in the dishwasher?" If Sasha's reply is, "Well, look who's talking, Miss-Can't-Put-the-Cap-on-the-Toothpaste," he is cross-complaining. At this point, the subject of the conversation will shift to the toothpaste cap, or Mia may offer a different cross-complaint.

Demand-withdrawal

The demand-withdrawal pattern can become a recurring pattern of conflict communication in long-term relationships (Caughlin & Huston, 2006). **Demand-withdrawal** is a conflict pattern in which one partner consistently demands while the other consistently withdraws. Typically, the person in the demanding position tends to be the less powerful and dissatisfied partner in the relationship, whereas the person in the withdrawing position is more powerful and happy with the status quo. If one person constantly demands to resolve a conflict while the other consistently ignores those demands, the result is an unhealthy escalation with no chance of resolution. For instance, imagine that Angelina, who is concerned about her husband's weight, introduces the topic by saying, "Kevin, I don't want to hurt your feelings, but you really need to lose a few pounds. It's not good for your health to be overweight. It's all the pop you drink and the bedtime snacks." Kevin, acting as though he did not hear a word Angelina has said, looks up from the computer and says, "Hey, we could get a great deal on a digital camera on eBay." He has met her demand with a withdrawal. If she switches topics, the issue of Kevin's weight may become fodder for a serial argument pattern in the relationship. Angelina may escalate, however, responding, "Kevin, quit with the eBay stuff. I'm talking to you. You need to lose weight while you're still young and it's relatively easy." Kevin may also escalate his withdrawal by getting up and walking out of the room in an attempt to end this episode. Angelina may follow him out of the room, yelling at his back more arguments about the relationship of health to weight until he stomps into the bathroom and slams the door. Since the issue really hasn't been discussed, Angelina is likely to raise it again.

Mutual Hostility

Perhaps the conflict pattern most damaging to relationships and to partners' self-esteem is **mutual hostility**, a conflict pattern in which partners trade increasingly louder verbal abuse, including inappropriate, unrelated personal criticism, name-calling, swearing, and sarcasm. Sometimes called "fighting," the pattern begins when one person interjects a hostile comment into a conflict conversation, which the other partner matches with one of his or her own. The longer this pattern continues, the more likely the conversation is to degenerate into hateful and bitter messages that can permanently damage a relationship as well as the mental and physical health of both participants (Roloff & Reznik, 2008). Most of us find conflict episodes that deteriorate into exchanges of mutual hostilities painful and shameful. We are hurt by our partner's comments and ashamed of the verbal abuse we inflict. Learning how to avoid and break patterns of destructive conflict can make us feel better about ourselves and our partners, while maintaining our personal health and the health of our relationships. Although destructive patterns are hard to break, we can learn strategies and skills for more effective conflict conversations.

Mutual hostility—a conflict pattern in which partners trade increasingly louder verbal abuse, including inappropriate, unrelated personal criticism, name-calling, swearing, and sarcasm

Guidelines for Effective Conflict Management

This section begins by identifying several recommendations to help you break a negative reciprocity cycle. Then we will describe how you can use the message skills learned in earlier chapters to create collaborative conflict conversations. Finally, we will discuss how you can repair relationships damaged by conflict.

Break Patterns of Destructive Conflict

You will recall that conflict can spiral into destructive patterns of negative reciprocity. Several strategies exist for breaking these negative patterns, including the following guidelines (Roloff & Reznik, 2008).

1. Avoid negative start-ups. The best way to break the cycle is not to start it in the first place. You can accomplish this in two ways. First, if you have developed a negative pattern with someone, have a conversation in which you set **ground rules**, mutually agreed on rules for behavior during conflict episodes. Examples of ground rules include no name-calling, no profanity or swearing, no interrupting, no walking out, paraphrasing your partner's comments before adding your own thoughts, and so forth. Ground rules are effective because both you and your partner agree to abide by them, so give the other person permission to remind you if you break a ground rule.

Ground rules—mutually agreed-on rules for behavior during conflict episodes

A second way you can avoid negative start-ups is to allow for some time to pass after the trigger incident and before the discussion. For example, Sarah and Katie Beth are sisters who go to the same college 200 miles away from their home. They share a car and drive back and forth for long weekends and vacations. Sarah prefers to do the driving because it keeps her from getting carsick.

Katie Beth understands this but thinks that Sarah drives too fast. The last few times the girls have driven home or back to school, they have ended up in a big argument. Last time it was so bad that they didn't speak for two weeks. Katie Beth, dreading the trip home at Thanksgiving, wants to avoid the demand-withdrawal pattern that characterizes their arguments during the trips. So three weeks before they are scheduled to leave for home, she calls Sarah and asks her to meet for coffee to discuss this issue and hopefully find a solution they both can live with. By removing the discussion from the actual trip, Katie is hoping that they can find a win-win solution.

2. Manage anger. The negative reciprocity spiral is usually fueled by the anger of one or both participants. So, managing your own and your partner's hostility can help. In conflict we often express our anger in ways that make our partners defensive. To protect themselves, partners often respond with angry messages of their own or by withdrawing. Two approaches can break this cycle.

First, during a conflict conversation, if you find your anger getting in the way of working cooperatively with your partner, take a break. Saying something like, "Excuse me, but I need to step back and get my emotions under control. I'd like to continue our conversation when I can be rational. So let's take a five- (or ten-, or twenty-, etc.) minute break while I regroup." Asking for breathing room can give you time to calm down and allow your partner a much needed break as well.

Second, a better long-term solution is to develop skills for constructively expressing anger in a way that doesn't make your partner defensive. In a heated conversation, directly describing your anger ("I'm really angry") can cause someone to become defensive. You may, therefore, want to choose synonyms for anger that will not be perceived as threatening. For example, if you say, "I am really mad at you for missing our date," your partner may become defensive. But if you say, "I'm totally frustrated. I thought we had a date, and when you didn't show up, I missed the opportunity to go to the movies with my roommate," your partner may feel guilty and apologize or calmly explain what happened. Trying to help, the typical response to someone's frustration differs from the typical response to someone's anger.

3. De-escalate the conflict. A dysfunctional conflict conversation tends to escalate: voices become louder, silences longer, nonverbal behaviors more exaggerated, messages more hostile, and positions more entrenched. One way to break this destructive conflict pattern is to prevent it from intensifying. There are four ways to do this. First, if this is a serial argument or if you have a history of dysfunctional conflict, you need to identify what triggers antagonism. We all have buttons that others can push. By reflecting on previous difficult conversations, we may discover what escalates the conflict—then, not do it. Second, noticing that a conflict is intensifying, we can try to calm our partners and ourselves. Sometimes simply acknowledging your partner's feelings and apologizing can have this effect: "Hey, wow, I can see you're getting upset. I'm sorry. I didn't mean to make you cry." At other times, taking a break from the conversation can help. Finally, injecting humor into the discussion can be an effective way to soothe and de-escalate, especially if that humor is self-directed or points out

▶ **OBSERVE AND ANALYZE**

Breaking Destructive Conflict Patterns

Think of a recent conflict you experienced in which a destructive pattern developed. Analyze what happened using the concepts from this chapter. What type of conflict was it? What conflict management style did you adopt? What was the other person's style? What triggered the pattern of negative reciprocity that developed? How might you change what happened if you could redo this conflict episode?

something about the conflict. If directed at your partner, however, it will increase, not decrease, negativity.

Create Collaborative Conflict Conversations

Collaboration is usually the most competent way to resolve interpersonal conflict. You can use the message skills you have learned to initiate, respond to, and mediate conflict. The following guidelines are based on work from several fields of study (Gordon, 1970; Adler, 1977; Whetten & Cameron, 2010).

Guidelines for Initiating a Collaborative Conflict Conversation

1. Mentally rehearse what you will say before confronting the other person. Initiating a collaborative conflict conversation requires us to be in control of our emotions. Yet, despite our good intentions to keep on track, our emotions can still get the better of us, and in the heat of the moment, we may say things we should not. We should, therefore, take a minute to practice, incorporating the guidelines listed here. Mentally rehearse a few statements you think will lead to productive conflict resolution.

2. Recognize and state ownership of the conflict. If a conflict is to be managed, it is important to acknowledge that you are angry, hurt, or frustrated about something that has occurred between you and your partner. Honestly own your ideas and feelings by using "I" statements. For example, suppose you are trying to study for a test in your most difficult course, and your neighbor's music is so loud that your walls are shaking to the point where you can't concentrate. You own your problem if you approach him, saying, "Hi. I'm trying to study for an exam."

3. Describe the conflict in terms of behavior (b), consequences (c), and feelings (f). Once you have owned the conflict as your problem, describe your perception of the issue to your partner using the b-c-f—behavior, consequences, and feelings—sequence: "When a specific *b*ehavior happens, specific *c*onsequences result, and I *f*eel (emotion)" (Gordon, 1971). Earlier you learned the message skills of describing behavior and describing feelings. Notice that the b-c-f sequence uses these skills. To return to our loud music example, you would follow up on your ownership of the problem, opening with the b-c-f sequence. You might say, "When I hear your music, I get distracted and can't concentrate on studying, and then I get frustrated and annoyed." The behavior is playing loud music; the consequences are distraction and inability to concentrate; the feelings are frustration and annoyance. Note that all of the statements here are I-centered: "When I hear your music, I get distracted," rather than "When you play your music so loud, you distract me"; and "I get frustrated and annoyed," rather than, "You frustrate and annoy me."

4. Do not blame or ascribe motives. Since your goal is to resolve the issue without escalating the conflict, be careful not to accuse your partner of bad motives or distort what the other person has done. You want to focus on what is happening to you.

SKILL BUILDER ▶ BEHAVIOR, CONSEQUENCES, AND FEELINGS (B-C-F) SEQUENCE

SKILL	USE	STEPS	EXAMPLE
Describing a conflict in terms of behavior, consequences, and feelings (b-c-f)	To help the other person understand the problem completely	1. Own the message, using "I" statements. 2. Describe the behavior that you see or hear. 3. Describe the consequences that result from the behavior. 4. Describe your feelings that result from the behavior.	Jason says, "I have a problem that I need your help with. When I tell you what I'm thinking and you don't respond (b), I start to think you don't care about me or what I think (c), and this causes me to get angry with you (f)."

5. Keep it short. Since collaboration requires interaction, it is important that you quickly engage the other person in the conversation. Effective turn-taking rather than dominating the exchange during its early stages will foster a problem-solving climate.

6. Be sure the other person understands your position. Even when you take the greatest care when briefly describing your needs, others may get the general drift of the message but underestimate the seriousness of the problem, or they may not understand you at all. The best way to check understanding is to ask your partners to tell you what they believe you have said. Their paraphrase should alert you to whether you need to follow up with additional explanation.

7. Phrase your preferred solution to focus on common ground. Once you have been understood and you have listened to your partner's position, suggest how you believe the issue can be resolved so that both of you benefit. If your solution is tied to a shared value, common interest, or shared constraint, your partner will see it as a viable solution. Returning to our example, you might say, "I think we both have had times when even little things got in the way of our being able to study. I realize I'm asking you for a favor, but I hope you can help me out by turning down your music for a couple of hours."

Guidelines for Collaborative Response to Conflict Initiation

Creating a collaborative climate is less difficult when responding to conflict that has been appropriately initiated. Your most difficult task as a responder is to take an ineffectively initiated conflict and turn it into a productive, problem-solving discussion. The following guidelines will help you respond effectively in these situations.

1. Put your shields up. Follow the example of the captains of the *Starship Enterprise*, when under attack, "Shields up!" When someone is overly aggressive in initiating a conflict, you must learn to raise your mental shields. This improves your capacity to listen and respond effectively rather than becoming defensive or counterattacking. One method for achieving this is to remember that the other person should be the one to own the problem, not you. In all likelihood, the anger being vented toward you is caused by accumulated frustration, only part of which directly relates to the current conflict. So put those shields up, take your time responding, and while you are doing so, think of your options for turning the attack into a problem-solving opportunity.

2. Respond empathetically with genuine interest and concern. A person who initiates a conflict, even with a bold order like, "Turn down that damn music!" will be watching you closely to see how you react. If you make light of the other person's concerns, become defensive, or counterattack, you will undermine the opportunity to solve the problem through cooperation. Even if you disagree with the complaint, you should demonstrate respect by being attentive and empathetic. Sometimes you can do this by allowing the other person to vent while you listen. Only when the other person has calmed down can problem solving begin. In our music example, the neighbor responding to your request to turn down the volume might first say, "I can see you're upset. Let's talk about this."

3. Ask questions to clarify issues and paraphrase your understanding of the problem. Since most people are unaware of the b-c-f sequence, you may want to paraphrase in a way that captures your understanding of the b-c-f issues or ask questions to elicit this information. For instance, let's suppose that you not only berate your neighbor, saying, "Turn down that damn music! Quit being such a jerk to others," but also ascribe motives to the behavior, saying, "You must enjoy deliberately disrupting everyone!" If information is missing, as with this initiating statement, then the neighbor could ask questions to fill in the missing information, such as "I'm not sure what you're upset about. Are you studying right now? Is that the issue?" Then, having all the information needed, the neighbor could paraphrase following the b-c-f framework: "Okay, so I take it you are upset (f) because my music is loud (b), and that's interrupting your ability to study (c). Is that right?" Verifying that the paraphrase is correct and that nothing else needs to been mentioned is also helpful. Sometimes people will initiate a conflict episode about a relatively minor issue without indicating what really needs to be considered.

4. Find common ground by agreeing with some aspect of the complaint. Regardless of how effective or ineffective the conflict initiation, once you have gotten to the stage of clarifying the issue, seek common ground. This does not mean giving in to the other person or pretending to agree. Instead, look for points on which you both can agree. You can agree with a complaint or criticism without accepting all of its implications (Adler, 1977). Useful alternatives include agreeing with part of the message, agreeing in principle (without agreeing that it applies to the current situation), agreeing that the initiator views the situation in a certain way, and agreeing that the initiator is having certain feelings.

The Power of *Wastah* in Lebanese Speech

BY MAHBOUB HASHEM

Mahboub Hashem is full professor and chair of the Mass Communication Department at American University of Sharjah, United Arab Emirates. His research interests are the effects of mass media on society and intercultural interpersonal communication.

"Do you have any *wastah*?" This was the only question that many of my Lebanese friends and relatives asked me when I applied for one of the Chair of Administrative Affairs positions at the Lebanese University [some years ago]. I replied that I ranked among the top five in the competency exam and they needed to hire at least ten people, so why would I need a *wastah*? They simply shrugged and warned, "Wait and you'll see."

To make the story short, I was passed over and more than 10 other people were hired. Every one of those who were hired had some type of *wastah*. I was hired three years later only after I had acquired strong *wastah*, which included several influential individuals, among them Suleiman Frangieh, the President of Lebanon at that time. . . .

By examining the *wastah* phenomenon in Lebanon and how it is practiced, one may be able to shed some light on this very important communicative behavior not only in Lebanon but also in the rest of the Middle East. This essay addresses the power of *wastah* (i.e., mediation), considered to be one of the most important communication patterns in the Lebanese cultural system. . . .

Wastah has been the way of life in Lebanon since before it became a republic. The term *wastah* means many things to many Lebanese people, including clout, connections, networking, recommendations, a "go-between" for two parties with different interests, and a type of contraception to prevent pregnancy.

Wastah can be used within various contexts, such as family, clan, government organizations, neighbors, villages, and nations. It is usually necessary to get a job, a wife, a date, a passport, a visa, a car, or any other commodity. It can also resolve conflicts, facilitate government decisions, or solve bureaucratic problems. For instance, I once had to wait three hours until I could find an influential person to help me pay the annual tag fee for my car. The common perception in the Arab world, particularly in Lebanon, is that "one does not do for oneself what might better be done by a friend or a friend's friend."

For instance, the neighbor can agree in part ("I know it's hard to study for a tough exam"), agree in principle ("You need a quiet place to study"), agree with perceptions ("I understand that you're having trouble studying with loud music in the background"), or agree with feelings ("I get that you're frustrated and annoyed")—all of which can occur without agreeing with the initiator's conclusions or solutions. By acknowledging whatever points of agreement exist, you create common ground for a problem-solving discussion.

5. Ask the initiator to suggest solutions. Once you are sure that the two of you have agreed on what the issue is, the final step is to ask the initiator for ways to handle the conflict. In response to the loud music conflict, the initiator's

HOW DOES THE PROCESS OF WASTAH WORK?

Wastah is mostly used to find jobs for relatives or close friends and to solve conflicts. The extended family acts as an employment agency by searching for a *wasit* to help get a job, preferably one with high social status in the family. The *wasit* is supposed to be well "wired up," an insider who can make things happen (Hall, 1984). He must also be able to use the language of persuasion . . . with the elite of the religious and political groups of the nation.

In conflict situations, the *wasit's* job is to conciliate rather than to judge. Conciliation is intended to lead disputants toward a compromise through mutual concessions, as well as to reestablish their relationship on the basis of mutual respect. The *wasit* tries to talk to each disputant separately, then brings them together to reach a possible compromise that presumes to save face for everyone involved and their extended families.

Lebanese people prefer mediators from the same family or business, depending on the type and context of the conflict. . . . [T]he role of a *wasit* is to create a supportive climate of communication wherein conflicting parties can modify their behaviors. When a conflict is between members from two different clans, however, a *wasit* on each side tries to prevail over his or her own clan members. These mediators then come together to conciliate.

For instance, when a conflict occurred between my father and a man named Tony Ayoub, one elderly person from the Hashem clan and another one from the Ayoub clan came together to mediate and negotiate a possible settlement. Then each of the two met with their clan member to discuss the results of their meeting(s) and what the two believed to be a fair solution. After several private meetings between the two mediators, my father and Tony were asked to personally participate in the final one to announce the settlement of the problem. The common ground among mediators of different families is the mutual desire to keep the government out of the clans' affairs as much as possible. Hence, mediators seem better qualified than government agencies to resolve certain conflicts. . . .

The knowledge of these styles and how they are used in various cultures promotes more awareness and understanding of ourselves and others and can consequently lead to more effective intercultural relationships.

Excerpted from Hashem, M. (2012). The power of *Wastah* in Lebanese speech. In A. González, M. Houston, & V. Chen (Eds.), *Our Voices* (5th ed., pp. 176–180). New York: Oxford University Press. Used with permission.

FOR CONSIDERATION:

1. How is the role of a *wasit* similar to or different from the role of a mediator?
2. Does having two *wasit*s negotiate a resolution to a conflict rather than the people who are directly involved in the conflict make sense? If so, why do you think this? If not, same question.
3. How comfortable would you be using a *wasit* to resolve an important conflict you had with someone else?
4. What characteristics would you want a *wasit* who represented you in a conflict to have?

solutions may be to turn the music down or turn it off completely. Since the initiator has probably spent time thinking about what needs to be done, your request for a solution signals a willingness to listen and cooperate. You may find that one of the suggestions seems reasonable to you (e.g., using earphones instead of turning it off). If none of the suggestions are reasonable, you may be able to craft an alternative that builds on one of the ideas presented: "I'd be happy to turn the volume down, but most people are done with their exams, so you might also think about working in the designated quiet area if someone else starts playing music loud." In any case, asking for suggestions communicates your trust in the other person, strengthening the collaborative climate.

Mediating a conflict takes skill, as Leonard on *The Big Bang Theory* learned when he attempted to mediate a conflict between Sheldon and Penny that began during a paintball game.

Mediator—a neutral and impartial guide who structures an interaction so that conflicting parties can find a mutually acceptable solution to an issue

Guidelines for Mediating a Conflict Conversation

In collectivist cultures, it is common to have a trusted and respected person mediate conflicts. In the "Diverse Voices" article, "The Power of *Wastah* in Lebanese Speech," the author explains how the Lebanese use powerfully connected individuals in this role. Although people in individualist cultures usually handle their conflicts without help, there are times when a mediator is sought, or where people choose to mediate conflicts that they observe between people they know. A **mediator** is a neutral and impartial guide who structures an interaction so that conflicting parties can find a mutually acceptable solution to an issue (Cupach & Canary, 1997). Working as a mediator, you can help friends and family repair relationships and communicate more positively by observing the following guidelines (Cupach & Canary, 1997; Whetten & Cameron, 2010).

1. Make sure that all people involved in the conflict agree to work with you. If one or both parties do not really want your help, you are unlikely to be able to do much good. You may be able to clarify this by saying, "I'm willing to help you work on this, but only if both of you want me to." If everyone does not agree to your serving as a mediator, bow out gracefully.

2. Establish ground rules. As the mediator, you are in a good position to have participants form ground rules that you can use later to return the conflict to a constructive conversation. You might begin this process by naming one ground rule you would like everyone to adhere to.

3. Probe until you identify the real conflict. Often people seem to be arguing about one thing when the true source of conflict has not been stated. Use clarifying questions, paraphrasing, and perception checking to probe the issue.

4. Remain neutral. Any perception of favoritism will test the patience of one of the parties and destroy the opportunity for successful mediation. Even if you believe one partner's position is stronger, you need to keep your opinions to yourself.

5. Keep the discussion focused on resolving the issue. If the conversation seems to drift to other issues than the conflict to be resolved, get the subject back on track with redirecting comments like, "I think we've gotten off topic. Let's get back to the issue."

6. Encourage equal talk time. It is important for the mediator to control the conversation in a way that gives both parties an equal chance to be heard. As mediator, you can do this by directing questions to the more reticent or withdrawn party and by reminding the more assertive partner of ground rules.

7. Establish an action plan and follow-up procedure. Once a solution has been agreed on in principle, the participants can work out the details unassisted. But taking the essential final step of making sure that the parties have an action plan with clearly agreed-to responsibilities is part of effective mediating. The plan should specify what each party is to do and how results will be measured and monitored.

Forgiveness: Repairing Relationships Damaged by Conflict

At times, no matter how hard you try, you will be unable to resolve a conflict so that it successfully meets the needs of both parties. Some conflicts are extremely deep and complex, and they cannot be managed using only the communication skills you have studied thus far (Sillars & Weisberg, 1987). These conflicts usually stem from one partner deeply hurting the other partner and damaging the offended partner's ability to continue trusting the transgressor. Examples include lying, stealing, infidelity, and other violations of relationship trust. In addition, our behavior during a mundane conflict can get out of line and hurt our partners. To repair the damage done to the relationship, partners need to seek and bestow forgiveness. **Forgiveness** is a communication process that allows you and your partner to overcome the damage done to your relationship because of a transgression. Scholars suggest that forgiveness interactions have seven steps (Waldron & Kelley, 2008).

1. Confession. The process of forgiveness begins when the offending partner acknowledges the wrong that has been done and accepts responsibility for it. For example: "Mom, I know I shouldn't have taken that money from your purse. It's my fault."

2. Venting. To forgive, offended partners may need to verbally and nonverbally express their negative emotions. The partner seeking forgiveness should listen to and affirm the other partner's feelings. Responding to her son's theft, the mother might say: "I am so angry with you. I needed that money to pay our utility bill, and I was so embarrassed when I got to the head of the line and didn't have the money." A validating response would be, "That must have been embarrassing. I can see why you would be so angry with me."

3. Understanding. During this phase of forgiveness, partners explore what motivated the transgression: "What were you thinking?" "I wanted to go out with my friends. I didn't have the money, and I knew if I asked you, you'd refuse. So I just took it."

4. Apologize. We all learned in childhood that an apology is "saying you're sorry." Social interactions are punctuated with brief apologies for minor impositions like bumping into or interrupting someone. But repairing damage to a relationship requires a more skillful approach to apology. The apology should acknowledge responsibility, express regret or remorse, and directly request forgiveness. "Mom, I'm truly sorry I took the money from your purse. Please forgive me." Assuming that you are sincere in your apology and work to avoid further transgressions, this type of apology provides a foundation for rebuilding the relationship.

5. Forgive. Forgiving explicitly or implicitly communicates to our partners that we absolve them from the consequences or penalties we have a right to impose. Sometimes forgiveness is direct, and the offended person will say, "I forgive you." In other cases, forgiveness is implied as offended partners choose

Forgiveness—a communication process that allows you and your partner to overcome the damage done to your relationship because of a transgression

What The Black? By Richard Harris Jr.

"Let me get this straight ... You're saying that I should apologize to you for not accepting your apology to me, fast enough?"

Cartoonstock www.Cartoonstock.com

SKILL BUILDER ▶ APOLOGIZING

SKILL	USE	STEPS	EXAMPLE
A direct request for forgiveness	To repair a relationship that your behavior has damaged	1. Directly acknowledge your transgression by owning what you did. 2. Express regret or remorse for your behavior and its effect on your partner. 3. Directly request that your partner forgive you.	"I did lie about where I was Friday night. I was out with another girl. I am so sorry that I lied, and I'm really sorry that I hurt you and destroyed your trust in me. Can you forgive me?"

not to punish the transgressing partner and continue the relationship as if nothing happened.

6. Set conditions. When a partner's behavior has violated an explicit or implicit rule of the relationship, part of forgiveness is to re-establish the rule or set new rules. Forgiveness is for past behavior, but resolving the conflict and rebuilding the relationship requires that the offending partner actually change. The mother might say, "I forgive you, but if it ever happens again, I won't let you stay home alone."

7. Monitor. To forgive is not to forget. Partners should monitor the relationship as they move past the incident. Have the transgressing partners really changed their behavior? Has the offended partner really recovered from the hurt inflicted? Since the purpose of forgiveness is to mend a relationship, partners should watch for signs that trust has been restored in the relationship.

THE SOCIAL MEDIA FACTOR

Conflict Online

Conflict can occur whenever people interact, whether in person or via social media. Although many of your conflict interactions will occur face-to-face, strategies for effective conflict and mediation are also useful when you need to manage conflict online. Unfortunately, digital communication also promotes certain kinds of conflict and inappropriate behavior. For example, posts on social networking sites can create conflict when one person reveals information that another considers private, or someone posts about an event, and others who were not invited realize they were excluded. In this section, we focus on flaming, cyberbullying, and cyberstalking, types of negative online behavior that create and sustain conflict, and how to respond effectively to each of these behaviors.

Flaming

Flaming is digital communication that displays hostility through insults, profanity, and other offensive language (O'Sullivan & Flanagin, 2003). Although this kind of communication does take place in face-to-face interactions, it is especially common online. For example, in a study of regular YouTube users, 80% reported often seeing flaming messages on the site (Moor, Heuvelman, & Verleur, 2010). There are many reasons why people flame. Certain personality traits, such as sensation seeking and verbal aggressiveness, may contribute to flaming. But characteristics of the digital environment are probably more important to consider. Online, it is possible for a person to interact without revealing much (if anything) of his or her true identity, which allows people to engage in aggressive communication with few (if any) real-life consequences. In addition, people online may engage in discussions of social or political issues that they would probably avoid in face-to-face interactions, and in the process encounter others whose views are different from their own. Given the controversial nature of such topics, disagreement can easily devolve into personal attack.

One explanation for this type of behavior is that, unlike in face-to-face interactions, online communication allows people to remain anonymous. When we are anonymous, our behavior is often less influenced by personal identities, or how we see ourselves as individuals, and more by our social identities, or the groups we identify with (SIDE Model; Lea, Spears, & de Groot, 2001). For this reason, someone who is usually open-minded and willing to hear different perspectives on political issues in person could easily become more dogmatic and antagonistic when speaking anonymously online and identifying with his or her group of choice, be it "Hispanic voters" or "business conservatives."

What can you do to reduce flaming and create more productive online exchanges? If you are tempted to flame another person because you dislike something they have said or done, stop and consider the impact of this behavior. First, hostility toward others, either in person or online, rarely produces meaningful changes in attitudes or behaviors. When you participate in flaming online, the people you are communicating with have little reason to agree with you or do what you want. If you want to change how another person thinks or acts, you need to persuade them, not insult them. Second, although flaming is sometimes wrongly perceived as humorous, and is the norm within certain online communities, more often than not observers view it as negative. In the study of YouTube users referenced above, most participants reported that flaming was annoying and not amusing (Moor et al., 2010). Increasingly, online communities are establishing procedures to identify and sanction flamers. For example, in the online gaming world League of Legends, which has 30 million players, users judge the worst cases of flaming (as identified by the game's behavioral profiling system) and those identified can be banned from participating. The players have determined that while swearing is allowed, swearing directed at another player is not (Hodson, 2013).

Flaming—digital communication that displays hostility through insults, profanity, and other offensive language

▶ **OBSERVE AND ANALYZE**

Examining Online Flame Wars

Think about the last time you were involved in or observed a flame war online. Was it in an online discussion group, a blog, or Facebook? If the comments are still available, go to that location. Spend some time looking through and reflecting on the postings. How would you describe the comments that people made on this page? How active were you in the flame war? What motivated you to comment? Looking at the comments, write a different response that might have helped to put out the fire.

If you are the target of a flame attack, what can you do? First, take a deep breath, and consider the following recommendations:

1. *Respond privately.* Craft an email or other private message that expresses your frustration with the poster's message. Direct your words at the content of the flame, not the flamer's character.
2. *Ignore the flame entirely.* Although your first impulse may be to privately or publicly respond to the poster, someone who flamed with the intention of being hurtful or humorous is unlikely to change just because you express your hurt or distaste. A return flame could be just what the poster wants, and in all likelihood, even a cool, reasoned response won't change the person's behavior or position. Instead, interact with others who are not flaming, and ignore the flamer.
3. *Respond in ways that non-flamers can support.* Rather than respond directly to the flame, speak against flaming, and support others whose contributions avoid flaming, even when their ideas differ from your own.
4. *Ask an authority to intervene.* In cases of flagrant flaming, you may consider sending a message to an appropriate authority such as a group moderator or site administrator. Save this for extreme cases of repeatedly abusive flames.

Cyberbullying

In face-to-face interactions, bullying occurs when a person is "exposed, repeatedly and over time, to negative actions on the part of one or more other persons" (Olweus, 1997). **Cyberbullying** is the extension of bullying behavior to electronic communication of any kind (Slonje, Smith, & Frisen, 2013). Unlike "traditional" bullying, cyberbullying is more likely to be anonymous, and may involve bullies and victims who are geographically distant. Cyberbullying includes a wide range of abusive behaviors, including insults, death threats, circulating rumors, creating polls to vote against a victim, distributing compromising or unflattering photographs or video of the target, distributing video of face-to-face bullying, and recruiting others to send threatening messages and engage in bullying.

A 2011 Pew Research Center study found that the majority of teens who use social media say other teens are mostly kind to one another. However, 19% of teens reported being bullied and most reported they had been bullied multiple times. 9% of teens report being bullied via text message, 8% through online media (such as email, social networking sites, or instant messaging), and 7% by phone calls. Girls were much more likely to report being bullied through electronic media than boys. In addition, 88% of teens who use social media reported witnessing someone else being mean or cruel on social media, 67% have witnessed others joining in, and 21% admitted that they had joined in. Also, 90% of those who have

Cyberbullying—the extension of bullying behavior to electronic communication of any kind

Cyberbullying can be devastating to the self-concept.

witnessed online bullying say they have ignored it. It ought to be noted that online cruelty is not limited to teens, however, as 69% of adult social media users say they have seen people being cruel and mean to others (Lenhart, Madden, Smith, Purcell, Zickhur, & Rainie, 2011).

If you find that you or someone you know is a victim of cyberbullying, experts recommend the following immediate steps (www.stopbullying.gov): (1) Don't respond to, or forward, cyberbullying messages. (2) Gather evidence of the cyberbullying: record dates, times, and descriptions, and save screenshots,

A QUESTION OF ETHICS ▶ WHAT WOULD YOU DO?

Kiara and Dion, a young African American couple, have been shopping at the outlet mall. After loading their purchases into the trunk of the car, they decide to move the car to a parking space closer to the next group of shops. As Kiara is backing out, she glances in the rearview mirror and cries, "She's going to hit us!" Kiara honks her horn, but the other vehicle, an SUV, continues backing up and bangs into Kiara's rear bumper. Kiara and Dion immediately hop out of the car to check out the damage.

Their hair covered by scarves, three conservatively dressed Arab women, who appear to be daughter, mother, and grandmother, slowly exit the SUV. Dion shouts, "What's wrong with you! Don't you know how to drive? Are you blind? Couldn't you see us or hear the horn?" Kiara tells Dion to shut up and turns to the driver, a young woman about her own age, and says, "Good grief! Just give me your information!" Rima, the other driver, turns to Dion and politely responds that she hadn't seen them or heard the horn. Then she tells the other two women to get back into the car. Finally, she turns to Kiara and explains that she needs to call her husband, hastily retreating into the SUV and pulling her cell phone out of her purse as she closes the door.

Kiara explodes, banging on Rima's window and shouting, "@#$^&$$ that. Why do you need to talk to your husband? He wasn't here! He doesn't have anything to do with this! Get back out here, now!" At this point, the second woman, apparently Rima's mother, cracks her window and quietly asks Kiara not to yell, to no avail. After a few moments, Rima rolls down her window and asks Kiara to speak with Rima's husband, who is on the phone.

Kiara yells that she has no intention of speaking to anyone and again demands that Rima produce her license and insurance information. Rima replies that she is going to call the police and rolls up the window. The three women sit in the SUV until a police car arrives.

After talking with Kiara and Dion, the responding officer explains to Rima that police don't intervene in traffic accidents on private property if there are no injuries unless there is a problem with the parties' exchanging information. Rima's grandmother interrupts to insist that Kiara's behavior had been profane, rude, and threatening. She demands that the officer make Kiara apologize for the affront to their dignity. The police officer replies that Kiara's behavior might have been aggressive, but her demand had been legal and was actually the proper procedure at the scene of this type of accident. Rima apologizes to the officer, adding that she had never had an accident before and had called her husband to find out what she should do. Because she was frightened by Kiara and Dion's intimidating behavior and because Kiara had refused to speak to him, Rima's husband had told her to call the police. So she obeyed. Had Kiara remained calm and been understanding, the officer would not have been inconvenienced.

FOR CONSIDERATION

1. Given what you have learned about cultural difference in conflict situations, was it ethical for each person in this situation to use the conflict style chosen? Justify your answer.
2. Are there ethical principles that transcend culture as human universals?

emails, and text messages. (3) Whenever possible, block those doing the bullying. Then, report cyberbullying to online service providers, law enforcement, and (when occurring between students) school officials.

Cyberstalking is a variation of cyberbullying that occurs when an individual repeatedly uses social media to shadow or harass others. Individuals who engage in this behavior often make threats or false accusations against another person or constantly view and access a person's Facebook profile. Cyberstalker behavior includes grooming minors for sexual exploitation. Cyberstalkers may also digitally gather information and then use that information to harass another person in a face-to-face setting. Those who constantly watch what their friends are up to on Facebook are sometimes called "Facebook creepers." If you frequently monitor the Facebook profiles of your friends to maintain an interpersonal connection, you are not necessarily engaging in cyberstalking if there is no malicious intent. If, however, Paul regularly monitors his ex-girlfriend's Facebook page to find out when she changes her relationship status to "In a Relationship," and then attacks her with rude, hurtful, and aggressive Facebook messages, Paul is engaged in cyberstalking. If you learn that you are the victim of a cyberstalker, defriend and block the person immediately, save any evidence you may have, and seek assistance from authorities.

> **Cyberstalking**—a variation on cyberbullying that occurs when an individual repeatedly uses social media to shadow or harass others

Summary

Interpersonal conflict is disagreement between two interdependent people who perceive that they have incompatible goals. Even in good relationships, conflicts are inevitable.

There are six types of interpersonal conflict: pseudo conflicts, fact conflicts, value conflicts, policy conflicts, ego conflicts, and meta conflicts. We manage conflict by withdrawing, accommodating, competing, compromising, or collaborating, each of which can be effective in certain circumstances. During a conflict, we are concerned not only with resolving the issue, but also with face needs. People from Western Hemisphere cultures tend to have a self-face orientation, whereas people from Eastern and Southern Hemisphere cultures tend to have other-face orientations. In America, ethnic and other co-cultural groups differ in their face orientations and conflict styles, which can complicate conflict resolution. Destructive patterns of conflict stem from negative reciprocity and include serial arguing, counterblaming, cross-complaining, demand-withdrawal, and mutual hostility. Several strategies can help you break these patterns. You can use the communication message skills you have learned to initiate, respond to, and mediate conflicts so that they are more likely to be resolved by win-win solutions. If conflict has damaged a relationship, however, we can attempt to repair it by seeking and granting forgiveness, for which apologizing is usually a prerequisite.

The anonymity of digital communication has increased the capacity for heated and often unproductive exchanges through social media—in blogs, emails, and through social networking sites. Flaming is hostile communication online, including insults, profanity, and other offensive language. Strategies for responding to flaming include responding privately, ignoring the flame, responding in ways that non-flamers can support, and asking an authority to intervene. Cyberbullying is engaging in repeated negative actions toward another person online, and cyberstalking is a variation of cyberbullying that involves digital "shadowing" and harassment. Important steps to take in response to cyberbullying and cyberstalking are not responding, gathering evidence, blocking, and reporting to authorities.

CHAPTER RESOURCES

Key Words

Flashcards for all of these key terms are available on the *Inter-Act* website.

Accommodating, pp. 323
Collaborating, pp. 324
Competing, pp. 323
Compromising, pp. 324
Counterblaming, pp. 329
Cross-complaining, pp. 330
Cyberbullying, pp. 342
Cyberstalking, pp. 344
Demand-withdrawal, pp. 330
Ego conflict, pp. 320

Face, pp. 326
Face negotiation theory, pp. 326
Fact conflict, pp. 320
Flaming, pp. 341
Forgiveness, pp. 339
Ground rules, pp. 331
Interpersonal conflict, pp. 318
Mediator, pp. 338
Meta conflict, pp. 321
Mutual hostility, pp. 331

Other-face orientation, pp. 327
Policy conflict, pp. 320
Principle of negative reciprocity, pp. 328
Pseudo conflict, pp. 320
Self-construal, pp. 328
Self-face orientation, pp. 326
Serial arguing, pp. 329
Value conflict, pp. 320
Withdrawing, pp. 322

Analyze and Apply

The following activities challenge you to demonstrate your mastery of the concepts, theories, and frameworks in this chapter by using them to explain what is happening in a specific situation.

11.1 Rewind/Rewrite

Now that you have read the chapter, hit "rewind" on the opening dialogue between Keisha, Sasha, and Tara and answer the following questions.

a. Use concepts from the chapter to explain the conflict between the sorority sisters. Policy and ego conflict, competing, self-face orientation, and the principle of negative reciprocity may be especially useful.

b. Rewrite how the dialogue could have unfolded if the sorority sisters had employed better conflict management skills.

c. Assume that Keisha and Tara ask Sasha to help them resolve their ongoing conflict with each other so that planning for future events goes more smoothly. What will Sasha need to do to be successful as a mediator? Or, using skills from Chapter 10, how might Keisha and Sasha approach Mrs. B. for help getting better food for the juniors?

11.2 Inter-Action Dialogue: Interpersonal Conflict

Interpersonal influence occurs when one person attempts to change another person's attitudes or behaviors. As you read the following dialogue, do a line-by-line analysis of this conversation and indicate where you see evidence of the participants' showing types of conflict, styles of managing conflict, and skills that promote successful conflict management. You can watch a video of this conversation on the Inter-Act website and use a form provided to write down your own analysis of the conversation.

DIALOGUE

Brian and Matt share an apartment. Matt is consistently late in paying his share of expenses. Brian has tolerated this for over six months, but he has finally had enough and decides to confront Matt.

Brian: Matt, I need to talk with you.

Matt: What's up?

Brian: Well, I have a problem. When I got home from class today, I tried to call my mom, and guess what? The phone's been disconnected.

Matt: You're kidding.

Brian: No, I'm not. And when I went next door and called the phone company, you know what they said?

Matt: I can guess.

Brian: They said the bill hadn't been paid and that this was the fourth month in a row that it was over two weeks late.

Matt: Look, man, I can explain.

Brian: Like you explained not paying the utility bill on time last month? We were just lucky that it was a cool week and that we didn't fry without air conditioning. The candlelit dinner was charming and all that, but I really resented having to go to the library to study for my test. Matt, I just can't go on like this. I mean, I gave you my share of the phone bill three weeks ago. I always give you my half of the utility bill the day it arrives. And I'm sick and tired of having to nag you for your share of the rent. For the last four months I've had to cover your share by taking money out of what I am saving to buy Angie's engagement ring. I know that you eventually pay me back, but I lose the interest, and it's just not fair.

Matt: Gosh, I didn't know that you were so upset. I mean, it's not like I don't pay. I always make good, don't I?

Brian: Yes, so far that's true, but every month it's later and later before you pay me back. And I'm not a lending agency. Why do you expect me to loan you money each month? We work at the same place, make the same money, and we've both got the same expenses. If I can come up with the rent and other expenses on time, you can, too.

Matt: Listen, I apologize about the phone bill. I thought I'd mailed it. So, I'll check it out with the phone company tomorrow morning. And the utility bill was just a mistake. I lost the bill and didn't realize it hadn't been paid. I know that I've not always had the money for the rent when you asked, but you usually ask me for it a week or more before it's due. You are really good at saving ahead, but I'm not. You say we have the same expenses, but that's not true. I have a car loan and you don't. And since I got that ticket last year, my car insurance has skyrocketed. Some months I'm living really close to the edge. I know it's no excuse, but I want you to understand that I'm not just some deadbeat who's trying to leech off of you.

Brian: Matt, I'm sorry that I said we have similar expenses. You're right. Yours are higher. And if I understood you correctly, our problems with the utility company and the phone company weren't caused by you not having the money but were because somehow the bills just slipped through the cracks?

Matt: Yeah. I'm never very organized, but right now things are chaos. Between work, school, and the stuff that's going on with my family, I don't know if I'm coming or going.

Brian: Well, I can understand that you are under a lot of pressure. And I hope you can understand that when you don't pay bills on time, it's not just you that suffers. Angie and I want to buy a house before we get married, so I'm really careful about paying bills on time so that I have a good credit rating. That's why I ask you for the rent so early. When you forget to pay the utility and phone bills, not only do we lose service, but since both of our names are on the bill, we both take a hit in our credit ratings. A poor credit rating will make it harder for me to get a loan. And it also will make it harder for you to get credit later. I know that you wouldn't intentionally do anything to hurt me, but the fact is, you have.

Matt: Whoa, I never really thought about it this way. Gee, I'm sorry.

Brian: Apology accepted. So how can we work this out?

Matt: Well, you seem to have thought more about it than I have. Do you have any ideas?

Brian: Yeah, as a matter of fact, a couple of alternatives come to mind. One, we could agree on a date each month to sit down and pay the bills together. That way, I'd know that the bills had been written and sent, and you could control my tendency to bug you for your half of the rent before it really needs to be sent. Or, with each paycheck, we could each put a certain amount into a joint account. Then when the bills come in I would just write the checks out of that account, and you wouldn't have to bother with it at all.

Matt: Maybe we could do a combination of those things.

Brian: What do you mean?

Matt: Well, I don't want to totally turn control over to you. I mean, I really need to learn how to be responsible for getting stuff done on time. But I'm really jammed for time right now. So how about if we set the date for paying the bills but also set up the joint account? That way, if something comes up, and I don't have the time to sit down with you and pay the bills, you can still get them done on time. But when I do have time, we can do it together. I think I can probably learn some good budgeting habits from you.

Brian: That's fine as long as you put in your share each pay period. I actually enjoy managing my personal finances, and I'd be glad to show you what I do. It may not work for you, but you might get some ideas that you can adapt to your style. In any case, I'm glad we talked. I was getting close to the breaking point with you, and now I'm feeling like things are going to be okay. So when can we get together for our bill-paying date and when should we set up the joint account?

11.3 Identifying Types of Conflict

Label the following conflicts as S (pseudo conflict), F (fact conflict), V (value conflict), P (policy conflict), E (ego conflict), or M (meta conflict). Then explain why you categorized each as you did.

_____ a. Joe wants to live with Mary, but Mary wants the two of them to get married.

_____ b. Stan believes that because he is an insurance salesman, Jerry should not dispute his position on annuities.

_____ c. George defends his failure to present an anniversary gift to Agnes by asserting that their anniversary is not today, May 8, but May 18.

_____ d. Martin calls to announce that he is bringing the boss home for dinner. His wife replies, "That will be impossible. The house is too messy to be seen, and I have nothing good enough in the fridge to serve guests."

_____ e. Jane says, "Harry, pick up your clothes. I'm not your maid!" Harry replies, "I thought we agreed that it's your job to take care of the house. I take care of the yard."

_____ f. When Jill and Vince argue about their finances, Vince gets agitated, raising his voice and essentially drowning Jill out. She responds by criticizing him for being domineering.

Answers: a., V; b., E; c., F; d., S; e., P; f., M

Skill Practice

Skill practice activities give you the chance to rehearse a new skill by responding to hypothetical or real situations. Additional skill practice activities are available at the companion Inter-Act website.

11.4 Initiating a Conflict

For each situation below, prepare a message that would effectively initiate a conflict.

a. _You observe your longtime romantic partner flirting with another person. Your partner's arm is around this person's waist, and they are laughing and periodically whispering in each other's ear._

Initiating Message:

b. _Your roommate borrowed your iPod and returned it late last night. You put it on your desk without really looking at it. This morning when you grab it to listen to at the gym, you notice that the display is cracked. You are certain it was not this way before your roommate borrowed it._

Initiating Message:

c. _Halfway through your shift, your manager calls you into the office to inform you that someone has called in sick and that you will have to stay until closing. You have a test tomorrow and need to study._

Initiating Message:

11.5 Responding to a Conflict

For each situation below, prepare a response that would move the conflict toward a collaboration.

a. *"I saw you yesterday, and boy, were you enjoying yourself. So I hope you really had fun because it's over between you and me. You can't cheat on me and expect me to take it."*

   Your Response:

b. *"I can't believe that you broke my iPod and then didn't have the guts to tell me."*

   Your Response:

c. *"There's no way I'm staying late again to close the store. You never even consider the fact that some of us have other things to do besides cover for you."*

   Your Response:

11.6 Apologizing

For each of the following situations, create an effective apology message.

a. *Your longtime romantic partner caught you flirting with someone else.*

   Your apology:

b. *You borrowed your roommate's iPod and returned it without telling your roommate that you had accidently dropped it, cracking the display.*

   Your apology:

c. *You told your best employee to stay until closing tonight because someone else could not make it to work. Although you didn't intend to anger your employee, you are afraid that this person is upset enough to quit.*

   Your apology:

Communication Improvement Plan: Conflict Management

Would you like to improve the following aspects of your conflict resolving behaviors, as discussed in this chapter?

- Initiating conflict

- Responding to conflict

- Mediating the conflicts of others

- Apologizing

Pick an aspect, and write a communication improvement plan. You can find a communication improvement plan worksheet on our website at www.oup.com/us/verderber.

COMMUNICATING IN INTIMATE RELATIONSHIPS: Long-Term Romantic Relationships, Family, and Friends

Josh and Sara have been married for six months. Both graduated from the same college and have good jobs. They are happy, but are beginning to realize that they have some differences when it comes to their immediate goals. Josh feels that his career is going well and wants to start a family right away, but Sara wants to get a promotion before having children. She has been working extra hours to impress her supervisor, whom Josh dislikes. This issue comes up over brunch with Josh's parents, Wes and Mauve.

Mauve (teasingly): So . . . I hear we may be waiting on our grandbabies a bit longer.

Sara (sighs and frowns at Josh): Well, yes, for a bit. I'd like to be earning more money before we start a family.

Wes (proudly): Josh makes a good salary. He can provide.

Josh: Thanks, Dad. That's what I keep saying.

Mauve: Yes, we raised Josh to know what his responsibilities are. My son puts family first.

Sara (quiet, but frustrated): Within a year or so I hope to be promoted, and then I'll feel comfortable starting a family.

Josh (petulant): I don't see the need to wait. Our friends are all starting their families now. And I don't like you having to butter up your boss!

(Continued)

351

Sara (irritated): It's not your career. How much leave are you going to take when the baby comes?

Wes (grumbling): Mauve stayed home with our kids. That's why they turned out so well.

Mauve (trying to soothe): Sara, you know we're always there to help if you need anything.

WHAT YOU SHOULD BE ABLE _TO EXPLAIN_ AFTER YOU HAVE STUDIED THIS CHAPTER:

▶ The characteristics of intimate relationships and interactions

▶ The characteristics of successful long-term romantic relationships

▶ The challenges in long-term romantic relationships

▶ Types of attachment and their implications for relationships

▶ Parenting styles and patterns of family communication

▶ Patterns of communication between siblings and across generations

▶ Three ways to improve family communication

▶ Communication skills that are especially important in friendships

▶ The influence of gender and sexual interest on friendships

▶ The dark side of intimate relationships

▶ Media multiplexity and hyperpersonal relationships

WHAT YOU SHOULD BE ABLE _TO DO_ AFTER YOU HAVE STUDIED THIS CHAPTER:

▶ Express gratitude and praise more effectively

P eople, it seems, are designed to be in relationships. We begin to understand the importance of relationships in infancy and early childhood, through interactions with our parents and other family members. As we grow older, we develop friendships and eventually romantic relationships. The closest of these relationships provide us with a "safe harbor." Here, we find support for our goals, comfort when things go wrong, and celebration for our successes. Yet even the closest relationships can be challenging. No matter how close you are to another person, you will still have some differences—in your ideas, goals, and ways of doing things. Effective communication helps manage these differences and keep relationships satisfying.

In this chapter, we will explore the role that communication plays in intimate relationships. We begin this chapter by exploring the concept of intimacy, what makes interactions and relationships intimate. The remainder of the chapter is devoted to understanding three types of intimate relationships: long-term romantic relationships, family, and friends. Our discussion will explain how communication can foster intimacy, relational satisfaction, and personal growth for the people involved in these types of relationships. We will also discuss difficulties that can arise in intimate relationships and suggest how these might be handled.

Intimate relationships—close relationships that have highly interdependent partners who are committed to each other, understand and trust one another deeply, and disclose in depth as well as breadth

Intimate Relationships and Interactions

You will recall that relationships vary in interdependence, commitment, understanding, trust, and self-disclosure. **Intimate relationships** are those that involve highly interdependent partners who are committed to each other, understand and trust each other deeply, and disclose in depth as well as breadth. We also learned in Chapter 6 that communication in relationships is both constitutive and indexical, which means that messages exchanged in a relationship make the relationship what it is, and also "take its temperature," or indicate how healthy the relationship is. Intimate relationships are constituted by repeated **intimate interactions**, series of conversations between partners that nurture interdependence, commitment, understanding, trust, and disclosure. For example, Jolie and Dylan are best friends. Their continued intimacy is created through their conversations where they plan activities together, their referencing the other as "my best friend" when talking with others, and sharing deeply personal information with each other. How frequently and consistently they talk in these ways provides an "index" for them and others as to how intimate their relationship is.

While intimate relationships require *repeated* intimate interactions, we can have an intimate interaction with someone and not have an intimate relationship. Consider the stranger on the airplane who discloses some deep problem, and you respond with supportive messages and then reciprocate by revealing a personal problem for which you receive this person's support. Once the flight is over, you go your separate ways, having had an intimate interaction. But if you never see the person again, you don't really have a relationship, let alone an intimate one. Similarly, not every interaction in an intimate relationship displays or contributes to feelings of intimacy. If Clarissa and her husband have a conversation for the purpose of making up their weekly grocery list, the conversation itself probably won't increase their intimacy. A long-term intimate relationship built on repeated intimate conversations can, and often does, withstand periods without them. For example, Sonia and Chas were best friends in high school, but when they became adults, their jobs and families took them to opposite ends of the country. They don't speak or see each other often, but they do communicate on Facebook, and get together once or twice a year. On Facebook, status updates and brief chats help them maintain a sense of connection, but when they are together they renew the intimacy of their relationship by disclosing intensely about their lives, goals, disappointments, and dreams. Without these opportunities to periodically talk face-to-face, they would most likely lose a sense of connection, and their relationship would become less intimate.

With this introduction to intimate relationships and interactions in mind, let's now turn our attention to understanding communication processes in three types of close relationships: marriages and long-term romantic relationships, family relationships, and friendships.

Intimate interactions—series of conversations between the partners that nurture interdependence, commitment, understanding, trust, and disclosure

▶ **OBSERVE AND ANALYZE**

Social Media in Intimate Relationships

How does your use of social media affect your intimate relationships? Review your emails, texts, and tweets for a recent three-day period, noting the percentage of each type of message you sent to and received from intimates. Analyze each message sequence to determine whether these interactions themselves can be classified as intimate. Did the intimate messages display all or some of the characteristics of intimate interactions? How would you characterize the mediated exchanges that were not intimate? Were they designed to share time and activities, or to communicate directions and requests? For each of the intimate partners you conversed with using social media, list the number of face-to-face conversations you also had during this time. Were these conversations more or less intimate than your mediated exchanges? What conclusions can you draw from this analysis?

Long-Term Romantic Relationships

Romantic relationships are those in which partners are sexually attracted to each other. We define **long-term romantic relationships (LTRRs)** as enduring romantic relationships that are intimate and in which partners have made some type of long-term commitment to each other. These include people who are engaged, co-habiting, "apart, together" in long-distance romantic relationships, and married. Despite declining rates of marriage in the United States, 85–90% of Americans are still projected to marry at some point in their lives (Cherlin, 2009). So, while singlehood is increasingly recognized as a positive, healthy choice (DePaulo, 2009), the majority of us will seek LTRRs to fulfill our needs for love, companionship, support, and sexual fulfillment. These relationships also provide the foundation for other important relationships, such as those with children, parents, in-laws, and close friends. Let's take a look at what characterizes successful LTRRs.

Long-term romantic relationships (LTRRs)—enduring romantic relationships that are intimate and where the partners have made some type of long-term commitment to each other

Characteristics of Successful Long-Term Romantic Relationships

What is the secret to a long and happy intimate romantic relationship? In an effort to answer what many consider to be the most important question about LTRRs, researchers have identified three common characteristics of married couples that have stayed together for more than fifty years (Dickson, 1995). We think that these characteristics apply not only to marriages, but also to other LTRRs.

1. Mutual respect. Respect is showing regard or consideration for your partner, that person's point of view, and that person's rights. Mutual respect occurs when both partners consistently are considerate of each other, value each other's views (especially when they differ), and honor and protect the legal and moral rights of the other. The "Learn About Yourself" activity in this chapter measures your respect for one of your partners.

2. Presence of a shared plan or life vision. The second characteristic of successful LTRRs is the presence of a shared plan or life vision. Successful LTRRs are based on mutual long-term goals in which partners picture each other as having a central role. Most couples will have periodic discussions of their shared plans, agreeing to modify them when circumstances change. Other couples may arrive at shared life plans or modify them without much discussion. One indication that a couple has a shared plan is when they discuss the future and talk about "we" and "us" rather than "I" or "me."

3. Comfortable level of closeness. Partners in LTRRs experience a comfortable level of closeness

Do you want a relationship that lasts a lifetime? How will you make that happen?

Take this short survey to learn something about yourself and your feelings about a partner in an intimate relationship. Answer the questions honestly based on your first response. There are no right or wrong answers. For each statement, select one of the numbers to the right that best describes your feelings.

_____ 1. My partner is trustworthy.
_____ 2. My partner fosters a relationship of mutual care.
_____ 3. My partner shows interest in me.
_____ 4. My partner is sensitive and considerate of my feelings.
_____ 5. My partner provides unconditional love.
_____ 6. My partner is open and receptive.
_____ 7. My partner is honest and truthful.
_____ 8. My partner fosters good two-way communication.
_____ 9. My partner is committed to me.
_____10. My partner is understanding and empathic.

1 = Always
2 = Often
3 = Sometimes
4 = Rarely
5 = Never

This is a test of your level of respect for a partner.

Scoring the Survey: Add the scores together for all ten questions. The score will range from 10 to 50.

The lower your score (closer to 10), the more you feel respect for your relationship partner. The higher your score (closer to 50), the less respect you feel for your relationship partner.

Adapted from Frei, J. R., & Shaver, P. R. (2002). Respect in close relationships: Prototype definition, self-report assessment, and initial correlates. *Personal Relationships, 9,* 121–139.

when they are satisfied with the amount and quality of their romantic encounters, affection displays, and time they spend together. The frequency of sexual activity and public displays of affection that are comfortable differ from couple to couple and over time with a single couple. Some couples like to be together constantly, whereas others are comfortable spending more time apart. Whatever level of closeness a couple is experiencing, what is important is not the amount of romance, sex, displays of affection, and time spent together, but whether both partners are satisfied with what is happening. However, because of relationship dialectics, closeness levels vary throughout LTRRs. Newer relationships are usually more intensely close, while longer relationships alternate through periods of intense closeness and periods of distance. However, successful couples are those who maintain mutually satisfying levels intimacy, affection, and sexuality over the long haul.

Challenges in Long-Term Romantic Relationships

Unfortunately, not all long-term romantic relationships will be satisfying and happy. Too often, communication problems lead to misunderstandings, conflicts, unhappiness, breakups, and divorces. If you are or have been in a long-term romantic relationship, you probably already recognize the importance of key communication skills like listening, providing emotional support, and managing conflict. In this section, we identify four challenges commonly experienced in long-term romantic relationships and the role that communication plays in each. These challenges are: maintaining intimacy; managing life transitions; negotiating an equitable distribution of work; and sustaining affection and desire.

Maintaining Intimacy

When you are falling in love with another person, you may think about them constantly, get a lot of pleasure from doing things to please them, and feel eager to share personal feelings and history. As relationships mature, it is not unusual for couples to begin taking their relationships and partners more "for granted." In one respect, this is a normal outgrowth of commitment. When Jamie and Chris were dating, forwarding funny YouTube videos, bringing each other flowers on Friday night, and sharing both painful and happy childhood memories were ways of saying "I want us to be together." Now that they have been living together for five years, however, they no longer feel the need to "court" each other. So they may become unconcerned about demonstrating their commitment. Yet, research on intimacy in LTRRs shows that commitment and satisfaction in a relationship will depend on continuing interactions and behaviors that demonstrate devotion. **Relational maintenance** is exchanging messages or behaving in ways that keep a relationship at a desired level of intimacy, satisfaction, and health (Dindia & Canary, 1993). So, when Jamie sends Chris flowers once a month to celebrate their first date, the flowers are a reminder of when everything was exciting and new in their relationship. At the same time, Jamie is assuring Chris that, even after five years of being together, Jamie still treasures the relationship.

People in LTRRs say and do many different kinds of things to maintain the intimacy in their relationships (Stafford, 2011). These include:

- Demonstrating positivity—optimistic, encouraging, and affirming messages and behaviors. Example: "Thank you for taking out the garbage, I know it was my turn. You're the best."
- Expressing assurance—messages and behaviors that express confidence and belief in the partner and the relationship. Example: "I know that if we try we'll be able to save enough money to get tickets to the concert."
- Continuing self-disclosure. Example: "Today at work, Jena was flirting with me. And I confess, it was tempting. Then I realized what I would be putting at risk and just ignored her."
- Demonstrating understanding—paraphrasing and supportive messages and behaviors. Example: "I can understand why you'd be tempted, and I'm glad you did what you did."

Relational maintenance—exchanging messages or behaving in ways that keep a relationship at a desired level of intimacy, satisfaction, and health

- Talking about the relationship—interactions devoted to discussing the state of the relationship. Example: "We've been together for five years, and while we've had some rough spots, I'm so glad you are still willing to put up with me."
- Integrating social networks—continuing to include the partner in interactions with one's colleagues, friends, and family. Example: "Hey, Amari, and Sasha—on my volleyball team—are having a cookout for all of us. I hope you haven't got something else planned because I'd love everyone to meet you."
- Task sharing—messages about how work is to be shared as well as engaging in joint work. Example: "I was thinking that since you're taking a full load at school and working part-time that I should take more responsibility for cooking."

Relational maintenance messages and behavior can be either routine or strategic. **Routine relational maintenance** happens when messages and behaviors that are performed without any deliberate intention to affect the relationship have the effect of preserving the intimacy. Rory and Jordan may do dishes together every night (an example of "task sharing") after dinner because they started doing it as newlyweds in a tiny apartment with no dishwasher. Neither of them is consciously trying to make their relationship better. Yet, by performing this chore together, they not only keep their kitchen clean, they also spend time in each other's company, which makes a space for routine conversations and, more importantly, for openness. **Strategic relational maintenance** happens when messages and behaviors are deliberately performed in order to maintain the level of intimacy in the relationship. After a heated argument, Quinn may make Val's favorite brownies in order to restore better feeling between them.

Both routine and strategic relational maintenance contribute to commitment and satisfaction in intimate relationships. Research suggests that positivity, assurances, and networking are especially beneficial to relationships (Ramierez, 2008). However, different kinds of maintenance are suited to specific partners, relationships, or circumstances. For example, although Hayden would prefer to stay home and work in the garden, Hayden accompanies Riley to out-of-state triathlons two or three times a year, providing emotional and practical support. Hayden's presence at the triathlons means a great deal to Riley because Riley knows that gardening is Hayden's primary way of relaxing, and instead of staying home, Hayden chooses to support Riley in this way. Even the simple act of viewing television can be transformed into relational maintenance when couples choose to watch the same show together, talk about topics prompted by the show, or work at joint tasks together (like folding the wash) while watching (Yoshimura & Alberts, 2008).

When you are fortunate enough to have a partner talk or behave in ways meant to maintain intimacy in your relationship, you can thank them through simple messages or reciprocal behaviors. One study confirmed that when you thank others for the things they do for you, they feel appreciated, and consequently are more likely to continue doing positive things (Grant & Gino, 2010).

Routine relational maintenance—messages and behaviors that are performed without any deliberate intention to affect the relationship but have the effect of preserving intimacy

Strategic relational maintenance—messages and behaviors are deliberately performed in order to maintain the level of intimacy in the relationship

In LTRRs, people who feel more appreciated by their romantic partners are more appreciative of their partners in turn, more responsive to their partners' needs, and more committed to their relationships (Gordon, Impett, Kogan, Oveis, Keltner, & 2012). But expressing gratitude and praising others is a skill. It begins by noticing the positive things that your partner does or says. In all likelihood, your romantic partner has done something recently that has helped to maintain your relationship. It might have been a small, routine behavior, like paying the bills or checking that all the doors are locked at bedtime. But it may have been more substantial, like forgoing a night out with friends to spend time with you. When you notice something for which you're grateful, the following guidelines can help you effectively praise your partner and demonstrate your gratitude: (1) describe specifically what the person said or did, (2) explain why that makes you grateful, (3) describe how you feel, and (4) allow your partner to respond to your message; don't immediately change the subject. You can increase the impact of your gratitude by writing your partner a thank-you note, sharing how grateful you are with others in front of your partner, or by reciprocating with your own words or actions. While we should express our gratitude when someone does something nice for us, we can also use the same skills to praise an action that does not directly affect us.

Managing Life Transitions

Life transitions—major events that not only affect one partner, but also require adaptation within the relationship

During LTRRs, partners can expect to encounter **life transitions**, or major events that not only affect one partner, but also require adaptation within the relationship. During transitions, how well partners communicate can make the difference between the relationship's thriving or dying. Transitions can be planned or unplanned, positive or negative, and created inside or outside the relationship. For example, imagine a couple has planned to have a baby, only to discover that one or both of them are infertile. What kinds of strains will that put on the

---

SKILL BUILDER ▶ **EXPRESSING GRATITUDE AND PRAISE**

SKILL	USE	STEPS	EXAMPLE
Sincerely describing the specific positive behaviors or accomplishments of another and their positive effects	To enhance your relationship with another person by verbalizing the positive effects of his or her behavior	1. Describe specifically what the person said or did. 2. Explain why that makes you grateful or is worthy of praise. 3. Describe how you feel. 4. Allow your partner to respond. Don't immediately change the subject.	"Dakota, thank you for doing the dishes tonight. I know you are as tired as I am. I really appreciate what you did. Thank you." "I am so amazed by you, Jordan! You were so kind to the server when he spilled water on you. I'm not sure I would have been able to keep my cool."

relationship? Alternatively, what strains do partners experience when they have a new baby? Suppose that one partner's parent has been diagnosed with Alzheimer's and can no longer live alone. What kinds of strain will providing for this parent put on the relationship?

Have you ever noticed that there is more tension or conflict in your relationships when transitions occur? Relational turbulence theory (Solomon & Theiss, 2010) posits that couples confront two kinds of problems during life transitions. One of these problems is **relational uncertainty**, which is lack of confidence in the relationship itself. During transitions, couples often question each other's involvement in the relationship and even what type of relationship they ought to have. For example, infertile couples who shared the dream of having biological children may question each other's commitment to the relationship. High school sweethearts who attend different colleges may wonder whether they should stay together or break up.

A second potential problem that may arise from life transitions is **interference**, when one partner's actions or choices create obstacles for the other. If one partner in a relationship takes a promotion that requires extensive travel, the other partner may have to assume more household responsibilities. Or one partner's decision to pay for an aging parent's medical care can result in a strain on the couple's budget. It is easy to imagine how such problems can create turbulence or instability in a relationship.

Relational turbulence theory indicates that relational uncertainty, interference, and turbulence are normal byproducts of transitions. Couples experiencing transitions can reduce turbulence by managing relational uncertainty and interference. Relational uncertainty can be alleviated through direct discussion about what the relationship means to them; for example, one partner might reassure the other that infertility does not change their commitment to their union. Likewise, couples can handle interference by agreeing to new ways of doing things. A couple facing caring for a relative might explore hiring a caregiver or downsizing to a smaller home in order to afford a care facility. Neither the conversations nor the changes that occur during a transition will be easy. However, with effective listening, support, reasoning, and collaboration, couples experiencing transitions in their long-term relationships can find ways to assure each other of continued affection and fidelity, and to meet each other's needs as they adapt to the new situation.

Interestingly, some couples report increased intimacy when they have successfully weathered a relationship "storm" (Theiss & Solomon, 2008). For example, a couple who works out how to care for one partner's aging parent are likely to feel pride in themselves and more capable of facing future challenges.

Relational uncertainty—lack of confidence in a relationship

Interference—the actions or choices of one partner that create obstacles for the other

Negotiating Equitable Distribution of Work

When people combine their living arrangements, finances, or responsibilities, this increase in interdependence creates opportunities for a better quality of life—as well as opportunities for disappointment, frustration, and conflict. Historically, in opposite sex long-term relationships, work was divided. Men were the more dominant partners, making most of the major decisions and having primary responsibility for the family finances, which they met by working outside the home. Women were more submissive, made fewer of the major decisions for the family, and were responsible for making a home and raising children. Relationships based on these separate role definitions still exist.

Today, in the United States, many women have careers that are of equal or greater status than those of their male counterparts. As a result of more women being in the workforce, there are more dual-income households, and co-habiting couples often share financial responsibilities. In this context, we would expect that decision-making and household chores should also be shared. Unfortunately, research suggests that this is not yet the reality for many couples. The norms of traditional marriages still permeate opposite sex long-term relationships. Even when women's careers and salaries are similar to those of their male partners, men continue to assume fewer responsibilities at home doing, on average, one-third of the household labor (LaChance-Grzela & Bouchard, 2010). Unfortunately, the pattern of inequity experienced in opposite sex relationships often intensifies when couples have children. Large-scale studies show that young women often experience a significant decline in satisfaction with their marriages after children are born, linked to unfair distributions of housework (and decreased leisure time with their husbands; Dew & Wilcox, 2011). Successful couples periodically talk about rebalancing shared household responsibilities so that each partner perceives equity in this facet of the relationship. Because each relationship is unique, each couple's allocation of tasks differs. Dwayne and

How do your parents divide household labor? How will you negotiate this with your life partner?

Cassandra may alternate cleaning the kitchen after dinner, while Allie and Noah handle kitchen clean-up together, and Anya always does the kitchen, trading off this chore with Jean-Paul for cleaning the bathrooms and washing the car.

Couples concerned about sustaining their relationships and supporting each other should have continuing conversations about the distribution of financial, household, and childcare responsibilities. The goal should be to achieve an **egalitarian relationship** where partners agree to what each will contribute to their shared life and that their individual contributions are equally valued (based on Steil, 2000, p. 128). Ongoing conversations about these issues require disclosure, feedback, collaboration, and negotiation, along with patience and commitment as partners adjust to changes. For example, while their children were young, Fran stayed home while Brad worked as an electrical contractor. During this time, Fran shopped, chauffeured the kids, kept house, and did the laundry, while Brad cooked dinner, did the yard work, paid the bills, and coached the kids' sports teams. Once the youngest child was in elementary school, Fran resumed her career, which required several days of out-of-town travel each month. Therefore, the couple rebalanced their household responsibilities. They decided that Brad would take over day-to-day chauffeuring and laundry. And on Saturday morning, Fran would clean up the house, while Brad did yard work. They also assigned daily and weekly chores to the children, based on age. The fairness and equity in egalitarian relationships contributes to happiness, contentment, stability, as well as relationship and sexual satisfaction (Hatfield, Rapson, & Aumer-Ryan, 2008).

> Egalitarian relationship—a relationship where partners agree to what each will contribute to their shared life and that their individual contributions are equally valued

Sustaining Affection and Desire

Affectionate communication expresses feelings of fondness and "intense positive regard" for another person (Floyd & Deiss, 2012). Some affectionate communication is nonverbal, such as kissing, hugging, touching, and smiling. Other affectionate communication is expressed through verbal messages that convey our positive emotion toward another person ("I love you" or "You make me so happy"), assurances of relationship commitment ("BFF!"), compliments, and gratitude or praise. Using idioms, expressions that are only meaningful to the couple, can also show affection. For example, when Ian does something that Gina finds peculiar and humorous but endearing, she smiles, points at him and says, "Awk-weird." To them this combination of "awkward" and "weird" means "You're odd, but I love you."

Your own experiences will tell you that affection "feels good," but research shows that giving and receiving more affectionate communication has benefits that range from greater happiness and self-esteem to reductions in blood pressure, cortisol (a stress hormone), and pain. In one study, one group of people in married and co-habiting (living together) relationships were told to kiss more over a six-week period, while another group received no instructions. At the end of the six weeks, the kissing group reported less stress and more relational satisfaction—and had healthier cholesterol levels (Floyd, Boren, et al., 2009). When you choose to kiss, gently touch, or smile at your significant other, share a private joke, comment on something positive the other person has done, or just say, "Hey . . . I love you! And I like you, too!" you are adding funds to what noted marriage scholar John Gottman has called your "emotional bank account." Affection exchange theory (Floyd, 2006) suggests showing affection is biologically adaptive for the human species because it sustains relationships necessary for reproduction and the survival of the species.

In long-term romantic relationships, partners also express affection through their sexual encounters. Extensive research indicates that in marriages and other LTRRs, sexual satisfaction is closely connected with love, relationship satisfaction, and commitment to the relationship (Sprecher, Christopher, & Cate, 2006). This finding probably doesn't surprise you, since good sex can be both physically and emotionally rewarding. Sex with a stranger may be physically satisfying as well, but most people agree that the most emotionally rewarding sex is experienced within intimate LTRRs.

Like most everything else in a relationship, couples can improve their sexual satisfaction through their communication during and outside of sexual encounters. One recent study found that people who used more nonverbal behavior to show pleasure during sex also reported more sexual satisfaction (Babin, 2013). Although even people in LTRRs may find it embarrassing to talk about sex, partners who talk about their likes and dislikes increase their sexual confidence and enjoyment (Faulkner & Lanutti, 2010). It's important for partners to tell each other what the other does that adds to or detracts from each's pleasure, and share what each enjoys doing or would prefer not to do. For example, Louisette might say to Evan, "I really like how slow you take it. I know it takes effort, but it makes me feel loved, not used." Similarly, Raquel might tell Oscar, "Hey, I know you're trying to make it great for me, but for whatever reason, playing with my ears just doesn't do much for me. If you nibbled on my neck, though. . . ." While the amount of sexual activity a couple engages in changes over time, most LTRRs need satisfying sexual encounters to thrive. Developing good communication about their sexual relationships also helps couples manage their changing needs.

Families

Families are also a place where we can experience intimate relationships. Traditionally, when people thought of a family, they generally were referring to opposite-sex married parents living with one or more of their children, and possibly with other biological relatives as well. Over time, the concept of family has changed. In 2015 the Supreme Court of The United States extended civil marriage and all of its benefits to include same-sex adults. A 2008 study found that married couples represented just 48 percent of American households (Pew Research Center, 2010). And although the term "family" is often thought of as including children, approximately 5 percent of married couples experience infertility, while other couples elect to remain childless. Nevertheless, these couples still consider themselves a family. Table 12.1 lists a variety of family configurations that are common to the United States.

TABLE 12.1 Common Family Structures

Traditional family: Family consisting of a man and a woman who are married and living with one or more children from their union.

Single-parent family: Family in which one parent lives with the children; the other is not present in the home and may or may not be actively parenting the children.

Shared-custody family: Family in which the parents have divorced; the children live alternately with each parent.

Blended family: Family consisting of two adults and one or more children, some of whom were born to those parents in previous relationships.

Common-law family: Family consisting of unmarried opposite-sex partners living with the children of their union.

Modern Family: Family consisting of two adults who are raising their children.

Extended family: Family consisting of multiple generations of related people living together.

Communal family: Family of unmarried people related by non-genetic factors who participate in a cooperative living arrangement.

Today, **family** can be defined as "a self-defined group of intimates who create and maintain themselves through their own interactions and their interactions with others; a family may include both voluntary and involuntary relationships; it creates both literal and symbolic internal and external boundaries, and it evolves through time" (Turner & West, 2013, p. 9). In other words, as people go through their lives, they create their families with various blood, legal, and emotional ties. They decide who is included in the family and who is not, and over time these choices may change.

Historically, families have been thought of as being anchored by an opposite-sex couple. But as prejudice declines and legal obstacles are diminished, families headed by same-sex partners are becoming increasingly visible (Suter, 2014). Even so, these families are more "discourse dependent" than the families of opposite-sex couples (Galvin & Patrick, 2009), meaning that they are especially reliant on communication to define themselves as a family, and defend themselves from attacks (Koenig-Kellas & Suter, 2012). As discussed in the "Diverse Voices" article, "Performing Commitment" by Jacqueline Taylor, this is especially true for same-sex families living in communities where they cannot legally marry or form a civil union.

In this section, we focus on parent–child communication because the quality of this type of interaction influences not only how the child relates to others during childhood, but also has lasting effects on the capacity of the child to form healthy adult relationships. In addition, we touch on communication in sibling relationships, and those of grandparents and grandchildren. We conclude the section with recommendations for improving communication in families.

Family—a self-defined group of intimates who create and maintain themselves through their own interactions and their interactions with others

Parent–Child Communication

Parent–child relationships are the most formative relationships in the lives of children. These relationships usually begin at birth and typically continue until

Performing Commitment

BY JACQUELINE TAYLOR

Families are structured in different ways. In this excerpt, the author describes how mundane daily activities as well as rituals and public ceremonies serve as performances of commitment in her family.

For over 13 years I have created family within the context of my commitment to Carol, my partner and longtime companion. The law says we are not a couple, but two single women. No church or state has blessed or ratified our union. Although our property and our finances are by this time as entwined as our hearts and lives, the state does not apply its joint-property laws to us or give us the right to inherit from each other in the absence of a will. I cannot include her on the family insurance benefits my university offers. The only place we can purchase a family membership is at the women's bookstore.

Eight years ago we became mothers together, with the adoption of our first daughter, Lucy. One year later we adopted Grace. The law recognized us not as one family, but as two—two single mothers living in the same house with our two adopted children. No blood ties unite any of the four of us. We are a family not because but in spite of the social and legal structures that refuse to name us so. Because our status as a family has been ignored or denied by the laws and customs of our society, our existence as a family can never be taken for granted but must be constantly created and recreated. That our family differs in some significant ways from conventional notions of what constitutes a family means that our creation of family must simultaneously affirm and critique familial structures. . . .

The process of knitting ourselves into a family has taken years and has been characterized more by daily and, yes, mundane performances of commitment than by rituals and ceremonies. Yet we have also participated in public rituals that have helped us to construct ourselves.

The arrival of our babies was greeted by four different showers thrown by friends. Each of our

death. Consequently, parents and children interact across a great deal of developmental change, and the nature of children's early interaction with their parents has profound effects on their emotional well-being, ability to form healthy relationships later in life, and children's own communication behaviors.

Effects of Early Attachment

Children, and the adults they become, understand and carry out relationships with others based on their earliest interactions with their parents and other adult caregivers. At birth, infants need their parents and caregivers to act as secure bases of comfort and safety. In other words, they need nurturing. Infants whose needs for nurturing are consistently met develop a **secure attachment**—strong, healthy emotional bonds with their parents and caregivers. This type of attachment teaches them to believe that they are worthy of care and that other people can be trusted to provide it. By consistently feeding ten-week-old Siobhan when she's hungry, changing her diaper, and talking softly to her while holding her

Secure attachment—a strong, healthy emotional bond between infants and their parents or caregivers based on the belief that they are worthy of care and that other people can be trusted to provide it

workplaces and two sets of friends organized parties. The various communities we participate in have worked hard to fill the gap between what the law and convention define as family and what our experience reveals. The four of us create our own rituals, as well. . . .

Carol reminds me that the most important performance of commitment is the daily care and love we give to our daughters. Parents communicate commitment every day through the constant and repetitive tasks that children's survival depends on—changing diapers, wiping up spills, kissing "owies"—and later on, supervising homework, chauffeuring to sports and music lessons, listening to their stories. For heterosexual families perhaps this is enough. But we gay and lesbian (and adoptive) families create family outside the context of the social and legal structures that allow traditional families to take themselves for granted, and so we must do more.

Thus, we have learned to use language consciously, carefully, and repetitively to define ourselves to each other and our social world. "Family" we say, over and over. "Thank you for carrying that package. You are helping our family." "This party is just for our family." "In our family, we don't hit."

Our family doesn't fit anybody's mold. But we are a family, held together by ties of love, loyalty, commitment, and daily life. Because our family does not conform to traditional definitions of family, the performances that connect us to the social fabric and to one another take on even greater importance. Through the anniversaries, ceremonies, rituals, and holidays that mark our years and the repeated mundane actions of commitment that mark our days, we perform the bonds that make us kin. . . . [F]amily is a group of people who live together and love each other, bound by their shared commitment to the health, growth, and welfare of all.

Excerpted from Taylor, J. (2002). Performing commitment. In J. N. Martin, T. K. Nakayama, & L. A. Flores (Eds.), *Readings in Intercultural Communication* (pp. 310–318). New York: McGraw-Hill.

FOR CONSIDERATION:

1. How does this article support the definition of family given in the chapter?
2. How might the changing legal landscape with regard to same-sex marriage affect premises of this article? Will married gay and lesbian couples no longer feel the need to engage in unique ritual behaviors?

tenderly, Siobhan's parents and nanny not only keep her physically healthy, but they also help her understand that she is deserving of care and teach her to view others as trustworthy. On the other hand, infants who are inconsistently nurtured are never sure whether their needs will be met. Such infants become highly attentive to the behavior of their parents or caregivers and may develop **anxious-ambivalent attachment**, anxiety stemming from worry that their needs will not be met, and ambivalence about whether others can be trusted. As these infants develop, they may come to see themselves as unworthy of nurturing. Finally, infants whose needs are consistently ignored develop **avoidant attachment**, the inability to trust others. If these babies survive such abusive treatment, they may come to reject attempts by foster parents and others to care for them. They may believe that they are worthy of care but typically view others as untrustworthy.

From infancy through childhood to adulthood, people carry these early attachment experiences with them. These become their **attachment styles**, the perceptions adults have about their self-worth and the trustworthiness of others

Anxious-ambivalent attachment—an anxiety-filled emotional bond between infants and their parents or caregivers stemming from worry that their needs will not be met and ambivalence about whether others can be trusted to care for them

Avoidant attachment—the inability of a child to emotionally bond with or trust others based on the belief that they are worthy of care but view others as untrustworthy, which results from experiencing severe neglect as an infant

Attachment styles—the perception of adults about their self-worth and the trustworthiness of others based on their relationships with their parents and caregivers during their infancy and childhood

How did your childhood interactions with parents and caregivers influence you?

Secure attachment style—the attachment style experienced by an adult who is able to easily form intimate relationships because they have high self-worth and trust others due to the secure attachments they experienced as infants and children

Dismissive attachment style—the attachment style experienced by a self-reliant and independent adult who has difficulty sustaining close relationships because, while they may have high self-worth, they don't trust others due to the avoidant attachments they experienced as infants and children

Preoccupied attachment style—the attachment style experienced by an adult who is excessively focused on how their relationship partners think about and behave toward them because they have low self-worth and high trust in others due to the anxious-ambivalent attachments they experienced as infants and children

Fearful attachment style—the attachment style experienced by an adult for whom it is difficult to form intimate relationships because they don't believe that they are worthy of a good relationship and they don't trust others to meet their relationship needs due to the anxious-ambivalent attachments they experienced as infants and children

based on their relationships with their parents and caregivers during infancy and childhood (Bartholomew & Horowitz, 1991). Infants with secure attachments to their parents and caregivers usually become adults with a **secure attachment style**. These people are able to easily form intimate relationships because they have high self-worth and trust others because of their childhood experiences. Neglected and abused infants with avoidant attachments typically become adults with a **dismissive attachment style**. These adults have high self-worth but don't often trust others. They are self-reliant and independent, but because of their inability to trust others, they can have difficulty sustaining close relationships. As adults, infants with anxious-ambivalent attachments usually develop one of two attachment styles. They may develop a **preoccupied attachment style**, which combines low self-worth with high trust in others. These adults are preoccupied with their relationships and excessively focused on how their relational partners think about and act toward them. The second adult attachment style that can evolve from anxious-ambivalent childhood attachments is known as the **fearful attachment style**, which is characterized by suffering from low self-worth and low trust in others. It is very difficult for these people to form intimate relationships, because they don't believe that they are worthy of good relationships and they don't trust others to meet their relationship needs. Fortunately, this style seems to be relatively rare.

Our attachment style influences our intimate relationships because it affects many different aspects of our communication, including how able we are to self-disclose, express our emotions, support others, and engage in other relationship-maintenance behaviors (Guerrero, Andersen, & Afifi, 2011). For example, if Skyler has a secure attachment style, she will be open about her life and her

TABLE 12.2 Attachment Styles and Communication Preferences

	Secure	Preoccupied	Fearful	Dismissive
Conflict Behavior	Most compromising and adept with problem solving	Demanding, exhibits dominating behavior, nagging, whining	Accommodating, responds passively	Withdrawing, less accommodating, more interrupting
Maintenance Behavior	Highest level of maintenance	High level of maintenance	Relatively low level of maintenance	Less maintenance overall, especially less romance and assurances
Emotional Expression	Readily expresses emotion in a direct, prosocial manner	Expresses negative emotions using aggression or passive aggression	Inhibits the expression of negative emotions	Experiences and expresses emotions (negative and positive) the least
Self-Disclosure	High levels of appropriate disclosure, able to elicit disclosure from others	High levels of disclosure that is sometimes inappropriate or indiscriminate	Low levels of disclosure, especially with strangers or acquaintances	Low levels of disclosure
Nonverbal Intimacy	Relatively high levels of facial and vocal pleasantness, laughter, touch, and smiling	Mix of positive and negative nonverbal cues, depending on the situation	Relatively low levels of facial and vocal pleasantness, expressiveness, and smiling	Relatively low levels of facial and vocal pleasantness, expressiveness, and smiling
Social Skill	Assertive, responsive to others, able to provide effective care and comfort	Overly sensitive, difficulty controlling emotional expression	Trouble expressing self and being assertive, exhibits anxiety cues such as lack of fluency and long pauses before responding	Trouble expressing self and comforting others

From Guerrero, Andersen, & Afifi, 2011, p. 171, used with permission.

emotions with her boyfriend at a relatively high but appropriate level. She will find it easy to comfort him when he needs it, and demonstrate her commitment to the relationship. Given these communication tendencies, it is not surprising that adults with secure attachment styles tend to be more satisfied with their romantic relationships than adults with other styles. This is especially true when "secures" are in relationships with other secures. Table 12.2 provides additional detail about communication behaviors associated with different attachment styles.

The type of attachment you experience in infancy can directly engender your adult attachment style, but it doesn't necessarily have to. Our relationships with our parents and other caregivers as well as our perceptions of these relationships can change throughout childhood and adolescence, revising the way we see ourselves and others (Le Poire, Shepard, & Duggan, 1999). An infant with a secure attachment might develop a preoccupied style in young adulthood if, for example, a bitter divorce causes either or both parents to become unreliable nurturers or caregivers during his adolescence. Or an abused or neglected child with an avoidant attachment might be adopted by a nurturing family who eventually instill in him the belief that others will be there for him when he needs help. The critical point is that parents' nurturing behavior communicates messages to children about their self-worth and the trustworthiness of others. The early messages of caregivers can have an enduring effect, beneficial or detrimental, on a person's ability to form satisfying relationships with others.

Parenting Styles

There are two fundamental dimensions of parents' communication with young children and adolescents: nurturing and controlling (Le Poire, 2006). **Nurturing messages**, including support, praise, affection, and attending to needs, encourage a child's physical, social, emotional, and intellectual development. **Controlling messages** are those that attempt to influence or regulate a child's behavior. When parents persuade, negotiate, discipline, and engage in conflict with their children, their messages assert parental control. Parents' messages can be both nurturing and controlling. For example, a mother who is teaching her preschooler how to hold a pencil correctly might say, "Nathan, if you move your fingers closer to the point, it will be easier to write." Her statement is controlling the child's behavior (where the pencil should be grasped) as she nurtures the child's capacity to write. There are three primary styles of parenting that differ in their approaches to nurturance and control (Baumrind, 1966, 2013).

High levels of control with low levels of nurturing characterize the **authoritarian parenting style**; order and tradition, respect, and obedience to parents is valued and reinforced through punishment. Parents expect children to unquestioningly obey rules and to respect adults. Authoritarian parents are generally unresponsive to children's efforts to reason or negotiate, even when those efforts are logical and polite. Authoritarian parental messages convey that it doesn't matter what children want, parents know best, and children should do as they are told. Authoritarian parents also express little affection, empathy, or support for their children.

The **permissive parenting style** is characterized by moderate to high levels of nurturing but little control over children's behavior. Creativity and freedom are valued, rules and demands are few, and children generally get what they want. On those few occasions when parents try to get children to do something or to stop misbehaving, they generally employ coercive strategies such as guilt ("Don't hit Carl. You don't want Mommy to get a bad headache, do you?") or diversion ("Stop hitting Carl. Can you find your ball?"). Permissive parental messages convey the idea that children are unique, creative, and special. Permissive parents don't want to quash their children's spirit so as long as they are safe; parents will typically support whatever their children choose to do.

Finally, the **authoritative parenting style** is characterized by firm control balanced with ample nurturing. Authoritative parents value socializing their children so that they become empowered and caring adults. Authoritative parents set and enforce high standards for their children, but they indicate *why* certain behaviors are better or worse with facts and reasoning. "If you hit Carl again,

Nurturing messages—messages of support, praise, affection, and attending to needs that encourage a child's physical, social, emotional, and intellectual development

Controlling messages—messages designed to influence or regulate a child's behavior

Authoritarian parenting style—a parenting style characterized by high levels of control with low levels of nurturing; order and tradition, respect, and obedience of parents is valued and reinforced through punishment

Permissive parenting style—a parenting style characterized by moderate to high levels of nurturing but little control over children's behavior; creativity and freedom are valued, rules and demands are few, and children generally get what they want

Authoritative parenting style—a parenting style characterized by firm control balanced with ample nurturing; socializing children to become empowered and caring adults is valued and reinforced by setting and enforcing high standards supported by facts and reasoning

you're going to time out. When you hit Carl, it hurts him. Would you like it if someone hit you? He won't want to play with you if you keep hurting him." They are also respectful of children's efforts to reason and negotiate, and whenever possible, reward positive behavior rather than punish negative behavior. Authoritative parental messages convey that it is a parent's job to set boundaries within which children have the freedom to explore, take reasonable risks, and learn; attempts at negotiation are typically met with respect.

Compared to children raised by authoritarian or permissive parents, children raised by authoritative parents have higher self-esteem and academic performance, and less conflict with their parents (LePoire, 2006). This is because authoritative parenting communicates love, value, and respect, while still guiding children toward more competent, mature behavior. These positive effects of authoritative parenting extend across cultures (Sorkhabi & Mandara, 2013).

Family Communication Patterns

Another way of understanding parent–child relationships is through their patterns of interaction. Families vary in two orientations toward communication: conversation orientation and conformity orientation (Fitzpatrick & Ritchie, 1994). **Conversation orientation** refers to the richness of family interaction. Families high in conversation orientation interact frequently and spontaneously, openly discuss a variety of topics, and include children in decision-making. Parents in these families work to socialize their children and to establish a rewarding family life through open and frequent communication. In contrast, families low in conversation orientation interact less frequently, discuss a limited range of topics, and restrict decision-making primarily to parents. Parents in these families may lack the time, energy, or skills necessary for establishing a family culture that encourages rich communication between members. Take, for example, the characters Sheldon and Leonard in the television sitcom *The Big Bang Theory*: both seem to have mothers who are low on conversational orientation. While very opposite in their parenting styles, neither mother seeks or seems to encourage frequent conversations. On the other hand, the Heck parents in the sitcom *The Middle* seem to foster openness, sharing, and disagreement among their very different children.

Conformity orientation refers to the extent of a family's willingness to listen to and value diverse ideas, and the degree to which family members are encouraged to think and behave independently. In families with a high conformity orientation, members are encouraged to share the same views, be mutually supportive of one another, and obey parents. When a family member expresses a differing viewpoint, he or she may be ignored or reprimanded ("Owen, you know better; in this family we don't talk about things like that"). Parents who believe in a hierarchical and cohesive family structure head such families. By contrast, in families with a low conformity orientation, members are encouraged to express their own views and act independently, even if such thoughts and actions differ from those of other members. Personal growth and individuality are prioritized, and relationships and activities outside of the family are encouraged.

Conversation orientation—the richness of family interaction, including how frequently and spontaneously members interact, sharing thoughts on many topics, and including children in decision-making

Conformity orientation—the extent of a family's willingness to listen to and value diverse ideas, and the degree to which family members are encouraged to think and behave independently

Parenting Styles and Family Communication Patterns

Select three families that you know well. Identify the parenting style(s) you observe dominating in each family. What observations led you to your conclusion? Based on your observations, how does parenting style affect the openness, willingness to disclose, ability to provide feedback, and supportiveness in the family? Do all of the parents in each family use the same parenting style, and if not, how do the different styles used by each parent affect the relationship they have with each other and with the children? Identify the family communication pattern that best describes each family. Do you see any relationship between parenting styles and family communication patterns?

What kind of conversation orientation and conformity orientation do you expect in this family?

The Duggar family from the reality show *19 Kids and Counting* are a clear example of a family with a high conformity orientation: all of the children are expected to adhere to the same religious beliefs and behavioral standards held by their parents, and activities usually involve the entire family or groups of family members. In contrast, the children of the sitcom *The Middle* are accepted for their idiosyncratic ideas and personalities even as their parents try to shield them from the effects these may have.

In families with a higher conversational orientation and a lower conformity orientation, children benefit in a variety of ways. Within such families, children experience more affection, self-disclosure, understanding, positive interaction, and relational satisfaction. They are also less aggressive, tend to have better conflict resolution skills, and are mentally and physically healthier than children from lower conversational and higher conformity orientations. Of the two orientations, conversation orientation has the stronger positive influence, indicating that it is especially important for parents to encourage expression and participation within the family, even if they work to shape children's beliefs and behaviors to align closely with their own (Schrodt, Witt, & Messersmith, 2008).

Modeling

Even when parents are not directly interacting with their children, they are providing a working model of communication for children to follow. For example, parents may be mortified to hear their toddlers innocently repeat profanity they've heard at home. But parental influence on their children's communication extends well beyond specific words or phrases. Parents serve as role models for virtually every aspect of communication, regardless of whether they want or intend to. For example, parents who use destructive conflict strategies with each other such as counterblaming and cross-complaining teach their children that this is how to handle conflict. Although some children and adolescents work to overcome their parents' modeling, they are likely to adopt the ineffective communication strategies modeled by their parents. For example, teenagers with parents whose interactions with each other are frequently rude, overly critical, sarcastic, insulting, and verbally abusive are significantly more likely to communicate in similar ways in their own romantic relationships and be unhappy in them (Whitton et al., 2008).

Fortunately, parents who model positive communication strategies like describing feelings, calmly discussing options, and supporting each other even during their disagreements not only nurture their own relationships but also provide an effective model for their children. If Courtney observes her parents listening attentively to each other's problems, providing sensitive comfort and measured advice to each other, she will be more likely to practice the same behavior when she interacts with siblings, friends, and other people in her life. If, however, she is exposed to her parents' dismissing each other's feelings, criticizing, and making fun of the other's distress, it is unlikely that she will learn how to comfort others.

Communication in Other Types of Family Relationships

Beyond your relationship with your parents, unless you are an only child, you also have relationships with your siblings. In many family configurations, there are "step" and "half" siblings, and in less traditional families, there are relationships for which there are currently no set terms. Some of these may even involve **fictive kin**, people who are considered family members even through there are no genetic or marital ties. You also have relationships with your extended family, including grandparents, aunts, uncles, and cousins. Each of these relationships creates its own communication opportunities, rewards, and challenges.

Often lasting from infancy to old age, sibling relationships can span more time than any other family relationship (Meyers & Kennedy-Lightsey, 2014). Although the sibling relationship is typically created through sharing at least one parent, the nature of the relationship at any given time depends on the quantity and quality of communication that occurs. Throughout childhood, siblings provide a training ground for many kinds of communication behavior, including affection and comforting but also persuasion and conflict. In young childhood, siblings are often playmates and competitors, or if there is a sufficient age difference, one sibling may act as caregiver for another. In early and middle adulthood, as siblings leave their family of origin and establish families of their own, the amount of contact between them and the intimacy of their relationship varies. Siblings' spouses and children can bring them closer together or, equally likely, create greater separation. As siblings establish their adult identities, the conflicts and rivalries from childhood may either persist or fade. Nevertheless, most siblings make some effort to maintain their relationships. Siblings whose behaviors and messages include positivity, openness, assurances, networks, and task behaviors have relationships with each other that are more loving, trusting,

Fictive kin—people who are considered family members even though there are no genetic or marital ties

committed and satisfying than sibling relationships where these behaviors and messages are lacking (Meyers, Goodboy, & Members of COMM 201, 2013). In later life, sibling relationships often become closer as siblings suffer bereavements (parents, spouses, and friends). Elderly siblings provide each other with companionship, practical help, and emotional support, which may take the form of reminiscing about the childhood they shared. Siblings also often find ways to resolve conflicts or rivalries that may have characterized their earlier relationships. With siblings, it is easy to see how communication constitutes the relationship, indexes intimacy, and serves as an instrument for accomplishing things.

Intergenerational relationships can also be rewarding, because they allow older family members to transmit cultural and family values, enabling younger family members to carry on family traditions. Still, elderly and younger family members may find it difficult to communicate with each other because of their different interests and values, the geographic distance between them, the fast pace of contemporary life, and societal stereotypes of youth and the elderly (Ryan, Pearce, Anas, & Norris, 2004). One of the most frequently reported communication problems between younger and older family members is how young adults speak to their elders. Gould (2004) found that when younger family members speak to elder ones, they often over-accommodate, excessively adapting their communication style to the perceived needs or desires of the older person. The younger family members inappropriately restrict topics, oversimplify their speech, talk too loudly, and repeat their remarks. Unless they are cognitively impaired, older family members recognize and resent this style of communication as limiting and patronizing and are consequently less satisfied with these interactions and relationships. Younger family members can improve communication by accommodating no more than necessary. For example, speak loudly to your great-aunt Bertha if she isn't wearing her hearing aid, but in normal tones to your grandfather whose hearing is unimpaired.

Guidelines for Improving Family Communication

Countless books and articles have been written on communicating in families. Although their recommendations vary, most would support the following guidelines for improving communication in the family.

1. Create opportunities for intimate communication. Many people spend very little time each day actually communicating in an intimate way with other family members. To sustain positive relationships with other family members, time needs to be set aside for talk that involves more than requests, orders, or mundane planning. One good time for families to talk is during the evening meal, and the benefits of these family dinners can be profound. A series of studies conducted by the National Center on Addiction and Substance found that the more dinners teenagers share with their family, the higher the quality of their relationships with their parents, and the lower their likelihood of using drugs (Feinstein, 2010). Unfortunately, many families allow work and activity schedules to prevent them from sitting down together, or they let mediated forms of

INTER-ACT WITH
SOCIAL MEDIA

Do you use social media to keep in touch with your parents or family members? If so, take a moment to review the digital messages that you exchange with them. Do you use one social media outlet more frequently than others to remain connected with certain individuals? How do you think social media influence the attachment you feel with your parent or loved one?

communication (television, Facebook, texting, etc.) replace meaningful face-to-face interaction with each other. Families who do not regularly share meals should consider scheduling these each week, assigning chores that family members do together, participating in hobbies or sports as a family, or having family "play dates." Whatever the means, families can improve their relationships by ensuring that they have time to interact in meaningful ways.

2. Recognize individual interests and accomplishments. Family relationships benefit from individual members' treating each other as important. Yet family communication can be marked by apathy when it comes to the interests and accomplishments of individual members. Sometimes individuals are overly concerned with differentiating themselves from other family members, such as children not wanting to be too much like their "uncool" parents, siblings asserting their individuality in relation to their brothers and sisters, or even parents viewing themselves as too sophisticated to be fully engaged with the "juvenile" pursuits of their children.

We can reward each other's accomplishments through celebratory support. When dad is recognized by his Kiwanis Club for volunteering, or when Naomi masters the Hebrew passage from *Torah* that she will read at her bat mitzvah, a family celebration is in order. It might be a simple family meal featuring the celebrant's favorite foods, or an elaborate bat mitzvah party. The point is to honor the accomplishment with a family celebration commensurate with the achievement. However, positive behavior that isn't as significant a milestone should also be celebrated with praise. Genuine praise increases feelings of affection and can strengthen relationships. It is also a powerful tool for reinforcing positive behavior and encouraging others to continue working toward a goal. When it comes to praising children, adults should use process-focused praise, which points out behavior or work ("Carson, you have worked hard on your scales and they sound much smoother this week"), rather than person-focused praise, which points out personal characteristics such as intelligence or talent ("Carson, you are so musically gifted"). Process-focused praise encourages children to adopt a flexible mindset, take on future challenges, and confront weaknesses. Person-focused praise can make children less flexible, enthusiastic, or motivated. Children praised in this way come to believe that their attributes should always make learning easy, and struggle when faced with more difficult tasks (Dweck, 2007).

When and why does praise fail? THE BUCKETS © 1997 Greg Cravens. Reprinted by permission of UNIVERSAL UCLICK for UFS. All rights reserved.

3. Recognize and adapt to change. Family members know each other so well that they may be quick to predict how a particular member will think, feel, or act in various circumstances. Because people change, these predictions will not always be accurate. However, family members are often the last to recognize a gradual transformation in another member of the family. Even as children grow and change in seemingly obvious ways, their brothers and sisters, and especially their parents, continue to see them as they once were, not as they are or are becoming. Likewise, children, especially adult children, have difficulty recognizing the changes that their parents are experiencing. For example, Mom may be more short-tempered during menopause and Dad may be distracted if he is worrying about retirement finances.

Friendships

As the saying goes, "Friends are the family we choose for ourselves." Regardless of how much people enjoy and value their familial relationships, they also value their friendships, especially their close friendships. **Friendships** are voluntary, platonic relationships characterized by equality and reciprocity. In other words, friends usually have relatively equal influence over each other and enjoy a pattern of equitable give-and-take that includes activities, resources, and communication (Samter, 2003).

Friendships are most likely to form between people who have the opportunity for frequent contact, who have similar demographic characteristics such as age, gender, and education, and who engage in the same kinds of activities. If you think about it, most of your friends are probably people you live near, work with, or do something with, such as attending the same religious services, taking your children to the same practice, or pursuing the same hobby. Because they are founded in contact and similarity, friendships are vulnerable to changes in life circumstances and often fade if friends are unable to see one another regularly or embark on very different life paths. If you've gone away to college and have high school friends who stayed in your hometown, you may have seen some of these friendships weaken. Close friendships, however, are more likely to be sustained over time and distance. With cell phones, email, texting, and social networking sites such as Facebook, friends motivated to stay in contact now have many means to do so.

Communication plays a significant role in the formation and maintenance of friendships. Five groups of communication skills appear especially important for friendships: initiation, responsiveness, self-disclosure, emotional support, and conflict management (Samter, 2003). As noted, each of these skills is discussed in more detail in a prior chapter.

- **Initiation.** Friendships begin and are maintained when you or your partner makes the first move to get in touch with the other or start a conversation. Competent initiations are smooth, relaxed, and enjoyable. We may laugh at the idea of rehearsed pick-up lines, yet friendships are unlikely to develop if neither partner is adept at

Friendships—voluntary, platonic relationships characterized by equality and reciprocity

beginning enjoyable conversations. (See Chapter 8 for a discussion of initiating conversations.)

- **Responsiveness.** Friends are sensitive and aware of their partners. Listening and responding skills help you focus on your friends' needs and react appropriately. It is difficult to form and maintain friendships with others who focus only on themselves, and for this reason, responsiveness is a key friendship competency. (See Chapter 7 for material on effective listening.)

- **Self-disclosure.** Because friends share personal information and feelings with each other, a friendship is unlikely to form if people discuss only abstract ideas or surface issues. The skill of self-disclosure—describing feelings and behaviors—is, therefore, important to maintaining friendships. (Self-disclosure skills are discussed in Chapter 6.)

- **Emotional support.** People expect their friends to comfort and support them. Thus, empathizing, comforting, and praising are important ways to provide the emotional confirmation your friends need. (Emotional support skills are explored in Chapter 9.)

- **Conflict management.** Friends will inevitably disagree about ideas or behaviors. Maintaining your friendships depends on how you handle these disagreements. The skills of collaboration and constructive criticism—both of which are types of conflict management—can help your friendship weather and even benefit from periods of disagreement. (Conflict management skills are described in Chapter 11.)

Gender Differences in Same-Sex Friendships

If you've noticed that friendships between women are conducted somewhat differently than those between men, you're not alone. Research indicates that men's friendships usually focus on shared activities (playing basketball, working on cars, or playing video games, for example) and the exchange of goods and practical assistance (loaning tools or helping each other move, for example). Men's conversations tend to take place during their shared activities and tend to center on their present activities, politics, work, current events, or sex rather than on disclosing thoughts or feelings, or exploring relationships. Women's friendships also incorporate plenty of shared activity, but women are more likely than men to spend time "just talking," self-disclosing, and emotionally supporting each other. These gender differences should not be exaggerated, like claims that men never just talk and women never do anything but just talk. These varied tendencies seem to persist, however, even as gender roles in society become more flexible.

One interpretation of these differences between men's and women's friendship behavior is that men's same-sex friendships are not as intimate as those of women. Indeed, studies have found that men rate their friendships as less close or intimate than women rate their friendships. It does seem that men may lack or choose not to make full use of their self-disclosure and emotional support skills in their friendships with other men. Men also commonly report that their

How is "covert intimacy" between men expressed during sports and other activities?

Covert intimacy—delivering messages that use mild insults, competition, or put-downs to signal closeness, trust, and equality

▶ **OBSERVE AND ANALYZE**

Men's and Women's Friendships

Interview two men and two women about their close friendships, using the following questions:

1. What makes a friendship a close friendship?

2. When you think about your closest friendships with other men or women, what are those relationships like?

3. When you spend time with your closest friends, what do you do? What do you talk about?

Compare the responses of your male and female interviewees. How well do they reflect what you have learned about typical friendships between men and between women? How different are their responses? Do you see any evidence that women's friendships are more intimate?

friendships with women are closer and more meaningful than their friendships with other men (Fehr, 1996).

Yet some argue that this research inappropriately judges men's friendships by feminine standards. Julia Wood argues that men create an "alternate path" to intimacy through their shared activities and favors, claiming that "covert intimacy" substitutes for the lack of self-disclosure and emotional support in men's friendships. **Covert intimacy** is delivering messages that use mild insults, competition, or put-downs to signal closeness, trust, and equality (Wood, 2010). With an acquaintance, these behaviors would signal distance, distrust, and even hostility, but in the context of a well-established male friendship, these messages usually convey affection. For example, Nick might playfully say to Alex, his childhood friend and now roommate, "Hey, idiot. Hasn't that girlfriend of yours realized yet that she can do better than you?" Alex might respond, "At least I have a girlfriend, loser. When are you going to stop creeping around the girls' dorm?" Such covert intimacy perhaps offers male friends a masculine way of communicating that they care about each other.

Friendship and Sex

Most of us have cross-sex friendships—platonic (non-romantic friendships with people of the opposite sex). In these relationships, partners may be valued for attributes and behaviors that are stereotypical for their sex. For example, Anna-Lisa may enjoy playing video games and skateboarding with Mark, while Ethan may appreciate Penny's help when shopping for clothes. Most of the expectations or rules for cross-sex friendships are similar to those in same-sex friendships. Like same-sex friends, cross-sex friends expect each other to keep commitments and confidences, help each other, disclose to each other but respect privacy, and stand up for each other (Felmlee, Sweet, & Sinclair, 2012).

One major complication that can arise in platonic friendships is sexual attraction. Sometimes people assume that there is a sexual component to a relationship when there is not one. At other times, we may need to sort out our own feelings ("Is what I feel just strong liking, or something else?"). Occasionally one partner may feel sexually attracted to the other (O'Meara, 1989). More often than not these complications are not a factor in most cross-sex friendships (Monsour, 1994); however, they can pose a significant challenge to the relationship if they arise. Research shows that platonic friends use different relational maintenance strategies to signal that they want the friendship to become romantic or sexual. They may find reasons to spend more time together, openly flirt, and provide more emotional and physical support. Friends who do not want the relationship to become romantic or sexual do not flirt or respond to the flirting of their partner, spend less time alone together, and talk about their romantic relationships with others (Guerrero & Chavez, 2005). When one friend discloses a romantic interest that is not reciprocated, the friendship is more likely to last if both partners acknowledge their different feelings, affirm the importance of the friendship despite the difference, continue with normal patterns of contact, and hold flirting in check. Tension in the relationship will also be reduced when the romantically interested friend can disclose a romantic interest in someone else (Motley, 2008).

In recent decades, we have seen a new development in friendships. **"Friends with benefits" relationships** are friendships that have a physical sexual component but are not intended to be romantic. People in these relationships report the primary advantage as being able to have sex with a trusted partner while avoiding commitment, and the primary disadvantage as developing unreciprocated romantic feelings for the other person (Bisson & Levine, 2009). Partners in these relationships usually explicitly negotiate expectations. Some friends with benefits develop rules in the effort to avoid getting hurt, including emotional detachment (don't get jealous or fall in love), honesty about other relationships, and continuing to do things together that highlight that the friendship is valued for more than just the sexual satisfaction each experiences. However, the difficulty in maintaining emotional balance in friends with benefits relationships results in many of the relationships' returning to non-sexual friendships, or evolving into romantic relationships (Hughes, Morrison, & Asada, 2005). Researchers are just beginning to examine the long-term implications of friends with benefits relationships, but those that do become romantic appear to have an equivalent chance of success compared with those that began more traditionally (Owen & Fincham, 2012).

"Friends with benefits" relationships—friendships that have a physical sexual component but are not intended to be romantic

The Dark Side of Intimate Relationships: Infidelity, Jealousy, and Possessiveness

Our intimate relationships are unique and valuable to us. We invest ourselves in them, and become emotionally attached. Consequently, we often react strongly when we believe that others threaten these relationships. In this section, we discuss infidelity, jealousy, and possessiveness. These issues arise when there are actual or perceived threats to our intimate relationships.

Infidelity

In most LTRRs, people expect their partners to be exclusive. In other words, they expect sexual behavior to occur within the relationship, and not with anyone else, and they also expect romantic feelings to be limited to the partner. **Sexual infidelity** occurs when people in LTRRs engage in sexual activity with someone other than their partners. **Emotional infidelity** occurs when one partner develops romantic feelings toward someone else. The two types of infidelity may occur separately, or together.

Infidelity is a serious threat to LTRRs. Yet, sexual infidelity occurs in 20–40% of romantic and co-habiting relationships, and 13–18% of marriages (Blow & Hartnett, 2005). Usually, the unfaithful partner is dissatisfied with the LTRR, or with the sexual aspect of the relationship, but sometimes other motives are involved, such as seeking excitement. As you would expect, it is regarded as one of the least forgivable acts in a relationship (Bachmann & Guerrero, 2006). More than half of married couples in which a partner is unfaithful will eventually separate or divorce (Allen & Atkins, 2012).

Recovering from infidelity is difficult, even when there is a desire to repair the relationship and with assistance from professional counselors (Fife, Weeks, & Stelberg-Filbert, 2013). The unfaithful partner has to demonstrate sincere remorse and renewed commitment, while rebuilding trust over time with a partner who is hurt, angry, and who may be struggling to understand or forgive. The best approach to managing infidelity is to prevent it. This requires maintaining an intimate, affectionate, and passionate relationship with your partner. You can boost your resistance to sexual temptation by talking about your commitment and trust, providing each other with consistent support, and spending time with friends who also value committed relationships. It can also be helpful to avoid people and situations that could lead to sexual attraction outside your LTRR, especially if you are going through a period of turbulence, dissatisfaction, or conflict (Nelson, Li, Eckstein, Ane, & Mullener, 2008).

Jealousy

Jealousy is an emotion people experience when they believe they might lose something they value to another person. **Relational jealousy** is an emotional reaction to the belief you might lose a valued relationship to a third party. In LTRRs, we experience relational jealousy when we think that someone (or something) else is a threat to the sexual or emotional exclusivity of the relationship. Relational jealousy also occurs in other types of intimate relationships. Sibling rivalries are a form of jealousy that stems from children's vying for parental attention and affection. Either parent may also succumb to jealousy if the children appear to favor Mom over Dad or vice versa, or parents may become jealous of the relationships that their older children develop with other adults. Jealousy can trouble platonic same-sex friendships if friends perceive that their partners are spending more time with others; and, of course, romantic relationships and life partnerships are also susceptible to jealousy.

Sexual infidelity—when people in romantic relationships engage in sexual activity with someone other than their partners

Emotional infidelity—when one partner develops romantic feelings toward someone else

Relational jealousy—an emotional reaction to the belief you might lose a valued relationship to a third party

Like other feelings, jealousy is inherently neither good nor bad. It can provoke appropriate concern when there is a legitimate threat to your relationship, and it can motivate you to talk with your partner about your feelings. But jealousy can also be a destructive force that may ruin your relationship if it becomes extreme possessiveness (Pelusi, 2006). **Possessiveness** is the desire to control another person to ensure that he or she is one's exclusive partner. Possessive behaviors can range from mild to severe, holding a partner's hand at a party to communicate to others that your partner "belongs" to you, for example, or physically or psychologically intimidating partners into compliance with your "ownership" of them.

Open, honest communication in the form of simple conversations between partners can reduce feelings of jealousy, prevent misunderstandings, and discourage possessive behaviors. If, for example, at a party Paul notices that his fiancée, Jocelyn, is spending most of the evening engrossed in conversation with a very handsome man whom Paul does not know, he may feel jealous. To prevent these feelings from deteriorating into possessiveness, he may politely interrupt the conversation, ask Jocelyn to dance, and confess his jealousy, diplomatically admitting, "Honey, I don't know who that guy is and what you're talking about with him, but I do know that I am feeling jealous." In doing so, he may learn that the mystery man is actually an old friend of her brother, and Jocelyn was enjoying stories of her brother's high school pranks.

Giving your partner feedback and describing his or her possessive behaviors in a tactful and sensitive way may discourage unreasonable jealousy. For instance, if Sarella and Cary have been seeing each other for several months and are getting serious, but Janette, Sarella's best friend and roommate, has begun to erase Cary's voice mail, Sarella may need to speak with Janette about this. She might broach the subject by saying, "Janette, during the past week I know that Cary has left three messages on the answering machine that weren't there when I got home. Can you help me understand what's happening?" This nonthreatening description may encourage Janette to confess her possessive feelings, opening the door to an extended conversation that deepens their understanding of and appreciation for the importance of their friendship.

These candid conversations can alleviate jealousy and possessive behaviors by building and restoring trust before the relationship is permanently damaged. Unfortunately, jealousy and possessiveness can in some instances become psychopathic, leading to stalking and harassment. If you find one of your intimates is crossing the line, moving from possessiveness to stalking, and if conversations have not helped, it may be time for you to distance yourself from the relationship and even seek help from law enforcement if this person persists.

> **Possessiveness**—the desire to control another person to ensure that he or she is one's exclusive partner

"Hello, remember me?" How do jealousy and possessiveness affect relationships?

Using Digital Communication Skills to Improve Relationships

The convenience, reach, and mobility of social media have altered how we practice interpersonal relationships with others. Texting, Facebook, Skype, and other services enable us to keep in constant contact with friends, rapidly respond to their messages, and ultimately strengthen our interpersonal connections.

Digital Communication Skills in Personal Relationships

One of the most important benefits of social media is the ability to easily maintain our interpersonal relationships. Even though we may regularly see many of our Facebook friends in face-to-face settings, we still use social media to strengthen those connections. Most relationships are characterized by **media multiplexity**—meaning that we carry out those relationships through more than one form of social media, and that those in closer relationships use more forms of social media (Haythornthwaite, 2005). Media multiplexity theory posits the presence of strong and weak social ties in an individual's relational network. Strong ties include relationships such as those with friends, romantic partners, and family members. These relationships exhibit behavior that reflects heightened emotion, interdependence, intimacy, and high levels of closeness. In contrast, weak ties are casual contacts that are more loosely connected to an individual's social network and are not characterized by intimacy (Haythornthwaite, 2005). According to media multiplexity theory, the number of different social media that friends use is strongly associated with whether a tie is weak or strong. Specifically, strong ties use several forms of social media, but weak ties use only one or two social media. Think about your best friend. You probably use many forms of social media to maintain this strong tie. You may interact on Facebook, text regularly, talk on the phone, and maybe even Skype several times a week. Now, think about a weak tie, perhaps an acquaintance from a large college class. If you are Facebook friends, you may comment on a wall post every now and then, but you probably rarely, if ever, talk on the phone, text, or Skype. Social media are important devices that enhance our strong social ties and give us the opportunity to maintain our weak social ties. Scan your Facebook friends list and identify your weak ties. Reach out to those people to strengthen your interpersonal connection.

Although people in close relationships use social networking sites to communicate with each other, most relationships maintained primarily through Facebook are actually weak. In fact, students report that, of their entire friends network on Facebook, only about one-third of those individuals are "real" friends (Baron, 2008; Ellison, Steinfeld, & Lampe, 2009). Even though social networking sites allow users to exchange synchronous and asynchronous messages, a vast majority of friends never seem to do this. The success of Facebook and other social networking sites as relationship-maintenance tools comes from

Media multiplexity—relationships carried out through more than one form of social media; people in closer relationships use more forms of social media

their wide but selective reach. Although you may keep in closer contact with strong ties, you can communicate with multiple weak ties simultaneously. Shelby can share the news of her engagement to all friends in a tweet or status update. Or she can choose who can receive the message in wall posts. If you are a frequent Facebook user, you probably share photos on a regular basis. Even though all your Facebook friends may not comment on your newly posted photos, simply having access to one another's updates on Facebook may facilitate some sense of interpersonal connection (Humphreys, 2007).

Social networking sites are also used to establish new relationships. Social networks are home to many latent ties—potential relationships within a social circle that are present but have not been activated, such as those with friends of friends on Facebook (Haythornthwaite, 2002). In addition, people may also explicitly seek new relational partners online through dating sites such as eHarmony.com and Match.com. Matchmaking is not new to social media, however. Ask your grandparents. Newspapers and magazines have always featured classified ads for people seeking romantic connections.

A QUESTION OF ETHICS ▶ WHAT WOULD YOU DO?

Jackie and Michael had been dating for a year and were talking about marriage when Michael's company transferred him to Columbus for six months. Two months into their separation, Jackie visited Michael's new city and had a chance to meet his co-workers at a party, including Veronica, a beautiful woman a few years younger than herself. Michael had talked to Jackie about all his new colleagues, including Veronica, but she had had no idea how attractive she was. As the evening went on, Jackie could sense that Michael and Veronica were forming a special friendship. She couldn't help but feel a twinge of jealousy for this woman who got to spend time with her boyfriend. Nevertheless, Michael seemed completely attentive to Jackie, and they had a wonderful visit.

A couple of weeks later, while on a business trip to Columbus, Gwen, an acquaintance of Jackie's, happened to see Michael and Veronica having dinner together at a restaurant. The day after her return, Gwen ran into Jackie at the grocery store and casually remarked that she had seen Michael with Veronica. When Jackie commented that Michael and Veronica were co-workers, Gwen hesitantly replied, "Well, they certainly seem to have a close working relationship." Jackie blanched. Trying to soothe her, Gwen said, "I'm sure there's an explanation for everything. I mean there could be lots of reasons for him to be holding her hand. I'm sorry I said anything." But Jackie did not feel better.

Later that evening, when Michael called, Jackie immediately confronted him by asking sarcastically, "So, how's Veronica?"

When Michael replied, "What do you mean?" Jackie went on, "Don't give me any of your innocent 'what do I mean' stuff—you were seen and you know it!"

"Oh, Gwen," said Michael. "So you'll take the word of some nosy troublemaker and judge me before you find out the real situation? If that's all the trust you have in me, then I'm not sure. . . ."

"Oh, sure, defend yourself by blaming Gwen. But she did see you. You're right about one thing, this is about trust."

FOR CONSIDERATION
1. What ethical issues are involved in this situation?
2. What could/should Jackie have said to her friend Gwen and to Michael?
3. How could/should Michael have responded?

Online relationship development has certain benefits, yet these interactions also present potential challenges. Communicating online, people can be more strategic in how they present themselves, compared to ordinary face-to-face conversations. If Andy is seeking a romantic relationship through eHarmony.com, he may post personal pictures from a time when he was thinner and regularly worked out at the gym. This ability to present yourself in a "better-than-real" way contributes to some online relationships' becoming **hyperpersonal**, or intense and intimate (Walther, 1996) beyond what would occur if the relationship were conducted face to face. When you interact with others online, remember to communicate ethically and avoid deceiving other people, while also remaining alert to the possibility that others may be presenting idealized or even false versions of themselves. Many ethical principles of face-to-face communication are still applicable to communication in digital contexts.

Hyperpersonal—intensity and intimacy experienced in an online relationship, beyond what would occur if the relationship were conducted face to face

Summary

Intimate relationships have highly interdependent partners who are committed to each other, understand and trust each other deeply, and disclose in depth as well as breadth. Intimate relationships result from intimate interactions, or conversations that nurture interdependence, commitment, understanding, trust, and disclosure. The three primary types of intimate relationships are long-term romantic relationships (which include marriages and other life partnerships), family relationships, and friendships.

Strong and enduring intimacy often occurs in long-term romantic relationships (LTRRs). In successful LTRRs, partners mutually respect each other, share a life vision, and have a comfortable level of closeness. Four challenges for LTRRs are maintaining intimacy, managing life transitions, negotiating an equitable distribution of work, and sustaining affection and desire.

Families come in many forms, and maintain themselves through their own interactions, as well as interactions with others. Depending on their caregivers' behavior, infants acquire secure, anxious-ambivalent, or avoidant attachments. Evolving from these infant experiences, adults develop attachment styles that are secure, dismissive, preoccupied, or fearful. Parental communication with children includes both nurturing and control. Parenting styles may be authoritarian, permissive, or authoritative, and family communication patterns may be high or low in conformity orientation and conversation orientation. Parents influence their children's communication skills through modeling. Communication in a sibling relationship changes over its lifespan, and intergenerational communication brings both opportunities and challenges. Family communication and relationships can be improved by creating opportunities for intimate communication, respecting individual interests and accomplishments, and recognizing and adapting to change.

Friendships are voluntary, platonic relationships characterized by equality and reciprocity. Friendships are most likely to form between people who have frequent contact, similar demographic traits, and engage in the same activities. Five groups of communication skills are especially important for friendships: initiation, responsiveness, self-disclosure, emotional support, and conflict management. Men's and women's same-sex friendships differ: men's relationships are more activity-focused, whereas women are more likely to engage in "just talking," self-disclosure, and emotional support. Although men's same-sex friendships may appear less intimate than women's, men may express their feelings of closeness through covert intimacy.

Infidelity, jealousy, and possessiveness occur when we encounter actual or perceived threats to our intimate relationships. Infidelity is a serious threat to LTRRs, so couples need to maintain relationship satisfaction, affection, and desire. Jealousy is a natural emotional reaction to relationship threats, but becomes destructive when it generates conflict or possessiveness. To reduce feelings of jealousy, engage in open, honest communications about your feelings. To curb a partner's possessiveness, provide feedback and describe the possessive behaviors.

CHAPTER RESOURCES

Key Words

Flashcards for all of these key terms are available on the *Inter-Act* website.

Anxious-ambivalent attachment pp. 365
Attachment styles pp. 365
Authoritarian parenting style pp. 368
Authoritative parenting style pp. 368
Avoidant attachment pp. 365
Conformity orientation pp. 369
Controlling messages pp. 368
Conversation orientation pp. 369
Covert intimacy pp. 376
Dismissive attachment style pp. 366
Egalitarian relationship pp. 361
Emotional infidelity pp. 378
Family pp. 363

Fearful attachment style pp. 366
Fictive kin pp. 371
"Friends with benefits" relationships pp. 377
Friendships pp. 374
Hyperpersonal pp. 382
Interference pp. 359
Intimate interactions pp. 353
Intimate relationships pp. 352
Life transitions pp. 358
Long-term romantic relationships (LTRRs) pp. 354
Media multiplexity pp. 380

Nurturing messages pp. 368
Permissive parenting style pp. 368
Possessiveness pp. 379
Preoccupied attachment style pp. 366
Relational jealousy pp. 378
Relational maintenance pp. 356
Relational uncertainty pp. 359
Routine relational maintenance pp. 357
Secure attachment pp. 364
Secure attachment style pp. 366
Sexual infidelity pp. 378
Strategic relational maintenance pp. 357

Analyze and Apply

The following activities challenge you to demonstrate your mastery of the concepts, theories, and frameworks in this chapter by using them to explain what is happening in a specific situation.

12.1 Rewind/Rewrite

Now that you have read the chapter, hit "rewind" on the opening dialogue between Sara, Josh, Wes, and Mauve, and answer the following questions.

a. Use concepts from the chapter to explain the tension in this interaction between Sara, Josh, and Josh's parents. Shared vision, relational maintenance, egalitarian relationship, conformity orientation, and relational jealousy may be especially useful.

b. Using skills from Chapters 10 and 11 (influence and conflict), how might Josh and Sara resolve their differences and plan for the future? Rewrite the dialogue assuming that they have done this. What do you think about Wes and Mauve's involvement in their son and daughter-in-law's relationship? Based on what you've learned about disclosure and privacy (Chapter 6), and influence (Chapter 10), what changes could they make in order to foster more positive interactions?

12.2 Improving Communication Among Family and Intimates

Assume that you write a personal advice column for an online newspaper. Respond to each of the letters asking for advice. In each response, preface your advice by explaining to the writer what you see happening, using the concepts and theories you have studied in this chapter.

a. Dear Doc. Comm,

I am a 21-year-old woman and have been dating a really fantastic man. He owns his own business and is very successful. Not only that, but he is really good looking with a fantastic body—in other words, a real catch. I think he likes me as much as I like him, but the problem is that while I am very open with him, he doesn't tell me much about his life. Whenever I ask about his family or other relationships he's had, he either politely changes the subject or ends the conversation, claiming to suddenly remember something that needs to be done at work. Is this normal for guys, or should I be concerned?

Signed,

Hanging in Helena

b. Dear Doc. Comm,

I am a 75-year-old man who has been forced to move in with my married daughter and her family. While I am grateful to her and her husband for taking me in, I am thoroughly disgusted by how my grandchildren behave. First, they seem to run the show. Both my daughter and her husband dote on the children. The kids, who are 5, 8, and 13, are allowed to do whatever they want. There is no set bedtime, no study time, and no household chores. The house is a complete disaster as the kids leave stuff all over, and neither my daughter nor her husband (who both work long hours) has the energy to pick anything up. Yesterday, the 8-year-old came into my room when I wasn't there and broke the remote control to my TV. I lost my cool, grabbed him by the arm, and dragged him out of my room, kicking and screaming. My daughter, hearing the commotion, came running and proceeded to fuss over the boy as though I had hurt him. Then she turned to me and said, "We don't believe in touching our children in anger. If you do this again, you will have to leave." I can't afford to live on my own, but I don't think I should have to put up with my grandchildren destroying my property. What can I do now?

Signed,

Grandpa in the Dog House

c. Dear Doc.Comm,

I am heartbroken. I just learned that my husband of twenty-five years is having an online affair with a woman in Hartford, CT (We live in Dallas, TX). Not only has he been corresponding with her for months, but it also appears that they have been sexting and she has sent him nude pictures of herself. When I confronted him with my discovery (which really happened accidently as he forgot to shut down his email and log out of his account on our home computer), he told me that it was "nothing to worry about. Everyone does this from time to time, and it was just a little online fun." I want to believe him. Is it normal for people to carry on with someone online? Should I just get over this? I thought we had a good marriage, but now I wonder. What do you advise?

> Signed,
>
> Devastated in Dallas

12.3 Understanding Digital Media Concepts

Read the following, and then answer the questions below to explain what is happening in this situation.

> *Eddie attends a college in a different state, about sixteen hours from his hometown. He only goes home for holidays. Midway through his first year, Eddie begins to realize how difficult it is to remain in touch with his friends from high school. It seems that they rarely communicate anymore. About once a month, Eddie posts a comment on the Facebook pages of his high school friends. He sees his college friends almost every day. Even though they see each other so often, they still text many times a day, talk on the phone, exchange emails, and interact on Facebook. Before Eddie comments on his roommate's Facebook status message, he notices that his roommate is Facebook friends with Caroline, a woman in Eddie's large biology class. He never talked to Caroline before, but he thinks she is attractive. He would like to get to know her more. Eddie sends Caroline a Facebook friend request and hopes for the best.*

a. Use media multiplexity theory to explain what is happening in this situation.

b. How might Eddie and Caroline's relationship become hyperpersonal?

Communication Improvement Plan: Intimate Relationships

Would you like to improve your use of the following aspects of intimate relationship communication discussed in this chapter?

- Communication in families
- Communication in friendships
- Communication in marriages or long-term romantic relationships

Choose one specific relationship that you would like to improve. Then, using the interpersonal communication skills you have studied in the course, write a communication improvement plan. You can find a communication improvement plan worksheet on our website at www.oup.com/us/verderber.

13

COMMUNICATION IN WORKPLACE RELATIONSHIPS

Riley has been the head of the sales division in a large company for just over a year. Alexi is her long-time co-worker and friend in the same division.

"Hi, Riley, are you busy?" asked Alexi as he poked his head into Riley's office.

"No, I'm available right now, but I do have a meeting in twenty minutes. What's up?"

"Well," Alexi continued as he slid into the chair in front of Riley's desk, "I want you to know that people are talking about you and Dominic. At least I would want to know if everyone was talking like that about me. . . ."

"Okay," Riley responded slowly. "What are people saying?"

"So, don't shoot me," Alexi began, clearing his voice. "But someone's brother saw you and Dominic having dinner at Campari's last Saturday night. And . . . kissing."

Riley exhaled loudly and scowled at Alexi. "Really? That's what you have to tell me?" She continued in a cold tone. "I have work to do, and so do you."

Alexi looked startled. "I'm sorry. I thought you wanted me to keep you informed about what goes on in the department."

"This is my business, not the department's," Riley said firmly.

(Continued)

Alexi frowned. "But Riley, you can't see him and be his manager too. I mean, that's against company policy, and besides, it's just not right. I'm your friend. What are you thinking?"

Riley shook her head and pointed to the door. "I'm your manager, not your friend. And you're way out of bounds. Now if you'll excuse me, I have a meeting."

WHAT YOU SHOULD BE ABLE *TO EXPLAIN* AFTER YOU HAVE STUDIED THIS CHAPTER:

▶ Effective communication in manager–employee relationships

▶ Communicating effectively in co-worker relationships

▶ Skillful communication with customers and vendors

▶ The value and challenges of informal relationships at work

▶ Adapting to cultural, gender, and generational diversity in the workplace

▶ How to improve workplace performance through feedback

▶ Responding assertively to the "dark side" of workplace communication

▶ Guidelines for digital communication in the workplace

WHAT YOU SHOULD BE ABLE *TO DO* AFTER YOU HAVE STUDIED THIS CHAPTER:

▶ Communicate more effectively with managers, co-workers, and customers

▶ Seek, give, and respond effectively to feedback and criticism

▶ Take appropriate action against bullying and sexual harassment

Most adults spend about half of their waking hours on the job. Thus, many of the relationships we maintain are with work colleagues. These relationships differ from friendships and family relationships because, for the most part, they serve different purposes and are not voluntary. Apart from deciding to take a specific job, you usually don't choose the people you work with or for. In this chapter we discuss several types of workplace relationships, each of which presents a unique setting for interpersonal communication. We begin with the relationship you develop with your manager, which is central to your experience and success at work. Understanding the nature of manager–subordinate relationships can help you to communicate more effectively with your manager, and manage your subordinates more effectively. Additionally, productive and pleasant co-worker and boundary-spanning relationships can be key to your satisfaction and effectiveness at work. But our relationships at work are not always formalized. Over the course of time, we can develop mentoring, friendship, and romantic relationships with others who are part of the same organization, which we will also explore. Finally, because many of us will work in organizations where our managers, co-workers, clients, and vendors are from a different culture than we are, we end the chapter by discussing how diversity plays out in workplaces.

Because finding a job brings its own challenges and demands a specific skill set, you can find a guide to searching for a job on the *Inter-Act* website in the Chapter 13 Resources.

Communicating in Formal Workplace Relationships

Think of the best and the worst job experiences you have had. What made one satisfying and the other dissatisfying? Or, what made you feel successful at one and unsuccessful at the other? For most of us, our best work experiences include communicating effectively. You probably knew what was expected of you, were praised and rewarded for good work, and formed positive work relationships, even friendships. Our worst work experiences often involve communication problems, including uncertain expectations, harsh criticism, and conflict. Good communication skills are universally recognized as essential for successful work relationships (Whetten & Cameron, 2005). In fact, employers often indicate that, although technical competencies are important in hiring decisions, the ability to communicate effectively is universally valued. Employers recognize that technical competency has limited use if an employee can't express ideas clearly, or get along with others. In order for an organization to thrive, it needs its members to not only do their jobs, but coordinate their work. Much of the time this coordination is achieved through person-to-person communication. Therefore interpersonal communication skills are necessary to developing and maintaining healthy relationships at work. These relationships include those with your managers or supervisors, co-workers, vendors, and customers or clients.

Communicating in Managerial Relationships

Managerial relationships develop over time and are maintained through communication and interaction. A **manager** is an employee who is responsible for planning, directing, and monitoring the work of other employees. To develop the type of relationship you would like to have with your manager, you need to understand how these relationships develop. Although a wide variety of educational and training programs are dedicated to helping current and future managers communicate with their employees, few programs exist to help employees communicate more effectively with their managers. Yet managing upward communication is key to your career.

Manager—an employee who is responsible for planning, directing, and monitoring the work of other employees

Understanding Manager–Employee Relationships

Because no two employees are alike, co-workers who report to the same manager will each have different relationships. Leader–member exchange theory explains these different types of relationships, along with their causes and consequences (Graen & Uhl-Bien, 1995). The model begins with the premise that managers are responsible for getting more work done than they have people to do it, even if everyone does their job. Therefore, managers seek subordinates who are willing to do more than what is normally expected of someone in their job, such as

Easy laughter exchanged with your boss may signal an in-group relationship. What other things might also signal a close working relationship?

In-group relationships—close working relationships between managers and employees who consistently take on work above that which is expected and are rewarded in a variety of monetary and non-monetary ways

Out-group relationships—difficult and strained working relationships between managers and employees who consistently do not work up to standards or get along with the managers

Mid-group relationships—relationships between managers and employees who perform their jobs acceptably, but not exceptionally well, so the manager usually doesn't think of them when looking for help with additional or special assignments

taking on more challenging assignments, doing tasks that are normally the manager's work, and acting as liaisons with other departments, all of which may require working longer hours.

Since we tend to reward people who help us, managers usually pay back or "exchange" with employees for their extra efforts. Occasionally managers are able to reward these workers with additional pay through bonuses or other financial reward programs. It is more likely, however that what the manager exchanges for the extra effort will be non-monetary. The exchange may take the form of frequent interactions, choice assignments, better office space, public praise (e.g., Employee-of-the-Month awards), and access to information not normally shared with people at the subordinate's level. The exchange may also include opportunities to influence the decisions that the manager makes (Lee, Park, Lee, & Lee, 2007). These employees may receive special treatment, such as being invited to meetings, or they may be able to negotiate special working arrangements, like working from home. Through these exchanges, subordinates and managers develop **in-group relationships**, close working relationships between managers and employees who consistently take on work above that which is expected and are rewarded in a variety of monetary and non-monetary ways. These relationships are characterized by open, trusting, supportive, and respectful interactions (Myers, Seibold, & Park, 2011).

Not all subordinates have in-group relationships. Some people have **out-group relationships,** difficult and strained working relationships between managers and employees who consistently do *not* work up to standards or get along with managers. Such employees are more likely to be defensive in interactions with managers, and dissatisfied with their jobs. If you recognize that you have an out-group relationship with your manager, you would be wise to try to improve your relationship, transfer to another group within your organization, or find another job in a different organization.

Many employees have **mid-group relationships,** relationships between managers and employees who perform their jobs acceptably but not exceptionally well, so managers usually don't think of them when looking for help with additional or special assignments. While these employees competently perform the work for which they are paid, when offered opportunities to do things outside of the normal job description, they may decline or accept the task reluctantly. Mid-group employees have less day-to-day and less personal contact with their managers, so they are less likely to have an accurate perception of what their managers think of them. Mid-group employees who do their jobs well will get good but not the top evaluations. They may get modest pay raises, but by simply performing the routine work expected of those at their level, they are unlikely to be promoted. Thus, the relationships that managers and employees develop exist on a continuum. At one end, some employees have close, collaborative, and highly productive relationships with their managers. At the opposite, employees have cursory or even contentious relationships (Graen & Uhl-Bien, 1995).

Guidelines for Effectively Communicating with Your Manager

To foster an effective working relationship with your manager, you need to understand your manager's responsibilities and communicate in ways that let your manager know that you understand them and that you are willing to help your manager be successful. The following guidelines can help you relate to and communicate with your manager.

1. Adapt to your manager's communication preferences. Managers differ in how they prefer to interact with their employees. Some "manage by walking around" and will stop by your work area to briefly chat, assign work, check on your progress, and give on-the-spot feedback. Other managers don't actively initiate conversations with their subordinates, but have an open-door policy and welcome employees who stop by to provide updates, ask questions, or seek help. Still other managers prefer that employees use the phone, email, or written status reports for day-to-day communications. Your manager's preferences may be due to his or her thinking style. Some managers are introverted thinkers who need to mull things over before they can effectively respond. These managers may respond most favorably when you put things in writing, explaining a problem or making a request. Likewise, when confronted with a complex issue in a face-to-face interaction, a manager with an introverted thinking style may tell you, "I'll get back to you." Other managers have extroverted thinking styles and need to talk through issues in face-to-face settings in order to arrive at the best plan. Your own thinking style may be naturally compatible with your manager's, or you may need to adapt your style.

2. Identify how you can help your manager effectively complete the work of your group. To establish a high-quality relationship with your manager, you must begin by assessing the skills and expertise you possess that can help your manager accomplish the work that falls outside the formal role prescriptions of your job. These skills may be those that are in short supply in your work unit, or those that your manager lacks. For instance, suppose your manager has a big presentation to give and needs to have a terrific PowerPoint to use with it. If you know your manager isn't very adept with presentation software, but you are a PowerPoint maven, you have a skill that is valuable to your manager. But unless you let your manager know about your skillfulness, it is useless to you and your group.

3. Volunteer for specific assignments and follow-through. Once you are aware of what skills and expertise you can bring to an exchange relationship, you need to communicate your willingness to perform extra assignments that require your talents and knowledge. For example, suppose your manager comments, "I'm dreading working on the presentation I have to give next week. I know what

▶ **OBSERVE AND ANALYZE**

Leader–Member Exchange Theory in Action

Interview someone who manages employees. Describe the Leader–Member Exchange Theory. Then ask the manager to describe how this model fits with his or her experiences. Use questioning to probe for details and examples. Then write a brief report describing this manager's experience and what you learned.

Employees who go above and beyond what is expected become more valuable to their managers. How might these employees rise above expectations?

I want to say, but it's going to take me forever to get the PowerPoint done and I really don't have the time." As a savvy employee, instead of just commiserating, you might directly volunteer for the job. "Barb, I took a PowerPoint class at the local high school last year. I love doing PowerPoints, and I'm good at it. Can I do this for you?"

4. Clarify assignments. Managers aren't perfect communicators. Sometimes when you are asked to do something or when you are in the midst of doing it, you will realize that you are not sure of what the assignment really calls for you to do. In these situations, you need to ask for clarification. You can do this by *asking questions, paraphrasing* what you understand the assignment to be, and *checking your perceptions* of your manager's nonverbal messages. So if your manager accepts your offer to prepare the PowerPoint and hands you a copy of the written report on which the presentation is to be based, you will still need to clarify details about the presentation itself. Questions like, "How much time do you have to make the presentation?" "How many slides were you wanting to show?" and "Is there specific information you want depicted?" can help you plan your work. Then you can use paraphrasing to check your understanding of the assignment. "Okay, you're giving a five-minute recap of this report to the executive committee next week, and you'd like seven colored slides to accompany what you are going to say. There should be a title slide and one or two slides to review your recommendations. Then there should be at least one slide that explains the process you used to come up with the recommendations, but the bulk of the slides will detail how you plan to implement the new program. And you'd like to see a draft of the slides tomorrow. At this point, is there anything else I should know?"

5. Seek feedback and use it to improve. Too often, employees believe that no news is good news, so they wait until formal performance reviews to hear feedback from their managers. Formal summary feedback may be helpful, but because it is based on your performance over a long period, it may not be specific enough to help you identify and correct performance problems that are affecting the quality of your current work. And it certainly doesn't allow you to make corrections during a task. If you want to develop a good working relationship with your manager, you need to ask for feedback in real time, and use it to improve your performance. For example, after giving your manager the draft of the PowerPoint slides, you might directly say, "Please tell me what you think. What things would you like me to handle differently?" If you receive praise for the work, that's terrific, but if your manager points out things to do differently, you need to view it as a chance for improvement, not as a put-down. In the section "Improving Workplace Performance Through Feedback," we discuss asking for feedback in more detail, along with responding to negative feedback (criticism) and giving constructive criticism.

Communicating in Co-worker Relationships

Co-workers are peers who work together, are at the same or similar levels in an organization's hierarchy, and have no formal authority over each other. Because we have several peers, for most of us, these relationships consume more of our time than any others. We may even spend more time with our co-workers than we do our family (Sias, 2009). Your co-workers may be other members of your work group, team, or department. They may be people in other departments that you interact with regularly on the job. Some co-workers report to the same manager, while others have different reporting relationships. Regardless, your co-workers influence both the quality of your job performance and your job satisfaction (Jablin & Krone, 1994).

Co-workers—peers who work together, are at the same or similar levels in an organization's hierarchy, and who have no formal authority over each other

Types and Functions of Co-worker Relationships

There are three types of co-worker or peer relationships (Kram & Isabella, 1985; Odden & Sias, 1997). **Informational peer relationships** are superficial in that interactions and conversations are devoted solely to work topics. There is no intimacy, little self-disclosure, or trust. Most relationships with co-workers are this type. **Collegial peer relationships** are work-based friendships in which a wider variety of topics are discussed, but boundaries are maintained and private personal information is not discussed. Partners offer social support to each other in problematic work situations, but spend little or no time together outside of work. **Special peer relationships,** equivalent to "best friend" relationships set within the work context, are rare and characterized by high levels of disclosure, trust, and social support. Such friends interact at work and outside of the work context.

Effective co-worker relationships serve important functions within organizations (Seis, 2009). First, co-workers can mentor each other (Isabella & Kram, 1985). A seasoned employee who has an "in-group" relationship with the manager can provide insight and information to help a new employee get up to speed more quickly. Second, co-workers function as sources of organizational information.

Informational peer relationships—relationships between co-workers that are superficial in that interactions and conversations are devoted solely to work topics

Collegial peer relationships—relationships between co-workers where a wider variety of topics are discussed and partners offer social support to each other in problematic work situations

Special peer relationships—equivalent to "best friend" relationships set within the work context; such relationships are rare and characterized by high levels of disclosure, trust, and social support

You may have many co-workers, but different relationships with each. Have you developed any close peer relationships at work?

Not only can they provide timely and useful task-related advice, but they can also give you the scoop on what is happening in other parts of the organization. As you might expect, the quality and type of information that co-workers share depends on their relationship. We tend to share more detailed information in collegial relationships (Sias, 2005). So, in general, the more collegial relationships you have with peers, the better informed you are. Third, co-workers exert power, control, and influence over each other through processes like collective bargaining and workgroup-developed rules. Alternatively, co-workers can implicitly exert power and control through subtler processes like informal workgroup norms around tasks and social behaviors (Barker, 1993). Finally, co-workers usually function as a source of social support. Being part of an organization can be stressful, so co-workers look to each other for help relieving stress. In fact, our co-workers can be more helpful in reducing work-related stress than our family members. When employees face a work-related problem, they usually turn first to a co-worker for support (Cahill & Sias, 1997).

Guidelines for Communicating in Co-worker Relationships

Like other relationships, your co-worker relationships are developed through your communication experiences. The following guidelines can help you in interactions with your co-workers.

　　1. Use positive nonverbal cues that make it easy for someone to approach you. Work is hard enough without having to deal with grumpy, distant, or irritable peers. Effective co-worker communication begins when we adopt nonverbal behaviors that put others at ease and invite interaction. A pleasant smile, head nod, and open body posture all communicate that you are ready for a productive interaction with your co-worker.

2. Share task-related information freely. Believing that knowledge is power, some people hoard what they know, intentionally misleading or withholding important information. This hurts the total work product of your group, and it alienates co-workers. While you should not share information imparted to you in confidence, you should share ordinary work information with all who ask. Be proactive; share information with co-workers who need it to perform well. Doing so builds credits with peers who will probably reciprocate.

3. Seek and provide peer feedback. Managers are not the only ones who can help you improve your work and understand the organization. More experienced co-workers can offer useful insights on a variety of issues. Not only can they provide assistance in task performance, but they can also help you better understand how you are perceived by others and the effect that your behavior is having on your relationships.

4. Manage conflict through collaboration and respect. As in other relationships, conflict between co-workers is inevitable. In fact, some conflict is built into the roles that co-workers play. This diversity of ideas and perspectives can benefit the organization when co-workers manage the conflict in a collaborative and respectful way. For example, engineers want a product to have an elegant design, while manufacturing wants a simple product that is efficient to produce. Although these goals may conflict, with collaboration that respects both needs, the team can create a product that is both simple and elegant, meeting the needs of both engineering and production. Even when you disagree on a work issue, you can show respect by demonstrating that you understand and appreciate differing perspectives.

5. Don't gossip about people in the organization. Destructive gossip wastes time in the workplace. If you hear it, don't pass it on. If you hear it and you think the concerns are valid, suggest that the person passing this on to you talk instead with the person who is the topic of the gossip. Or you can talk with this person yourself and, using the guidelines for giving feedback, provide them with constructive advice. If the gossip is not valid, politely correct the person who is gossiping. As a rule of thumb, you should always support a person who is not present and is being talked about. Doing so sends the message to others that you can be relied on to have their backs as well.

6. Be a good team member. Today, much of the work that goes on inside organizations occurs in teams (Eisenberg & Goodall, 2004). A **workplace team** is a formally established group with a clear purpose and appropriate structure in which members know each other's roles and work together to achieve goals (Conrad & Poole, 2005). In team meetings, members help the team work productively by coming to meetings prepared and sharing in task roles such as initiating a discussion of issues, offering and soliciting information and opinions during discussion, analyzing what is said, and orienting the group to keep the discussion moving on track. They also share maintenance roles that foster a positive work climate. These include ensuring that everyone has a chance to speak,

Workplace team—a formally established group with a clear purpose and appropriate structure in which members know each other's roles and work together to achieve goals

verbally encouraging and supporting others, relieving group tension, and managing group conflict. They work hard to remain focused and avoid multitasking and other distractions like text messaging. After team meetings, they review their notes and incorporate their assignments into their calendars.

Communicating in Customer and Vendor Relationships

Boundary spanning—the process of communicating with people outside of an organization in a mutually beneficial relationship

Some of us spend most of our workdays communicating with other members of our organization, while others spend most of their time communicating with people who are not members of their organization. **Boundary spanning** is the process of communicating with people outside of an organization in a mutually beneficial relationship. Boundary spanners are the face of the organization to customers and clients, vendors (suppliers), and other entities that affect or are affected by the organization (such as government agencies, competitors, etc.). The two most common types of external boundary-spanning relationships are those with customers and clients, and those with vendors. **Customers and clients**

Customers and clients—the people, groups, or organizations that use an organization's goods or services

are the people, groups, or organizations that use an organization's goods or services. Inside and outside sales representatives, store clerks, customer service representatives, service technicians, delivery people, social workers, caregivers, medical personnel (doctors, nurses, technicians, orderlies, etc.), and public accountants are examples of people who span the boundary between an organization and its customers or clients. **Vendors** are the people, groups, or organizations that supply an organization with necessary raw materials or other goods and services. Purchasing agents, accounts payable staff, and personnel recruiters are examples of jobs that work with vendors.

Vendors—the people, groups, or organizations that supply an organization with necessary raw materials or other goods and services

You may notice that, although the educational requirements for these positions vary, for the most part, these are entry-level jobs. So organizations look for people with excellent communication skills and then train the new hires to effectively manage their boundary relationships. When boundary spanners are well trained, the organization benefits by having effective customer and vendor relationships. How often have you called a customer service hotline only to be greeted by someone who can't solve your problem, gives you incorrect information, can't answer your question, or is disrespectful or rude to you? How does that behavior affect what you think of and say to others about that organization? In many cases, this type of ineffective behavior occurs because people have not been trained in the communication skills that are key to their success. When you are in a boundary-spanning position, it is important to recognize that the people you talk to see you as your organization, and how you treat them will affect their future decisions about doing business or working with your organization.

Guidelines for Communicating in Boundary-Spanning Relationships

Communicating with customers, clients, and vendors can be stressful because, while you are responsible for interacting with these important people, you probably have little or no control over the policies you have to follow and communicate. The following guidelines can help you be more effective in these relationships.

Customer service representatives spend most of their time boundary spanning. What communication skills are especially important in these jobs?

1. Listen to understand. In most cases, your boundary-spanning conversations will center on how you can fulfill the other party's expectations. Sometimes these conversations will occur before you do business; at other times, the conversations will occur after expectations have not been met. In either case, the key to a successful interaction begins by listening to understand. This means not only *paraphrasing* what you have heard, but also *asking questions to clarify* what needs to be done. Assuming that we understand what someone else needs can create problems. For example, when Karen informed a sales clerk, "I need to return this blouse," the clerk glared at her and asked caustically, "Did you not read our sign?—Exchanges provided with receipt. Absolutely no returns." Karen actually wanted to exchange the blouse for another size, but instead of *asking a question to clarify* these intentions, the clerk publicly humiliated her. Consequently, the store lost Karen as a customer and probably several others whom she told about the incident.

2. Demonstrate empathy and provide comfort. When you are boundary spanning with clients or customers who are having problems, you need to empathize and offer emotional support, even when you can't solve their problem. For example, as Cassie was complaining about her new printer, the tech support responded empathetically with short *perception checking* and *supportive* comments like, "Wow, I can see that you're really frustrated. I would be, too." Then the tech apologized for not being able to answer her questions but identified people who could: "I'm so sorry. I'd really like to help, but I don't know anything about your printer. If you can tell me your printer brand, though, I can give you the number of your printer's tech support. Sorry." Although the tech couldn't solve

The Customer Experience

Recall two recent customer experiences that you have had: one that was positive and one that was negative. Compare them using the guidelines for boundary-spanning communication. What made the greatest difference in how you experienced each encounter?

the problem, the empathy and support that Cassie received made her a walking advertisement for her computer company.

3. When turning down a request, honestly explain the reasoning behind a company policy as well as the limitations of your authority. People are more willing to accept an unfavorable outcome if they realize the policy has a rational basis, which is explained to them before a problem arises. Many discount chains give cashiers a script to use as they ring up sales: "We cannot accept returns and keep our prices low, so be sure to check the merchandise before you leave." In addition, you should clearly state the boundaries of your authority in representing your organization: "I wish I could refund your money, but without a receipt, the only thing I can do is make an exchange."

4. Clearly communicate expectations for vendors. Nothing is more frustrating than working hard to fulfill a customer request, only to find out that the customer left out critical requirements. When you are dealing with a vendor, you are responsible for making sure that you understand and clearly communicate all the requirements that the vendor needs to meet. Most effective organizations recognize the importance of establishing and maintaining mutually rewarding relationships with vendors. How you react when a problem arises can either cement or damage your relationship.

Communicating in Informal Workplace Relationships

Our formal relationships at work are dictated by the work we do, whom we have to work with in order to complete our tasks, our position in the organization, and the person to whom we report. But there are other informal workplace relationships that can affect our careers and our satisfaction at work. These may or may not involve people with whom we have a formal working relationship. Three of the most common informal relationships are mentoring relationships, workplace friendships, and workplace romantic relationships. Let's take a brief look at each.

Mentoring Relationships

Mentoring relationship—a developmentally oriented relationship between a mentor, a more experienced and often older person, and a protégé, a less experienced and often a younger person

A **mentoring relationship** is a developmentally oriented relationship between a mentor, a more experienced and often older person, and a protégé, a less experienced and often younger person (Eby et al., 2013). In an effective mentoring relationship, the protégé's skills, knowledge, and insight are developed through the guidance and learning opportunities provided by the mentor. While some organizations have formalized mentoring programs where the organization pairs mentors and protégés, informal mentoring, arranged individually between mentor and protégé, is more typical and often more successful (Eby, Rhodes, & Allen, 2010).

Good mentoring can be highly beneficial for protégés, with positive outcomes that include higher compensation, more promotions, and greater career satisfaction and commitment (Dougherty, Turban, & Haggard, 2010). Mentors also receive benefits, including personal satisfaction derived from helping a younger colleague, a renewed motivation prompted by the protégé's fresh perspective and enthusiasm, and the opportunity to influence the future (Ramaswami & Dreher, 2010). In addition, good mentors who develop a number of successful protégés increase their own influence within the organization because the protégés often reflect the values and support the goals of their mentor.

When seeking a mentor, it is useful to consider both your own qualities and those of your potential mentor. Protégés report greater support and relationship satisfaction with mentors they view as similar to themselves. Likewise, mentors are more likely to accept (or seek) protégés whom they view as similar to themselves (Dougherty, Turban, & Haggard, 2010). However, mentors also prefer protégés with demonstrated ability and willingness to learn. If you are uncomfortable asking someone directly for a mentoring relationship, or uncertain whether the person will be a good mentor for you, start by asking for advice or a small amount of assistance, or by offering your assistance. A mentoring relationship can develop from these kinds of initial exchanges (Kalbfleisch, 2008).

Mentoring relationships are developed, maintained, and repaired through communication (Kalbfleisch, 2008). In early meetings with your mentor, you should discuss specifically what you would like to get out of the relationship. Do you want help improving your performance on specific job tasks? Do you want help understanding how office politics work? Do you want career advice? Once you have established the relationship, set up a regular meeting schedule with specific goals for each meeting. Be open with your mentor, share problems, weaknesses, and fears, and solicit feedback on your performance. Be non-defensive when your mentor gives you constructive feedback. As your relationship develops, you and your mentor may begin to discuss personal as well as work issues. This is fine as long as you are comfortable sharing, but be ready to politely define a boundary if you feel the conversation is becoming too personal.

Both mentors and protégés benefit from conflict management skills, as over time, disappointments and disagreements are likely to arise. One significant source of conflict in mentoring relationships is mentors' requests for help from the protégé (Kalbfleisch, 2008). Although some mentors will provide assistance without any "strings attached," others may expect you to reciprocate in some way. For example, Cate might ask Carmen to attend a meeting in her place, freeing up her schedule for other responsibilities, but also offering Carmen access to others that he would not normally have the chance to associate with. Rather than being put off by mentors' requests, protégés should plan from the outset to negotiate the assistance they provide, seeking a collaborative solution that benefits themselves and their mentors.

A good mentoring relationship can help build career success for you, and in turn, help you learn to successfully mentor others. This is one way that interpersonal communication and interpersonal relationships build strong organizations, communities, and societies.

Cartoonstock www.Cartoonstock.com

Workplace Friendships

Many co-workers remain informational peers with interactions limited to work topics and small talk. Yet, other co-workers become collegial peers or friends, and a few become special peers or very close friends. These workplace friendships are sources of support and resources that help people do their jobs, and do them more happily. Research shows that friendships improve work satisfaction and commitment, increase cohesion, and reduce intentions to leave a workplace (Morrison, 2009). They also can improve the workplace atmosphere and communication, making difficult jobs better, increasing productivity, and bridging racial divides (Berman, West, & Richter, 2002). Friendships can also create a welcoming culture that attracts new employees and encourages more supportive and collegial relationships overall (Cooper-Thomas & Morrison, 2013).

Research on the development of workplace friendships shows that the processes of relationship development operate similarly in the workplace as they do in our non-working social lives (Sias, 1998). Not surprisingly, co-workers are most likely to become friends when they work in close proximity and share tasks on a regular basis. This gives them the opportunity for frequent interaction and the development of interdependence. Socializing outside of work also contributes to these friendships, creating opportunities for disclosure that separate a person from their work role. For example, Wes and Mark, who have adjacent cubicles, are often assigned to the same work teams, and join the company softball team are more likely to become friends than Wes and Larson, who do similar work but have cubicles on different floors and don't interact outside of work. Casual work friends use each other as sounding boards to discuss work-related problems and enjoy bantering about purely social topics such as sports, celebrity news, or current events. While they may share personal information such as the recent antics of their children or weekend activities, they generally won't disclose deeply about their lives and personalities. Wes and Mark may know where the other went to college, be able to name each other's children, and identify each other's favorite sports teams, but as casual friends they are unlikely to know each other's financial or marital worries.

Some co-workers will not just become collegial peers or friends, but will develop such a friendship into a special peer relationship or close friendship. A significant life event or work-related problem can create a turning point in these relationships, prompting deeper disclosures and more interdependence in their personal as well as professional lives. Special peers also pursue more joint non-work activities. For example, once a week, Wes and Mark leave work and grab lunch at a local restaurant where they can talk openly, or they may go see a basketball game together. Close friends at work sometimes achieve the status of best friend, though research indicates that they are usually referred to as "best friend at work" or "almost best friend," with the title of "best friend" reserved for non-work friendships (Sias, 1998). This suggests there is a degree of intimacy reserved for relationships that do not have a work dimension. However, best friendships at work are still highly intimate relationships, developed over long periods of time with extensive, detailed self-disclosure, socializing outside the organization, sharing life events, and helping each other with work-related problems.

Work friendships sometimes create problems for the organization, other employees, or the friends themselves. These include promoting office gossip, distracting people from their work, encouraging inappropriate conduct, and facilitating workplace romances (Berman, West, & Richter, 2002). Workplace friends can manage some of these issues by limiting personal talk during work hours, getting others involved in decision-making so that they are not inappropriately influenced by friends, and behaving professionally at all times. Supervisors who befriend subordinates need to be especially careful about fairness to all employees. In their own relationships, workplace friends need to manage conflict so that it doesn't affect work performance. It is also wise to be more cautious about self-disclosure with workplace friends than with friends outside of work, especially when the relationship is new, and with information that could damage your reputation or career.

Romantic Relationships at Work

Workplace romance is a mutually desired relationship between two employees of the same organization who become sexually attracted to each other (Pierce & Aguinis, 2001; Wilson, 2013). The mutual desire for the intimate relationship distinguishes it from sexual harassment, which is discussed later in the chapter. Workplace romances are not unusual. A 2011 survey by CareerBuilder.com found that 40% of respondents had dated a co-worker, and one-third of those had married the person they dated. Many people spend long hours at work and have little free time in which to meet other partners. In addition, the same processes that create workplace friendships can lead to workplace romances when co-workers are open to sexual attraction.

Despite their frequency, workplace romances remain controversial and problematic. Concerns about these relationships include whether the relationship is being used for career advantage, whether organizational information is inappropriately shared (during "pillow talk"), how co-workers will be affected, and what will happen if the relationship ends (Wilson, 2013). These concerns are especially strong when the relationship is between a superior and a subordinate, and when one or both parties have marriages or other relationships threatened by the workplace romance. Given these concerns, some organizations (Walmart, for example), attempt to prohibit or strongly regulate workplace romance. Yet others (like Southwest Airlines), recognize that romance is nearly inevitable and important in their employees' lives, so they accept the relationships that form (Budak, 2012). In 2006, about 30% of companies had written policies on workplace romances, and many require the reassignment of one employee if a romantic relationship develops between a manager and an associate (Parks, 2006).

Before you opt into a workplace romance, you should carefully consider the effect this will have on your job and long-term career ambitions. When deciding whether to date a colleague, first consider reviewing and following your

Workplace romance—a mutually desired relationship between two employees of the same organization who become sexually attracted to each other

company's policies on workplace romances. If the policy allows co-workers to date, the partners should agree on standards for appropriate verbal and nonverbal communication with each other while at work, and they should continue to self-monitor their communications to maintain professionalism in the workplace at all times. If the policy forbids dating other employees, both partners need to seriously consider the risks and consequences of being discovered. In addition, potential romantic partners should consider the likelihood that managers and co-workers will have issues with the relationship, as well as the possibility that the relationship could end badly, ultimately making it difficult to continue working with each other. If you become romantically involved with your manager or someone else at a higher level in the organization, you may face having others devalue your accomplishments, and the recognition you receive may be seen as favoritism. Research indicates that subordinates, and women, tend to experience more negative outcomes from workplace romance, and should be especially thoughtful about their choices.

Communicating in a Diverse Workplace

Today's workplace reflects the increasing diversity of our country as women and men of differing races, ethnicities, sexual orientations, ages, socioeconomic status, political persuasions, religious traditions, and countries come together to work side by side. This means that success in the workplace depends increasingly on your ability to understand, get along with, and clearly communicate with people who differ from you. You may face various challenges at work stemming from the diversity of our workforce, including negotiating differences in culture-based work styles, gendered communication, and intergenerational work values and practices. Let's take a brief look at each of these.

Culture-Based Work Style

In addition to the cultural differences that we have already discussed, some cultures value work over relationships, while others value relationships over work. Moreover, some cultures value a sequential approach to large tasks, while others favor a holistic approach. When we go to work, we bring these cultural preferences with us, and when our co-workers are from other cultures, culture-based work style differences can cause conflict (Varner & Beamer, 1995).

Results-oriented organizational culture—an organizational culture that is individualistic and, like the dominant culture of the United States, prioritizes results over building relationships at work

Relationship-oriented organizational culture—an organizational culture that is collectivist, like those of Japan, Spain, and Mexico, and prioritizes building relationships at work over results

A **results-oriented organizational culture** is individualistic and, like the dominant culture of the United States, prioritizes results over building relationships at work; whereas a **relationship-oriented organizational culture** is collectivist, like those of Japan, Spain, and Mexico, and prioritizes building relationships at work over results (Varner & Beamer, 1995). Employees from results-oriented cultures see little need to spend time establishing or maintaining relationships, preferring to get right down to business. They view time as precious, and their ultimate goal is to get the job done. Getting to know customers or business associates on a personal level before doing business with them is not considered essential. In fact, anything believed to distract from the professional

How would you adapt to working in a relationship-oriented, or collectivist, organizational culture? What about a results-oriented, individualist culture?

objective would be seen as inefficient or counterproductive. In contrast, employees from relationship-oriented cultures see the quality of their personal relationships with customers and business associates as the primary business concern. People from these cultures prefer not to conduct business until they have established or refreshed a personal relationship.

A second culture-based work style difference is the way people prefer to approach large or complex tasks. A **sequential task-completion culture** is a culture where large or complex tasks are broken into separate parts and completed one part at a time and in order; that is, Step A is finished before beginning Step B and so on, until the task is completed. In contrast, a **holistic task-completion culture** is an organizational culture where large and complex tasks are completed by simultaneously working on all parts of the task; sometimes focusing on one part, then another, then back to the first, in an iterative fashion. As you can imagine, when teammates from sequential task-completion cultures work with those from holistic cultures, problems arise. For example, suppose that department store assistant managers Greg (a typical Canadian sequential task completer) and Chun-Hae (a typical Korean holistic task completer) have been asked by their boss to work together to develop a plan for displaying the store's new fall merchandise. Chun-Hae would be inclined to look at the whole problem at once, talking for a few minutes about what to put where, then bouncing around her ideas about how to physically handle the moving process, then describing how possibly to involve the sales associates in the plan, and finally returning to discussing new ideas about what to put where. Although another holistic task completer would be comfortable with this approach, Greg is likely to become confused and

Sequential task-completion culture—an organizational culture where large or complex tasks are broken into separate parts and completed one part at a time and in order

Holistic task-completion culture—an organizational culture where large or complex tasks are completed by simultaneously working on all parts of the task; sometimes focusing on one part, then another, then back to the first, in an iterative fashion

Kaigi: Japanese Style Business Meetings

BY KAZUO NISHIYAMA

Kazua Nishiyama is emeritus Professor of Communication at the University of Hawaii, Manoa. Team roles and decision-making styles are greatly influenced by culture. In this excerpt, the author describes how interdependence leads to a climate of agreement and decision making based on consensus in Japanese groups.

Unlike their counterparts in Western business organizations, Japanese executives and managers are not really independent decision makers. Rather, the group of people who would be involved in implementing the decision makes the decision. So the process through which this is done is very different than the typical way group decisions are made in Western business organizations.

Decision-making in Japanese organizations begins with the *ringi,* which is a series of informal discussions among key people that emphasizes interpersonal harmony, cooperation, and consensus. These discussions provide a sounding board for unofficially testing the responses to a proposal without the risk of a loss of face for anyone. It also means that no one person can accept credit or blame for the outcome of a proposal.

Once there is a fairly positive reaction, a lower or middle level manager drafts a detailed written proposal. The written proposal is circulated to every executive and manager who carefully review and hopefully approve it. The proposal is circulated so that lower level managers review and sign off before higher-level managers review it. Finally it will be sent to the President of the organization for the last sign off.

In Western business organizations meetings are used to facilitate decision making in face-to-face situations. The *kaigi* in Japanese business organizations outwardly appears to be similar. However, it is quite different. A *kaigi* is the occasion to formally confirm what has been already decided informally. In many instances, Japanese participants go through the ritual of asking questions and debating certain points. But, in fact, they are merely saying what has been discussed and agreed upon beforehand. In addition, they do not want surprise questions or strong objections from anyone of the participants during the actual meeting.

In Western cultural contexts it is acceptable to change one's mind about what has been informally agreed upon prior to the meeting, if a much better idea or new compelling evidence is presented. In the Japanese cultural context, however, such changing of one's mind is a serious social infraction and a betrayal of interpersonal trust. Any agreement that has been reached during informal consultations is considered a firm commitment. It is different from the tentative commitment or personal opinion that Western businesspeople usually try to obtain when going through the process of "touching bases."

The role of each Japanese participant in a *kaigi* is different from that of his Western counterpart. The Japanese chairperson's main role is not to aggressively take direct control over the decision-making process, but to mediate the consensus-building process among all participants. In fact, the second ranking person will do most of the talking and direct other participants to contribute to the ongoing discussion in a predetermined order. Each of the junior ranking participants presents a brief report prepared in advance and seeks everyone's approval. The participants seldom disagree with others during face-to-face meetings because they have probably talked about their reports informally and obtained everyone's concurrence beforehand. There may be a few questions for clarification but open arguments or heated discussions will not be permitted.

If a junior participant wishes to voice his opinion he will preface his remarks by saying, "I may be making this comment based on my limited experience and I may be wrong, but . . ." or he may say, "Please tell me if you think I'm wrong but . . ." He needs to take a tentative approach and also show humility in order not to cause loss of face among any of the participants. Other participants will also hesitate to voice frank opinions or disagreement because they fear even their constructive criticisms could be taken as personal attacks or insults. They all tend to look for subtle verbal and nonverbal cues and try to understand how the other participants feel about what is being discussed.

But Japanese business people do exchange frank, honest opinions and comments. They do so, however, by intentionally creating informal opportunities outside of the conference rooms. They frequently go out together for drinking and dining, where they exchange their true feelings. An unhappy participant may even complain bitterly, pretending that he has had too much to drink, but he is allowed to do so because this is one of the ways to appease the dissatisfied member. The Japanese call this method of communicating while drinking alcohol "*nomini-cation*" (drink and communicate). Even in this *nomini-cation* context it is still important for all the participants to remember their position in the organizational hierarchy. A so-called "drunk person" is expected to apologize to his senior members on the following morning for his misbehavior. He might say, "I am sorry I was so drunk last night. I don't even remember what I said," even when he remembers clearly what he complained about.

Unlike the Japanese counterpart, an American chairperson controls the discussion of a conference and encourages active participation from the participants. He might even challenge every participant to voice his or her own opinions and comments openly. And the participants feel free to exchange constructive criticism and objections based on their knowledge and experience without fear of being ostracized or alienated.

Westerners, particularly Americans, are often frustrated when they attend meetings in Japan. They often are dismayed because they expect that the Japanese participants will act the same way they do. They usually find it difficult to read subtle verbal and nonverbal cues offered by the Japanese participants. For example, the Japanese might say, "Yes, yes," and nod their head in agreement, but in most instances these verbal and nonverbal cues do not mean they are agreeing at all. They may mean, "I hear what you are saying," "Please explain more," or "I will pretend I agree with you for now, but I still have objections." Another problem is that in the Japanese language, they can say, "Yes, I don't agree with you," which literally means, "Yes, you are right, I don't agree with you" (Nishiyama, 2000).

In order to accurately assess what the Japanese counterparts mean by what they say, it is often necessary for the Americans to go out drinking and dining with a few of their Japanese counterparts. Perhaps one of the Japanese may help them "interpret" what has transpired during the conference. He may divulge certain important information off the record during after-hours *nomini-cation*.

There are eight guidelines Westerners can follow to help them overcome the communication difficulties that can arise in Japanese–Western meetings:

1. *Maintain close personal contacts*. In Japan, business decisions are often made on the basis of personal preference rather than objective data, so it is important to cultivate and maintain close relationships with those who are in charge.

2. *Do not rush Japanese counterparts*. In Japan deadlines are flexible, so especially when the Japanese company is the customer, they expect the seller, who has lower status, to abide by his customer's deadlines.

3. *Do not consider the* ringi *negative because it is slow and cumbersome*. The process is longer, but implementation of the decision is swift once it is made.

4. *Bring gifts for Japanese counterparts*. Gift giving is an important custom in establishing amicable interpersonal relationships. It does not have to be expensive but it should be a token of friendship.

5. *Successful participation in decision-making conferences is predicated by a good understanding of Japanese culture and social customs*. Knowing your status in the conference and therefore where to sit and when to speak may be key to your effectiveness.

6. *Do not talk too much and do not dominate the discussion*. Being verbally dominant may win the argument but lose the deal. When English is used as the medium for communication in the meeting, remember that your Japanese counterparts may need more time to think in Japanese first and translate their thoughts into English. Never try to help your Japanese counterparts with English by putting words into the speaker's mouth.

7. *Be patient and disregard Western time orientation*. Westerners tend to be clock oriented while Easterners are more person oriented. This means that Japanese are inclined to adjust the handling of time based on who is speaking.

8. *If at all possible, prepare visual aids in Japanese*. The Japanese usually want to have written documentation that covers important data and information. Visual aids in Japanese help them to better understand what is being explained orally in English.

Excerpted from Nishiyama, K. (2014). Japanese style of decision making in business organizations. In L. A. Samovar, R. E. Porter, E. R. McDaniel, & C. S. Roy (Eds.), *Intercultural Communication: A Reader* (14th ed., pp. 266–272). Boston, MA: Cengage Learning. The original essay first appeared in the 12th edition.

FOR CONSIDERATION

1. What part of the decision-making process in Japan would you find most difficult to adapt to?

2. What types of problems can you anticipate might occur if American and Japanese business people attended a meeting without being aware of their cultural differences?

3. What is the most important thing you have learned from this article?

frustrated, wishing Chun-Hae would focus on one issue, work through it, make decisions, and then move on to the next topic. Likewise, if Greg initiates the discussion and tries to hold Chun-Hae to his step-by-step process, she is likely to become annoyed and bored.

Effective business communication depends on mutual awareness of and sensitivity to cultural differences in work styles without assuming some approaches are better than others. It is also important to realize that a person from a particular culture may or may not communicate in the style typical of that culture, so you should not assume that, for instance, all Americans are results-oriented and sequential or that all Koreans are relationship-oriented and holistic. A strategy for dealing with cultural differences is to acknowledge and communicate about respective cultural styles. Parties working across cultural boundaries may benefit from talking about their preferred ways of doing business and negotiating an agreement between the business partners. As workplaces become more culturally diverse, employees need to be flexible with their natural work style and learn alternate styles. For another example of how cultural styles vary, see this chapter's "Diverse Voices" box in which Kazuo Nishiyama explains how Japanese business decision making and meetings differ from their Western counterparts'.

Gendered Linguistic Style in the Workplace

Linguistic style—the patterned way in which a person uses language to communicate

Your **linguistic style** is the patterned way in which you use language to communicate. Because of the different ways that they were socialized, most men and women have different linguistic styles; patterns they also, not surprisingly, use at work. How we talk can have profound effects not only on how we are perceived, but also on how we perceive others, as we use our own style to help us interpret the pragmatic and sociolinguistic meaning of others' messages. Specifically, we tend to value those who talk like we do. In most organizations, where men are overrepresented in more powerful positions, women can be at a disadvantage, not because they are less competent at performing their jobs, but because their communication style unconsciously encourages the male managerial decision makers to view them as less competent. Some scholars believe that this is a major reason why women encounter the "glass ceiling," an invisible yet real barrier that prevents deserving employees from advancing. Let's take a closer look at how the communication styles of men and women differ in linguistic usage, attention to social dynamics, conversational rituals, and communicating authority, and how these differences play out at work (Tannen, 1995).

Women and men tend to differ in how they use language to communicate their meanings. It is critical to note that, although extensive evidence supports the existence of different linguistic styles, this does not mean that all women or any particular woman has a "feminine style" or that all men and or any particular man has a "masculine style." Women can and do develop masculine linguistic styles, and men can and do develop feminine linguistic styles. Nevertheless, understanding these can help us as we try to separate a person's communication style from their actual performance in the workplace.

A feminine linguistic style uses indirect language when giving orders to an employee. A female manager might give an assignment by saying, "Could you get me the budget report needed by the V.P. by noon on Friday?" Whereas, her male peer manager might say, "You need to prepare an expected-to-realize year-to-date budget update for me and have it on my desk by tomorrow at 10:00." Men tend to use indirect language, however, to acknowledge a mistake or problem: "There was a problem in estimating our telecommunications budget needs, and I will make sure this doesn't happen again." A woman, on the other hand, would be more likely to acknowledge the mistake was hers and apologize: "I made a mistake when I estimated our telecommunications budget needs. I am so sorry." Women and men also differ in their personal pronoun use. Women tend to use inclusive first-person plural pronouns (*we, our, ours*) and men first-person singular and third-person pronouns (*I, he, she, they*). She says, "In our department we've done a good job and are actually below our anticipated budget," whereas he says, "I've really been watching the budget like a hawk, so I'm happy to report that my department is below my anticipated budget." What is the effect of these differences? Managers predominantly of one gender could perceive a different gendered style inaccurately. A female manager may view her male employees as too direct and self-serving, while a male manager may view his female employees as unable to exercise authority, incapable of assuming leadership, and not particularly competent.

Men and women also are sensitive to different language dynamics. Men tend to be attuned to the power dynamic communicated by how something is said. When speaking, they try to maintain a one-up position and avoid more tentative, one-down messages; they prefer to make assertive statements rather than ask questions. Women, on the other hand, tend to be attuned to the relationship or rapport dynamic in an interaction, forming messages that save face or buffer the face threats of others. When speaking to an assistant, for example, he says, "Get John on the phone," while she says, "Would you please get John on the phone for me. Thanks." "His speak" asserts his right to command and his more powerful status. "Her speak" attends to her assistant's face needs, putting her legitimate demand in the form of a request rather than simply ordering her subordinate to do her bidding.

A number of conversational rituals also differ in gendered ways that affect workplace perceptions, including the use of apology, giving and understanding feedback, giving compliments, and the use of ritual argument. First, women use an apology as a ritual way of comforting. When she says, "I'm so sorry that you missed the deadline," she is not apologizing for causing you to miss the deadline but rather expressing empathic sorrow. Men, however, who view an apology as a one-down power position, generally don't offer this kind of support.

Second, women begin giving feedback by praising something positive, then communicating constructive criticism. The criticism will probably be duly noted by other women but possibly missed by male employees, who are attuned to the praise. Male managers who do not use this ritual, providing direct criticism without acknowledging positive aspects of a performance, are likely to hurt the morale of female employees.

Third, female conversations are marked by a ritual exchange of compliments. A woman who praises the way you managed the work team meeting expects you to compliment her in return. If you don't, she might prime you by asking a question that invites a compliment: "What did you think of my argument about reducing costs by using temps?" A man may not recognize this question as part of a ritual compliment exchange, providing instead honest feedback that points out the flaws in her proposal.

Fourth, men may vigorously argue as a ritual, not because they are fundamentally opposed to another's assertions but as a way of testing the strengths and weaknesses of various positions and options. What looks adversarial is really cooperative, and no damage is done to their relationship. Heated arguments between women, however, typically mean that they are, indeed, opposed to another's position or adamant about their own. Such arguments are considered a breach of the relationship that will require repair through a forgiveness process.

The final gendered difference in linguistic style involves perceptions of confidence and authority. Men are more likely to seek out and spend time with upper managers, seizing the opportunity, for instance, to sit with top managers at luncheons or other social occasions and spotlight their recent accomplishments. Women, on the other hand, are likely to consider this behavior overly forward, even intrusive. Socialized to be self-effacing, they are less likely to talk up their achievements with upper managers even when given the chance. Consequently, male upper managers tend to view male employees as more accomplished than the women.

At this point in the evolution of our workplaces, men are disproportionately represented in the ranks of upper management, a situation that puts women at a disadvantage because of their linguistic style. Regrettably, little can be done to alter this situation—other than being aware of these differences and their consequences. Women, for example, who adopt a masculine style are generally seen negatively and labeled "pushy," "bitchy," or "ball-busting." Men, however, can also suffer if they violate traditional expectations for gendered communication. Men who employ a feminine linguistic style may be seen as even more indecisive and overly sensitive than women (who are expected to be this way).

Intergenerational Communication Issues

There is no mandatory retirement age in many countries, including the United States. As a result, the age range in an organization's workforce may span four decades. Consequently, the possibility of age-based misunderstandings occurring in the workplace has increased. Scholars have found that older and younger employees tend to differ in their views of authority, approach to rules, priorities regarding work versus leisure, and competence with technology (Zemke, Raines, & Filipczak, 2000).

In general, people sixty or older tend to have greater respect for authority. They grew up in a time when our culture valued greater power distance. The frequent use of formal titles and other deferential behavior demonstrated respect for more powerful figures whose authority was seldom openly questioned.

In contrast, people under the age of thirty tend to be more skeptical of and less formal when dealing with authority figures. They grew up in an era of greater equality in a society that commonly challenged the status quo. Consequently, they are more likely to question their managers, openly disagree with their decisions, and call them and co-workers by their first names.

Older individuals tend to adhere more strictly to company rules and expect others to do the same, believing that employers have the right to make the rules and that employees have the responsibility to follow those rules as a condition of employment. They may even find company regulations reassuring because they promote predictability. Many younger co-workers, however, may see rules as suggestions to be followed or not, depending on their own analysis of a situation. Having been raised with situational ethics, younger people may believe that extenuating circumstances call for flexibility, thus allowing them to ignore or bend the rules. Such differences in perspective may cause us to judge one another, thereby impeding team cohesiveness at work.

For many older individuals, work always takes priority over family and leisure. In fact, many older Americans consider a strong work ethic one of a person's most respectable personality traits. In contrast, many individuals under thirty, who have not yet experienced the challenges of providing for a family or who have seen the toll that work has taken of their parents, may place a higher priority on leisure. Co-workers of different ages also differ regarding their use of and competence with technology. For many older employees, the challenges of learning to use new technology can cause anxiety. For younger people who are "digital natives," adapting to ever-changing technology is expected and relatively effortless.

How can you communicate effectively across generations and other differences at work?

It is important to keep in mind that there is no right or wrong set of generational values. Nevertheless, generational differences in values and behaviors can create enormous challenges for workplace communication. The more we understand and are sensitive to age-related differences in workplace behavior, the more we can communicate with flexibility across the age gap. The interpersonal skills of assertiveness, questioning, perception checking, describing behavior, and owning feelings may also prove useful in preventing or managing intergenerational communication conflicts at work.

Improving Workplace Performance Through Feedback

To improve as an employee and grow in your career, it is essential to seek and learn from feedback, both positive and negative. You also need to give feedback to others, whether they are your peers, your subordinates, or even your superiors. In Chapter 12, we focused on skills for conveying gratitude and praise. Both of these are feedback skills because they show that you think positively of another person's behavior or accomplishments, and they are just as essential in workplace relationships as in personal relationships. When you sincerely thank your manager for the updates to the break room, you encourage him or her to continue thinking of ways to make employees' jobs easier, and when you praise your co-worker's work during a team meeting, you build her confidence. Others who hear you being grateful and appreciative of others will recognize you as a positive person to work with, and may be inspired to follow your example.

In this section, we continue to emphasize the importance of feedback, but with emphasis on criticism, or negative feedback. We begin with how to solicit feedback, how to criticize constructively, and how to respond to negative feedback.

Asking for Feedback

In some cases, we know with certainty whether we have done something well or poorly. But there are many situations in which success or failure is a matter of meeting the standards of those around us. You may have learned how to write newsletters in a college composition class, but will your article on the new employee cycling club satisfy the Vice President for Human Resources? Alternatively, you may have been a mediocre cold-caller for your campus fundraising campaign, but have your two years as assistant to a lead recruiter in the Development office improved those skills? The only way to find out is by getting feedback. Some of this feedback will come unsolicited, but at other times we will want to prompt others to disclose things they have observed about us.

Asking for feedback—the skill of eliciting observations from others about your behavior

Asking for feedback is the skill of eliciting observations from others about your behavior. It's important to think of feedback as being in your best interest. No one likes to be criticized, and some people are embarrassed by praise, but through personal feedback we often learn and grow. When you receive a different appraisal from the one you expected, you have learned something about yourself that you did not previously know. Whether you will do anything about the feedback is up to you, but the feedback you have solicited allows you to consider aspects of your behavior that you might not have discovered on your own. Before you ask, make sure that you are ready for an honest response. If you ask for feedback, don't expect others to lie to you just to make you feel better. If you don't want an honest response, don't ask the question. For example, if you ask a friend, "What do you think of my speaking skills?" expect an honest reply, even if it is negative, such as, "Well, you tend to ramble a bit." If others realize that when you request personal feedback, you are typically fishing for a compliment, honest appraisals will not be forthcoming in the future.

Follow these guidelines when asking for personal feedback:

1. Specify the kind of personal feedback you are seeking. Rather than asking general questions about ideas, feelings, or behaviors, ask specific questions. If you say to your co-worker, "Colleen, is there anything you don't like about my ideas?" she probably won't know how to respond. But if you say, "Colleen, do you think I've given enough emphasis to the marketing possibilities?" you will encourage Colleen to speak openly about the specific issue.

SKILL BUILDER ▶ ASKING FOR FEEDBACK

SKILL	USE	STEPS	EXAMPLE
Asking others for their reaction to you or to your behavior	Helping you understand yourself and your effect on others	1. Specify the kind of personal feedback you are seeking. 2. Ask neutral questions. 3. Listen and paraphrase what you hear.	Lucy asks, "Tim, when I talk with the boss, do I sound defensive?" Tim replies, "I think so—your voice gets sharp and you lose eye contact, which makes you look nervous." "So you think that the tone of my voice and my eye contact make the boss perceive me as defensive?" "Yes." "Thanks, Tim. I've really got to work on this."

2. Ask neutral questions. You can't expect honest personal feedback if you ask loaded questions that invite a particular answer. For example, if you say, "I did a great job on that, didn't I?" or "I screwed that up, right?" the person you ask isn't given full rein to provide honest feedback.

3. Listen and paraphrase what you hear. By paraphrasing the personal feedback you receive, you ensure that you do not overgeneralize what you have heard. For example, if Joshua asks his classmate to comment on his presentation but mentally boils down the specific comments to simply "good" or "bad," he is not going to learn anything constructive from the feedback he requested. Instead, Joshua could say "Okay, I hear you saying that I could do a better job of signposting, so the audience has a clearer sense of my organization."

Constructively Criticizing

To complement your skills at requesting and responding to feedback, it's important to develop your own ability to give feedback. You have already learned how to offer praise, but it is equally important to learn when and how to offer criticism. Unfortunately, most of us are far too quick to criticize others and in ways that are less than constructive. At times we overstep our bounds by trying to help others become better people when they aren't interested in hearing from us. Even when the time is right for disclosing negative feedback, we may not always do a good job of expressing it. Although research shows that constructive criticism can actually strengthen relationships and improve interactions in the long run, criticism not empathetically grounded or otherwise poorly communicated is likely to hurt relationships and lead to defensiveness (Tracy, Dusen, & Robinson, 1987).

In organizations we are expected to provide both positive and negative feedback to our subordinates, peers, and even occasionally our managers.

Although the word "criticism" can mean "harshly judgemental," the skill of constructive criticism is not based on blaming or mean-spirited faultfinding. **Constructive criticizing** is the feedback skill of diplomatically describing the specific negative behavior of your partner and its effects on others. When your sincere purpose is to help the other person improve their performance and behavior, your criticism, if well expressed, can prevent someone from failing at their job or in their career. The constructive criticism process begins by empathizing with the other person and by forecasting how she or he will react to the feedback. Then we should work to formulate a personal feedback message that accurately communicates our meaning while attending to the face needs of our partner. The following guidelines can help you effectively disclose constructive criticism:

1. Criticize in private. Only under the direst and most life-threatening circumstances should you criticize someone in front of managers, colleagues, or subordinates. It is far more face-threatening to be the recipient of criticism when you have an audience and are aware that they may be internally judging you as well. When you have criticism to deliver, try to do it one-on-one. Sometimes you may need to give criticism in a group context, such as feedback for a work team. In this case, look for ways to avoid singling people out: prepare equal amounts of criticism for everyone present, or convey that the criticism is useful for everyone in the group. For example, "I'm going to talk with each of you in turn about strengths and where to improve, but my feedback is intended to benefit the whole team."

2. Ask for permission. Unless you are in a position of authority, make sure that your partner is willing to hear your feedback. There are times when people have acted poorly, and they know it. They don't really need others to remind them. At other times, people may be overloaded with emotional issues, and hearing any negative feedback would be counterproductive. So before you disclose negative feedback, you should seek your partner's permission and willingness to hear what you have to say. Even when you are in a position of authority, you can still reduce resistance by getting assent: "I'd like to talk with you about improving this situation." Most often people will agree to hear you out. But sometimes the response will be, "No," "Not now," "I already know what you're going to say, and I don't want to hear it," and so forth. With peers who respond this way, you should probably hold back. As someone in authority, however, you can choose another time, or respond with, "I'm sorry. I really think the issue is important and we need to tackle it now."

3. Whenever possible, preface a negative statement with a positive one. One way to address your partner's face needs is to begin your comments by praising some related behavior. Of course, common sense suggests that superficial praise followed by crushing criticism will be seen for what it is. But criticism prefaced with valid praise can reduce defensiveness. Suppose that Dan asks Ryan, "What did you think of my presentation of a fundraising plan for the

Constructive criticizing—the feedback skill of diplomatically describing the specific negative behavior of your partner and its effects on others

fraternity?" Ryan, who has several reservations about what Dan is proposing, might begin his feedback by saying, "I think the idea of the guys doing spring cleanup work for a daily fee is really creative." Here the praise provided is relevant and balances the negative feedback that follows.

4. Be specific about the behavior and why it is problematic. The more specifically you describe the behavior you are going to criticize, and why it's a problem, the more effectively a person will be able to understand what needs to change and how to change it. In addition, focusing on the behavior avoids attacking the person or evaluating his or her general worth, which would result in losing face. In our example, it would not be helpful for Ryan to say only, "Some of your ideas won't work," or "It's not going to make us much money." The first statement is so general that Dan will have no idea what Ryan thinks he should change, and the second asserts a negative outcome without explaining why this will occur. Instead, Ryan might say, "Well, I think the idea of the guys' doing spring cleanup work for a daily fee is really creative, but I think the plan to have us sell magazines could be a problem. The rowing team just did that last month and made only one-third of their goal. They found that college students don't have extra money for magazine subscriptions." This criticism tells Dan exactly what Ryan thinks is wrong, and why, without attacking Dan as a person.

SKILL BUILDER ▶ CONSTRUCTIVELY CRITICIZING

SKILL	USE	STEPS	EXAMPLE
Diplomatically describing the specific negative behaviors or actions of another and their effects on others	To help people see themselves as others see them	1. Criticize in private. 2. Ask for permission. 3. Whenever possible, preface a negative statement with a positive one. 4. Be specific about the behavior and why it is a problem. 5. When appropriate, suggest how the person can change the behavior or action.	Carol says, "Bob, I've noticed something about your behavior with Jenny. Would you like to hear it?" After Bob assures her that he would, Carol continues: "Although you seem really supportive of Jenny, there are times when Jenny starts to relate an experience and you interrupt her and finish telling the story. You did this a few times while Jenny was trying to talk about her trip to Colorado, and she looked a little hurt. She's pretty sensitive about being interrupted, so you might want to let her finish her stories the rest of this evening or she might get upset."

Seeking, giving, and responding appropriately to feedback are essential skills in the workplace.

5. When appropriate, suggest how the person can change the behavior or action. Since the focus of constructive criticism is helping, suggestions that might lead to positive change are important. In responding to Dan's request for feedback, for example, Ryan might also have added, "Maybe we could find out what school supplies or personal care products are most often purchased and sell those instead." By including a positive suggestion, you not only help the person but also show that your intentions are constructive.

Responding to Negative Feedback (Criticism)

Even when we ask for feedback, it can be difficult to receive negative evaluations from others. When negative feedback comes without warning, or seems unduly harsh, you may be inclined to flee the situation, attack with a counter-criticism, or ignore what was said. None of these is a good way to respond however, especially in a work environment where aggressive communication or failure to improve your performance can be costly. The following guidelines will help you respond gracefully to criticism and allow you to make the most of negative feedback.

1. Show gratitude for the feedback you receive. Regardless of how the feedback makes you feel, start your response by sincerely thanking people for their feedback. No one likes to be asked for feedback and then be ignored after providing what they were asked for. In some cases, showing gratitude may cause a critic to revise his or her opinion, or restate it more kindly. If showing gratitude for a mean-spirited critique is too much of a stretch, or will seem sarcastic, you should at least avoid negative nonverbal reactions such as scowling or sighing.

2. Agree with everything you can. Drop your defenses, take a deep breath, and consider that the negative feedback may be entirely correct. If so, agree: "You're right. I haven't been careful to arrive on time for team meetings." If appropriate, add an apology: "I'm sorry about disrupting the meetings by arriving late." Or, "I see what you mean, my writing isn't as readable as it could be." Sometimes, this is the right thing to do even if you don't completely agree. You may think that your writing is clear and engaging, but it's your manager's opinion that matters when it comes to you getting a raise or a promotion.

However, as we discussed in Chapter 11, when you don't think a criticism is entirely accurate, there are at least four useful ways of agreeing without accepting all of a criticism's implications (Adler, 1977). You can agree with part of the message. For example, if you think that timeliness is a recent issue rather than a consistent one, you might agree that "I have been late to the last two meetings." You can agree in principle, without agreeing that it applies to you: "I know readability is very important for the newsletter." You can agree that your critic sees the situation in a particular way: "I understand. It must seem to you that I am not being responsible about team meetings." And, you can agree that the initiator is having certain feelings: "You're really frustrated with my writing." Each of these strategies is respectful of the critic and shows willingness to engage with the criticism, without giving complete agreement.

3. Ask for more detail. Show that you are taking the criticism seriously by asking follow-up questions. You can seek more information about the critic's perspective, or what they suggest you do to improve. For example, you might ask, "Have I misunderstood the newsletter style completely, or are there specific things I should tackle?" or "Do you think it's a matter of adding more stories and quotes, or something else?"

4. Take responsibility. When you accept responsibility for what has happened, and show that you intend to do something about it, you often disarm your critic and encourage them to help you. You shouldn't take responsibility for things that aren't your fault, but you do need to show that you understand how you've contributed to the problem, and demonstrate your commitment to fixing it. You might say, "It's my job to make this newsletter as fun to read as possible. I'll ask people which articles they enjoyed reading most in past issues." If your critic has made suggestions for improvement, show that you will use them: "I'll be sure to

---

SKILL BUILDER ▶ RESPONDING TO NEGATIVE FEEDBACK

SKILL	USE	STEPS	EXAMPLE
Responding gracefully and effectively to criticisms or concerns expressed by others	To get the greatest value from others' feedback and maintain a positive relationship with a critic	1. Show gratitude for the feedback you receive. 2. Agree with everything you can. 3. Ask for more detail. 4. Take responsibility.	"Thank you for sharing your concerns with me. I understand why you need me to be more of a team player. Should I start helping more on recruitment, or training? I apologize for not contributing as much as I could have, and I promise to turn this situation around." "I really appreciate you taking the time to talk with me. I never meant my behavior to offend you, but I can see that you are hurt and unhappy with me. How can I make this right with you? I want to help us be friends again."

get more quotes for future articles, as you suggested." In the process of taking responsibility, you can provide information that clarifies where you are not responsible, and where you need help to meet your critic's expectations. For example, you might say, "I've been late to the last two team meetings because I recently lost my babysitter and have to get my kids to school, but I'm looking for a new sitter. In the meanwhile, is there anything you'd like me to do?"

The Dark Side of Workplace Communication

While most exchanges at work are task-related or intended to foster positive working relationships, two types of communication can damage people, their workplace relationships, and their performance: aggression and sexual harassment.

Aggression at Work

Workplace aggression is any counterproductive behavior at work intended to hurt someone else (Rai, 2002). Aggression can be active or passive, verbal or physical, direct or indirect (Baron & Neuman, 1996). When Joe, for example, chooses to ignore an email from Thom that asks for a copy of last quarter's sales figures by tomorrow, Joe's behavior is passive, verbal, direct aggression: passive because he has hurt Thom's ability to do his job by avoiding responding to his request, verbal because he is not providing the report, direct because his behavior is aimed squarely at hurting Thom. Workplace aggression also varies in whether it is verbal, behavioral, or physical.

Verbal aggression is sending verbal messages intended to hurt someone. It includes incivility, rudeness, teasing, brushing people off, name-calling, and verbal fighting. Gossiping, spreading rumors, and slandering others at work are also forms of verbal aggression. Verbal aggression can occur face-to-face, over the phone, or through electronic means like flaming emails, text messages, and so forth. Some verbal aggression stems from the inability to be assertive and resorting instead to a verbally aggressive message when frustrated, angry, or defensive. If you are the target of verbal aggression, you should respond assertively. Suppose you are trying to explain to a co-worker that as a result of his incomplete research, you were unable to submit a report on time. His response is verbally intimidating: "Oh, you're just such a perfectionist. Nothing anyone does is ever good enough for you. Well, you can just shove it because you're not my boss, and I don't have to listen to this s***." Using your interpersonal assertiveness skills, you might respond: "I know it must be hard to hear that the research was insufficient, but I haven't done anything to deserve this outburst, and I am really disappointed in you. Do you understand why I would feel this way?" Then listen. Sometimes a verbally aggressive person is overwrought about issues unrelated to the immediate situation. Once you have identified the real area of conflict, you can use a collaborative approach to solve the problem.

Behavioral aggression is a nonverbal act intended to hurt someone. It includes brushing people off, shunning, withholding resources, and sabotaging others' work products. For example, at the quarterly management meeting, when people were

---

Workplace aggression—any counterproductive behavior at work intended to hurt someone else

Verbal aggression—sending verbal messages intended to hurt someone

Behavioral aggression—nonverbal acts intended to hurt someone

told to break into groups to discuss next quarter's goals, Maddie purposefully turned her back on Karin, who was waving and walking toward her. This was behavioral aggression. It would have been honest and not aggressive for Maddie to simply set a boundary, politely telling Karin that she didn't wish to work with her on this task. When you feel that someone is being behaviorally aggressive, you can use your assertiveness skills to teach the other person how you expect to be treated.

Physical aggression is a nonverbal act of violence against another person with the intent to do bodily harm. It includes gross violations of personal space (getting in your face), pushing, hitting, threatening with a weapon, and so forth. If you experience or witness physical aggression in your workplace, you should report it to your manager (unless the manager is the violent person) and to Human Resources. Even if the person who behaved this way seems contrite and promises to never do it again, you need to report the behavior. When you do this, be careful to describe the exact sequence of events without evaluating the cause or attributing motives, of which you may not be aware.

> **Physical aggression**—nonverbal acts of violence against another person with the intent to do bodily harm

In some instances, aggression is an aberration. It happens rarely. Or an individual is aggressive toward others in general, without any consistent target. These forms of workplace aggression are problematic, yet workplace bullying presents an even greater challenge. **Bullying** is persistent, highly aggressive behavior directed by the aggressor, or bully, toward a specific person or persons, or target(s) (Lutgen-Sandvik & Tracy, 2012). Workplace bullies often have allies, or people who help them bully, and bullies also benefit from the silence of observers who do nothing to stop the abuse, usually due to fear. Common bullying behaviors include foul language, yelling and screaming, constant criticism, spreading rumors, and public humiliation. Although we normally think of bullying as a schoolyard phenomenon, studies indicate that workplace bullying is widespread, with approximately one in ten U.S. workers experiencing bullying in a given year, 30–40% experiencing bullying at some point in their working lives, and an additional 10% witnessing bullying without being direct targets (Namie & Lutgen-Sandvik, 2010).

> **Bullying**—persistent, highly aggressive behavior directed by the aggressor, or bully, toward a specific person or persons, or target(s)

Workplace bullying damages targets' mental and physical health; contributes to depression, anxiety, and suicide; and also affects organizational outcomes such as productivity, absenteeism, and turnover. Yet, unlike sexual harassment or racial discrimination, bullying isn't necessarily illegal, and companies often lack policies to prevent or punish it. Workplace bullies often have some degree of power over their targets, such as supervising them or having greater seniority in the company, and in some companies, their aggressiveness is (mistakenly) valued as "competitiveness." For these reasons, people in a position to do something about bullying often minimize the seriousness of the problem, fail to believe the target, and even blame the target for the bully's actions. Awareness of workplace bullying and motivation to eliminate it is increasing, due to organizations like the Workplace Bullying Institute (WBI) and its efforts to promote anti-bullying laws in multiple states. However, currently only about one-third of complaints are resolved to the target's satisfaction (Namie & Lutgen-Sandvik, 2010).

The problem of bullying is unlikely to be resolved with simple solutions (Gardner et al., 2013). A great deal of research shows that avoiding or placating the bully usually perpetuates the abuse, and confronting one is also generally ineffective and can provoke increased abuse. Some bullies succeed in using confrontations to get targets labeled as unstable, or as bullies themselves. The bleak reality of bullying in the workplace is that efforts to stop bullies often fail. Bullying experts, such as those at the WBI, recommend that targets make finding another job and taking care of their own emotional needs the highest priority. They reason that if people in the organization were able or motivated to control the bully, they would probably already have done so. This is why anti-bullying policies and laws are so important.

However, targets may be able to take effective action against the bully, or at least remove themselves from the bully's range, by preparing a case that can be presented to upper management or Human Resources, or others who might be motivated to help. In some cases, legal action can be taken (usually, this requires evidence of sexual harassment or racial discrimination). Preparing a case means having a coherent, credible report of what has happened, with detailed documentation of specific abusive incidents. Table 13.1 describes what reports should (and should not) contain to be as credible as possible (Tracy, 2007). Your chances of a successful outcome within the organization improve if others also report the bully, or support your claims, and if you can show that the bully is reducing profit or affecting other company outcomes (see the WBI website for more tips on how to do this at www.workplacebullying.org). If one of your friends is bullied, your social support may be more important than you realize for helping them cope and succeed. Nonjudgemental listening and support will not only help improve their esteem, but you may be able to help them create a more effective case against the bully.

TABLE 13.1 Credible Reports of Workplace Bullying
1. Have a clear beginning, middle, and end
2. Identify the bully and focus on the bully's destructive behavior
3. Give details about the bullying, including quotes, times, places, and people present
4. Avoid issues not relevant to the bullying
5. Anticipate objections and others' perspectives
6. Portray the cost of the abuse, without being excessively emotional
7. Contain examples or metaphors for the abuse that others will find familiar
8. Refer to others who have been bullied
9. Show the effects of bullying on the target's peers and workplace productivity
10. Depict the target as a survivor, not a victim

Source: Lutgen-Sandvik & Tracy, 2012.

Sexual Harassment

Sexual harassment is unwanted verbal or physical sexual behavior that interferes with work performance. More specifically, according to U.S. Equal Employment Opportunity Commission (EEOC), **sexual harassment** is a form of sex discrimination including unwelcome sexual advances, requests for sexual favors, and other verbal or physical conduct of a sexual nature that explicitly or implicitly affects an individual's employment, unreasonably interferes with an individual's work performance, or creates an intimidating, hostile, or offensive work environment. It is behavior that violates Title VII of the Civil Rights Act of 1964. According to the EEOC, the sexual harasser may be a woman or a man, the victim's supervisor, an agent of the employer, a supervisor in another area, a co-worker, or a non-employee. The key is that the harasser's conduct is unwelcomed by their target. Sexual harassment may be a direct sexual advance or an indirect result of other's behaviors. The victim may or may not be of the opposite sex. Finally, sexual harassment may or may not have resulted in economic injury or employment termination of the victim.

Prevention is the best way to eliminate sexual harassment in the workplace. Employers create a safe working environment by clearly communicating to employees that sexual harassment will not be tolerated. They should hand out a policy statement that defines and gives examples of sexual harassment, provide training that helps employees both identify and avoid sexual harassment, establish an effective complaint or grievance process, and take immediate and appropriate action when an employee complains.

If you perceive that you are the target of sexual harassment in the workplace, or if you are experiencing a hostile work environment because of another's inappropriate sexual behavior, two principal communication strategies are useful. First, begin by directly informing the harasser that his or her conduct is unwelcome and must stop. You should privately document the first incident of harassment. Date, sign, and keep it for possible future use. It may also be wise to email a copy to yourself so that the date you recorded the incident can't later be called into question. Second, decide whether to use the employer complaint mechanism or grievance system available to you. If you perceive the first instance of sexual harassment to be extremely offensive or serious, immediately make a formal complaint. On the other hand, if you consider the first instance to be only mildly offensive, you may want to refrain from making a formal complaint, trusting that the behavior will not continue. If the offensive behavior does continue after you have communicated to the harasser that his or her conduct is unwelcome, you should inform the harasser of your intention to file a formal complaint and then follow through using the appropriate channels. Once a formal complaint has been made at work, it is the organization's responsibility to investigate and provide resolution. If your complaints are dismissed, if you are retaliated against, or if you are dismissed from your job, contact the EEOC for their advice.

Sexual harassment—a form of sex discrimination including unwelcome sexual advances, requests for sexual favors, and other verbal or physical conduct of a sexual nature that explicitly or implicitly affects an individual's employment, unreasonably interferes with an individual's work performance, or creates an intimidating, hostile, or offensive work environment

Digital Communication Skills in Professional Relationships

Relationships with professional colleagues may compose the bulk of our interpersonal relationships. Being an effective communicator with your colleagues and supervisors can lead to promotions and other important career opportunities (Whetten & Cameron, 2005). Therefore, by learning how to take advantage of opportunities provided by social media and understanding how to avoid drawbacks of new technologies, you can better position yourself for professional success. Social media can influence potential professional relationships long before you actually start a full-time position. It is important to understand how you can develop professional relationships through social media while simultaneously serving as an effective manager of your online identity. You must also become familiar with guidelines for digital communication etiquette (sometimes referred to as "netiquette").

Using Social Media Responsibly and Effectively

While social media can be a great way to stay connected, the tremendous reach, mobility, and interactivity of social media blurs the line between our personal and professional lives. We are technically "available" anywhere, anytime (Kleinman, 2007). Since we may always be connected to the office through our smart phones, we are just one call, text, or email away. One way to describe this new reality created by mobile and tablet devices is "Always on and always with" (Park 2014).

How are digital messages at work different from those we exchange with our friends?

Sometimes we become slaves to our electronic devices, sacrificing personal and family time to check and answer email as it is received. Many companies today encourage their employees to seek work–life balance, and part of establishing this balance is to set appropriate boundaries between work and home. One such boundary is intentionally choosing to stop monitoring your electronic devices when at home.

Social media permit us to manage multiple conversations while on the job. When you are browsing Facebook at your desk, your computer may ding with a new email, your iPhone may alert you to an incoming text, and Skype may ring with an incoming video call. As you learn to manage multiple conversations at work, remember that each person deserves your full attention. Client relationships, profits, and your job may be on the line. Many of us believe that we can multi-task just fine; however, overwhelming (and growing) research shows that multi-tasking doesn't really work: you get less done, not more, and you make mistakes in the process. In one study, multitasking negotiators were seen as less trust-worthy and less professional, and achieved lower payoffs overall (Krishnan et al., 2014). The lesson here is simple: avoid multitasking if you can, and focus on one thing at a time. If that means putting your phone down, logging off Facebook, or closing your email, do it. You will be more effective.

Using Social Media Strategically and Wisely

A common practice for employers now is to search for information about their potential new hires through social media. Those pictures of you at a party may be funny to you and your friends, but they may make you look less than profes-sional to a potential employer. Scan your Facebook page for any potentially in-criminating photos that may lead a potential employer or co-worker to draw inaccurate perceptions about your professionalism. If you regularly use Twitter, be careful what you tweet to your followers. If you say some not-so-nice things about a colleague or your company, that brief message could make its way into the hands of your supervisor. You don't want to lose a potential job, raise, or promotion over 140 rude and hastily typed characters.

If you have not done so already, immediately begin preparing your digital image for the job search. Increase your Facebook privacy settings, remove any questionable photos from your web page, and think twice about what you post online. Begin to regularly google your name and versions of it. You need to be fa-miliar with what appears in the list of search results. When you look at the list of search results, count the number of personal hits relating to aspects of your non-work life and the number of professional hits relating to aspects of your career life. For example, when Dylan googled his name, he found six professional hits: items pertaining to his work as a writer for the university's newspaper. He also discovered two personal hits: questionable photos from a recent fraternity social event. He quickly emailed the fraternity's webmaster and asked him to remove the pictures from the website. Consider the ratio of professional-to-personal hits when scanning search results. You always want more professional items appearing in a search. If you find yourself in the unfortunate situation of having more personal items appear in an online search, work to repair that image immediately.

**INTER-ACT WITH
SOCIAL MEDIA**

The digital persona that you present through social media can positively or negatively affect a potential employer's perception of your professional competence. Conduct an audit of your social media presence. Scan each platform on which you actively participate, including Facebook, Twitter, Instagram, Vine, YouTube, and any news forums. If employers looked across your various postings, what conclusions would they draw? If your current image is a problem, what steps can you take to change it?

Using Social Media Professionally

Social media have drastically changed how colleagues interact in professional settings. Email, instant messages, tweets, video chats, blogs, podcasts, and wikis, used individually or in combination, allow team members to communicate easily, regularly, and inexpensively as they seek to accomplish professional goals. Appropriately integrating social media into your professional relationships with colleagues and clients is an essential skill. One study of social media policies in major organizations found that they currently emphasize three issues: (1) visibility and persistence, (2) editability, and (3) association (Vaast & Kaganer, 2013).

Visibility and Persistence

One of the key things companies want their employees to remember while using social media is that our posts are both visible and persistent. The reality of social media is that people can and will see the stuff we post, and it will potentially stay around for a long time. Our professional (and for that matter, personal) communication via social media should reflect an awareness of this. For example, Faegre Baker Daniels, an international law firm, has guidelines for social media that include, "Remember that the Internet is not anonymous, nor does it forget" (Vaast & Kaganer, 2013).

Editability

While the things we post are both visible and persistent, information online can also be edited by others or ourselves. The rules of thumb are if it needs to be changed, change it; if it was changed, admit it; and if it shouldn't be changed, consider whether and how it should be released. One example of company policies on editability comes from clothing retailer Nordstrom's: "Be sure to correct any mistake you make immediately and make it clear what you've done to fix it" (cited by Vaast & Kaganer, 2013).

Association

Finally, thriving companies value relationships, both within and outside of their organizations. Creating a strong network with co-workers and clients is important, but it is also important to make a clear distinction between personal and professional communications. Sometimes inappropriate or blurred-line communications have resulted in someone's being fired or disciplined. One example of a company policy on association comes from Cap Gemini, an international consulting, technology, and outsourcing company. "When you discuss [Cap Gemini] Group-related information online, be transparent by giving your name and role and mentioning that you work for the Group. If you have an individual site that refers to or has an impact on the Group, use a disclaimer such as 'the views expressed on this site are my own and not those of Cap Gemini'" (cited by Vaast & Kaganer, 2013).

In addition to these guidelines, consider these three things:

1. Match your purpose with your media. Media Synchronicity Theory (Dennis, Valacich, Speier, & Morris, 1998) tells us that some media serve our purposes better than others, depending on our goals. So if your team is preparing and revising an executive summary of your committee's work, it would be inefficient to email a draft to the team for each member to comment on and separately email those revisions back to the team leader. Instead, consider using a wiki where users can collaboratively add and edit content. On the other hand, if you are trying to patch over hard feelings with a client, a phone call may be better for conveying your emotions than an email or text.

2. Respond in a timely fashion. Timely responses to emails and other messages are appreciated. Although the burden of responding to multiple messages can be great, try to give each message the attention that it deserves. Do not put off responding to a colleague, who may be waiting on you for approval or insight.

3. Give praise where appropriate. Finally, social media are powerful because of their reach and speed. You can easily share good news about yourself through Facebook or Twitter (without going overboard, of course). But more than that, social media are even more effective when you praise others and give them a

A QUESTION OF ETHICS ▶ WHAT WOULD YOU DO?

Caleb had been working for Kim Imports as a shift manager for almost a year. While the owner, Mr. Kim, was polite to him, he noticed that other employees, who were Chinese, seemed to have a closer working relationship with Mr. Kim. One man, Han Lee, seemed especially close to Mr. Kim. Recently Mr. Kim had told the employees that some merchandise was unaccounted for. Mr. Kim had voiced his concern and his fervent wish to resolve the problem as soon as possible. To Caleb, it sounded like someone was stealing from the company.

One evening, Caleb went into the warehouse to check on a recent order. Upon entering the building, he overheard Han Lee speaking in Chinese to another man. Caleb noticed that the other man didn't work at Kim Imports, and that they were loading a pallet of goods into the back of a van. Stepping into their view, Caleb raised his hand and greeted Han Lee, explaining that he had come to check on an order. Han Lee looked at the ground, then stared at Caleb before quietly saying something to the other man in Chinese. The man dropped what he was doing, climbed into the van, and drove away. Caleb quickly retreated to his office and contemplated what he should do next. After thinking about it, he wrote the following email to Mr. Kim:

Dear Mr. Kim,

I am sorry to report that I have discovered who is stealing our inventory. Tonight I confronted Han Lee speaking in Chinese to a man I had never seen before who was loading merchandise into a van. When I approached them, they stopped and the other man quickly left. I hope that this information will help put an end to the thefts.

The next evening, Caleb found a letter addressed to him on his desk. It was a note from Mr. Kim expressing his regret that the business could no longer afford to employ him as a shift manager. Enclosed with the letter was a check amounting to two weeks' salary.

FOR CONSIDERATION
1. What cultural factors might account for what happened to Caleb?
2. Was it ethical for Caleb to accuse Han Lee of stealing? Explain your position.
3. If what Caleb did was unethical, what should Caleb have done instead? Explain your conclusion.

moment in the spotlight. If Jenny surpassed her sales quota for the month, tweet it to the entire company, if appropriate. Here you can use social media's reach to congratulate a colleague and quickly share her good news with others.

Summary

Most adults spend more time with people at work than they do with their friends and family. In organizations we have both formal and informal relationships. The most important relationship that we have is with our manager, because our manager influences or controls the work we are assigned, the evaluations that determine our rewards, and the progress we can make in our career. Leader–member exchange theory explains that managers form in-group, middle-group, and out-group relationships with subordinates, depending on the work and quality of work that the subordinate performs. In exchange for the additional work taken on, in-group members enjoy choice career-advancing developmental assignments, non-monetary perks, and greater access to the manager. Because so much of your success depends on developing a good working relationship with your manager, you should: adapt to your manager's communication preferences, identify how you can help your manager effectively complete the work of your group, volunteer for specific assignments and follow-through, ask questions to clarify assignments, and seek feedback and use it to improve.

Co-workers are peers who work together, are at the same or similar level in an organization's hierarchy, and have no formal authority over each other. People develop three types of co-worker relationships: informational, collegial, and special. Co-worker relationships serve important functions within organizations, including mentoring, information sharing, exerting peer power and control, and providing social support. Boundary spanning is the process of communicating with people outside of an organization in mutually beneficial relationships. Some members of an organization form relationships with customers and vendors. In addition to the formal work relationships that are dictated by the work that is done, who has to work together in order for tasks to be accomplished, the position one holds in an organization, and the person whom one reports to, we also have informal work relationships. Mentoring relationships are developmentally oriented, with a mentor providing knowledge, insight, guidance, and learning opportunities to a younger or less experienced protégé. We also develop workplace friendships, which provide sources of support and resources to help us do our jobs better and more happily. Some people develop romantic relationships at work. While workplace romances are more common than we might expect, those who enter into them need to carefully consider an organization's policies and the effect that the relationship might have on their careers.

Diversity in the workforce means that we are interacting with people of different cultures, genders, and generations, a situation that requires varied and flexible approaches to communication in the workplace. We can improve our own and other's performances at work by skillfully asking for feedback, constructively criticizing others, and responding appropriately to negative feedback.

There are "dark side" issues that must be dealt with at work, including workplace aggression, both verbal and behavioral, which sometimes becomes bullying, and sexual harassment. Today, we are increasingly using social media at work, so we need to develop digital communication skills to use in managing our professional relationships. These include skills that help us use social media responsibly, effectively, strategically, wisely, and professionally.

CHAPTER RESOURCES

Key Words

Flashcards for all of these key terms are available on the *Inter-Act* website.

Asking for feedback pp. 410
Behavioral aggression pp. 416
Boundary spanning pp. 396
Bullying pp. 417
Co-workers pp. 393
Collegial peer relationships pp. 393
Constructive criticizing pp. 412
Customers and clients pp. 396
Holistic task-completion culture pp. 403
In-group relationships pp. 390
Informational peer relationships pp. 393

Linguistic style pp. 406
Manager pp. 389
Mentoring relationship pp. 398
Mid-group relationships pp. 390
Out-group relationships pp. 390
Physical aggression pp. 417
Relationship-oriented organizational culture pp. 402
Results-oriented organizational culture pp. 402

Sequential task-completion culture pp. 403
Sexual harassment pp. 419
Special peer relationships pp. 393
Vendors pp. 396
Verbal aggression pp. 416
Workplace aggression pp. 416
Workplace romance pp. 401
Workplace team pp. 395

Analyze and Apply

The following activities challenge you to demonstrate your mastery of the concepts, theories, and frameworks in this chapter by using them to explain what is happening in a specific situation.

13.1 Rewind/Rewrite

Now that you have read the chapter, hit "rewind" on the opening dialogue between Riley and Alexi, and answer the following questions.

a. Use concepts from the chapter to explain what happened in this incident. The concepts from leader–member exchange theory, mentoring, types of co-worker relationships, office romance, and giving feedback may be especially relevant

b. Rewrite the dialogue so that Alexi does a better job of recognizing the relationship dynamics and more closely follows the guidelines for giving feedback. Suppose you are Riley's confidante and she has shared with you what Alexi reported. Assuming you have also heard the same thing through the grapevine, write a dialogue you would have with her after she told you of her conversation with Alexi.

13.2 Application Scenarios

a. Your friendship with a co-worker has turned into romance. How should you handle this development?

b. A friend of yours has now come to you three or four times with stories of rude treatment by a senior co-worker. What can you recommend for your friend to do?

c. You recently switched departments. Your new supervisor seems a little too interested in how you look and what you do after hours. What can you do?

Skill Practice

Skill practice activities give you the chance to rehearse a new skill by responding to hypothetical or real situations. Additional skill practice activities are available at the companion website.

13.3 Asking for Feedback

For each situation below, prepare a skillful message asking for feedback.

a. Situation: You walk into your manager's office and hand him a status update on the project that you have been working on for several weeks. Without looking up, he extends his hand while shaking his head side to side.

b. Situation: After a contentious team meeting in which you have argued with another member of the team about work-load equity, you approach another member of your team who seemed to be upset by the heated discussion.

c. Situation: You are walking back to your office with your mentor, who just watched you give a major presentation to your clients. During the presentation, you noticed her shaking her head side to side and looking disheartened.

13.4 Constructive Criticizing

For each situation below, prepare a skillful message that offers constructive criticism.

a. Situation: Your cubicle mate returns from her performance review and tells you that she received a poor performance evaluation from your manager because she has not been completing projects on time. You have noticed that she spends at least an hour a day talking with her family, shopping online, or perusing Facebook. She says to you, "I just don't know how I can possibly get everything done that he expects of me. What do you think?"

b. Situation: You have just returned from a company-sponsored leadership seminar that required you to be out of town for three weeks straight, including weekends. As a single parent with no family in town, you were forced to pay for a caregiver to stay with your children while you were away. While your company reimbursed you for travel, lodging, and meals, your biggest expense, childcare, is not a reimbursable expense. You get a call from the Director of Employee Development, who asks how the conference went and whether you would like to be considered for a follow-up session.

c. Situation: You are part of a six-person team who is to give a 30-minute presentation to your Vice President. During the team's first rehearsal, one of your teammates took 15 minutes to present his material, primarily due to the 32 very complex PowerPoint slides he developed. While all of the information he is presenting is good, it is probably more detail than your Vice President needs to hear.

13.5 Responding to Negative Feedback

For each situation below, prepare a skillful message that responds to the negative feedback.

a. Situation: Your mentor invited you to lunch with several of her peer managers. You thoroughly enjoyed the luncheon and the opportunity it provided for you to showcase your knowledge of the new IT system that was being implemented in the company. While driving back to the office with your manager, she turned to you and said, "I was very uncomfortable with how you acted at lunch today. I had hoped that you would temper your tendency to toot your own horn and would use this as a 'listen and learn' opportunity. As it was, you spent a lot of time telling people things they already knew. I'm not sure it reflected well on you or on me."

b. Situation: Once again you are arriving five minutes late for your shift because the bus schedule has changed. Your head nurse intercepts you and gives you a verbal warning about your tardiness. She indicates that the next time you are late, she will have to give you a written warning.

c. Situation: On your most recent performance evaluation, your manager gave you a low score on the category "Works well with others" and wrote, "Not a team player." While it's true that you prefer to work alone, you're not sure what your manager means by "not a team player."

Communication Improvement Plan:
Workplace Communication

Would you like to improve the following aspects of your work relationships?

- Relationship with your manager
- Relationship with your co-worker[s]
- Relationships with your customers/clients/vendors
- Dealing with aggression
- Dealing with sexual harassment

Pick an aspect of your work relationships, then, using the interpersonal communication skills you have studied in the course, write a communication improvement plan. You can find a communication improvement plan worksheet on our website at www.oup.com/us/verderber.

Glossary

Accommodating resolving a conflict by satisfying the other person's needs or accepting the other person's ideas while neglecting one's own needs or ideas

Acoustic space the area over which your voice or other sounds can be comfortably heard

Active listening the skillful, intentional, deliberate, conscious process of attending to, understanding, remembering, critically evaluating, and responding to messages that we hear

Advice recommendation about action to take in response to a problem

Affection need our desire to love and be loved

Affiliation the appreciation or esteem one person has for another

Analytical listening style a personal listening style that focuses on gathering information and thinking carefully about what is said

Anxious-ambivalent attachment an anxiety-filled emotional bond between infants and their parents or caregivers stemming from worry that their needs will not be met and ambivalence about whether others can be trusted to care for them

Appraisal theories of emotion theories that hypothesize that what we feel arises from what we think

Appropriate messages messages that conform to the social, relational, and ethical expectations of the situation

Argumentativeness defending our own ideas or attacking the reasoning of others while according them respect

Artifacts the objects we use to adorn our territory

Asking for feedback the skill of eliciting observations from others about your behavior

Assertiveness the skill of sending messages that declare and defend personal rights and expectations in a clear, direct, and honest manner while still respecting the preferences and rights of others

Assimilation the tendency to force new information to fit a memory structure, or filtering it out because it doesn't fit

Asynchronous communication that occurs when participants are not co-present and where there are delays between sending, receiving, interpreting, and responding to messages

Attachment styles the perception of adults about their self-worth and the trustworthiness of others based on their relationships with their parents and caregivers during their infancy and childhood

Attending the process of willfully striving to perceive selected sounds that are being heard

Attention the process of focusing more closely on some of the stimuli in your environment

Attributions explanations we think of for why a particular person is behaving a certain way

Authoritarian parenting style a parenting style characterized by high levels of control with low levels of nurturing; order and tradition, respect, and obedience of parents is valued and reinforced through punishment

Authoritative parenting style a parenting style characterized by firm control balanced with ample nurturing; socializing children to become empowered and caring adults is valued and reinforced by setting and enforcing high standards supported by facts and reasoning

Authority heuristic being influenced by what knowledgeable professionals believe or advocate during peripheral processing of persuasive messages

Automatic social cognition arriving at conclusions about others, ourselves, or a situation without much consciousness, intention, or awareness of their future impact

Autonomy the desire to act and make decisions independent of your relationship partner

Avoidant attachment the inability of a child to emotionally bond with or trust others based on the belief that they are worthy of care but view others as untrustworthy, which results from experiencing severe neglect as an infant

Back-channel cues verbal and nonverbal signals that indicate you are listening and attempting to understand the message

Behavioral aggression nonverbal acts intended to hurt someone

Behavioral flexibility the capacity to react in a variety of ways to the same or similar situations

Benign violation the idea that humor is created from behavior that is unexpected, but not harmful

Blatant stereotyping when people who have extremely negative views of out-groups, express and promote those views, and readily apply their stereotypes to members of the out-groups

Blind pane a pane of the Johari window that contains the information that your relationship partner knows about you, but of which you are unaware

Body language the intentional or unintentional movement of various body parts that sends nonverbal messages

Body orientation your position in relation to another person

Boundary management discussion of who is allowed to co-own private information

Boundary spanning the process of communicating with people outside of an organization in a mutually beneficial relationship

Boundary turbulence interpersonal difficulty associated with violation of a privacy boundary

Bullying persistent, highly aggressive behavior directed by the aggressor, or bully, toward a specific person or persons, or target(s)

Canned plan a learned communication strategy for a specific type of situation

Capitalization the process of sharing our successes and leveraging the good feelings that come from them by telling others, with the expectation that they will celebrate with us

Celebratory support the skill of helping others capitalize on their success

Central route consciously processing persuasive messages by critically evaluating the logic, credibility, and emotional appeals of the sender

Change requests messages that direct others how to change their behavior to show greater respect for our rights or expectations

Chronemics the study of how perception of time differs between individuals and cultures

Claims simple statements of belief or opinion

Clarifying question a response designed to get further information or to remove uncertainty from information already received

Closed-ended questions questions that can be answered with "yes," "no," or a few words

Closedness the desire to maintain privacy

Co-cultures cultures that exist side by side with the dominant culture and comprise smaller numbers of people who hold common values, attitudes, beliefs, and orientations that differ from those of the dominant culture

Codeswitch to alter linguistic and non-verbal patterns to conform to the dominant or co-culture depending on the topics or the participants in a conversation

Coercive power the potential to influence rooted in our ability to physically or psychologically punish our partner

Cognitive component of emotion the meaning or interpretation of the emotion-provoking event

Cognitive-emotional theory of esteem support messages the theory that support providers can help restore

self-esteem and promote problem-solving by encouraging more positive reappraisals

Collaborating resolving a conflict by using problem solving to arrive at a solution that meets the needs and interests of both parties in the conflict

Collapsed contexts the merging of public and private contexts as a consequence of social media

Collectivist culture a culture that values community, collaboration, shared interests, harmony, the public good, and avoiding embarrassment

Collegial peer relationships relationships between co-workers where a wider variety of topics are discussed and partners offer social support to each other in problematic work situations

Commitment a dimension of relationships that gauges how dedicated or loyal partners are to each other

Communication competence another person's perception that your messages are both effective and appropriate in a given relationship

Communication context the set of background conditions surrounding an interaction, including the physical, social, historical, psychological, and cultural contexts

Communication context the set of background conditions surrounding the interaction

Communication privacy management theory (CPM) a framework for understanding the decision-making processes people use to manage private information

Communication skills combinations of goals, plans, and scripts that are effective and appropriate for specific messages, interactions, and relationships

Communication skills the combinations of goals, plans, and scripts that are effective and appropriate for specific types of messages, interactions, and relationships

Communication theories systematic and research-based explanations of how communication works

Competence the perception that speakers are credible because they are well-qualified to provide accurate and reliable information

Competing resolving a conflict by satisfying one's own needs or advancing one's own ideas with little concern for the needs or ideas of the other person or for the relationship

Complaint a message telling someone that what is or has occurred is unacceptable because it has violated your rights or expectations

Complementary message one that is the opposite to the dominance or submission implied in the partner's previous message

Compromising resolving a conflict by bargaining so that each partner's needs or interests are partially satisfied

Co-narration specific type of conversational sequencing in which people finish each other's sentences because they have intimate knowledge of the topic and each other's style

Concrete language words that describe something that can be sensed

Conformity orientation the extent of a family's willingness to listen to and value diverse ideas, and the degree to which family members are encouraged to think and behave independently

Connection the desire to link your actions and decisions with those of your relationship partner

Connotation the feelings or evaluations we personally associate with a word

Consistency heuristic being influenced by our past active, voluntary, and public commitments during peripheral processing of persuasive messages

Constitutive function the messages exchanged in a relationship form the relationship

Constructive criticizing the feedback skill of diplomatically describing the specific negative behavior of your partner and its effects on others

Content paraphrase a feedback message that conveys understanding of the denotative meaning of a verbal message

Controlled social cognition consciously and intentionally stopping to think about something because you realize that how you think will affect what happens

Controlling messages messages designed to influence or regulate a child's behavior

Control need our desire to influence the events and people around us and to be influenced by others

Conversational coherence the extent to which the comments made by one person relate to those made previously by others in a conversation

Conversational maxims specific rules that cooperating partners count on others to follow

Conversation an interactive, extemporaneous, locally managed, and sequentially organized interchange of thoughts and feelings between two or more people

Conversation orientation the richness of family interaction, including how frequently and spontaneously members interact, sharing thoughts on many topics, and including children in decision-making

Conversation purpose what the conversation is intended to do

Conversation tone emotional and relational quality, or how it feels "inside" the interaction

Cooperative principle the pragmatic principle that states that conversational partners are able to understand what the other means to do with their verbal messages because they assume that their partners are collaborating by sharing verbal messages in line with the shared purpose of the conversation

Counterblaming a conflict pattern in which you blame your partner for what he or she has accused you of doing, shifting responsibility and leaving the original issue unresolved

Covert intimacy delivering messages that use mild insults, competition, or put-downs to signal closeness, trust, and equality

Co-workers peers who work together, are at the same or similar levels in an organization's hierarchy, and who have no formal authority over each other

Credibility the extent to which your partner believes in your competence, trustworthiness, and likability

Critical listening style the personal listening style that focuses attention on the accuracy and consistency of speakers' messages

Critically evaluating the process of determining how truthful, authentic, or believable you judge the message and the speaker to be

Cross-complaining a conflict pattern in which partners trade unrelated criticisms, leaving the initial issue unresolved

Cultural context the set of beliefs, values, and attitudes common to the specific cultures of each participant that influence how each interprets what is happening in a conversation

Cultural identity that part of your self-image that is based on the cultural group or groups with which you most closely associate and align yourself

Culture shock the psychological discomfort you experience when you must interact in a new culture

Culture the system of shared values, beliefs, attitudes, and orientations learned through communication that guides what is considered to be appropriate thought and behavior in a particular segment of the population

Customers and clients the people, groups, or organizations that use an organization's goods or services

Cyberbullying the extension of bullying behavior to electronic communication of any kind

Cyberstalking a variation on cyberbullying that occurs when an individual repeatedly uses social media to shadow or harass others

Dark-side messages messages that are not ethical and/or appropriate

Decoding making sense of the messages we receive

Demand-withdrawal a conflict pattern in which one partner consistently demands while the other consistently withdraws

Denotation the direct, explicit meaning of a word found in a written dictionary of the language community

Describing feelings the skill of verbally owning and explaining the precise feelings you are experiencing

Dialect a form of a more general language spoken by a specific culture or co-culture that, while differing from the general language, shares enough commonality that most people who belong to a particular language community can understand it

Dialectic of certainty the tension between wanting your partner to behave in predictable ways versus wanting your partner to act in new and delightfully surprising ways

Dialectic of expression the tension we feel between sharing intimate thoughts with a partner and maintaining our privacy

Dialectic of integration the tension between the desire to be connected to your partner versus being independent from your partner

Digital communication literacy the ability to critically attend to, analyze, evaluate, and express digital messages

Digital communication the electronic transmission of messages

Direct verbal style language that openly states the speaker's intention and message content that is straightforward and unambiguous

Discrimination acting differently toward a stereotyped group or individual

Dismissive attachment style the attachment style experienced by a self-reliant and independent adult who has difficulty sustaining close relationships because, while they may have high self-worth, they don't trust others due to the avoidant attachments they experienced as infants and children

Display rules rules about when, why, and how different emotions are to be expressed (or not)

Dispositional attribution an explanation that puts the cause of a behavior within the control of a person

Diversity variations between and among people

Dominance the degree to which one person attempts to control the behavior of another; the opposite of submission

Dominant culture the learned system of values, beliefs, attitudes, and orientations held by the majority of people in a society

Effective messages messages that achieve the goals of their senders

Egalitarian relationship a relationship where partners agree to what each will contribute to their shared life and that their individual contributions are equally valued

Ego conflict disagreement that results when both parties insist on being the "winner" of the argument to confirm their self-concept or self-esteem

Elaboration likelihood model (ELM) of persuasion a theory that posits people will use either heuristics or more elaborate critical thinking skills when processing persuasive messages

Electronic word of mouth (eWOM) information, opinion, or advice about an organization's products or services that is electronically shared by an individual consumer

Emblems gestures that substitute completely for words

Emotional appeals persuasive messages that influence others by evoking strong feelings in support of what the speaker is advocating

Emotional infidelity when one partner develops romantic feelings toward someone else

Emotional intelligence the ability to monitor your own and others' emotions and to use this information to guide your communications

Emotions the positive and negative sensations we experience as a result of perceiving something in our environment that supports or threatens our well-being, which result in uncontrolled physical reaction expressed through verbal and nonverbal behaviors that motivate us to take action

Empathic responsiveness also called empathic distress, is the "warmest" or most emotional form of empathy, involving personally experiencing an emotional response that is parallel to the other person's actual or anticipated display of emotion

Empathy the cognitive and affective process of perceiving the emotions others are feeling and then acting on our perception

Encoding creating messages that convey our meanings and goals by selecting words and behaviors that we believe represent our ideas and feelings

Encouraging reappraisal offering information, observations, and opinions that help the support recipients reframe the situation so that they see it in a different light that is not associated with strong emotion

Ethical dialogue a conversation characterized by authenticity, empathy, confirmation, presentness, equality, and supportiveness

Ethics a set of moral principles held by a society, a group, or an individual that provides guidelines for acceptable behavior

Ethnicity a classification of people based on shared national characteristics such as country of birth, geographic origin, language, religion, ancestral customs, and traditions

Ethnocentrism being focused on one's own culture and viewing it as more important than the cultures of others

Ethnorelativism the point of view allows you to see the value in other cultural perspectives

Evidence facts, expert opinions, and personal narratives that support the truth of your reason

Expectancy violations behaviors that are different from what we expect

Expert power the ability to influence rooted in someone's subject-specific knowledge and competence

Extemporaneous uttered in the spur of the moment without lengthy preplanning

External noise physical sights, sounds, and other stimuli that draw people's attention away from intended meaning

Eye contact using eye focus to signal attention, respect, emotional reactions, or dominance

Face how we want our partners and other who are present to view us, our public self-image

Face negotiation theory proposes that in conflict settings we prefer conflict styles consistent with our cultures and the face-orientations most consistent with those cultures

Face our public self-image, or how we want others to view us

Facial expression arranging facial muscles to communicate emotion or provide feedback

Fact conflict disagreement that is caused by a dispute over the truth or accuracy of an item of information

Facts statements whose accuracy can be verified or proven

Family a self-defined group of intimates who create and maintain themselves through their own interactions and their interactions with others

Feared self-concept the set of ideas about yourself that you don't want to have

Fearful attachment style the attach-ment style experienced by an adult for whom it is difficult to form intimate

relationships because they don't believe that they are worthy of a good relationship and they don't trust others to meet their relationship needs due to the anxious-ambivalent attachments they experienced as infants and children

Feedback information about how a message was interpreted by its recipient, conveyed in a subsequent message

Feedback providing verbal and nonverbal responses to relationship partners and/or their messages

Feeling component of emotion the positive or negative sensations that we recognize as happiness, anger, anxiety, contempt, pride, surprise, and so on

Feelings paraphrase a feedback message that conveys understanding of the emotional meaning behind a speaker's verbal message

Feminine culture a culture in which people regardless of sex can assume a variety of roles depending on the circumstances and their own choices

Fictive kin people who are considered family members even through there are no genetic or marital ties

Flaming digital communication that displays hostility through insults, profanity, and other offensive language

Flaming sending an aggressive message using social media

Forgiveness a communication process that allows you and your partner to overcome the damage done to your relationship because of a transgression

Formality degree to which a conversation follows scripted norms, rules, and procedures

Free information information volunteered during conversation rather than specifically required or requested

Friendships voluntary, platonic relationships characterized by equality and reciprocity

"Friends with benefits" relationships friendships that have a physical sexual component but are not intended to be romantic

Fundamental attribution error the tendency to believe that others' negative behaviors result from their choices, whereas our own negative behaviors stem from conditions over which we have no control

Furnishings furniture and other decorative accessories for a house or room, which can be arranged to affect the space between people, and consequently convey messages about identity and interaction

Gesture using hand, arm, and finger movement to replace, complement, and augment a verbal message

Goals-Plans-Action theory a theory of message production that posits that goals motivate us to communicate, but planning determines what we actually say

Gossip discussion of people who are not present for the conversation

Ground rules mutually agreed-on rules for behavior during conflict episodes

Haptics of or relating to the sense of touch

High-context culture a culture in which much of the real meaning of a message is indirect and can only be accurately decoded by referring to unwritten cultural rules and subtle nonverbal behavior

High power-distance culture a culture in which both high- and low-power holders accept the unequal distribution of power

High uncertainty-avoidance culture a culture characterized as having a low tolerance for and a high need to control

unpredictable people, relationships, or events

Historical context the background provided by previous communication episodes between the participants

Holistic task-completion culture an organizational culture where large or complex tasks are completed by simultaneously working on all parts of the task; sometimes focusing on one part, then another, then back to the first, in an iterative fashion

Hyperpersonal intensity and intimacy experienced in an online relationship, beyond what would occur if the relationship were conducted face to face

Ideal self-concept the set of ideas about who you *would like to be*

Idiolect our personal symbolic system that includes our active vocabularies, our pronunciation of words, and our grammar and syntax when talking or writing

Idioms expressions used by members of a language or speech community whose meaning differs from the usual meanings associated with that combination of words

Immediacy behaviors nonverbal actions that signal warmth, communicate availability, decrease distance, and promote involvement between people

Implicit personality theory a specific kind of schema that connects a set of personality traits and behaviors

Impression formation the judgment process of developing an initial concept of another person

Impression management our attempt to protect our self-concept by influencing the perception that others have of us

Inclusion need our desire to be in the company of other people

Incongruence a situation in which there is a gap between perception and reality

Independent self-concept culturally based self-perceptions in which people see themselves as distinct from others with separate characteristics and abilities

Indexical function the interaction between relationship partners indicates what the relationship is like, including the partners' dominance and affiliation toward each other

Indirect verbal style language that masks the speaker's true intentions and roundabout, vague message content whose real meaning is embedded in the social or cultural context

Individualistic culture a culture that values personal rights and responsibilities, privacy, voicing one's opinion, freedom, innovation, and self-expression

Inferences claims or assertions based on the facts presented

Informational peer relationships relationships between co-workers that are superficial in that interactions and conversations are devoted solely to work topics

Information co-owners people who share private information because one person has shared it with the other, or both have shared the same experience

In-group relationships close working relationships between managers and employees who consistently take on work above that which is expected and are rewarded in a variety of monetary and non-monetary ways

Instrumental function the communication messages exchanged in a relationship are the means through which we accomplish our personal and our relationship goals

Interaction coordination the activities participants in a conversation perform to adjust their behaviors to those of their partners

Interaction goals the things a message sender wants to accomplish through communication

Interactivity the ability of a communication tool to facilitate social interaction between groups or individuals

Intercultural communication interactions that occur between people whose cultures are so different that the communication between them is altered

Intercultural competence effective and appropriate behavior and communication in intercultural situations

Interdependence a dimension of relationships that gauges the extent to which partners rely on each other to meet their needs

Interdependent self-concept culturally based self-perceptions in which people view their traits, abilities, and characteristics within the context of a particular relationship

Interference the actions or choices of one partner that create obstacles for the other

Internal noise thoughts and feelings that interfere with producing or interpreting meaning

Interpersonal conflict disagreement between two interdependent people who perceive that they have incompatible goals

Interpersonal influence the act of changing the attitudes or behaviors of others

Interpersonal needs theory the premise that all of us have inclusion, affection, and control needs that we try to meet through our relationships, although our need for each of these varies in degree from person to person

Interpersonal trust a dimension of relationships that gauges the extent to which partners believe that they know what to expect from each other, know how they are supposed to act, and know that they want to act according to expectations

Intimate interactions series of conversations between the partners that nurture interdependence, commitment, understanding, trust, and disclosure

Intimate relationships close relationships that have highly interdependent partners who are committed to each other, understand and trust one another deeply, and disclose in depth as well as breadth

Intonation the variety, melody, or inflection of a person's voice

Involuntary relationship a relationship in which we have no choice about the other people with whom we interact

Jargon technical terminology whose meaning is understood by only a select group of people in a specialized speech community based on shared activities or interests

Johari window a visual framework for understanding how self-disclosure and feedback work together in a relationship

Judgment evaluating people and their behaviors

Kinesics the study of body language

Language a symbolic system used by people to communicate verbal or written messages

Language community all people who can speak or understand a particular language

Lean media media that rely heavily on language and other symbols, such as emoticons or emojis, to convey meaning

Leave-taking cues nonverbal behaviors that indicate someone wants to end the conversation

Legitimate power the potential to influence others rooted in the authority granted to a person who occupies a certain role

Lexicon the collection of words and expressions in a language

Life cycle the process and pattern of changes in a relationship

Life transitions major events that not only affect one partner, but also require adaptation within the relationship

Likability the perception that speakers are credible because they are congenial, friendly, and warm

Liking heuristic being influenced to believe or do what people we like advocate during peripheral processing of persuasive messages

Linguistic sensitivity using language that respects others while avoiding language that offends

Linguistic style the patterned way in which a person uses language to communicate

Listening apprehension the anxiety we feel about listening that interferes with our ability to be effective listeners

Listening style your favored but usually unconscious approach to attending to your partner's messages

Listening the process of receiving, constructing meaning from, and responding to spoken and/or nonverbal messages

Local management the way that conversational partners produce and monitor every aspect of the conversational give-and-take

Long-term romantic relationships (LTRRs) enduring romantic relationships that are intimate and where the partners have made some type of long-term commitment to each other

Low-context culture a culture in which message meanings are usually encoded in the verbal part of the message

Low power-distance culture a culture in which members prefer power to be more equally distributed

Low uncertainty-avoidance culture a culture that tolerates uncertainty and is less driven to control unpredictable people, relationships, or events

Macro skills broader communication skills that apply to certain types of interactions and relationships and help us generate longer sequences of messages

Manager an employee who is responsible for planning, directing, and monitoring the work of other employees

Masculine culture a culture in which men and women are expected to adhere to traditional sex roles

Masspersonal a term used to describe media such as Facebook that disseminate personal messages to a large audience

Maxim of manner the assumption that others will say things in an orderly way

Maxim of quality the assumption that others will tell the truth

Maxim of quantity the assumption that others will provide an appropriate amount of information, neither too little nor too much

Maxim of relevance the assumption that others will respond in coherent ways to what has been previously said,

in line with the topic or purpose of the interaction

Meaning the significance that the sender (speaker) and the receiver (listener) each attach to a message

Media multiplexity relationships carried out through more than one form of social media; people in closer relationships use more forms of social media

Media richness theory the proposition that certain media are better suited than others for some types of messages due to differences in how accurately they reproduce intended meanings

Mediator a neutral and impartial guide who structures an interaction so that conflicting parties can find a mutually acceptable solution to an issue

Memories recollections of specific people and events that happened in the past

Mentoring relationship a developmentally oriented relationship between a mentor, a more experienced and often older person, and a protégé, a less experienced and often a younger person

Message a performance that uses words, sentences, and/or nonverbal behaviors to convey the thoughts, feelings, and intentions of the speaker

Message interpretation process what we think and do to decode a message

Message interpretation the process of understanding a message you have received

Message planning identifying one or more message strategies you can use that will accomplish your interaction goals

Message production process what we think and do to encode a message

Message production the process of encoding a message for the person you are talking with

Meta conflict disagreement over the process of communication itself during an argument

Microaggressions everyday insults, indignities, and demeaning messages sent to a member of a stereotyped group by well-intentioned others who are unaware of the hidden messages being sent

Micro skills very specific communication skills for producing certain types of messages or brief sequences of messages

Mid-group relationships relationships between managers and employees who perform their jobs acceptably, but not exceptionally well, so the manager usually doesn't think of them when looking for help with additional or special assignments

Mindfulness the process of drawing novel distinctions

Minimal effective response what you need to feel that your rights and expectations are respected, not everything you might want

Mnemonic device a learning technique that associates a special word or short statement with new and longer information

Monochronic a time orientation that views time as being small, even units that occur sequentially

Motivational component of emotion the action that emotion encourages us to take

Motor component of emotion the expression of emotion through nonverbal and verbal behaviors

Mutual hostility a conflict pattern in which partners trade increasingly louder verbal abuse, including inappropriate, unrelated personal criticism, name-calling, swearing, and sarcasm

Neutralization the strategy of dealing with dialectical tensions by compromising between the desires of those in the relationship

Noise any stimulus that interferes with shared meaning

Nonverbal communication all human communication that transcends spoken or written words

Novelty the desire for originality, freshness, and uniqueness in your partner's behavior or in your relationship

Nurturing messages messages of support, praise, affection, and attending to needs that encourage a child's physical, social, emotional, and intellectual development

Olfactory cues messages sent through smells and scents

Open-ended questions questions that require answers with more elaboration and explanation

Openness the desire to share intimate ideas and feelings with your relationship partner

Open pane a pane of the Johari window that contains the information about you that both you and your relationship partner know

Other-face orientation the inclination to uphold and protect the self-images of our partners and other people affected by the conflict, even at the risk of our own face

Other-generated social media cues items that other people post on our page like comments on Facebook or Twitter

Ought self-concept the set of ideas about what you *think you should be*

Out-group relationships difficult and strained working relationships between managers and employees who consistently do not work up to standards or get along with the managers

Paralanguage using the voice to convey meaning

Paraphrase an attempt to verify your understanding of a message by putting it into your own words and sharing it with the speaker

Passive-aggressive behavior messages that indirectly express hostility

Passive approach concealing your feelings rather than voicing your rights and expectations to others

Passive listening the effortless, thoughtless, and habitual process of receiving the messages we hear

Perception checking sharing your perception of another's behavior to check its accuracy

Peripheral route automatically processing persuasive messages by using shortcut heuristics that save time and mental energy

Permissive parenting style a parenting style characterized by moderate to high levels of nurturing but little control over children's behavior; creativity and freedom are valued, rules and demands are few, and children generally get what they want

Personal identity the traits and characteristics that, taken as a whole, distinguish you from other people

Personal space the area that surrounds a person, moves with that person, and changes with the situation as well as moment-to-moment

Perspective taking empathizing by using everything we know about our partners and our partners' circumstances to help us understand how they are feeling

Persuasion the use of verbal messages designed to influence the attitudes and behaviors of others

Phonology the sounds used to pronounce words

Physical aggression nonverbal acts of violence against another person with the intent to do bodily harm

Physical appearance how you look to others, including your race, gender, body type, facial features, clothing, personal grooming, and body art or tattoos

Physical context the setting of a communication episode

Pitch the rate of vibration of your vocal cords

Platonic relationship a relationship in which partners are not sexually attracted to each other or choose not to act on their sexual attraction

Policy conflict disagreement caused by differences over a preferred plan or course of action

Politeness language strategies that show concern for face

Polychronic a time orientation that views time as a continuous flow

Possessiveness the desire to control another person to ensure that he or she is one's exclusive partner

Possible self-concept a set of ideas about what you *are capable of being*

Posture the position and movement of the whole body

Power distance the extent to which members of a culture expect and accept that power will be unequally shared

Power the potential that you have to influence the attitudes, beliefs, and behaviors of someone else

Pragmatic meaning meaning of a verbal message that arises from understanding the practical consequences of an utterance

Precise words words that identify a smaller grouping within a larger category

Predictability the desire for consistency, reliability, and dependability in your partner's behavior or in your relationship

Predicted outcome value theory the claim that in our early conversations with potential relationship partners, we gather information to predict whether the benefits of future interactions will outweigh the costs

Prejudice the emotional reaction to a stereotyped group or individual from that group

Preoccupied attachment style the attachment style experienced by an adult who is excessively focused on how their relationship partners think about and behave toward them because they have low self-worth and high trust in others due to the anxious-ambivalent attachments they experienced as infants and children

Primacy effect the tendency to remember information that we heard first over what we heard in the middle

Primary goals needs, wants, or other desires motivating a person to communicate that direct the person to a specific canned plan

Primed attending to things that have recently been thought about

Principle of negative reciprocity the proposition that we repay negative treatment with negative treatment

Privacy withholding confidential or secret information to enhance autonomy or minimize vulnerability

Probing questions questions that search for more information or try to resolve perceived inconsistencies in a message

Proxemics the study of personal space

Pseudo conflict disagreement that is caused by a perceptual difference between partners and is easily resolved

Psychological context the moods and feelings each person brings to an interpersonal encounter

Qualifying language language that indicates where a statement applies and does not apply, or indicates appropriate uncertainty about where it should apply

Quality the sound of a person's voice

Rate the speed at which a person speaks

Reach the ability to connect with people in distant places

Reappraise revise one's perspective

Reasons statements that provide valid evidence, explanations, or justifications for a claim

Recency effect the tendency to remember information that we heard last over what we heard in the middle

Reciprocity heuristic being influenced by a perceived debt or obligation to someone else during peripheral processing of persuasive messages

Referent power the potential to influence rooted in liking, respect, or admiration

Reframing the strategy of dealing with dialectical tensions by changing perceptions about the level of tension

Relational dialectics the conflicting pulls or tensions that exist in relationships as well as within each individual in a relationship

Relational jealousy an emotional reaction to the belief you might lose a valued relationship to a third party

Relational listening style a personal listening style that focuses on what messages tell us about our conversational partners and their feelings

Relational maintenance exchanging messages or behaving in ways that keep a relationship at a desired level of intimacy, satisfaction, and health

Relational self-concept the set of ideas you have about yourself

Relational uncertainty lack of confidence in a relationship

Relationship a set of expectations that two people have for their behavior with respect to each other, based on the pattern of interaction between them

Relationship costs negative outcomes to a relationship, including the time and energy we spend developing a relationship and the negative experiences that may arise, like hurt feelings, conflict episodes, jealousy, etc.

Relationship exists when two individuals are interdependent, so that each person's behavior affects the other

Relationship-oriented organizational culture an organizational culture that is collectivist, like those of Japan, Spain, and Mexico, and prioritizes building relationships at work over results

Relationship rewards positive outcomes to a relationship, including having basic relationship needs for affection, control, and inclusion met

Relationship transformation continuing to interact and influence a partner through a different type of relationship after one type of relationship has ended

Religion a system of beliefs, rituals, and ethics based on a common perception of the sacred or holy

Remembering the process of moving information from short-term memory to long-term memory

Responding the process of providing feedback to your partner's message

Results-oriented organizational culture an organizational culture that is individualistic and, like the dominant culture of the United States, prioritizes results over building relationships at work

Reward power the potential to influence rooted in our ability to provide something our partner values and cannot easily get from someone else

Rich media media where meaning can be conveyed through both verbal and nonverbal behavior

Risk–benefit analysis weighing advantages and disadvantages (of disclosing private information)

Ritual question a question about the other person or the situation that is easy to answer and doesn't pry into personal matters

Romantic relationship relationships in which partners act on their mutual sexual attraction to each other

Routine relational maintenance messages and behaviors that are performed without any deliberate intention to affect the relationship but have the effect of preserving intimacy

Salient directing attention at people or things because they stand out in the social context, differ from our expectations, or are related to our goals

Scarcity heuristic being influenced by the rarity or availability of something during peripheral processing of persuasive messages

Schema a memory structure that connects something or someone to its related qualities

Script a sequence of communication behaviors or messages designed to carry out a plan

Scripted highly routinized

Secondary goals motivations that affect the specific script chosen to accomplish a primary goal

Secret pane a pane of the Johari window that contains all those things that you know about yourself, but have chosen to keep private from your relationship partner

Secure attachment a strong, healthy emotional bond between infants and their parents or caregivers based on the belief that they are worthy of care and that other people can be trusted to provide it

Secure attachment style the attachment style experienced by an adult who is able to easily form intimate relationships because they have high self-worth and trust others due to the secure attachments they experienced as infants and children

Self-concept a very large schema in memory that is the collection of all of the ideas you have about yourself, including your abilities, personality traits, and roles

Self-construal how you see yourself

Self-disclosure verbally sharing personal ideas and feelings with others

Self-disclosure verbally sharing personal, private information, and feelings

Self-esteem our positive or negative judgment of the characteristics we think we have

Self-face orientation the inclination to uphold and protect our self-image in our interactions with others

Self-fulfilling prophecies predictions that become true because we act in ways consistent with the prediction

Self-generated social media cues items of information that people post on their own profiles, such as status updates and profile pictures

Self-schema the qualities of yourself that you see as in defining or understanding who you really are

Self-talk the messages we send to ourselves through our thoughts

Semantic meaning meaning of a verbal message derived from the language itself

Semantic noise words in a message that distort or interfere with the interpretation of the meaning of a message

Sequential organization the identifiable beginnings (openings), middles (bodies), and ends (closings) of conversations

Sequential task-completion culture an organizational culture where large or complex tasks are broken into separate parts and completed one part at a time and in order

Serial arguing a conflict pattern in which partners argue about the same issue two or more times

Sexual harassment a form of sex discrimination including unwelcome sexual advances, requests for sexual favors, and other verbal or physical conduct of a sexual nature that explicitly or implicitly affects an individual's employment, unreasonably interferes with an individual's work performance, or creates an intimidating, hostile, or offensive work environment

Sexual infidelity when people in romantic relationships engage in sexual activity with someone other than their partners

Shared meaning when the receiver's interpretation of the message is similar to what the speaker thought, felt, and intended

Situational attribution an explanation that puts the cause of the behavior outside the control of a person

Slang the informal vocabulary developed and used by particular co-cultural groups in a society

Small talk a type of conversation focused on inconsequential topics such as the weather, uncontroversial news topics, harmless facts, and predictions

Social class a level in the power hierarchy of a society whose membership is based on income, education, occupation, and social habits

Social cognition how we make sense of other people, ourselves, and our social world

Social context the type and closeness of the relationship that may already exist between the participants

Social cues verbal and nonverbal features of a message that offer more information about the context, meaning, and the identities of the involved parties

Social exchange theory the premise that we continue to develop a relationship as long as we feel that its rewards outweigh its costs and we perceive that what we get from a particular relationship is more than we would be able to get if we invested elsewhere

Social media technologies that facilitate communication and interaction

Social network a group of individuals who are connected by friendship, family ties, common interests, beliefs, or knowledge

Social penetration theory the premise that self-disclosure is integral to all stages of relationships, but the nature and type of self-disclosure change over time, as people move from being strangers to being intimates

Social presence your personal sense that in a particular moment your conversational partners are immediately available to you even if they aren't

Social projection overestimating the similarity between our preferences, traits, opinions, and concerns and those of others

Social proof heuristic being influenced by what others think or do during peripheral processing of persuasive messages

Sociolinguistic meaning the meaning of a verbal message that varies according to the language norms and expectations of a particular cultural or co-cultural group

Somatic component of emotion the physical experience of a feeling

Special peer relationships equivalent to "best friend" relationships set within the work context, such relationships are rare and characterized by high levels of disclosure, trust, and social support

Specific language language in an utterance that uses concrete and precise words, as well as details and examples, combining them in accord with the rules of grammar and syntax for that language

Speech act the action that the speaker takes by uttering a verbal message; often implies how the listener should respond

Speech community the members of a larger language community who speak a common dialect with a particular style and observe common linguistic norms or scripts

Stereotype a schema in which the central concept is a category or group of people

Stereotyping applying a stereotype to a particular individual, and treating that person as though he or she embodies all the characteristics associated with that stereotype

Storage and replicability the extent to which a type of digital communication is preserved, can be continually accessed by others, and traced as to the time and place that a message was sent and who the participants in the exchange were

Strategic relational maintenance messages and behaviors are deliberately performed in order to maintain the level of intimacy in the relationship

Subtle stereotyping when people who are minimally aware that they are basing their interaction on stereotypes nonetheless act toward someone on the basis of that stereotype

Supportive climate a conversational environment in which recipients will feel comfortable disclosing their problems and feelings

Supportive interactions conversations in which the goal is to provide emotional support for one partner

Symmetrical message one that matches the dominance or submission implied in a partner's previous message

Sympathetic responsiveness empathizing by feeling concern, compassion, or sorrow for another person because he or she is in a distressing situation

Synchronous communication that occurs when participants are co-present and exchange messages in real time

Syntax and grammar the rules for combining words to form larger units of expression

System-generated social media cues pieces of information that the system provides, such as the number of friends we have on Facebook

Talk time the share of time participants each have in a conversation

Temporal selection the strategy of dealing with dialectical tensions by choosing one side of a dialectical opposition while ignoring the other for a period of time

Temporal structure the time it takes to send and receive messages or the time that elapses during a communication interaction

Territory the space over which we claim ownership

Theory of conversationally induced reappraisals the theory that having our emotions recognized and understood results in relief, which allows us to look for other explanations for how we feel and steps we can take to make the situation better

Topical segmentation the strategy of dealing with dialectical tensions by choosing certain areas in which to satisfy one side of a dialectical tension while choosing other areas to satisfy the opposite side

Touch putting part of the body in contact with something or someone

Transactional style the personal listening style that prefers speakers to remain on task and "get to the point"

Transcorporeal communication a process through which a living person sends a digital message to a deceased person through a website or social networking site

Trustworthiness the perception that speakers are credible because they are dependable, honest, and acting for the good of others

Turning point any event or occurrence that marks a relationship's transition from one stage to another

Turn-taking alternating between speaking and listening in an interaction

Uncertainty avoidance the extent to which the people in a culture look for ways to predict what is going to happen as a way of dealing with the anxiety caused by uncertain situations or relationships

Understanding accurately decoding a message so you comprehend the semantic, pragmatic, and socio-linguistic meaning of a message

Understanding and predictability a dimension of relationships that gauges how well partners understand and can predict each other's behaviors

Unknown pane a pane of the Johari window that contains information about which neither you nor your relationship partner is aware

Value conflict disagreement caused by differences in partners' deep-seated moral beliefs

Values the commonly accepted preference for some states of affairs over others

Vendors the people, groups, or organizations that supply an organization with necessary raw materials or other goods and services

Verbal aggression sending messages that attack another person's self-esteem or express personal hostility for perceived violations of rights or expectations

Verbal aggression sending verbal messages intended to hurt someone

Verbal message a message that is conveyed using a language

Viral message a message whose reach is at a level unanticipated by its original sender

Vocal interferences extraneous sounds or words (fillers) that interrupt fluent speech

Volume the loudness of a person's vocal tone

Voluntary relationship a relationship in which we freely choose the people with whom we interact

Withdrawing resolving a conflict by physically or psychologically removing yourself from the conversation

Words the arbitrarily chosen symbols used by a language or speech community to name or signify

Working self-concept the set of ideas about yourself that you are actively remembering

Workplace aggression any counter-productive behavior at work intended to hurt someone else

Workplace romance a mutually desired relationship between two employees of the same organization who become sexually attracted to each other

Workplace team a formally established group with a clear purpose and appropriate structure in which members know each other's roles and work together to achieve goals

References

Chapter 1

Andersen, P. (2000). Cues of culture: The basis of intercultural differences in nonverbal communication. In L. A. Samovar & R. E. Porter (Eds.), *Intercultural Communication: A Reader* (9th ed., pp. 258–266). Belmont, CA: Wadsworth.

Baym, N. K. (2010). *Personal Connections in the Digital Age*. Malden, MA: Polity Press.

Berger, C. R. (1997). *Planning Strategic Interaction: Attaining Goals through Communicative Action*. Mahwah, NJ: Lawrence Erlbaum.

Berger, C. R. (2002). Goals and knowledge structures in social interaction. In M. L. Knapp & J. A. Daly (Eds.), *Handbook of Interpersonal Communication* (pp. 181–212). Thousand Oaks, CA: Sage.

Berscheid, E., & Peplau, L. A. (1983). The emerging science of relationships. In H. Kelley, E. Berscheid, A. Christensen, J. Harvey, T. Huston, G. Levinger, . . . D. Peterson (Eds.), *Close Relationships* (pp. 1–19). New York: Freeman.

Burgoon, J. K. (1998). It takes two to tango: Interpersonal adaptation and implications for relationship communication. In J. S. Trent (Ed.), *Communication: Views from the Helm for the 21st Century* (pp. 53–59). Boston: Allyn & Bacon.

Burleson, B. R. (2010). The nature of interpersonal communication: a message-centered approach. In C. R. Berger, M. E. Roloff, & D. R. Roskos-Ewoldsen, (Eds.), *The Handbook of Communication Science* (2nd ed., pp. 145–163). Thousand Oaks, CA: Sage.

Daft, R. L., & Lengel, R. H. (1984). Information richness: A new approach to managerial behavior and organizational design. *Research in Organizational Behavior, 6*, 191–233.

Dillard, J. P. (2015). Goals-plans-action theory of message production: Making influence messages. In D. Braithwaite & P. Schrodt (Eds.), *Engaging Theories in Interpersonal Communication: Multiple Perspectives* (pp. 63–74). Thousand Oaks, CA: Sage.

McLaren, R. M., & Solomon, D. H. (2015). Relational framing theory: Drawing inferences about relationships from interpersonal interactions. In D. Braithwaite & P. Schrodt (Eds.), *Engaging Theories in Interpersonal Communication: Multiple Perspectives* (pp. 115–127). Thousand Oaks, CA: Sage.

Salovey, P., & Meyer, J. D. (1990). Emotional intelligence. *Imagination, Cognition, and Personality, 9*, 185–211.

Spitzberg, B. H. (2000). A model of intercultural communication and competence. In L. A. Samovar & R. E. Porter (Eds.), *Intercultural Communication: A Reader* (9th ed., pp. 375–387). Belmont, CA: Wadsworth.

Spitzberg, B. H., & Cupach, W. R. (2007). Disentangling the dark side of interpersonal communication. In B. H. Spitzberg & W. R. Cupach (Eds.), *The Dark Side of Interpersonal Communication* (2nd ed., pp. 3–29). Mahwah, NJ: Lawrence Erlbaum.

Terkel, S. N., & Duval, R. S. (Eds.). (1999). *Encyclopedia of Ethics* (p. 122). New York: Facts on File.

Chapter 2

Benet-Martínez, V., & Haritatos, J. (2005). Bicultural identity integration (BII): Components and psychological antecedents. *Journal of Personality, 73*, 1015–1050.

Chen, G. M., & Starosta, W. J. (1998). *Foundations of Intercultural Communication*. Boston: Allyn & Bacon.

Ekman, P., & Cordaro, D. (2011). What is meant by calling emotions basic. *Emotion Review, 3*(4), 364–370.

Fiske, S. T., & Taylor, S. E. (2013). *Social cognition: From brains to culture*. Thousand Oaks, CA: Sage.

Lazarus, R. S. (1991). *Emotion and adaptation*. New York: Oxford University Press.

Levenson, R. W. (2011). Basic emotion questions. *Emotion Review, 3*(4), 379–386.

Markus, H. R., & Kitayama, S. (1991). Culture and the self: Implications for cognition, emotion, and motivation. *Psychological Review, 98*, 224–253.

Miczo, N., & Burgoon, J. K. (2008). Facework and nonverbal behavior in social support interactions within romantic dyads. In M. T. Motley (Ed.), *Studies in applied interpersonal communication* (pp. 245–265). Thousand Oaks, CA: Sage.

Moors, A. (2009). Theories of emotion causation: A review. *Cognition and Emotion, 23*, 625–662.

Mruk, C. (2006). *Self-Esteem: Research, Theory, and Practice* (3rd ed.). New York: Springer.

Rayner, S. G. (2001). Aspects of the self as learner: Perception, concept, and esteem. *International Perspectives on Individual Differences, 2*, 25–52.

Roseman, I. J., Antoniou, A. A., & Jose, P. E. (1996). Appraisal determinants of emotions: Constructing a more accurate and comprehensive theory. *Cognition and Emotion, 10,* 241–277.

Sue, D. W., Capodilupo, C. M., Torino, G. C., Bucceri, J. M., Holder, A., Nadal, K. L., & Esquilin, M. (2007). Racial microaggressions in everyday life: implications for clinical practice. *American Psychologist, 62*(4), 271–286.

Tong, S. T., Van Der Heide, B., Langwell, L., & Walther, J. B. (2008). Too much of a good thing? The relationship between number of friends and interpersonal impressions on Facebook. *Journal of Computer-Mediated Communication, 13*(3), 531–549.

Utz, S. (2010). Show me your friends and I will tell you what type of person you are: How one's profile, number of friends, and type of friends influence impression formation on social network sites. *Journal of Computer-Mediated Communication, 15*(2), 314–335.

Walther, J. B., Van Der Heide, B., Hamel, L. M., & Shulman, H. C. (2009). Self-generated versus other-generated statements and impressions in computer-mediated communication: A test of warranting theory using Facebook. *Communication Research, 36*(2), 229–253.

Weiten, W., Dunn, D., & Hammer, E. (2011). *Psychology applied to modern life: Adjustment in the 21st century.* Belmont, CA: Cengage Learning.

Wyer Jr., R. S., & Carlston, D. E. (1994). The events of persons representation. In R. S. Wyer Jr., & T. K. Srull (Eds.), *Handbook of Social Cognition* (Vol. 1: Basic Processes, pp. 41–97). New York: Lawrence Erlbaum.

Chapter 3

Anatole, E. (May 28, 2013). Generation Z: Rebels with a cause. Retrieved 9/23/13 from http://www.forbes.com/sites/onmarketing/2013/05/28/generation-z-rebels-with-a-cause/.

Andersen, P. A., Hecht, M. L., Hoobler, G. D., & Smallwood, M. (2003). Nonverbal communication across cultures. In W. B. Gudykunst (Ed.), *Cross-Cultural and Inter-cultural Communication* (pp. 73–90). Thousand Oaks, CA: Sage.

Bonvillain, N. (2003). *Language, Culture and Communication: The Meaning of Messages* (4th ed.). Upper Saddle River, NJ: Prentice Hall.

Chen, G. M., & Starosta, W. J. (1998). *Foundations of Intercultural Communication.* Boston: Allyn & Bacon.

Chuang, R. (2004). An examination of Taoist and Buddhist perspectives on interpersonal conflict, emotions and adversities. In F. E. Jandt (Ed.), *Intercultural Communication: A Global Reader* (pp. 38–50). Thousand Oaks, CA: Sage.

Deardorff, D. K. (2006). The identification and assessment of intercultural competence. *Journal of Studies in International Education, 10,* 241–266.

Doi, T. (1973). *The anatomy of dependence.* Tokyo: Kodansha International.

Ellis, D. G. (1999). *Crafting Society: Ethnicity, Class and Communication Theory.* Mahwah, NJ: Lawrence Erlbaum.

Emelo, R. (Jun. 21, 2013). Forget Gen Y. Get ready for Gen Z. Retrieved 9/23/13 from http://www.astd.org/Publications/Blogs/Human-Capital-Blog/2013/06/Forget-Gen-Y-Get-Ready-for-Gen-Z.

Grosjean, F. (2010). *Bilingual: Life and reality.* Cambridge, MA: Harvard University Press.

Hall, E. T. (1976). *Beyond Culture.* New York: Anchor/Doubleday.

Hofstede, G. (1980). *Culture's Consequences.* Beverly Hills, CA: Sage.

Hofstede, G. (1998). (Ed.). *Masculinity and Femininity: The Taboo Dimension of National Cultures.* Thousand Oaks, CA: Sage.

Hofstede, G. (2000). The cultural relativity of the quality of life concept. *Academy of Management Review, 9,* 389–398.

Klyukanov, I. E. (2005). *Principles of Intercultural Communication.* New York: Pearson.

Kim, Y., Sohn, D., & Choi, S. M. (2011). Cultural difference in motivations for using social network sites: A comparative study of American and Korean college students. *Computers in Human Behavior, 27*(1), 365–372.

Kottak, C. (2012). *Anthropology: The Exploration of Human Diversity* (14th ed.). New York: McGraw-Hill.

Luckmann, J. (1999). *Transcultural Communication in Nursing.* New York: Delmar.

Marshall, T. C., Chuong, K., & Aikawa, A. (2011). Day-to-day experiences of *amae* in Japanese romantic relationships. *Asian Journal of Social Psychology, 14*(1), 26–35.

Matsumoto, D., Yoo, S. H., & Fontaine, J. (2008). Mapping expressive differences around the world: The relationship between emotional display rules and individualism versus collectivism. *Journal of Cross-Cultural Psychology, 39,* 55–74.

Neuliep, J. W. (2006). *Intercultural Communication: A Contextual Approach* (3rd ed.). Thousand Oaks, CA: Sage.

Niiya, Y., Ellsworth, P. C., & Yamaguchi, S. (2006). Amae in Japan and the United States: An exploration of a "culturally unique" emotion. *Emotion, 6*(2), 279.

Prensky, M. (2001). *Digital Natives, Digital Immigrants. On the Horizon* (Vol. 9, No. 5). West Yorkshire, England: MCB University Press. Retrieved from http://www.marcprensky.com/writing/Prensky%20-%20Digital%20Natives,%20Digital%20Immigrants%20-%20Part1.pdf.

Qiu, L., Lin, H., & Leung, A. K. (2013). Cultural differences and switching of in-group sharing behavior between an American (Facebook) and a Chinese (Renren) social networking site. *Journal of Cross-Cultural Psychology, 44*(1), 106–121.

Rogers, E. M., Hart, W. B., & Miike, Y. (2002). Edward T. Hall and the history of intercultural communication: The United States and Japan. *Keio Communication Review, 24*, 3–26.

Samovar, L. A., Porter, R. E., McDaniel, E. R., & Roy, C. S. (2013). *Communication between Cultures* (8th ed.). Boston, MA: Wadsworth Cengage Learning.

Smedley, A., & Smedley, B. D. (2005). Race as biology is fiction, racism as a social problem is real: Anthropological and historical perspectives on the social construction of race. *American Psychologist, 60*(1), 16–26.

Ting-Toomey, S., Yee-Jung, K., Shapiro, R., Garcia, W., Wright, T., & Oetzel, J. G. (2000). Cultural/ethnic identity salience and conflict styles. *International Journal of Intercultural Relations, 23*, 47–81.

U. S. Census Bureau. (n.d.). Hispanic Americans by the numbers. Retrieved 9/23/2013 from http://www.infoplease.com/spot/hhmcensus1.html.

Wood, J. T. (2012). *Gendered Lives: Communication, Gender, and Culture* (10th ed.). Boston, MA: Wadsworth Cengage Learning.

Zemke, R., Raines, C., & Filipczak, B. (2013). *Generations at Work* (2nd ed.). New York: AMACOM.

Chapter 4

Chaika, E. (2007). *Language: The Social Mirror* (4th ed.). Boston: Heinle ELT/Cengage.

Cvetkovic, L. (Feb. 21, 2009). *Serbian, Croatian, Bosnian, or Montanegren, or "Just our language."* Retrieved 9/21/15 from http://www.rferl.org/content/Serbian_Croatian_ Bosnian_or_Montenegrin_Many_ In_Balkans_Just_Call_It_Our_ Language_/1497105.html.

Daft, R. L., & Lengel, R. H. (1984). Information richness: A new approach to managerial behavior and organizational design. *Research in Organizational Behavior, 6*, 191–233.

Freed, A. F. (2003). Reflections on language and gender research. In J. Holmes & M. Meyers (Eds.), *The Handbook of Language and Gender* (pp. 699–721). Malden, MA: Blackwell Publishing.

Grice, H. P. (1975). Logic and conversation. In P. Cole & J. L. Morgan (Eds.), *Syntax and Semantics: Volume 3. Speech Acts.* New York: Academic Press.

Higginbotham, J. (2006). Languages and idiolects: Their language and ours. In E. Lepore & B. C. Smith (Eds.), *The Oxford Handbook of Philosophy of Language* (pp. 140–150). Oxford: Oxford University Press.

Korta, K., & Perry, J. (2008). Pragmatics. In E. N. Zalta (Ed.), *The Stanford Encyclopedia of Philosophy* (Fall 2008 edition). Retrieved 9/21/15 from http://plato.stanford.edu/archives/fall2008/entries/pragmatics/.

Langer, E. J., & Moldoveanu, M. (2000). The construct of mindfulness. *Journal of Social Issues, 56*, 1–9.

Lewis, M. P. (Ed.). (2009). *Ethnologue: Languages of the World* (16th ed.). Dallas, TX: SIL International. Retrieved 9/21/15 from http://www.ethnologue.com/.

Lim, T.-S., & Bowers, J. W. (1991). Facework: Solidarity, approbation, and tact. *Human Communication Research, 17*(3), 415–450.

Motley, C. M., & Craig-Henderson, K. M. (2007). Epithet or endearment? Examining reactions among those of the African diaspora to an ethnic epithet. *Journal of Black Studies, 37*, 944–963.

O'Grady, W., Archibald, J., Aronoff, M., & Rees-Miller, J. (2001). *Contemporary Linguistics* (4th ed.). Boston: Bedford/St. Martin's.

Peter, J., Valkenburg, P. M., & Schouten, A. P. (2005). Developing a model of adolescent friendship formation on the internet. *Cyberpsychology and Behavior, 8*(5), 423–430.

Saeed, J. I. (2003). *Semantics* (2nd ed.). Malden, MA: Blackwell Publishing.

Stewart, L. P., Cooper, P. J., Stewart, A. D., & Friedley, S. A. (2003). *Communication and Gender* (4th ed.). Boston: Allyn & Bacon.

Ting-Toomey, S., & Chung, L. C. (2005). *Understanding Intercultural Communication.* New York: Oxford University Press.

Walther, J. B. (1996). Computer-mediated communication: Impersonal, interpersonal, and hyperpersonal interaction. *Communication Research, 23*(1), 3–43.

Walther, J. B., Loh, T., & Granka, L. (2005). Let me count the ways: The interchange of verbal and nonverbal cues in computer-mediated and face-to-face affinity. *Journal of Language and Social Psychology, 24*(1), 36–65.

Wright, R. (2010). *Chinese Language Facts.* Retrieved 9/21/15 from http://www.languagehelpers.com/languagefacts/chinese.html.

Chapter 5

Axtell, R. E. (1998). *Gestures: The Do's and Taboos of Body Language Around the World* (rev. ed.). New York: Wiley.

Burgoon, J. K., & Bacue, A. (2003). Nonverbal communication skills. In J. O. Greene & B. R. Burleson (Eds.), *Handbook of communication and social interaction skills* (pp. 179–220). Mahwah, NJ: Erlbaum.

Burgoon, J. K., Guerrero, L. K., & Manusov, V. (2011). Nonverbal signals. In M. L. Knapp & J. A. Daly (Eds.), *The Sage*

Handbook of Interpersonal Communication (Vol. 4, pp. 239–282). Thousand Oaks, CA: Sage.

Chen, G. M, & Starosta, W. J. (1998). *Foundations of Intercultural Communication: Color Blindness and Equal Opportunity*. Boston: Allyn & Bacon.

DiTomaso, N., Parks-Yancy, R., and Post, C. (2003). White views of civil rights: Color blindness and equal opportunity. In A. W. Doane & E. Bonilla-Silva (Eds.), *Whiteout: The Continuing Significance of Racism*. New York: Routledge.

Dovidio, J. F., Hebl, M., Richeson, J. A., & Shelton, J. N. (2006). Nonverbal communication, race, and intergroup interaction. In V. Manusov & M. L. Patterson (Eds.), *The Sage handbook of nonverbal communication* (pp. 481–500). Thousand Oaks, CA: Sage.

Eagly, A. H., & Koenig, A. M. (2006). Social role theory of sex differences and similarities: Implication for prosocial behavior. In K. Dindia & D. J. Canary (Eds.), *Sex differences and similarities in communication* (2nd ed., pp. 161–177). Mahwah, NJ: Erlbaum.

Hall, E. T. (1969). *The Hidden Dimension*. Garden City, NY: Doubleday.

Henley, N. M. (1977). *Body Politics: Power, Sex and Nonverbal Communication*. Englewood Cliffs, NJ: Prentice-Hall.

Kleinman, S. (2007). *Displacing Place: Mobile Communication in the Twenty-first Century*. New York: Peter Lang.

Knapp, M. L., & Hall, J. A. (2006). *Nonverbal Communication in Human Interaction* (6th ed.). Belmont, CA: Wadsworth/Thomson Learning.

Lo, S.-K. (2008). The nonverbal communication functions of emoticons in computer-mediated communication. *Cyberpsychology and Behavior, 11*(5), 595–597.

Martin, J. N., & Nakayama, T. K. (2006). *Intercultural Communication in Contexts* (4th ed.). New York: McGraw Hill.

Matsumoto, D., Yoo, S. H., & Fontaine, J. (2008). Mapping expressive differences around the world: The relationship between emotional display rules and individualism versus collectivism. *Journal of Cross-Cultural Psychology, 39*, 55–74.

Pearson, J. C., West, R. L., & Turner, L. H. (1995). *Gender and Communication* (3rd ed.). Dubuque, Iowa: Brown & Benchmark.

Samovar, L. A., Porter, R. E., McDaniel, E. R., & Roy, C. S. (2013). *Communication between Cultures* (8th ed.). Boston, MA: Wadsworth Cengage Learning.

Schmidt, K. L., Cohn, J. F., & Tian, Y. (2003). Signal characteristics of spontaneous facial expressions: Automatic movement in solitary and social smiles. *Biological Psychology, 65*(1), 49–66.

Ting-Toomey, S., & Chung, L. C. (2011). *Understanding intercultural communication* (2nd ed.). New York: Oxford.

Tracy, J. L., & Matsumoto, D. (2008). The spontaneous expression of pride and shame: Evidence for biologically innate nonverbal displays. *Proceedings of the National Academy of Sciences, 105*(33), 11655–11660.

Wood, J. T. (2013). *Gendered lives* (10th ed.). Boston, MA: Cengage.

White, C. H. (2015). Expectancy violations theory and interaction adaptation theory: From expectations to adaptation. In D. O. Braithwaite & P. Schrodt (Eds.), *Engaging theories in interpersonal communication: Multiple perspectives* (pp. 217–228). Thousand Oaks, CA: Sage.

Chapter 6

Altman, I., & Taylor, D. (1973). *Social penetration: The development of interpersonal relationships*. New York: Henry Holt.

Baxter, L. (1982). Strategies for ending relationships: Two studies. *Western Journal of Speech Communication, 46*, 223–241.

Baxter, L. A., & Bullis, C. (1993). Turning points in developing romantic relationships. In S. Petronio, J. K. Alberts, M. L. Hecht, & J. Buley (Eds.), *Contemporary Perspectives on Interpersonal Communication* (pp. 358–374). Chicago: Brown and Benchmark.

Baxter, L. A., & Erbert, L. A. (1999). Perceptions of dialectical contradictions in turning points of development in heterosexual romantic relationships. *Journal of Social and Personal Relationships, 16*, 547–569.

Baxter, L. A., & Montgomery, B. M. (1996). *Relating: Dialogues and Dialectics*. New York: Guilford Press.

Baym, N. K., & boyd, d. (2012). Socially mediated publicness: An introduction. *Journal of Broadcasting and Electronic Media, 56*(3), 320–329. doi: 10.1080/08838151.2012.705200

Berger, C. R., Calabrese, R. J. (1975). Some exploration in initial interaction and beyond: Toward a developmental theory of communication. *Human Communication Research, 1*, 99–112.

Boon, S. D. (1994). Dispelling doubt and uncertainty: Trust in romantic relationships. In S. Duck (Ed.), *Dynamics of Relationships* (pp. 86–111). Thousand Oaks, CA: Sage.

Bryant, E. M., & Marmo, J. (2012). The rules of Facebook friendship: A two-stage examination of interaction rules in close, casual, and acquaintance friendships. *Journal of Social and Personal Relationships, 29*(8), 1013–1035.

Canary, D. J., Stafford, L., & Semic, B. A. (2002). A panel study of the association between maintenance characteristics and relational characteristics. *Journal of Marriage and Family, 64*, 395–406.

Canary, D. J., & Dainton, M. (2002). Preface. In J. C. Canary & M. Dainton (Eds.), *Maintaining Relationships Through Communication: Relational, Contextual and*

Cultural Variations (pp. xiii–xv). Mahwah, NJ: Erlbaum.

Cupach, C. R., & Metts, S. (1986). Accounts of relational dissolution: A comparison of marital and nonmarital relationships. *Communication Monographs, 53,* 311–334.

Dindia, K., & Baxter, L. (1987). Strategies for maintaining and repairing marital relationships. *Journal of Social and Personal Relationships, 4,* 143–158.

Duck, S. (1987). How to lose friends without influencing people. In M. E. Roloff & G. R. Miller (Eds.), *Interpersonal Processes: New Directions in Communication Research* (pp. 278–298). Beverly Hills, CA: Sage.

Fehr, B. (2008). Friendship formation. In S. Sprecher, A. Wenzel, & J. Harvey (Eds.), *Handbook of Relationship Initiation* (pp. 29–54). New York: Psychology Press.

Gumpert, G., & Drucker, S. J. (2007). Mobile communication in the twenty-first century, or "Everybody, everywhere, at any time." In S. Kleinman (Ed.), *Displacing place: Mobile communication in the twenty-first century* (pp. 7–20). New York: Peter Lang.

Knapp, M. L., Vangelisti, A. L., & Caughlin, J. P. (2014). *Interpersonal Communication and Human Relationships* (7th ed.). New York: Pearson.

Knapp, M. L., & Vangelisti, A. L. (2011). Relationship decline. In K. M. Galvin, *Making Connections* (5th ed., pp. 273–278). New York: Oxford University Press.

Knobloch, L. K., & Miller, L. E. (2008). Uncertainty and relationship initiation. In S. Sprecher, A. Wenzel, & J. Harvey (Eds.), *Handbook of Relationship Initiation* (pp. 121–134). New York: Psychology Press.

Knobloch, L. K., & Carpenter-Theune, K. E. (2004). Topic avoidance in developing romantic relationships associations with intimacy and relational uncertainty.

Communication Research, 31(2), 173–205.

Luft, J. (1970). *Group Processes: An Introduction to Group Dynamics.* Palo Alto, CA: Mayfield.

Parks, M. R. (2007). *Personal Relationships and Personal Networks.* Mahwah, NJ: Lawrence Erlbaum Associates.

Pearce, W. B. (1974). Trust in interpersonal communication. *Communication Monographs, 41*(3), 236–244.

Petronio, S., & Durham, W. T. (2015). Communication privacy management theory: Significance for interpersonal communication. In D. O. Braithwaite & P. Schrodt (Eds.), *Engaging theories in interpersonal communication: Multiple perspectives* (pp. 335–347). Thousand Oaks, CA: Sage.

Samovar, L. A., Porter, R. E., McDaniel, E. R., & Roy, C. S. (2013). *Communication between Cultures* (8th ed.). Boston, MA: Wadsworth Cengage Learning.

Schutz, W. (1966). *The Interpersonal Underworld.* Palo Alto, CA: Science & Behavior Books.

McLaren, R. M., & Solomon, D. H. (2015). Relational framing theory: Drawing inferences about relationships from interpersonal interactions. In D. Braithwaite & P. Schrodt (Eds.), *Engaging theories in interpersonal communication: Multiple perspectives* (pp. 115–127). Thousand Oaks, CA: Sage.

Smyth, J. M., Pennebaker, J. W., & Arigo, D. (2012). What are the health effects of disclosure? In A. Baum, T. A. Revenson, & J. Singer (Eds.), *Handbook of health psychology* (2nd ed., pp. 175–192). New York: Taylor & Francis.

Sunnafrank, M. (1990). Predicted outcome value and uncertainty reduction theories: A test of competing perspectives. *Human Communication Research, 17,* 76–103.

Taylor, D. A., & Altman, I. (1987). Communication in interpersonal relationships: Social penetration theory. In M. E. Roloff &

G. R. Miller (Eds.), *Interpersonal Processes: New Directions in Communication Research* (pp. 257–277). Beverly Hills, CA: Sage.

Thibaut, J. W., & Kelley, H. H. (1986). *The Social Psychology of Groups* (2nd ed.). New Brunswick, NJ: Transaction Books.

Wood, J. T. (2000). Dialectical theory. In K. M. Galvin & P. J. Cooper (Eds.), *Making Connections: Readings in Relational Communication* (pp. 132–138). Los Angeles: Roxbury Publishing Company.

Chapter 7

Bodie, G. D., St. Cyr, K., Pence, M., Rold, M., & Honeycutt, J. (2012). Listening competence in initial interactions. I: Distinguishing between what listening is and what listeners do. *International Journal of Listening, 26*(1), 1–28.

Bodie, G. D., & Worthington, D. L. (2010). Revisiting the Listening Styles Profile (LSP-16): A confirmatory factor analytic approach to scale validation and reliability estimation. *The International Journal of Listening, 24*(2), 69–88.

Bostrom, R. N. (2006). The process of listening. In O. Hargie (Ed.), *Handbook of Communication Skills* (3rd ed., pp. 267–291). New York: Routledge.

Brownell, J. (2006). *Listening: Attitudes, Principles, and Skills* (3rd ed.). Boston, MA: Allyn & Bacon.

Ellinor, L., & Gerard, G. (1998). *Dialogue: Rediscover the Transforming Power of Conversation.* New York: Wiley.

Estes, W. K. (1989). Learning theory. In A. Lesgold & R. Glaser (Eds.), *Foundations for a Psychology of Education* (pp. 1–49). Hillsdale, NJ: Erlbaum.

Halone, K. K., & Pecchioni, L. L. (2001). Relational listening: A grounded theoretical model. *Communication Reports, 14,* 5.

Kanalley, C. (March 10, 2011). Charlie Sheen not dead, but virus spreads on Facebook. *The Huffington Post.*

Retrieved from: http://www
.huffingtonpost.com/2011/03/10/
charlie-sheen-not-dead_n_834092
.html. July 28, 2015

Lenhart, A. (Apr. 9, 2015). Teens, social
media and technology overview,
2015. Retrieved 9/21/15 from
http://www.pewinternet.org/2015/
04/09/teens-social-media-
technology-2015/#fn-13190-2.

O'Shaughnessey, Brian. (2003). Active
attending, or a theory of mental
action. *Consciousness and the World,
29*, 379–407.

Przybylski, A. K., & Weinstein, N.
(2013). Can you connect with me
now? How the presence of mobile
communication technology
influences face-to-face conversation
quality. *Journal of Social and
Personal Relationships, 30*(3),
237–246.

Purdy, M. (1996). What is listening?
In M. Purdy & D. Borisoff (Eds.),
*Listening in Everyday Life: A
Personal and Professional Approach*
(2nd ed., pp. 1–20). New York:
University Press of America.

Sargent, S. L., & Weaver, J. B. (2007).
The Listening Styles Profile. In
R. A. Reynolds, R. Woods, and
J. D. Baker (Eds.), *Handbook of
Research on Electronic Surveys
and Measurements* (pp. 335–338).
Hershey, PA: Idea Group
References.

Steil, L. K., Barker, L. L., & Watson,
K. W. (1983). *Effective Listening*.
Reading, MA: Addison-Wesley.

Watson, K. W., Barker, L. L., &
Weaver, J. B., III (1995). The
listening styles profile (LSP-16):
Development and validation of an
instrument to assess four listening
styles. *International Journal of
Listening, 9*, 1–13.

Weaver, III, J. B., & Kirtley, M. D.
(1995). Listening styles and
empathy. *The Southern Communication Journal, 60*(2), 131–140.

Wheeless, L. R. (1975). An investigation of receiver apprehension
and social context dimensions
of communication apprehension.
The Speech Teacher, 24, 261–268.

Wolvin, A. D., & Coakley, C. G.
(1992). *Listening*. Dubuque, IA:
Wm. C. Brown.

Chapter 8

Alberts, J. K., & Drzewiecka, J. A.
(2008). Understanding the
communication and relational
dynamics of humor. In M. T. Motley
(Ed.), *Studies in applied interpersonal
communication* (pp. 229–244).
Thousand Oaks, CA: Sage.

Biocca, F., Harms, C., & Burgoon, J. K.
(2003). Toward a more robust
theory and measure of social
presence: Review and suggested
criteria. *Presence, 12*(5), 456–480.

Duck, S. (2007). *Human Relationships*
(4th ed.). Thousand Oaks, CA: Sage.

Engdahl, S. (Ed.). (2007). *Online
Social Networking*. New York:
Thompson Gale.

Fraley, B., & Aron, A. (2004). The effect
of a shared humorous experience
on closeness in initial encounters.
Personal Relationships, 11, 61–78.

Gabor, D. (2001). *How to start a
conversation and make friends
(revised and updated)*. New York:
Simon & Schuster.

Garner, A. (1997). *Conversationally
Speaking* (3rd ed.). Los Angeles:
Lowell House.

Goldsmith, D. J., & Baxter, L. A.
(2006). Constituting relationships
in talk: A taxonomy of speech
events in social and personal
relationships. *Human Communication Research, 23*, 87–114.

Gudykunst, W. B., & Matsumoto, Y.
(1996). Cross-cultural variability
of communication in personal
relationships. In W. B. Gudykunst,
S. Ting-Toomey, & T. Nishida (Eds.),
*Communication in Personal Relation-
ships Across Cultures* (pp. 19–56).
Thousand Oaks, CA: Sage.

Johannesen, R. L, Valde, K. S., &
Whedbee, K. E. (2008). *Ethics in
Human Communication* (6th ed.).
Long Grove, IL.: Waveland Press.

Kennedy, C. W., & Camden, C. T.
(1983). A new look at interruptions.
*Western Journal of Speech
Communication, 47*, 45–58.

Maki, S. M., Booth-Butterfield, M., &
McMullen, A. (2012). Does our
humor affect us? An examination
of a dyad's humor orientation.
Communication Quarterly, 60(5),
649–664.

McGraw, A. P., & Warren, C. (2010).
Benign violations making immoral
behavior funny. *Psychological
Science, 21*(8), 1141–1149.

McLaughlin, M. L. (1984). *Conversation: How Talk Is Organized*.
Newbury Park, CA: Sage.

Nofsinger, R. E. (1991). *Everyday
Conversation*. Thousand Oaks,
CA: Sage.

Sakamoto, N. M. (1995). Conversational ballgames. In R. Holton
(Ed.), *Encountering Cultures*
(pp. 60–63). Englewood Cliffs, NJ:
Prentice-Hall.

Sandstrom, G. M., & Dunn, E. W.
(2014). Is efficiency overrated?
Minimal social interactions lead to
belonging and positive affect. *Social
Psychological and Personality
Science, 5*(4), 437–442.

Sawyer, R. K. (2001). *Creating
Conversations: Improvisation in
Everyday Discourse*. Cresskill, NJ:
Hampton Press.

Chapter 9

Barbee, A. P., & Cunningham, M. R.
(1995). An experimental approach
to social support communication:
Interactive coping in close
relationships. In B. R. Burleson
(Ed.), *Communication Yearbook 18*
(pp. 381–413). Thousand Oaks,
CA: Sage.

Brock, R. L., & Lawrence, E. (2010).
Support adequacy in marriage:
Observing the platinum rule. In
K. T. Sullivan & J. Davila (Eds.),
*Support processes in intimate
relationships* (pp. 3–25). New York:
Oxford University Press.

Burleson, B. R., & Goldsmith, D. J.
(1998). How the comforting
process works: Alleviating
emotional distress through
conversationally induced
reappraisals. In P. A. Andersen &
L. K. Guerrero (Eds.), *Handbook of

Communication and Emotion: Research, Theory, Applications, and Contexts (pp. 248–280). San Diego, CA: Academic Press.

Burleson, B. R. (2003). The experience and effects of emotional support: What the study of cultural and gender differences can tell us about close relationships, emotion, and interpersonal communication. *Personal Relationships, 10,* 1–23.

Chentsova-Dutton, Y. E., & Vaughn, A. (2011). Let me tell you what to do: Cultural differences in advice-giving. *Journal of Cross-Cultural Psychology, 43,* 687–703.

Degroot, J. M. (2012). Maintaining relational continuity with the deceased on Facebook. *OMEGA—Journal of Death and Dying, 65*(3), 195–212.

Eisenberg, N., & Fabes, R. A. (1990). Empathy: Conceptualization, measurement, and relation to prosocial behavior. *Motivation and Emotion, 14,* 131–149.

Feng, B., & Feng, H. (2013). Examining cultural similarities and differences in responses to advice: A comparison of American and Chinese college students. *Communication Research, 40,* 623–644.

Gable, S. L., Reis, H. T., Impett, E., & Asher, E. R. (2004). What do you do when things go right? The intrapersonal and interpersonal benefits of sharing positive events. *Journal of Personality and Social Psychology, 87,* 228–245.

Gable, S. L. Gonzaga, G. C., & Strachman, A. (2006). Will you be there for me when things go right? Supportive responses to positive event disclosures. *Journal of Personality and Social Psychology, 91,* 904–917.

Goldsmith, D. J. (2000). Soliciting advice: The role of sequential placement in mitigating face threat. *Communication Monographs, 67,* 1–19.

Holmstrom, A. J., & Burleson, B. R. (2011). An initial test of a cognitive-emotional theory of esteem support messages.

Communication Research, 38(3), 326–355.

Holmstrom, A. J., Russell, J. C., & Clare, D. D. (2013). Esteem support messages received during the job search: A test of the CETESM. *Communication Monographs, 80*(2), 220–242.

Kunkel, A. W., & Burleson, B. R. (1999). Assessing explanations for sex differences in emotional support: A test of the different cultures and skill specialization accounts. *Human Communication Research, 25,* 307–340.

Langston, C. A. (1994). Capitalizing on and coping with daily-life events: Expressive responses to positive events. *Journal of Personality and Social Psychology, 67,* 1112–1125.

Leathers, D. G. (1997). *Successful Nonverbal Communication: Principles and Applications* (3rd ed.). Boston: Allyn & Bacon.

Legacy.com. (2011). About Legacy.com, Inc. Available at http://legacy.com/NS/About.

Lyons, R. F., Sullivan, M. H. L., Ritvo, P. G., & Coyne, J. C. (1995). *Relationships in chronic illness and disability.* Thousand Oaks, CA: Sage.

MacGeorge, E. L., Feng, B., & Thompson, E. R. (2008). Good and bad advice: How to advise more effectively. In M. T. Motley (Ed.), *Studies in Applied Interpersonal Communication* (pp. 553–575). Los Angeles, CA: Sage.

MacGeorge, E. L., Feng, B., & Burleson, B. R. (2011). Supportive communication. In M. L. Knapp & J. A. Daly (Eds.), *The Sage handbook of interpersonal communication* (4th ed., pp. 317–354). Thousand Oaks, CA: Sage.

MacGeorge, E. L., Guntzviller, L. M., Hanasono, L. K., & Feng, B. (2013). Testing advice response theory in interactions with friends. *Communication Research*, advance online publication. doi: 10.1177/0093650213510938

Mirivel, J. C., & Thombre, A. (2010). Surviving online: An analysis of

how burn survivors recover from life crises. *Southern Communication Journal, 75,* 232–254.

Omdahl, B. L. (1995). *Cognitive Appraisal, Emotion, and Empathy.* Mahwah, NJ: Erlbaum.

Plumb, T. (Aug. 31, 2006). Websites offer mourning for youths online. *The Boston Globe.*

Preston, S. D., & de Waal, D. B. M. (2002). Empathy: Its ultimate and proximate bases. *Behavioral and Brain Sciences, 25,* 1–72.

Segrin, C. (1998). Disrupted interpersonal relationships and mental health problems. In B. H. Spitzberg & W. H. Cupach (Eds.), *The dark side of close relationships* (pp. 327–365). Mahwah, NJ: Erlbaum.

Smith, C. A., & Kirby, L. D. (2009). Putting appraisal in context: Toward a relational model of appraisal and emotion. *Cognition and Emotion, 23*(7), 1352–1372.

Stiff, J. B., Dillard, J. P., Somera, L., Kim, H., & Sleight, C. (1988). Empathy, communication, and prosocial behavior. *Communication Monographs, 55,* 198–213.

Stingl, J. (Feb. 20, 2007). Grief finds expression electronically. *Milwaukee Journal Sentinel.*

Weaver, III, J. B., & Kirtley, M. B. (1995). Listening styles and empathy. *Southern Communication Journal, 60,* 131–140.

Wright, K. B. (2015). Computer-mediated support for health outcomes: Psychological influences on support processes. In S. S. Sundar (Ed.), *The handbook of the psychology of communication technology* (pp. 488–506). Malden, MA: Wiley-Blackwell.

Chapter 10

Alberti, R. E., & Emmons, M. L. (2001). *Your Perfect Right: Assertiveness and Equality in Your life and Relationships* (8th ed.). San Atascadero, CA: Impact Publishers.

Carnegie, D. (1936). *How to Win Friends and Influence People.* New York: Simon & Schuster.

Chu, S.-C., & Kim, Y. (2011). Determinants of consumer engagement in electronic word-of-mouth (eWOM) in social networking sites. *International journal of Advertising, 30*(1), 47–75.

Cialdini, R. B. (2001). Harnessing the science of persuasion. *The Harvard Business Review.* October 2001. 70–80.

Cialdini, R. B. (2009). *Influence: Science and Practice* (5th ed.). Boston: Pearson Education.

Dillard, J. P., & Knobloch, L. K. (2011). Interpersonal influence. In M. L. Knapp (Ed.), *The SAGE Handbook of Interpersonal Communication* (pp. 389–422). Los Angeles, CA: Sage.

Eskin, M. (2003). Self-reported assertiveness in Swedish and Turkish adolescents: A cross-cultural comparison. *Scandinavian Journal of Psychology, 44*(1), 7–12.

French, Jr., J. R. P., & Raven, B. (1968). The bases of social power. In D. Cartwright & A. Zander (Eds.), *Group Dynamics* (3rd ed., pp. 259–269). New York: Harper & Row.

Gratereaux, A. (Mar. 23, 2011). I'm not gonna preach, I'm a role model. *Fox New Latino.* Retrieved online May 17, 2011, at http://latino.foxnews.com/latino/entertainment/2011/03/23/bruno-mars-cocaine-bust-im-gonna-preach-im-a-role-model/.

Guerrero, L. A., Andersen, P. A., & Afifi, W. A. (2013). *Close encounters: Communication in relationships* (4th ed.). Thousand Oaks, CA: Sage.

Hample, D. (2003). Arguing skill. In J. O. Greene & B. R. Burleson (Eds.), *Handbook of Communication and Social Interaction Skills* pp. (439–477). Mahwah, NJ: Erlbaum.

Hinken, T. R., & Schriesheim, C. A. (1980). Development and application of new scales to measure the French and Raven (1959) Bases of Social Power. *Journal of Applied Psychology, 74,* 561–567.

Infante, D. A., & Rancer, A. S. (1996). Argumentativeness and verbal aggression: A review of recent theory and research. In B. R. Burleson (Ed.), *Communication yearbook, 19* (pp. 319–351). Thousand Oaks, CA: Sage.

Jorgensen, P. E. (1998). Affect, persuasion, and communication process. In P. A. Anderson & L. K. Guerrero (Eds.), *Handbook of Communication and Emotion: Research, Theory, Applications, and Contexts* (pp. 403–422). San Diego, CA: Academic Press.

Martin, M. M., Anderson, C. M., & Horvath, C. L. (1996). Feelings about verbal aggression: Justifications for sending and hurt from receiving verbally aggressive messages. *Communication Research Reports, 13*(1), 19–26.

Meuter, M. L., McCabe, D. B., & Curran, J. M. (2013). Electronic word-of-mouth versus interpersonal word-of-mouth: Are all forms of word-of-mouth equally influential? *Services Marketing Quarterly, 34*(3), 240–256.

Niikura, R. (1999). The psychological process underlying Japanese assertive behavior: Comparison of Japanese with Americans, Malaysians, and Filipinos. *International Journal of Intercultural Relations, 23,* 47–76.

O'Sullivan, P. B., & Flanagin, A. J. (2003). Reconceptualizing "flaming" and other problematic messages. *New Media and Society, 5*(1), 69–94.

O'Sullivan, P. B. (2005). *Masspersonal communication: Rethinking the mass interpersonal divide.* Paper presented at the 55th Annual Convention of the International Communication Association, New York, NY.

Petty, R. E., & Briñol, P. (2011). The elaboration likelihood model. In P. A. M. V. Lange, A. W. Kruglanski, & E. T. Higgins (Eds.), *The handbook of theories of social psychology* (Vol. 1, pp. 224–245). Thousand Oaks, CA: Sage.

Rakos, R. F. (2006). Asserting and confronting. In O. Hargie (Ed.), *The Handbook of Communication Skills* (3rd ed.). New York: Routledge.

Samovar, L. A., Porter, R. E., McDaniel, E. R., & Roy, C. S. (2013). *Communication between Cultures* (8th ed.). Boston, MA: Wadsworth Cengage Learning.

Chapter 11

Adler, R. B. (1977). *Confidence in Communication: A Guide to Assertive and Social Skills.* New York: Holt, Rinehart, & Winston.

Brake, T., Walker, D. M., & Walker, T. (1995). *Doing business internationally: The guide to cross-cultural success.* New York: Irwin.

Caughlin, J. P., & Golish, T. D. (2002). An analysis of the association between topic avoidance and dissatisfaction: Comparing perceptual and interpersonal explanations. *Communication Monographs, 69,* 275–295.

Caughlin, J. P., & Huston, T. L. (2006). Demand/withdraw patterns in marital relationships: An individual differences perspective. In R. M. Dailey & B. A. LePoire (Eds.). *Applied Interpersonal Communication Matters: Family, Health, and Community Relations* (pp. 11–38). New York: Peter Lang.

Cupach, W. R., & Canary, D. J. (1997). *Competence in Interpersonal Conflict.* New York: McGraw-Hill.

Garcia, W. R. (1996). Respecto: A Mexican base for interpersonal relationships. In W. Gudykunst, S. Ting-Toomey, T. Nishida (Eds.), *Communication in Personal Relationships Across Cultures* (pp. 137–155). Thousand Oaks, CA: Sage.

Gordon, T. (1970). *Parent Effectiveness Training.* New York: Peter H. Wyden.

Gordon, T. (1971). *The Basic Modules of the Instructor Outline for Effectiveness Training Courses.* Pasadena, CA: Effectiveness Training Associates.

Guerrero, L. A., Andersen, P. A., & Afifi, W. A. (2013). *Close encounters: Communication in relationships* (4th ed.). Thousand Oaks, CA: Sage.

Hodson, H. (2013). Online juries help curb bad gamer behaviour. *New Scientist, 218*(2912), 18.

Lea, M., Spears, R., & de Groot, D. (2001). Knowing me, knowing you: Anonymity effects on social identity processes within groups. *Personality and Social Psychology Bulletin, 27*(5), 526–537.

Lenhart, A., Madden, M., Smith, A., Purcell, K., Zickuhr, K., & Rainie, L. (Nov. 9, 2011). Teens, kindness, and cruelty on social network sites. Retrieved from http://www.pewinternet.org/2011/11/09/teens-kindness-and-cruelty-on-social-network-sites/. July 28, 2015

Moor, P. J., Heuvelman, A., & Verleur, R. (2010). Flaming on YouTube. *Computers in Human Behavior, 26*(6), 1536–1546.

Olweus, D. (1997). Bully/victim problems in school: Facts and intervention. *European Journal of Psychology of Education, 12*(4), 495–510.

O'Sullivan, P. B., & Flanagin, A. J. (2003). Reconceptualizing "flaming" and other problematic messages. *New Media and Society, 5*(1), 69–94.

Roloff, M. E., & Cloven, D. H. (1990). The chilling effect in interpersonal relationships: The reluctance to speak one's mind. In D. D. Cahn (Ed.), *Intimates in Conflict: A Communication Perspective* (pp. 49–76). Hillsdale, NJ: Erlbaum.

Roloff, M. E., & Johnson, K. L. (2002). Serial arguing over the relational life course: antecedents and consequences. In A. L. Vangelisti, H. T. Reis, & M. Fitzpatrick (Eds.), *Stability and Change in Relationships* (pp. 107–128). Cambridge, UK: Cambridge University Press.

Roloff, M. E., & Reznik, R. M. (2008). Communication during serial arguments: Connections with individuals mental and physical health. In M. T. Motley (Ed.), *Studies in Applied Communication* (pp. 97–119). Thousand Oaks, CA: Sage.

Sillars, A. L., & Weisberg, J. (1987). Conflict as a social skill. In M. E. Roloff & G. R. Miller (Eds.), *Interpersonal Processes: New Directions in Communication Research* (pp. 140–171). Beverly Hills, CA: Sage.

Slonje, R., Smith, P. K., & Frisén, A. (2013). The nature of cyberbullying, and strategies for prevention. *Computers in Human Behavior, 29*(1), 26–32.

Spears, R., & Lea, M. (1992). Social influence and the influence of the "social" in computer-mediated communication. In M. Lea (Ed.), *Contexts of computer-mediated communication* (pp. 30–65). Hemel Hempstead: Harvester Wheatsheaf.

Thomas, K. W. (1976). Conflict and conflict management. In M. D. Dunnette (Ed.), *Handbook of Industrial and Organizational Psychology* (pp. 889–935). Chicago: Rand-McNally.

Ting-Toomey, S., & Chung, L. C. (2011). *Understanding intercultural communication* (2nd ed.). New York: Oxford.

Ting-Toomey, S., Oetzel, J., & Yee-Jung, K. (2001). Self-construal types and conflict management styles. *Communication Reports, 14,* 87–104.

Waldron, V. R., & Kelley, D. L. (2008). *Communicating Forgiveness.* Thousand Oaks, CA: Sage.

Whetten, D. A., & Cameron, K. S. (2010). *Developing Management Skills* (8th ed.). Upper Saddle River, NJ: Prentice Hall.

Zhang, Q., Ting-Toomey, S., & Oetzel, J. G. (2014). Linking emotion to the conflict face-negotiation theory: A US–China investigation of the mediating effects of anger, compassion, and guilt in interpersonal conflict. *Human Communication Research, 40*(3), 373–395.

Chapter 12

Allen, E. S., & Atkins, D. C. (2012). The association of divorce and extramarital sex in a representative US sample. *Journal of Family Issues, 33*(11), 1477–1493.

Babin, E. A. (2013). An examination of predictors of nonverbal and verbal communication of pleasure during sex and sexual satisfaction. *Journal of Social and Personal Relationships, 30*(3), 270–292.

Baron, N. S. (2008). *Always on: Language in an Online and Mobile World.* New York: Oxford University Press.

Bartholomew, K., & Horowitz, L. M. (1991). Attachment styles among young adults: A test of a four-category model. *Journal of Personality and Social Psychology, 61,* 226–244.

Baumrind, D. (1971). Current patterns of parental authority. *Developmental Psychology Monographs, 4,* 99–102.

Baumrind, D. (2013). Authoritative parenting revisited: History and current status. In R. E. Larzelere, A. S. Morris, & A. W. Harrist (Eds.), *Authoritative Parenting: Synthesizing Nurturance and Discipline for Optimal Child Development* (pp. 11–34). Washington, DC: American Psychological Association.

Bevan, J. L. (2013). *The Communication of Jealousy.* New York: Peter Lang.

Bisson, M. A., & Levine, T. R. (2009). Negotiating a friends with benefits relationship. *Archives of Sexual Behavior, 38*(1), 66–73.

Blow, A. J., & Hartnett, K. (2005). Infidelity in committed relationships. II: A substantive review. *Journal of Marital and Family Therapy, 31*(2), 217–233.

Cherlin, A. (2009). *Marriage, divorce, remarriage.* Cambridge, MA: Harvard University Press.

DePaulo, B. M. (2007). *Singled out: How singles are stereotyped, stigmatized, and ignored, and still live happily ever after.* New York: Macmillan.

Dew, J., & Wilcox, W. B. (2011). If Momma ain't happy: Explaining declines in marital satisfaction among new mothers. *Journal of Marriage and Family, 73*(1), 1–12.

Dickson, F. C. (1995). The best is yet to be: Research on long-lasting marriages. In J. T. Wood & S. Duck (Eds.), *Under-Studied*

Relationships: Off the Beaten Track (pp. 22–50). Thousand Oaks, CA: Sage.

Dindia, K., & Canary, D. (1993). Definitions and theoretical perspectives on maintaining relationships. *Journal of Social and Personal Relationships, 10*, 163–173.

Ellison, N. B., Steinfield, C., & Lampe, C. (2007). The benefits of Facebook "friends": Social capital and college students' use of online social network sites. *Journal of Computer-Mediated Communication, 12*(4), 1143–1168.

Faulkner, S. L., & Lannutti, P. J. (2010). Examining the content and outcomes of young adults' satisfying and unsatisfying conversations about sex. *Qualitative Health Research, 20*(3), 375–385.

Fehr, B. (1996). *Friendship Processes.* Thousand Oaks, CA: Sage.

Feinstein, E. (Sep. 2010). *The Importance of Family Dinners, VI.* The National Center on Addiction and Substance Abuse at Columbia University. Available at http://www.casacolumbia.org/upload/2010/20100922familydinners6.pdf

Fife, S. T., Weeks, G. R., & Stellberg-Filbert, J. (2013). Facilitating forgiveness in the treatment of infidelity: An interpersonal model. *Journal of Family Therapy, 35*(4), 343–367.

Fitzpatrick, M. A., & Ritchie, L. D. (1994). Communication schemata within the family: Multiple perspectives on family interaction. *Human Communication Research, 20*, 275–301.

Floyd, K. (2006). *Communicating affection: Interpersonal behavior and social context.* New York: Cambridge University Press.

Floyd, K., Boren, J. P., Hannawa, A. F., Hesse, C., McEwan, B., & Veksler, A. E. (2009). Kissing in marital and cohabiting relationships: Effects on blood lipids, stress, and relationship satisfaction. *Western Journal of Communication, 73*(2), 113–133.

Floyd, K., & Deiss, D. (2012). Better health, better lives: The bright side of affection. In T. J. Socha & M. Pitts (Eds.), *The positive side of interpersonal communication* (pp. 127–142). New York: Peter Lang.

Frei, J. R., & Shaver, P. R. (2002). Respect in close relationships: Prototype definition, self-report assessment, and initial correlates. *Personal Relationships, 9*, 121–139.

Gordon, A. M., Impett, E. A., Kogan, A., Oveis, C., & Keltner, D. (2012). To have and to hold: Gratitude promotes relationship maintenance in intimate bonds. *Journal of Personality and Social Psychology, 103*(2), 257.

Gould, O. (2004). Telling stories and getting acquainted: How age matters. In M. W. Pratt & B. H. Fiese (Eds.), *Family Stories and the Lifecourse* (pp. 327–351). Mahwah, NJ: Erlbaum.

Grant, A. M., & Gino, F. (2010). A little thanks goes a long way: Explaining why gratitude expressions motivate prosocial behavior. *Journal of Personality and Social Psychology, 98*(6), 946–955.

Guerrero, L. K., & Chavez, A. M. (2005). Relational maintenance in cross-sex friendships characterized by different types of romantic intent: An exploratory study. *Western Journal of Communication, 69*(4), 339–358.

Guerrero, L. A., Andersen, P. A., & Afifi, W. A. (2013). *Close encounters: Communication in relationships* (4th ed.). Thousand Oaks, CA: Sage.

Haythornthwaite, C. (2002). Strong, weak, and latent ties and the impact of new media. *Information Society, 18*, 385–401.

Haythornthwaite, C. (2005). Social networks and Internet connectivity effects. *Information, Communication & Society, 8*, 125–147.

Heiman, J. R., Long, J. S., Smith, S. N., Fisher, W. A., Sand, M. S., & Rosen, R. C. (2011). Sexual satisfaction and relationship happiness in midlife and older couples in five countries. *Archives of Sexual Behavior, 40*(4), 741–753.

Hughes, M., Morrison, K., & Asada, K. J. K. (2005). What's love got to do with it? Exploring the impact of maintenance rules, love attitudes, and network support on friends with benefits relationships. *Western Journal of Communication, 69*(1), 49–66.

Humphreys, L. (2007). Mobile social networks and social practice: A case study of dodgeball. *Journal of Computer-Mediated Communication, 13*(1), 341–360.

Knobloch, L. (2015). Relational turbulence theory. In D. O. Braithwaite & P. Schrodt (Eds.), *Engaging theories in interpersonal communication* (pp. 377–387). Thousand Oaks, CA: Sage.

Koenig Kellas, J., & Suter, E. A. (2012). Accounting for lesbian-headed families: Lesbian mothers' responses to discursive challenges. *Communication Monographs, 79*, 475–498.

Lachance-Grzela, M., & Bouchard, G. (2010). Why do women do the lion's share of housework? A decade of research. *Sex Roles, 63*(11–12), 767–780.

Le Poire, B. A., Shepard, C., & Duggan, A. (1999). Nonverbal involvement, expressiveness, and pleasantness as predicted by parental and partner attachment style. *Communication Monographs, 66*, 293–311.

Myers, S. A., Goodboy, A. K., & Members of COMM 201 (2013). Using equity theory to explore adult siblings' use of relational maintenance behaviors and relational characteristics. *Communication Research Reports, 30*(4), 275–281.

Myers, S. A., & Kennedy-Lightsey, C. D. (2014). Communication in adult sibling relationships. *The SAGE Handbook of Family Communication* (pp. 220–234). Thousand Oaks, CA: Sage.

Nelson, J. A., Li, C.-S., Eckstein, D. G., Ane, P., & Mullener, W. (2008). Antidotes for infidelity and prescriptions for long-lasting relationships: Four couples' activities. *The Family Journal, 16*(4), 375–378.

Owen, J., & Fincham, F. D. (2011). Effects of gender and psychosocial factors on "friends with benefits" relationships among young adults. *Archives of Sexual Behavior, 40*(2), 311–320.

Pelusi, N. (July 6, 2006). Jealousy: A voice of possessiveness past. *Psychology Today,* 34–35.

Ramirez, A. (2008). An examination of the tripartite approach to commitment: An actor-partner interdependence model analysis of the effect of relational maintenance behavior. *Journal of Social and Personal Relationships, 25*(6), 943–965.

Ryan, E. B., Pearce, K. A., Anas, A. P., & Norris, J. E. (2004). Writing a connection: Intergenerational communication through stories. In M. W. Pratt & B. H. Fiese (Eds.), *Family Stories and the Lifecourse* (pp. 375–398). Mahwah, NJ: Erlbaum.

Samter, W. (2003). Friendship interaction skills across the life span. In J. O. Greene & B. R. Burleson (Eds.), *Handbook of communication and social interaction skills* (pp. 637–684). Mahwah, NJ: Erlbaum.

Schrodt, P., Witt, P. L., & Messersmith, A. S. (2008). A meta-analytical review of family communication patterns and their associations with information processing, behavioral, and psychosocial outcomes. *Communication Monographs, 75*(3), 248–269.

Sorkhabi, N., & Mandara, J. (2013). Are the effects of Baumrind's parenting styles culturally specific or culturally equivalent? In R. E. Larzelere, A. S. Morris, & A. W. Harrist (Eds.), *Authoritative parenting: Synthesizing nurturance and discipline for optimal child development* (pp. 113–135). Washington, DC: American Psychological Association.

Stafford, L. (2011). Measuring relationship maintenance behaviors: Critique and development of the revised relationship maintenance behavior scale. *Journal of Social and Personal Relationships, 28*(2), 278–303.

Steil, J. M. (2000). Contemporary marriage: Still an unequal partnership. In C. Hendrick & S. S. Hendrick (Eds.), *Close relationships: A sourcebook* (pp. 124–136). Thousand Oaks, CA: Sage.

Suter, E. A. (2015). Communication in gay and lesbian families. In L. H. Turner & R. West (Eds.), *The SAGE Handbook of Family Communication* (pp. 235–247). Thousand Oaks, CA: Sage.

Theiss, J. A., & Solomon, D. H. (2008). Parsing the mechanisms that increase relational intimacy: The effects of uncertainty amount, open communication about uncertainty, and the reduction of uncertainty. *Human Communication Research, 34*(4), 625–654.

Turner, L. H., & West, R. (2013). *Perspectives on family communication* (4th ed.). New York: McGraw-Hill.

Walther, J. B. (1996). Computer-mediated communication: Impersonal, interpersonal, and hyperpersonal interaction. *Communication Research, 23,* 3–43.

Whitton, S. W., Waldinger, R. J., Shultz, M. S., Allen, J. P., Crowell, J. A., & Hauser, S. T. (2008). Prospective associations from family-of-origin interactions to adult marital interactions and relationship adjustment. *Journal of Family Psychology, 22,* 274–286.

Wood, J. T. (2012). *Gendered Lives: Communication, Gender, and Culture* (10th ed.). Boston, MA: Wadsworth Cengage Learning.

Yoshimura, C. G., & Alberts, J. K. (2008). Television viewing and relational maintenance. In M. Motley (Ed.), *Studies in Applied Interpersonal Communication* (pp. 287–307). Thousand Oaks, CA: Sage.

Chapter 13

Adler, R. B. (1977). *Confidence in communication: A guide to assertive and social skills.* New York: Holt, Rinehart, & Winston.

Baron, R. A., & Neuman, J. H. (1996). Workplace violence and workplace aggression: evidence of their relative frequency and potential causes. *Aggressive Behavior, 22,* 161–173.

Berman, E. M., West, J. P., & Richter Jr., M. N. (2002). Workplace relations: Friendship patterns and consequences (according to managers). *Public Administration Review, 62*(2), 217–230.

Budak, J. (2012). Embracing office romance. Retrieved June 25, 2015, from http://jasminebudak.com/2012/05/17/embracing-office-romance/.

Cahill, D. J., & Sias, P. M. (1997). The perceived social costs and importance of seeking emotional support in the workplace: Gender differences and similarities. *Communication Research Reports, 14*(2), 231–240.

Cooper-Thomas, H. D., & Morrison, R. L. (2013). Maximizing the good and minimizing the bad: Relationships in organizations. In R. L. Morrison & H. D. Cooper-Thomas (Eds.), *Relationships in Organizations: A Work Psychology Perspective* (pp. 1–7). New York: Palgrave MacMillan.

Dennis, A. R., Fuller, R. M., & Valacich, J. S. (2008). Media, tasks, and communication processes: A theory of media synchronicity. *MIS Quarterly, 32*(3), 575–600.

Dougherty, T. W., Turban, D. B., & Haggard, D. L. (2007). Naturally occurring mentoring relationships involving workplace employees. In T. D. Allen & L. T. Eby (Eds.), *The Blackwell handbook of mentoring: A multiple perspectives approach* (pp. 139–158). Malden, MA: Wiley-Blackwell.

Eby, L. T., Allen, T. D., Hoffman, B. J., Baranik, L. E., Sauer, J. B., Baldwin, S., . . . Curtis, S. (2013). An interdisciplinary meta-analysis of the potential antecedents, correlates, and consequences of protégé perceptions of mentoring. *Psychological Bulletin, 139*(2), 441.

Eby, L. T., Butts, M. M., Durley, J., & Ragins, B. R. (2010). Are bad experiences stronger than good ones in mentoring relationships? Evidence from the protégé and mentor perspective. *Journal of Vocational Behavior, 77*(1), 81–92.

Eisenberg, E. M., & Goodall, H. L. (2004). *Organizational Communication: Balancing Creativity and Constraint.* New York: Bedford St. Martin's.

Graen, G. B., & Uhl-Bien. M. (1995). Relationship-based approach to leadership: Development of leader-member exchange (LMX) theory over 25 years: Applying a multi-level multi-domain perspective. *Leadership Quarterly, 6*(2), 219–242.

Gumpert, G., & Drucker, S. J. (2007). Mobile communication in the twenty-first century; or "Everybody, everywhere, at any time." In S. Kleinman (Ed.), *Displacing place: Mobile communication in the twenty-first century* (pp. 7–20). New York: Peter Lang.

Jablin, F. M., & Krone, K. J. (1994). Task/work relationships: A life-span perspective. In M. L. Knapp & G. R. Miller (Eds.), *Handbook of Interpersonal Communication* (2nd ed., pp. 621–675). Thousand Oaks, CA: Sage.

Kalbfleisch, P. J. (2007). Mentoring enactment theory: Describing, explaining, and predicting communication in mentoring relationships. In B. R. Ragins & K. E. Kram (Eds.), *The handbook of mentoring at work: Theory, research, and practice.* Thousand Oaks, CA: Sage.

Kram, K. E., & Isabella, L. A. (1985). Mentoring alternatives: The role of peer relationships in career development. *Academy of Management Journal, 28*(1), 110–132.

Krishnan, A., Kurtzberg, T. R., & Naquin, C. E. (2014). The curse of the smartphone: Electronic multitasking in negotiations. *Negotiation Journal, 30*(2), 191–208.

Lee, H. E., Park, H. S., Lee, T. S., & Lee, D. W. (2007). Relationships between LMX and subordinates' feedback-seeking behaviors. *Social Behavior and Personality: an International Journal, 35*(5), 659–674.

Lee, R. T., Brotheridge, C. M., Cooper-Thomas, H., Gardner, D., O'Driscoll, M., Catley, B., . . . Trenberth, L. (2013). Neutralizing workplace bullying: the buffering effects of contextual factors. *Journal of Managerial Psychology, 28*(4), 384–407.

Lutgen-Sandvik, P., & Tracy, S. J. (2012). Answering five key questions about workplace bullying how communication scholarship provides thought leadership for transforming abuse at work. *Management Communication Quarterly, 26*(1), 3–47.

Morrison, R. L., & Nolan, T. (2009). I get by with a little help from my friends . . . at work. *Kōtuitui: New Zealand Journal of Social Sciences Online, 4*(1), 41–54.

Myers, K., Seibold, D., & Park, H. (2011). Interpersonal communication in the workplace. In M. L. Knapp & J. A. Daly (Eds.), *The Sage Handbook of Interpersonal Communication* (4th ed., pp. 527–562). Thousand Oaks, CA: Sage.

Namie, G., & Lutgen-Sandvik, P. E. (2010). Active and passive accomplices: The communal character of workplace bullying. *International Journal of Communication, 4*, 343–373.

Odden, C. M., & Sias, P. M. (1997). Peer communication relationships, psychological climate, and gender. *Communication Quarterly, 45*, 153–166.

Park, S. (2013). Always on and always with mobile tablet devices: A qualitative study on how young adults negotiate with continuous connected presence. *Bulletin of Science, Technology & Society, 33*(5–6), 182–190.

Parks, M. (2006). Workplace romance. Retrieved June 25, 2015, from http://www.shrm.org/research/surveyfindings/documents/2006%20Workplace%20Romance%20Poll%20Findings.pdf.

Rai, S. (2002). Preventing workplace aggression and violence—a role for occupational therapy. *Work, 18*(1), 15–22.

Ramaswami, A., & Dreher, G. F. (2007). The benefits associated with workplace mentoring relationships. In T. D. Allen & L. T. Eby (Eds.), *The Blackwell handbook of mentoring: A multiple perspectives approach* (pp. 211–232). Malden, MA: Wiley-Blackwell.

Sias, P. M. (2005). Workplace relationship quality and employee information experiences. *Communication Studies, 56*(4), 375–395.

Sias, P. M., & Cahill, D. J. (1998). From coworkers to friends: The development of peer friendships in the workplace. *Western Journal of Communication, 62*(3), 273–299.

Tannen, D. (1995). The power of talk: Who gets heard and why. *Harvard Business Review, 75*(5), 138–148.

Vaast, E., & Kaganer, E. (2013). Social media affordances and governance in the workplace: An examination of organizational policies. *Journal of Computer-Mediated Communication, 19*(1), 78–101.

Varner, I., & Beamer, L. (1995). *Intercultural Communication in the Global Workplace.* Chicago: Irwin.

Whetten, D. A., & Cameron, K. S. (2005). *Developing Management Skills* (6th ed.). Upper Saddle River, NJ: Prentice Hall.

Wilson, F. (2013). Love is in the air—Romantic relationships at work. In R. L. Morrison & H. D. Cooper-Thomas (Eds.), *Relationships in Organizations: A Work Psychology Perspective* (pp. 8–27). New York: Palgrave MacMillan.

Zemke, R., Raines, C., & Filipczak, B. (2000). *Generations at Work.* New York: AMACOM.

Photo Credits

Chapter 1

Page 2, ©Jdnyim/Moment/Getty Images; **5,** Jim Cummins/Media Bakery; **10,** ©iStockphoto/Aleksej Vasic; **16,** AP Photo/Alessandra Tarantino; **17,** wavebreakmedia/Shutterstock.com; **18,** Courtesy of Randy Glasbergen; **18,** AP Photo/Matt Sayles; **21,** JB Lacroix/WireImage/Getty Images; **27,** Courtesy of CoxandForkum.com

Chapter 2

Page 34, ©iStock.com/ttueni; **39,** ©iStock.com/Neustockimages; **39,** ©iStock.com/drbimages; **40,** Park Street/PhotoEdit; **41,** ©iStock.com/Kuzma; **43,** Cartoonstock www.Cartoonstock.com; **49,** Flirt/Alamy; **50,** ©iStock.com/monkeybusinessimages; **54,** igor.stevanovic/Shutterstock.com

Chapter 3

Page 64, ©iStock.com/PeopleImages; **67,** Cartoonstock www.Cartoonstock.com; **68,** David Price/Arsenal FC via Getty Images; **72,** ColorBlind Images/Iconica/Getty Images; **73,** ©iStock.com/Juanmonino; **73,** ©iStock.com/Shmulitk; **74,** Dmitry Naumov/Shutterstock.com; **76,** Paul Austring Photography/First Light/Getty Images; **83,** ©Francis Dean/Dean/The Image Works; **84,** Ilya S. Savenok/FilmMagic/Getty Images

Chapter 4

Page 96, ©iStock.com/Peter Burnett; **102,** Courtesy of Chris Madden; **104,** Andrew Burton/Getty Images; **105,** Cartoonstock www.Cartoonstock.com; **108,** michaeljung/Shutterstock.com; **110,** John Roman Images/Shutterstock.com; **114,** Vgstockstudio/Shutterstock.com; **117,** jiris/Shutterstock.com;

121, Celia Mannings/Alamy; **124,** ©iStock.com/bo1982

Chapter 5

Page 130, ©iStock.com/onebluelight; **133,** Cartoonstock www.Cartoonstock.com; **135,** ©iStock.com/Francesco Cantone; **136,** AP Photo/Charles Sykes, Invision, File; **136,** Photo by Frank Micelotta/Invision/AP Images; **137,** ©iStock.com/Anantha Vardhan; **139,** Jupiterimages/Photolibrary/Getty Images; **140,** Courtesy of Linda Causey; **141,** ©iStock.com/Rich Legg; **142,** ©iStock.com/mediaphotos; **143,** Cartoonstock www.Cartoonstock.com; **155,** rvlsoft/Shutterstock.com; **155,** Perfect Vectors/Shutterstock.com; **156,** graphicgeoff/Shutterstock.com; **156,** veronchick84/Shutterstock.com; **156,** yuoak/Digital Vision Vectors/Getty Images

Chapter 6

Page 160, Kena Betancur-Pool/Getty Images; **170,** Mike Powell/Stone/Getty Images; **173,** ©Kevin R. Morris/Corbis; **178,** Courtesy of Ariel Skelley; **185,** SW Productions/Stockbyte/Getty Images; **188,** Cartoonstock www.Cartoonstock.com; **191,** Brand New Images/Stone/Getty Images

Chapter 7

Page 196, Jagodka/Shutterstock.com; **199,** ©iStockphoto/Lise Gagne; **204,** Cartoonstock www.Cartoonstock.com; **205,** ©iStockphoto/monkeybusinessimages; **207,** Justin Sullivan/Getty Images; **209,** Cartoonstock www.Cartoonstock.com; **212,** ©iStockphoto/fotostorm; **213,** ©iStockphoto/Deborah Cheramie; **214,** ©iStockphoto/Aleksej Vasic

Chapter 8

Page 222, ©iStockphoto/Mark Massel; **225,** ©iStockphoto/Olivier Lantzendorffer; **228,** Cartoonstock www.Cartoonstock.com; **230,** ©iStockphoto/kaspiic; **231,** Jon Furniss/Getty Images; **232,** Oli Scarff/Getty Images; **233,** Blend Images/Shutterstock.com; **235,** Cartoonstock www.Cartoonstock.com; **237,** Cartoonstock www.Cartoonstock.com; **247,** ©Alan Carey/The Image Works

Chapter 9

Page 252, Monkey Business Images/Shutterstock.com; **257,** Ermolaev Alexander/Shutterstock.com; **263,** Copyright/Nicky Niederstrasser/Corbis/AP Images; **264,** Izabela Habur/Getty Images; **266,** Rob Hyrons/Shutterstock.com; **267,** Ghislain & Marie David de Lossy/Getty Images; **270,** ©iStockphoto/ImagineGolf; **271,** Cartoonstock www.Cartoonstock.com; **273,** Zia Soleil/Getty Images

Chapter 10

Page 282, ThinkStock/Superstock; **286,** ©iStockphoto/Sean Locke; **288,** ©iStockphoto/diego_cervo; **290,** Cartoonstock www.Cartoonstock.com; **293,** Radius Images/Getty Images; **296,** Eky Studio/Shutterstock.com; **299,** SpeedKingz/Shutterstock.com; **301,** ©iStockphoto/Joselito Briones; **307,** © 2/Ocean/Corbis

Chapter 11

Page 316, Cultura RM/Andreas Pollok/Getty Images; **320,** Stockbyte/Matin Bahadori/Getty Images; **321,** AFP/Emmanuel Dunnand/Getty Images; **322,** ©iStockphoto/Bjoern Meyer; **324,** Cartoonstock www.Cartoonstock.com;

Index

Note: Page numbers followed by f and t refer to figures and tables, respectively.